CALIFORNIA

VEGETABLE PATCH

& SEED SOURCE

THE ORGANIC GARDENER'S COMPLETE REFERENCE ALMANAC

BY

DUANE NEWCOMB AND KAREN NEWCOMB

HarperCollins*West*

A Division of HarperCollinsPublishers

Other books by Duane Newcomb
The Postage Stamp Garden Book
Rx for Your Vegetable Garden
The Backyard Vegetable Factory
Growing Vegetables the Big Yield/Small Space Way

Other books by Duane and Karen Newcomb
The Complete Vegetable Gardener's Sourcebook

HarperCollins West and the authors, in association with The Basic Foundation, a not-for-profit organization whose primary mission is reforestation, will facilitate the planting of two trees for every one tree used in the manufacture of this book.

FIRST EDITION

Library of Congress Cataloging-in-Publication Data

Newcomb, Duane G.

California vegetable patch and seed source : the organic gardener's complete reference almanac / Duane Newcomb and Karen Newcomb. -- 1st ed.

p. cm.

ISBN 0-06-258554-1 (alk. paper)

1. Vegetable gardening—California. 2. Organic gardening—California. I. Newcomb, Karen. II. Title.

SB324.3.N4935 1995

635'.0484—dc20   94-17780
                                                              CIP

95 96 97 98 99 ❖ RRD(H) 10 9 8 7 6 5 4 3 2 1

This edition is printed on acid-free paper that meets the American National Standards Institute Z39.48 Standard.

CONTENTS

INTRODUCTION		1
CHAPTER 1	HOW TO PLAN YOUR VEGETABLE GARDEN	3
CHAPTER 2	HOW TO GET YOUR SOIL READY	11
CHAPTER 3	WHEN AND HOW TO PLANT: AN OVERALL GUIDE	33
CHAPTER 4	WATERING	49
CHAPTER 5	WHAT'S BUGGING YOUR GARDEN?	57
CHAPTER 6	DEALING WITH VEGETABLE DISEASES	69
CHAPTER 7	WEATHERING THE ELEMENTS	79
CHAPTER 8	MOTHER NATURE'S PUZZLERS	85
CHAPTER 9	INDIVIDUAL VEGETABLES, GROWING TIPS, AND SEED SOURCES	101
APPENDIX A	SEED CATALOG SOURCES	385
APPENDIX B	COUNTY FARM ADVISORS	391
APPENDIX C	VEGETABLE PLANTING GUIDE	395

INTRODUCTION

SO YOU WANT TO GROW VEGETABLES

Every year on the first warm day of spring, Duane would rush outdoors to spade up the backyard and plant as many kinds of vegetables as possible. Afterwards, he would stand at the edge of the freshly raked garden and visualize the profusion of peas, carrots, tomatoes, and other vegetables that would soon be growing there.

Unfortunately (until a few years ago), that's when reality set in. For although Duane was good at visualizing vegetables, he was not very good at growing them. He tried. He'd earned degrees in both botany and forestry. He read the latest scientific bulletins on vegetable gardening. He knew what the inside of a carrot looked like, how to develop new varieties of plants from old, what macro- and micronutrients were, and the names and symptoms of all the major plant diseases. He had superior knowledge, yet he couldn't grow a vegetable garden worthy of the name.

He recalls: "Beets came up in clumps, then died. The carrots either didn't show up at all or turned out small and spindly. Bean pods shriveled up at the ends. The birds ate all the baby cucumber plants, and many of the vegetables that did grow were stunted."

In short, Duane had a brown thumb.

On the other hand, I spent my early years on a farm where the planting was done by others and when you wanted a vegetable, you simply went out and picked one. My thumb was greener, but not by much. Together, Duane and I created some vegetable garden disasters.

Of course, there was a turnaround point in our failing gardening endeavors. Duane discovered Intensive Gardening (explained in chapter 1), began to apply some very basic garden rules, and went on to write several books about small space gardening. Yet, even after discovering what had been going wrong, and learning how to remedy the errors, it's taken many years of practice to perfect our gardening skills. Also, we discovered we had to buy and read numerous books on individual gardening subjects just to get the knowledge we needed. We discovered that these books, frequently written by Eastern gardeners, didn't help us in California much. California is indeed an enigma. The state is huge, home to 24 individual macroclimates and many variations within these. We found that it was necessary to understand our particular climate well to grow varieties that suited the lengths and temperatures of the growing seasons. For example, for the past 15 years we've gardened at a 1,600-foot elevation in the Sierra Nevada foothills. In this unique setting, some tomato varieties recommended on a national basis didn't ripen until just before the first frost; the beefsteak tomatoes (which we really wanted to grow) were a virtual disaster. That's when we decided to compile one book that would bring together a lot of fundamental information. While every variety listed in this book can be grown in California, not every variety can be grown in every climate without special care. The cultural requirements listed in chapter 9 of this book give California gardeners a tool to help match individual climates with vegetable varieties (see the inside of the book's back cover). Whether you choose to grow a conventional row garden or try the intensive method, vegetable gardening doesn't have to be a dilemma. We know that anyone who can turn over a shovelful of dirt can grow almost any edible. Give us a season and you'll know it, too.

—Karen Newcomb
Grass Valley, CA 1994

CHAPTER ONE

HOW TO PLAN YOUR VEGETABLE GARDEN

Garden dreamers make dozens of drawings of what their new garden is going to look like before they buy seeds or turn over a spadeful of soil. We suggest you do the same. A good plan keeps your mistakes to a minimum by giving you a preliminary idea of where to put your garden, what to plant in it, how much space to allocate, and what shape it should have. We suggest you sketch your plan to scale on graph paper. Don't just estimate the number of plants needed; actually measure the spacing of rows and the distance between plants to get an exact count. (See Appendix C for spacing and the number of plants needed per person.)

Of course the first thing to do in planning your garden is to decide where to locate it.

These are the main placement considerations:

• Place your garden where it gets at least six hours of direct sun a day, since most vegetables need at least this much.

• Keep your garden bed at least 20 feet from shallow-rooted trees such as elms, maples, and poplars. Not only will the foliage of these trees block the sun, but their roots will compete for water and nutrients. Generally, tree roots take food from the soil in a circle whose radius is the tree's widest-reaching branches, and as a result, plants usually do poorly within this area.

• Keep your garden out of depressions where standing water collects and away from downspouts where the force from a sudden rain can wash out your plants.

• Try to situate your garden near a water outlet. This eliminates having to drag a hose long distances. Also, try to place your garden as near to your tool storage as possible.

Conventional Gardens

Conventional vegetable gardens are planted in rows with spacing between the individual vegetables making up the rows, and a 1–3-foot interval between the rows. Garden size depends primarily on the space available. Ideally, the plot should measure no less than 100 square feet (10x10 feet). With a garden this size, you can plant as many as 15 vegetables, including corn, lettuce, beets, radishes, carrots, tomatoes, and green beans. A 25x40-foot garden, properly tended, can provide all the fresh vegetables a family of four can eat.

- Place tall plants at the north end so they don't shade other vegetables in your garden.

- Place large plants against a fence whenever possible. Fences make nice trellises for climbing plants such as cucumbers, green beans, and squash.

Intensive Gardens

Intensive gardens use all available garden space by eliminating rows and growing most vegetables a few inches apart across the entire bed. We combine small intensive/planted garden squares (from 4x4 to 6x6) in part of our garden and wide rows (4 feet wide by any length you want) in another section. In a 1-square-foot intensive garden you can grow about as many carrots as you can in a 12-foot row in a conventional garden. Other vegetables give similar yields depending on the spacing. It's easy to produce an abundant crop of your favorite vegetables in a space so small that ordinarily you wouldn't even consider it adequate for gardening.

The following intensive planting rules will help you obtain maximum results.

- Plant the tallest vegetables on the north side of your garden to avoid shading the other vegetables, and plant the other vegetables—in descending order of height—toward the south end of the garden (Figure 1-1).

- Use all the space in your garden, then thin out the seedlings (the small plants) as they come up. Space transplants (plants transferred from a container into the garden) the same distance apart in all directions. See page 36 for correct spacing. The leaves of plants should touch one another on all sides (Figure 1-1).

- If your plot is large—say, 10x2 feet or 8x8 feet—you can plant vegetables in separate square, rectangular, or even circular beds. In plots more than 5–6 feet wide, you'll need to have pathways to reach all your plants. However, if the plot is narrow or small, simply block out irregular groups of vegetables and fill in the spaces any way you wish (Figure 1-1).

- Root vegetables (such as carrots and beets), leafy vegetables (such as lettuce and spinach), and corn need special planning. Divide the areas chosen for each of these vegetables into thirds or fourths, and plant each of these subsections a week to 10 days apart. As one subsection finishes bearing mature vegetables, another begins.

- Use the airspace above your garden as much as possible. Train indeterminate tomatoes, vine cucumbers, and other trailing plants up trellises, fences, poles, or whatever structure you can create, so these tricky vines won't be running all over your garden bed and crowding out the other plants. The better you get at this vertical growing, the more vegetables you'll be able to pack into your intensive garden. Experiment with a variety of support systems.

- Besides vegetables, include some flowers, especially marigolds, and herbs in your garden. You'll love the fragrance and color they add. You can even plant edible flowers, such as nasturtiums.

figure 1-1

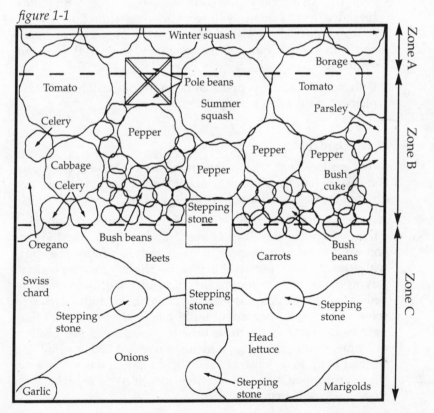

Zone A is a 6- to 15-inch strip at the north end of the garden; zone B occupies the next 2 to 4 feet; zone C occupies the remainder of the garden. The vegetables are planted in each zone by height.

Flower Bed Gardens

Who says you have to grow a formal vegetable garden? These days, anything goes. A lot of gardeners believe flower beds are actually the natural places to grow vegetables because some flowers enhance vegetable growth or protect vegetables against insects.

Here are some helpful guidelines to "vegetablize" flower beds:

- To give your garden an especially lush look, plant vines such as cucumbers and small melons against a wall; beans can sprout there, too, or you can stake them.

- Use lettuce (especially leaf lettuce) and Swiss chard as a flower bed edging. Grow head lettuce just behind this border. If your summer weather is too warm for lettuce, shelter it beneath the taller plants in the front row.

- Plant small sections of root crops about every 10 days to ensure a continuous harvest. See individual vegetable listings in chapter 9 for details.

- Plant flowering cabbage or even regular cabbage when you're looking for a show-off.

- Plant corn in a good sunny corner. A 4x6-foot plot with plants spaced 8 inches apart will accommodate approximately 10 stalks. Choose a variety that bears more than one ear per stalk and you'll have quite a harvest. (See chapter 9 for seed sources.)

- Both hot and sweet peppers come in myriad colors and complement many other plant palettes.

Boxed Gardens

Boxed gardens spark the imagination. They're small, neat, clean, and easy to handle. You can walk all the way around them. You can thin the plants without having to get dirty.

A boxed garden is not really a true box with a bottom; it's more of a frame. To make one all you have to do is measure out the area you want to enclose, prepare the soil, and then frame the space with standard 2x10 redwood planks, set slightly into the earth to stay in place. For greater stability, you can nail the corners together. A box like this is so easy to handle that it appeals to one's sense of energy conservation! Build one box, plant it, and then over the next few weeks create the entire garden, adding one box at a time. Boxes can easily be made into raised beds by building the planks up to the desired height, and topping them with a flat plank board to make a seat (convenient while you're picking out those few weeds that might occur).

Generally, plant one or two vegetables per bed, with corn planted in three separate beds about two weeks apart (Figure 1-2). Split most beds in two, planting a different vegetable in each section. These split sections can also be subdivided into thirds and planted two weeks apart. Plant all root and leafy vegetables this way. Train cucumbers, cantaloupe, beans, and other vines and trailers up stakes or trellises. (In California we can't plant winter crops such as cabbage, onions, carrots, or lettuce in hot summer areas, but we can use these split sections in our winter garden.)

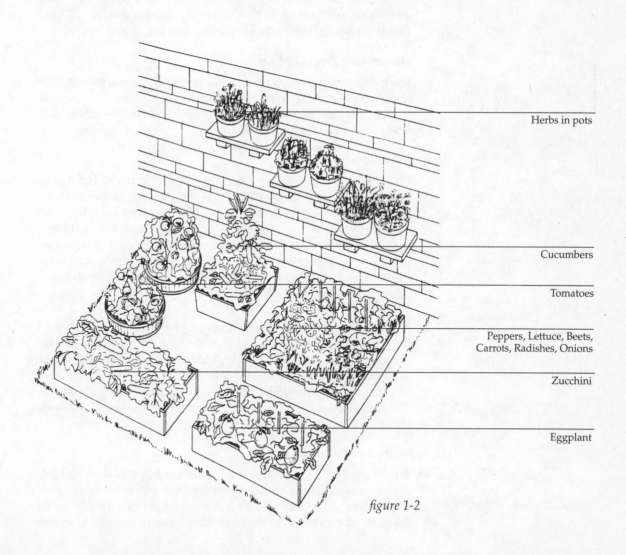

Herbs in pots

Cucumbers

Tomatoes

Peppers, Lettuce, Beets,
Carrots, Radishes, Onions

Zucchini

Eggplant

figure 1-2

Planning Tips

Lay It Out

During the planning stage, most gardeners like to lay out the beds directly on the ground so they can get an idea of what the finished garden will look like. Square or rectangular beds can be marked with wooden or plastic stakes and strings.

For a round bed, drive a peg into the ground; attach a cord with another peg on the loose end, and draw a circle as though you were using a compass.

Garden Measure

If you don't have a measuring tape, substitute a tough cord that will not stretch (such as clothesline cord) with knots every 10 feet. This is especially useful for measuring bed width and length.

Minimizing Frost Damage

Frost damage in the spring can be especially destructive to vegetable crops in some areas of California. To minimize loss, avoid sloping sites against solid fences, walls, and hedges since frost tends to form at the base of these.

Microclimates

Planning becomes easier when you know the microclimates in your garden. They vary on the sides of the house, at the northern sides of bushes, and in other places. To plot your own little climates, use a thermometer and a light meter and take readings around the yard. These readings can help you decide where to put heat- and light-loving plants (tomatoes, squash) and even those vegetables that need shade during hot summers (lettuce).

How Much Time?

Smart gardeners estimate the amount of time they are going to have to spend putting in and maintaining their gardens before they decide on size. As a rough guide, figure on spending about 40 minutes to spade up a 100-square-foot area. Allow 45 minutes to plant it and 30 minutes to an hour per week for cultivation. You will also need 30 minutes for changing the water. It will take about nine times longer for a 30x30-foot garden.

Year-Round Gardening?

It pays to plan for a fall garden (or winter in many parts of California) as well as for the spring. Often you can plant in July, August, September, and October for an autumn harvest (see the California Climate Map, inside back cover). Your county extension service can usually give you the latest planting date in your area for a fall harvest.

For the Whole Yard

Consider working your vegetables into small plots in front of your shrubbery. Some vegetables can be grown in flower beds, others in containers on a patio or front porch.

Dividing the Garden

Dividing the garden into sections helps to facilitate the rotation of crops. It also aids in keeping records of what is planted from season to season and from year to year.

Oops!

Don't forget to make your fence openings wide enough for the equipment you need. The width of a wheelbarrow is measured from knuckle to knuckle when you grip the wheelbarrow handles; the width of a clothes basket from elbow to elbow when carrying the basket. These measurements determine the width of gates, passageways, and other openings.

CHAPTER TWO

HOW TO GET YOUR SOIL READY

The condition of your garden soil can make or break the productivity of the garden. Yet, what most people see when they look at their soil is a lot of dirt. It's the stuff that comes into the house on our clothes, shoes, fingernails, and dogs. However, soil is much more than that.

The organic material in the soil or the raw material that you deposit there—leaves, grass clippings, garbage, and so forth—contains essential elements that plants can use to foster their own growth. Unfortunately, these elements are tied up in such a way that our vegetables can't touch them. Fortunately for our plants, every square foot of soil swarms with millions of bacteria and other microorganisms, and these bacteria rip into the organic material in the soil, breaking it down and converting it to forms that plants can gobble up.

How fast the soil bacteria act on this raw material depends on the nature of the material itself, the temperature, the amount of air available, and the soil moisture. In the spring, when the soil warms up, both the numbers of bacteria in the soil and the bacterial action increase tremendously. When you add fresh organic material, the bacteria immediately attack it, breaking it down into food for your plants.

What gardener doesn't dream about having perfect soil—crumbly, well-aerated, sweet-smelling stuff that would grow 10-foot-high corn, elephant-size watermelons, and even lip-smacking tomatoes? Technically, the perfect garden soil contains 50 percent solid matter and 50 percent "pore" space (the space that allows absorption of liquid). Moisture occupies about half the pore spaces, soil air the other half. Of the solid matter, roughly 45 percent should be mineral matter, 5 percent organic. The water in this soil carries the dissolved nutrients easily to plants' roots, and the air in the soil provides a constant supply of oxygen while at the same time carrying off carbon dioxide. It also contains all the nutrients necessary to make your plants healthy.

Know Your Soil

Most garden soils are far from perfect, yet many gardeners plant without making any improvements and then wonder why their vegetables are far from ideal. They drool enviously over the vegetables pictured in advertisements for plant food, but those luscious vegetables started out in good soil. Most backyard soils are going to need a little help. If you look in your own garden, you're likely to find clay, sand, and silt.

Clay soil is composed of fine, flat, waferlike particles that fit together tightly and take in water slowly. Chemically, clay is chiefly silicon and aluminum, with small amounts of sodium, magnesium, iron, calcium, and potassium. When you sprinkle a clay bed, the water runs off instead of sinking in. If the clay particles do absorb moisture, they hold it too tightly for the plants to use much of it. When it's rubbed between the fingers, wet clay soil feels smooth, soft, and slippery.

When clay dries, it often has the consistency of brick. The particles are so compressed that there isn't any space for air to penetrate, and plant roots have great difficulty forcing their way down. Plants grown in untreated clay soil are often stunted and have pale green or yellow leaves.

Sandy soil is at the opposite end of the scale. It is lighter than clay but has particles 25 times larger. While sand is easy to dig in, it has almost no capacity to store water, which moves freely through the soil and quickly leaches out the nutrients. Sandy soils warm up faster than clay soils and reflect a considerable amount of heat. Most sandy soils, however, contain enough clay and silt to retain some water and nutrients.

Sandy soil rubbed between the fingers feels grainy and gritty; gravelly soils are self-evident. Plants grown in sandy or gravelly soils frequently have yellow or pale green leaves.

Silt falls somewhere between clay and sand. It consists of medium-size gritty particles that pack down hard almost like clay and is seldom very fertile. If a silt topsoil covers a layer of heavy clay, the plants may be stunted because the clay layer traps and holds water. Silty soil rubbed between the fingers feels slippery but has a grainy texture. Plants grown in silty soils often have pale green or yellow leaves.

Loam is the kind of soil every gardener wants, and although it isn't the theoretical ideal described earlier, it's close enough to grow great vegetables. Loam is crumbly granular soil that has close to even quantities of different-size particles and a good supply of humus (decomposed organic material). A combination of root growth, worms, and bacteria gives this soil's grains a good structure, enabling both adequate retention of water and proper drainage. Similarly, air moves freely through this soil, so roots can find their proper depth. Technically, the U.S. Department of Agriculture considers loam to consist of 7 to 27 percent clay, 28 to 50 percent silt, and 20 to 45 percent sand. Plants grown in loam are usually vigorous, healthy, and green.

Deciding What You Have

In addition to the touch-and-feel tests for clay, sand, and silt, you can take your own soil sample and then send it to a lab or conduct a quart-jar test at home that will give some quite sophisticated results.

To take a soil sample, follow these steps:

1. Select eight to 15 spots throughout the garden area. A zigzag pattern is best.

2. With a soil probe or garden spade, take a sample from each area, 8 inches deep.

3. Discard the top inch of surface.

4. Place the samples in a plastic bag and mix thoroughly.

5. Take one cup of the mixed soil and put it in a small plastic bag if you are shipping it to a lab. You can also use some soil from this mixture to carry out a test yourself.

To conduct your own test, follow these steps:

1. Place a soil sample in a quart jar and fill the jar with water until it's two-thirds full.

2. Shake well and let the contents settle for a few hours.

3. Examine the soil layers. At the bottom you'll find coarse sand and pebbles, fine sand and silt next, then clay, with the water at the top.

4. Take a ruler and measure from the bottom of the jar to the top of the clay layer; this is the height of the entire soil column. Determine the percentage of each of the three soil components, by dividing the height of each layer (in inches)—clay, silt and fine sand, pebbles and coarse sand—by the height of the entire soil column (Figure 2-1).

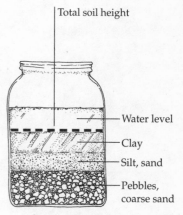

figure 2-1

You can also estimate the percentage of each material visually, but using a ruler will give precise amounts. For example, if the total soil column measures 4 inches and there is a 1-inch clay layer, divide 4 into 1 to obtain the percentage of clay (25 percent). When you have done this for all three layers, compare your results with the USDA's percentages for loam.

Improving Soil Structure

You can improve clay, silty, and sandy soils by adding massive amounts of organic material. We like to shovel 6–8 inches of compost, ground bark, sawdust, leaf mold, manure, or peat moss over the top of the garden area (adding nutrients according to the formulas on page 19) and then spade or rototill this layer into the soil.

Organic particles in clay soil hold the compacted clay particles apart while acting as a kind of glue to hold the fine clay particles together in crumbs. This opens up the soil and allows air and water to circulate freely, which gives vegetables a fighting chance.

Heavy clay soils can also be improved by adding 40 to 50 pounds of gypsum (available at nurseries) per 1,000 square feet. The positive calcium ions in the gypsum neutralize the negative sodium ions in the clay and allow the clay particles to group together, or flocculate, into bigger soil crumbs that create larger air spaces and permit good water and air penetration.

Adding fine-textured organic material to sandy soil fills the spaces among the grains and helps retain water both by stopping the flow and by absorbing some of it. As you get to know your soil, you may discover other structural impediments, such as rocky or shallow soil. If rocks are your problem, you'll have to bring in a foot or two of topsoil and do your gardening in raised beds or pick out the rocks a few at a time with a spading fork. Neither solution is easy or fun.

Shallow soil is a problem because there may be an impenetrable layer a foot or so below the soil surface that holds water, creating a kind of swamp in which it's virtually impossible to grow vegetables. This condition can produce stunted plants with pale green or yellow leaves. The problem can sometimes be solved by punching holes in the obstructing layer with an auger to let the water drain out.

To facilitate the best possible vegetable growth, the roots must be provided with plenty of space straight down. Some of these plants have roots that try to reach China. Tomato roots, for instance, often reach a depth of 10 feet or more; cabbage, 7–8 feet; and carrots, 5 feet (Figure 2-2). To provide for these root systems, you'd have to remove the impenetrable layers and replace them with topsoil. What a job that would be! Since most vegetables can survive in a depth of 1–2 feet, however, gardeners with shallow soil are best advised to avoid crops such as tomatoes, cabbage, and the like.

If you decide to go the raised-bed route, plant your garden in a bed that's 8–12 inches high and filled with equal parts loam, sand, and organic material (compost, rotted manure, and similar matter). These raised beds provide beneficial drainage, give the roots a good growing medium, and warm up faster in the spring than regular garden beds.

figure 2-2

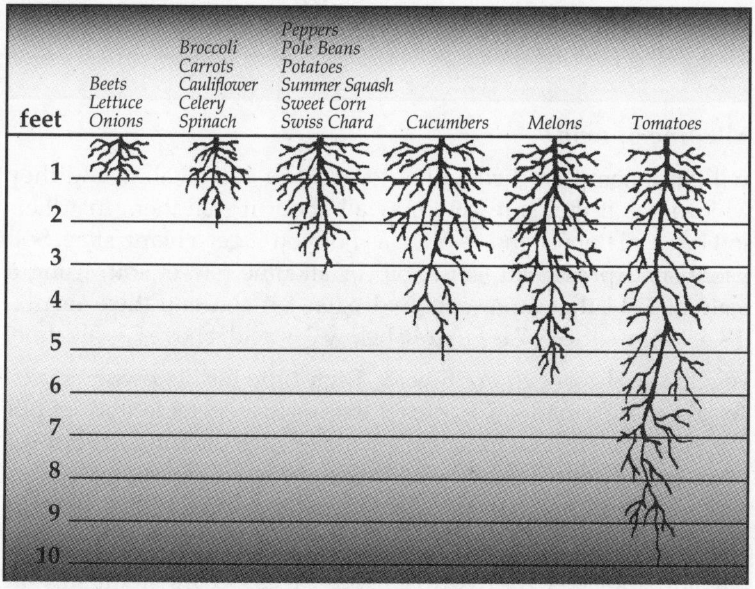

| feet | Beets Lettuce Onions | Broccoli Carrots Cauliflower Celery Spinach | Peppers Pole Beans Potatoes Summer Squash Sweet Corn Swiss Chard | Cucumbers | Melons | Tomatoes |

The Ultimate Intensive Bed

This method uses principles developed by Alan Chadwick (formerly at the University of California, Santa Cruz) for creating biodynamic beds. The quality of the resulting soil is excellent, but you must double-dig by hand, so it is several times the work of other methods. Here's how to do it.

1. Cover the entire bed with 6–8 inches of an organic and nutrient mixture.

2. Dig a trench along one entire side, about one spade wide and one spade deep (a spade is about 9–10 inches). Put the excavated topsoil (which contains the organic-nutrient mix) just outside the bed; you'll need it in step 6.

3. Loosen the subsoil in the trench that you just created, digging down another 9–10 inches. Don't turn this soil over; just loosen it with your shovel. This will give you a fairly coarse mixture at the bottom and a fine mixture at the top.

4. Remove one spade depth of topsoil (including the organic-nutrient mix) from a strip of bed paralleling the trench that you opened, filling in this first trench as you go.

5. In the newly created trench, loosen the subsoil as before, then fill it with the topsoil and organic-nutrient mixture from the third strip, and so on.

6. When you reach the last row of the bed, fill in this trench with the topsoil plus organic mixture that you laid aside from the first trench.

7. Allow the soil surface to stay rough for a few days so that air can get into the bed. Then, using a spade and a rake, work the topsoil until it has a fine texture. Make sure that you break up all clods.

Alkaline or Acid?

Tell gardeners that their soil is too acid or too alkaline and they will nod as if they already know all about it. Tell them that their soil has a pH of 5.7 and as often as not you'll get a blank stare. Soil scientists express acid (sour soil) or alkaline (sweet soil) using a scale of 1–14 that represents hydrogen-ion concentration, or pH. It's actually simple: 7 is neutral; below 7 is acid; above 7 is alkaline.

Vegetables, however, are finicky. Each type has its own particular pH requirements. Chapter 9 lists each vegetable and its pH range. Since it isn't practical to make one planting section of your garden one pH and another section a different pH, most gardeners compromise on a slightly acid to neutral soil (pH 6.5–7).

Soils turn acid when calcium and magnesium ions are leached out and replaced by hydrogen ions. This occurs frequently in areas of heavy rainfall. Soils become more alkaline as calcium, manganese, and sodium ions accumulate and replace hydrogen ions. This often occurs in areas of low rainfall and poor drainage, as well as in regions where there are natural limestone deposits. The soil in the Southwest tends to be alkaline; in the Northeast it tends to be slightly acid.

If your soil is too alkaline, your plants may show yellow leaves, stunted growth, and leaf margins that appear burnt. Alkaline soils are sometimes too salty, and, in extreme cases, heavy brown or white salt deposits are left on the soil surface. Acid soil is not easy to detect visually and will generally require some sort of pH test.

Testing pH is a simple task. The easiest device to use is a soil-test tape (which costs about $3.50). To find the pH of your garden, just press the tape against the soil and compare the color of the tape with the colors on the pH chart. A pH test kit (about $7) works on the same principle but utilizes liquid instead of the tape. A battery operated pH meter (about $50) automatically registers the pH when its prongs are placed in the soil.

If you need to make a number of pH tests on a continuing basis, a pH meter is the most convenient device. If you'll be making only a few tests in a small plot, a soil-test tape or pH test kit will do the job.

To counteract acidity, add ground or dolomitic lime at the rate of about 4 pounds per 100 square feet for each unit of pH below 6.5. Some gardeners also use hydrated (burned) lime, but it leaches away rapidly and can burn your hands. To correct alkaline soil, add sulfur at the rate of about 4 pounds per 100 square feet for each unit of pH above 7. Gypsum and soil aluminum sulfate can also be used. Follow the directions on the package.

The California Soil Map (inside front cover) will give you a general idea of the soil conditions in your area.

Plants Get Hungry, Too

Although nutrition is as important to plants as it is to people, many gardeners simply ignore the issue. Then they wonder what's wrong with their vegetables.

Vegetables generally need 15 nutrients for maximum growth. Three elements—oxygen, carbon, and hydrogen—come from air and water. The other 12 exist in the soil. Nitrogen, phosphorus, and potassium are the major macronutrients needed by vegetables in large amounts.

Nitrogen, a major element in plant nutrition, produces leaf growth and gives leaves a vibrant dark green color. It helps generate a healthy root system, increases the set of fruit, and nourishes soil microorganisms. It is especially important for such leafy vegetables as cabbage, lettuce, spinach, and collards. Nitrogen deficiency causes yellow leaves and stunted growth. Excess nitrogen delays flowering, produces excessive growth, reduces the quality of fruits, and renders crops less resistant to disease.

Blood meal contains 7 to 15 percent nitrogen. It can be mixed as a liquid fertilizer, using one tablespoon to a gallon of water. Hoof and horn meal contains 7 to 15 percent nitrogen. Cottonseed meal has 6 to 9 percent. Fish meal and fish emulsion contain up to 10 percent nitrogen and nearly as much phosphorus. Bonemeal may contain up to 3 percent nitrogen. Follow directions on package.

Phosphorus stimulates early root formation, hastens maturity, and is important for the development of fruit, flowers, and seeds; it also helps provide disease resistance and winterkill protection. A phosphorus deficiency causes dark or bluish green leaves followed by bronzing, reddening, or purpling, especially along veins and margins. Lower leaves are sometimes yellow, drying to greenish brown or black. Plants are often stunted, spindly, late to mature. Excess phosphorus produces iron and zinc deficiencies in corn, beans, tomatoes, and other plants.

Phosphorus fertilizers include bonemeal, averaging 20 to 25 percent phosphoric acid, and phosphate rock, a finely ground rock powder that contains about 30 to 33 percent phosphoric acid, plus minor and trace elements.

Potash (potassium) is important in plants' ability to manufacture sugar and starches. It improves the color of flowers and the length of time fruit is edible. Potash promotes vigorous root systems and is essential in growing good root crops. It produces strong stems, reduces water loss, increases vigor, combats disease, and reduces winterkill. Potash deficiency causes dry or scorched leaves, and there may be small dead areas along the margins and between the leaf veins. Plants are sometimes stunted and appear rusty while their fruit is often small and thin-skinned. Excess potash produces coarse, poorly colored fruit. Nitrogen, phosphorus, and potash (potassium) are provided in standard commercial fertilizers.

Potassium is supplied by granite dust (up to 8 percent potash), hardwood ashes (up to 10 percent), softwood ashes (about 5 percent), and greensand (up to 9 percent).

You should add humus and these three nutrients to your garden before you replant. You can add dry fertilizers to the soil in the form of a packaged, preblended organic mix or you can mix your own from organic ingredients. Every two to four weeks, give your entire garden a supplemental feeding of fish emulsion. Crops that are heavy feeders will especially benefit from these supplements.

TABLE 2-1 NATURAL PLANT FOODS

TYPE	SOURCE	COMPOSITION (%)		
		NITROGEN	PHOSPHORUS	POTASSIUM
Animal Manure (fresh)	cattle	0.53	0.29	0.48
	chicken	0.89	0.48	0.83
	horse	0.55	0.27	0.57
	sheep	0.89	0.48	0.83
Animal Manure (dried)	cattle	2.00	1.80	3.00
	horse	0.80	0.20	0.60
	sheep	1.40	1.00	3.00
Animal Tankage	dried blood meal	9–14	-	-
	bonemeal	1.6–25	23–25	-
	dried fish scrap	6.5–10	4–8	-
	fish emulsion	5–10	2.0	2.0
Pulverized Rock Powder	rock phosphate	-	38–41	-
	greensand	-	1.35	4.1–9.5
Vegetable	cottonseed meal	6.7–7.4	2–3	1.5–2.0
	seaweed	1.7	0.8	5.0
	soybean meal	6.0	1.0	2.0
	oak leaves	0.8	0.4	0.2
	wood ashes	-	1.5	7.0

Organic Fertilizers

You can buy a good organic fertilizer from a nursery or garden center or order one from many catalog seed firms. You can also mix a worthy organic fertilizer yourself. Here are three formulas.

FORMULA ONE	FORMULA TWO	FORMULA THREE
2 pints blood meal 4 pints bonemeal 3 pints greensand	4 pints cottonseed meal 4 pints bonemeal 3 pints greensand	2 pints blood meal 4 pints bonemeal 2 pints wood ashes

You can substitute for any nutrient in a formula as long as you keep the same nitrogen: phosphorus: potassium ratio. For instance, cottonseed meal contains 7 percent nitrogen as compared to the 15 percent found in blood meal; this means you will need roughly twice as much cottonseed meal as blood meal. Store your mixture in small plastic bags to use when you make up your garden beds. Pints are easy units to handle, but you can make up these mixes in any quantity as long as you create the same relationship among the ingredients. For the average garden, use 1½ gallons per 100 square feet.

Micronutrients

Magnesium, manganese, copper, zinc, iron, sulfur, calcium, molybdenum, and boron are secondary nutrients, or micronutrients, and are needed only in extremely small quantities. However, it's important to understand what each of these elements does for vegetables and how to tell if any are missing.

Magnesium is important in chlorophyll production. It promotes early and uniform maturity and is important in fruit growth. Magnesium deficiency causes yellowing of the lower leaves at the margins, tips, and between the veins. The leaves wilt from the bottom up until only the top leaves appear normal. Magnesium deficiency in corn shows up on the leaves as yellow stripes. Excess magnesium may produce a calcium deficiency. Magnesium deficiency can be corrected with a fertilizer containing magnesium sulfate or Epsom salts—about 1 pound per 1,000 square feet of garden space.

Manganese is important for green plant development. It is essential to both respiration and normal chlorophyll formation. Manganese deficiency causes stunted growth and mottled yellowing of the lower leaves. Excess manganese may produce small dead areas in the leaves with yellow borders around them. A deficiency can be corrected with manganese sulfate. Follow the instructions on the package. Organic matter also contains manganese.

An enzyme activator, **copper** plays vital roles in both chlorophyll and protein formation. Copper deficiency produces dark green, grayish-olive, or blue leaf edges that curl upward. Flowering and fruit development is checked, while carrots are poorly colored and bitter. Excess copper stunts roots and prevents the uptake of iron. Copper deficiency can be corrected by applying about 6 ounces of copper sulfate per 1,000 square feet. You can also apply seaweed to the leaves or add well-rotted manure.

Another enzyme activator, **zinc** is necessary for normal chlorophyll production and cell division. Zinc deficiency brings about mottling, yellowing, or scorching of the tissues between veins. Satisfy this need by applying 8 ounces of zinc sulfate per 1,000 square feet. Ground phosphate rock also contains trace elements of zinc.

Iron promotes chlorophyll production. Insufficient iron causes mottling, yellowing, or scorching of the tissues between veins. A deficiency can be corrected by using a soluble organic iron complex, iron sulfate, or chelated iron. Seaweed also adds iron.

Sulfur helps maintain the dark green color of plants. It is also a constituent of proteins and growth-regulating hormones. If soil doesn't have enough sulfur, young leaves turn pale green or yellow while the older leaves remain green (yellowing in nitrogen-deficient plants starts with the older leaves). Plants become dwarfed and spindly. Most soils contain adequate sulfur, but if there is a lack, ammonium sulfate can be added.

Calcium promotes early root formation, improves general vigor, and increases resistance to disease. Calcium deficiency causes distortion in young stems, and stem tips die. Excess calcium can cause a deficiency (reduced intake) of potassium and magnesium. Inadequate amounts of calcium can be corrected by spraying plants with calcium nitrate or adding calcium sulfate (gypsum) to the soil. Follow the directions on the package.

Chlorophyll and sugar are formed with **molybdenum,** which is important for seed development and required by the nitrogen metabolism of all plants, although only in minute quantities. Insufficient molybdenum leads to stunted, crinkled leaves that are pale green or yellow and malformed. Remedy this deficiency by applying sodium or ammonium molybdate (1 pound per acre—about a teaspoonful per 1,000 square feet). You can also plant vegetables, and turn under at maturity.

Calcium utilization and normal cell division require **boron,** which also influences the conversion of nitrogen and sugars into more complex substances. A deficient amount of boron is shown in the scorching of tips and margins of younger leaves. Excess boron turns leaves yellowish red. Boron deficiency can be corrected by spraying plants with a borax solution (1 teaspoon per gallon).

The availability of all nutrients needed for plant growth also depends on the soil's pH, so keep that in mind when you consider the possible causes of a problem. In addition, the amounts given here for correcting micronutrient deficiencies are minimum ones. Severe deficiencies demand larger quantities of individual nutrients. To determine exact amounts, have the soil tested. Soil labs are listed in the phone book.

Table 2-2 provides a quick summary of the preceding information. Armed with this, you should be able to diagnose and treat many of the problems described in this chapter.

TABLE 2-2 SOIL AND NUTRITION PROBLEMS AT A GLANCE

WHAT's WRONG? WHAT TO LOOK FOR	POSSIBLE CAUSES	CURES
SOIL		
Stunted plants; pale yellow leaves.	Clay soil, soil too heavy (use the jar test).	Turn a 6–8-inch layer of organic material into the soil.
Yellow or pale leaves.	Sandy soil, soil too light (use the jar test).	Turn a 6–8-inch green layer of organic material into the soil.
Yellow or pale green leaves.	Silty soil (use the jar test).	Turn a 6–8-inch layer of organic material into the soil.
PH		
Stunted growth; burned leaf margins; yellowing leaves.	Soil too alkaline (test for pH).	Add sulfur at the rate of about 4 pounds per 100 square feet for each unit of pH above 7.
PH tests below 6.5.	Soil too acid (test for pH).	Add lime at the rate of about 4 pounds per 100 square feet for each unit of pH below 6.5.
NUTRITION		
Yellow leaves starting with the lower leaves; stunted growth.	Nitrogen deficiency.	Apply blood meal at the rate of 10 ounces per 100 square feet.
Bluish green leaves followed by bronzing or purpling, drying to a greenish brown or black.	Phosphorus deficiency.	Apply phosphate rock at the rate of ¾ pound per 100 square feet, or test soil and follow recommendations.
Dry or scorched leaves; dead areas along margins; plants stunted; rusty appearance.	Potash (potassium) deficiency.	Apply wood ashes or greensand at the rate of 1¼–1½ pounds per 100 square feet, or test soil and follow recommendations.
Mottling of lower leaves at margins, tips, between veins; leaves wilt from bottom up.	Magnesium deficiency.	Use 1 pound of Epsom salts per 1,000 square feet, or test soil and follow recommendations.
Mottled yellowing leaves; stunted growth.	Manganese deficiency.	Use manganese sulfate, or test soil and follow recommendations; large quantities of organic matter adds manganese.
Dark green, olive-gray leaf edges; edges curl upward.	Copper deficiency.	Use 6 ounces of copper sulfate per 1,000 square feet, or test soil and follow recommendations; spray liquid seaweed on leaves; well-rotted manure also adds copper.

TABLE 2-2 *(continued)*

WHAT'S WRONG? WHAT TO LOOK FOR	POSSIBLE CAUSES	CURES
NUTRITION *(continued)*		
Mottling, yellowing, or scorching of the tissues between veins.	Zinc deficiency.	Use 8 ounces of zinc sulfate per 1,000 square feet, or test soil and follow recommendations; ground phosphate rock contains traces of zinc.
Yellow leaves; green veins.	Iron deficiency.	Use a soluble iron complex, iron sulfate, or chelated iron, or test soil and follow recommendations; seaweed adds iron.
Young leaves turn pale green to yellow; older leaves remain green.	Sulfur deficiency.	Most soils contain adequate amounts of sulfur; if not, test soil and follow recommendations.
Stem tips die; distortion of young stems.	Calcium deficiency.	Spray plants with calcium nitrate or add calcium sulfate (gypsum), or test soil and follow recommendations.
Leaves pale green or yellow; leaves crinkled, stunted.	Molybdenum deficiency.	Use 1 teaspoon of sodium ammonium molybdate per 1,000 square feet, or test soil and follow recommendations; plant vegetables and turn under on maturity.
Scorching of tips and margins of younger leaves.	Boron deficiency.	Spray plants with borax solution (1 teaspoon per gallon), or test soil and follow recommendations.

Adding Organic Matter

Compost, a mixture of decomposed organic materials, is the best form of organic matter for your garden. It's a kind of humus, but the chemical breakdown takes place outside of the soil in a compost pile. When compost is introduced to garden soil, all of its nutrients are available to the plants.

Leaf mold, another fine soil amendment, is made of decomposed leaves. A recent study by the University of Arkansas found that 3 inches of well-decomposed leaf mold tilled into the upper 6 inches of soil can increase the production of most vegetables by 35 to 150 percent. (This study was conducted in experiment station beds.) To obtain this soil conditioner, you can put leaves in your compost pile, shred them with a leaf shredder or lawn mower, or buy leaf mold from a nursery.

Sawdust is an excellent soil conditioner. It is easy to use, costs little, and aerates the soil. However, unless you use thoroughly composted sawdust, you must add nitrogen; fresh sawdust will rob the soil of nitrogen during decomposition.

Peat moss consists of the decomposed remains of prehistoric plants that were compressed for thousands of years at the bottoms of bogs and swamps. Peat moss has good aeration and the highest water retention of all soil conditioners. You do not need to add nitrogen.

Animal manures are vital to a garden. Different manures have their own properties and amounts of nitrogen, phosphorus, and potassium. Chicken, horse, sheep, and rabbit manures are known as "hot" manures because of their high nitrogen content. Cow and swine manures are called "cold" manures because they are low in nitrogen and break down fairly slowly.

Use rotted manure, not fresh. The bacteria in soil needs extra nitrogen to break down fresh manure, and this can divert nitrogen from your plants. Manure that has already decomposed is in a form your plants can use immediately.

Creating Compost

Since compost improves soil texture and adds nutrients, every gardener should prepare compost and turn it into the soil each spring. A compost consists of organic matter that has been piled up and allowed to decompose to a point where plants readily can absorb its elements. Decaying materials such as leaves, sawdust, manures, grass clippings, food scraps (no meat), and similar items form compost. You can build your compost pile on open ground, in a bin, even in a garbage can.

Basics

Good composting depends on particle size, the amount of nitrogen available, the heat produced, the moisture in the pile, and how often the pile is turned.

The smaller the particle size, the faster the decomposition, because the decomposers (bacteria) have more surface area to work on. If the leaves, stems, and other materials are shredded before being added to the compost pile, they'll decay faster and be ready sooner.

The bacteria in the pile need nitrogen. If there is too much carbon-rich organic material in proportion to the available nitrogen, the bacteria will not work as fast, and the decomposition will go slowly. You will notice low heat production in the compost pile.

While leaves make one of the best organic conditioners, they are sometimes hard to compost because they consist primarily of carbon, with little nitrogen. Correct this imbalance by adding nitrogen in the form of blood meal, chicken manure, or massive amounts of grass clippings.

A mixture of about two parts carbonaceous material (leaves, straw, wood chips, and food scraps) and one part nitrogenous material (grass clippings, kitchen vegetable waste, weeds, and manure) keeps the action going. If the pile doesn't heat up, add large amounts of grass clippings, dried blood meal, or steamed bonemeal.

Compost must heat up to 140–160°F for fruitful bacterial action to occur. Smaller compost piles lose heat easily, which slows bacterial action. A minimum size for a "quick-cooking" open-air pile is 3 cubic feet.

Moisture is also essential for decomposition to take place. Make sure the pile remains about as damp as a squeezed-out wet sponge. Just put your hand inside and feel—but be careful because it can be surprisingly hot. If necessary, add water until the matter has the right consistency, but remember that too much water reduces the oxygen available to the bacteria.

These are the steps to creating a compost pile:

1. Clear off an area of ground that's 5–6 feet square.

2. Put down a 6-inch layer of fairly coarse material such as twigs, brush, and cornstalks. This provides ventilation underneath the pile.

3. Start building the pile in layers. Put down a 6-inch layer of vegetation, grass clippings, leaves, weeds, vegetable remains, and table scraps.

4. Sprinkle this 6-inch layer of organic material with a fertilizer that has a high concentration of nitrogen. Use 2 pounds (1½ pints) of dried blood meal or 1 pound bonemeal (1½ cups) for every square foot of surface.

5. Add about an inch of soil. The soil contains bacteria that will break down the organic material.

6. Repeat this layering procedure until the pile is 5 feet high.

7. Water down the pile until it is moist but not saturated.

8. Mix the compost once a month using a manure fork. Turn the top and side materials into the center. Most of the bacterial action takes place there because it is the hottest spot in the pile.

A bin (Figure 2-3) makes composting neat and easy. A bin in its simplest form is any sort of container that surrounds the compost, such as a chicken-wire structure, a large construction-wire loop, four window screens nailed together, or a wall of rocks or cement blocks. The most elaborate bins have separate compartments for fresh compost, partially decomposed compost, and ripe compost. Bins range in size from about 3 feet square and 3 feet high to 5 feet in diameter and 3–4 feet in height.

Build your compost pile within the bin just as you would if there were no enclosure. Keep it moist and turn it with a spading fork until it's ripe.

The Green Machine

Some gardeners grow plants to be plowed or tilled under as "green manure." Green-manure crops reach deep into the subsoil, absorbing valuable nutrients into their tissues. When the crop is turned under, it improves the soil's texture by increasing the humus content and building up the available nutrients in the topsoil. Common green manures include alfalfa, clover, buckwheat, millet, rye, and grass.

Many of these crops are an excellent source of nitrogen, especially legumes (such as peas and beans), which have the ability to turn nitrogen from the air into soil forms that plants can use. Experiments with green manures show that they increase the yields of potatoes, corn, and beans tremendously. For most gardeners, green manuring can reduce fertilizer needs by 50 percent.

Earthworms: Mother Nature's Soil Arrangers

Organic gardeners have long known that the earthworm is the best thing that can happen to a garden. Earthworms improve soil as they burrow through it. They ingest and grind the soil, mix it with calcium carbonate, and send it on through to be digested by enzymes. The resultant earthworm castings contain nitrogen, phosphorus, and potash. The earthworms' work augments air space and root access while improving water absorption.

Gray-pink earthworms (*Helodrilus caliginosus* and *Helodrilus foetida*) do the best work. They can't be introduced in hard clay soils because they'll leave, but they'll make a fairly good soil even better. The fishworm (*Eisenia foetida*) is a good addition to compost piles.

Crop Rotation

In addition to adding compost and other ingredients to your garden soil each growing season, you should rotate the crops. Some vegetables make heavy demands on the soil (they're called heavy feeders), others take out very little (light feeders), while legumes (beans and peas) actually restore soil fertility. Moving the kinds of vegetables around keeps the soil in good shape throughout the years and even adds to its vigor.

Heavy feeders should be followed when possible by legumes. After the legumes, plant the light feeders. In an intensive garden, this rotation is a little difficult because the taller plants are on the

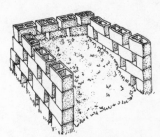

Cement-block bin

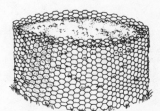

Chicken-wire bin

Closed wooden bin

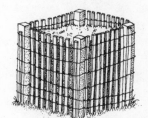

Picket-fence bin

Rough stone bin

north side and the smaller plants on the south side. But if you want to give the soil a break, you must restore the balance whenever possible.

When you create the right soil conditions at the start and infuse the soil with nutritional supplements each growing season, you wind up with a soil that will continually grow sound, healthy vegetables with only a minimum of additional effort.

LIGHT FEEDERS	HEAVY FEEDERS	SOIL RESTORERS
beets	broccoli	beans
carrots	brussels sprouts	peas
onions	cabbage	
radishes	cauliflower	
rutabagas	corn	
turnips	cucumbers	
	eggplant	
	kale	
	lettuce	
	melons	
	mustard greens	
	New Zealand spinach	
	okra	
	peppers	
	spinach	
	squash	
	Swiss chard	
	tomatoes	

Soil and Composting Tips

These Top 30 suggestions from California gardeners will help save time or solve soil and composting problems.

Quick Soil Typing

To quickly identify the type of soil in your garden, grab a handful of moist soil, squeeze it tightly, then release it. If it keeps its shape, some clay is present. If you can model with it and it feels smooth, it contains a lot of clay. If it crumbles, feels gritty, and stains your hand, it is a mixture of sand and clay. A silty soil feels smooth but cannot be modeled. A very sandy soil slips through your fingers.

Soil Temperature Management

Most gardeners measure the gardening season from the last frost in the spring to the first frost in the fall. In reality, it runs from the time the soil temperature hits 45°F until it falls below 45°F. (The soil bacteria that make the nitrogen available to roots only become active as the soil approaches 40°F.) Check the temperature with a soil thermometer.

Preconditioning

To wake up your garden in the spring, apply an even layer of compost, rotted manure, or dry organic fertilizer over the soil and proceed with a shallow rototilling or spading (4–6 inches deep). This helps break up soil chunks, mixes in dead plants, aerates the soil, and starts bacterial action. Leave the bed alone for a few weeks, then seriously work it.

Quick Check

You can't spade or rototill soggy soil. To determine when to go to work, pick up a clod and press it with your thumb. Soil that is ready for work falls apart. If it won't break apart easily, give it some time to dry.

Mother Nature's Help

Mother Nature will help you break up heavy soil if you let her. In the fall, pile the sod to form ridges and furrows in your garden. This exposes the soil to frost and rain; the weather action will break up the particles over time to make them more workable.

Improving Heavy Soil

The best way to tame heavy soil is to mix sand and weathered ashes (ashes left outside for several months) into the bed. This improves drainage and makes the soil easier to work.

Rock Screen

The easiest way to handle rocky soil is to sift it through a screen. Build a 4x4-foot screen using two-by-fours, and prop it over the bed. Starting with a 4x4-foot section of the bed, put all the soil through the screen; remove the rocks to a depth of about 6 inches. Move the screen down to the next section of the bed and repeat.

Quick Additive

Soil additives don't have to be long-lasting to be effective. Sawdust, for instance, which breaks down fairly quickly, may be more directly beneficial to vegetables than more durable additives. (Remember that sawdust robs plants of nitrogen initially, so you need to add blood meal or a similar nitrogenous fertilizer to the soil.)

Compost Helpers

To enrich your soil the easy way, try adding Red Wiggler earthworms, which you can buy from any worm farm. They excel at breaking down compost. To keep the Red Wiggler working and multiplying, you must add generous amounts of fresh manure or compost. Otherwise they will disappear from your bed.

Spading the Garden

There's a right way and a wrong way to spade your garden. If you cut the soil straight down, you can then turn it over without difficulty. But if you cut at an angle, you won't penetrate deeply enough to be able to turn the clods completely over.

Tilling Heavy Soil

If you rototill an especially heavy clay soil that is slow to dry out below the surface, it will become lumpy and extremely hard as it dries. To solve this, till 3–4 inches down and let the bed dry for a day. Then till again to the full depth.

Cutting Down on Weeds

To minimize the weed problem, till the soil thoroughly and let it sit for a day or two. Then till it again and let it sit four to five days. Besides killing the roots of grasses and weeds, this procedure also aerates the soil far better than a single effort can.

Leaf Mold

To improve vegetable yields, try leaf mold. In a loamy garden soil, 2–3 inches of leaf mold have increased yields of broccoli, eggplant, and cucumber 25–50 percent.

Keeping the Soil Light

Newly cultivated beds often compact easily when gardeners walk on them to weed or plant seedlings. To keep the soil fluffy while you're working in the garden, place boards at least 6 inches wide across the beds. This distributes your weight evenly across a larger area to prevent compression.

Garden Drainage

Here's a simple test that will indicate the quality of drainage in your garden. Dig a hole 2 feet square and 2 feet deep at the lowest part of your garden. One week after a period of heavy rain, check the hole. No standing water means you have good drainage. If some water is pooled at the bottom, the drainage is good enough for plants with shallow roots.

Water-Saving Mulch

An effective water-saving mulch is one that is thick enough to create dead air space. This means a 1–2-inch layer of mostly ½-inch bark particles or a 3-inch layer of larger bark pieces.

Leaf Mold Mulch

A thin layer of leaf mold makes a great mulch. It conserves soil moisture and controls weeds that haven't emerged by depriving them of sunlight and air. Leaf mold also helps prevent organic fertilizers from leaching out of the soil. To create leaf mold, pick the leaves up in your lawn mower bag and place them in a leaf compost pile. The shredding speeds up decay.

Newspaper Mulch

Shredded newspapers (as well as sheets) make an excellent mulch. For protection from cold weather, spread about 6 inches over the bed toward the end of the season. But don't use colored pages because the ink contains lead, which should be nowhere near a food garden.

Biodegradable Mulch

To get all the advantages of a plastic-type mulch without having to pick it up in the spring, try the special biodegradable paper mulches. This thick, dark material holds weeds down for a season; it can then be tilled into the soil where it will rot away. Cost is around 9¢ a square foot.

Lawn Mower Shredder

A good way to speed up compost action is to chop leaves and plant material with a rotary mower. Just run over the debris a few times, collect it in the mower bag, and throw it on the pile. You can also dump chopped material directly onto the garden bed in the fall and rototill it in the soil. The bed will be ready to plant by spring.

Oil Drum Compost

An empty oil drum can be a good container for compost. Cut a 20x12-inch slit in the bottom of a 50-gallon oil drum, and hinge the lid. Toss in coffee grounds, eggshells, peelings, greens, and a limited amount of grass clippings. Add a shovelful of soil and mix together. The compost will be ready to use in six to eight weeks.

Compost in a Trash Can

The advantage of making compost in a trash can is that it won't have the smell of an open pile or bin. Use a galvanized trash can, punch about 10 holes in the bottom, scrape off the ground, and set the can 1 inch into the ground. Fill it up with grass clippings, leaves, soil, peat moss, and kitchen scraps. The compost will be ready in about six weeks. (Figure 2-4).

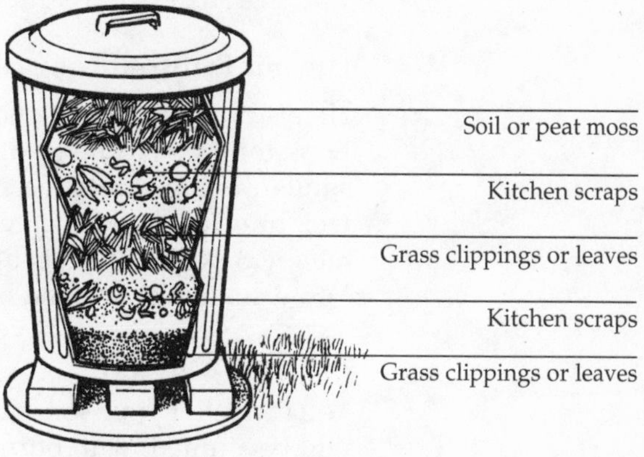

Soil or peat moss

Kitchen scraps

Grass clippings or leaves

Kitchen scraps

Grass clippings or leaves

figure 2-4

Spot Composting

You can improve the soil for growing tomatoes, eggplant, and peppers by spot composting. In the fall, bury kitchen scraps 3 inches deep in 18–20-inch-diameter holes wherever you expect to plant the seedlings. These spots will be usable garden space the following spring.

Long-Term Compost

If you have brush that's too coarse or woody to compost quickly or to shred, heap it in a long-term compost pile. It usually takes several years to break down, but this pile will allow you to get rid of material you can't handle any other way. Birds will like the pile, but if *you* don't you can hide it behind some shrubs or a fence.

Inner Compost Temperature

Most gardeners hate checking the inner temperature of their compost pile. Make it easy by mounting a candy thermometer on a 6-foot pole. This allows you to reach into the pile (to make sure it is heating up) without burning your fingers.

Compost Pile Solutions

Here are the most common problems that gardeners have with compost.

- The compost has a bad odor. The problem: Not enough air. The solution: Turn it.

- The center of the pile is dry. The problem: Not enough water. The solution: Moisten materials while turning the pile.

- The compost is damp and warm in the middle, but nowhere else. The problem: The pile is too small. The solution: Build a bigger pile.

- The heap is damp and smells sweet but won't heat up. The problem: Lack of nitrogen. The solution: Mix in a nitrogen source such as grass clippings, fresh manure, or blood meal.

Organic Fertilizer Language

Here's how to calculate how much nitrogen is in your fertilizer. Look for the percentage of nitrogen on the sack of blood meal or similar organic fertilizer. Multiply that percentage times the weight of the sack's contents. For example, 10 pounds of blood meal (13 percent nitrogen) contains 1.3 pounds actual nitrogen. You want about 1 pound of nitrogen per 1,000 square feet of soil.

Alkaline Soil

You can tell if your soil is too alkaline without testing. The plants will be stunted, with burned leaf margins and yellowing leaves. The solution is to add sulfur.

Foliar Feeding

Anytime you notice signs of nutrient deficiency in your plants, foliar feeding is a quick answer. Make up a weak solution of seaweed or fish emulsion (follow the directions on the container), and spray it on the leaves.

Liquid Manure

To make a quick liquid fertilizer, soak cattle or sheep manure in water until it just colors the water. Drain this liquid through a cloth, and pour it into a container to use on your garden vegetables.

CHAPTER THREE

WHEN AND HOW TO PLANT:
AN OVERALL GUIDE

Vegetables are divided into warm season and cool season crops. Different classes of vegetables require different amounts of heat in order to grow.

Generally, plants that we harvest for their fruit (the part of the plant in which seeds are produced), such as tomatoes, squash, peppers, eggplant, melons, and lima beans, need ample heat and long days. Even when there's no longer any danger of frost, there must be enough heat during the day to satisfy a plant's requirements, or it will just sit there and do nothing. Tomatoes planted in April may not grow for quite a while. Then the days turn warm and the plants suddenly take off. Furthermore, the plants set out early in the season never seem to catch up with the plants set out later; cool weather impedes development.

Cool season plants, on the other hand, do well when the temperature is on the low side. Generally speaking, these are the leafy and root vegetables, such as carrots, beets, spinach, cabbage, and lettuce. Peas qualify as a cool season plant even though the fruit is harvested. When the weather is cool and the days short, these plants put all their energy into forming leafy or root materials, but when the days warm up, they stop this activity and start going to seed. As a result, you usually have to plant cool season vegetables early so that they can achieve the right size before the weather becomes too hot. You can also plant them late in the growing season so they mature in the cooler days of fall.

In addition to warm season and cool season vegetables, there are early and late varieties of most vegetables. The early varieties require less heat to mature than the late ones. If you want to get to work on your vegetables early, you can start with an early variety, then follow with later varieties of that particular vegetable—all season long.

If you live in an area where the temperature never rises above the 70s during the summer, you might want to plant only early varieties. (Chapter 9 provides seed sources for each vegetable and includes all early and late varieties.) It is important to choose varieties that are right for your growing season.

All this means that you have to learn the heat requirements of particular plants in order to know when to plant in your area. Experienced gardeners know exactly when to plant for best results. The California Climate Map (inside back cover) will help you make these decisions.

If you want to fool your friends into thinking you're a veteran gardener, just look for some of Mother Nature's best clues. The blooming of fairly common plants will signal the times to start planting far more accurately than arbitrary planting rules. Watch for these developments, then go to work:

CONDITION	PLANT
Development of color in flowers from spring bulbs, such as tulips or narcissus	Beets, carrots, leaf lettuce, onions, peas, radishes, and spinach
Appearance of plum and cherry blossoms	Head lettuce
Appearance of apple, quince, and strawberry blossoms	Everything else—cucumbers, melons, squash, tomatoes, etc.

For quick reference, vegetables can be divided into three categories:

1. Cool season crops (adapted to 55–70°F) tolerant of some frost: asparagus, beets, broccoli, brussels sprouts, cabbage, kale, mustard greens, New Zealand spinach, onions, radishes, rutabagas, spinach, turnips.

2. Cool season crops intolerant of some frost at maturity: carrots, cauliflower, endive, lettuce, peas, rhubarb, Swiss chard.

3. Warm season crops (requiring 65–80°F day and night) readily damaged by frost: beans, corn, cucumbers, eggplant, melons, okra, peppers, squash, tomatoes.

Planting With a California Climate Map

California is such a big, diverse state that it comprises 24 separate climate zones and almost every growing condition you can imagine. Spring planting times for vegetables are generally linked to the date of the last frost. (See chapter 9 for the planting times of individual vegetables.) The following list offers approximate dates for the last spring frost and first fall frost in the major areas of California.

REGION	LAST SPRING FROST	FIRST FALL FROST
Central Valley	March 1	November 15
Imperial Valley	January 30	December 20
North Coast	February 28	December 1
South Coast	January 30	December 15
Mountains	April 20	September 1

Fine-tune this information by referring to the California Climate Map (inside back cover). Within each of the 24 zones you'll find numerous microclimates where the average date of the last killing frost varies. Spring nighttime temperatures, for instance, are warmer near the ocean, cooler in inland valleys, and still cooler at higher elevations inland. Geographical points only a few miles apart may have radically different temperatures. Coming up with absolute dates isn't possible. The approximate frost dates and the climate map, however, can help you decide roughly when to plant spring and fall gardens.

To find out the last frost dates in your area, contact your county extension agent (farm advisor). See Appendix B for the addresses and phone numbers.

Planting by Moon Cycles

Some gardeners swear by this method. It's true that both the moon and the sun affect the tides and that the gravitational pull of the moon is greater at certain times than at others. If you closely observe the growth of your garden in relation to various phases of the moon, you'll notice some startling connections. Spurts of growth seem to coincide with the new moon and the full moon.

Here are some rules old-timers use:

1. Plant vegetables that grow above ground (such as tomatoes, squash, and lettuce) two nights before the new moon or in the first quarter of the new moon. You can also sow when the moon is waxing from half to full.

2. Plant root crops (such as carrots, beets, radishes, and onions) in the third quarter of the waning moon.

3. Transplant during the waning moon. The root will take imme-
    diately.

Giving Plants Their Space

No matter where the moon is, you had better know where your
plants are. If you are setting up a conventional garden (in rows),
follow the spacing instructions in chapter 9 or the directions on the
seed packets.

Spacing is even more important in an intensive bed. The object is
to arrange the plants so their outer leaves just touch one another
when the plants are about three-quarters mature, so the leaves car-
pet the bed when the plants are fully mature. The plants then
shade their own root zones, allowing the bed to retain moisture
(calling for less watering) and ensuring that almost no weeds come
through. The area beneath the leaves becomes its own fertile microclimate. At maturity, there's virtually a little greenhouse under
those leaves. Wind bounces off the foliage and sunshine glances
off. The area doesn't become too hot, too cold, or dried out by the
wind. Many gardeners believe that this microclimate is extremely
important to successful intensive beds.

When planting vegetables in an intensive garden, space the plants
a little closer together than is typically recommended on seed
packets or in instructions for seedlings. Corn, for instance, does
quite well planted 8 inches apart in intensive gardens, as opposed
to the 12-inch separation recommended for traditional gardens.

INTENSIVE PLANT SPACING IN INCHES

asparagus 12	cucumbers (caged) 4	onions..........................2–3
beans (bush).................4	eggplant...........................25	peas (supported)...........2
beans (pole)............6–10	kale 16	peppers 12–24
beets 2–3	lettuce (butterhead).......4–5	radishes..........................2
broccoli 15	lettuce (head) 10	rutabagas 6
brussels sprouts.........16	lettuce (leaf).................5–10	spinach 6
cabbage 12	melons (supported)...12–24	squash (bush) 18
carrots 1–2	mustard greens 4	Swiss chard...................6
cauliflower 16–30	New Zealand spinach.......8	tomatoes (caged).........18
corn..............................8	okra...................................15	turnips...........................3

How to Start Vegetables

You have a choice.

- For some vegetables, such as carrots, beets, and other roots, you should sow seeds directly in the ground.

- For broccoli, cabbage, cauliflower, lettuce, onions, tomatoes, and several other vegetables, you can buy seedlings from the nursery and transplant them directly into your garden.

- For most vegetables, you can plant seeds in containers indoors and then later transplant the resultant seedlings outdoors when the weather warms up.

Sowing Seeds Directly

For certain plants, you must start with seeds to get good results. Such plants as bush beans, beets, carrots, dwarf peas, radishes, rutabagas, spinach, and turnips don't transplant well, so you'll want to sow their seeds into the garden bed. Follow these steps:

1. Soak the soil the day before planting.

2. For a conventional garden, stake out the rows with string, and space the seeds according to the package directions. For an intensive bed or wide rows (4 feet wide), scatter the seeds evenly across the bed (or a portion of it), trying not to miss the corners. Aim to space the seeds roughly according to the spacing table. The bigger seeds, such as those for radishes and spinach, won't be any problem: you can see exactly where they are, and if you get too many in one spot, you can just move them around. For tiny seeds you might want to practice first with ground coffee. (Chapter 9 offers handy hints for planting the seeds of each vegetable.)

3. Cover the seeds with fine soil. Seeds for different kinds of vegetables need to be at different depths below the soil surface.

4. If too many plants come up later, crowding one another, simply thin them out a bit; pull up a number of the plants so the remaining ones are more evenly distributed, according to the desired spacing.

Some seeds won't come up. Germination is never 100 percent, for a few seeds in any collection will be sterile. Furthermore, soil moisture, depth of planting, and other imperfect conditions affect the germination of even fertile seeds.

Unused seeds can be saved for the next year. The germination rate will drop only slightly. Reseal the seed packets with tape so they're airtight, and store them in a cool, dry place.

Buying Seedlings and Transplanting

Broccoli, brussels sprouts, cabbage, cauliflower, eggplant, peppers, tomatoes, and some other vegetables seem to get off to a better start if they are transplanted into the garden as seedlings. In general, transplanting provides a head start because you have little plants already developed by the time it's warm enough to plant outdoors. It also means you won't have to thin any plants; you space out the seedlings directly. If you decide to buy vegetables as small plants, you can probably find most of the popular varieties at your local nursery.

When planting seedlings, avoid bending or squeezing the root mass by digging big enough holes. Try to disturb the roots as little as possible when transferring each seedling to the ground, and once the plant is in, make sure the soil is firm but not packed around the roots.

figure 3-1

You can probably get by with just a small trowel for transplanting, but some other tools can be useful. One of the best is a pointed stick—a small dowel with a rounded point (Figure 3-1). Use it in one hand to poke into the soil. With your other hand, hold the seedling in the hole, and then use the stick to push the soil back around the roots.

Starting Seeds Indoors in Containers

Why bother to grow your own seedlings when it's much easier to go down to the nursery, pick out some seedlings, come back, and plunk them in your garden? The reasons for developing your own seedlings are psychological as well as practical. Growing plants from the moment of germination will bring you joy and feelings of accomplishment. The plants are entirely yours. On the practical side, seeds are cheaper than seedlings. And nurseries offer only a relatively small selection of vegetable varieties, so if you want to experiment with unusual or new varieties, you must grow your plants from seeds.

Whether you grow them yourself or purchase them from a nursery, seedlings are a great advantage for such warm weather crops as cucumbers, melons, squash, and tomatoes, which don't do well until outdoor temperatures begin to hover in the 60s or above. By growing them indoors early and transplanting them later, you can get a jump on the weather.

Metal Foil Pans. Here's one easy way to start vegetables indoors:

1. Get some foil pans from a variety or grocery store. Make up a soil mix of equal parts sand, loam, and compost or peat moss. (You can also buy potting soil from your local nursery.) Screen this mixture so that the particles are fairly small.

2. Plant the seeds an inch or two apart in the soil mixture, and cover them with soil or vermiculite. Vermiculite—light mineral granules that can be bought packaged at any nursery—is best because it holds moisture well.

3. Place the containers in a warm place (60–65°F) where they will be in full sun or under a fluorescent grow light for about 12 hours a day, if possible. For fast germination of the seeds of eggplant, peppers, and tomatoes, you'll need a soil temperature of 75–85°F. Within a couple of weeks, most plants will be poking through the soil.

figure 3-2

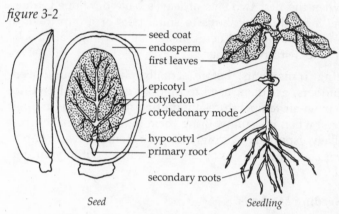

seed coat
endosperm
first leaves

epicotyl
cotyledon
cotyledonary mode

hypocotyl
primary root

secondary roots

Seed *Seedling*

4. When the second pair of leaves opens (Figure 3-2), move each plant to a separate small pot or paper cup, or space the plants 3 inches apart in another loaf pan.

5. Transplant the seedlings outside when all threat of frost is past or according to the planting dates in your area.

Peat Pots. Small individual pots, square or round, made of compressed peat moss or other nourishing materials are available at nurseries. Some types are already supplied with soil; others you must fill with potting soil. Sow a seed or two into each pot. When the plant is several inches tall, transplant both pot and contents to the garden bed. The roots will grow through the walls of the pot, and the plants won't suffer any shock. Other advantages are that you don't lose any soil from around the roots and the necessary nutrients are built right into the container. Peat pots are especially good for cucumbers, melons, and squash, because disturbing their roots during transplanting tends to check their growth.

Starter Kits. For a method that's simpler than using peat pots, buy one of the starter kits for tomatoes and other vegetables. These kits have container, soil, and seed already put together. All you have to do is take the lid off the container and water the soil. Some kits come with packets of seeds that you have to plant in the container yourself. This seedling system is a great way to

figure 3-3

Upside-down coffee can. Take off on warm, sunny days.

Large paper cups.

Punch holes in the sides of milk cartons to allow air to circulate.

Newspaper tent weighed down with bricks or stones.

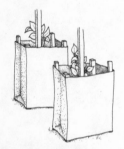

Bottomless paper bags.

Plastic jug. Remove bottom to convert to a mini-greenhouse.

introduce children to gardening. Some seed companies make complete gardening kits for kids.

Flats. You can also start seeds in a 14x24x3-inch box called a flat. Use a soil mix of equal parts sand, loam, and compost or peat moss, or buy packages of planting mix. Thoroughly soak the soil. Scatter small seeds gently over the surface, then press in. For larger seeds, make furrows with a pencil (the furrows should be 2 inches apart and have the depth required for particular vegetables); then drop in your seeds and cover them with soil. Place the flat in a warmly lit spot—like that described for seedlings in foil pans. When the first two sets of leaves have developed, transplant the individual seedlings to small pots or group them in other flats 3 inches part. When transferring seedlings, always be careful not to disturb the roots.

Hardening Transplants. Before actually planting young seedlings outdoors, get them used to outdoor conditions. Introduce them to open-air temperatures by putting them outside (in their containers) when it's sunny. Bring them indoors whenever frost seems likely, especially overnight. Expose them to lower temperatures for about two weeks before setting them out in your garden bed.

Other Seeding Methods

It's possible to plant seeds outdoors before the weather becomes warm enough for safe exposure to the elements. However, you have to be a truly dedicated gardener who doesn't mind some extra work and has the patience to watch over those tiny plants.

To grow melons, for instance, you can make small frames or boxes, each 1x1 foot and 3–4 inches high, with a clear plastic cover, and place them on your prepared garden bed. Plant 8–10 seeds within each frame. Remove the cover on warm days; replace it on cold days and nights. Do not remove the cover permanently until all danger of frost has passed.

You can also make simple seedling protectors in various ways, such as by cutting off the bottoms of plastic gallon jugs and setting these over your planted seeds (Figure 3-3). You can purchase commercial plant protectors called "hot caps" made out of a waxed-paper-like product from any nursery. Plastic sheets can even be made into a miniature greenhouse. All of these methods will give your seedlings a speedy start. Just make sure you remove the caps, jugs, or plastic sheets on warm days, or the young plants may burn under the intensified heat.

Wall of water

Stretching Your Crops

Any gardener can learn little tricks that make Mother Nature work overtime. These miracle "crop stretchers" are intercropping, succession planting, and catch cropping.

Intercropping simply involves planting quick-maturing crops between slower-maturing crops. You can plant quick-maturing radishes, green onions, or leaf lettuce between corn or tomatoes. Because you plant the corn and tomatoes far apart, you will harvest the crops between them before the corn and tomato plants have grown big enough to crowd the smaller plants out. That's getting double duty out of your intensive beds.

Succession planting consists of planting a crop as soon as you take out an early one. (Make sure you add compost, manure, bonemeal, and wood ash, or appropriate substitutes, before you replant.) For instance, you can harvest spinach and then plant beans or take out broccoli and then plant corn. Or you can successively plant early season, midseason, and late season varieties of the same kind of vegetable. Any combination of early and late varieties expands the productivity of your garden.

Catch cropping is planting quick-maturing plants in places where you just harvested larger, slower-growing vegetables. You can harvest a couple of broccoli plants in late summer, for instance, and then grow radishes or green onions in the same space. The basic rule for catch cropping is: Don't leave bare ground unplanted.

Seed Planting-Transplanting Tips

No-Spill Seed

If you are tired of seeds spilling out of your pocket while you're bent over planting, use a spring-clamp clothespin to hold the packet closed. Simply fold the envelope over and clip. The remaining seeds will stay put.

Canned Seeds

To save seed from one season to another, and to preserve a high rate of germination, store unused seeds—in their original packets—in a sealed canning jar in your refrigerator. Seeds survive best when the temperature is 32–40°F. Put a packet of silica gel (available in drugstores) in the bottom of each jar to absorb moisture.

Vegetable Seed Life

How many years can you keep seed until it goes bad?

• Garlic, okra, onion, parsnip, salsify, and shallot seed are viable for one year.

- Leeks, peppers, and rhubarb are viable for two years.
- Asparagus, broccoli, carrots, celery, collards, corn, peas, and spinach will endure three years.
- Beans will last three to five years.
- Beets, brussels sprouts, cabbage, cauliflower, chard, eggplant, kale, radishes, rutabagas, squash, and tomatoes will last four years.
- Cucumbers, kohlrabies, and melons are good for five years.
- Lettuce is viable for six years.

Seed Test

To find out whether your stored seed is still good, give it the towel test. Count out 10 seeds of one variety on a damp paper towel. Wrap the paper towel in a wet terry-cloth hand towel, and place this in a plastic bag. Six days later, unwrap the seeds and see how many have sprouted. If eight out of 10 seeds sprouted, you have an 80 percent germination rate. If the germination rate is 50 percent or below, your seeds have flunked the test. Throw them on the compost heap, and order fresh seed.

Unscrambling Instructions

What do the instructions on seed packages mean by "plant as soon as the soil can be worked in the spring"? Obviously, frozen soil can't be worked. When thawing, it's too wet. Usually, about two weeks of sunny, breezy, above-freezing weather dries the earth enough to make it ready. A trusty rule of thumb is to walk on the garden: If mud sticks to your shoes, wait another week. If your shoes stay clean, plant now.

Be Time Flexible

Some gardeners plant on the same date every year as if planting charts were etched in stone. The truth is, planting dates are made of rubber. The growing season broadly is the period between the last frost of spring and the first frost of winter. Yet some areas warm up quickly after the last frost, and others take a while. Moreover, the growing season may last 220 days one year and 160 days another. Use seasonal charts as a guide, but vary your planting dates from year to year according to the prevailing weather conditions.

Fine-Tuning the Season

Some seeds like wet soil for germination; others prefer it semi-dry. This is known as the "soil moisture range."

- Cabbage, carrots, cucumbers, muskmelons, onions, peppers, radishes, squash, sweet corn, tomatoes, turnips, and watermelon germinate over the full moisture range from wilting to field capacity (the maximum amount of moisture the soil can hold).

- Beets, endive, lettuce, lima beans, peas, and snap beans germinate best in the upper half of the soil moisture range.
- Celery germinates only when the soil moisture is near or above field capacity.
- Spinach and New Zealand spinach germinate best in the lower two-thirds of the soil moisture range.

Sanded Seed

Such seeds as okra and asparagus sprout easily if you crack their tough coats. The easiest way to do this is to roll the seeds gently between two blocks of sandpaper until their ridges are worn down; then soak them overnight before planting. This technique will shave days off their germination time.

Work Up a Lather

To sprout parsley, parsnip, and beets, scrub them in a pint of warm water. If the water is hard, add half a cup of vinegar. Lather your hands with mild bath soap (not detergent), rub the seeds in your hands, and rinse them in this acidified water. Then soak the seeds overnight in this same water. Next day, drain the seeds on a towel and plant them before they dry out.

Sinking Seeds

Spring rains sometimes sink tiny seeds too deeply into the soil for germination, resulting in crop failure. To prevent this, simply unroll inexpensive paper toweling in your planting rows. Scatter the seeds on top of the paper, and cover lightly with soil. The toweling keeps the seeds at the right depth while it slowly decomposes.

Seed Depth

There's a handy rule of thumb for seed depth. Plant at a depth four times the diameter of the seed. In wet weather or heavy soils plant a little more shallowly; in light or sandy soils, plant a bit deeper.

Presprouting Magic

Here's how to make some sprouting magic. Put a cup of moist, shredded sphagnum moss in a paper bag, add a pinch of seeds, and shake to mix. Roll in a towel, moisten this, and wring it out. Twist and fold the top of the bag over, and seal it with tape or a rubber band. Place the bag in a warm place. Plant the sprouts when about half the seeds have pushed out roots or shoots (from

3–4 days to several weeks depending on the vegetable and the temperature). Don't worry about the sprouts being upside down or sideways in a furrow because they will twist and turn to orient themselves.

Small Seed Spacing

To space small seeds, mix them with white sand in a saltshaker, and sprinkle along down the furrow. This allows you to see where they go and to adjust the flow.

"Fore"

If you have trouble bending over to plant seeds, buy a golf club shaft protector. This plastic tube is about 3 feet long and costs about 25¢. Place one end of the tube on the ground in a planting row, then drop the seeds through the other end. You can space your seed evenly without straining.

Difficult Seed Sowing

Trying to sow a fall garden in the heat of summer? Here are four methods gardeners use to get their fall crop up and growing fast.

- Cover the rows of seeds with one-by-fours or one-by-sixes. Lift the boards daily to check for sprouting. Once a few seedlings break through the ground, remove the boards.

- Cover the rows with strips of porous cloth mulch. You can water directly through this. Remove the cloth once the seeds germinate.

- A thin layer of grass clippings preserves moisture and helps seed germinate quickly. The clippings stay in place while the plants grow to maturity.

- Cover your seeds with a thin layer of potting soil. This prevents crusts from forming and retains water while the seeds germinate.

Surefire Germination

To germinate seeds like tomato, pepper, and eggplant directly in the ground, dig a shallow trench 3–4 inches and cover it with plastic film. Angle the plastic so water can run off. The seed will not only germinate quickly but will continue to grow rapidly.

Perfect Choice

When selecting seedlings from a nursery, choose well-established plants with at least four true leaves and a healthy green color. Eggplants, peppers, and tomatoes should be wider than tall. Protruding roots means the plant is root-bound; premature fruiting means the pot is stressing the plant; leggy, leaning plants were grown in inadequate light.

Easy Picking

Chopsticks make a good planting tool when you want to use cell paks (growing containers) or small pots. Wooden chopsticks work best. After you get the hang of it, the process of picking up the seeds and twisting them into the soil goes quickly. Push the soil back over the holes to cover the seeds.

Seedling Problems

If you have trouble with damping-off (a disease caused by fungi that makes seedlings wilt or rot) when starting seeds in pots or flats, try planting them first in vermiculite. Sow the seeds ¼–½ inch deep in a pot or flat filled with moistened vermiculite. Pat the vermiculite firm, water lightly, and slip the seedlings into a plastic bag. This keeps them moist when the first true leaves form. Transplant them to pots or peat pots. This process almost guarantees success.

Quick Transplant

Before planting seeds in pots, cut some plastic bags into squares, poke holes in the bottom of the plastic (for drainage), and place one square inside each pot. Fill the pots with soil and seed. When transplanting time comes around, just lift the plastic squares out and your plants can be gently settled into the ground.

Handle Carefully

Seeds that have sprouted in flats need to be picked out and placed in another container as soon as the seedlings are large enough to handle. Use a pointed stick to lift the seedling from under its roots. Always handle seedlings by the leaf, not the stem. A new leaf will soon replace a damaged one, but it's impossible to replace a stem.

Speedy Germination

Heating devices accelerate germination and make flats comfortable for seedlings. You can buy many types of heaters, from soil warming mats to heated seed flats. Most elaborate are plastic tabletop greenhouses equipped with soil heater cables. This method sometimes cuts germination time in half. Studies at the University of California, Davis, show that radish seeds take an average of 29 days to germinate at 41°F, but they germinate in just three days at 86°F. Carrots germinate in about 50 days at 41°F and only six days at 86°F.

The Traveling Gardener

Avid gardeners often acquire new plants, seeds, and cuttings when they travel. But if you attempt to bring home plants from outside the United States (and even from other states), they will be confiscated. The safest bet is to collect seeds. To find out exactly what you can bring into your home state, write to: Travelers Tips, Animal and Plant Health Inspection Service Information, 732 Federal Building, Hyattsville, MD 20782.

Tips on Protecting Seedlings

Stop the Shock

A number of tricks can alleviate transplant shock so your seedlings suffer little setback or delay in growth.

- Start with small seedlings. Four to six leaves are enough.
- Transplant at sundown or on a cloudy day.
- Wet the soil thoroughly around the seedlings' roots a few hours before you go to work so the plants will be plump with water.
- Dig the holes before you uproot any seedlings. Fill the holes with water, and let it soak in.
- Move the seedlings with as much soil around their roots as possible.
- Move one plant at a time, but do it quickly. Don't delay.
- Immediately soak the soil around each transplant. Don't wait until you have completed a row. Sprinkle the transplants daily.
- Transplanting experts often move little clumps of plants at a time so as not to damage roots by pulling individual plants apart. After the plants have taken you can thin them out.

Quick Recovery

To make transplants from a flat look vigorous and healthy, cut the potting soil around the seedlings into squares a day or two before setting out. This severs roots that would be broken during transplanting. Since they will have started to recover before you set them out, they hit the garden already growing at full speed.

Protecting from Wind Damage

Wind can wilt or break off small seedlings, and once this happens, the plant never truly recovers. Shelter your seedlings from the wind with a box, a piece of plywood, or a piece of plastic stretched over a wire frame (Figure 3-4). Another option is to locate them in a sheltered corner of your garden. This saves the plants and gives your seedlings a little extra help.

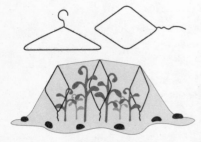

figure 3-4

Quick Seedling Protection

To protect seedlings against frost, almost anything will do: homemade paper hats, clear plastic cake covers, a milk carton cut in half, some flat cardboard folded over, a cardboard box with both ends cut out and the top end covered with clear polyethylene. Just use your imagination (Figure 3-5).

figure 3-5

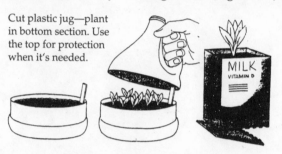

Cut plastic jug—plant in bottom section. Use the top for protection when it's needed.

Cut-off milk cartons make excellent transplant containers.

Perforate around the bottom for easy removal when transplanting time comes.

Open-ended can with plastic cover protects seeds, seedlings from bugs and cold.

Odds and Ends Protection

In a pinch, you could even use a bottomless paper bag or a bottomless box with a lid to protect your transplants from wind, cold nights, and hot sunshine. Stakes in each corner will hold bags open.

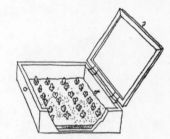

Plastic covers wooden frame. Lower flap for protection on cold nights.

Portable Greenhouse

A child's plastic wagon makes an excellent portable greenhouse. Just fill it with soil, plant your seeds, and cover it with a sheet of glass. Whenever necessary, you can easily move it to sunny, shady, warmer, or cooler spots. Best of all, once warm weather arrives, you can pull the wagon through the garden as you plant the seedlings.

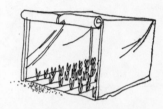

Bottomless box with plastic top can be moved around the garden and eliminates transplanting.

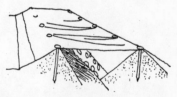

Plastic film protects seeds in furrow and is held in place by nails.

CHAPTER FOUR

WATERING

Water is an essential ingredient in all plant growth, for almost every botanical process takes place in its presence. Water is necessary in plants' food-manufacturing process (photosynthesis), is the main constituent of living cells, and abounds in young plant tissues. It keeps stems and leaves stiff. And water is the main ingredient in most of the vegetables we eat, comprising, for example, 91 percent of asparagus, 87 percent of beets, 95 percent of cucumbers, and 94 percent of tomatoes.

These facts might suggest that all you have to do in order to grow sumptuous vegetables is pour on the water. Unfortunately, Mother Nature doesn't work that way. Too much water is just as harmful as too little.

The Ideal Soil/Water Relationship

Water in the soil carries dissolved nutrients that are absorbed by plants' roots. Soil air provides a constant supply of oxygen while carrying off carbon dioxide. An ideal soil for plant growth generally contains 50 percent solid matter and 50 percent pore space (the space that allows absorption of liquid). Moisture should occupy about half of the pore space.

When you swamp the pore space (complete fullness is called field capacity), you cut off the oxygen supply and stop root growth. The longer the air is blocked, the greater the damage. Once the roots are damaged, organisms that cause rot enter; root rot frequently sets in.

When you water so much and/or so often that you keep more than 50 percent of the pore space filled yet don't keep the soil quite saturated enough to cut off the plant's oxygen, you generally create lush leaf growth at the expense of fruit development. This happens to tomatoes, eggplant, and peppers that are only slightly overwatered. The symptoms are lots of green leaves but little fruit.

On the other hand, when water occupies less than 50 percent of the pore space, the plant must work harder to grow. A plant that doesn't get a full quota of H_2O, say agronomists, is under "water stress." Water stress affects vegetable plants in different ways. A cucumber stops growing; a tomato ripens all its fruit; muskmelons lose their sweetness during the ripening period. Once a vegetable experiences water stress, it can't be salvaged. The first symptom is wilting leaves.

Yet another cause of problems is an uneven water supply. When the soil dries out completely, is watered, dries out again, and is watered, the plants suffer. In fact, damage can occur if this happens only once. Carrots can crack, cabbage heads can split.

TABLE 4-1 CRITICAL WATERING PERIODS

Vegetables need a constant water supply for best growth. Inadequate water, however, affects vegetable quality most during the following periods.

VEGETABLE	CRITICAL PERIOD
asparagus	spear development
beans	pollination/pod development
broccoli	head development
cabbage	head development
carrots	root enlargement
cauliflower	head development
corn	tassel/ear development
cucumbers	flower/fruit development
eggplant	flower/fruit development
lettuce	head development
melons	flower/fruit development
onions	bulb enlargement
pumpkins	flower/fruit development
squash	flower/fruit development
tomatoes	flower/fruit development

How Much Water?

To keep your vegetables growing at their fastest rate, water until your particular soil type is filled to field capacity in the main root zone (about 1 foot deep for most vegetables, about 2 feet deep for corn, tomatoes, and a few other large vegetables); don't water again until most of the available water has been used.

The amount of water your plants use depends on temperature, wind, rainfall, and individual needs. The amount of water your soil holds depends on its texture. Sandy soil holds less water than clay, yet clay holds water so tightly that some of it is unavailable for plant use. Loam makes adequate amounts of water readily available to your vegetables.

If you know what kind of soil you have, you can estimate roughly when your soil is saturated, or has reached field capacity (Table 4-2). If you have loamy soil, approximately 1 inch of water will saturate the first foot. To help with gauging this, place a large transparent measuring cup in the garden. When an inch of water has accumulated in the cup, the top foot of your garden has all the water it can hold.

TABLE 4-2 SOIL WATER-HOLDING CAPACITY
(INCHES OF WATER NEEDED PER FOOT OF SOIL DEPTH)

SOIL TYPE	APPROXIMATE WATER-HOLDING CAPACITY
Sandy	.8
Loam	1.0
Clay	1.5

Table 4-3 is a general guide to average daily water use. An example will clarify how to estimate your vegetable garden's need for water. Let's say you have loam soil and live in an area where the summers are warm. According to Table 4-2, loam holds 1 inch of water, so you turn on the sprinkler until the measuring cup holds that amount. It will take about two hours to saturate that first foot of soil. If you're raising tomatoes or corn, you'll want to water twice as long.

Furthermore, let's say it's early summer. Looking at Table 4-3, you decide your plants are using a quarter inch of water a day. So the available water in the first foot of saturated soil will be depleted in about four days. Therefore, you should water most vegetables about two hours every four days. This is only a quick appraisal, of course. Changing weather conditions mean that vegetables may use twice the normal amount of water from one day to the next.

TABLE 4-3 WATER USE GUIDE
(INCHES OF SOIL WATER USED PER DAY IN A VEGETABLE GARDEN)

SEASON	WARM WEATHER (80°F AND ABOVE)	COOL WEATHER (BELOW 80°F)
Summer	.25-.35	.15-.2
Spring/Fall	.1-.2	.1-.15

A fail-safe watering method that maintains the correct degree of soil moisture is to water deeply for two to four hours, and then wait until the soil dries out to a depth of 4–8 inches before watering again. Check this with a trowel.

How to Water

Home gardeners generally water overhead or use some sort of drip system. Californians are urged to use a drip system to conserve water, but many continue to water both ways. The chief advantage of overhead watering is that it's easy. The principal disadvantages are that a great deal of water is lost through evaporation and that it makes the garden more susceptible to disease.

There are five types of overhead watering devices. One is a **pulsating sprinkler.** Water strikes an arm to move the pulsating, or "rainbird," type of sprinkler in a 50–75-foot radius. These are available in brass or less expensive plastic and can be used with an underground pipe system or on a portable spike or sled base. One pulsating sprinkler will water a medium-size garden and can be adjusted to operate in a full or partial circle. These sprinklers have almost no disadvantages.

The arm of an **oscillating sprinkler** moves back and forth to water a square or rectangular area of about 50–60 feet. These devices can be adjusted to water only a portion of this space. Oscillating sprinklers, like the pulsating type, have few disadvantages.

A spray of water propels the rotating arms or blades of a **rotating sprinkler.** It will water in a circle with a 5–50-foot diameter. Some of the larger rotating sprinklers can travel down a hose laid across the garden and will water an area of up to 1,500 square feet. Some water is wasted by a rotating sprinkler, since it cannot be adjusted. Also, you may have to move it several times to water your entire vegetable garden.

Stationary sprinklers have holes that spray water in circles, squares, or rectangles of up to 100 square feet. There are no moving parts. These sprinklers must be moved several times to water a garden of average size.

Spray heads are made from plastic or brass and are usually connected to an underground pipe system. The head sprinkles in several patterns, including quarter, half, three-quarter, and full circles. The underground pipe used in this system makes cultivating the garden difficult.

Besides sprinkler watering, some gardeners like to water by hand. There are a variety of hose nozzles, including hand-held nozzles, fan sprays, and ground bubblers. Wands 24–52 inches long permit watering underneath the leaves. Hand watering is fine for small gardens but can become tedious for gardens of more than 100 square feet.

In general, exercise some prudence whenever you overhead water. Remember to water early in the morning to enable the leaves to dry off quickly; lingering moisture can create a mildew problem. In addition, the leaves of some plants, such as squash, may burn if the plants are watered during the heat of the day. Water tomatoes overhead only until the fruit begins to ripen; then, to keep the fruit from cracking, water on the ground until you have harvested the plants.

Drip irrigation is the frequent, slow release of water into the soil through small mechanical devices called emitters. The system consists of three main parts: basic controls, a main line or lines, and emitters with small extension tubes.

The basic controls include a shutoff valve, a pressure regulator, and a filter. The shutoff valve turns the system on and off. The pressure regulator reduces water pressure in the household water line from 50-80 pounds per square inch to the low rate of 5–25 pounds per square inch needed by most drip systems. The filter screens out sediment and other particles that could plug the small emitter openings.

The main line is made of ⅜–½-inch black polyethylene hose that carries water from a garden hose or water outlet either across the top portion of the garden (the main header) or up and down the rows (the laterals).

Emitters are small plastic nozzles that plug into the main lines and deliver a measured ½, 1, 2, 3, or 4 gallons of water per hour directly to the vegetables. An emitter can be connected to the main line by very small tubes (spaghetti tubing) or it can be plugged directly into the main line, with spaghetti tubing used to deliver water to individual plants.

There are at least 50 kinds of emitters on the market today. Drippers, for instance, are small plastic devices with a barb at one end that snaps into the main-line hose while the other end dispenses water. Standard drippers are best for bringing water directly to large plants that are spaced 1–3 feet apart, such as tomatoes and eggplant.

Perforated or drip tubing, another form of emitter, is 10–30-foot-long plastic tubing with holes spaced 12, 18, or 24 inches apart along its length. One kind of drip tubing is plugged into a main line placed across the top of the garden; each perforated tube is laid down an individual garden row and dispenses water along its entire length. Most kinds of perforated tubing deliver 2–6 gallons of water per hour for every 10 feet of tubing. Drip tubing is especially suitable for watering closely spaced crops such as carrots, beets, and radishes.

Follow the same basic guidelines for drip irrigation as for other kinds of watering. Turn your system on for about 30 minutes, and then check with a trowel to make sure the water has penetrated the first foot of soil. If it hasn't, continue watering until it does. After that, check the soil daily with a trowel, and don't water again until it has dried to a depth of 4–8 inches.

Drip systems are available in kit form or as individual components at nurseries and plumbing-supply stores. You can put your own system together; they are usually easy to install in average-size gardens.

Drip irrigation is by far the most efficient watering method for California vegetable gardens. Only a key area of soil is watered, little or no water is lost to evaporation and surface runoff, and there is no sprinkler overshoot. In the future, as water becomes more expensive and water conservation even more important, many vegetable gardeners will use this method exclusively.

Foolproof Watering

You can take a lot of guesswork out of watering by hooking your system (either overhead or drip) to an electric timer or a moisture sensor. A simple timer may involve a clock that turns the water on for a given number of minutes a day. Sophisticated timing devices can be programmed for several days ahead and set to deliver different amounts of water to separate parts of your garden.

Moisture sensors keep soil water at a safe level. The sensing device is buried in the garden 8–10 inches deep, and water is turned on when the sensor dries out. The requisite moistness may be dialed into some sensors, which will turn the water on when the soil drops below that level. The major drawback to a moisture sensor is its high cost, but it is nevertheless the ultimate assurance that your vegetables will get exactly the degree of moisture they need at all times.

Mulching Means Moisture

Gardeners can also use mulch to ensure adequate soil moisture for vegetable plants. A mulch is any material spread on the garden bed that shades the ground completely, reduces soil evaporation, and helps retain moisture. Many organic materials will make a good mulch; you can try wood chips, sawdust, grass clippings, horse manure, or compost.

Place organic mulches around your plants' stems, and cover the ground completely. Since organic material cools the soil, mulch in late spring after the soil temperature has warmed to at least 65°F. The best time to spread an organic mulch is immediately after a rain, as it keeps the moisture in the soil for an extended period of time.

Water has such importance in the garden that it is worth repeating the fail-safe approach: Water deeply for two to four hours, and then don't water again until the soil dries to a depth of 4–8 inches. Test it with a trowel. If you follow this rule and garden in well-drained soil, you will probably be able to deal with conditions ranging from drought to several days of rain.

CHAPTER FIVE

WHAT'S BUGGING YOUR GARDEN?

The pests that do the most damage to your vegetables are divided into four categories:

1. Chewers are beetles, caterpillars, and other pests that chew holes in the leaves of vegetable plants.

2. Sucking insects are aphids, true bugs, and whiteflies; they suck plant juices.

3. Borers are insects that bore into leaves and fruit.

4. Soil insects attack from below.

Most of these insects go through developmental stages. An adult beetle, fly, or moth lays eggs that hatch larvae, which eat everything in sight. The larva of a beetle is a grub; the larva of a fly is a maggot; the larva of a moth or butterfly is a caterpillar. When the larva reaches its maximum size, it stops feeding and enters the dormant stage. The adult insect emerges from this pupa. Both the mature and the larval stages can be extremely destructive.

Chewing Insects

Both beetles and caterpillars will gobble up your plants, leaving holes in leaves and fruit. These holes may be tiny pinpoints or larger, irregular perforations. You may even discover that whole leaves have been devoured and chunks of fruit have been munched away. Regrettably, you should get to know the major chewers in your garden.

Beetles, as every experienced gardener knows, are obnoxious insects with biting mouths and hard front wings. They can make short work of your vegetables. A number of beetles would like to call your vegetable garden home for at least part of the year.

Colorado potato beetle

Striped blister beetle

Cowpea curculio

Japanese beetle

Mexican bean beetle

Asparagus
beetle

Bean leaf
beetle

Flea beetle

Spotted
cucumber
beetle

Striped
cucumber
beetle

Weevil

Asparagus beetles are slender, ¼ inch long, and brownish in color. Both adults and larvae eat the new shoots and leaves of asparagus. As soon as asparagus appears, the beetle lays eggs on the tips. Within a week, the eggs hatch and start to feed. After 10 to 14 days, these larvae burrow into the ground to become yellow pupae.

Bean leaf beetles have a reddish or yellow coloring, black spots on their backs, and black margins around their front wings. The ¼-inch-long adult beetles, which are found throughout the United States, nibble irregular holes into the leaves of all kinds of beans.

Flea beetles are tiny bronze or black beetles. The mature beetles jump like fleas when disturbed and eat what looks like tiny shot holes in leaves. The white ¼-inch larvae feed on the roots or seeds of germinating plants. They do the most damage when cool temperature delays germination, giving them time to eat more seeds. They are found throughout the United States.

Spotted cucumber beetles (of the genus *Diabrotica*) are about ¼ inch long, yellow, and have black spots on their backs. Also known as the southern corn rootwork, the adult chews large, irregular holes in foliage. The larva tunnels through the roots of cabbages, corn, cucumbers, melons, peas, and other vegetables. Adults and larvae both spread bacteria that cause cucumber and corn wilts. When the temperature rises above 70°F, these beetles start to feed and lay eggs at the bases of stems. The newly hatched larvae feed underground.

Striped cucumber beetles are about ¼ inch long and either yellow or black, with three stripes on their wing covers. The larvae are slender and white, becoming brownish at the ends. Adults eat the leaves, stems, and fruits of tender young plants. These beetles pass the winter on the ground beneath the leaves of plants. After feeding on foliage for several weeks, they lay eggs in the soil. The larvae then bore into roots and stems. This pest also spreads bacteria that engender cucumber wilt and cucumber mosaic (a viral disease).

Vegetable weevils are grayish-brown beetles with a light-colored "V" on their wing covers. The larvae are light green with light yellow heads. Both adults and larvae feed on the leaves and roots of many vegetables.

Caterpillars are the extremely destructive larvae of moths and butterflies. Most of these pests go through four stages: egg, larva, pupa, and adult. The larval stage, or caterpillar, is the most troublesome for gardeners. After hatching from eggs, caterpillars feed almost continuously on vegetables until they enter a dormant pupal state. All adults have wings.

Cabbage loopers are pale green, 1½-inch-long caterpillars that are sometimes called measuring worms because they fold into a loop and then stretch to full length as they crawl. They chew irregular holes in the leaves of many vegetables. The adult, a 1-inch-long, brown-gray moth, emerges in spring and lays single eggs on the upper surface of leaves. The eggs hatch in about two weeks; four or more generations may appear in a single year.

Cabbage looper

Corn earworms, also called tomato fruitworms, are a corn lover's nightmare. The 2-inch-long green or brown caterpillar feeds on corn kernels for about a month, then drops to the ground and tunnels several inches into the earth to pupate. Adults emerge two weeks later as green or brown moths. Unfortunately, each female moth can lay as many as 3,000 eggs. Besides corn, this pest also attacks beans, lettuce, potatoes, tomatoes, and other vegetables.

Corn earworm

The **Imported cabbageworm** preys on all members of the cabbage family, including brussels sprouts, cabbage, cauliflower, collards, kale, and radishes, as well as lettuce. These 1-inch-long green caterpillars chew through outer leaves and tunnel inside cabbage and cauliflower heads. They pupate in cocoons suspended from plants and in garden refuse. The resultant white cabbage butterfly, marked by black spotted wings, is born in early spring. The females lay several hundred eggs underneath leaves, which hatch into caterpillars in less than a week.

Cabbageworm

Cutworms are 1½–2 inches long, smooth, dull gray to black in color, and usually found just under the surface of the soil during daylight. At night they feed on plants near the soil's surface or crawl up the plants to feed on foliage. You know cutworms are working in your garden when you find the stems of your favorite vegetables cut off at ground level. This pest spends the winter as a naked pupa in the soil, and the adult emerges early in spring. The female lays 60 or more eggs in patches on leaves, tree trunks, and brush. In a few days, the eggs hatch into ravenous worms.

Black cutworm

Garden webworms, after having spun themselves protective silken coverings, chomp on the stems, leaves, and fruits of beans, corn, cowpeas, peas, soybeans, and other plants. This pale green caterpillar grows to about 1 inch long and then spends the winter in a pupal stage in the soil. In spring, the small buff-colored females lay clusters of eggs on plants' leaves. Caterpillars hatch in a week, spin a webbed shelter, and feed for a month.

Pickleworm

The ferocious-featured **tomato hornworm** always looks as though it's ready to attack any gardener who dares come too close. Despite the horn projecting from its hind end, this 3–4-inch green caterpillar is harmless to humans; it cannot sting or bite. It does, however, chew hunks out of the foliage of tomatoes,

Tomato hornworm

Earwig

Grasshopper

Snail and slug

Aphid

eggplant, peppers, potatoes, and related vegetables. If let alone, it will sometimes strip a plant bare of leaves. This pest spends winter underground in a brown, hard, spindle-shaped shell. Moths with 5-inch wingspans emerge in early summer to lay single yellow-green eggs on the undersides of leaves.

Some chewing pests are neither beetles nor caterpillars, but they can be just as destructive. Watch especially for earwigs, grasshoppers, slugs, and snails.

Earwigs are ugly nocturnal feeding insects with pincers at the ends of their abdomens. They feed on leaves at night, then hide in the soil and other dark places during the day.

Grasshoppers don't usually attack vegetable beds, but when they do they can be pernicious. Those found in gardens are 1–2½ inches long and colored dark gray, green, brown, or black. The female buries her eggs about 1 inch below the soil's surface.

Slugs and **snails** can be a terrible nuisance for they devour many kinds of young shoots and seedlings and chew large, round holes in leaves near the ground. These pests feed at night and on cool, overcast days, hiding themselves on warm, sunny days. They leave a telltale trail of silvery slime everywhere they go.

Sucking Insects

A number of insects, including aphids, whiteflies, leafhoppers, and spider mites, suck plants' juices, causing a spotty or yellow discoloration of leaves and shoots. This damage can be difficult to spot at first, but a severe infestation may result in the wilting and curling of leaves and shoots. All sucking insects except leafhoppers congregate in large groups.

Aphids are the bane of every gardener. Tiny (1/16–1/8 inch long) and pear-shaped, they come in numerous colors—green, yellow, orange, black, gray, pink, brown, and white. The saliva of some species stunts plant growth and makes leaves wilt and curl. All aphids secrete honeydew (plant sap enriched with sugars and amino acids), which attracts ants.

Aphids have a strange life cycle. Wingless females emerge from eggs as nymphs, which mature and—without being fertilized—give birth to living young. The young reproduce in the same way for several generations until some develop wings and fly away to other plants. In the fall, winged males as well as females are born. Aphids generally produce 20 or more generations each season.

The diminutive (1/30-inch-long) **whitefly** pierces the leaves or stems of vegetables and draws out the sap. It has two pairs of wings covered with a waxy powder. Large numbers of whiteflies are often present on the undersides of leaves but go unnoticed until the plant is disturbed, when they take off in a cloudlike swarm. Whiteflies secrete a sticky honeydew that becomes a growing surface for sooty black fungus. The female whitefly lays about 25 eggs that hatch into nymphs. After feeding for some time, the nymphs enter a pupal stage, from which they emerge as adults.

Whitefly

Leafhoppers are strange-looking, slender, wedge-shaped insects that may grow to be ½ inch long. They pierce plants to suck their sap. Vegetables attacked by leafhoppers often have discolored, crinkled, curled leaves as well as wilting or browning leaf tips and margins, which is called hopper burn. Eggplant, celery, lettuce, potatoes, and rhubarb are especially susceptible. Adult leafhoppers migrate south in the winter and return in the spring.

Active, needle-thin, black or straw-colored **thrips** have two pairs of slender wings edged with long hairs. Species are named for the plants they attack; thus there are onion thrips and bean thrips. Thrips can damage carrots, cabbage, cauliflower, celery, cucumbers, melons, squash, tomatoes, turnips, and other vegetables by sucking plant juices. Female thrips insert eggs into leaves and stems, and pale, hungry nymphs hatch in about a week. Several generations are born in a year, but thrips are most numerous in late spring and midsummer.

Leafhopper

Several species of **mites** attack vegetables, but the one commonly found in home gardens is the red spider or two-spotted spider mite. This pest is about as small as a speck of pepper, and despite its name, it is more often green, yellow, or brown. To determine whether your plants are under siege, place a piece of white paper under a small plant and shake the plant; if mites are present, some will fall onto the paper and you'll see the specks moving. Mites lower plants' vitality by destroying leaf tissue and sucking out nutrients. They assail a number of garden vegetables, including tomatoes. The affected leaves turn pale green and may show blisters on the upper sides.

Thrip

Mites construct silver webs over flower buds and leaves as well as between stalks. Females attach 100 or more eggs to webs on the undersides of leaves. Mites have a one- to two-week life cycle, and as many as 17 generations develop in a year's time. Spider mites are found everywhere in North America.

Spider mite

True Bugs

People commonly refer to all insects as "bugs," but entomologists put true bugs in a distinct class by themselves. They are ⅒–⅜ inch long with forewings that thicken toward the base and long, slender beaks that suck sap from vegetables. Young true bugs are smaller versions of the adults. The most mischievous of these creatures are squash bugs and tarnished plant bugs.

Squash bug

Tarnished
plant bug

Squash bugs are ⅝ inch long, black or brown on top, and yellow underneath. Leaves attacked by squash bugs wilt rapidly, becoming black and crisp. All vine crops, particularly squash and pumpkins, are subject to attack. Squash bugs spend the winter under dead leaves, boards, and similar materials. In spring, the females lay yellow eggs on the undersides of leaves. The nymphs that emerge are bright green and molt several times before becoming winged adults. There is generally only one generation a year.

Tarnished plant bugs are ¼ inch long, flat, oval, and streaked with brownish, yellow, or yellow-black blotches. Also, the lower third of each side of a tarnished plant bug is marked by a clear yellow triangle with a black dot. The nymphs are yellow-green with black dots. By injecting fluid into the plant, the bug causes deformed leaves on beets and chard, wilted and discolored stems on celery, and blackened shoot tips, dwarfing, and pitting on beans. These true bugs attack many other vegetables a well.

Borers

Borers are either grubs that become beetles or caterpillars (moth larvae) that feed within stems. Some borers eat the tissues of swelling buds and fruits; others attack roots or stems.

European corn borers are flesh-colored caterpillars up to 1 inch long with rows of brown spots. Adult moths have a 1-inch wingspan and are yellow-brown with wavy, dark bands. The corn borer is the most destructive corn pest known. Caterpillars first eat holes into the leaves and then bore into the stalks and ears. Bent stalks and castings outside of tiny holes in the stalks indicate that borers are at work. The female moth lays about 400 eggs on the bottom sides of corn leaves; the caterpillars hatch in about a week and spend winter in old stalks left in the garden.

European corn borer

Potato tuberworms are ¾-inch-long pink or pinkish white worms with brown heads. They destroy potatoes and will also attack eggplant and tomatoes. The adult is a narrow-winged gray-brown moth. The larvae mine leaves and stems, causing shoots to wilt and die. They will migrate down stems to potatoes and burrow in many directions through the flesh. After they have fed, they pupate in dirt-covered cocoons on the ground. Adult moths lay their eggs one at a time on leaves' undersides or in potatoes' eyes.

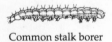

Common stalk borer

Squash vine borers are 1-inch-long wrinkled, white caterpillars with brown heads; they bore holes in the stems of vine crops. The adult resembles a wasp, with clear copper-green forewings

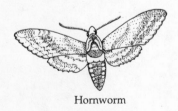

Hornworm

(1½ inches across) and an orange-and-black abdomen. The insect winters in the soil in a black cocoon. When vines start to produce runners, the moth emerges. The female pastes eggs on stems and leaf stalks near the ground. Larvae hatch in about a week.

Spinach leaf miners are pale green maggots that tunnel inside plant leaves, giving them a blistered appearance. They will beset beets and chard as well as spinach. The adult is a thin, gray ¼-inch-long fly. It lays up to five oval, white eggs on the underside of a leaf. The maggots eat for one to three weeks before dropping from the plant to spin cocoons in the soil. The mature fly emerges two to four weeks later.

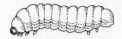

Squash vine borer

Adult squash vine borer

Soil Pests

Marauding plant destroyers include root maggots (fly larvae), grubs (root-feeding beetle larvae), wireworms (the larvae of click beetles), and cutworms (a type of caterpillar discussed previously, as were grubs). Most of these pests destroy vegetables by boring into bulbs, large roots, and stems.

Maggots are the larvae of flies (resembling the common housefly). These white or yellow, legless, wormlike creatures leave irregular pits in the bulbs and roots of many vegetables.

Cabbage maggots are the ⅓–inch-long, wedge-shaped larvae of the cabbage-root fly. Plants attacked by cabbage maggots may be stunted and pale, and their roots are often honeycombed with slimy, curving tunnels. The female fly deposits tiny, white eggs on plant stems near the soil. In a few weeks, the maggots emerge and storm the plants.

Wireworms are click beetles' larvae. They are shiny, yellow or brown creatures that grow up to ⅝ inch long. They bore into seeds, potato seed pieces, potatoes, and other root crops. Adult click beetles are about ½ inch long, black, and slender. When placed on their backs, they snap onto their feet with a clicking sound. If wireworms bore into a developing plant, it comes up but grows thin and patchy. These pests can do great damage to corn. Each generation requires two to three years to mature.

White grub

Black cutworm

Wireworm

Click beetle

Get Physical with Those Pests

There are a number of effective ways to deal with garden invaders. Some can simply be stopped by hand. The easiest way to get rid of beetles or caterpillars is to pick them off your vegetables and drop them into a jar of water. Let the jar stand for a few hours; then pour the contents into a hole and cover it with dirt. This method works well unless you're confronted with an all-out attack.

You can use a garden hose to spray sucking insects such as aphids with water. They may come back, but many times this simple treatment stops them in their tracks.

Traps and Tricks

Many insects feed at night and keep themselves hidden during daylight hours. You can trap them by placing rolled-up newspapers or a few boards around the garden; then burn the papers or boards or squash the trapped insects. Sticky squares of paper placed among garden rows often trap maggots and a few other pests; use either Tanglefoot (a commercial product available at most nurseries) or molasses to make them stick. A saucer of beer will attract and drown snails and slugs.

Unroll aluminum foil on the ground around your plants with the shiny side up to repel aphids, leafhoppers, and thrips. The key to aphid protection is brightly reflected sun. Therefore you should plant your seedlings far enough apart so the leaves won't shade the soil. The intensified heat also causes many crops to mature earlier.

Twelve-inch-square boards painted orange or bright yellow, coated with mineral oil or Tanglefoot, and placed near infested plants attract great numbers of whiteflies along with aphids, leafhoppers, blackflies, moths, and gnats. Hang white sticky squares near the top of eggplant, tomato, or pepper foliage to trap flea beetles.

Oily and Sudsy Sprays

Two common nontoxic substances will control many insects. The first, a light oil spray that gardeners call mineral oil, works by smothering slow-moving insects. It can effectively control the corn earworm. You can purchase this oil spray at garden centers.

The second is soapy water, which works wonders on such persistent hangers-on as aphids. Mix about 20 tablespoons of soap flakes in 6 gallons of water, and squirt your plants with a spray gun. It won't hurt the plants.

Insecticidal soaps, sold through seed catalogs and by most nurseries, are effective on leafhoppers, thrips, scale insects, soft-body insects, mealybugs, whiteflies, mites, earwigs, tent caterpillars, and others.

Use Aromatic Sprays

Many gardeners swear by a variety of foul-smelling homemade plant sprays. Here are three to try.

1. Gather plants with disagreeable odors, such as chives, garlic, and marigolds. Put the cloves, petals, and leaves in a pot or pan, add enough water to cover the ingredients, and bring the mixture to a boil. Strain off the solid particles, and dilute the liquid with five times as much water. As soon as this brew cools, you're ready to spray.

2. Boil tomato stems and leaves in water. Cool, then strain off the solid particles. Spray the liquid on your vegetables. It is said to repel a number of pests.

3. Cut up a pound of rhubarb leaves. Boil them in 1 quart of water for 30 minutes, then strain out the leaves and store the liquid in a bottle. To help the solution stick to plants' leaves, add a dab of liquid soap when it has cooled. The oxalic acid in this mixture is effective for controlling aphids.

Turn the Good Guys Loose

A number of predatory insects are ready to fight on your side. (You can order some for your garden from the seed catalogs in Appendix A.)

The **ladybug,** an age-old symbol of good luck, is familiar to most people with its spotted, orange-red, hemispherical shell. It eats two and a half times its own weight each day in aphids, mealybugs, moth eggs, and spider mites. The ladybug larva is a blackish, spiny-bodied creature with six short legs and red, blue, or yellow spots. It also consumes a number of insects before it grows up.

Ladybug larva

The **praying mantis,** a funny-looking, walking-stick-like insect, consumes huge quantities of beetles, caterpillars, and grasshoppers. The young mantises eat aphids, flies, and other small insects.

Praying mantis

Lacewings (sometimes known as stinkbugs) are those fragile-looking, light green insects most gardens host from time to time. The lacewing adult is mainly a nectar lover. The lacewing larva has a gluttonous appetite for aphids, mealybugs, mites, leafhoppers, thrips, and other insects.

Lacewing larva

Robber fly

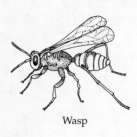

Wasp

Syrphids, flies that look something like bees, are also fond of nectar, but their larvae will gobble up aphids, scale insects, and soft-bodied bugs. **Robber flies** look like bumblebees with long, whiskered faces and long abdomens. They eat everything from grasshoppers to flies and bees. Finally, **wasps** are raised commercially for pest control. They lay their eggs inside more than 200 garden pests, including cutworms.

If you plan to use predators, you'll have to order a large number of good insects. Many gardeners recommend a combination of ladybugs, lacewings, and praying mantises. Don't be surprised if they immediately take off to the garden next door. You'll be most likely to keep them if you do three things: provide water, plant a variety of flowering plants along with your vegetables, and keep something growing in the garden the entire season.

Biological Warfare

You can battle several types of insects in your garden by using bacteria. Here are the major ones to try.

Bacillus thuringiensis (sold under the names Dipel, Thuricide, Biotrol, and Agritrol) produces a toxin that is especially effective at controlling leaf-munching worms (caterpillars) such as the cabbage looper, the imported cabbageworm, the European corn borer, and the tomato hornworm. This insecticide won't store too long because the live bacteria spores usually die within several months to two years. Mark the date on the package, and try to use it within a few months.

Grasshopper spore contains the spore of a natural parasite that attacks grasshoppers. Dust it over your plants. When insects eat the spore, they lose interest in feeding and become lethargic. The results come slowly at the beginning, but this product will reduce the grasshopper population noticeably over a couple of seasons.

Botanical Sprays

Though they won't harm birds, animals, or humans, *organic* botanical sprays can be deadly to insects.

Pyrethrum is a material derived from the dried-flower extracts of a particular chrysanthemum (a Kenyan and Ecuadoran cousin of the garden chrysanthemum). Proper doses will kill insects on contact and are especially potent against aphids, leafhoppers, caterpillars, thrips, and leaf miners.

Rotenone is an insecticide derived from the roots (and sometimes the stems) of tropical shrubs and vines of the genera *Derris* and *Lonchocarpus*. Rotenone not only acts on contact but is a digestive poison, so it can exterminate many sucking and chewing insects, including beetles, caterpillars, thrips, aphids, and leafhoppers.

Ryania is a naturally occuring insecticide derived from the stems and roots of a South American shrub found in Trinidad and the Amazon basin. Like rotenone, ryania is both a contact insecticide and a stomach poison. It is a special enemy of the European corn borer but also quells a wide variety of other insects.

Made from the seeds of a Mexican lily plant, **sabadilla** is another natural insecticide that kills on contact as well as through ingestion. It will annihilate squash bugs in particular.

CHAPTER SIX

DEALING WITH VEGETABLE DISEASES

Plant pathologists consider a vegetable to be sick when it doesn't develop or produce normally because it is under attack by some living organism. A leaf or stem infection typically exhibits a sunken, brown center bordered by a tan or yellow area; this in turn is surrounded by a pale green border into which the disease is spreading (Figure 6-1). Infected fruit shows similar color zones. Although leaf and fruit discoloration may occur from insect damage, these hues do not appear in definite zones.

figure 6-1

The Vegetable Destroyers

Here's a rundown of the most common diseases that can assail your plants. Table 6-1 will help you make a speedy diagnosis if your vegetables are exhibiting specific symptoms.

Bacteria are mostly single-celled plants that swarm through every inch of your soil. By estimate, 1 pound of garden soil contains more than 2 million bacteria. The thought is staggering, yet fortunately, most bacteria are harmless and many actually help to break down organic matter in the soil. Some, however, kill vegetables or make them inedible. The most visible characteristic of a bacterial infection in vegetables is a gelatinous fluid oozing from the tainted area. You might find any of three kinds of bacterial damage in your garden: bacterial spots, soft rots, and wilts (Figure 6-2).

figure 6-2

Bacterial spots, or blight, may start as dark green spots or streaks on leaves and stems that later turn gray, brown, or reddish brown and exude a liquid jelly. The spots sometimes drop out, leaving ragged holes, and the leaves may wither and die. Scabby or

TABLE 6-1 VEGETABLE DISEASES AT A GLANCE

TYPE/DISEASE	WHAT TO LOOK FOR	PREVENTION/CONTROL
BACTERIA		
Bacterial spots	Dark green spots or streaks that later turn gray, brown, reddish; can ooze gelatinous fluid.	Rotate crops; keep plants vigorous by fertilizing.
Bacterial soft rot	Infected areas on leaves, branches, or fruit, bordered by yellow or tan area; advanced infection causes large, sunken, dark areas, frequently oozing gelatinous fluid.	Avoid planting in undrained soil; alternate crops on long rotation. Destroy affected plants.
Bacterial wilt (spread by insects)	Wilting and death; symptoms identical to fusarium and verticillium wilt.	Destroy infected plants; grow resistant varieties.
FUNGI		
Mildew	Grayish patches on upper surfaces of leaves (powdery mildew); pale green or yellow areas on upper surfaces, light gray or purple below (downy mildew).	Rotate crops; avoid overhead sprinkling; plant resistant varieties.
Rust	Yellow, orange, red, or brown pustules on undersides of leaves and stems.	Destroy nearby weeds that show rust; collect and destroy infected plants.
Rot	Mushy and spongy stems, leaves, roots, and/or fruits.	Plant in well-drained soil; destroy infected material and plant debris; keep fruit off soil.
Canker	Sunken or swollen discolored areas on stems that sometimes girdle stems.	Destroy infected plants; use four-year rotation; purchase healthy-looking plants.
Scab	Roughened raised or sunken crusts on leaves, stems, fruits, roots, and tubers.	Practice long crop rotation; plant resistant varieties; remove weeds.
Fungal leaf spots/blight	Spots on leaves; centers may fall out; spots may enlarge.	When severe, collect and burn infected material.
Wilt	Leaves turn pale green to yellow; plants wilt and die.	Use resistant varieties; practice long rotation; collect and destroy infected plants.
Smut/sooty mold	Dark brown to black sooty-looking masses inside swollen white blisters.	Pick off and burn infected parts before blisters open; grow resistant varieties.
VIRUSES		
	Distortion of leaves, flowers, and fruit; stunted plants; yellow streaking or mottling.	Destroy diseased material; control weeds.
NEMATODES		
	Yellowing, stunting, wilting, dieback; knots on roots.	Destroy infected plants; plant resistant varieties; rotate plantings.

sunken brown spots or blotches caused by bacteria are generally called blights.

Bacterial soft rot may infect the leaves, branches, and fruit of plants. A lighter yellow or tan area usually borders the infected area. Advanced infection causes large, sunken, dark, oozing areas on the fruit.

Bacterial wilt occurs when the microorganisms (usually spread by insects) invade and plug up the plant's water-conducting tubes. If you slice the stem of an infected plant, a gelatinous fluid will seep out. These bacteria can make seemingly healthy, vigorous plants simply dry up and wilt overnight, much to the gardener's dismay.

Bacterial diseases can't be controlled chemically except through the treatment of vegetable seeds before planting. Certain insects, such as the flea beetle and the cucumber beetle, carry bacterial disease in their digestive tracts. When these beetles have lunch in your garden, they spread disease.

Fungi are minute nongreen plants that exist everywhere in garden soil. One pound of soil contains up to 225 million of them. Like bacteria, some fungi decompose organic matter into nutrients that can be used by vegetables. Other fungi, however, attack live plants. With the exception of rots, fungal diseases tend to start with a sunken, dark area that is later bordered by yellow, tan, or light green. Eight general types of fungal infections can appear in your garden: mildews, rusts, rots, cankers, scab, spots, wilts, and smuts (Figure 6-3).

Mildews fall into two groups, powdery mildew and downy mildew. Powdery mildew shows up as superficial white to light gray patches on the upper surfaces of leaves and on buds. Plants infected with downy mildew have pale green or yellow areas on the tops of leaves, with light gray or purplish patches below. Mildewed leaves wilt, wither, and die. Seedlings may wilt and collapse. Both mildews affect numerous kinds of vegetables. Mildew attacks are most severe in cool, humid, or wet weather and commonly occur in areas with cool nights and warm days.

Rust sometimes appears as bright yellow, orange, red, reddish brown, or black powder pustules on the undersides of leaves. This is a complicated disease, since the forms that attack vegetables require two different plants (called alternate hosts) to complete the fungi's life cycle. The rust that attacks corn completes its life cycle on oxalis. In extreme cases, plants troubled by rust shrivel and die.

Rot is a term that covers several diseases. Plants with root rot may gradually or suddenly lose vigor, their leaves turning pale or yellow; the roots may be mushy and spongy (a decay

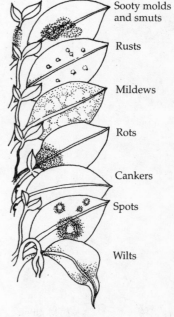

Sooty molds and smuts

Rusts

Mildews

Rots

Cankers

Spots

Wilts

figure 6-3

caused by both fungi and bacteria. In many cases, nematodes (microscopic worms) provide the wound by which root-rotting fungi and bacteria enter. When seedlings rot, wilt, collapse, and die before or after they emerge, the condition is called damping-off. Fruit rot often starts as one or more spots that enlarge to include a portion or all of the fruit. Rots can attack practically every vegetable in your garden.

Cankers are dead areas on plants' stems. They are oval or irregular in shape, often sunken or swollen, and typically discolored. Some completely girdle the stem. Plants with canker are often stunted. One of the more serious vegetable diseases, blackleg of cabbage falls within the canker category.

As its name suggests, scab usually manifests roughened, crust-like, raised or sunken areas on leaves, stems, fruit, roots, or tubers. Affected leaves may wither and drop early. A few bacteria and a wide range of fungi cause scab.

Fungal leaf spots vary in size, shape, and color. The centers of the spots may fall out or enlarge into blotches. Wet seasons, high humidity, and water splashed on foliage increase the incidence of leaf spots. Specific spot diseases include black spot, tar spot, and anthracnose.

Wilt is basically three diseases. Each type invades and blocks the water- and food-conducting vessels inside plants. Hence wilts are sometimes confused with root rot.

Bacterial wilt was discussed earlier in this chapter. Fusarium and verticillium wilt are caused by fungi. Plants attacked by either verticillium or fusarium wilt are usually stunted and yellow. The wilting starts at the base of stems and proceeds upward.

Smuts and sooty molds produce massive amounts of black, sooty spores. Smut is a fungal disease that begets dark brown to black sooty-looking spore masses inside swollen, whitish blisters. Sooty mold shows up as unsightly, superficial, dark brown or black blotches on leaves, fruit, and stems. Easily removed by rubbing, sooty mold causes little damage.

Viruses are complex single molecules that behave like living organisms. More than 200,000 of these marauding molecules inhabit a square inch of soil. To identify viruses, plant pathologists usually group them by what they do to plants. Viral diseases may distort (pucker or curl) leaves, flowers, or fruits; stunt plants; cause yellow streaks; or mottle leaves (Figure 6-4).

A few of the viruses that affect vegetables are aster yellows (plants are stunted and yellow), curly top (plants are dwarfed, with bunched, curled leaves), mosaic (leaves have mottled yellow or light green areas), ring spot (plant tissue has yellow or

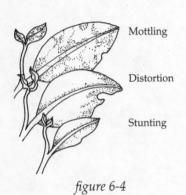

Mottling

Distortion

Stunting

figure 6-4

brown concentric rings), and yellows (plants are uniformly yellow, they may wilt and die). Viruses that assail individual vegetables will be covered in greater detail in chapter 8.

Good cultivation practices and the use of virus-resistant vegetables provide the best protection from these diseases. Since many viruses are spread by sucking insects such as aphids and leafhoppers, you can also limit the viral diseases in your garden by controlling insects that spread them (see chapter 5).

Parasitic nematodes are vigorous, slender, tiny roundworms that attack plants. They are usually considered a plant disease because they cause similar symptoms. Most nematodes are harmless because they feed on decomposing organic material and other soil organisms. But nematodes that attack living vegetables suck out the plants' green color and cause stunting of their vegetables, wilting, and dieback (the death of peripheral parts).

The root-knot nematode brings out galls on the roots of many vegetables. The first indication of nematode injury in a garden or field is often the appearance of small circular or irregular areas of stunted plants with yellow or bronzed foliage. This area gradually enlarges. A number of nonchemical methods can protect your vegetables from nematodes.

Preventing Vegetable Diseases

Before vegetables can fall prey to either insects or disease, the plants must be susceptible to them. That is, the garden must have the right environmental conditions (such as abundant moisture or an optimum temperature) and a disease-causing organism or insect ready to pounce. If any of these elements is missing, your plants will remain healthy. Use the following basic preventive measures to maintain this health.

1. Choose a garden site where water drains off easily. Avoid heavy clay soils that retain moisture or add organic material to create good drainage. Excess soil moisture provides precisely the right conditions for root rots and increases the chances of damping-off among your seedlings. Standing water or excess moisture will also stunt plant growth.

2. Keep your garden clean. Pick up piles of trash as they accumulate. Even more important, remove crop residues when you harvest your vegetables, as dead fruit provides a perfect egg depository or winter lodgings for some insects. In many cases, cleanup alone will drastically reduce the possibility of an insect problem, which in turn prevents the diseases transmitted by insects.

3. Disease spreads quickly through clusters of a single type of

vegetable. Therefore, it's a good idea to mix crops within each row. Since favorable conditions can help a disease to move quickly through the entire garden, destroy infected plants or plant parts as soon as you discover them. Also, avoid working in the garden immediately after a rain or when the plants are wet with dew. Disease organisms that cling to your clothing and hands are more easily transferred to your vegetables at this time.

4.　　If you smoke, wash your hands with soap and water before working in the garden. This helps stop the spread of to-bacco mosaic, a viral disease that is a problem in some areas.

5.　　Choose vegetable varieties that are resistant to one or more diseases. Varieties have varying degrees of immunity, rang-ing from tolerance to partial resistance to complete immu-nity. (Chapter 9 covers all vegetable varieties so you can select the right ones for your garden. You can then order seeds or transplants from a seed catalog or go to your local nursery. Chances are, the nursery won't have the variety you want but may carry a variety right for your area.)

First, identify garden problems (such as wilt or blight); then select varieties that resist these diseases. If you have a choice of several resistant varieties, base your decision on size, color, and your own growing area's needs.

You can also call your county's agricultural extension ser-vice (listed in Appendix B) to ask which diseases are a prob-lem locally. Request a list of recommended vegetable varieties. Select resistant varieties from this list, matching them with the problem diseases.

6.　　Start healthy to stay healthy. Buy disease-free seed and ro-bust transplants. Certified disease-free seed is grown in arid parts of the western United States and can be purchased through seed catalogs and at garden centers.

Most reputable nurseries sell only healthy transplants, but you should check for yourself. Select vigorous-looking plants with no spots on their leaves.

7.　　Remember this rule: Dig deep, dig early. If you spade your garden deeply in early spring, you can destroy the larvae of beetles and the pupae of many caterpillars that overwinter in the soil. They'll never have a chance to emerge and attack your crops.

8.　　Practice crop rotation. Plant each type of vegetable in a dif-ferent spot every year. If you put your annual garden plan on paper and save it, you won't have to worry about re-membering where things were. If possible, move the entire garden every three or four years. Cabbage maggots, veg-etable weevils, seed corn maggots, and other insects live in the ground adjacent to their host plants and redouble their efforts the next season if their favorite plants stay nearby. Eggplant, tomatoes, and all members of the cabbage clan are especially susceptible to disease if planted in the same spot each year.

9. Time your planting of particular vegetables to avoid peak insect buildups. In some areas, flea beetles destroy radishes, turnips, and similar crops planted in mid-May. If they're planted after June 15, however, they will suffer little damage because the adult stage will have passed.

10. Let other plants help. The clever gardener selects plants that influence insect pests. Some, called trap crops, attract insects to divert them from the main crop. For example, yellow nas-turtiums lure black aphids away from beans and tomatoes.

   Certain plants repel pests because of inherent chemical com-pounds that are either obnoxious or toxic to insects. Both French and African marigolds excrete compounds that poi-son nematodes. When grown in soil infested with these par-asitic worms, they reduce the nematode population and the severity of any attack.

   Some gardeners swear by companion planting to control in-sects. Experiment station tests, however, have failed to prove whether this method works. You may still want to try it in your garden. If it succeeds, you're way ahead. If it does not, you have planted some extremely useful herbs and some beautiful flowers.

11. Give your vegetables elbowroom. Individual plants com-pete with each other for water, nutrients, and growing space. Each vegetable has its own optimal spacing. Cab-bages spaced 18–24 inches apart produce larger heads than those spaced 12 inches apart. Studies show that cucumbers spaced 12 inches apart yield more than those spaced either 6 or 18 inches apart. Vegetables planted directly in the seedbed (rather than being transplanted) must be thinned out to provide growing room. Crowded vegetables are fre-quently small and spindly—carrots twist around each other, radishes won't form bulbs, lettuce won't head—as well as more liable to be threatened by insects and disease. (Chapter 9 provides information about the favored spacing of specific vegetables.)

12. Fertilize regularly. Apply fertilizer before planting your vegetables. Spread horse manure 4–6 inches deep on the bed, then spade it into the top 8–12 inches of soil. Add bonemeal (4 pounds per 100 square feet) and wood ash or rock phosphate (3 pounds per 100 square feet).

    Healthy, well-nourished plants are less prone to sickness and insect attack than those growing in soil that lacks the required nutrients.

13. Remove those weeds. Weeds harbor insects, host disease, and reduce access to air and sunlight, creating conditions conducive to disease development. Weeds also compete directly with vegetables for water, nutrients, light, and space.

    Control weeds within the garden plot by scraping the ground with a hoe blade nearly parallel to the soil surface and less than 1 inch deep. This method will keep you from injuring vegetable roots that lie near the surface. It isn't necessary to be so careful when removing weeds outside vegetable beds.

    You can also control weeds with black polyethylene mulch, weed cloths (a black fabric that prevents weed growth), or an organic mulch. Apply organic mulch 4–6 inches deep so that weeds cannot peek through.

14. If you must water overhead, do it early in the morning so that the leaves dry off quickly. Late-afternoon and evening watering mean that the leaves will remain damp for longer periods. Because spores of disease-producing fungi need moisture to germinate, water on the leaves facilitates the rapid development of leaf spot, downy and powdery mildew, rust, and other foliage diseases.

15. Plan ahead. Many gardeners find that following a smart schedule is all that's necessary to keep their vegetables relatively free of both insects and diseases season after season. Cleanup should take place throughout the gardening season and immediately following harvest. Deep spading to control larvae and pupae should be handled in early spring. Plan crop rotation several seasons ahead. Other gardening chores should be handled at the appropriate times. A summary of preventive measures appears in Table 6-2.

TABLE 6-2 CONTROL PRACTICES FOR DISEASES

	CROP ROTATION	DISEASE-FREE SEED	GARDEN CLEANLINESS	HEALTHY TRANSPLANTS	RESISTANT VARIETIES	SITE SELECTION	WEED CONTROL
BACTERIA							
Spots/blight	🌿	🌿🌿	🌿	🌿🌿🌿	🌿		
Bacterial wilt	🌿			🌿🌿🌿		🌿	
OTHER DISEASES							
Canker	🌿🌿🌿		🌿				
Mildew				🌿🌿🌿	🌿		
Rot	🌿	🌿	🌿	🌿🌿🌿		🌿	
Rust				🌿🌿🌿	🌿		
Scab	🌿		🌿		🌿🌿		
Smut			🌿		🌿🌿		
Spots		🌿🌿	🌿		🌿🌿		
Wilt	🌿			🌿🌿🌿	🌿🌿🌿		
Viruses		🌿🌿🌿		🌿🌿🌿	🌿🌿		🌿

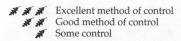

🌿🌿🌿 Excellent method of control
🌿🌿 Good method of control
🌿 Some control

CHAPTER SEVEN

WEATHERING
THE ELEMENTS

Nature's peculiarities often alter the growth and quality of homegrown vegetables. Temperatures that are too high or too low, summer hail, and too much or too little sun may damage crops. While we can't control Mother Nature, we can learn to cooperate or compensate so that our gardens have a better than even chance.

Germination Gems of Wisdom

Most vegetables germinate seed, grow, and set fruit within a surprisingly narrow temperature range. Each vegetable seed has individual requirements regarding soil temperature. Lettuce and onion, for example, tolerate soil temperatures down to 32°F; germination at such low temperatures is slow, but the seed will survive and will sprout as the soil temperature warms up. Bean and sweet corn seeds, on the other hand, will rot if left in the ground more than a few days at temperatures below 55–60°F.

Vegetable seeds also cease germinating when the temperature rises too high—somewhere between 86 and 104°F, depending on the vegetable. During hot weather, surface soil temperatures often climb far above this range. Thus, even if the seed has germinated, the seedlings (especially carrots and beets) can die of heat injury at the soil surface. Gardeners can aid germination and seedling survival during hot weather by spreading 2 inches of organic material (such as compost) over the soil after the seeds have been planted. This protective layer reduces soil temperature and holds in moisture.

TABLE 7-1 SOIL TEMPERATURES FOR VEGETABLE SEED GERMINATION

VEGETABLE	MINIMUM	OPTIMUM	MAXIMUM
asparagus	50	75	95
beans (lima)	60	80	85
beans (snap)	60	85	95
beets	40	85	95
broccoli	40	85	95
cabbage	40	85	95
carrots	40	80	95
cauliflower	40	80	95
celery	40	80	95
cucumbers	60	95	105
eggplant	60	85	95
endive	32	75	75
lettuce	32	75	75
melons	60	95	105
okra	60	95	105
onions	32	80	95
parsley	40	80	95
parsnips	32	70	85
peas	40	75	85
peppers	60	85	95
pumpkins	60	95	105
radishes	40	85	95
spinach	32	70	75
squash	60	95	105
sweet corn	50	85	105
Swiss chard	40	85	95
tomatoes	50	85	95
turnips	40	85	105

To ensure good seed germination, plant vegetables when the soil is within the proper temperature range as shown in Table 7-1. A soil thermometer, available at most nurseries, is a handy tool to have.

Warm and Cool Season Crops

It's important to repeat that vegetables are generally either warm season or cool season crops. Plants harvested for their fruit, such as tomatoes, melons, eggplant, peppers, and squash, need copious heat and long days to grow well and form fruit. Leafy and root vegetables, including carrots, beets, spinach, and cabbage, flourish when the weather is on the cool side.

Within these wide categories, each vegetable has its own temperature range for growing. Radishes will develop when the temperature is between 40 and 75°F, while corn wants it between 50 and 95°F.

Hardy and Tender Crops

Vegetables can also be categorized by the time span between when they are planted and the last spring frost. There are three major designations: very hardy (planted four to six weeks before the last frost), hardy (planted two to four weeks before the last frost), and tender (planted on, or a week or two after, the last frost).

In addition, vegetable varieties have individual temperature ranges. Early varieties require a smaller amount of heat to mature than midseason varieties. Most miniature vegetables need less cumulative heat than other vegetables.

If you live in an area of cool summers (below 70°F), you can grow crops that require a longer or hotter season (such as melons) by planting the earliest varieties available. Those with the fewest days to maturity have the lowest heat requirements.

You can plan by using some estimated dates for the first fall and last spring frost in different regions of California: Central Valley, November 15/March 1; Imperial Valley, December 20/ January 30; North Coast, December 1/February 28; South Coast, December 15/January 30; Mountains, September 1/April 20.

However, it's possible to extend the season and protect all plants from frost and wind by covering them with hot caps, bottomless plastic jugs, or other protective devices.

Fruit Set

Eggplant, peppers, tomatoes, beans, and peas start to form fruit when the male parts of their flowers successfully pollinate the female parts. The success or failure of this pollination depends greatly on the temperature. The determining factor for such vegetables as peppers and tomatoes is the nighttime, not the daytime, temperature. To set fruit, most tomatoes require temperatures above 55°F for at least part of the night. Night temperatures above 75°F inhibit fruit set and cause blossoms to drop.

Misshapen tomato fruit and puffiness can result from high or low temperature extremes, which interfere with the growth of pollen tubes and normal fertilization of the flower's ovary. In addition, catfacing (puckering and scarring of the blossom end of the fruit) can occur when cool weather at flowering time makes the blossom stick to the small fruit. Many of these problems can be averted by placing clear polyethylene covers over the plants when temperatures fall below 60°F.

The Long-Day/Short-Day Factor

As a rule, vegetables need a minimum of six to eight hours of direct sunlight a day. The length of daylight (called day length) they receive also makes a difference. In fact, vegetables are categorized according to the day length they need to produce flowers and fruit. Some, such as spinach, Chinese cabbage, and corn, start to flower in late spring as they begin to receive more than 12 hours of light each day. These are called long-day plants. Gardeners want corn to flower (to tassel and produce ears), but it exasperates them when the lengthening days of late spring trigger the flowering of Chinese cabbage or spinach long before the plants are ready to harvest.

Short-day plants produce flowers only when they receive less than 12 hours of daylight. Still other vegetables, such as tomatoes, are day-neutral or intermediate-day plants; they will flower and fruit in a wide variety of day lengths.

Day length can also influence the bulbing of onions. Some varieties need a long day (more than 12 hours of daylight) to induce bulbing while others bulb only when days have less than 12 hours of light.

Too Much Sun

Cool weather crops do poorly when the summer sun is intense, as the exposed parts of fruits can become 20° hotter than the shaded parts. This contributes to uneven ripening and blotchy fruit. If the sun is hot enough (over 90°F), the exposed parts of plants frequently show sunscald—that is, a yellow or white patch on the side of the fruit facing the sun. This spot may remain yellow or it may shrink and form a flattened, grayish white spot. Varieties of peppers and tomatoes that have little foliage commonly suffer from sunscald. (Hence you can reduce the chances of sunscald for tomatoes, peppers, and similar crops by selecting varieties that grow heavy foliage.)

Protect cool weather vegetables such as lettuce by providing partial shade. A lath frame supported on 2-foot-high posts works fine. Many gardeners are using shadecloth (a plastic screening that cuts sun intensity), which can be found at most garden centers. It can be installed over garden beds on a plastic pipe-frame support.

Shadecloth that casts 30 percent shade is preferable when temperatures are below 85°F. When temperatures rise above 85°F and the sun is intense, use 47 percent shadecloth. During summer in desert climates, 55 percent shadecloth is best. Cool season vegetables do not need shading in areas that are normally overcast.

Too Little Sun

Plants that receive much less than six hours of direct sun a day (as distinct from day length) can become spindly, unproductive, and taller than normal. If certain sections of your garden receive less than six hours, you can supplement the natural light with a reflector panel. Make these panels by stapling or gluing aluminum foil to large pieces of cardboard or plywood—4x4 feet, 4x6 feet, and 5x8 feet are good sizes—mounted on a wood frame. Light reflectors should be set up on the east, west, or north side of your garden, or on all three. Experiment to determine the size and placement that work best for your garden.

Wind and Hail

Plants subjected to strong winds divert energy from setting and bearing fruit to self-protection, and harvests under blustery conditions are usually poor. Shield your plants from this stress with protective milk cartons anchored by wire, bottomless sacks, or a 2-foot-high plastic wall running along the windward side.

Hail, which sometimes accompanies summer, spring, or fall thunderstorms, can destroy cucumbers, squash, and beans. Lettuce will be reduced to a pulpy mass but will come back. Shredded corn will produce a crop as though nothing had happened. Carrots and asparagus will not be affected. You can protect the delicate plants for short periods by covering them with a clear polyethylene sheet.

CHAPTER EIGHT

MOTHER NATURE'S PUZZLERS

This chapter covers the general and specific environmental troubles that befall vegetables. It begins with a chart that will help you quickly identify general conditions and what to do about them. A series of charts, each devoted to an individual vegetable, follows. These offer similar information about the potential environmental problems that could affect certain vegetables.

GENERAL GARDENING PROBLEMS AFFECTING ALL VEGETABLES

WHAT'S WRONG? WHAT TO LOOK FOR	POSSIBLE CAUSES	CURES
Darkened areas on stems and leaves; young plants turn brown, die.	Fertilizer burn (fertilizer placed directly on plants or leaves, or too much fertilizer in soil).	Mix 4–6 inches of animal manure into the soil before planting. Make sure fertilizer does not touch plants.
Stunted growth; sickly yellow color.	1. Soil may have a deficiency. 2. Soil is compacted or isn't draining properly. 3. Overwatering. 4. Low soil pH. 5. Insects or disease.	1. Work 4–6 inches of animal manure into soil. If problem does not clear up, test for trace element deficiency. 2. Add 5–6 inches of organic matter to soil. Turn in thoroughly to a depth of 8–12 inches. 3. Do not keep soil soggy. Water for 2–3 hours, then do not water again until soil is dry 4–8 inches deep. 4. Test soil for lime. Identify and use control measures. 5. See insect or disease chart.
Weak, spindly plants.	1. Too much shade. 2. Plants spaced too closely. 3. Too much nitrogen.	1. Move garden or plants to a location that has at least 6–8 hours of sunlight daily. 2. Thin to the spacings suggested on seed packets. 3. Avoid excess fertilization.
Dark or bluish green leaves, followed by bronzing, reddening, purpling; stunted.	1. Phosphorus deficiency. 2. Low temperatures.	1. Add rock phosphate or bonemeal at the rate of 2–4 pounds per 100 square feet. 2. Plant at recommended times or shelter plants with protective devices.
Scorching, browning, or bronzing of leaf margins (older leaves affected first); plants appear rusty.	Potassium deficiency.	Add wood ash or greensand at the rate of 2–4 pounds per 100 square feet.
Wilting plants.	1. Poor drainage, excess water in soil. 2. Lack of moisture in soil. 3. Lack of moisture in soil.	1. Turn 5–6 inches of organic matter into the soil to a depth of 8–12 inches. 2. Cover the soil with 2–3 inches of organic material. 3. Water 2–3 hours at a time. Don't water again until the soil is dry to a depth of 4–5 inches. This keeps the moisture within a safe range.
Many blossoms drop off before fruit forms; failure to set fruit.	1. Low moisture supply in soil; blossoms drop when exposed to hot, dry winds. 2. Low night temperatures. 3. High temperatures.	1. Use a 2–3-inch organic mulch around plants. 2. Solutions are discussed under individual vegetables. 3. Solutions are discussed under individual vegetables.

GARDENING PROBLEMS AFFECTING SPECIFIC VEGETABLES

VEGETABLE	WHAT'S WRONG? WHAT TO LOOK FOR	POSSIBLE CAUSES	CURES
ARTICHOKES	The bract (the edible part of the artichoke) becomes tough and leathery.	Summer heat opens the buds.	Harvest buds when they are still tightly closed.
ASPARAGUS	Yellowing plants, including leaves.	1. Consistent overwatering. 2. Soil pH is below 6.5.	1. Water carefully. A good rule of thumb: Water 2–3 hours, then wait until the soil has dried to a depth of 4–8 inches. 2. Test the pH level. (Consult chapter 2.)
	Brown or discolored spears, soft consistency.	Crop comes up too early in the spring, and some spears freeze. (This becomes more obvious as the temperature warms up.)	Discard early spears or insulate with protective devices.
	Crooked, curved, or misshapen spears.	1. Windblown sand injures spears. 2. Cramped cultivation leads to nicked spears.	1. Shield spears. 2. Be careful not to damage spears when weeding beds.
BEANS (all types)	Seedlings fail to emerge.	1. Soil temperatures below 55–60°F cause seeds to rot. 2. Soil is heavy or crusted. Seedlings break off or can't push through. 3. Beans planted in the spring 2 or more inches below ground often rot and fail to come up. Beans planted later, 1 inch or less deep, may dry out and die before emerging.	1. Delay planting until the soil has warmed enough. 2. Apply a light mulch of compost, sawdust, or similar material over the bed. 3. Plant beans about 1 inch deep in early spring, 2 inches deep later in the season.
	Poor flower and bean production.	1. Lack of nutrients in the soil (beans must produce strong, early growth before flowering starts). 2. A few old pods left on the vines greatly reduces the development of new beans.	1. Mix organic material into the soil before planting. 2. Pick snap beans off vines during the young, succulent stage.
	Baldhead: bean plants have no growing tips. No new leaves or buds develop.	An injury to the seed damages the embryo (infrequently caused by insect and disease attack).	Buy seed from major growers. Remove plants from row and replant.
	The first few seeds develop; the rest of the pod shrivels to a tail (called a pollywog).	Lack of moisture in the soil.	Layer 2–3 inches of organic material on top of the bed. Water beans 2–3 hours at a time. Don't water again until the soil is dry to a depth of 4–5 inches.
	Vines flower, but flowers drop off without producing beans.	Temperature jumps from cool to 90°F and above, or weather is dry and especially windy.	Avoid planting Blue Lake, Kentucky Wonder, and pole limas (they are especially susceptible). Plant faster maturing varieties.

GARDENING PROBLEMS AFFECTING SPECIFIC VEGETABLES

VEGETABLE	WHAT'S WRONG? WHAT TO LOOK FOR	POSSIBLE CAUSES	CURES
BEANS (all types) (continued)	Sunscald: reddish or pale brown spots and streaks on the pods.	Pods are exposed to hot sun following cool, overcast weather.	Plant in well-drained soil.
BEETS	Stringy, tough roots; bland flavor.	1. Exposed to temperatures over 85°F. 2. Excessive competition from weeds or other beets. 3. Dried out soil slows down growth. (Beets need to grow at full speed without a single letup.) 4. Beets remaining in the ground more than 10 days after they reach edible size.	1. Grow in early spring or fall, when temperatures are lower. 2. Keep beds weeded. Space a minimum of 2–3 inches apart. 3. Place 3–4 inches of organic material on top of the bed. Follow the fail-safe watering schedule. 4. Harvest at about 2 inches in diameter.
	Spotty germination; many seedlings failing to emerge.	When temperatures are too high at planting time, seeds fail to germinate.	If the weather turns unexpectedly hot, place 1 inch of compost or other organic material over the seedbed. Water twice a day, 2–3 hours at a time, until the seedlings are well established.
	Red color on leaf margins or tips that spreads to entire surface; dying leaf tips; crinkled middle and older leaves; corky spots at surface of beet or near growth rings.	Boron deficiency. Acid soil (pH 6.5 or below) makes beets especially sensitive to boron deficiency.	Check the soil's pH level. If below 6.5, add 5 pounds of lime per 100 square feet for each pH unit (e.g., from 5.5 to 6.5 is one unit).
	White ring (whitish rings inside the beet).	Drought or heavy rains that follow an extended hot period.	There's no cure for heavy rains. Keep soil from drying out during drought conditions.
BROCCOLI	Small, scattered heads form prematurely.	Young plants are subjected to temperatures below 40°F before or shortly after planting.	Insulate small plants with protective devices.
	Buds stop appearing. Some older buds have little, yellow flower heads.	As soon as some heads flower, the plant stops producing young buds.	Keep your crop harvested. Pick the developing buds every 3 days as long as the plant continues to produce.
	Premature flowering (good growth followed suddenly by sprouting yellow flowers).	Temperatures over about 85°F.	Plant early varieties to mature ahead of the heat, or plant broccoli in midsummer for a fall crop.
BRUSSELS SPROUTS	Large, leafy, loose sprouts.	Temperature too high. (Brussels sprouts need temperatures below 75°F to produce compact sprouts.)	Time your planting so the crop matures in fall.
	Wartlike projections the size of pin heads on leaves and stems.	Tissue injured by soil particles blown against leaves.	Protect plants on the windward side. (Although the injury is conspicuous, it does not affect production.)

GARDENING PROBLEMS AFFECTING SPECIFIC VEGETABLES

VEGETABLE	WHAT'S WRONG? WHAT TO LOOK FOR	POSSIBLE CAUSES	CURES
CABBAGE (collards, Chinese cabbage)	Grows well, then suddenly starts to flower (also sometimes flowers and goes to seed just before harvest stage).	Exposure to 40–50°F temperatures for 3–4 weeks. (Cabbage planted to overwinter often fails to produce heads.)	Plant slimmer, pencil-size transplants. This problem is especially serious when larger transplants are used or when cabbage is planted in the fall for spring growth (mild winter areas only).
	Heads start to split.	Plants are allowed to dry out and then watered; as a result, the center and outer portions develop at different speeds. The heads of early varieties often split soon after they mature in warm weather.	Stop watering, or rotate the whole plant about half a turn (to break off some roots and slow growth).
	Browning along margins of old leaves; bitter, tough heads; water spots in core and stem.	Boron deficiency.	Test the soil. To correct, apply 8 ounces of borax for every 1,000 square feet of garden space.
CARDOON	Pithy, tasteless leafstalks.	Slowed growth.	Keep the soil moist. Place a 2–3-inch layer of organic material over the bed, or water the plant for 2–3 hours and not again until the soil dries to a depth of 4–8 inches.
CARROTS	Sprouts appear in sparse clumps or don't come up at all.	1. Seed isn't planted deeply enough. If the weather turns hot and dry, seed is parched and fails to germinate well. 2. The soil forms a hard crust that prevents the sprout from breaking through.	1. Cover seed with 1 inch of vermiculite, compost, or sawdust to retain moisture. Cover the seedbed with clear plastic to prevent evaporation; remove plastic as soon as the seedlings peek through the soil. 2. Prevent the soil surface from drying out, as described above.
	Twisted or forked roots.	1. Rocks or clods in the soil cause roots to twist around them or to fork. 2. Plants are too close together. (Those grown less than 1 inch apart tend to be misshapen and tough.) 3. Soil contains too much manure, causing rough-branching carrots.	1. Pick out rocks and clods. 2. Space carrots 1–2 inches apart. 3. Mix only fine, well-rotted manure into the bed.
	Longitudinal cracks; sometimes leaves are yellow and malformed.	1. Boron deficiency. 2. Dry weather is followed by heavy rain, or the soil dries out completely and then is watered heavily.	1. Test the soil. If deficient, apply 2 ounces of borax per 1,000 square feet. 2. Place 2–3 inches of organic material on top of the soil. Don't water until the soil is dry to a depth of 4–5 inches. (Check with a trowel.)
	Carrot tops (shoulders) turn green.	Overexposure to light causes chlorophyll to develop, making shoulders green and inedible.	Cover the shoulders with soil.

VEGETABLE	WHAT'S WRONG? WHAT TO LOOK FOR	POSSIBLE CAUSES	CURES
CARROTS (continued)	Roots are long, thin, and spindly, or short and stumpy.	Soil temperatures are too high or too low. Roots that develop at 40–50°F become long and pointed. Roots that develop at 70–80°F are short and stumpy.	Plant and cultivate when soil is 60–70°F. If soil temperatures regularly rise above 70°F, grow carrots during the cooler days of spring or fall.
	Pale orange roots.	Prolonged exposure to air temperatures below 65°F. (These carrots lose some of their nutritional value.)	Plant later in the spring so carrots can grow in temperatures of 65°F and above, or grow them under protective devices.
	Flower heads resembling Queen Anne's lace develop on the plants.	Prolonged exposure to low temperatures (below 65°F).	Plant later in the spring.
	Bitter flavor.	Exposure to hot, dry weather.	Cover the soil with 2–3 inches of organic material to keep it cooler and to reduce moisture loss.
	Seed stalks appear early in the season.	Exposure to below-freezing temperatures early in the season.	Shield young plants with protective devices.
CAULIFLOWER	Loose, yellowish heads.	Exposure to the sun.	Tie the lower "wrapper" leaves over the developing heads. The best heads are grown in the fall under cool, moist conditions.
	Curds gradually turn brown.	Boron deficiency.	Have the soil tested. Apply ½ ounce of borax for every 24 square feet.
	Leaves become long and narrow ("whiptail"); plants may not produce heads.	Molybdenum deficiency in very acid soil.	Test the soil for pH and trace elements. Apply lime to neutralize soil. Add ½ ounce of ammonium molybdate per 500 square feet. Plant resistant cauliflower varieties.
CELERY	Ragged crosswise cracking of stems; stiff, brittle, sometimes bitter stems; edges of young leaves may be streaked; browning leaves.	Boron deficiency (common in heavily alkaline soils).	Test the soil. If deficient, apply 2 ounces of borax per 30 square yards. Plant resistant varieties.
	Streaking and scorching of tips and leaf margins of both celery and celeriac.	Magnesium deficiency.	Have the soil tested. Use magnesium chelates; follow manufacturer's instructions. Plant resistant varieties.
	Lots of leaves but no stalks appear.	Sudden fluctuations in temperature during early stages of growth (up to about 4 inches high).	Cover plants with translucent gallon milk jugs or similar protective devices. Remove when the weather becomes warmer.

GARDENING PROBLEMS AFFECTING SPECIFIC VEGETABLES

VEGETABLE	WHAT'S WRONG? WHAT TO LOOK FOR	POSSIBLE CAUSES	CURES
CORN	Ears are only partially filled with ripe kernels.	Each kernel must be pollinated individually. (Wind-borne pollen from the male tassels floats into the female cob.)	Plant corn in blocks of 2–3 rows, rather than in a single row, to increase the likelihood of pollination.
	Purple margins develop on the leaves, starting with those at the bottom; the entire plant may be dark green and stunted.	Phosphorus deficiency.	Sprinkle bonemeal on the bed before planting (2–3 pounds per 100 square feet).
	Leaf edges roll inward.	Inadequate watering (corn needs moisture to make rapid growth just as the ears start to mature).	Place 2–3 inches of organic material on top of the bed to reduce moisture loss. Water corn 2–3 hours at a time, then withhold water until the soil dries to a depth of 4–8 inches.
	Small ears.	Plants are too close together.	Space early varieties at least 8 inches apart. Space later varieties 12–15 inches apart.
	Popped kernels (they look like popcorn).	Seed coats break at the weakest point.	No cure exists. Plant another variety.
CUCUMBERS	Early flowers don't produce fruit.	1. Female flowers (necessary for the production of cucumbers) may not have appeared. The first flowers are male.	1. Be patient. The plants will soon produce flowers of both sexes. You can also grow the all-female cucumber hybrids. (Each seed package contains a few seeds of male flower-bearing plants so there is something to pollinate the female blossoms. The package clearly states that the variety is an all-female hybrid.)
		2. An insufficient number of insects (mostly bees) to carry out pollination.	2. Play bee. Pick off a male flower (the ones without little cucumbers) and rub the fuzzy inside part on the tip of the tiny cucumbers.
	Bitter cucumbers.	1. Uneven watering or temperatures that vary more than 20°F from day to day.	1. Place 2–3 inches of organic material on top of the bed to hold down moisture loss. Use the fail-safe watering method.
			2. Grow a bitter-free variety of cucumber.
	Few cucumbers.	Plants are spaced too closely.	Space cucumbers 8–12 inches apart. (Plants set closer or farther apart than this produce fewer mature cucumbers.)
	Plants stop producing.	Old cucumbers aren't picked off. (Even a few fruit left on the vine to mature will halt production.)	Pick cucumbers from the vines as they reach usable size.

GARDENING PROBLEMS AFFECTING SPECIFIC VEGETABLES

VEGETABLE	WHAT'S WRONG? WHAT TO LOOK FOR	POSSIBLE CAUSES	CURES
EGGPLANT	Blossoms appear but fall off without producing fruit.	Eggplant blossoms drop at temperatures below 58°F and above 70°F.	Plant early eggplant varieties that are unaffected by these temperatures.
	Lush foliage, little fruit.	Too much water.	Water 2–3 hours at a time. Don't water again until the soil has dried out 4–8 inches deep. Check with a trowel.
	Stunted plants.	Temperature dips below 40°F.	Set the plants out when the air temperatures are staying above 65°F, or protect the plants with plastic bottomless jugs or other insulating devices.
KALE	Growth practically stops; leaves don't look crisp or fresh.	Temperature rises above the high 60s.	Plant kale in mid- or late summer for a fall crop. (The flavor improves noticeably after a few nights of frost.)
LETTUCE AND SALSIFY	Seed planted in midsummer for a fall harvest often fails to germinate well.	It's too warm. (Lettuce seed has a germination rate of 99 percent at 77°F. The rate drops to 12 percent at 86°F.)	After planting, place a 2–3-inch layer of organic material over the seedbed to reduce the soil temperature. Or plant tolerant varieties.
	Lettuce flowers and goes to seed before it is ready to eat.	Long, hot summer days and warm nights.	Plant in spring, 2 weeks before the last frost, or plant in late summer for a fall crop, or shade the garden with gauze or shadecloth to reduce light and heat. Plant heat-resistant varieties.
	Brown lettuce-leaf tips that look burned.	Intense light. (This frequently happens in midsummer when the garden receives full sun for the entire day.)	Give your lettuce partial shade with shadecloths, or plant where bushes will shade the lettuce bed for part of the day.
	Failure to form good heads.	Plants are crowded together.	Thin head lettuce to stand 12–14 inches apart.
	Loose-leaf varieties grow nothing but small, bitter outside leaves; the tender material in the middle fails to form.	Plants are too close to each other.	Thin loose-leaf lettuce to stand 6–10 inches apart.
	Romaine doesn't form hearts.	Seed is planted too deeply.	Drop seeds on bed and cover with ½ inch of soil only.
MELONS (cantaloupe, Persian, honeydew, crenshaw, watermelon)	Dark, dry, leathery areas on the blossom ends of fruit.	A sudden change in soil moisture (as when rains are followed by a dry spell).	Try to maintain an even supply of moisture in the soil. Place 2–3 inches of organic material on top of the bed. Water on the fail-safe schedule.

VEGETABLE	WHAT'S WRONG? WHAT TO LOOK FOR	POSSIBLE CAUSES	CURES
MELONS (cantaloupe, Persian, honeydew, crenshaw, watermelon) (continued)	Cantaloupes have a mushy or very bitter taste.	Uneven watering. (Gardeners who claim this happens because their cantaloupes cross-pollinate with their cucumbers are incorrect. That does not occur.)	Maintain an even supply of moisture in the soil, following the instructions under "Cures" for blossom end rot in peppers (see page 94).
	Unripe melons.	The gardener isn't familiar with the subtle signs that melons are ready to pick.	*Cantaloupes*: If the stem slips off easily, the cantaloupe is near maturity. The blossom end softens, and the netting becomes corky. *Persians and crenshaws*: They smell sweet when mature. *Watermelon*: When the light spot on the underside turns from white to yellow, the melon is probably ripe. The "thump" test is unreliable.
	Failure to ripen before frost.	Insufficient time to mature. (Most require 75 warm—above 70°F—days or more. Persians, crenshaws, and casabas require up to 115 days.)	Grow early short season varieties.
MUSTARD	Plants flower and go to seed.	Temperature rises regularly above 80°F.	Plant 2 weeks before the last spring frost. Or, if spring temperatures regularly rise above 80°F, plant in late summer for a fall crop.
	Leaves develop a peppery tang; the flavor is especially strong in older leaves.	Hot weather, with temperatures above 85°F.	Grow mustard in spring and early fall, when the temperatures are below 65°F. (Cool weather improves the flavor.)
OKRA	Seeds don't germinate; plants fail to come up.	The seeds rot when the soil isn't warm enough (at least 70°F) at planting time.	Plant seeds when the soil temperature has reached at least 70°F. Sprouting can be improved by soaking seeds in water at least 24 hours beforehand.
	Bud drop (the buds and flowers drop off before pods start to form).	Hot, dry weather (above 95°F) or sudden temperature drops.	Wait until the weather becomes more conducive to pod formation.
	Woody or tough okra.	Failure to pick pods regularly.	Pick plants clean of pods over 1½–2 inches long.
ONIONS (onions, garlic, leeks, shallots, chives)	Plants go to seed and produce flabby, hollow bulbs.	Sets (small bulbs) planted in late fall or winter. (The nutrients that should go into bulb production go into seed production instead.)	Keep the flower buds picked off, or harvest the onions as soon as you detect flower stalks and use them as green onions or leeks.
	Bulbs split and may look as if they are trying to form two bulbs.	Uneven watering.	Place 2–3 inches of organic material on top of the bed to retain moisture. Water onions according to the fail-safe method.

GARDENING PROBLEMS AFFECTING SPECIFIC VEGETABLES

VEGETABLE	WHAT'S WRONG? WHAT TO LOOK FOR	POSSIBLE CAUSES	CURES
ONIONS (onions, garlic, leeks, shallots, chives) (continued)	Garlic plants produce many leaves but no bulbs.	Improper temperature conditions. (Homegrown garlic cloves—divided bulbs—must be exposed to temperatures of 32–50°F for 1–2 months before planting to induce bulb formation.)	Place garlic cloves in the refrigerator for 1 month before planting.
	Small garlic bulbs.	Started from undersize cloves.	Plant the large cloves from the outside of garlic bulbs. Use the small, slender cloves from the center for cooking.
PARSNIPS	Poor flavor.	Insufficient exposure to below-freezing temperatures. (Parsnip roots develop sweetness only under cold conditions.)	Allow parsnips to remain in the ground until the second or third hard frost.
PEAS	Lush vine growth but few blossoms.	This is one of nature's mysteries.	Pinch off the stems' growing tips. This usually checks the growth and encourages flower production.
	Profuse blossoms that don't produce pods.	Pollen isn't being transferred from the flowers' male parts to their female parts.	Shake the pods a little. (Although peas are self-pollinating, they sometimes need a little help.)
	Hard pods and woody peas.	The pods are left on the vines too long.	Pick peas just as they fill out, while they are still tender.
	Brown cavity on inner surface of pea; marshy spot.	Partial deficiency of available manganese in alkaline soils.	Spray the foliage with a 1 percent manganese sulfate solution at flowering time and 2–3 weeks later. Seaweed also supplies manganese.
PEPPERS	Blossoms form but fall off without producing fruit.	The temperature drops much below 60°F or rises above 75°F.	Plant early varieties.
	Few blossoms, few fruits.	Plants are blooming and producing fruit while they are too small. They will remain stunted.	Don't purchase small nursery seedlings that have started to bloom.
	Blossom end rot (a dark, leathery area on the blossom end of the fruit).	1. This is often caused by too much, then too little moisture in the soil (especially severe when temperatures rise above 90°F and when fruit is exposed to full sun). Sometimes a calcium deficiency is a related cause. 2. Overwatering. 3. Temperatures are too high or too low. 4. Insufficient pollination.	1. Keep the soil moist at all times. Place 2–3 inches of organic material on top of the bed. Water peppers 2–3 hours at a time, then refrain from watering again until the soil is dry to a depth of 4–8 inches. 2. Keep soil moisture even by following instructions above. 3. Increase night temperatures by placing plastic covers over wire cages. 4. Attempt to increase pollination by lightly tapping or jarring the plants.

VEGETABLE	WHAT'S WRONG? WHAT TO LOOK FOR	POSSIBLE CAUSES	CURES
PEPPERS (continued)	Sunscald: soft, light-colored areas that become sunken as they dry.	Exposure to direct, hot sunlight.	Control leaf spot that causes leaf loss. Use shade-cloth if peppers are being damaged.
POTATOES	Knobby potatoes.	Uneven supply of moisture.	Place 2–3 inches of organic material on top of the bed to hold down moisture loss. Water potatoes mindfully, according to the fail-safe schedule. Avoid planting varieties that tend to be excessively knobby, such as Green Mountain and Russet Burbank.
	Cavities near the center of the potato ("hollow heart").	Rapid, uneven growth of tubers.	Space potatoes close together. Cut down on water. Avoid planting varieties that develop hollow heart: Chippewa, Katahdin, Mohawk, Irish Cobbler, Sequoia, Russet rural, and White Rose.
	All tops and no potatoes.	Nights are too warm. (Potatoes need night temperatures below 55°F for good tuber formation.)	Time your planting so potatoes grow during cool weather. In hot areas, plant in midsummer to mature in fall.
	Green potatoes (sunburn).	Sun exposure during growth or after digging.	Keep potatoes covered with soil. Store in complete darkness.
	Leaflets become light green, wilt, then dry up (sunscald); tubers become watery and turn brown to a considerable depth.	Exposure of plant or tubers to hot sun and drying winds following cloudy weather.	Place a sunscreen over the plants during extremely hot weather. Don't leave tubers in the sunshine.
	Yellowing of leaflets' tips and margins; gradual dying and browning or blackening of foliage; possible death of more than half the foliage (similar to leafhopper burn).	Excessive loss of moisture during hot, dry weather.	Cover the bed with 2–3 inches of organic material.
	Irregular brown spots scattered throughout the flesh.	Hot, dry weather during growing season; lack of soil moisture.	Layer bed with 2–3 inches of organic material and water on the fail-safe schedule.
	Marble-size potatoes grow directly from potato eyes.	Excessive concentration of cell sap in tubers.	Plant potatoes later in the season. Don't store seed potatoes in light at temperatures of 90°F or higher.
	Irregular dead streaks on potato stems.	High levels of soluble manganese in acid soils.	Grow resistant varieties.

GARDENING PROBLEMS AFFECTING SPECIFIC VEGETABLES

VEGETABLE	WHAT'S WRONG? WHAT TO LOOK FOR	POSSIBLE CAUSES	CURES
POTATOES (*continued*)	Tuber tissue looks wet when dug up and brought into a warm area; later it becomes infected with a bacteria.	Freezing causes this injury.	Harvest your crop before the ground freezes.
	Dead tissue (necrosis) in tubers.	Potatoes remain in hot soil after vines begin to die.	Keep the soil moist and shaded, or dig the tubers up as soon as the vines start to die.
	Dark brown stippling of leaves' upper surfaces (most severe on older leaves).	Pollution damage from ozone in the air.	No cure currently exists. Resistant varieties are being developed.
RADISHES	Taste hot.	Soil is too dry. Soil temperature rises above 90°F.	Keep soil cool with a 2–3-inch layer of organic material. Water radishes for a period of 2–3 hours, then don't water again until the soil has dried to a depth of 4–8 inches (the fail-safe method).
	Leaves form, but bulbs do not.	Plants are too close together.	Thin radishes to stand about 2 inches apart.
	Woody, pithy radishes.	Plants are harvested at the wrong time.	Dig up your radishes as soon as the bulbs reach an edible size.
SPINACH	Leaves turn yellow; in severe cases, entire leaves have a sulfur color.	Nitrogen deficiency. (Spinach is very sensitive to this.)	Add blood meal to the soil.
	Spinach rushes into flower (bolts) before the leaves reach eating size (this stops the production of usable foliage).	Long spring days with temperatures in the 40s during the first few weeks of growth, immediately followed by temperatures in the 80s.	Plant varieties that resist early flowering, or plant spinach in late summer so the plants mature in fall.
SQUASH (summer squash, winter squash, pumpkins)	Some seeds fail to come up.	A certain percentage of all squash seeds naturally resist the water uptake that triggers sprouting, so this is inevitable to some extent.	Increase germination and slightly decrease sprouting time by soaking seeds in tepid water for 24 hours. Dry the seeds on a paper towel before planting.
	Dark brown, leathery areas on the fruit's blossom end (blossom end rot).	Uneven soil moisture. (Intermittently wet and dry soil seems to promote blossom end rot.)	Place 2–3 inches of organic material on top of the soil to maintain steady moisture. Water squash according to the fail-safe method.
	Small squash start to form, then rot or dry up.	Female flowers blossom before male flowers appear to pollinate the plants.	Wait patiently until the male flowers blossom. They will then pollinate the female flowers, and fruit will grow.
	Too much squash fruit on the plant.	Unpollinated fruit aborts in a self-pruning process.	Keep zucchini fruit picked to sustain production.

GARDENING PROBLEMS AFFECTING SPECIFIC VEGETABLES

VEGETABLE	WHAT'S WRONG? WHAT TO LOOK FOR	POSSIBLE CAUSES	CURES
SQUASH (summer squash, winter squash, pumpkins) *(continued)*	Few flowers form fruit, even when both male and female flowers are present.	Not enough bees. (The percentage of flowers setting fruit increases when many bees pollinate the flowers. The average size of a pumpkin or squash also increases when the vines are pollinated by numerous bees.)	Play bee. Using an artist's brush, transfer pollen to female flowers (those with tiny squash at the base). Dust the pollen on the tip of the squash fruit above the flower (stigma).
SWEET POTATOES	Elongated, slender tubers.	1. Too much water. 2. Heavy clay soils.	1. Don't let the soil become saturated. Water deeply for 2–3 hours, then don't water again until the soil has dried 4–8 inches deep. 2. Spade 6 inches of organic material into your sweet potato bed.
	Some transplanted sprouts die or fail to produce vines.	1. Thin succulent sprouts planted (lacking the moisture to survive until roots form). 2. Sprouts planted vertically.	1. Plant larger sprouts with thick stems. 2. Plant slips horizontally, 2–3 inches deep with 5 nodes underground and only the tips showing.
	Poor flavor.	Harvested after the soil temperature has dropped below 55°F.	Harvest before the soil temperature dips below 55°F (check with a soil thermometer), or harvest on a mild day within a week or two of the first expected frost.
	Roots rot after harvesting.	Wounds at either end (caused by harvesting) fail to close.	Set sweet potatoes out in a room that's about 75°F, and cover them with newspapers to keep the humidity high (80–90 percent). They'll be ready in about a week. Now wrap them in newspapers; store at 55°F.
	When cooked, part or all of the sweet potato is hard.	Storage in near-freezing temperatures or in the refrigerator.	Store sweet potatoes at about 55°F.
TOMATOES	Blossoms form but fall off without producing fruit (blossom drop).	Night temperatures are too low (below 55°F) or too high (much above 75°F).	Increase night temperatures by using plastic covers over wire cages. You may hasten pollination and fruit production by lightly tapping or jarring the plants.
	A dark, leathery area on the blossom end of the fruit (blossom end rot).	The soil is too moist, then too dry (especially severe when temperatures rise above 90°F and when the fruit is exposed to full sun). Sometimes also related to calcium deficiency.	Keep the soil moist at all times. Place 2–3 inches of organic material on the bed to hold down moisture. Use the fail-safe watering method. Mulch with black plastic to reduce moisture fluctuation. Test the soil; if deficient in calcium, add soluble calcium.
	Yellowish patches on fruit (sunscald) that later form large, grayish white spots.	Too much direct exposure to the sun and temperatures of 90–100°F.	Grow varieties with heavy leaf cover.

WHAT'S WRONG?

VEGETABLE	WHAT TO LOOK FOR	POSSIBLE CAUSES	CURES
TOMATOES (continued)	Malformed fruit with ugly scars between the segments (catfacing).	Cool, cloudy weather at the time of blossoming may cause the blossoms to stick to the small fruits, tearing and distorting them.	Pull blossoms off when the fruit is small. Plant varieties that resist catfacing.
	Swollen fruit with puffy inner air spaces.	Puffiness occurs when the temperatures during pollination are below 55°F and sometimes at temperatures above 90°F.	Increase temperatures by placing plastic covers over the cages. Provide shade in very hot weather.
	Radial cracking from the top toward the bottom of the fruit; concentric cracking around the fruit stem.	Uneven soil moisture—too dry or too wet. (This occurs frequently during rainy periods when the temperatures are 85–90°F.) Also, tomatoes exposed to full sun develop more cracks than those covered with dense foliage.	Place 2–3 inches of organic material on top of the bed to retain moisture. Water by the fail-safe method. Mulch with black plastic to reduce moisture fluctuation. Plant in well-drained soil.
	Fruits take on strange, distorted shapes.	Exposure to temperatures below 55°F during blossoming.	Increase the night temperatures by putting plastic covers over the tomato cages. Grow early varieties.
	Zipper streak: a brown, dashed scar down the side of the tomato.	Cool, wet weather causes the blossom to stick to the tiny fruit. The blossom tears off to leave a zipperlike scar. This scar enlarges as the fruit grows.	Pull off the flower parts when the fruit are tiny.
	Blotchy, uneven ripening.	Overexposure to intense sunlight. (The exposed parts of a fruit can become 20 degrees hotter than its shaded parts.)	Plant varieties with good foliage for protection.
	Lush foliage, little fruit.	1. Overwatering. 2. Temperatures are too low. 3. Inadequate pollination.	1. Water 2–3 hours at a time; don't water again until the soil has dried to a depth of 4–8 inches. Check with a trowel. (This is the fail-safe method.) 2. Increase night temperatures by using plastic covers over the wire cages, or fill water jugs and place them around the plants. 3. Try to increase pollination and fruit production by tapping or jarring the plants.
	The leaves' edges roll inward, starting with the lower leaves; the leaves may cup and overlap (leaf roll).	Prolonged rains lead to accumulated moisture in the soil.	Spread black plastic over the bed to keep out excess moisture.
	Gray to grayish brown blotches on the surface of green fruit; internal browning.	Low light intensity; low temperatures; high soil moisture; excessive compaction in soil.	Grow tomatoes in well-drained soil. Avoid heavy fertilization, which produces heavy foliage. Plant resistant varieties.

GARDENING PROBLEMS AFFECTING SPECIFIC VEGETABLES

VEGETABLE	WHAT'S WRONG? WHAT TO LOOK FOR	POSSIBLE CAUSES	CURES
TURNIPS, RUTABAGAS, KOHLRABIES	Turnips and rutabagas go to seed before good roots form.	Too many days of exposure to 40°F temperatures causes the plants to flower, making the roots unusable.	Plant in the spring, 4–6 weeks before the last frost. In areas where late spring and summer days are often 80°F and higher, plant for a fall harvest.
	Turnips and kohlrabies become pithy, fibrous, and bitter.	The plants remain in the ground too long. (Woody fibers appear as they become older.)	Harvest turnips and kohlrabies when they are about 2 inches in diameter.

CHAPTER NINE

INDIVIDUAL VEGETABLES, GROWING TIPS, AND SEED SOURCES

A well-planned and properly tended vegetable garden can be an extremely rewarding experience for anyone. When conditions are right, this garden will continuously supply you with fresh, nutritious, pesticide-free (should you choose this method) vegetables and will be a source of exercise and relaxation.

Yet how well the garden does in any particular year depends on a number of variables beyond the gardener's control: the weather, seeds that don't sprout, insect infestations, birds that eat seedlings, gophers, and so on. While you have no choice about many of these developments, this chapter will provide some gardening expertise to make your work a little easier, increase the yields of your crops, and solve troublesome gardening problems. The chapter will proceed vegetable by vegetable, in alphabetical order. Some vegetables have more tips than others.

This section also lists the numerous varieties of each vegetable, so that you can make informed choices for your garden. A large number of seed catalogs were used to obtain the greatest selection. Each seed catalog has been coded with the first three initials of the company's name, or the first four if names are similar.

Appendix A supplies the names and addresses of these seed catalogs, along with a brief description of each catalog and the price, if any. The companies are from all over the United States and Canada.

Any vegetable variety listed here can be grown in California. Once you know your climate zone (see California Climate Map, inside back cover), you can choose among the varieties suited to your climate. But don't limit yourself to the varieties that usually grow in your area. Adjust what you grow to the time of the season.

For instance, to keep tomatoes growing from early to late in the season, gardeners in the Sacramento Valley and surrounding foothills start out with a short season variety. They can find a short season variety in catalogs from Montana, Oregon, Idaho, or Canada. Territorial Seed Company (TER) is based in Oregon, High Altitude Gardens (HIG) is from Idaho, and Garden City Seeds (GAR) is from Montana; they will all offer short season varieties that grow in their states.

To continue with this example, midseason tomatoes in the Sacramento Valley can be the standard varieties known as California tomatoes, such as Ace, Campbell, and Heinz. Many gardeners insist on cultivating the big, late varieties, such as beefsteak, which don't ripen until almost the end of the season. As you don't want to wait the entire growing season for a tomato, experiment with different varieties in your garden. Plant short season varieties along with middle and late types. This goes for all vegetables. Don't restrict yourself. Try something new.

Varietal Terms

All-American Selections: Vegetable varieties chosen each year by the All-American Selection organization as the winners of the All-American medals. The bronze, silver, and gold awards are based on results of tests conducted in test gardens across the United States. To be selected for All-American honors, a vegetable must have superior qualities and be adapted to a wide range of seeds and climates. Trial rows of All-American entries are grown side by side with popular varieties. All-American Selections are noted as AAS in seed catalogs.

Gynoecious Cucumbers: These varieties bear only female flowers for heavier production. Seeds of a pollinator are included in all gynoecious variety seed packets to ensure good fruit set. They are identified in seed catalogs as gyn.

Heirlooms: Non-hybrids that were introduced prior to 1940. After 1940 hybrids began to displace these traditional varieties. Many heirloom varieties date from the 1600s. Family heirlooms are varieties that have been handed down within families for generations.

Hybrids: A cross between two parents of different types. Each parent imparts its own particular qualities. The seeds of hybrid varieties will not retain the varieties' characteristics.

Open Pollinated (OP): Non-hybrid varieties that retain the in-bred characteristics of the parents.

Plant Variety Patented (PVP): Hybrid varieties developed by breeders and protected under the Variety Protection Act, which prohibits unauthorized propagation of these varieties for sale.

ARTICHOKES

BOTANICAL NAME: *Cynara scolymus*

DAYS TO MATURITY: Artichokes bear one year after planting, sometimes the first summer.

PLANTING TIME: Plant root divisions during the spring. You can also sow seeds indoors at 70°F about three months before the last frost. Set them out in a protected area with southern exposure.

SOIL: Light, sandy, well-drained.

NUTRIENTS: In summer, apply a fish emulsion at 10-day intervals.

WATER: Water well and often through spring and summer. Never allow roots to dry.

LIGHT: Full sun.

SPACING: Space plants 3 feet apart.

HARVEST: Cut the unripened flower heads before the bracts begin to separate.

STORAGE: Artichokes can be stored in a refrigerator drawer only a few days.

Artichoke Growing Tips

Better Taste

When summers are especially hot, the heat will open the leaf buds, causing the edible part of the artichoke (the leaf bract) to become tough and leathery. To avoid this, harvest the buds when they are still closed tight. At this stage, they'll be absolutely succulent.

Summer Artichokes

Gardeners in hot areas sometimes have trouble growing artichokes because they dry out. Spreading lawn clippings around the roots will retain moisture and keep the artichokes happy.

ARTICHOKES

VARIETY	HEADS/PLANTS	DESCRIPTION	SOURCES (p. 385)
ARTICHOKES			
GREEN GLOBE	Large flower heads, 4-foot plants with 6-foot spread.	Edible flower buds are made up of thick, fleshy scales and solid centers. Best harvested young, it's not hardy.	COM DEG GLE GUR HEN LED NIC RED SEE TER TIL WILL
GREEN GLOBE IMPROVED	Large flower heads, 5–6-foot plant.	Standard variety; reduced sharp spines.	BOU PAR PIN VER
PURPLE ARTICHOKE (Purple Sicilian)	4-foot plant, purple flower bracts.	Similar to Green Globe.	ORN PIN
VIOLETTO	Elongated; purple heads.	Italian variety.	GLE ORN SEE
ARTICHOKES (OTHER TYPES)			
CHINESE ARTICHOKES	Grow 12–18 inches tall.	Keep plant moist to produce a good crop of pearly white 2-inch roots. Use in salads or on relish trays; stir-fry or pickle them.	SUN

ASPARAGUS

BOTANICAL NAME: *Asparagus officinalis*

DAYS TO MATURITY: The first crop will come during the third year if the plant is grown from seeds. It will take two years if it's started from year-old roots.

PLANTING TIME: Sow seeds indoors in midwinter or in a hotbed in early spring. Transplant the seedlings outdoors in the spring when all danger of frost has passed.

SOIL: Sandy loam; pH 6.0–8.0.

NUTRIENTS: In early spring, feed with a "complete" organic fertilizer (page 22). Fertilize again in the summer with fish emulsion (follow the directions on the bottle) after harvesting the spears.

WATER: Do not irrigate during winter months. Soak the roots thoroughly whenever the soil begins to dry out.

LIGHT: Full sun.

SPACING: Dig a trench 8–10 inches deep and 12 inches wide. Then form a shallow ridge 8 inches high at the base. Space the crowns 12–18 inches apart with the small, stringy roots spread over both sides of the ridge. Cover the crowns with 2–3 inches of soil.

HARVEST: As the young plants grow, fill in the trench little by little. Don't harvest any spears the first year. During the second year, when the foliage turns brown in late fall, cut the stems to the ground.

STORAGE: Use fresh.

Asparagus Growing Tips

Cut Low

To keep asparagus growing at top speed year after year, cut the stalks to within 2 inches of the ground after the first fall frost. Do this after the leaves turn yellow but before the berries on the female plants fall. If the berries are allowed to drop, they will produce seedlings that will compete with the established plants and reduce overall production.

Straight Spears

When gardeners cultivate too vigorously with a hoe, they wind up with misshapen, crooked, or curved asparagus spears. Slow down and take care not to nick the spears when you weed. These nicks affect the spears' growth.

More Asparagus

Cutting back asparagus foliage always reduces the next crop. To make your asparagus go that extra mile, support the growing foliage with stakes and wires. This keeps the bed tidy and ensures the biggest crop possible each year.

Better Production

To increase your asparagus yield almost immediately, strip off the green peppercorn-size berries as they appear on the fronds of the female plants.

New Varieties

The new hybrid asparagus produce many times the yield of the old Washington types. Jersey Giant and UC 157 F-2 are two of the best. Trials comparing 11 kinds of asparagus, held in Davis and Stockton, California, Yuma, Arizona, and Prosser, Washington, declared UC 157 the hands-down winner, with Jersey Giant a close second. Each produced at least one-third more than the third-place competitor.

ASPARAGUS

VARIETY	HEADS/PLANTS	DESCRIPTION	SOURCES (p. 385)
ASPARAGUS			
ARGENTEUIL (OP) (Precoce d'argenteuil)	Green with purple tips.	French variety; thick, white stems.	HIG LEJ ORN SEE
CONNOVER'S COLOSSAL	Dark green shoots.	Grown from seed, this variety requires 3–4 years to establish a crop. It's best to use the seed in a bed that's already established.	BOU
GLEN SMITH	Dark green shoots.	Improved Viking; heavy producer; good for freezing.	WILL
JERSEY GIANT (hybrid, SYN 4–57)	½-inch diameter.	Widely adapted; rust-resistant; tolerant of fusarium wilt. All plants are male.	BURP JUN SHE THO TWI
JERSEY KNIGHT (hybrid)	Green, up to 4 inches around.	All-male plant; vigorous grower; highly disease-resistant; will grow in poor, salty, or alkaline soil; hardy in subzero weather.	BURG FAR GUR HEN PAR
LARAC (hybrid)	Uniform spears, white to green.	French disease-resistant variety; takes 3 years to establish from seed.	GOU JUN PIN TER
MARTHA WASHINGTON	Large, tight spears are green with a purple cast.	Resistant to fusarium rust and tolerant to fusarium wilt.	ORN
MARY WASHING-TON (hybrid)	Medium, green tips.	A prolific variety that's rust-resistant.	ALL BURG BURP BUT DEG FAR FIS GAR GUR HEN HIG JUN LED MEY PIN RED ROS SEE TILL VER
MARY WASHING-TON UC 72	Tight heads with green stalks, no purple tinge.	Earliest of the Mary Washingtons.	BURR
NEW JERSEY CENTENNIAL	Green.	Mainly male plants.	COM
ROBERTS IMPROVED	Bright green spears.	Matures early; never tough or woody; tender and crisp whether fresh, canned, or frozen.	GUR HEN
UC 72	Large, dark green spears with purple cast.	High yields; good tolerance to fusarium wilt and rust.	TWI WIL
UC 157 (hybrid)	Deep green, smooth spears; uniform scales.	Tendency to form clusters of 3–5 spears; vigorous growth.	BURP DEG POR SHE TER
UC 157 F-2 (hybrid)	Dark green spears.	Keeps tight cylindrical heads even in higher temperatures.	BURR TER TWI
VIKING KB3 (OP)	Heavy green stalks.	Hardy; rust-resistant; fusarium-tolerant.	STO
WALTHAM (hybrid)	Tighter heads than most other varieties.	Consistently high quality; easy to grow; rust-resistant.	GUR HEN

BEANS, GREEN

BOTANICAL NAME: *Phaseolus vulgaris*

DAYS TO MATURITY: 40–80, depending on variety.

PLANTING TIME: Plant after the ground has warmed to at least 60°F. You can also start them under glass or polyethylene two to four weeks before the last frost date. For a continuous supply, plant every two weeks.

SOIL: Do not plant beans where other beans have grown in the past three years; pH 6.0–7.5.

NUTRIENTS: With the help of soil bacteria, beans draw nitrogen from the air for growth. Feed plants every three to four weeks with fish emulsion.

WATER: Water regularly and thoroughly all season. Avoid overhead watering.

LIGHT: Full sun.

SPACING: Sow seeds 1–1½ inches deep, 3 inches apart. If you are growing pole green beans, place them 6 inches apart along fences or bean poles.

HARVEST: Pole beans are best harvested when young. Bush beans can be picked at any stage but have a better flavor when young. By keeping the beans picked, you will extend the season.

STORAGE: Use fresh, canned or frozen.

Green Bean Growing Tips

Bush Pole Beans

To magically turn pole beans into bushy vines, pinch off the growing tips every time they exceed 12 inches. This keeps the plants at easy-picking height and doubles the crop over comparable bush beans.

Bean Tower Power

Beans go crazy when properly supported by a bean tower. A tower of bean power grows up to 20 pounds of Kentucky Wonder string beans a season. Construct the tower from ¾-inch PVC pipe. Drill ⅛-inch holes 6 inches apart in the bottom crosspieces. By hooking them up to a hose, you can irrigate the plants' root zones below ground.

Bean Jungle

You can double the harvest of beans per vine by growing them up a trellis or large-mesh wire fencing rather than up wires or strings. Sow seeds 1 inch deep, 3 inches apart, after the soil temperature exceeds 60°F. Although this creates a jungle of foliage, the beans can be picked easily at all levels.

BEANS, GREEN

Protecting Beans

Radishes planted around both pole and bush beans enhance the beans' flavor and repel bean beetles. Radishes are ready every 24 to 30 days, so reseed every 10 days or so.

The Snap Test

To pick green beans when they're first-rate, apply the snap test. If a pod breaks in half with a succulent crack, it is ripe. If the older pods are not diseased, throw them into the compost.

Bean Sculpture

To create a unique bean tower, nail two old 26-inch bicycle wheels to a fence or post. Plant pole beans 6 inches apart along the base of the first wheel. The beans will eventually grow in and out, up and sideways, along the spokes, creating some unusual patterns.

VARIETY	DAYS	DESCRIPTION	SOURCES (p. 385)
POLE SNAP BEANS (GREEN)			
BLACKCOAT (Blackcoat runner bean)	100	Immature pods are edible. This ancient Mesoamerican species has coal black seeds.	SEED
BLUE LAKE (Black Seeded)	55–63	Round, straight, 6–7 inches long; 6-foot vines.	SEED
BLUE LAKE (OP) (White Seeded, White Creaseback)	55–66	Dark green pods are oval, straight, and 5½–6 inches long. Seeds are white. Use this stringless, vigorous 5–6-foot plant canned, fresh, or frozen.	ABU ALL BOU BURG BURR GAR GUR HEN JLH JUN PAR PON POR ROS SEE SHE STO TER THO TIL VER WILL
BUTLER	60	Red flowered, runner bean has 12-inch-long pods. Stringless and meaty, it sets well in hot weather.	BOU
DESIREE	55	10–12-inch pods; white flowered runner; stringless. This prolific variety has exceptional flavor and is more productive under dry weather conditions.	BOU THO
EARLIPOL	55	A good early pole bean for cold climates, it's high yielding and stringless. Mature seeds are medium brown with a dark brown eye. Performs well in northern states.	SOU
EMERITE	55	Pencil-slim French variety; 7–9-inch filet green pod; resistant to common mosaic viruses.	COO GOU ORN PIN SHE STO
EMPEROR	60	Red flowered, edible runner bean from England.	COO
ENORMA	60	20-inch, slender pods; heavy yields; good flavor.	THO
FORTEX	60	Dark green, round pod is over 11 inches. Walnut brown seeds; stringless. Pick at 7 inches for filet bean. Use fresh or freeze.	JOH ORN TER
GARRAFAL ORO (Garafal Oro)	65	9-inch, flat bean; prolific French variety; rarely grows more than 4 feet; freezes well.	PIN

VARIETY	DAYS	DESCRIPTION	SOURCES (p. 385)

POLE SNAP BEANS (GREEN) *(continued)*

VARIETY	DAYS	DESCRIPTION	SOURCES (p. 385)
GENUINE CORNFIELD (Scotia, Striped Creaseback)	70–80	5–7-inch, round, medium green pod; buff-colored seeds with brown stripes. Harvest before the seed fills the pod.	PIN RED SEE VER
GOLIATH (Prizetaker)	65	Reliable 20-inch runner bean with red flowers; a heavy cropper and good freezer.	THO VER
GRAMMY TILLEY	70	This flavorful white runner bean, suitable for the north, is a good substitute for limas where they don't do well.	PIN
GREEN ANNELINO	60	Italian heirloom variety; small, crescent-shaped bean with Romano flavor.	COO
HELDA	60	9-inch-long, broad, light green pods; disease-resistant, making it especially good for greenhouse culture.	WILL
HICKMAN'S SNAP	80–90	Virginia heirloom variety produces a 12-foot vine of snap beans with uniquely colored seeds—gray, brown, white, and black.	SEED
HUNTER	60	Stringless 8-inch, flat bean is disease-resistant and suited for greenhouse growing.	WILL
IVANHOE	65	A runner bean with 18-inch-long, straight pods; stringless; scarlet flowers, with lilac-pink seed.	THO
KENTUCKY BLUE	57–65	This All-American winner—with 7-inch, round, extra straight pods—combines characteristics of its Kentucky Wonder and Blue Lake parents (but is sweeter than Kentucky Wonder).	ALL BURP FAR FIS GUR HEN HIG JOH JUN LED MEY NIC PAR PIN SOU TER THO TIL TWI VER
KENTUCKY WHITE WONDER	63	6–8-inch, straight, dark green pods; stringless, highly productive, white seeded variety; sets pods from base to top of vine; rust-resistant and well-adapted to Pacific Coast.	DEG PON VER
KENTUCKY WONDER (OP) (Old Homestead, Texas Pole, Green Pod)	58–74	7–9-inch, oval, silvery green pod; 1850s heirloom variety; brown seeded; hardy climber; stringless. Peas are meaty and tender with fine flavor and texture, good fresh or frozen.	ABU ALL BURG BURR BUT COM DEG FAR GAR GUR HEN HIG MEY NIC ORG PIN POR ROS SEE SEED SOU STO TER THO TIL VER WIL WILL
KWINTUS	70	Long, flat pods stay tender and flavorful no matter how large they get. A European climbing bean bred for greenhouses, it's also good outdoors.	COO
LADY DI	65	Seeds in the 12-inch, dark green pod of this high-quality runner bean develop slowly. Plant is vigorous and adaptable, good for freezing and for exhibition.	THO
LANDFRAUEN	55	The 5–6-inch-long, light green pods have purple mottling. Stringless, Zebra-type bean is excellent fresh, frozen, or dried.	PAR
MC CASLAN	61–66	7½-inch, flat dark green pods; white seeds; 1930s variety; stringless, fleshy, and brittle with good flavor. Use as a fresh or dry shell bean.	RED SOU VER
MUSICA	55–67	9–10x3¼-inch, flat bean; "Sward bean" type used in Continental cookery; resistant to common bean mosaic.	TER THO

VARIETY	DAYS	DESCRIPTION	SOURCES (p. 385)

POLE SNAP BEANS (GREEN) *(continued)*

VARIETY	DAYS	DESCRIPTION	SOURCES (p. 385)
NECKARKONIGIN	60	9-inch, slim, green pod; stringless German variety; French slicing.	WILL
NORTHEASTER (OP)	55–65	8-inch, flat, medium green pod with rich flavor; stringless; strong vine; can be grown in greenhouse.	GAR HIG JOH
OREGON BLUE LAKE	60	6½-inch oval, round pods; stringless. Small white seeds are good as dry beans. Use fresh, canned, or frozen.	NIC
OREGON GIANT PAUL BUNYAN BEAN (OP) (Cascade Giant Pole)	55–68	Mottled red, 12-inch pod keeps its flavor. This prolific climber is also good as a shell bean.	ABU GAR ORG SEED
PAINTED LADY	68	9–12-inch runner bean with red and white flowers; good for freezing.	BOU
PARK'S EARLY RISER	40–45	8–10-inch-long, dark green pod; stringless. Italian flavor complements pasta and tomato sauces.	PAR
POTOMAC	67	This 6½-inch-long, slightly curved bean dates from 1860 Virginia but has also been grown in Tehama County, California, for 125 years. Flowers are lavender-pink. Seeds are purple-black and germinate well in cool soil.	SOU
PRISCILLA POLISH	75	This heirloom variety with 5-inch pods is similar to Kentucky Wonder but has a longer season. Seeds dry to light tan with black stripe. Use as a snap or soup bean.	SEED
PRIZE WINNER	70	Improved strain of Scarlet Runner has scarlet flowers, good flavor, and large pods; cool weather variety.	NIC VER
RATTLESNAKE	73–85	7-inch, round pod; buff-colored seeds with purple streaks; heavy producer in hot, humid climates.	PIN PLA SOU VER
RED KNIGHT	70	British runner bean has long, flat pods, scarlet flowers, and stringless beans. Vines grow up to 12 feet. Use fresh or as a dry bean. Attracts hummingbirds.	SHE
RED PLUM	60	Runner bean with 6–8-inch, almost stringless pod; resistant to halo blight; very heavy yields in organic gardens.	THO
ROMANO (OP) (Italian Pole)	64–70	5½-inch-wide, flat pods; brown seeded; good in Italian cooking, canned, and frozen.	ABU ALL BURP BUT COM DEG FAR GAR HEN LED NIC ORG PIN PON RED SEE SEED THO TIL VER WILL
ROYAL STANDARD	65	20-inch-long, smooth, bright green pods set well under adverse conditions. Plant is very heavy yielding.	THO
RUTH BIBLE	67	This 1832 Kentucky heirloom's 3½-inch pods have strings and brownish tan seeds. It's a good cornfield bean, best picked when tender.	SOU
SCARLET EMPEROR	75–120	Runner bean with 16-inch, smooth pods and scarlet flowers; heavy cropper; good freezer.	BOU ORN SEED TER

VARIETY	DAYS	DESCRIPTION	SOURCES (p. 385)

POLE SNAP BEANS (GREEN) *(continued)*

VARIETY	DAYS	DESCRIPTION	SOURCES (p. 385)
SCARLET RUNNER (OP)	65–70	Very productive runner bean has 6–inch, flat pods and scarlet flowers. Vines grow to 12 feet.	ABU ALL COM DEG GAR JLH LED PIN PLA RED SEE SOU STO TIL VER WILL
SELMA STAR	60	7–8-inch, straight pod; stringless; good fresh, canned, or frozen.	PAR
SPANISH GIANT ROMANO	70	Long Romano-type bean.	ORN
STREAMLINE	75	A runner type with 16-inch pods, its flavorful beans are born in clusters.	THO
SULTAN'S EMERALD CRESCENT	75	Each pod curls.	SEE
TURKEY CRAW	70	Heirloom seed from Virginia, North Carolina, and Tennessee; 3½-inch-long pods; stringless; often used as a cornfield bean; good for freezing or drying.	SOU
WESTLAND	70	European type with 4–5-inch-long pod; stringless; good yields; freezes well.	WILL
WHITE DUTCH RUN-NER (Oregon Lima)	70	Large, white bean is not a true lima; short season variety; strong climber.	ABU SEE WILL
WHITE KNIGHT	73	British runner bean has white flowers and 9–12-inch pods. Vines grow up to 12 feet. If these thick, stringless green beans are left to grow, large beans can be used as shell beans.	SHE
WILD MEXICAN POLE	80	Pod grows to 4 inches but is best eaten when 2 inches. Vines grow to 10 feet or more.	RED
WINGED BEAN	150	Pods and foliage are edible. Tropical climber grows to 8 feet and is best grown as a greenhouse crop.	JLH SUN
YARD LONG BEANS (green pod, black seeded) (Dow Guak, Dow Ghok, Asparagus Bean, Vigna sesquipedalis, Orient Wonder, and China Long)	80	Deep green pod, black seeded variety grows 2–4 feet long; should be picked at 12–15 inches. Isolate from cowpeas and other types of asparagus beans by a minimum of 35 feet.	SEE SOU SUN
YARD LONG BEANS (green pod, red seeded) (Dow Guak, Dow Ghok, Asparagus Bean, Vigna sesquipedalis, Orient Wonder, and China Long)	80	Pick the green pod, red seeded variety at 12–15 inches. Seeds are maroon-brown with darker brown streaks. Isolate from cowpeas and other types of asparagus beans by a minimum of 35 feet.	BURP COM GLE LED LEJ NIC RED SEE SOU STO SUN TIL VER WILL

POLE SNAP BEANS (YELLOW AND PURPLE)

VARIETY	DAYS	DESCRIPTION	SOURCES (p. 385)
ALABAMA NO. 1	67	A 1930 heirloom variety, the pod is silver-green tinged with purple, while seed is black. Stringless when young, plant tolerates shade and resists nematodes.	SOU

VARIETY	DAYS	DESCRIPTION	SOURCES (p. 385)

POLE SNAP BEANS (YELLOW AND PURPLE) *(continued)*

VARIETY	DAYS	DESCRIPTION	SOURCES
BLACK KNIGHT	60	Solid black English selection runner bean is very large and prolific, with red flowers.	ABU
BLAUHILDE	60	The 9-inch blue bean turns green when cooked; it's stringless and fleshy, a high yielder.	WILL
BLUE COCO	59	Flattened purple pods grow to 6 inches and produce crunchy, excellent beans.	SEE SOU
CASCADE GIANT	58–70	Northwest heirloom "improved" Oregon Giant has thin 8–12-inch stringless pods with scarlet-purple stripes.	SEED TER
DOW PURPLE POD	75–80	Northwest heirloom's pods are flat and purple. It will germinate in cold weather.	ABU VER
FRIMA	60	Yellow, Romano-type bean; abundant yields; meaty flavor.	COO
GOLDMARIE	40–45	8–10-inch golden pod; flattened and stringless; Italian flavor.	PAR TER
JEMINEZ	67	7–8-inch, flat, oval, dark green pods with purple-red streaks that are good cooked as a snap bean or fresh as a shell bean.	JOH
KENTUCKY WONDER WAX ROUND POD (Golden Podded Wax)	60–68	7–9-inch, slightly curved pod with brown seeds; almost stringless; meaty and brittle.	ALL COM GUR HEN JUN MEY STO VER
LOUISIANA PURPLE POD	67–70	Southern heirloom variety has 7-inch bright purple pod. Entire plant is purple-green with textured leaves and bright purple flowers. Harvest when young and stringless. Seeds are light to medium brown.	ABU PIN SOU
NECKARGOLD	60	Stringless, white seeded variety has a 9-inch, round, deep yellow pod. Don't plant until the soil warms.	WILL
PURPLE POLE (OP)	65	Flat, 8-inch, red-purple pods turn green when cooked. This heirloom variety is stringless, meaty, and thick.	BUT GAR HEN PLA PON VER
SULTAN'S GOLDEN CRESCENT	65	Golden pod curls.	SEE
VIOLET POD (Violet Snap, Trionfo Violetto)	60	These are stringless, long, smooth, flat purple beans. Seed sprouts when soil is cool.	COO ORG TER
YELLOW ANNELINO	60	Italian heirloom with distinctive flavor and unique shape, crescents, and curls produces 3–4-inch yellow pods.	COO ORG

BUSH BEANS (SNAP/SLICING)

VARIETY	DAYS	DESCRIPTION	SOURCES
ADMIRES	65	Tasty, 1-inch-wide pods; resistant to mosaic and anthracnose.	WILL

VARIETY	DAYS	DESCRIPTION	SOURCES (p. 385)

BUSH BEANS (SNAP/SLICING) *(continued)*

VARIETY	DAYS	DESCRIPTION	SOURCES
AIGUILLE VERT	65	Very thin, dark green, French-style bean.	LEJ
ARAMIS (OP)	65–68	Disease-resistant European variety is stringless, with 7–9-inch pods. Must be picked young for best flavor.	GAR WILL
ASTREL	55–60	Pods of stringless baby French filet bean plant should be picked when they are 4–5 inches. Compact plants with concentrated pod sets are resistant to anthracnose and mosaic virus.	JUN
ASTRO (Round Pod)	50–60	Upright, vigorous plant with deep green pods is a good canner.	ALL
ATLANTIC	50	6½-inch medium green pods; considered the best processing and second early market bean in the Northeast; mottled colored seed	STO
BACCICIA	70	This Italian variety produces a 14-inch bush and rose-colored seeds.	SEED
BAFFIN	60	Like a true French haricot vert but stringless, these pencil-slim, short beans have outstanding flavor. Do not sow too early.	BOU
BAHALORES	47	Harvest these 4–5-inch, French-filet-type beans when the pods are immature and still stringless.	PIN SEE
BE205	53	Round pods; heavy yielder at tops of plants.	PIN
BLACK VALENTINE (Resistant Asgrow)	70	6½-inch, slightly flattened pod of heirloom variety; heavy yielder; tolerant of drought, cold, and poor soils; edible fresh or canned.	ABU PLA SEE VER
BLACK VALENTINE RESISTANT	50	An 1855 heirloom variety with a 6½-inch, straight, round, dark green pod; stringless; good for soup.	SOU
BLUE LAKE BUSH	52–60	6½-inch, round, dark green pod; stringless, white-seeded, 18-inch plant with good flavor; freezes well.	ABU ALL BURR DEG FIS HIG MEY ORN POR ROS STO TIL
BLUE LAKE 264	58	5½–6½-inch, round to creased back pods; white seeded; disease-tolerant; All-American winner.	COM
BLUE LAKE 274 (OP)	55–60	5–6-inch, round, dark green pod; white seeded; resistant to mosaic and New York 15 virus.	BURP DEG FAR GAR GUR HEN JUN LED MEY PAR PIN TWI VER WIL WILL
BOUNTIFUL	48–51	This 6–7-inch, flat, green, all-purpose bean is a good freezer.	ALL COM LED MEY ORG PIN SEE SOU VER WIL
BROWN DUTCH	60	Flat, light green pod; tan seed; use as a French haricot type bean or as a dried bean.	BOU
BURPEE'S STRINGLESS	56	6-inch, medium green pod; all-purpose bean with brown seed; good canner.	ALL DEG FAR MEY
BURPEE'S STRING-LESS GREEN POD	50	5–6-inch, slightly curved, deep green pod with a tender, brittle bean; good canner or freezer.	BURP DEG POR VER WIL

VARIETY	DAYS	DESCRIPTION	SOURCES (p. 385)
BUSH BEANS (SNAP/SLICING) (continued)			
BURPEE'S STRING-LESS GREEN POD IMPROVED	53	6-inch, nearly round, slightly curved, fiberless pod.	ROS
BURPEE'S TENDERPOD	50	These flavorful 5½-inch, round, curved pods are tender, meaty, brittle, stringless, and fiberless. Use fresh, canned, or frozen.	BURP
BUSH ROMANO	50–60	Use the 5–6-inch, flat, Italian-type beans fresh, canned, or frozen. The 18-inch plant has oval, white seeds.	STO
CAMILE	60	Filet-type bean comes from a straight, thin pod. Harvest promptly and frequently. Vigorous plants are resistant to mosaic virus.	COO
CANADIAN WONDER	60	Old-fashioned variety is vigorous, hardy, prolific, and bushy.	BOU
COMMODORE (New Dwarf Kentucky Wonder)	58–63	Easy-to-pick, round, dark green pod; stringless; heavy yielder.	MEY POR ROS SEE
COMMODORE IMPROVED	58	A 6½–7-inch, curved, dark green pod comes from this vigorous, medium-size plant.	DEG WIL
CONTENDER	42–55	5–7-inch, round, oval, medium green pod; stringless; widely adapted; bushy, mosaic-resistant.	BOU BURR DEG FAR HEN LED PON POR RED SOU STO VER WIL
CYRUS	50	Very prolific; produces slim, round, straight pod with excellent flavor.	ORG
DAISY	55	The 5–7-inch, medium green pods are set above the foliage for easy picking. Seeds are slow to mature.	LEJ THO
DANDY	54	Pick round, dark green pods when 4 inches long for gourmet eating.	DEG NIC MEY TWI
DECIBEL	50–56	5½-inch, very thin, French filet bean; stringless; white seeded; disease-tolerant.	COM ORN STO TWI
DERBY	55–57	This All-American winner's 7-inch, dark green pod ripens very slowly. The variety is tolerant to mosaic, and Plant Variety Patented (PVP).	BOU BURP COM GUR HEN JUN LED MEY NIC PAR POR STO THO TWI VER WILL
DIEUL FIN PRECOCE	60	Old favorite Petit Gris; crops well; fine flavor.	BOU
DUCHESS	50	Even in less than desirable planting conditions, this dependable bean with 5½-inch, dark green pods and dark brown seeds produces abundantly. It's disease-tolerant and Plant Variety Patented (PVP).	BURR
DWARF BEES	55	A true bush runner bean, it has brilliant scarlet flowers that attract hummingbirds. You can harvest beans 2 weeks after flowering starts.	ORN TER VER
EARLI-SERVE	41–47	4-inch, slender, straight pod; big yields on 18-inch plant; white seeded; tolerant to bean mosaic.	BURR GUR HEN HIG STO VER

VARIETY	DAYS	DESCRIPTION	SOURCES (p. 385)

BUSH BEANS (SNAP/SLICING) (continued)

VARIETY	DAYS	DESCRIPTION	SOURCES (p. 385)
EARLY CONTENDER	49	6–7-inch, oval pod; stringless; buff-colored seeds; vigorous and heat-tolerant; resistant to mosaic and powdery mildew.	GUR POR
EMPRESS	55	5¾-inch, straight, dark green pod; plump, white seeds; stringless; an excellent freezer.	GUR
E-Z PICK BLUE LAKE BUSH	60–75	The 6–6½-inch dark green pods are concentrated and set high for easier picking; they are good for canning and freezing. The plant grows to 22–25 inches.	FAR FIS JOH PAR STO TER VER
FINAUD	60	Pick straight, slender pods at 4–6-inch stage.	COO
FIN DE BAGNOLS	63	Heirloom variety is a 14–16-inch plant that forms 6–7-inch, slim pods. Filet French beans should be picked at about 4 inches.	COO GOU LEJ
GATOR GREEN 15	55	6–7-inch, round, slender, medium green pod; white seeded; high yields on upright plant; resists mosaic and New York 15 virus; Plant Variety Patented (PVP).	MEY TWI
GATOR GREEN IMPROVED	48	Upright plant keeps 6-inch pods off the ground. It's mosaic-tolerant and white seeded.	STO
GREENCROP (OP)	42–55	8x½-inch, flat, dark green pod; stringless and brittle; white seeded; best for frenching.	GAR POR SEE STO VER WIL WILL
GREEN ISLE	55	6–8-inch pod; resistant to most diseases.	FAR PIN VER
GREEN LANTERN	53	8-inch, round, straight, dark green pod; white seeded; excellent tolerance to most mosaics and some strains of fall rust.	STO
GREEN RULER	51	Romano-type bean, it develops an 18-inch, spreading, bushy vine, with long, very flat pods that freeze well.	DEG
GREENSLEEVES	56	Round, dark green pod; white seeded; resistant to common and New York 15 mosaic; good freezer.	BURP
GULLIVER	60	Stringless, high-yielding runner bean has 9–10-inch-long straight, smooth pods.	THO
HAMMOND DWARF SCARLET RUNNER	55	Edible blossoms; 18-inch plant.	ORN
HARVESTER TEEPEE	51	8-inch, slender pod; has tepee growth habit (grows into a tent shape); produces over a long period.	BURR PIN WIL WILL
IDAHO REFUGEE	50	Old-time, midseason bean.	SEE
JADE	53–58	Large, upright plant forms 7-inch, rich green pods and pale green seeds. It tolerates bean mosaic virus.	JOH LED VER
JUMBO BUSH	55–60	Romano-type gourmet bean with 12x1-inch dark green pod; nearly seedless; stringless; heavy bearing and quick podding; Plant Variety Patented (PVP).	FIS GUR HEN JOH NIC PAR PIN POR TER VER WIL

VARIETY	DAYS	DESCRIPTION	SOURCES (p. 385)

BUSH BEANS (SNAP/SLICING) *(continued)*

VARIETY	DAYS	DESCRIPTION	SOURCES
KEBARIKA	70	Kenya variety, 18-inch plant; 6-inch pod; 5 purple mottled seeds in each pod; tolerates heat and drought.	SEED
KENTUCKY WONDER BUSH (Commodore)	65	A bush version of the Kentucky Wonder pole, it produces crisp, meaty, 8-inch, round pods. Keep it picked to induce big yields.	GUR PAR SEE THO VER
KENTUCKY WONDER BUSH 125	58	Upright, 20-inch plant gives high yields of 6–7-inch, flat, oval, medium green pods. It's Plant Variety Patented (PVP).	BURR DEG HEN JUN PAR TWI
LABEL	55	Baby French-type bean; 4½–5½-inch, slender, green pod; stringless, unless stressed; white seeded; tolerant to bean diseases.	GOU NIC ORN PIN SHE STO TWI
LANCER	59	Erect plant holds its 6-inch, slender, round pods off the ground. It's resistant to bean mosaic and New York 15 virus.	COM
LANDRETH	55	1894 variety; meaty and stringless.	JLH SEE
LIMELIGHT	38	Thick, broad pod; 12–15-inch plant; fiberless; heavy cropper if picked regularly; good to freeze.	THO
MAGPIE	65	Thin, 7-inch pod; black-and-white seed; heirloom variety.	SEED
MARBEL	54	This French variety produces a compact, upright plant with 7x¼-inch, dark green pods streaked with violet. Tan seed is streaked dark purple.	JOH ORN STO
MASAI	60	Ultra slim pod; high yielding, cold- and disease-tolerant filet variety.	THO
MINI GREEN	52	This true baby bean's 4-inch-long pods need no snapping. Pick beans as they mature.	PAR
MONTANA GREEN	50	6–7-inch, round, medium green pod; stringless; light buff seeds.	HIG
MONTANO	50	5-inch, round, straight, dark green pod; slow seed development; erect plant with concentrated pod set; resistant to most bean diseases; good canner, freezer.	WILL
NOORDSTER	50	Most beans of this short season, stringy variety mature at the same time.	WILL
OREGON LAKE BUSH	55	Vigorous, multibranched bush.	NIC
OREGON TRAIL BUSH	58	Vigorous and productive plants with 7-inch pods.	TIL
PLENTIFUL STRINGLESS	50–65	16–18-inch plant; 6–7-inch, flat pod; beetle-resistant.	SEED
PODSQUAD	45	6-inch, round, medium green pod; slow seed development; white seeded; resistant to common bean mosaic virus; Plant Variety Patented (PVP).	STO
PRELUDE	45	Stringless, green pod.	WILL

VARIETY	DAYS	DESCRIPTION	SOURCES (p. 385)

BUSH BEANS (SNAP/SLICING) *(continued)*

VARIETY	DAYS	DESCRIPTION	SOURCES
PRIMO	51	Slim Romano bean in 5¾-inch, medium green pods; white seeded; tolerant to bean virus 1-A; Plant Variety Patented (PVP).	STO
PROVIDER (OP)	52–55	5¼–6-inch, round pod; purple seeded; heavy yields; resistant to mosaic and powdery mildew.	ABU ALL GAR HEN JOH MEY PIN SEED STO VER
RADAR	57	Slim, stringless pod from Holland.	GOU
RAPIER (OP)	63	Gourmet cooks will love this plant, loaded with finger-length pods. Pick at pinkie length.	GAR TER
REGALFIN	60	Very thin, French slicing bean.	LEJ
REMUS MR	40	Fiberless 10-inch, round pods hang from the top of the 18–20-inch plant, which is resistant to common bean mosaic. The beans freeze well.	PAR
RESISTO	56	Round, straight, medium green pod; slow seed development; high yields; rust-resistant.	WIL
ROMA (Italian Bean)	53–59	4½-inch, wide, flat, thin, green pod; white seeded; resembles pole Romano; good fresh or frozen.	ALL GUR TIL
ROMA II	59	Use the 4½-inch, flat, medium green pods fresh, canned, or frozen. The plant gives big yields, is resistant to common bean mosaic virus, and is Plant Variety Patented (PVP).	BURP COM JUN LED MEY ORN PAR POR TWI VER WIL
ROMANETTE	60	5–6-inch, broad, flat, medium green pod; white seeded; 16–18-inch, upright plant; resistant to common bean mosaic.	DEG
ROMANO 14	56	5½–6-inch, broad, flat, medium green pod; tan seeds; true Romano flavor; good canned, fresh, or frozen.	SOU WIL
ROMANO BUSH	50	6-inch, extra wide, medium green stringless pod; distinctive flavor; white seeded; Plant Variety Patented (PVP).	GUR ORG PIN STO
ROYALNEL (Fin de Fin)	50	French slicing bean.	LEJ
SLENDERETTE	53	Erect plant holds huge crop of 5-inch, slender dark green pods off the ground. Good fresh, canned, or frozen. This Dutch variety has white seeds.	PAR PLA SHE VER
SPECULATOR	48	The 18-inch plant holds 4-inch, straight, dark green pods off the ground. The seeds are white.	STO
SPRING GREEN	46	4–6-inch, dark green pod; white seeded; stringless; 18-inch, upright plant; mosaic-tolerant; good canned or frozen.	STO
STRIKE	45	5½-inch, round, slender, straight, medium green pod; white seeded; tolerant to bean mosaic and New York 15 virus.	ORN STO WIL

VARIETY	DAYS	DESCRIPTION	SOURCES (p. 385)

BUSH BEANS (SNAP/SLICING) *(continued)*

VARIETY	DAYS	DESCRIPTION	SOURCES
STRINGLESS GREEN POD (Landreth's)	52–54	The 20-inch, upright plant is heavy bearing and able to tolerate drought. It has 5–6-inch, round, green pods and brown seeds.	POR SEE VER
SUNRAY	58	5–6-inch, round, straight pod; brown seeded; high yields.	PIN
TAVERA	54	4–5-inch, round, slender, dark green pod; stringless; small, white seed; medium-size plants.	JOH
TENDERCROP	52–61	5–5½-inch, straight, round pod; dark seed; stringless; good yielder; resistant to pod mottle, mosaic, and New York 15 virus.	GUR HEN NIC PAR PON VER WIL
TENDERETTE	55	5½–6-inch, straight, rich green pod; white seeded; stringless and fiberless; good fresh, canned, or frozen.	GUR HEN MEY SEE VER
TENDERGREEN (Asgrow Stringless)	52–57	The stringless 6–7-inch, round, dark green pod is a good canner. The 14–18-inch plant is resistant to mosaic.	ABU ALL BOU BUT COM DEG LED PIN POR
TENDERGREEN IMPROVED	53–56	This mosaic-resistant variety has 6–7-inch, round pods and purple-mottled, tan seeds.	BURR FAR GUR HEN JUN STO VER WIL WILL
TENDERLAKE	51	Low-fiber Blue Lake type; pods tolerant to rust and brown spot; white seeded; Plant Variety Patented (PVP).	HEN STO
TENDERPICK	54	Vigorous, 20-inch plants are heavy producers of 5½-inch-long, dark green pods with curving tips. This white-seeded variety is highly recommended for fresh use, canning, and freezing.	BURP
TENDERPOD	50	4½–5½-inch, light green pod; highly productive, good canning bean; All-American winner.	BURP GUR LED
TENNESSEE GREENPOD BUSH	50	This 6–7-inch, medium-dark green pod is recommended for hot, dry growing conditions and can also be left to dry as a baking bean.	VER
THE PRINCE	55	18-inch, oval pod; widely adapted 14-inch plant; excellent for freezing.	BOU
TOPCROP	48–52	5½–6-inch, medium green pod; stringless; 16-inch plant with good yields; mosaic-resistant.	BURR DEG FAR FIS GUR HEN JUN MEY PIN PON POR ROS SOU TWI VER WIL
TOTEM	65	8–10-inch filet version of Blue Lake bush.	TER
TRIOMPHE DE FARCY	48–59	3–7-inch-long, ¼-inch-wide, straight, thin pod with purple mottling; heirloom variety; 17–18-inch plant with good yields.	BURP COO GOU JOH LEJ
TRIUMPH	56	5¾-inch, slightly curved pod; 18–24-inch, heavy yielding plant; Plant Variety Patented (PVP).	TWI
VENTURE (OP)	48–50	6½-inch, somewhat lumpy, green pod; white seeded; high yields; widely adapted and easy to grow.	GAR HIG JOH LED PAR TER VER

VARIETY	DAYS	DESCRIPTION	SOURCES (p. 385)

BUSH BEANS (SNAP/SLICING) *(continued)*

VARIETY	DAYS	DESCRIPTION	SOURCES
VERNANDON	55	6-inch, round, slim, deep green pod; classic French filet bean; easy to grow; resistant to bean virus and anthracnose.	ORN SHE
WADE BUSH	54	6-inch, round, slender pod; red-brown seeds; stringless; resistant to mosaic and powdery mildew.	FAR VER
WHITE HALF RUNNER (Mississippi Skip Bean)	60	4-inch, round, light green pod; fibrous when full-grown; use as fresh or shell bean.	BURP SOU VER
WHITE HALF RUNNER (Mountaineer)	52	This early half runner has a round, oval, light green pod. Use these as string or shell beans.	HEN MEY PAR POR WIL
WIDUCO IMPROVED	50	5–6-inch, round, green pod; disease-resistant; good freezer.	WILL

WAX BUSH BEANS

VARIETY	DAYS	DESCRIPTION	SOURCES
BEURRE DE ROCQUENCOURT (OP) (Golden Rocky, Beau de Reaucancourt)	46–60	The 12–16-inch, upright plant yields 6–7-inch, yellow, oval, round pods and black seeds. The beans are stringless. This variety is recommended where nighttime temperatures drop below 60°F.	ABU GAR GOU PIN SEE SEED TER WILL
BRITTLE WAX (Round Pod Kidney Wax)	50–58	Mildly flavored, 6–7-inch, yellow pod; stringless; white seeded; good canned, fresh, or frozen.	BURP FAR GUR PON TIL
CHEROKEE (Golden All American, Valentine Wax)	49–58	6–6½-inch, oval, golden pod; black seeded; stringless; dependable during poor weather conditions; resistant to mosaic and New York 15 virus.	ABU BURR COM DEG FAR GUR HEN LED MEY PON SEED STO VER
DORABEL	44	4½-inch, round, Baby French Wax; stringless; white seed; tolerant to common bean mosaic virus, anthracnose, and halo blight; Plant Variety Patented (PVP).	COO PIN STO TWI
DRAGON LANGERIE (OP)	57–65	Dutch variety with long, flat, creamy yellow, striped purple pod; high yielding; fine flavor.	COO GAR ORN PIN SEE VER
EARLIWAX GOLDEN YELLOW BEAN	54	For fresh or processed beans.	VER
GOLDCROP	45–54	The 5–6½-inch, shiny yellow pods are set at outer edges of foliage. Stringless, white seeded variety is good fresh, canned, or frozen.	ALL BURP FAR GUR JUN STO THO
GOLDEN BUTTER (Mont D'Or)	60	Medium golden pod; black seeded; stringless.	BOU
GOLDEN ROD	54–56	High yielding, vigorous, upright plant forms 5–6-inch, round, medium yellow pods. White seeds develop slowly. Plant is tolerant to common bean mosaic. Use beans fresh or canned. Plant Variety Patented (PVP).	JUN STO
GOLDEN WAX	50–60	5¼-inch, heavy, flat pod; stringless; very productive; rust-resistant; good freezer.	BUT FIS HEN LED WIL

VARIETY	DAYS	DESCRIPTION	SOURCES (p. 385)

WAX BUSH BEANS (continued)

VARIETY	DAYS	DESCRIPTION	SOURCES (p. 385)
GOLDEN WAX IMPROVED	51	Flat, oval, light golden yellow pod; white seeded; good yields of brittle, stringless beans.	ALL COM DEG GUR POR ROS VER
GOLDEN WAX TOP NOTCH	50	5-inch, flat, straight, yellow pod; white seed with brown eye.	MEY
GOLDKIST	59	For best flavor, harvest the slender, golden yellow pods when young. Variety offers good yields.	LED
GOLD MINE	47	5-inch bright yellow pod; Gold Rush type with less fiber; white seeded; tolerance to common bean mosaic virus, brown spot, and sometimes halo blight; Plant Variety Patented (PVP).	STO
GOLD RUSH	54	Straight, yellow pods hang in clusters around the main stem of this excellent freezer bean. It's resistant to common bean mosaic virus.	STO
HONEY GOLD	40	5½-inch, short, straight, round pod; stringless; 12–14-inch plant; heavy yielder; resistant to bean mosaic.	STO
KENTUCKY WONDER WAX	68	7½-inch, yellow pod; slow to mature; same flavor as Kentucky Wonder.	HEN SEE
KINGHORN (Butter Wax, Improved Brittle Wax)	50–56	White seeded, vigorous French variety develops 5–6-inch, creamy yellow pods that are good for canning and freezing.	GUR HIG SEE WILL
PENCIL POD BLACK WAX	52–55	This black-seeded, stringless variety has 6–7-inch, round, slightly curved, golden yellow pods and can withstand temperature changes better than most.	ALL FAR JUN SEE SOU TIL VER WILL
PENCIL POD WAX (OP) (Butter Bean)	51–58	5–6-inch, deeply curved, rich yellow pod; black seeded; stringless, tender, and brittle.	COM DEG GAR ORG PIN
ROCDOR (OP) (Roc D'Or)	50–57	Pick the black-seeded French filet bean's 6½-inch pods when young. This variety tolerates cooler, wetter conditions and resists mosaic virus and anthracnose. Use beans fresh, canned, or frozen.	GAR JOH NIC ORN SEED SHE STO
SLENDERWAX	58	20-inch plant; 5-inch, golden yellow pod.	VER
SUNGOLD	45–56	5–6-inch, round, straight, bright yellow pod; white seeded; slow seed development; resistant to bean mosaic; good choice for high-altitude gardens.	FIS HEN HIG STO
SUNRAE	55	6-inch, golden yellow pod; heavy yields; vigorous plant.	PAR
TOP NOTCH GOLDEN WAX	50	Nearly flat pod; variety resembles Golden Wax, but pods are longer; stringless beans.	FAR
WAX ROMANO	59	Flat, bright yellow pod; similar to Roma II; high-yielding, disease-resistant.	BURP

VARIETY	DAYS	DESCRIPTION	SOURCES (p. 385)
BUSH BEANS (PURPLE/YELLOW/OTHER—NON-WAX)			
MINI YELLOW	52	Same as Mini Green. Pick 4-inch pods as they mature. The beans are good fresh, frozen, canned, or pickled.	PAR
PURPLE QUEEN	55	Purple pods turn green when cooked. Seed is light brown. This variety is an improved Royalty Purple Pod. It tolerates cold well.	ORN
PURPLE TEEPEE	51–55	The 5–6-inch, purple pod turns green when cooked. Compact plant is easy to pick. Beans are excellent fresh, canned, or frozen.	HIG PAR PIN THO
REGAL SALAD	52	5–6-inch, curved, bronze pod; slightly fuzzy texture and outstanding flavor; erect plant.	PIN
ROYAL BURGUNDY	50–60	The 5½–6-inch, round, curved, purple pod turns green when cooked and is good fresh or frozen. Stringless, 12–15-inch plant is a good variety for colder soils. Plant Variety Patented (PVP).	BURP COM COO DEG GUR HEN JUN LED SEE SHE STO TER TIL TWI VER WILL
ROYAL DUKE	50	Round, purple pods turn green when cooked.	FIS
ROYALTY PURPLE POD (OP) (Scarlet Emperor)	50–60	The 5-inch, round, curved pod cooks green and has an unusual, rich flavor. This stringless variety with buff-colored seed is good for colder soils. Freeze beans or use fresh.	ABU ALL BUT FAR GAR JLH JOH PLA SEED SOU WIL
SEQUOIA	55–65	Great Romano flavor; deep purple color.	COO

BEANS, LIMA

BOTANICAL NAME: *Phaseolus lunatus*

DAYS TO MATURITY: 60–90.

PLANTING TIME: Sow outdoors about four weeks after the last frost.

SOIL: Light, warm, and sandy; pH 6.0–7.5.

NUTRIENTS: Lima beans supply their own nitrogen. Feed them every three or four weeks with fish emulsion.

WATER: Avoid overhead watering. Keep moist and don't allow a crust to form over the soil surface. Don't overwater.

LIGHT: Full sun.

SPACING: Sow seeds 1–1½ inches deep. Thin bush beans to 3 inches apart. Thin pole beans to 6 inches apart.

HARVEST: Pick the pods of limas as soon as they begin to look lumpy and before they turn yellow.

STORAGE: If you have too many beans, dry them for future use by letting the pods mature on the vine and turn beige. Remove the dried beans and heat them in a 130°F oven for an hour

BEANS, LIMA

BEANS, LIMA

to kill any weevils. Store them in sacks or sealed jars in a dry place. Some varieties can be frozen.

Lima Bean Growing Tips

Peak Flavor

The large white or speckled lima beans are at their peak flavor when the beans are fully formed in the pods. To test, simply shell several pods that seem to be full, then choose pods with a similar feel. This test will not work for baby limas or baby butter beans.

Early Harvest

You can gain a couple of weeks on the season by sprouting lima bean seeds on a windowsill inside wet paper towels. When they start to sprout, set them outside. Stick the sprouting seeds with sprout tips showing in the ground the minute the soil warms up.

VARIETY	DAYS	DESCRIPTION	SOURCES (p. 385)
POLE LIMA BEANS			
AUBREY DEANE	87	This pre-1890 family heirloom from Greene County, Virginia, is especially productive under hot, dry conditions. Seeds are buff-colored and splashed with red-maroon.	SOU
BURPEE'S BEST (Dreer's Improved Challenger, Potato Lima)	87–92	4½x1¼-inch, broad, straight pod; plump potato-type seed; strong climber, reaching 10–12 feet; high yields.	MEY
CAROLINA (Sieva, Southern Running Butterbean)	79	3½x2-inch, flat, medium green pod; white seeded; heavy yields.	BURP HEN MEY PIN RED WIL
CHRISTMAS POLE (Large Speckled Christmas, Calico, Giant Florida Pole)	80–88	A high-quality, vigorous, 10-foot climber, this long season bean has 5–6-inch, flat, raised area of dark red pods that turn pink-brown when cooked. The cream-colored seed has irregular red stripes.	NIC ORN PAR POR ROS SEE SOU VER WIL
FLORIDA BUTTER (Florida Speckled Butter, Speckled Butter)	85	3½-inch, medium green, slightly curved pod; 8-foot vine; light buff-colored seeds splashed with maroon; good tolerance for hot, humid weather.	ORN POR ROS SOU VER WIL
FORDHOOK	92	4½x1¼x¾-inch pod; 3–5 potato-type beans per pod; may grow to 12 feet.	BURP ROS WILL
ILLINOIS GIANT	86	This hybrid of Christmas and Dr. Martin is drought- and heat-resistant. Its large seeds are light green with speckles and splashes of maroon-red. The beans are easy to shell.	SOU
KING OF THE GARDEN (White Pole Lima)	88–90	A long season producer, it climbs to 10 feet and forms 5–8-inch dark green pods, good for shelling or freezing. Seeds are thick, flat, and ivory white to pale green.	COM DEG GUR JUN LED MEY PAR PON RED SEE SOU STO TWI VER

VARIETY	DAYS	DESCRIPTION	SOURCES (p. 385)

POLE LIMA BEANS (continued)

VARIETY	DAYS	DESCRIPTION	SOURCES (p. 385)
PRIZETAKER (Big Six)	90	6x1½-inch pod; excellent flavor, fresh or frozen.	BURP LED MEY
RED SPECKLED POLE (Speckled Calico)	78–88	Large, colorful, red-speckled beans; grows 6–7 feet tall; excellent quality.	HEN
WHATCOM LIMA	80	Not a true lima, this is an expansive form of White Dutch Runner.	ABU
WORCHESTER INDIAN RED POLE	80	A prolific producer under adverse conditions, it sets medium-size limas. Seeds range from dull red to dull maroon-red. The plant is heat- and drought-resistant.	ʿSOU

BUSH LIMA BEANS (PLUMP SEEDED)

VARIETY	DAYS	DESCRIPTION	SOURCES (p. 385)
BURPEE'S BUSH IMPROVED	70–75	5½x1¼-inch, flat, oval, medium green pod; white seeded; easy to shell; high-quality.	ALL BURP BURR DEG FAR JUN MEY VER
DIXIE WHITE BUTTERPEA	70–76	The pod is broad, oval, and lightly curved; seed is white. This strong, 2-foot plant will set even under hot conditions.	PAR POR VER
DIXIE SPECKLED BUTTERPEA	76	Similar to Dixie White butterpea, the dark green pod is 3½x½ inches and slightly curved. Brownish red seed is speckled with darker brown. The 16–21-inch plant is productive in hot weather.	LED PAR VER WIL
EXCEL NORTHERN FRESH	65–72	2-foot bush; plump, light green baby lima.	SEED
FORDHOOK IMPROVED	75	3–4-inch, pale green pod; good yields in hot weather; excellent fresh, canned, or frozen.	FAR
FORDHOOK 242 (Potato Lima)	75–85	Heat-resistant plants set their 3–4-inch pods even under adverse conditions. Beans are good fresh, canned, or frozen.	ALL BURP BURR COM DEG GUR HEN JOH JUN LED MEY ORN PAR PON POR SEE STO TWI VER WIL
HOPI YELLOW	110	The medium-large, flattened, true lima's basic color is warm "old gold," with some streaking. It's an heirloom variety.	ABU SEED
SIMMON'S RED STREAK	100	Short runner plant produces flat, red and white limas.	SEED

BUSH LIMA BEANS (SMALL SEEDED)

VARIETY	DAYS	DESCRIPTION	SOURCES (p. 385)
BABY BUSH (Evergreen Bush)	67–72	Producing bright green pods, this variety endures hot weather well. Pod becomes creamy white when mature.	BUT
BABY FORDHOOK BUSH	67–70	2¾x¾-inch dark green, slightly curved pod; 14-inch plant.	BURP MEY VER
EASTLAND	68–75	Flat, 3–4-inch, medium green pod; greenish white seed; upright plant, resistant to downy mildew; good fresh, canned, or frozen.	BURR PAR SEED STO

VARIETY	DAYS	DESCRIPTION	SOURCES (p. 385)

BUSH LIMA BEANS (SMALL SEEDED) *(continued)*

VARIETY	DAYS	DESCRIPTION	SOURCES (p. 385)
GENEVA	85	Light green pod; tolerates cool soil; good for freezing.	JOH
GREEN SEEDED BABY HENDERSON (Thorogreen Baby Lima)	67	The 3-inch, flat, pale green pods form in clusters. Seeds stay green in all stages. Prolific plant grows to be 14–16 inches.	BOU FAR GUR HEN JUN LED MEY NIC ORN VER WIL
HENDERSON BUSH	65–81	1889 heirloom variety with a 3-inch, flat, dark green, slightly curved pod; small erect plant; good freezer and canner.	ALL BURP GUR MEY PAR PIN POR ROS SEE TWI VER WIL
HENDERSON BUSH IMPROVED	65	Dependable heirloom variety.	DEG RED
JACKSON WONDER (Calico, Speckled Bush)	65–83	3¼-inch-long pod; purple-mottled buff-colored seed; 24-inch plant; heavy yields; use fresh or dried.	GUR ORN PAR POR ROS SOU VER WIL
THAXTER (All Green)	67	3¼-inch, small, flat pod; 15–16-inch plant; tolerant of downy mildew.	COM
WILLOW-LEAF WHITE	86	The 1891 heirloom variety's 3-inch, dark green pod contains 3 chalky white seeds.	SOU

BEANS, DRIED or SHELL

BOTANICAL NAME: *Phaseolus vulgaris*

DAYS TO MATURITY: 90–125.

PLANTING TIME: Plant outdoors when the soil has warmed to 65–70°F and all danger of frost is past.

SOIL: Well-drained; pH 6.0–7.5.

NUTRIENTS: These legumes supply their own nitrogen. Apply fish emulsion every three or four weeks during the growing season.

WATER: Water weekly to a 1-inch depth.

LIGHT: Full sun.

SPACING: Sow seeds 1–1½ inches deep, 3 inches apart. For row planting, space 2 feet apart. For pole beans, space 6 inches apart.

HARVEST: Pick pods in the fall when plants' leaves have fallen. Dry on a screen or hang plants upside down. Shell by threshing in a burlap sack or by hand.

STORAGE: Keep the dried beans in a capped jar.

BEANS, DRIED or SHELL

VARIETY	DAYS	DESCRIPTION	SOURCES (p. 385)

SHELL BEANS (FAVA BEANS—"ENGLISH BROADBEAN")

VARIETY	DAYS	DESCRIPTION	SOURCES
ALBINETTE	80	Small, white-seeded type's pods grow in bunches for a heavy yield. Sow in early spring.	WILL
APROVECHO SELECT	75–85	Developed in Oregon with unusually large seeds and sweet flavor; hardy to below 20°F.	ABU SEED
AQUADULCE CLAUDIA	90	Pale green pod; 3–4-foot plant; hardy to 12°F.	ORN THO
AQUADULCE VERY LONG POD	85–90	12–14-inch, pearl green pod; hardy, productive 36–40-inch plant.	ABU DEG LEJ NIC PIN SEE
BANNER	140	Small seeds; 6-foot plant.	ORN
BONNIE LAD	75	15-inch plant with 5–6-inch pods; small, light green beans.	SEED
BROAD LONG POD (Fava Long Pod)	85–90	Used as a substitute for limas in northern climates, it develops a 7-inch, oblong, flat, light green pod. Do not grow this variety in hot weather.	ALL BURP COO PLA POR SOU SUN VER
BROAD LONG POD IMPROVED	85–90	7-inch, flat, oblong pod; use as green shell bean or as dry bean.	LED WILL
BRUNETTE	72	Each 4–5-inch pod contains 7 medium-large beans. The plant grows to 18–24 inches.	ABU
BUNYARDS EXHIBITION	85	Each 12–14-inch pod has 7 beans. The mature plant is 24–40 inches.	ABU
CHAK'RUGA	110–140	A Bolivian variety, the 3–4-foot, multibranched plant is drought-tolerant.	SEED
EQUINA	85	Small seeds.	SEE
EXPRESS	71	Each 36-inch, winter-hardy plant forms 34 7–8-inch pods. They freeze well.	THO
IMPERIAL GREEN LONGPOD	84	9 large, green-seeded beans per 15–20-inch pod; good freezer.	THO
IPRO (OP)	78	The 3½-foot plant is heat-resistant and tolerant to top yellow virus.	GAR JOH
SWEET LORANE	90–100	Small seeded; hardy in cold weather.	SEED
TOTO	63	Dwarf upright plant holds its 8-inch, pendant-shaped, medium green pods off the ground and yields abundantly. Seed is beige.	STO
WINDSOR LONG POD (OP) (Broad Windsor)	65–75	Fat, flat pod containing up to 6 beans; 3½-foot, frost-hardy plant; dependable variety.	ABU BOU GAR HIG SEED STO TIL WILL

VARIETY	DAYS	DESCRIPTION	SOURCES (p. 385)
SHELL BEANS (HORTICULTURAL)			
BERT GOODWIN'S	75	The 7-inch pod holds large, mottled brown beans that are good for freezing. This variety sends out a few runners but is a bush plant.	PIN
COCO RUBICO	80	Exceptionally large, horticultural-type shell bean.	SEE
DWARF HORTICULTURAL (Kievits, Long Pod, Wren's Nest)	65	5–6-inch, thick pod; carmine color at maturity.	BURP FIS LED PIN WILL
FRENCH DWARF HORTICULTURAL	60–65	Long, straight pod; 14–18-inch plant; use as green snap bean or dry.	ALL COM
FRENCH HORTICULTURAL (October Bean)	64–90	Heirloom bean; 18-inch plant; reaches dry-bean stage in 90 days; hardy and disease-resistant.	SEED STO VER
HORTICULTURAL SHELL	85	16-inch plant; beige-white seeds with red markings.	SEED
KING MAMMOTH HORTICULTURAL	70	Large, shelly bean.	SEE
SCARLET BEAUTY ELITE	70	Beans are elongated with shades of purplish brown and beige. There are 7 beans per pod.	PIN
SPECKLED BALE	75	Heirloom variety; plump horticultural bean from Oregon.	ABU
TAYLOR'S DWARF HORTICULTURAL (Speckled Bays, Shelley)	64–95	The 14–18-inch semirunner comes from 1800s heirloom seed. The pod is 5½–6 inches, oval, and cream colored. The buff-colored seed is splashed red.	COM GAR GUR HEN MEY SEE SOU TIL TER VER WIL
TONGUE OF FIRE	70	This variety produces 6–7-inch, flat, red-streaked, ivory pods. Large, round beans have great flavor and texture. From Tierra del Fuego.	ABU GAR GOU ORN SEE VER
VERNEL	70	French import with pale green, oval pods; medium-size bean—use as dry or shell bean.	GOU ORN
WORCESTER HORTICULTURAL	70	A 7-inch, flat, splashed-red pod is set by this mammoth form of old-fashioned Horticultural Shell or Speckled Cranberry Bean. It's a pole bean.	ALL
SHELL BEANS (SOYBEANS)			
AGATE	90–95	Bicolored soybean has yellow-gold ring around a brown center. The small plant is a Japanese variety from Sapporo.	SEED
BLACK JET	104	Medium-size, jet black pod; 2–2½-foot plant; short season variety; high yielding; use thin-skinned bean as a dry bean.	ABU JOH
BUTTERBEANS	90	3 beans per pod; 2–2½-foot stocky, prolific plant; good freezer.	JOH

VARIETY	DAYS	DESCRIPTION	SOURCES (p. 385)

SHELL BEANS (SOYBEANS) *(continued)*

VARIETY	DAYS	DESCRIPTION	SOURCES
EDIBLE SOY BEAN (Vegetable Soy Bean)	80–103	Plant in spring or summer for a 20-inch plant with oval, bright green pods. Use young seeds as green shell beans. Use mature seeds to prepare soy milk or bean curd.	SUN
ENVY	75	Pod is bright green inside and out. The 2-foot plant is high yielding. Use as fresh green or dried bean.	JOH
FRISKELY V	70–91	The 18-inch, upright plant has buff-yellow pods and beige seed. It does not produce abundantly but can be grown in short season areas.	STO
HAKUCHO EARLY	95	Use the beans of this bush type as green shell beans or as you would limas.	WILL
LAMMER'S BLACK	104	Large plant; black soybeans; heirloom variety.	SEED
MIDNIGHT	90	This vigorous heavy-yielder's seeds go from light green to red to black when mature.	PIN
PRIZE	85–105	Erect bush forms large, oval pods. Use as a green shell or lima bean.	DEG LED ORN
VINTON 81	90	Yellow seeded; good for tofu, fresh, or as shell bean; vigorous producer; 36-inch plant.	PIN
WHITE LION	75	Large, dark green pod; 3 seeds per pod; 2-foot plant.	GLE

SHELL BEANS (KIDNEY)

VARIETY	DAYS	DESCRIPTION	SOURCES
AZTEC RED KIDNEY	90	Large, dark red kidney matures fairly late; heirloom variety; bush plant.	ABU
CANNELONE BEAN	70–90	Highly productive 1800s Italian heirloom sets a white kidney bean that's great for baking.	COO
DARK RED KIDNEY	95	Large, flat, waxy green pod; used as a dry cooking bean.	ABU JUN
MONTCALM	105	This upright, nonsprawling plant is very productive.	TER
RED KIDNEY (OP)	95–100	The 20–22-inch plant sets large, flat, green pods. Seed color is pinkish red to mahogany.	ALL BUT COM DEG FAR GAR GUR HEN LED PAR PON VER WILL
WHITE KIDNEY	100	24-inch plant with large pods.	VER

SHELL BEANS (MISCELLANEOUS)

VARIETY	DAYS	DESCRIPTION	SOURCES
ADVENTIST	90	Small, golden bean; very prolific; excellent for soups and stews.	ORG
ADZUKI (Chinese Red Bean, Red Ball)	90–125	Its 5-inch pod's dark red, rounded seeds have a distinctive, nutty flavor. The 2½-foot, bushy plant likes acid soil and cool nights.	JLH JOH PIN RED SUN VER

VARIETY	DAYS	DESCRIPTION	SOURCES (p. 385)

SHELL BEANS (MISCELLANEOUS) *(continued)*

VARIETY	DAYS	DESCRIPTION	SOURCES (p. 385)
AGATE PINTO	95	Rectangular, buff-colored; mottled bean; no habit of sprawling.	JOH TER
AMISH GNUTTLE	90	5-inch pod; small, pink and tan seeds with purple specks; short vines.	ORG
ANASAZI (Jacob's Cattle Bean, Trout Bean, Coach Dog Bean, Dalmation Bean)	90–95	Heirloom variety is traced back to ancient cliff-dwelling people. Beans are red and white mottled, and good for baking.	ABU PLA SEED VER
APPALOOSA	90–110	Bush plant sends off runners; it sets a white bean with maroon and black mottling.	ABU PLA
ATLAS	72	6-inch-long, flat, broad, light green, red-striped pod; buff seeds with red blotches.	VER
BEAUTIFUL	85	Medium-size, round beans are creamy white with a maroon design that looks painted on. They're easy to digest, producing little gas.	GAR
BLACK BEAN	90	Small black beans used in Mexican cooking.	JLH
BLACK COCO	95	Plump, black, quick-cooking bean.	TER
BLACK TURTLE SOUP BEAN	85	This dwarf bush gives 7–8 black beans per pod. The beans have been used in black turtle soup for more than 150 years.	VER
BLUE SPECKLED	85	This tepary bean is a staple in the Sonoran Desert. The drought-tolerant, viney bush has a medium-size seed.	SEED
BOLITA	100	Great-granddaddy of the pinto bean, this low bush plant sends out runners. Harvest beans when pods are dry.	PLA
BORLOTTO	68	Italian heirloom's pods are stippled bright rosy red and cream. Grow these like regular bush beans.	SHE
BOX	90	English variety's beans are purple on white.	ABU
BUCKSKIN	85	Oregon heirloom with buff-colored seed can be used as snap or dry bean.	ABU GAR
CANNELLINI	75	These Italian dry or shell beans are white and kidney shaped.	PIN
CLIFF DWELLER	90	This Southwest heirloom is heat- and drought-resistant, with 3–4 seeds per pod. Buff seeds are splashed black or dark wine at edges. Vines are vigorous and productive in the Southwest.	SOU
CLUSTER BEAN BARASATI	90	Productive 2–6-foot, upright plant likes sandy soil. Beans are used in East Indian cooking.	JLH
DUTCH BROWN	83	Pennsylvania Dutch heirloom variety; brown seeded; for dry use; 20-inch plant.	SEE VER WILL
EXPRESS	118	Vigorous, upright plant forms small, shiny, dark red Adzuki variety beans.	JOH

VARIETY	DAYS	DESCRIPTION	SOURCES (p. 385)

SHELL BEANS (MISCELLANEOUS) *(continued)*

VARIETY	DAYS	DESCRIPTION	SOURCES
FLAGEOLET (Chevier Vert)	65–100	Heirloom French, dry soup bean; 14-inch plant; pure white seed.	COO ORG PIN SHE
FLAMBEAU (French Flageolet)	76	Long, slender pod with 8–10 vivid mint green beans; prolific; excellent freezer.	JOH NIC
FRIJOL EN SECO	90	Bush pinto that tolerates drought and poor soil. From New Mexico.	PLA
GARBANZO (Chick-Pea)	65–100	Large, tan seed has distinctive chestnut flavor. Erect bush plant is suited to droughty areas.	ABU JLH LED PLA VER
GARBANZO	90	Black seeded; Ethiopian origin.	ABU JLH
GARBANZO	90	Green seeded; native to India.	ABU
GARBANZO, SARAH	100–110	Brown seeds; 2 beans per pod.	SEED
GAUCHO	90	Heirloom variety from Argentina has rich, tan-colored beans.	ABU
GOLD NUGGET (OP)	85	1920s bean originally from New Mexico. 5–8 golden brown beans per pod; light green plant.	GAR
HORSE HEAD	90	Heirloom variety is a bush. Violet seeds are used in soups and stews.	ORG
HUMASON'S BEST	90	Dry shelling bean with orange mottling.	ABU
HUTTERITE SOUP	78–85	This heirloom variety makes a thick, creamy soup. (Hutterites are a Mennonite sect that came to the U.S. in the 1760s.)	SEED
IMPROVED PINTO	90	Large, plump bean; heavy producer.	POR
IRELAND CREEK ANNIE	90	Pale buff-yellow bean resembles buckskin.	ABU
KABULI BLACK	95	Good-size black bean; frost-tolerant.	GAR JLH
KENEARLY BAKING BEAN	95	Nova Scotian strain forms a white bean with a yellow-brown eye.	VER
KILHAM GOOSE	90	Shiny, round-seeded "goose" pea bean; purple-on-white coloring; bush.	ABU
LENTIL MASOOR (Egyptian Lentil, Red Lentil)	90	Its small seed, with dark skin and salmon-orange interior, cooks quickly.	JLH
LIMELIGHT	46	Short, compact bush plant produces 3–4-inch, broad, flat, lime green pods.	ABU FIS
LOGAN GIANT	68	West Virginia heirloom's seeds are large, slightly flattened, and brown with cream frosting on one end; they're good dried beans. There are 6 beans per pod on the 15-foot vine.	SOU

VARIETY	DAYS	DESCRIPTION	SOURCES (p. 385)

SHELL BEANS (MISCELLANEOUS) *(continued)*

VARIETY	DAYS	DESCRIPTION	SOURCES (p. 385)
MAINE YELLOW EYE (OP) (Sulphur, Dot Eye Bean, Golden Cranberry, China Yellow, Stuben Yellow Eye)	85–92	The curved, light green pod holds a plump, yellow-tan dry bean with a squashlike flavor—good for baking. The 18-inch plant is dependable and prolific.	ABU ALL GAR JOH ORG RED SEE SOU VER
MARFAX	89	Round pod; popular baking bean; dependable yielder.	ABU
MIDNIGHT BLACK TURTLE (OP) (Black Turtle, Black Mexican)	85–104	A small black bean for soup or refried beans. An heirloom variety with heavy yields, the tall bush does not sprawl.	ABU GAR JOH ORG PIN RED SEE SHE
MITLA BLACK BEAN	70–90	Beige seed with blue speckles; nutty flavor; high yielding variety from Mexico; tepary bean used in soup.	PLA SEED
MITLA SPECKLED TEPARY BEAN	70–90	Variety is similar to the Black Tepary, but seeds are beige with blue speckles and have a nutty flavor.	PLA
MONEY	90	Red speckled bean from England; high yielding.	ABU
MOTH BEAN	95	In India, young pods are eaten as a vegetable. High-protein dried beans are used like lentils. Sprawling, mat-forming plant is for very warm climates.	BOU JLH
MUNG (Look Dow)	120	Small, olive green pod; does well in warmer weather; excellent as sprouts.	BOU COM DEG LED STO SUN VER
OAHU COMMON FIELD	90	These small tan, brown, and black beans from Hawaii flourish in tropical weather. Green pods are eaten like snap beans; mature beans can be dried and used in soups and stews.	JLH
OAHU ISLAND COMMON LIMA	90	Flat or plump beans are brown, red, black, purple, tan, and white; many are spotted and bicolored. Use these like regular limas. Known since pre-Columbian times, this variety prefers warm temperatures but will tolerate cool weather, drought, and poor soil.	JLH
PAINT DRY	100	Short season dry bean; offshoot of Yellow Eye bean.	SEED
PAWNEE SHELL	85	Deeply marked, brown-on-beige seed.	SEED
PINK BEAN	85	True bush; similar to Red Mexican.	VER
PINTO	85–90	Pod is 5 inches, oval, and broad. Seed is light buff speckled with greenish brown. Pintos are popular in Mexican cooking.	ABU DEG HEN LED PAR PIN POR SEE VER WIL
RED MEXICAN	85	Medium green pod; 1855 California heirloom bean; 14-inch plant; great in soup or baked.	RED
RICE BEAN	85	This small, slender, dark red bean is from tropical Asia. Use dried seeds in soups, stews, or sprouted. Variety likes warm, humid climates.	JLH

VARIETY	DAYS	DESCRIPTION	SOURCES (p. 385)
SHELL BEANS (MISCELLANEOUS) *(continued)*			
SANTA MARIA PINQUITO	90	Pink, square bean.	NIC RED SEE SOU
SCOTCH	90	Butterscotch-colored, flattened pole bean for dry use.	ABU
SIX NATIONS SHELL	80	14-inch plant with medium-size, white-speckled, red seeds.	SEED
SOLDIER (OP) (Johnson)	85–90	New England heirloom bean; white bean with a maroon blotch on the eye; flavor similar to kidney; 18-inch, drought-resistant plant.	ALL GAR GUR JOH RED SEE VER
SONORAN TEPARY BEAN (Sonoran Gold Bush)	70–110	Native to Sonoran Desert; 30 percent crude protein; 3-inch pod; small, gold bean.	PLA RED SEED
SWEDISH BROWN BEAN (OP)	85–92	Dark tan, oval bean with small, white eye is a good baking bean. Semivining, heavy-yielding plant is hardy and widely adapted.	ABU GAR ORG SEED VER
URDI BLACK (Urd, Black Gram)	85	Popular in India, the small black bean is used for soups and sauces or ground into meal.	JLH
VAL DAL	90	This hyacinth bean has white seeds and white flowers. Young pods and leaves can be cooked as a vegetable. Use dry beans in sauces, soups, and stews.	JLH
WALCHERSE WHITE	90	White bean used for soups and baking.	WILL
WORCHESTER INDIAN RED POLE	90	Heirloom variety seeds range from dull red to dull maroon-red; they're a medium-size lima-type bean. Plant produces prolifically under adverse conditions.	SOU
YELLOW EYE	70–90	Vermont heirloom variety grows an 18-inch, high-yielding plant. Plump, oval bean—white with a yellow eye—is used for soups, stews, and baking.	COO SEE
YELLOW FLAGEOLET	90	3-inch pod; same as Green Flageolet.	SEE

SHELL BEANS (NAVY)

VARIETY	DAYS	DESCRIPTION	SOURCES
LUCAS' NAVY	90	Small, white bean grown in the Puget Sound area of Washington.	ABU
NAVY (Pea Bean, White Wonder, Soup Bean, Sanilac, French, Fleet Wood)	85–95	Long, off-green pod; small white seeds; standard dry soup bean; heavy yielder.	COM GAR LED SEE VER

SHELL BEANS (RED, PURPLE, CRANBERRY)

VARIETY	DAYS	DESCRIPTION	SOURCES
CRANBERRY BEAN	60	Egg-shaped, thick, flat pod; beans splashed red at maturity.	ABU ORN

VARIETY	DAYS	DESCRIPTION	SOURCES (p. 385)

SHELL BEANS (RED, PURPLE, CRANBERRY) *(continued)*

VARIETY	DAYS	DESCRIPTION	SOURCES (p. 385)
GRAMMA WALTERS	70	Heavy-bearing, speckled Cranberry type.	ABU
JACOBS CATTLE (OP) (Trout Bean, Dalmation Bean, Coach Dog Bean)	65–85	Oblong beans are red on pure white—good for baking, with a clear, spicy flavor. This heirloom variety's 24-inch plant is ideal for cold climates.	ABU ALL COO GAR PIN RED SEE SEED VER
LOWE'S CHAMPION	65–72	Heirloom bean; 4–5-inch, rounded, flat, green pod; mahogany brown seed; 18–24-inch plant.	JOH
MEXICAN RED BEAN (OP)	85	Round, medium green pod; maroon beans; 14-inch plant; excellent baking bean.	GAR VER
MONTEZUMA	95	Red baking bean; bush plant.	NIC
RED PEANUT BEAN	50	The 14-inch plant's 4-inch pods turn red at maturity. Variety is ideal for dry climates.	VER
SPECKLED BALE	90	Plump Cranberry type from Oregon.	ABU
SPECKLED CRAN-BERRY EGG (Wren's Egg, King Mammoth)	65	5-inch, wide, thick pod; very productive pole bean; disease-resistant; good fresh shelled or frozen.	SEE VER
VERMONT CRAN-BERRY BUSH (Old Fashioned, King's Early)	60–90	Heirloom soup bean; maroon seed with rose tan streaks; bush plant; tastes like steak, good for meat substitute.	COO PIN RED VER
VERMONT CRAN-BERRY POLE	60–90	Possesses same characteristics as Vermont Cran-berry Bush; use as shelling bean; does well in all climates.	ABU VER

SHELL BEANS (WHITE)

VARIETY	DAYS	DESCRIPTION	SOURCES (p. 385)
AURORA	85	This is the Cadillac of baking beans; its long, narrow pods carry pure white beans. The bush plant grows well in cool weather.	VER
AZTEC (Dwarf White)	55	Known as a potato bean, it has large, plump, white seeds the size of limas. Plant has short 3-foot runners and can withstand hot days and cool nights.	PLA SEED
CANNELLINI	80	Very large, white beans have flavor of green beans when dry.	SEE
GREAT NORTHERN WHITE (OP) (Montana White)	85–90	5-inch, flat pod; big, white beans; 1907 heirloom bean; semi-vining; use as soup or baking bean.	BURP DEG FAR GAR GUR HEN JUN SEE VER
HOPI WHITE	80	Small, white bean, resembling Navy.	ABU
OREGON WHITE LIGHT LIMA	70	Each pod has 5–6 white seeds that look like limas but are common beans. Good cold tolerance in this 18-inch plant.	SEED
WARIHIO WHITE	92	Medium-size, flattened, white tepary bean is a good baker. Small plant with green, pointed leaves is prolific in hot, dry weather. This heirloom variety's pods are 4½–5 inches, flat, and straight.	SEED

VARIETY	DAYS	DESCRIPTION	SOURCES (p. 385)

SHELL BEANS (WHITE) *(continued)*

| WHITE MARROW (White Marrowfat) | 68–100 | 4½–5-inch, flat, straight pod; white seed; navy type; good baker; heirloom variety. | STO VER |

BEETS

BOTANICAL NAME: *Beta vulgaris*

DAYS TO MATURITY: 48–80.

PLANTING TIME: The first sowing should be done two to four weeks before the last spring frost date. Sow additional crops every two weeks or so.

SOIL: Light, loamy, and well-drained; pH 6.0–7.5.

NUTRIENTS: When seedlings are 3–4 inches high, feed them with fish emulsion. A light application of organic nitrogen is the only fertilizing they need.

WATER: In dry weather, water thoroughly to prevent wilting. Water overhead to keep both the tops and the roots crisp.

LIGHT: Full sun.

SPACING: Beet seeds come in clumps containing three or more seeds. Sow these clumps ½ inch deep and 1 inch apart; stamp on the soil after the seed has been covered. Rows should be 14–16 inches apart. For intensive beds, you can plant about 20 beets per square foot.

HARVEST: Start harvesting beets when they are ¾ inch in diameter. Most varieties lose their flavor if they are allowed to grow larger than 3 inches in diameter.

STORAGE: Beets should be used fresh or pickled.

Beet Growing Tips

Redder Beets

To produce bright red beets, sprinkle the bed lightly with table salt—about a spoonful per foot. This improves the growth and color of the roots and eliminates white rings.

Tough Beets

Tough beets are often caused by insufficient water or irregular watering. Water beets when the soil is dry 2 or more inches down (check with a trowel). Do not let the soil dry out at any time during the growing period.

BEETS

Winter Beets

Every good cook likes to grow a few beets to pop into winter salads. Space 30 beet seeds in an 8-inch pot filled with potting mix. Keep this watered and on a windowsill. Thin to 10 well-spaced plants. Use the beet greens and roots when needed.

VARIETY	DAYS	DESCRIPTION	SOURCES (p. 385)
BEETS (GLOBE-SHAPED)			
ACTION	60	Dark red; resistant to bolting; exceptionally sweet; good choice for greens.	PIN
BOLTHARDY	58	This deep red Dutch variety has stringless, sweet flesh.	THO
BURPEE'S RED BALL	60	Dark red; medium-tall tops; 3-inch-diameter beet.	BURP
CRIMSON GLOBE	60	An old variety; 3-inch, globe-shaped roots; deep crimson, slightly zoned; grows quickly.	BOU
DARK RED CANNER	59	Dark red; 12–14-inch tops; small but exceptional canner.	HEN
DETROIT 6 (hybrid)	53	5-inch diameter; deep red, smooth skin; no bolting.	THO
DETROIT DARK RED IMPROVED	65	Dark red, smooth skin; small taproot.	COM
DETROIT DARK RED MEDIUM TOP (OP)	55–60	Introduced in 1892; 3-inch diameter, dark red; 12-inch, dark, glossy tops; resistant to downy mildew and widely adapted; good fresh, canned, or frozen.	ABU ALL BURP BURR DEG FAR GAR GUR HEN LEJ ORG PIN PON POR SEE SEED SOU STO TIL TWI VER WIL WILL
DETROIT DARK RED SHORT TOP (OP)	60	Root is deep red with minimal zoning. Tops are dark green with maroon tinge.	FIS JUN MEY PAR STO
DETROIT SUPREME	59–65	Dark red; does not tend to form interior rings; fine taproot.	HEN STO TER
GARNET	55–60	Garnet color, completely free of zoning; clean roots and short tops.	FAR
GLOBE DARK RED	65	Dark red; recommended for dehydration and pickling.	GLE
KING RED	52	Dark red, smooth-skinned, and uniform; good canner.	DEG
LITTLE EGYPT	34	Deep red roots and short tops; transplanting type.	STO
MONOPOLY	45	Deep red Dutch variety with nice leafy tops; no thinning needed; good for freezing.	SHE
NERO	60	Improved Detroit type; dark red, free from zoning; for all uses.	WILL
PACEMAKER III (hybrid)	50	Bloodred, with 16–17-inch tops; tolerant to leaf spot; good fresh or canned.	POR STO TWI

VARIETY	DAYS	DESCRIPTION	SOURCES (p. 385)

BEETS (GLOBE-SHAPED) (continued)

VARIETY	DAYS	DESCRIPTION	SOURCES (p. 385)
PERFECTED DETROIT DARK RED	58	Deep dark red with no rings or streaks; great canner.	GUR HEN ROS
RED ACE (hybrid)	51–53	Deep red, smooth, round roots; 14-inch tops; good fresh or canned.	COM JOH JUN LED MEY PAR PIN STO TER TIL TWI VER
SANGRIA (hybrid)	55	Red, smooth roots have vigorous 10–12-inch tops. Harvest early for baby beets or later at full maturity. Beets have no corkiness.	FAR HEN SHE

BEETS (SEMI-GLOBE)

VARIETY	DAYS	DESCRIPTION	SOURCES (p. 385)
BIG RED (hybrid)	55	Deep red, top-shaped, all-purpose beet; high yields.	COO JUN POR STO
CROSBY'S EGYPTIAN (Early Crosby Egyptian)	42–60	Dull red, 3–5-inch, flattened roots; 1880 variety.	GOU LEJ SEE SEED SOU VER
EARLY WONDER (OP) (Green Top)	48–55	This dark red, all-purpose beet with 16–18-inch tops stores well.	ABU ALL BURP BURR BUT COM COO DEG FAR FIS GAR GLE GUR HIG JOH LED MEY PIN PLA PON SOU TER TIL TWI VER WIL WILL
LONG SEASON (Winter Keeper, Lutz Green Leaf, Always Tender)	60–80	Deep red heirloom variety; large and rough looking but fine keeper; all-purpose beet.	ABU BURP COM COO GAR GUR HEN JLH LED NIC ORG PAR PIN PLA SEE SEED SOU STO TER
REPLATA	60	This bright red, improved, flat-topped Egyptian type can be transplanted.	ORN
RUBY QUEEN	52–60	All-American winner; dark red, somewhat elongated roots; short tops; good canner.	BURR COM DEG FAR GUR HEN JUN LED MEY PAR PIN PON RED SEE STO TWI VER WIL

BEETS (CYLINDRICAL)

VARIETY	DAYS	DESCRIPTION	SOURCES (p. 385)
CYLINDRA (OP) (Butter Slicer)	55–60	Dark red, up to 8 inches long, 2–3 inches across; good slicer.	BURP BURR COM FAR FIS GAR GOU HEN JUN PAR PIN PON SEE SHE TIL TWI WILL
FORMANOVA (Cylindra Improved, Cooks Delight)	50–60	Dark red, 6–8x2½-inch roots; good for pickling or freezing.	BOU COO JOH NIC STO VER
FORONA	54–70	Danish variety, high-quality elongated beet with short tops and a high sugar content.	TER
MACGREGOR'S FAVORITE	59	Elongated, bloodred-maroon, 3-inch roots; old Scottish variety.	COO GAR ORN

VARIETY	DAYS	DESCRIPTION	SOURCES (p. 385)
BEETS (BABY)			
DWERGINA	58	Dark red, round, free of zones; Dutch variety; small taproots.	COO GOU JOH ORN
GLADIATOR	54	Crimson, golf-ball-size roots; perfect pickler.	GUR
LITTLE BALL (Kleine Bol, Little Mini Ball)	43–58	Red 3-inch-diameter ball forms rapidly. Harvest this Dutch variety when 1–1½ inches. Plant densely in succession for crops all season.	BURP HIG ORN PAR PIN SEE SHE STO TER TIL TWI WILL
SPINEL BABY BEET	52–60	Red, 1½-inch beet is great canned or pickled.	NIC
BEETS (OTHER COLORS)			
ALBINO VEREDUNA (Albino White Beet, Snowwhite)	50–60	Pure white, globe-shaped, large, 1–3-inch roots; paddle-shaped leaves; good pickler with extra-sweet, mild flavor.	COO GOU ORN SEE STO TER
CHIOGGIA (Candy Stripe, Dolce Di Chioggia)	50–55	Italian heirloom variety has a candy red exterior, with rings of cherry red and creamy white interior.	COO JOH NIC ORN PIN SEE SEED SHE SOU
GOLDEN BEET	50–60	Golden orange, small, round beet; good pickler; won't bleed.	ABU BURP COO FIS GLE GUR HIG JUN LED NIC ORN PIN PON SEE SHE STO SOU WILL
BEETS (FOR GREENS)			
BEETS FOR GREENS	57	Grown for tops.	ALL
GREEN TOP BUNCHING	65	A multipurpose strain, its round, bright red roots maintain good interior color. Medium-size tops stay bright green during unfavorably cool weather.	DEG STO

BROCCOLI

BOTANICAL NAME: *Brassica oleracea italica*

DAYS TO MATURITY: 47–90.

PLANTING TIME: Broccoli can be started indoors or in a hotbed two to three months before the last spring frost. Plant seedlings in the ground four to six weeks before the last frost. Broccoli does best when temperatures remain between 40 and 70°F through the growing season.

SOIL: Rich, heavy; pH 6.0–7.0.

NUTRIENTS: Broccoli is a heavy feeder. Nourish once a month with fish emulsion or with an organic liquid nitrogenous fertilizer, such as 1 tablespoon of blood meal mixed with 1 gallon of water.

WATER: Never allow its roots to dry during the summer months. Neither should you waterlog broccoli. A light mulching will help keep the soil moist.

LIGHT: Full sun.

SPACING: Sow ½ inch deep, 1–1½ feet apart. For a traditional row garden, space rows 3 feet apart.

HARVEST: The plants are ready for picking just before the buds begin to open. Harvest them with a knife, cutting the stems 6 inches beneath the bud clusters. Some varieties produce edible side branches; others produce a central head with no side shoots.

STORAGE: Use broccoli fresh.

Broccoli Growing Tips

Fully Packed

Broccoli often produces premature, small, scattered heads when young plants are subjected to temperatures below 40°F before or shortly after planting. Shield your plants in early spring with hot caps or other protective devices.

Broccoli Factory

Some gardeners continuously produce edible broccoli buds like they're running a production line. Their secret: after harvesting the main head, you must pick the developing buds every three or four days as long as the plant continues to produce. Once you let a few developing buds flower, the action stops, and you're out of business until next season.

Firm Anchor

To stop mature broccoli plants from tipping over, make a hole with a trowel. Plant each seedling so the base of its leaves is only a finger's breadth above the soil surface. Since the plant develops a heavy superstructure, this extra depth provides firmer anchorage.

BROCCOLI

VARIETY	DAYS	DESCRIPTION	SOURCES (p. 385)
BROCCOLI (CENTRAL HEAD, SIDE SHOOTS)			
BONANZA (hybrid)	55	3–5-inch-diameter head; tight buds on central head; lots of side shoots; good freezer.	BURP
CALABRESE (OP) (Green Sprouting Calabrese, Italian Green, Italian Green Sprouting)	70–85	5–6-inch-diameter bluish green head; many side branches; 2½–3-foot plant; good freezer.	ABU BOU FAR JLH NIC PIN RED SEE SOU

VARIETY	DAYS	DESCRIPTION	SOURCES (p. 385)

BROCCOLI (CENTRAL HEAD, SIDE SHOOTS) *(continued)*

VARIETY	DAYS	DESCRIPTION	SOURCES (p. 385)
CRUISER (hybrid)	58	High yielding; does well in hot, dry conditions; blue-green head; prolonged side shoots.	STO VER
DIA GREEN (hybrid)	43	Up to 8-inch head; good side shoots.	PIN
EARLY EMERALD (hybrid) (Early Green)	50	5–6-inch-diameter blue-green head; heavy production of side shoots.	ORG PAR
EMERALD CITY (hybrid)	82	Main season variety has blue-green, 7-inch heads, small beads, and smooth skin.	JOH STO
EMERALD SPRING	55	Large blue-green head; many side shoots after main head is cut.	SEED
EMPEROR (hybrid)	58–80	8-inch, tight, deep green head; widely adapted and highly tolerant of black rot and downy mildew; good side shoots.	JOH PAR STO TWI
EUREKA (hybrid)	87	Main season variety has dark green 8-inch head and tolerates black rot and downy mildew.	STO
EVEREST (hybrid)	55	Small bead size; medium-size plants with good tolerance to downy mildew, brown bead, and head rot.	JOH
GALLEON (hybrid)	75	A shorter, earlier version of Packman; semidomed, 6¾-inch head with medium-size beads.	STO TWI
GOLIATH	55–75	10–12-inch, blue-green head; many sizable side shoots; 15-inch plant.	BURP FIS GUR JUN PON STO WILL
GREEN MOUNTAIN	60	Large, compact, dark green head; large side shoots through the season.	LEJ
GREEN SPROUTING DE CICCO	60–70	3–6-inch, flat green head; 1890 Italian heirloom variety; some heat tolerance.	ALL COM DEG HIG JOH ORG ORN SOU TIL WILL
GREEN VALIANT (hybrid)	70	Dense, blue-green head; good side shoot production; frost-resistant for fall harvest.	JOH STO TER TWI
LEGEND (hybrid)	86	Harvest this main season variety in cool weather. It grows a blue-green head and midsize beads. It's tolerant to downy mildew.	STO
LEPRECHAUN (hybrid)	74	7-inch, domed head, medium-size beads.	STO
MARINER (hybrid)	77	Mid- to late summer harvest; good heat tolerance; fairly small, dark green beads; tolerant to bacterial leaf spot, downy mildew, hollow stem, and black rot.	STO TWI
PACKMAN (hybrid)	58–80	10–inch head, midsize beads; excellent side shoots.	DEG GUR HEN JOH JUN LED LIB MEY NIC PAR PIN POR STO TER TWI WILL
PINNACLE	58	Large, dome-shaped, blue-green head.	LIB
SAGA (hybrid)	57	A heat-tolerant variety with medium-size, dark green, firm heads and heavy stems, this plant makes a healthier crop when stressed by heat and/or humidity.	JOH

VARIETY	DAYS	DESCRIPTION	SOURCES (p. 385)

BROCCOLI (CENTRAL HEAD, SIDE SHOOTS) *(continued)*

VARIETY	DAYS	DESCRIPTION	SOURCES
SHOGUN (hybrid)	93	Japanese variety with 6-inch head; tolerance to downy mildew, black rot, and weather; 5 side shoots per plant; harvest in fall.	SHE TER
SOUTHERN COMFORT (hybrid)	80	Japanese variety with rapid side shoot growth and thin skin.	TER
SPARTAN K EARLY (OP)	47–55	6–8-inch, bluish green head; short, compact plant.	SEE
SULTAN (hybrid)	85	Large, 8-inch, high-domed, blue-green head; small beads; some tolerance to downy mildew.	STO
TOP STAR (hybrid)	65	7–8-inch-diameter head; good side shoot production well into fall.	PIN
UMPQUA (OP)	55–80	6–7-inch head; good side shoot production.	PIN SOU TER
WALTHAM (OP)	60–95	A variety with a large, compact head and good side shoot production, it withstands cold and short dry spells.	SEEDS VER
WALTHAM 29 (OP)	74–80	4–8-inch, slate green head; lots of side shoots; low, compact plant.	ABU ALL BURR BUT COM DEG LED LIB MEY ROS SEE SOU TIL

BROCCOLI (CENTRAL HEAD, FEW BRANCHES)

VARIETY	DAYS	DESCRIPTION	SOURCES
ATLANTIC	65	Medium-size head; short, compact plant.	LED MEY SOU
BRIGADIER (hybrid)	75	Midseason variety with slightly domed head; 26-inch plant.	BURR LED
EVEREST (hybrid)	83	6-inch, dome-shaped, small-beaded head; good tolerance to downy mildew.	STO
GALAXY (hybrid)	85	Plant in spring, summer, or fall; medium to large, domed, blue-green head; short, full plant.	WIL
GREEN COMET	40–78	All-American winner; 6–9-inch, blue-green head; holds shape well and resists disease; 12–16-inch plant; good fresh or frozen.	BURP COM COO FAR GUR HEN JUN LED LIB MEY PAR PIN PON POR THO TWI VER WILL
GREEN DUKE (hybrid)	69–88	7–8-inch, domed head; 22–24-inch plant; for spring or summer planting.	DEG
GREEN HORNET	78	7–8-inch, bright green head; no side branches; good fresh or processed.	STO
MEDIUM-LATE 423	423	Plant this biennial broccoli as you would any other overwintering broccoli, and harvest in February or March. It's recommended for coastal climates and Northern California.	TER
MERCEDES (hybrid)	58	7–8-inch, flat, finely beaded, blue-green head; good raw, cooked, or frozen.	SHE
OKTAL (hybrid)	80	Dutch variety has long-stemmed florets.	ORN

VARIETY	DAYS	DESCRIPTION	SOURCES (p. 385)

BROCCOLI (CENTRAL HEAD, FEW BRANCHES) *(continued)*

VARIETY	DAYS	DESCRIPTION	SOURCES (p. 385)
PARAGON (hybrid)	75	8-inch, blue-green head; extralong spear; good fresh or frozen.	STO
PREMIUM CROP (hybrid)	58–82	9–10-inch, blue-green head; 16–18-inch plant; disease-resistant; All-American winner.	ALL COM FAR HEN LED LIB MEY NIC PAR PIN POR SHE SOU STO TWI
SPRINTER (hybrid)	60–72	With a midsize dark green head, this variety performs well in high temperatures and is highly disease-tolerant.	HIG VER
SUPER DOME (hybrid)	58	Resistant to downy mildew, it produces a very large head—7 inches across.	VER

BROCCOLI (OTHER TYPES/COLORS)

VARIETY	DAYS	DESCRIPTION	SOURCES (p. 385)
EARLY PURPLE SPROUTING (Early Purple Sprouting Red Arrow)	110–220	Medium-size head turns green when cooked. The 3-foot plant is prolific and frost-hardy.	ABU BOU THO
EARLY WHITE PEARL	80	Fine, white curd; hardy plant; weather-tolerant.	GLE
FAT SHAN WHITE (Chinese Broccoli)	80	Japanese, cool weather variety has a delicate flavor. Thick main stem can be cooked along with flower buds.	GLE RED
ITALIAN SPROUTING (OP) (Calabria)	80	Heavy yields of large central heads; medium-size side shoots.	STO
KING ROBERT PURPLE	57	Large head turns green when cooked. This variety also freezes well.	GLE
LATE PURPLE SPROUTING	220	English purple variety, bred for overwintering; large bush.	BOU COO TER THO
LATE RAPONE PIZZMO	90	Harvest in fall for slender flowering shoots, tops, and spicy greens.	COM
MINARET (hybrid)	102	Romanesco type; pointed spiral clusters; 4–5-inch, light green head; uniform growing habit.	COO JOH TER
RAAB (Rapa, Italian Turnip, Early Pugliese, Rapini, De Rapa)	50–100	This heirloom variety features lots of branching but no central head. Cut before the plant flowers. It has a pungent flavor; never serve raw.	BURP COM JLH LED NIC PIN SEE SHE
RAPINE (Spring Raab)	70	Completely unlike regular broccoli, this early European branching variety looks like mustard, with many green, dime-size buds and no head. It bolts rapidly.	DEG JOH LED STO TWI
ROMANESCO	50–100	The 3-foot plant produces conical spirals with loads of little apple green spears that can be snapped off individually or together. It's an Italian heirloom variety.	ABU BOU JLH LEJ NIC ORN SEE SHE THO
ROSALIND (OP)	60–65	This purple broccoli performs best during cooler fall weather.	TER

VARIETY	DAYS	DESCRIPTION	SOURCES (p. 385)

BROCCOLI (OTHER TYPES/COLORS) *(continued)*

VARIETY	DAYS	DESCRIPTION	SOURCES
SALADE (Fall Raab)	60	For tender, dark greens in spring or summer, plant this variety, which has turnip-green-type leaves with ¼-inch florets. Overwinter to produce midsize florets in early spring.	STO
SPIRAL POINT	70	A cross between cauliflower and broccoli, this Italian variety has olive green, spiral, pointed curds.	GLE
VIOLET QUEEN (hybrid)	70	Large Japanese plant has an 8-inch head. Deep purple florets turn green when cooked.	ORN
WHITE SPROUTING	105–120	Small, white head looks like cauliflower and freezes well. The 3-foot plant is a heavy cropper.	BOU
WHITE SPROUTING LATE	250	Has some cauliflower genes; creamy white color; English variety.	TER THO

BRUSSELS SPROUTS

BOTANICAL NAME: *Brassica oleracea gemmifera*

DAYS TO MATURITY: 80–140.

PLANTING TIME: Sow seeds 120 days before the first expected fall frost. The minimum soil temperature is 40°F.

SOIL: Almost any kind of soil is fine, although they don't like overly acidic conditions; pH 6.0–7.5.

NUTRIENTS: Fertilize the plants three times during the growing season. Apply fish emulsion or use 1 tablespoon blood meal mixed into 1 gallon of water.

WATER: Sprouts need plenty of water.

LIGHT: Full sun.

SPACING: Sow seeds ¼ inch deep. For rows, plant 3 feet apart.

HARVEST: When the sprouts are firm and deep green, snap or trim them from the stalk. They have the best flavor when they are 1–1½ inches in diameter. Mild frost improves the flavor. Pick the lower leaves off when you harvest the sprouts but don't remove the top leaves.

STORAGE: They are best used fresh.

Brussels Sprouts Growing Tips

From Bottom to Top

To harvest brussels sprouts properly, start at the bottom, snapping them off as you go up. Always remove the leaves below

BRUSSELS SPROUTS

the picked sprouts. Leave the small top sprouts and any that are smaller than 1½ inches in diameter.

Hungry Birds

The birds in your garden probably love brussels sprouts as much as you do. Save these vegetables for yourself by pulling wire or plastic netting over the top of each row (leave the ends open). This stops the birds' feasting and lets you harvest the entire crop without interference.

Good Anchorage

To stop brussels sprouts from tipping over just before harvest time, shore up the soil around the plant stem one month after planting. This anchors the plant firmly.

VARIETY	DAYS	DESCRIPTION	SOURCES (p. 385)
BRUSSELS SPROUTS			
ADONIS (hybrid)	110	Excellent yields; buttonlike sprouts all the way up the stem.	THO
ANAGOR	90	Cold-resistant.	GOU
BEDFORD FILLBASKET	84–95	Biennial heirloom variety is a 3–4-foot plant that produces large, solid sprouts.	SEED
BUBBLES (hybrid)	110	Dark green, round sprouts are well spaced on stems. Variety has some tolerance to drought and powdery mildew.	LED STO
CONTENT (hybrid)	105	Under normal rainfall conditions, this plant produces round, deep green, uniform, medium-grade sprouts. There is some tolerance to leaf spot and yellow leaves in the fall.	STO
DOLMIC	102	European variety with dark green, oval sprouts, ready in late August; good yields.	STO
EARLY DWARF DANISH (OP)	95–105	Large sprouts on short plant; suitable short season variety.	GAR
EARLY HALF TALL	90	Heavy crop; ready by mid- to late autumn.	BOU
ICARUS (hybrid)	100	Large, very solid sprouts are ready for harvest from October to February. Variety is cold-resistant and disease-tolerant.	THO
JADE CROSS (hybrid)	80–95	The 24-inch plant yields copiously. Oval, blue-green sprouts grow all the way up to the stalk; they have excellent flavor and freeze well.	COM GUR HEN JUN PAR PIN PON POR STO WILL
JADE CROSS E	90–97	The 26-inch plant produces twice as many sprouts as open pollinated types. Its sprouts are oval and dark blue-green.	ABU LIB MEY NIC STO TWI VER WIL
LONG ISLAND	90–95	Fall frost improves flavor of these 1½-inch sprouts.	FAR

VARIETY	DAYS	DESCRIPTION	SOURCES (p. 385)
BRUSSELS SPROUTS (*continued*)			
LONG ISLAND IMPROVED (Catskill)	85–95	Abundant 1¼-inch sprouts cover most of the 20-inch, upright plant. It will produce several pickings.	ABU ALL BURR BUT COM DEG FIS GAR HIG LED LEJ LIB MEY PON RED ROS SEE SOU TIL WIL WILL
LUNET (hybrid)	115	Dutch variety with medium-large, firm sprouts; high yields for harvest from November to December.	TER
OLIVER (hybrid)	90	Medium green, smooth ¾-ounce sprouts; vigorous in diverse climates.	JOH STO
PEER GYNT (hybrid)	140	Dark green sprouts grow from stem base to the top. Harvest from September to December.	THO
PRINCE MARVEL (hybrid)	90–97	The 35-inch plant sets smooth, firm, rounded, well-spaced sprouts and has improved tolerance to bottom and center rot.	PAR STO TER VER
RIDER (hybrid)	95	Variety is high yielding. Sprouts stand well away from the stalk for easy harvest.	COO TER
ROODNERF LATE SUPREME (OP)	100	Medium-tall plant yields tasty sprouts.	TER
ROYAL MARVEL (hybrid)	85	This earlier Jade Cross type has high tolerance to bottom rot and tip burn. Tight sprouts resist insect damage.	POR TWI
RUBINE RED	90–105	Red foliage and red sprouts won't fade when cooked. Variety has distinct flavor and loves cool weather.	BOU COO GLE GUR HEN ORN PAR PIN SEE VER WILL
SEVEN HILLS	95	Sprouts are ready early in winter.	BOU
TARDIS (hybrid)	130	Abundant yields from Christmas to March.	TER
TAVERNOS (hybrid)	160	Evenly sized, bright green sprouts; good standing ability.	THO
VALIANT (hybrid)	110	Rot- and burst-resistant, Dutch variety gives heavy yields of buttonlike sprouts. Harvest late fall through winter.	POR SHE STO
VINCENT (hybrid)	200	Dark green, round, well-spaced sprouts; sturdy, 22-inch plant.	TER
WIDGEON (hybrid)	120	Smooth, midsize, dark green sprouts are widely spaced on tall plants. Harvest this cold-tolerant English variety from midfall through winter.	JOH

CABBAGE

CABBAGE

BOTANICAL NAME: *Brassica oleracea capitata*

DAYS TO MATURITY: 45–120.

PLANTING TIME: Set out transplants four to six weeks before the last frost. In mild winter areas, plant in fall or winter.

SOIL: Medium light, well-drained; pH 6.0–7.5.

NUTRIENTS: Apply fish emulsion every three to four weeks or use 1 tablespoon of blood meal mixed in 1 gallon of water.

WATER: Never let cabbage wilt. Mulch helps keep the soil moist and cool.

LIGHT: Full sun.

SPACING: Sow seeds ½ inch deep, 2–2½ feet apart. Plant rows 3 feet apart.

HARVEST: When the heads are firm, cut cabbages off at the base of the stalk.

STORAGE: Use fresh, ferment for sauerkraut, or store in a cool place.

Cabbage Growing Tips

Cut-and-Come-Again

You can easily turn your cabbage plants into a vegetable factory. When you remove a head, cut squarely across the stem, leaving four or more leaves. Then cut a shallow slit across the top of the stump. The cabbage plant will produce up to five smaller cabbage heads within six weeks after this cutting.

Bolting Solution

Nothing is quite so frustrating as cabbage that grows furiously in the spring and then suddenly changes from the leafy to the flowering stage (bolt). This frequently occurs when young plants are exposed to temperatures below 50°F for two to three weeks. The larger the transplants, the faster they seem to flower. To avoid this, select and plant seedlings with stems about the size of a lead pencil.

Super Cabbages

To create colossal cabbages, try this technique before transplanting. Dig or rototill 4 inches of dried horse manure into the top 6 inches of the bed soil. When you're finished, spread out 10 pounds of wood ashes per 50 square feet of bed. Rake the bed smooth and put in the transplants. This helps increase the size and weight of the heads.

Variety Soil Typing

Veteran gardeners select their cabbage varieties to fit the type of soil they have. Early cabbages (those that mature in about 75 days) do best in light soil. Fall/winter cabbages (those that need at least 110 days to mature) do best in heavy, damp soil.

Color Coding

Purple is your clue when it comes to selecting cabbage transplants in the spring. A purple coloring on green cabbage indicates that the seedlings have been properly hardened off (conditioned to outside temperatures) and will be able to survive spring conditions in the garden.

Plate-Size Cabbage

To produce dinner-plate-size cabbages, space plants 8–10 inches apart. Although the closer spacing means the heads will be smaller, you will produce more pounds of cabbage in the same soil.

Head Start

Give your cabbage transplants a head start: dig the hole deeper than usual—at least 12 inches deep—and fill it with peat moss. The roots can then spread out and grow down. If cabbage transplants are placed in a shallow hole, the roots grow toward the surface and the plants develop slowly.

Doubling Up

An experienced gardener likes to get double and triple duty out of every garden. To double up in the cabbage patch, plant leaf lettuce between your cabbage transplants. When the cabbage begins to squeeze out the lettuce, pull out the lettuce plants and allow the cabbages to take over.

Put Them on Hold

If too many cabbage heads are ready at the same time, pull up the extra heads with their roots and place them head down on a bed of straw, hay, or dry leaves. An alternative is to hang the plants upside down on a nail or wire. Either way, they will keep well into winter.

Bird Attack

You can protect cabbage seedlings from marauding birds by covering them completely with a few wire loops and netting. When the plants are about 8 inches high, remove the netting.

CABBAGE

VARIETY	DAYS	DESCRIPTION	SOURCES (p. 385)
CABBAGE (ROUND, GREEN) **EARLY SEASON**			
BALBRO (hybrid)	60	2½-pound, bright green head; no tolerance of yellows.	STO
BINGO (hybrid)	60–65	Recommended for organic growers, this vigorous plant develops very large, heavy heads and good leaf cover. It's tolerant of mosaic virus.	THO
BLUE VANTAGE	71	Midsize plant with blue-green leaves is resistant to tip burn and yellows as well as tolerant to black rot. Sturdy root system handles water stress well.	LIB
CASTELLO (hybrid)	68	2-pound, 5-inch-diameter head; good thrip tolerance; not yellows-tolerant.	STO
CENTRON (hybrid)	72	A yellows-tolerant version of Castello, it produces 6½-pound, blue-green heads and also has good tolerance to splitting.	STO
CHARMANT (hybrid)	52–65	2½–3 pounds; Stonehead type; deep green; vigorous grower; resistant to yellows and tip burn.	LIB TER TWI
CHEERS	72	Resistant to fusarium yellows and tolerant to black rot.	LIB
COPENHAGEN MARKET	68	3½ pounds; all-purpose cabbage; suited to small gardens.	BURP BURR COM DEG GUR HEN HIG LEJ MEY STO TIL WIL
DARKRI (hybrid)	42–67	6–8-inch-diameter head; short exterior leaves; high yields in less space; high quality even in summer.	PAR
EARLIANA	60	2-pound, 4½–5-inch head; Golden Acre type.	BURP WILL
EARLY DUTCH ROUND	70–72	4–5-pound, 7-inch head; not yellows-resistant.	SEE
EARLY MARVEL (OP) **(Early Ditmarsh)**	59–65	3–4-pound, 5-inch, dark green, round head; short core; not tolerant to yellows.	STO
ELISA (hybrid)	48	The large glossy head is completely round. This Japanese variety holds well in the garden without splitting and tolerates excessive moisture.	VER
EMERALD ACRE (OP)	61	3–4-pound, 4-inch, medium green head; good tolerance to bolting; not yellows-tolerant.	STO
EMERALD CROSS **(hybrid)**	62–67	4–5-pound, 7-inch, blue-green head; Japanese variety with characteristics of Copenhagen Market; space-efficient plant.	WILL
FERRY'S EARLY DUTCH ROUND	70–75	Blue-green head is 4–5 pounds and 7 inches in diameter.	WIL
FLASH (hybrid)	65	2–3-pound, round, deep green head; short core; stocky plant; resistant to fusarium yellows; recommended for short season areas.	BURR WILL
GOLDEN ACRE **(Derby Day)**	58–65	2–3-pound, gray-green head; disease-resistant; short-stemmed.	ABU ALL BURR DEG FAR FIS GAR GUR JUN LED LEJ LIB PON ROS SEE STO TER TIL WIL
GOLDEN ACRE RESISTANT	70	Some yellows tolerance.	MEY

CABBAGE (ROUND, GREEN)
EARLY SEASON (continued)

VARIETY	DAYS	DESCRIPTION	SOURCES (p. 385)
GREENBOY (hybrid)	75	5-pound, 7-inch, blue-green, compact head (ball head) with short core; fair tolerance to black speck.	TWI WIL
GRENADIER (hybrid)	52–63	A Dutch variety with 3–5-pound, 8-inch heads, it prefers spring and fall growth and is not yellows-tolerant.	SHE STO
KRAUTMAN (hybrid)	78	Very dependable; high yielding; resistant to splitting.	PIN
LUNA (hybrid)	60–75	2-pound, light green head; Japanese variety; designed for short season areas.	HIG
MARNER ALFROH (OP)	60–70	3-pound, compact, round head; German variety summer cabbage.	BOU
MINSTREL (hybrid)	52	Fast growth; solid interior and good size; resists splitting.	PIN
PACIFICA (hybrid)	63	3-pound, 6-inch head; dense interior; short core; tolerant to yellows, black rot, and tip burn.	STO
PERFECT ACTION (hybrid)	73	2–4-pound, dark green, round, dense head; yellows- and split-resistant.	JOH
POLAR GREEN (hybrid)	56	Compact plant with 2½–3-pound, light green head has good tolerance to tip burn and low temperatures but not to yellows.	STO
PRIMAX	60–63	A larger strain of Golden Acre with a short stem, this variety resists splitting. Its head weighs 2–4 pounds.	GAR HIG JOH
PRIME CHOICE (hybrid)	74	The 2½–5-pound, 6½-inch, blue-green head doesn't split easily. Plant is yellows-tolerant.	STO
PRIME PAK (hybrid)	74	3–4-pound, 5–6-inch, blue-green head; resistant to yellows.	BOU
PUMA (hybrid)	64	2–4-pound head; extrashort core; compact plant; yellows-resistant.	JOH LIB
REGALIA (hybrid)	64	2–3-pound head; solid interior; short core; tolerant to yellows, tip burn, and black rot.	STO
ROCKET (hybrid)	65	3–4-pound, blue-green head; small-framed plant; tolerant to yellows.	TWI
SALARITE	57	5½-inch-diameter, deep green head; compact plant; not recommended for home gardens.	NIC STO TER
STOKES EARLY 711 (hybrid)	56	2-pound, perfectly round head; no yellows tolerance.	STO
STONEHEAD (hybrid)	50–70	The firm, blue-green head is 3½ pounds and 6 inches in diameter. This all-purpose cabbage produces well in a small area.	COM FAR GUR HEN JUN LED LIB NIC PIN POR STO VER
SUPERETTE (hybrid)	66	3–7½-pound, 8-inch, silvery blue-green head; yellows-resistant.	LIB STO

VARIETY	DAYS	DESCRIPTION	SOURCES (p. 385)

CABBAGE (ROUND, GREEN)
EARLY SEASON (continued)

VARIETY	DAYS	DESCRIPTION	SOURCES
TUCANA (hybrid)	62	Variety's heads weigh 3 pounds and will split if not harvested at maturity. Plant requires proper moisture for larger heads.	STO

CABBAGE (ROUND, GREEN)
MIDSEASON

VARIETY	DAYS	DESCRIPTION	SOURCES
ALL SEASONS (Wisconsin All Season)	80–90	7–10-pound, 10–11-inch, solid, light green, compact head; resistant to heat and drought.	DEG FAR GUR VER
BLUE PAK (hybrid)	76–78	2¼–4-pound, deep blue-green head; solid interior; resistant to fusarium yellows.	STO
BLUE VANTAGE (hybrid)	76	Ball-head type; 3½–4-pound, deep blue-green head; short core on medium plant; resists yellows and tip burn; tolerant to black rot.	TWI
CAVALIER (hybrid)	88	3–5-pound, dark blue-green, solid head; must be sprayed for thrips.	STO
CHEERS (hybrid)	80	4½–5½-pound, dark blue-green, uniform, round head; tolerant to yellows and black rot.	STO
COPENHAGEN MARKET	72	4–4½-pound, 6½-inch, solid head; white interior; heavy yields.	SEE
ERDENO (hybrid)	88	4–8-pound, blue-green head with dense interior. Frost-tolerant Danish variety; adapted to fertile soils.	SHE
FORTUNA (hybrid)	80–85	2–3-pound, blue-green head; good resistance to black rot, tip burn, and fusarium yellows.	LED NIC
GENESIS (hybrid)	75	Large, round, short-cored head; resistant to fusarium yellows and black rot.	BURR
GLORY OF ENK-HOUSEN (Enkhuizen)	75	6–10-pound, dark green head; moderately dense interior.	GAR SEE WILL
GOURMET (hybrid)	75	3–5-pound, 5–6-inch, blue-green, round to flat head; resistant to yellows.	LIB STO WIL
GRAND PRIZE (hybrid)	75	4–6-pound, 6–7-inch, blue-green head; good holding ability; resistant to yellows.	LED
GRAND SLAM (hybrid)	82	7–8-inch, blue-green head; resistant to fusarium yellows.	LED TWI VER
GREENBOY (hybrid)	85	Ball-head type, 7½ inches across, with a short core; gray-green head; grows in all areas.	TWI
GREEN CUP (hybrid)	77	3–6-pound, globe-shaped, blue-green head; adapted to lower-fertility conditions; black-rot tolerant and yellows-resistant.	JOH LIB
GREEN GLITTER (hybrid)	80	3½-pound, dark green head; holds up well during chilly fall weather.	NIC
HERCULES (hybrid)	83–98	8–10-inch head; resists splitting; all-purpose cabbage.	WIL

VARIETY	DAYS	DESCRIPTION	SOURCES (p. 385)
CABBAGE (ROUND, GREEN)			
MIDSEASON (*continued*)			
KING COLE (hybrid)	68–74	4–10-pound, 7–8-inch, blue-green head; resistant to yellows.	LED LIB MEY
LITTLE ROCK (hybrid)	84–86	The 2½–7-pound, 6–7-inch ball head can be harvested small or large; it resists splitting. Variety is yellows-resistant.	LIB STO
MARION MARKET	70–80	5½–7-pound, 8-inch, blue-green head; yellows-resistant; good for sauerkraut.	BURR DEG LED
MULTIKEEPER (hybrid)	86	Tolerant to many diseases; good for short-term storage; tolerant to thrips.	STO
PERFECT ACTION (hybrid)	77	2–4-pound, dark green, round, dense head with split resistance; yellows-resistant.	JOH
PERFECT BALL (hybrid)	80	Dark blue-green, short, cored head; summer or fall crop; resistant to yellows.	JOH ORN
PRIME CHOICE	74	The 2½–5-pound, 6½-inch, dark blue-green head does not split easily. Plant is yellows-tolerant.	STO
QUICKSTEP (hybrid)	52–57	Rock hard head with fine interior; for summer harvest.	THO
RIO VERDE (hybrid)	79–92	5-pound, 7-inch, slightly flattened, blue-green head; yellows-resistant; fairly tolerant of cold.	LIB MEY TWI WIL
ROUNDUP (hybrid)	76–80	3–9-pound, slightly flattened head; all-purpose cabbage; resistant to yellows.	LIB STO
ROYAL VANTAGE	75	Variety with 3–4-pound, round, blue-green head is tolerant to adverse weather conditions, stress, and poor soil as well as resistant to yellows and black speck.	LIB
SOLID BLUE 780 (hybrid)	78	3½–4-pound, 7½-inch head; short core; medium to large frame; disease-tolerant.	TWI
SOLID BLUE 790 (hybrid)	79	The 3½–4-pound, 6–7-inch round head has a short to medium core. Plant tolerates black rot and yellows.	TWI
SURVIVOR (hybrid)	85	This all-purpose, disease-tolerant cabbage has a 3-pound, dark blue-green head that can be stored for short periods.	STO
TENACITY (hybrid)	88	4-pound, 7-inch, blue-green head; tolerant to black rot; recommended for late fall harvests only.	STO
TROPIC GIANT	75	The 12-inch heads weigh up to 15 pounds.	PAR
CABBAGE (ROUND, GREEN)			
LATE SEASON			
ALBION (hybrid)	110	5–6-pound, shiny green, slightly flattened head; upright plant; good thrip and yellows tolerance.	STO
APEX (hybrid)	95	3–5-pound head; holds for weeks without cracking; short core; good frost resistance.	JOH

VARIETY	DAYS	DESCRIPTION	SOURCES (p. 385)

CABBAGE (ROUND, GREEN)
LATE SEASON (continued)

VARIETY	DAYS	DESCRIPTION	SOURCES
APRIL GREEN	99	Dark green Dutch variety; Langedijker type; short-stemmed.	SEE STO
ATRIA (hybrid)	95	Round, dark green head; yellows-tolerant.	STO
AVALON (hybrid)	95	Blue-green head; yellows-tolerant.	STO
BURPEE'S DANISH ROUNDHEAD	105	5–7-pound, 7–8-inch head; heirloom variety; good winter keeper; all-purpose cabbage.	BURP
CUSTODIAN (hybrid)	95	4–6-pound, bright green head; good for storage; tolerates frost and black rot.	JOH
DANISH BALLHEAD (True Hollander)	100–105	This all-purpose cabbage with 3–8-pound, dark green heads grows well in mountain sections and keeps well.	BURR COM FAR FIS GAR JUN LED LIB PIN SEE TER TIL WILL
DECEMA (Langedijker Late Winter-Keeper)	95–120	Heavy-yielding Dutch variety; light green head; holds color well during storage.	WILL
GALAXY (hybrid)	110	Very round head with short core; long-term storage.	STO
GENESIS	95	Blue-green, round, short-cored head; resistant to yellows and black rot.	LED
GENEVA (hybrid)	105	10-pound, blue-green head; good tolerance to thrips and yellows; medium-long storage.	STO
HILTON (hybrid)	105	6–8-pound head; upright plant with large frame; good thrip tolerance; yellows-tolerant.	STO
HISTAR (hybrid)	125	12-pound, 10–16-inch head with white interior; Dutch variety, bred for sauerkraut.	TER
HOUSTON EVERGREEN	94	Very firm; retains green color in storage.	STO
LATE DANISH (hybrid)	100	Round, firm, blue-green head; short stem.	BUT
PENN STATE BALLHEAD	90–110	4–8-pound, 7–9-inch head with short stem and white interior; sauerkraut cabbage; good winter keeper.	GAR
PIXIE	190	Grow this variety, which has a small, dense, solid head, for early spring cabbage.	THO
QUICK GREEN STORAGE (OP)	90	Medium-length storage type; compact plant.	STO
SAFEKEEPER (hybrid)	95	Heavy frame and wrapper leaves; storage type; no yellows tolerance.	STO
SAFEKEEPER II (hybrid)	98	Variety has a better tolerance to fall rains and its head is less egg-shaped than Dutch hybrids. It is tolerant to yellows and black rot.	STO
SANIBEL (hybrid)	90–92	10-pound, 10–11-inch, medium green head; all-purpose cabbage.	BURR JUN LIB

VARIETY	DAYS	DESCRIPTION	SOURCES (p. 385)

CABBAGE (ROUND, GREEN)
LATE SEASON *(continued)*

VARIETY	DAYS	DESCRIPTION	SOURCES
SPRINGTIME (hybrid)	230	Hardy, bolt-resistant ball-head type; solid, 3-pound head.	TER
STONAR (hybrid)	96	8¾-pound head; long-term storage cabbage; yellows- and thrips-tolerant.	STO
STRUCKTON (hybrid)	98	Blue-gray, storable cabbage; tolerant to thrips and yellows.	STO
SUPERGREEN (hybrid)	95	Uniform, round, solid head with medium stem and nice wrapper leaves; must be sprayed for thrips; tolerates yellows and pepper spot; short-term storage.	STO
TUNDRA (hybrid)	150	Hardy in winter; an improved Celtic.	THO
WINTERSTAR (hybrid)	130	Gray-green, flattish, round head with a short stem.	TER
WISCONSIN HOLLANDER NO. 8	105–110	Excellent for storing; resistant to yellows.	ROS

CABBAGE (SMALL)

VARIETY	DAYS	DESCRIPTION	SOURCES
FIRST EARLY MARKET 218	240	1–1½-pound, pointed, loose head; hardy to below 10°F; English variety.	TER
FLASH (hybrid)	65	2–3-pound, deep green head; short core; disease-resistant; tolerance to fusarium yellows.	LED PIN

CABBAGE (FLAT)

VARIETY	DAYS	DESCRIPTION	SOURCES
ALL SEASONS	85–90	12-pound, 10–12-inch head for winter storage; all-purpose cabbage; resistant to yellows.	DEG
BRUNSWICK	85–90	This old variety is for sauerkraut or fresh use. Its 6–9-pound, flattened head stores well.	GAR GLE
EARLY FLAT DUTCH	84–95	This pre-1875 heirloom variety's 6–10-pound, 11-inch head is good for kraut.	FIS MEY ORN SOU
LATE FLAT DUTCH	100–110	15-pound, 6-inch, bluish green head; European variety; good winter keeper	DEG GUR LED LIB ORN ROS
LATE PREMIUM DUTCH FLAT	100–105	This 1840 heirloom variety grows slowly and does best in cool weather. The head grows to 8–14 pounds, 12 inches.	FAR HEN MEY SEE SOU TIL WIL
RIO VERDE (hybrid)	85	6–7-inch, blue-green, flat head; medium-long core; large, vigorous plant.	BURR
SAVONARCH (hybrid)	110	9–10-inch, light green, flat-topped, dense head.	TER
STEINS EARLY DUTCH FLAT	75–85	5½–6-pound, 8–9-inch head; good winter keeper.	SEE

VARIETY	DAYS	DESCRIPTION	SOURCES (p. 385)
CABBAGE (POINTED HEAD)			
CHARLESTON WAKE-FIELD (Long Island Wakefield)	70–75	The 4–5-pound, 8-inch-diameter, dark green, conical head holds well.	MEY SEE
CUORE DI BUE (Ox Heart)	75	Unusual Italian variety has tight, pointed, compact, dark green head. Sow seeds in early spring for summer or fall harvest.	JLH
EARLY JERSEY WAKEFIELD	62–70	2–3-pound, dark green, tight, cone-shaped head; 1840 heirloom variety; reliable and well-adapted.	ABU BURP BURR BUT COM COO DEG FAR FIS GAR JLH JOH LED LEJ LIB MEY NIC ORG PON POR ROS SEE SOU TIL VER WIL
EXPRESS	60	Green, firm, crisp, and tender.	WILL
GREYHOUND	64	Average flavor.	BOU SEE
JERSEY WAKEFIELD	58–75	2–3-pound head; compact plant; resistant to yellows.	FAR
CABBAGE (SAVOYED)			
BEST OF ALL	85	Extralarge head; endures cold well.	BOU
BLUE MAX	85	3–4-pound head; blue and lime green colors; tender texture.	HIG ORN SEE
CANADA SAVOY	73	3½-pound, dark green, small head; not yellows-tolerant.	STO
CHIEFTAIN SAVOY (OP)	80–90	This 1938 variety is an All-American winner that tolerates late frost. Its 5–7-pound, 8-inch, blue-green, flat heads are good for coleslaw.	ABU COM GAR HEN LED MEY SOU STO TER TIL VER
DES VERTUS	75	An all-around excellent variety that can stand heat, it produces a 3-pound, deep blue-green head.	SHE
DRUMHEAD SAVOY	90	Firm, crisp head.	ALL
GENUINE (hybrid)	72	3–3½-pound, 6-inch, small, semiround, medium green head with a medium-long core and well-textured interior; tolerant to tip burn.	TWI
JANUARY KING	100–110	Sweeter than most savoys, this variety will stand light frost. Heads are 1½–5 pounds and dark bluish green outside, pale green inside. Leaves turn bright pink with cool weather.	ABU BOU ORG SEE TER
JULIUS (hybrid)	75	4–5-pound, blue-green, globe-shaped head; short core; vigorous and uniform.	JOH TER
LANGEDIJKER EARLY (Kapperties Kool)	65	Fine, curled, green heads for summer use.	WILL
LANGEDIJKER WINTER KEEPER	80	Light green; hardy.	SEE WILL
MIDVOY (hybrid)	77	3½-pound, medium green, slightly savoyed head; no yellows tolerance.	STO

VARIETY	DAYS	DESCRIPTION	SOURCES (p. 385)
CABBAGE (SAVOYED) *(continued)*			
NOVUM, ORIGINAL	80	Very dark green, heavily crinkled cabbage for summer and fall use.	WILL
ORMSKIRK EARLY	80	Large, round, dark green head with flowerlike leaves; hardy to 10°F.	BOU
PRIMAVOY (hybrid)	98	3½-pound, dark blue-green, well savoyed head; no yellows tolerance.	STO
PROMASA (hybrid)	60	1-pound, oval head with short stem.	NIC TER
SAVOY KING (hybrid)	82–120	4–5-pound, dark green, semiflat head; tolerates heat well; All-American winner.	DEG LIB NIC PAR PON TWI WILL
SAVOY QUEEN	88	Nearly the same as Savoy King, with 5-pound head; yellows-tolerant.	STO
SPEEDY SAVOY (hybrid)	75	An improved, darker blue-green version of Savoy Ace; good tip burn and yellows tolerance.	STO
SPIVOY	50	4–6-inch head; long standing and hardy.	PAR
TALER (hybrid)	85	Blue-green, round head; some frost tolerance; no yellows tolerance.	STO
TARVOY (hybrid)	105	Dense, dark green head; outstanding performer in difficult conditions.	THO
TESTA DI FERRO (Iron Head)	90	Italian variety's deep green, crinkled leaves form a loose head.	JLH
VANGUARD	70	Sweet and tender.	FIS
WIVOY	160	Dutch variety; medium green, highly savoyed head; cold-resistant to 7°F.	TER

CABBAGE (RED)

VARIETY	DAYS	DESCRIPTION	SOURCES
APRIL RED (hybrid)	95	6-pound, dense, round heads are well wrapped. Sow seed in late April or May.	STO
BLACK HEAD	95	2–4-pound, deep red head.	SEE
FIRE DANCE (hybrid)	90	3½–5-pound, deep red head for short storage; yellows-tolerant.	STO
LANGEDIJKER DARK RED WINTER KEEPER	100	Solid, red head with strong storage quality.	WILL
LANGEDIJKER RED, EARLIEST	100	2-pound head; ideal for small gardens.	WILL
LANGEDIJKER RED WINTER KEEPER, ORIGINAL 218	100	Firm, oblong head; good keeper.	WILL

VARIETY	DAYS	DESCRIPTION	SOURCES (p. 385)

CABBAGE (RED) (continued)

VARIETY	DAYS	DESCRIPTION	SOURCES (p. 385)
LASSO (OP)	70–75	Very firm 2–4-pound heads are on the small side. Dependable import from Denmark stands well without splitting.	GAR HIG JOH PIN SEE
MAMMOTH RED ROCK	90–95	An all-purpose cabbage, its 5–8-pound, red-purple head stores well.	ABU GAR LED LEJ MEY VER WIL
METEOR (OP)	80–110	6–8-inch, deep purple head; Dutch variety with good cold tolerance.	STO TER
PIERRETTE	78	3½-pound, 6-inch head; tolerant to splitting.	STO
PREKO	75	2½-pound, bloodred, compact head.	STO
RAVEN (hybrid)	75	2½-pound, bright red, round head with nice interior color; tolerant to yellows.	STO
RED ACRE	75–85	2–5-pound, 6–7-inch, reddish purple head; short stem.	ALL BURR COM FAR FIS GUR HEN HIG LIB PON POR ROS SEE SOU TIL
RED DRUMHEAD	95	Sow February through May for this 7–8-inch, round head that's good for pickling. Plant is yellows-resistant.	BOU WILL
RED RODAN	140	8–10-inch, hard head; Danish variety; large, vigorous plant.	TER
RED ROOKIE (hybrid)	78	3-pound, 6-inch head; semi-open frame; short to medium core, well filled; widely adapted.	LIB TWI VER WIL
REGAL RED (hybrid)	85	4½x4-inch head; short-term storage; no yellows tolerance.	JOH STO
RIO GRANDE RED (hybrid)	88	6x5-inch, well-colored head; some tip burn tolerance, but no yellows tolerance.	STO
RONA RED (hybrid)	98	Excellent for storage; some tip burn tolerance, but no yellows or black rot tolerance.	STO
ROOKIE	68	Deep red color throughout.	LIB
RUBY BALL (hybrid)	65–80	3–6-pound head; Japanese variety; very dependable All-American winner.	BURR COO DEG LED LIB MEY NIC PIN POR TER VER
RUBY PERFECTION (hybrid)	83–85	3–5-pound, 6-inch-diameter, deep red, round head; stores well.	JOH TWI
SCARLET O'HARA (hybrid)	72	2–3½-pound head with red-burgundy color; Japanese variety; storable.	ORN SHE
SOLID RED 831 (hybrid)	83	3½–4-pound head with a medium length core; yellows and tip burn tolerance.	TWI
SOLID RED 841 (hybrid)	84	3½–4-pound, 6-inch, dark red, round head with deep interior color and medium length core; widely adapted.	TWI

VARIETY	DAYS	DESCRIPTION	SOURCES (p. 385)

CABBAGE (RED) *(continued)*

VARIETY	DAYS	DESCRIPTION	SOURCES (p. 385)
SOMBRERO (hybrid)	67	Dutch variety with round, compact head; high disease resistance.	JUN PIN
SUPER RED (hybrid)	80	Round, dark red head; some tolerance to thrips and tip burn; no yellows tolerance.	STO

CABBAGE (OTHER TYPES)

VARIETY	DAYS	DESCRIPTION	SOURCES
CABBAGE-SPROUTS	90	A crossbreed of Golden Acre cabbage and brussels sprouts, it produces a 2–3-pound head.	FIS
COUVES (Portuguese Cabbage)	100	Slow-growing, cabbagelike plant; loose leaves have large midribs; use like celery.	COM

CABBAGE (ORIENTAL, HEADING-LONG)

VARIETY	DAYS	DESCRIPTION	SOURCES
CHIHILI	73	White heads with fringed edges are 18–20 inches tall and 3½ inches thick.	TIL
GREEN ROCKET (hybrid)	70	Heads are 18 inches tall, cylindrical and 4–5 pounds. Variety is tolerant to most diseases.	VER
JADE PAGODA (hybrid)	72	16-inch-tall, 5-inch-thick, deep green, broad, compact, uniform head; relatively slow to bolt.	LED MEY PAR POR STU
MICHIHILI (OP) (Slobolt)	70–78	Head is 4–6 pounds, 18x4 inches. Dark green plant resembles celery and cos lettuce.	ABU ALL BURR BUT COM DEG FAR GAR GUR JUN LED MEY NIC PIN POR ROS SOU STO SUN TWI WIL WILL
MONUMENT (hybrid)	70–80	17–18-inch head; white interior; tolerant of speckling; bolts quickly in spring.	ORN STO TWI
PE-TSAI	75	Head is 12 inches long and pale green. Sow in midsummer.	BOU
SOUTH CHINA EARLIEST	45	1-pound, 10x14-inch, creamy white, tender, compact head; tolerates summer heat and bad weather; Japanese variety.	GLE JOH RED
TWO SEASONS (hybrid)	62	Variety matures quickly to form large, savoy-cabbage leaves, and solid, 10x7½-inch head. Plant will stand a long time before bolting to seed.	BURP

CABBAGE (ORIENTAL, SQUAT, NAPA-BARREL-TYPE HEAD)

VARIETY	DAYS	DESCRIPTION	SOURCES
BLUES (hybrid)	65	4½-pound, broad, squat head; slow to bolt; resistant to alternaria leaf spot, bacterial soft rot, downy mildew, and viruses.	JOH PAR TWI
CHINA PRIDE (hybrid)	68	5½-pound head; adapted to cooler temperatures; high tolerance to downy mildew, bacterial soft rot, and tip burn.	ORN STO TWI

VARIETY	DAYS	DESCRIPTION	SOURCES (p. 385)

CABBAGE (ORIENTAL, SQUAT, NAPA-BARREL-TYPE HEAD) (continued)

VARIETY	DAYS	DESCRIPTION	SOURCES
CHINESE EXPRESS (hybrid) (China Express)	60–80	4–5-pound, stocky, broad, barrel-shaped head; slow to bolt.	TER VER
EARLY HYBRID G	55	12–18-inch, medium green, deeply savoyed head with slightly spreading outer leaves; good for spring planting.	LIB
HYBRID 50 DAY	50	3–4-pound, small to medium, pale green head with white interior; endures heat fairly well.	TWI
HYBRID WR60	60	12x8-inch, uniform head; very slow bolting.	WILL
KASUMI	64	5-pound head; good tolerance to bolting and tip burn.	STO
KYOTO NO. 3	70–80	Virus-resistant, this variety doesn't mind wind and produces a 15-pound, 12-inch head. Sow in late summer or early spring.	RED WILL
NAGODA (hybrid)	50	3–5-pound head; tolerant of cool weather and summer heat.	FIS
NERVA (hybrid)	55	Dutch variety; bolt-resistant; solid, crisp head.	TER
NOZAKI EARLY	55	Light green head; for late spring sowing.	ABU
ORIENT EXPRESS	43	Small, solid, oblong head; heat-resistant.	BURP
ORANGE QUEEN (hybrid)	80	The 4.8-pound lemon yellow head will turn light orange when exposed to sunlight. Variety bolts easily.	STO
SPRING A–1 (hybrid) (Takii's Spring A–1)	60–75	3–4-pound, small, pale green head; slow to bolt and not sensitive to temperature changes.	NIC PIN VER
SPRINGTIDE (hybrid)	43	10–11-inch-long, deep green head; strong resistance to bolting; tolerant to soft rot and black speck.	JOH
SPRINGTIME II (hybrid)	57	10-inch-long, 3½-pound head; slow to bolt; tolerant to viruses, downy mildew, white spot, and alternaria leaf spot.	STO
SPRING TRIUMPH (hybrid)	70–75	5–7-pound head; sow in spring or summer.	SUN
SUMMERTIME II (hybrid)	67	6-pound head; slow to bolt during heat waves; sow in July; tolerant to viruses, downy mildew, white spot, and alternaria.	STO
TREASURE ISLAND (hybrid)	85	6-pound head with vivid green interior; disease-tolerant; grows well in low temperatures.	NIC
TROPICAL DELIGHT (hybrid) (Louisiana Lettuce)	58	3–4-pound, light yellow-green head; suited to hot weather (bolts in cool weather); Japanese variety.	TWI
TROPICAL 50 (hybrid)	50–55	3–4-pound, oval head.	SUN
TROPICAL PRIDE (hybrid)	50–55	Head is 3–4 pounds. Sow in summer.	SUN

VARIETY	DAYS	DESCRIPTION	SOURCES (p. 385)

CABBAGE (ORIENTAL, SQUAT, NAPA-BARREL-TYPE HEAD) *(continued)*

VARIETY	DAYS	DESCRIPTION	SOURCES
2-SEASON	62	10-inch, oval head with savoyed leaves; resists soft rot and bolting.	GUR
WINTER GIANT	80–85	Head is 10 pounds. Sow in summer.	SUN
WONG BOK (OP)	80	5–7-pound, 7–10-inch, light green head; drought-resistant; sow in spring or summer.	COM DEG NIC SUN
WR 60 (hybrid)	60	Head is 4 pounds, 12x8 inches. Very slow bolting variety shows tolerance to mosaic virus, soft rot, and mildew.	WILL
WR SUPER 90 (hybrid)	90	Barrel-shaped, firm, 7-pound head; tolerant to common diseases; Japanese variety.	VER

CABBAGE (ORIENTAL, LOOSE HEADING)

VARIETY	DAYS	DESCRIPTION	SOURCES
LETTUCE TYPE	45	The 3-pound, 11–12-inch, cylindrical head looks like a big head of romaine lettuce.	JOH
SHANTUNG (OP)	55–65	4–5-pound head with loose, frilly leaves.	SUN

CARDOON

BOTANICAL NAME: *Cynara cardunculus*

DAYS TO MATURITY: 110–140.

PLANTING TIME: Plant the seeds in late spring.

SOIL: Rich and moist.

NUTRIENTS: In late summer, feed them weekly with fish emulsion.

WATER: From late spring to early autumn, water well.

LIGHT: Full sun.

SPACING: Sow groups of 3–4 seeds in a trench 1 inch deep, at 1½-foot intervals.

HARVEST: Allow a month of blanching before harvesting cardoon. To blanch, wrap long strips of thick, brown paper around the plants, starting at the bottom, then pack soil around the bottoms. If you don't want to blanch them at the end of summer, you can wait until winter and simply eat them as you want them.

STORAGE: Cardoon must be kept in a completely dark place.

CARDOON

Cardoon Growing Tips

Taste Treat

Pamper cardoon with a cup of fish emulsion or a diluted chicken-manure solution every two to three weeks as they grow. This prevents the leaf stalks from becoming pithy and tasteless due to sluggish growth. At the same time, make sure the plants never dry out.

Black Plastic Magic

If you can't wait for a bite of cardoon, wind black plastic mulch around the stems, leaving the leafy tops exposed, and tie with brown cord. The stalks will be blanched and ready to eat in about four weeks compared to the six to eight weeks required when you use other materials.

VARIETY	DAYS	DESCRIPTION	SOURCES (p. 385)
CARDOON			
CARDOON	110	When leaves are almost fully grown, tie them together near the top; pile straw around the head and dirt against the straw to blanch. Full sun and rich, moist soil are needed.	NIC RED SEE
LARGE SMOOTH	110-180	Fine, smooth stalk; requires rich soil.	DEG

CARROTS

BOTANICAL NAME: *Daucus carota sativa*

DAYS TO MATURITY: 50–110.

PLANTING TIME: Sow carrots in the ground two to four weeks after the last frost. Continue to sow at three-week intervals. In warmer regions, where winter temperatures rarely fall below 25°F, sow in late summer for a fall/winter crop.

SOIL: Light, sandy loam that's free of rocks; pH 6.0–7.0.

NUTRIENTS: Fertilize twice during the growing season. Apply fish emulsion. Push soil up around carrot base to prevent the root tops from turning green.

WATER: Maintain even soil moisture.

LIGHT: Full sun.

SPACING: Sow ½ inch deep, about 4 seeds per inch. Space rows 14–17 inches apart.

HARVEST: Carrots store well in the ground; dig them up as you need them. You can also keep carrots between layers of dry sand in a box that you should put in a frost-proof shed (cut off the tops and pack them evenly) or store them outside covered with straw.

STORAGE: Leave in ground; use fresh, canned, or frozen.

Carrot Growing Tips

Sprout Them Fast

To ensure uniform germination, try covering your seedbed with a sheet of clear plastic. Carrots are a cool weather crop but won't germinate well in early spring when the soil temperature is below 40°F. The plastic covering heats up the soil and maintains moisture. Uncover the seedbed on warm, sunny days to keep the soil temperature from exceeding 95°F.

Scorched Earth

Home gardeners who have weed problems should take a tip from commercial growers. Wait seven or eight days after sowing your carrot beds, then scorch the earth lightly using a small propane tank equipped with a nozzle (hardware stores sell them). This kills the weeds to give the growing carrots a better chance.

Mix and Match

To grow a great carrot crop in less-than-perfect soil, you'll need to match the carrot variety to the soil type. In rocky or shallow soil, plant Oxheart or Nuggets. In heavy, clay soil, plant short to medium carrot varieties such as Red Cored Chantenay, Royal Chantenay, or Nantes. In light, sandy soil, plant long, slender varieties such as Imperator or Gold Pak.

Pot Magic

To take the guesswork out of growing carrots, try starting them in clay or plastic pots. Fill several 4–6-inch pots with a good potting mix to within 1 inch of the rim. Sow 10–12 seeds evenly over the surface. Water the soil thoroughly, and keep it damp until the seeds sprout. When each plant has two to three fernlike leaves, thin until you have around seven evenly spaced seedlings per pot. When the plants are 6–9 inches high, remove the entire root mass from the pot and plant this intact in the garden. The contents of 10 pots planted close together (intensive style) yield about 70 carrots.

Speedy Germination

Carrots take twice as long to germinate as most other vegetables. To shorten the process, pour a teakettle of boiling water

CARROTS

over the seeds before covering them with soil. This makes them sprout in about half the usual time and increases overall germination.

Automatic Spacing

To avoid the backbreaking work of thinning carrots by hand, rake the carrot bed with a steel rake when the baby carrots are 2–3 inches high. You'll save a lot of effort and space out the carrots automatically. A few plants will be squashed, but they will recover in a day or two.

The Perfect Carrot

Want to grow long, slender carrots like you see in the supermarket? Sow the seeds of Imperator or Gold Pak ½ inch deep and cover them with ¼ inch of compost or peat moss. Keep this layer moist until the seeds germinate. When the plants are about an inch tall, withhold watering until they start to wilt, then resume normal watering until harvest. This tactic encourages fast downward growth and produces appealing carrots.

Warm Weather Solution

When hot weather makes germination impossible, one solution is to sow carrot seeds along a pencil-size ¼-inch furrow, then cover them with ¼ inch of soil. The trick is to plant these fragile seeds deep enough so they won't dry out yet shallow enough so they can break through easily. Water with a fine mist so the seeds won't wash away.

VARIETY	DAYS	DESCRIPTION	SOURCES (p. 385)
CARROTS (LONG, SLENDER—GOLD PAK)			
CELLOBUNCH (hybrid)	80	7–10 inches long and more than 1 inch thick; uniform, cylindrical shape; high quality; high yields.	WIL
GOLD PAK	65–80	8½x1 inches; deep orange; improved Imperator strain; good quality.	COM DEG GUR HEN PON POR
GOLD PAK 28	69–77	10x1¼ inches; reddish orange; small, indistinct core.	JUN STO
JAPANESE IMPERIAL LONG	90–100	Thin roots are 9–12 inches or longer. Color is dark orange.	SEED
MOKUM (hybrid)	60	This 6–10-inch, deep orange, sweet root can be pulled early as a baby carrot. It's also a good variety to can or freeze.	COO TER
ORLANDO GOLD (hybrid)	65–80	9–11 inches long; orange; crack-resistant; no green shoulders; small core; bolt-resistant.	COM DEG HEN JUN LED POR WILL
SCARLET WONDER	70–110	12 inches; deep scarlet; sweet and tender.	SEE VER

VARIETY	DAYS	DESCRIPTION	SOURCES (p. 385)

CARROTS (LONG, SLENDER, BROAD SHOULDERS—IMPERATOR)

VARIETY	DAYS	DESCRIPTION	SOURCES
A PLUS (hybrid)	65–73	7–8 inches; deep scarlet; adapted for organic and mineral soils.	JUN NIC ORN PAR PIN
ARISTO PAK (hybrid)	70	8–8½ inches long, bright orange, inside and out.	WIL
AVENGER (hybrid)	62	10 inches; bright orange; tolerant to powdery mildew; grow in heavy soil or sand.	STO
CANADA GOLD (hybrid)	73	8–9-inch-long, smooth, tapered carrot; grow in deep, smooth soil.	FAR NIC
CANDY PACK (hybrid)	75	8–10-inch, bright orange, sweet, tender carrot.	JUN
CHEYENNE (hybrid)	63	8–10 inches; smooth, cylindrical, and slightly tapered; tolerant to alternaria.	STO
CHOCTAW (hybrid)	67	10 inches; tolerant to alternaria and cercospora.	STO
DISCOVERY (hybrid)	62	10 inches long, deep orange; tolerant to alternaria; for shallow muck or sand.	STO
HURON (hybrid)	67	This 10-inch, cigar-shaped, dark orange carrot contains Super Sweet gene; tolerant to alternaria and leaf spot.	STO
IMPERATOR	64–80	10 inches long and 1½ inches thick; orange red; popular variety.	BURP FAR LED MEY PON ROS VER
IMPERATOR, LONG	77	10x2 inches; orange; finely grained and tender.	ALL SEE
IMPERATOR 58	58–77	10x1 inches; rich orange; uniform interior color and fine grain; tender.	BURR DEG POR STO TIL WIL WILL
IMPERATOR 58 IMPROVED	75	10x½ inches; dark orange; crisp and coreless.	HEN
KING MIDAS (hybrid)	65	Dark orange, inside and out. The carrot grows to 8–9 inches but can be used for baby carrots at 3–4 inches.	SHE
LEGEND (hybrid)	65	9 inches; dark orange; grow in sand or muck.	STO
LONG ORANGE IMPROVED	88	Mature carrot is 12x2¾ inches. Plant this 1620 Dutch heirloom variety in loose soil.	SOU
ORANGE SHERBET (hybrid)	60	10x1¼ inches; bright orange; tolerance to blight.	STO
ORANGETTE (hybrid)	62	For muck or sand, this improved Six Pak II type produces a 7–10-inch, deep orange carrot.	STO
PAK MOR (hybrid)	60	6–10 inches; bright orange.	FAR
SAVORY (hybrid)	68	This carrot has 40 percent more vitamin A than Imperator.	PIN
SEMINOLE (hybrid)	66	Yielding a 9-inch, dark orange carrot, the variety contains Super Sweet gene and is tolerant to many leaf diseases.	STO

VARIETY	DAYS	DESCRIPTION	SOURCES (p. 385)
CARROTS (LONG, SLENDER, BROAD SHOULDERS—IMPERATOR) *(continued)*			
SWEETNESS (hybrid)	62	The 6–8-inch, bright orange carrot grows well in all types of soil.	LED JUN WILL
TANGERINE DELIGHT (hybrid)	60	8½–9 inches; tolerance to rusty root and leaf blight; for shallow muck or sandy soils.	STO
TENDERSWEET	60	Heavy producing variety grows 10x2-inch, orange red, sweet, tender carrots.	GUR HEN
VITA SWEET BRAND VARIETY 691 (hybrid)	69	9–10 inches; bright orange interior; tolerant to alternaria.	TWI
VITA SWEET BRAND VARIETY 711 (hybrid)	71	The 9–10x1¼-inch, dark orange, almost coreless carrot can grow in deep soils, whether muck or mineral.	TWI
VITA SWEET BRAND VARIETY 781 (hybrid)	78	9–10x1¼ inches; bright orange exterior and interior.	TWI

CARROTS (MEDIUM SLENDER, TAPERING—DANVERS)

VARIETY	DAYS	DESCRIPTION	SOURCES
CAMBERLEY	74	This 6–7-inch, uniformly deep red carrot will grow in heavy soil and can overwinter well in the ground.	BOU GAR
CONDOR (hybrid)	67	8½ inches long; bright orange; high sugar content; good tolerance to alternaria leaf spot.	STO
DANVERS	70–75	6–7½x1½ inches; deep orange; adapted to all types of soils; very productive.	TER
DANVERS HALF LONG	73–85	This deep orange, nearly coreless 1871 heirloom variety is widely adapted and suited for heavy soil. The 8x2-inch carrot stores well.	ALL BURP DEG FAR FIS GAR GUR HEN LEJ MEY PIN PON ROS SEE SOU THO TIL WILL
DANVERS HALF LONG IMPROVED	75	Bright orange with a red core; produces well in almost any soil.	COM
DANVERS NO. 126 (OP)	65–80	6–7½x2 inches; good processing carrot; excellent interior color; outstanding variety for heavier soils.	ABU BURR DEG LED POR SOU STO VER WIL
DANVERS NO. 126 IMPROVED	75	The 6–8-inch, orange red carrot will store well. Variety gives heavy yields. Tops are heat-resistant.	TWI
DESS-DAN (hybrid)	67	7–9½ inches; deep orange; processing carrot.	STO
GOLDEN STATE (hybrid)	70	7x1¾ inches; bright orange; sweet and tender.	PAR
PROCESSOR II (hybrid)	67	9 inches long; intense orange; high-quality processing carrot.	STO

CARROTS (MEDIUM PLUMP, BLUNT END—SPARTAN)

VARIETY	DAYS	DESCRIPTION	SOURCES
ORANGE SHERBET	60	10x1¼ inches; bright orange; tolerant to blight.	STO

VARIETY	DAYS	DESCRIPTION	SOURCES (p. 385)

CARROTS (MEDIUM PLUMP, BLUNT END—SPARTAN) *(continued)*

VARIETY	DAYS	DESCRIPTION	SOURCES
SPARTAN BONUS (hybrid)	70–77	7x2 inches; deep orange.	FAR
SPARTAN PREMIUM 80	67	9 inches; good tolerance to leaf blight and rusty root.	STO

CARROTS (MEDIUM PLUMP, TAPERING—CHANTENAY)

VARIETY	DAYS	DESCRIPTION	SOURCES
AUTUMN KING	70	Fine variety for winter storage; heavy yields.	BOU
AUTUMN KING IMPROVED	70	All-purpose carrot is 10 inches long and good for winter storage.	THO
BURPEE'S GOLDINHEART	70–72	5½x2¼ inches; good to can or freeze.	BURP
CHANTENAY (OP) (Rouge Demi-Longe de Chantenay)	68–72	6x2¼ inches; bright orange with a red core.	ALL BOU LEJ NIC SEE
CHANTENAY HALF-LONG RED CORED IMPROVED	70	Deep orange with a red core; all-purpose carrot.	LED
CHANTENAY IMPROVED	70	7 inches; red core; robust growth.	COM
CHANTENAY LONG	68–72	7x2 inches; deep orange.	DEG VER
IMPERIAL	75	5 inches; adaptable, unfussy variety; reliable in heavy clay or sticky soils.	SHE
KURODA (Kurota)	60–70	This 7–8x2-inch, deep orange, storable carrot grows in poorer soil. Variety is heat- and disease-resistant.	COO HIG NIC PAR SEED
RED-CORED CHANTE-NAY (Supreme Long)	68–72	The 6x2-inch, red-orange carrot retains its color when cooked. This 1829 heirloom variety grows even in heavy soil.	ABU DEG FAR FIS GAR GUR HEN JUN MEY NIC PIN PON ROS SEED SOU TIL WIL WILL
ROYAL CHANTENAY (OP)	68–70	An all-purpose carrot that's easy to grow, it's 6½x2½ inches, red-orange, and coreless.	BURP BURR PAR POR STO TER WILL
TOKITA'S SCARLET	70	7-inch, orange carrot; Japanese variety.	PIN

CARROTS (MEDIUM CYLINDRICAL, BLUNT END—NANTES)

VARIETY	DAYS	DESCRIPTION	SOURCES
ARMSTRONG (hybrid)	65	7–8-inch, rich orange carrot; slow to crack.	TER
BERLICUMMER	69	9x1¾ inches; almost no cracking or splitting.	PIN WILL
BERTAN (hybrid)	70	6 inches; bright orange; stays sweet a long time; high-yielding.	THO
CARROT FLY AWAY (hybrid)	72	Fly-resistant; good flavor.	THO

VARIETY	DAYS	DESCRIPTION	SOURCES (p. 385)

CARROTS (MEDIUM CYLINDRICAL, BLUNT END—NANTES) *(continued)*

VARIETY	DAYS	DESCRIPTION	SOURCES (p. 385)
CHRISMA (hybrid)	70	7–9x1½-inch, cylindrical, medium orange carrot with a blunt tip; bolt- and crack-resistant.	VER
CLARION (hybrid)	60	7 inches; orange; sweet and aromatic; good eating quality.	JOH
CORELESS AMSTERDAM	55	6–7-inch, salmon red, sweet, and crisp carrot; Dutch variety.	STO
DANRO	70	A Dutch variety, the 6–7x1½-inch, intensely orange, high-fiber carrot grows in heavier soils and keeps longer in the soil.	ORN
EAGLE (hybrid)	56	8½ inches; orange; high quality for slicing or canning.	STO
EARLY NANTES	60	Almost coreless; good in heavy soils.	BOU
ESTELLE (hybrid)	75	7–10 inches; rich orange color; good yields.	TER
FAKKEL MIX	90	6–7 inches; good for juice.	TER
FALCON II (hybrid)	60	7 inches; good interior color.	STO
FLAKKEE LONG RED GIANT	65	2 feet; red core; excellent for storing.	SEE WILL
INGOT (hybrid)	66	7–9 inches; contains Super Sweet gene; all-purpose carrot.	JOH MEY NIC POR THO
JAMES SCARLET INTERMEDIATE	60	A half-long variety; perfectly symmetrical; rare variety.	BOU
JUWAROT	90	All-purpose 5–8-inch, deep red carrot is full of vitamin A and will keep through winter.	BOU THO
KLONDIKE NANTES	56	7–8-inch, deep orange carrot with high sugar content; good fresh or frozen.	STO
LUCKY B (hybrid)	67	7 inches; good interior color; exceptionally sweet.	JUN
NANCO (hybrid)	57	7-inch-long, deep orange carrot with a small core; high yields.	STO
NANDOR (hybrid)	66	8–10-inch, orange-red, coreless, tender, and sweet carrot; high yields.	PAR
NANTAISE TIP TOP (Nantes Tip Top)	73	Dutch variety; 7 inches; deep orange; low fiber; adapts well to wide range of soils.	SHE WILL
NANTES	68–70	6x1½ inches; red hue; flavorful.	COM DEG HEN LEJ MEY ORG PIN SEE SEED
NANTES FANCY	65	7 inches; adapted to wide range of soils; excellent for storing.	GAR
NANTES FORTO	60	Longer and somewhat heavier than Nantes; coreless; good freezer.	WILL

VARIETY	DAYS	DESCRIPTION	SOURCES (p. 385)
CARROTS (MEDIUM CYLINDRICAL, BLUNT END—NANTES) *(continued)*			
NANTES IMPROVED CORELESS	68	Bright orange; small core; crisp and tender; good variety for frame culture.	BURR
NANTES SLENDERO	70	This Dutch variety's 6–9-inch, bright orange carrot holds well in the ground without cracking.	TER
NANTES STUMP ROOTED	69	7x1¼ inches; bright orange.	ROS
NAPOLI (hybrid)	58	The 7-inch carrot has nice color and taste. Plant tolerates alternaria blight.	JOH
NAROVA (hybrid)	56	All-purpose 7½-inch-long carrot is 8.5 percent sugar.	STO
NAVAJO (hybrid)	67	9 inches; deep orange; tolerance to alternaria and leaf spot.	STO
PIONEER (hybrid)	67	8 inches; deep orange; good yielder.	COM
PRESTO (hybrid)	52	8 inches long; Europe's most popular Nantes.	STO
PRIMO (hybrid)	55	Easy-to-pick French variety has no green shoulders and is also good as a baby carrot.	HIG
RONDINO (hybrid)	64	All-purpose, 7-inch, orange carrot with an indistinct core.	JOH
RUMBA	72	6–7 inches; deep orange; adapted to a wide range of soils.	JOH
SCARLET NANTES HALF LONG (OP) (Early Coreless, Nantes Coreless)	68–70	All-purpose 8x1½-inch, deep orange, coreless carrot; good standard variety.	ABU ALL BURP DEG FAR FIS GAR GUR HIG JLH JOH LED PAR PON SEED SOU STO TIL TWI VER WIL
SPARTAN PREMIUM 80 (hybrid)	57	9 inches; good tolerance to leaf blight and rusty root.	STO
SPECIAL NANTES 616	62	7 inches; well colored; good for storage.	STO
SWEETNESS (hybrid)	65	This 8-inch, orange-gold carrot is especially good fresh.	GUR HEN NIC
TAMINO (hybrid)	90	Grow this Dutch variety in loamy or humus-rich soil. The 10x1½-inch carrot will hold all winter in the ground without losing quality.	TER
TOUCHON	58–75	7x1½-inch, red-orange carrot; heirloom variety; excellent quality.	ABU COO DEG FAR GUR HEN HIG LEJ NIC SEE STO
TOUCHON DELUX	58	7 inches; brilliant orange; smooth and uniform.	STO
TOUDO (hybrid)	70	The 7½x1½-inch root can be pulled as a baby carrot. It resists splitting.	BURP

VARIETY	DAYS	DESCRIPTION	SOURCES (p. 385)
CARROTS (ROUND)			
ORBIT	50	1-inch-diameter; highly tolerant to splitting and yellowing.	TIL VER
PARISIAN (Parisian Market, Parisian Rondo)	50–60	This 2x1½-inch, deep orange, very sweet heirloom variety grows well in shallow soil.	BOU PIN SEE
PARMEX	50	Ball-shaped; 1–1½ inches in diameter; bright orange.	HIG ORN
PLANET	55	Beet-shaped; 1½ inches in diameter; deep red-orange; French variety.	ORN SHE
SWEET CHERRY BALL	50	1½-inch, orange, bite-size carrot.	GLE
THUMBELINA	60	Round carrot is ½ inch in diameter. Roots are smooth. All-American winner is good for heavier soils.	ALL BURP COM COO FAR GAR GUR JOH JUN LED NIC PAR PIN POR STO TWI WILL
CARROTS (SMALL)			
AMCA (OP)	50	3–3½ inches; deep orange; blunt tips; tolerant to alternaria.	TWI
BABY FINGER NANTES (Baby Nantes)	50	Can or pickle this 3x¾-inch, rich orange carrot.	HEN
BABY LONG	65	6–7 inches; good color throughout.	NIC
BABY ORANGE (OP)	53	Bright orange; good processing variety.	STO
BABY SPIKE	52	Variety holds its dainty size (3–4x½ inches) well past maturity. It has an excellent internal orange color.	GUR HEN PAR POR
BABY SWEET (hybrid)	49	Bright orange with rich interior color; slow to bolt.	STO
BOLERO (hybrid)	73	Nantes variety with good internal and external color; highly tolerant to alternaria; well-adapted to stressful conditions.	TWI
CARAMBA	75	3–5 inches; Dutch variety; Amsterdam Forcing type; perfect miniature carrot when picked early.	SHE
CARROT SUCRAM	70	3–4 inches; Nantes type; very sweet; good for processing.	NIC SEE
KINKO 4"	55	Harvest this 4-inch, red-orange carrot when young. It's for shallow soils.	GAR JOH
KINKO 6"	50–55	The 6-inch, cone-shaped roots are crack-resistant. Variety grows well in adverse conditions.	GAR HIG
LADY FINGER	60–95	5-inch, almost coreless, gourmet carrot.	DEG FAR HEN PAR TIL
LITTLE FINGER (Early Scarlet Horn)	50–65	This gourmet Nantes type is 2–3x⅜ inches, with a small core and extrasweet taste.	BOU COM GUR JLH JUN ORN PIN VER

VARIETY	DAYS	DESCRIPTION	SOURCES (p. 385)

CARROTS (SMALL) *(continued)*

VARIETY	DAYS	DESCRIPTION	SOURCES
MINICOR (Baby Nantes)	55	Harvest the 6–7-inch, orange carrot when just 3–4 inches. Tip is blunt and rounded.	COO GAR GUR JOH STO TIL WILL
OX HEART (Guernade)	70–75	6x4 inches; deep orange; easily dug up; heavy yields in thin soil.	ABU FIS GAR SEE
PRIMO (hybrid)	60	Improved Nantes; gourmet baby carrot with lush top.	ORN
SHORT 'N SWEET	68	Bright orange; good in heavy soils.	FAR LED
TANGERINE (hybrid)	51	7 inches when fully mature; blunt ends; dark orange.	STO

CARROTS (UNUSUAL TYPES)

VARIETY	DAYS	DESCRIPTION	SOURCES
AFGHAN PURPLE	65	Bicolored: yellow core surrounded by royal purple flesh; 9 inches long and tapered; wild carrot flavor; low in sugar; use as an accent vegetable.	SOU
BELGIUM WHITE (White French)	75	White 1885 heirloom variety with mild flavor.	BOU NIC
INDIAN LONG RED	75	Long and tapered.	GLE
JUMBO	80	This holds the record as the longest and heaviest carrot.	THO
KINTOKI EARLY STRAIN	70	8x1½ inches; true red; Japanese variety; tender and sweet.	GLE
LONG RED SURREY	75	Carrots are 5–6 times as long as they are broad. This 1834 heirloom variety keeps well in the ground and is drought-tolerant in sandy soil.	BOU
MERIDA	75	Overwintering, Nantes type carrot; resistant to bolting; good for juice; Dutch variety.	TER
SCARLET IMPERIAL LONG	77	3-foot-long, salmon orange carrot; Japanese variety.	GLE
TOP WEIGHT	75	A New Zealand variety, the orange-red carrot will stand in the soil for 6 months without cracking or splitting.	GLE

CARROTS (FORCING VARIETIES)

VARIETY	DAYS	DESCRIPTION	SOURCES
AMSTERDAM FORCING	60–72	Deep orange, stumpy roots.	ABU SEE WILL
AMSTERDAM FORCING MAXI	55	6x1 inches; orange-scarlet; coreless type for outdoors and cold frame; good for freezing.	WILL

CAULIFLOWER

CAULIFLOWER

BOTANICAL NAME: *Brassica oleracea botrytis*

DAYS TO MATURITY: 30–180.

PLANTING TIME: Plant in spring four weeks before the last frost. For a fall harvest, plant in late spring. In hot areas where winters are mild, plant in late summer for a winter crop.

SOIL: Light and rich; pH 6.0–7.5.

NUTRIENTS: Feed the plants every three to four weeks with fish emulsion or use 1 tablespoon of blood meal in 1 gallon of water.

WATER: Always keep the soil moist.

LIGHT: Full sun.

SPACING: Sow seeds ½ inch deep, 18–24 inches apart. If row gardening, space rows 3 feet apart.

HARVEST: Be sure to blanch the heads by pulling a few outer leaves together over the buds and securing them. Harvest the heads when they are still tight; cut the stalk just below the head.

STORAGE: Use cauliflower fresh.

Cauliflower Growing Tips

Blanching Made Easy

To blanch cauliflower easily, cover each head with aluminum foil when it is about the size of a softball. First, crinkle up a square of aluminum foil that's approximately 14x14 inches. Unfold the square and loosely place it over a cauliflower head, allowing as much air space as possible. Tuck the edges around the head. At harvest time, your cauliflower will be pleasingly white.

Healthy Cauliflower

Select seedlings that have about four green leaves; a short, straight stem; and plenty of root. Reject seedlings with a bluish tinge (since they will produce only small curds), seedlings with six or more leaves (they have matured too quickly and will die), and blind seedlings (those with no growing points).

Easy Storage

It's a snap to store cauliflower. Pull up the entire plant, and hang it upside down in a cool, dark place. While cauliflower plants are in storage, spray them with water every night.

VARIETY	DAYS	DESCRIPTION	SOURCES (p. 385)
CAULIFLOWER (EARLY SEASON)			
ALERT	52–55	Self-blanching type; very dense head, short stem, and large leaves.	GAR HIG PAR
CASHMERE (hybrid)	52	Dome-shaped, 2¼-pound head; heat-tolerant.	JOH STO
EARLY SELF BLANCHE	55	Large, very white, firm, smooth head.	LIB
EARLY SNOWBALL (Snow Drift)	55–65	6–7¼ inches in diameter; close, compact, creamy white head; for short season growing.	ABU BUT DEG JLH PIN PON RED
EARLY SNOWBALL A	55	Ivory white; short season variety.	BURR
EARLY WHITE (hybrid)	52	8–9-inch, pure white head; good all-purpose variety.	BURP PIN
EXTRA EARLY SNOWBALL	50	Snow white; good curd protection.	SEE STO
GARANT	59	The 3–4-inch heads have fine texture. This English variety is a good choice for miniature cauliflower and for freezing.	BOU
MILKYWAY (hybrid)	45	2-pound, 8-inch-thick, solid, smooth head; quick growth; all-purpose variety.	PAR
MONTANO (hybrid)	53	This Dutch variety gives a 6–7-inch, dome-shaped head with tender, creamy white curds. It produces even in areas with short springs and summers.	SHE
POLAR EXPRESS	50	2-pound, dome-shaped head with purple tinge.	STO
RUSHMORE (hybrid)	51	2¼-pound, 6¼-inch, high domed head with very white curds.	STO
SILVER CUP 40 (hybrid)	40	Small, 12–14-ounce, white head.	PIN
SILVER CUP 45 (hybrid)	45	Cousin to Silver Cup 40, with a 16–18-ounce, white head.	PIN
SNOWBALL T–3	51	Compact, domed head; tolerates adverse conditions.	GAR
SNOW CROWN (hybrid)	50–68	Snowball type with 2-pound, 5–9-inch head; good fresh or frozen; All-American winner.	BURP COM FAR JOH JUN LED LIB MEY NIC ORN PIN PON POR STO TER TWI VER WILL
SNOW GRACE	53	Similar to Snow Crown.	LIB
SNOW KING (hybrid)	45–60	Snowball type with 5½–9-inch-thick head; heat-tolerant; good freezer.	GER HEN JUN LIB VER WIL WILL
STOKES EXTRA EARLY SNOWBALL	55–60	This very solid head with good curd protection is widely adapted to different soils.	STO
SUPER SNOWBALL (OP) (Burpeeana, Early Snowball A)	55–60	6½-inch, ivory head; short season variety.	ALL BURP FAR FIS HEN
WHITE BISHOP	52	2¼-pound, deep, heavy head; tolerant to purple tinge.	STO

VARIETY	DAYS	DESCRIPTION	SOURCES (p. 385)

CAULIFLOWER (EARLY SEASON) *(continued)*

VARIETY	DAYS	DESCRIPTION	SOURCES
WHITE CORONA (hybrid)	30	Perfect for a small garden, these 3–4-inch heads have pure white, smooth, compact curds.	PAR
WHITE KNIGHT	55	2¼ pounds, 6¾ inches; tolerance to purple tinge.	STO
WHITE QUEEN (hybrid)	54	Snow Crown type with dome-shaped head.	STO

CAULIFLOWER (MIDSEASON)

VARIETY	DAYS	DESCRIPTION	SOURCES
ALL YEAR ROUND	70	Large head remains in good condition for a long time. This is a good one to freeze.	BOU
ALPHA BEGUM	75	Large Dutch variety with excellent flavor.	TER
ALPHA FORTADOS	67–70	Well-domed head.	TER
ANDES	65–70	6½-inch-deep head; tolerant of heat and cold.	HIG JOH STO
ARBON (hybrid)	120–140	Large, tender, snow white curds; for growing only in the maritime Northwest.	TER
CANDID CHARM (hybrid)	75	7–9-inch-deep, pure white, tightly packed head with no purple cast.	HIG LIB TWI
DOK ELGON	65	Undemanding variety can overwinter and freezes well.	BOU
DOMINANT	68	Head is large, firm, and white. Extensive root system provides some drought tolerance.	GAR SEE STO
EARLY GLACIER (hybrid) (Snowflake)	105	2-pound, pure white, dome-shaped head.	LIB
ELBY (hybrid)	70	Heads have heavy, large, deep, dense curds. Variety will tolerate rough handling, drought, and excessive wet.	THO
ELGON (hybrid)	60	Widely adapted, does well in hot or cool weather.	VER
INCA	70	2-pound head; overwintering variety; good frost tolerance.	TIL
INCLINE (hybrid)	76	7½-inch-thick, heavy, dense, pure white, high-domed head; tolerance to hollow stem.	STO
LERCERF	68	European variety; solid, white, self-protecting head.	WILL
MAJESTIC (hybrid)	66	7–8-inch, slightly domed, pure white head.	TWI
PRECOCE DI TOSCANA (Tuscany Early)	70	Italian variety with large, creamy white head.	JLH
RAVELLA (hybrid)	70	Fancy grade, extrawhite type covers heads with its own leaves. This Dutch variety resists bolting and does well in warm climates.	PAR TER

VARIETY	DAYS	DESCRIPTION	SOURCES (p. 385)

CAULIFLOWER (MIDSEASON) *(continued)*

VARIETY	DAYS	DESCRIPTION	SOURCES (p. 385)
SELF-BLANCHE (OP) (Snowball Self-Blanching)	68–71	6½–8-inch-thick, white, self-wrapping variety.	FAR FIS GAR GUR HEN JUN LIB MEY PON SEE
SERRANO (hybrid)	63	7-inch, deep, dome-shaped head with smooth curds.	STO
SIERRA NEVADA	68	Andes type with deep, round, smooth, pure white curds.	STO
SIRIA (hybrid)	65	7-inch-deep head; tolerant to hollow stems and heat; protect from secondary black rot infections.	STO
SNOWBALL (hybrid)	65–80	Medium-large, deep, solid head.	ALL LEJ
SNOWBALL A IMPROVED	60	Large head is a good freezer.	WILL
SNOWBALL X	60–64	6–7-inch head with small, firm, pure white curds.	BOU BURR TER
SNOWBALL Y	65–70	6½-inch head; reliable under adverse conditions.	LIB MEY
SNOWBALL Y IMPROVED (OP)	68–70	Medium-large, snow white head; widely adapted.	BURR DEG JUN ROS WIL
SNOW GIANT	110	5-pound, snow white head; grows under adverse conditions.	GLE
SNOW PAK (hybrid)	62–85	9–12-inch, white head; Plant Variety Patented (PVP).	BURR LED WILL
SNOW'S OVER-WINTERING WHITE	110	16 inches across; sow in late spring for December harvest; cold-tolerant.	SEED
SOLIDE	67	Deep, very white head with heavy curds; slowly grows during hot periods.	STO
STARBRITE Y (hybrid)	68	7–8-inch, medium-large, domed head; good holding ability.	TWI
TAIPAN	66	Self-wrapping spiral leaves provide good ventilation and coverage of the white curds.	STO
VERNON	75–95	This Dutch variety's deep, almost globe-shaped head has smooth curds with fine florets.	TER
WHITE FOX (Witte Vos)	68	8-inch, smooth, uniform, creamy white head; Dutch variety.	ORN PIN STO
WHITE ROCK (OP)	69–100	6½ inches thick; good curd protection; Dutch variety; Plant Variety Patented (PVP).	SHE STO TER TWI
WHITE SAILS (hybrid)	68	7½ inches thick; self-wrapping leaves; excellent heat tolerance.	STO
WHITE SUMMER (OP)	65	6–7 inches thick; self-wrapping type; Plant Variety Patented (PVP).	STO TWI
WHITE TOP	70–90	Self-wrapping Dutch variety with strong root system.	STO

VARIETY	DAYS	DESCRIPTION	SOURCES (p. 385)

CAULIFLOWER (MIDSEASON) *(continued)*

VARIETY	DAYS	DESCRIPTION	SOURCES
YUKON (hybrid)	71	7¼-inch, high-domed, dense, heavy head; use fresh or process.	STO

CAULIFLOWER (OTHER COLORS)

VARIETY	DAYS	DESCRIPTION	SOURCES
ALVERDA	75	Medium-size head has bright lime green curds; European variety.	COM JOH TER
BURGUNDY QUEEN (hybrid)	70	6½-inch-thick, 19-ounce, purple head; heat-tolerant; good variety to freeze.	ORN STO
GREEN HARMONY (hybrid)	80	Crossbreed of broccoli and cauliflower; pale green, midsize head.	GLE
ITALIAN PURPLE BRONZE	110	Head turns dark green when cooked.	COM
PURPLE CAPE	200	Hardier than the white cauliflowers, this English 1834 heirloom variety is bright purple. Treat this vegetable like broccoli.	BOU TER
PURPLE GIANT	75	Rich purple head turns green when cooked and freezes well.	LED SEE
PURPLE HEAD	70–110	Large, compact purple head tastes like broccoli and turns green when cooked.	WILL
ROMANESCO	75	Conical-shaped, creamy green head is 7 inches thick at its base and 6–7 inches high. It's filled with spears that are easily pulled apart.	COM PAR
SICILIAN PURPLE	85	Purple curds; mild flavor; good freezer.	ABU NIC
VERDE DI MACERATA	80	Apple green, midsize head turns light green when cooked and has excellent flavor.	JLH
VIOLET QUEEN (hybrid)	55–65	Purple curds; grown like broccoli, without tying; recommended for short season areas.	JOH LIB NIC STO TIL VER

CAULIFLOWER (MINIATURE)

VARIETY	DAYS	DESCRIPTION	SOURCES
MINI CORGILL	82–86	These vigorous, easy-to-grow plants don't mature all at once.	THO

CAULIFLOWER (OTHER TYPES)

VARIETY	DAYS	DESCRIPTION	SOURCES
CHARTREUSE II (hybrid)	62	Grow this broccoli-cauliflower crossbreed like early-spring or late-fall broccoli or cauliflower. Harvest in fall, not in midsummer.	STO

CELERIAC

BOTANICAL NAME: *Apium graveolens rapaceum*

DAYS TO MATURITY: 110–120.

PLANTING TIME: Germination of celeriac seed requires a soil temperature of 60°F. Sow seeds or seedlings in spring.

SOIL: Rich and well-drained; pH 6.0–7.0.

NUTRIENTS: Fertilize every two to three weeks during the growing season with fish emulsion or use 1 tablespoon of blood meal mixed into 1 gallon of water.

WATER: Water frequently but don't saturate.

LIGHT: Full sun.

SPACING: Space transplant seedlings 1 foot apart. Rows should be 12–15 inches apart.

HARVEST: Pull up the plants, and cut off their tops. If you plan to store, don't lift them until the hard frost makes it necessary.

STORAGE: The roots can be stored in damp sand for several weeks.

Celeriac Growing Tip

Starting Celeriac

Gardeners whose local nurseries don't carry celeriac as seedlings can order celeriac seeds from most garden catalogs. Prepare a seed tray with planting mix, and sow the seeds evenly and thinly across it. Water the surface, then cover the tray with black plastic, and place it in a warm place to germinate. After germination, replace the black plastic with a clear plastic bag.

VARIETY	DAYS	DESCRIPTION	SOURCES (p. 385)
CELERIAC (CELERY ROOT)			
ALABASTER	120	The large, white, 4-inch-thick root is similar to celery and good in vegetable soup.	TIL
BRILLIANT	100	Medium-large roots are round and relatively smooth with buff-colored skin and a white interior. Variety resists pithiness.	JOH TER
CELERIAC (Knob Celery)	110–120	This 2–3-inch-wide celery stores well; turnip-rooted.	SUN VER
CEC010	120	Large, thick, pure white roots; can store through winter.	LED
DOLVI	150	Vigorous, nearly round roots resist many diseases and have fine texture and flavor.	NIC

VARIETY	DAYS	DESCRIPTION	SOURCES (p. 385)
CELERIAC (CELERY ROOT) *(continued)*			
GIANT SMOOTH PRAGUE	110–120	4-inch-thick, smooth root.	COM DEG JUN MEY PIN STO WIL
MAGDENBURGER	110	Large, white roots with white interior.	LEJ
MENTOR (hybrid)	110	High-yielding Dutch variety without hollow hearts or discoloration.	SHE
MONARCH	120	These large roots' firm, white flesh does not discolor.	WILL
MONOSTORPALYI	200–240	Hungarian variety with small to midsize roots.	RED
PRAGUE	120	Large roots.	SEE
ZWINDRA (hybrid)	140	Lacy tops; European delicacy.	ORN

CELERY

BOTANICAL NAME: *Apium graveolens dulce*

DAYS TO MATURITY: 60–140.

PLANTING TIME: Plant celery seedlings in the garden two to four weeks before the last frost. Since celery seeds require a temperature of 55–61°F for germination, sow them in peat pots 10 to 12 weeks before planting time.

SOIL: Rich, light, and sandy; pH 6.0–7.0.

NUTRIENTS: Feed every two to three weeks during the growing season with fish emulsion or use 1 tablespoon blood meal mixed into 1 gallon of water.

WATER: Water frequently, never allowing the soil to become dry.

LIGHT: Full sun.

SPACING: Plant seedlings 6–8 inches apart. For row planting, space rows 2½ feet apart.

HARVEST: Blanch celery first. When the plants are about 12 inches high, begin putting earth up around them. Lift winter celery as required during autumn and winter. The summer varieties are ready earlier.

STORAGE: Use fresh as needed.

Celery Growing Tips

Coffee-Can Blanching

For whiter celery, cover the lower two-thirds of the stalks with

CELERY

coffee cans or gallon milk cartons with the bottoms removed. The celery is blanched and ready to harvest in about a month.

Speeding Up Production

Here's how to speed up production and blanch the stalks at the same time. In the spring dig a trench one spade deep and 12–15 inches wide. Turn well-rotted manure and/or compost into this trench and let it settle before setting out the plants 6 inches apart. Fill the soil around the stalks as the plants grow.

Planting Close Together

An easy alternative way to blanch celery is to plant your seedlings close together (about 12 inches apart) in a square or rectangle. Erect a framework of stakes around this. Cover the stakes with a sheet of black plastic. Move both the stakes and the plastic in around the celery as it is harvested.

Finicky Seed

To safeguard the germination of celery seed planted in spring, pay close attention to the light conditions in your celery bed. When the seed is kept in complete darkness, it won't germinate if the soil temperature is above 50°F. But give celery seed a little light, even diffuse light (by covering it with clear plastic or a very thin layer of organic material instead of soil) and the seeds will germinate in soil that's as warm as 70°F.

VARIETY	DAYS	DESCRIPTION	SOURCES (p. 385)
CELERY (GREEN)			
CUTTING LEAF CELERY	80	Dwarf-size celery; strong taste; recommended for drying. Use to flavor soups and stews.	SEE WILL
EA SPECIAL STRAIN	80	Tall Utah type with upright, glossy, bright green stalks more than a foot long; good disease resistance, slow to bolt.	BOU
FENLANDER	105	An autumn variety with stringless, pale green stalks.	THO
FLORIDA 683	120–125	22–24-inch-tall plant; 10½-inch stalks; excellent heart formation; resistant to mosaic.	STO WIL
FORDHOOK GIANT	120	Short, stocky, dark green plant.	SEE
FRENCH CELERY DINANT (Chinese Celery)	55	Resistant to light frost, this plant sends out a multitude of narrow stalks that can be dried.	NIC SEED
GIANT PASCAL (Winter King)	134–140	Tall, stringless, thick stalks that keep well.	COM PON SEE SEED

VARIETY	DAYS	DESCRIPTION	SOURCES (p. 385)
CELERY (GREEN) *(continued)*			
GREEN GIANT (hybrid)	95	Medium-tall plant with many upright leaves; resistant to blight.	DEG
HERCULES	85	Tall Utah type with huge, crisp, dark green stalks.	TER
MATADOR	105	Dark green, midsize plant; tolerant to yellows; Plant Variety Patented (PVP).	STO
PICADOR	100	Must be planted in fusarium-infected soil (grows too tall on regular land); yellows-tolerant.	STO
STARLET (OP)	120	Tall Utah type with tolerance to fusarium wilt; slow to bolt; 25–27-inch-tall plant.	TWI
SUMMER PASCAL (Tall Fordhook)	115–125	26–28 inches tall with extrathick stalks; resistant to blight.	MEY
SUMMIT	100	10-inch-long, dark green, medium ribbed stalks; fusarium-tolerant.	ORN STO
TALL GREEN LIGHT	100	21-inch plant with 10-inch, medium green stalks; freedom from chlorosis (a disease marked by yellowing or blanching).	DEG
TALL UTAH	90–125	Compact, medium green, 23-inch plant with large heart, long stalks.	ROS SEED
TALL UTAH 52–70 R	52–70	Resistance to mosaic and boron deficiency.	DEG
TALL UTAH 52–70 R IMPROVED	52–70	Compact, 24-inch-tall plant with dark green, 11–12-inch stalks; tolerates boron deficiency.	BURP BURR PAR TIL TWI
UTAH (Salt Lake, Utah Early Green)	100–125	Stocky plant with a full heart and thick stalks.	FAR FIS SEE
UTAH 52–70 HK	98	Dark green, uniform, compact plant; less pithy than other Utah strains.	STO
VENTURA	80–100	Tall Utah type grows to 13–28 inches with 13-inch stalks. Variety has some tolerance to yellows.	JOH STO

CELERY (GOLDEN)

VARIETY	DAYS	DESCRIPTION	SOURCES
GOLDEN PLUME (Wonderful)	85–118	Self-blanching and stringless.	STO
GOLDEN SELF-BLANCHING (American, Fall Dwarf Strain)	80–118	Compact, delicate plant.	ALL BOU BUT DEG FAR JUN LIB MEY NIC PIN PON ROS SEE SEED TER VER WILL
GOLDEN SELF-BLANCHING	110–120	This 20–30-inch plant is highly resistant to disease.	RED
LATHOM BLANCHING-GALAXY	120	Self-blanching; stays stringless longer than most; stands ready to harvest a long time.	THO

VARIETY	DAYS	DESCRIPTION	SOURCES (p. 385)
CELERY (PINK/RED)			
GIANT PINK	120	Stalks are pink to red (redder in winter).	ORN
PINK CELERY	120	This English variety blanches easily and quickly. The color remains after cooking.	GLE SEE
RED CELERY	120	English heirloom variety; bright red.	GLE SEE SEED
CELERY (WHITE)			
SOLID WHITE	120	Solid, crisp stalks with fine flavor.	BOU
CELERY (ORIENTAL)			
CHINESE GOLDEN MEDIUM EARLY	90	Light green leaves with long, hollow stalks; fragrant aroma.	SUN
CHINESE KAN-TSAI	60	Long, slender, dark green stems with strong flavor; easy to grow.	ABU HIG
CRISPY SPEARS	45	Chinese origin; 18-inch stalks; easy to grow.	PAR
HEUNG KUNN (Chinese Celery)	90	Aromatic and delicious; can be grown indoors; grows best in cool, moist soil.	THE
KINTSAI ORIENTAL WILD (Kintsai Soup Celery)	40–50	Slender stalks have strong, sharp flavor and are widely used in Asian cooking.	GLE

CHARD

BOTANICAL NAME: *Beta vulgaris cicla*

DAYS TO MATURITY: 50–60.

PLANTING TIME: Sow seeds two to three weeks before the last frost. If your area's winter temperatures don't fall below 25°F, sow seeds in fall for a winter crop.

SOIL: Any well-drained garden soil; pH 6.0–7.5.

NUTRIENTS: Feed every four to six weeks with fish emulsion.

WATER: Never let chard wilt. Mulch helps keep the soil moist and cool.

LIGHT: Sun to partial shade.

SPACING: Sow seeds 1 inch deep; thin to 8 inches apart. For row planting, space rows 18–24 inches apart.

HARVEST: Use as needed when the outer leaves are 6–10 inches tall. Cut leaves near the base of the plant with a sharp knife.

STORAGE: Use chard fresh.

CHARD

Chard Growing Tip

Rejuvenating Chard

To rejuvenate chard, cut off the leaves an inch or two above the crowns. The whole plant will take on new life in a few weeks and produce an abundance of fresh, tender shoots and leaves.

VARIETY	DAYS	DESCRIPTION	SOURCES (p. 385)
CHARD (DARK GREEN, CRUMPLED)			
ARGENTATA	55	This Italian heirloom variety has silvery white midribs and deep green, broad, savoyed leaves. Plants will endure a wide variety of weather conditions.	SHE
DARK GREEN WHITE RIBBED (Large White Ribbed, Silver Ribbed)	55–60	Broad, white-ribbed, crumpled, dark green leaves.	FAR JLH LED
DORAT	60	Danish variety with wide, white stalks and pale, yellow-green, savoyed leaves.	ORN TER
FORDHOOK	58	Dark green, savoyed leaves.	BUT PIN
FORDHOOK GIANT (Dark Green Lucullus, Burpee's Fordhook Giant)	50–60	Snow white midribs and heavily crumpled leaves; yields until frost.	ABU ALL BURP COM FIS GAR HIG JOH MEY ORN PON RED ROS SEE STO TER TWI VER WIL
FRENCH GREEN	60	Thick, white stalks and crumpled leaves; some resistance to heat and cold.	ABU
LARGE WHITE RIBBED	60	Smooth, dark green leaves with silvery white, fleshy, broad stems.	BURR DEG
PAROS	55	French variety with dark green, crinkled leaves; won't bolt in hot weather.	SHE
SILVERADO	55	Dwarfed, upright, slim, white stalks with dark green, savoyed leaves; refined Lucullus type.	STO
WHITE KING	55	Upright plant with celerylike, thick, white stalks and dark green, savoyed leaves.	STO
CHARD (RED)			
CHARLOTTE	55–65	Bright scarlet.	COO
RAINBOW	60	Red, orange, purple, yellow, and white stems.	BOU
RHUBARB CHARD (Ruby Red)	55–60	Crimson stalks with heavily crumpled, green leaves.	ABU ALL BURP BURR COM DEG FAR FIS GAR JOH LED NIC ORG ORN PIN SEE SEED SHE STO TER TIL TWI VER WILL
VULCAN	60	Bright red stems with dark green, savoyed leaves.	PAR

VARIETY	DAYS	DESCRIPTION	SOURCES (p. 385)

CHARD (DARK GREEN, SMOOTH LEAVES)

VARIETY	DAYS	DESCRIPTION	SOURCES
ERBETTE	55–65	Smooth greens that make a great cut-and-come-again plant.	COO
FRENCH SWISS CHARD	60	18-inch-tall plant with thick, white stalks and large, smooth leaves.	NIC
GENEVA SWISS CHARD	60	Large ribs; can withstand severe weather and will grow year-round.	PAR
GREEN	60	Smooth, green leaves and small stalks; also called a spinach beet.	WILL
JAPANESE SWISS CHARD (Nihon)	60	With thick, light green stalks, this chard resembles smooth, round-leaved spinach.	SUN
LARGE SMOOTH WHITE RIBBED	60	Broad, white ribs; very productive.	SEE TWI
MONSTRUOSO	60	Very productive Italian strain with broad, white stalks.	COO
PERPETUAL (Perpetual Spinach)	50	Very little midrib. New leaves are produced until fall. This productive plant resists heat, drought, and frost.	COO

CHARD (LIGHT GREEN)

VARIETY	DAYS	DESCRIPTION	SOURCES
GIANT LUCULLUS	50	Yellow-green, crumpled leaves; 24–28-inch-tall plant.	COM
LUCULLUS	50–60	Large, white midribs in crumpled leaves.	ABU ALL FAR GUR HEN JUN LED PAR SEE TIL VER WILL
SAN FRANCISCO WILD	60	Originally from Italy, this chard—light green stems with 9-inch leaves—now grows wild around San Francisco Bay. It's never tough or bitter.	RED

CHICORY

BOTANICAL NAME: *Cichorium intybus*

DAYS TO MATURITY: 55–110.

PLANTING TIME: Sow in early summer.

SOIL: Rich, with well-rotted manure.

NUTRIENTS: If soil is supplied with plenty of manure beforehand, there is no need for additional feeding.

WATER: Keep the bed well watered.

LIGHT: Full sun.

SPACING: Plant ½ inch deep; thin to 9–10 inches apart.

CHICORY

HARVEST: During the summer, use the outer leaves in salads as needed. In autumn, remove the soil down to the point where the heart joins the roots. Cut the heart off with a sharp knife, or pull the plant up and trim the heart afterwards. The roots of some varieties should not be lifted and stored, while other varieties may be stored in boxes.

STORAGE: Store the roots in boxes of moist sand. These roots can be forced for a second season of chicory.

VARIETY	DAYS	DESCRIPTION	SOURCES (p. 385)
CHICORY (RADICCHIO, SEMI-HEADING AND HEADING)			
ADRIA	75	This Italian chicory's crimson heads mature to 5½ inches across and weigh 9 ounces. Veins are white.	STO TWI
ALTO	60	Heavy, relatively uniform variety with improved heat tolerance; for spring, summer, and fall.	JOH
AUGUSTO	70	Deep burgundy head; frost-tolerant variety of Italian chicory.	HIG JOH
CARMEN	75	Improved Chioggia type; 5½-inch-wide, 9-ounce, crimson head with white veins.	STO
CASTELFRANCO	85	This Italian heirloom variety has marbled red and white coloring. Heads do not need cutting back to produce well.	COO
CESARE	90–110	Non-forcing radicchio; red and white heads; green outer leaves.	LED
CRYSTAL HAT	70	Long, oval heads resemble romaine lettuce. This non-forcing variety withstands heat and frost.	NIC
EARLY TREVISO	80	If heads don't form by Labor Day, cut it back to 1 inch above the crown when cool weather begins.	COO
GIULIO (Guilio)	60–100	Full-size, deep burgundy heads with white veins; does best in mild climates.	COO HIG JOH NIC ORN SHE
LIVRETTE	90	Similar to Guilio; for fall planting.	ORN
MADGEBURG (Coffee Chicory, Large Rooted, Cicoria Sicliana)	55–100	Plant grows to 15 inches; roots are 14–16 inches. This chicory can be ground into coffee substitute.	COM RED SEE STO TIL WILL
MEDUSA (hybrid)	65	Medium-size, dark red, round heads; for all cropping periods.	JOH
MILAN (Milanse)	90	Traditional Italian radicchio; 8-ounce, round, burgundy-red head.	LED
MITADO	90	Sow this German forcing variety in May, lift roots in late autumn.	NIC

VARIETY	DAYS	DESCRIPTION	SOURCES (p. 385)

CHICORY (RADICCHIO, SEMI-HEADING AND HEADING) *(continued)*

VARIETY	DAYS	DESCRIPTION	SOURCES (p. 385)
NERONE DE TREVISO (hybrid)	90	Italian non-forcing variety; grow through summer, harvest in cool fall weather; red-edged leaves with creamy white bases.	SHE
PAIN DE SUCRE (Sugar Loaf, Sugarlof)	90	18–20-inch, upright, green plant with a twisted head; mildest of all chicories; easy to grow.	BOU
PALLA ROSSA	90	This heirloom variety is for fall planting. Non-forcing radicchio has dark green exterior leaves, red interior, and pure white ribs.	ORN
PAN DI ZUCCHERO (Poncho)	89	Italian variety with a tight, oblong, yellow-green head.	SHE
RADICHETTA (Asparagus, Dentarella, Catalonga, Ciccoria)	52–75	Italian variety; toothed, curled, and green; 1½–3-inch-wide stalks.	COM COO LED NIC SEE STO VER
RED BELGIUM	90	French Witloof type bears slender, finished heads.	GOU
RED "C"	80	Witloof type for fall harvest; delightfully pungent, broad leaves.	DEG
RED TREVISO (Rossa Di Treviso)	85	Italian heirloom variety; 8x3–4-inch head; forcing type.	COO GAR GLE HIG NIC ORN RED SEE SHE
ROSSA DI CHIOGGIA	80	White with red speckles after blanching.	ORN
ROSSA DI VERONA	85	Dark red Italian heirloom variety; slightly bitter.	ABU BOU VER
ROSSANA RADICCHIO (hybrid)	90	Well-defined, softball-size, dark crimson head; dark wine leaves with pearly white midribs; very heat-resistant.	SHE
ROUGE DE VERONE (Verona Red, Italian Greens)	85–95	Heirloom variety; forcing type; recommended for northern gardens.	BURP COM COO DEG GLE GOU HIG JLH NIC ORN SEE
RUBICO	90	This Italian Chioggia type has round, red and white heads. Sow seeds directly into the garden soil after mid-July.	WILL
SAN PASQUALE (All Seasons, Italian Dandelion)	70	Similar to Radichetta; small and tender; light green, finely cut leaves.	LIB MEY TWI
TRILOF	90	Uniform, 6-inch head; forcing type.	WILL
TURBO (hybrid)	110	Biennial; 6-inch, uniform head.	GOU HIG STO
WITLOOF CHICORY (French Endive, Large Brussels, Belgium Endive)	70–140	Forcing variety with solid, 4–6-inch-long heads.	COM HIG LED PIN RED SEE WILL
WITLOOF IMPROVED	110	5–6-inch head; broad leaf stalks.	STO
WITLOOF ROBIN	60–150	Pale pink after forcing.	COO
WITLOOF ZOOM (hybrid)	110	French forcing variety.	COO WILL

VARIETY	DAYS	DESCRIPTION	SOURCES (p. 385)

CHICORY (ENDIVE, NOT CURLED—ESCAROLE)

VARIETY	DAYS	DESCRIPTION	SOURCES (p. 385)
BATAVIAN FULL HEARTED (Deep Heart, Escarole, Florida Deep Heart, Wivol)	85–90	Slightly crumpled, dark green leaves with a 12-inch spread; white rib and tender heart.	BOU GAR LED PIN STO TIL TWI
BROAD LEAVED BATAVIAN	90	Large, broad, slightly twisted leaves with a 16-inch spread; full heart.	ALL BURP FIS MEY WILL
BROADLEAVED FULL-HEART WINTER	95	The extralarge head needs to be tied for a tender, yellow heart.	WILL
CORNET D'ANJOU	80	This heading escarole is a variety from Anjou, France. Its shape resembles the mouth of a horn.	COO
CORNET DE BORDEAUX (Little Horn of Bordeaux)	90	Lobed leaves are not deeply cut. Plant grows upright, with white ribs.	RED
GROSSE BOUCLEE (Bouchlee)	70	Large variety with a tight, long, self-blanching heart; resistant to bolting.	DEG GOU HIG PIN WIL
SINCO	83	French variety; dark green, broad, slightly crinkled leaves; closely bunched, well-blanched heart.	SHE

CHICORY (ENDIVE, CURLED—FRISEE)

VARIETY	DAYS	DESCRIPTION	SOURCES (p. 385)
FINE CURLED	50	Can be used as a cut-and-come-again salad leaf or left to head up.	COO
FRISAN	98	17-inch head; full, blanched center; tolerant to low temperatures.	STO
GALIA	45–60	Small head size makes it suitable for small gardens.	COO DEG
GREEN CURLED (Green Fringed Oyster, Green Curled Ruffec)	90	16–18-inch-wide, finely cut, green, curled leaves.	ALL BOU BURP JUN LED NIC RED SEE STO TWI WILL
LORCA	60	Large, thick heads; very curly.	DEG
NEOS	45	Extrafrilly, deep-hearted, and self-blanching; mildly bittersweet; slow to bottom rot.	JOH
NINA	42	The gray-green leaves are deeply cut and chewy. Forms a mass of tender, white leaves at the heart.	JOH
NUVOL	55	Large head of wavy, dark green, broad leaves; self-blanching, creamy yellow to white heart; slow to bolt.	JOH
PRESIDENT (Giant Green Curled)	80	Large endive with a dense, full heart; withstands adverse weather in the fall.	SEE
SALAD KING	46–100	Deep green, frilly, toothed leaves with a 22–24-inch spread; slow to bolt and not harmed by frost.	BURR HIG JOH MEY STO

VARIETY	DAYS	DESCRIPTION	SOURCES (p. 385)

CHICORY (ENDIVE, CURLED—FRISEE) (continued)

VARIETY	DAYS	DESCRIPTION	SOURCES
TRAVIATA	42	Distinct endive from France; deep, self-blanching head of especially curly leaves.	JOH
TRES FINE MARAICHERE	48	French variety; green, frilly outer leaves with crunchy, white ribs.	GOU HIG SHE

CHICORY (CUTTING CHICORY)

VARIETY	DAYS	DESCRIPTION	SOURCES
BIONDISSIMA TRIESTE	40	Harvest when the leaves are 4–6 inches high.	COO
CERIOLO (Grumulo)	120	Low-growing, rosette-type, spring chicory; 2–3 inches across head.	COO NIC
PUNTARELLA	120	This spring salad plant with twisted, succulent stems will overwinter in all but the coldest areas.	COO
SPADONA (Lingua di Cane, Dog's Tongue)	40	These smooth leaves are for cutting. Harvest at 4–6 inches tall.	COO

COLLARDS

BOTANICAL NAME: *Brassica oleracea acephala*

DAYS TO MATURITY: 45–80.

PLANTING TIME: Where winter frost is expected, sow seeds in early spring as soon as the soil can be worked. Where winter temperatures rarely drop below 25°F, sow seeds anytime from late summer to early fall.

SOIL: Medium light, well-drained; pH 6.0–7.5.

NUTRIENTS: Feed collards every three to four weeks with fish emulsion or use 1 tablespoon blood meal mixed in 1 gallon of water.

WATER: Collard roots lie close to the surface of the soil. Keep them moist.

LIGHT: Full sun.

SPACING: Sow seeds ½ inch deep; thin to 3 feet apart. If you want rows, space them 3 feet apart.

HARVEST: When you're picking the leaves, do not disturb the central bud.

STORAGE: Use fresh.

COLLARDS

VARIETY	DAYS	DESCRIPTION	SOURCES (p. 385)
COLLARDS			
BLUE MAX (hybrid)	68	Large, blue-green, crinkled leaves; fast grower.	ORN POR TWI
CHAMPION	60–80	Large, dark green leaves; plant has a 34-inch spread; widely adapted.	JOH MEY ORN STO TER TWI
FLASH (hybrid)	78	Broad, flat, blue-green leaves; slow to bolt.	LIB STO
GEORGIA (Georgia Green, Georgia Blue, Creole, Southern)	70–80	Non-heading; blue-green crumpled leaves with white veins; 1880 heirloom variety; 2–3-foot spread.	BOU BUT COM DEG FIS GAR LED LEJ MEY NIC PAR POR ROS SEE SOU TWI WIL
GREEN BLAZE	79	Non-heading and slow bolting; bright green, smooth leaves; 30–34-inch spread; pre-1860 heirloom variety; best grown in warm coastal climates.	SOU
HICROP (hybrid)	75–80	Slightly savoyed leaves; 15-inch spread; heavy yielding; slow to bolt.	PAR
MORRIS CAROLINA HEADING	80	Low-growing; smooth leaf; 1½–2-foot spread.	MEY
MORRIS HEADING	85	Wavy green, savoy-style leaves; 30–40-inch spread; slow to bolt.	POR SOU
MORRIS HEADING IMPROVED	85	Slightly savoy-style, dark green leaves; compact heads on short stems.	SEE
SOUTHERN SHORT STEM (North Carolina Short Stem)	80	2-foot spread; will thrive under conditions that are usually unfavorable to cabbage.	SEE
TOP BUNCH (hybrid)	67	Blue-green leaves; high quality.	TWI
VATES (Vates Non-heading)	55–80	Smooth leaf; plant has a 1½–2-foot spread; will endure light frost.	ABU BURR COM DEG HEN LED LIB MEY SEE SOU STO TIL TWI WIL WILL

CORN

BOTANICAL NAME: *Zea mays*

DAYS TO MATURITY: 58–110.

PLANTING TIME: The germination temperature for corn is 50–59°F. Sow in late spring.

SOIL: Sandy, somewhat fertile; pH 6.0–7.0.

NUTRIENTS: Feed the plants at least twice during the growing season with fish emulsion. Corn needs some nitrogen fertilizer only during its early growth.

WATER: Water the plants whenever they show any signs of wilting, and keep them moist when the tassels appear because that means the ears are forming.

LIGHT: Full sun.

SPACING: Sow seeds 2 inches deep; thin to 10–14 inches apart. For row planting, sow in rows 30–36 inches apart. Be sure to plant in blocks since corn is pollinated by the wind. Never plant super sweet varieties next to regular corn.

HARVEST: Never leave the ears on too long before harvesting. To pick, pull each ear down and twist it free.

STORAGE: Corn is definitely best when it has just been picked. Some varieties can be frozen, canned, or pickled.

Corn Growing Tips

Baby Corn

If your mouth waters for those 3-inch ears of corn used in Chinese cooking, don't bother to plant special varieties. Just place the corn seed close together (6 inches or so), then harvest the tiny ears when the silks start to emerge from the husks; at this point the cobs will have barely developed but perfect kernels.

Peak Flavor

To pick corn at the peak of its flavor, try this test. Pop a kernel 2 inches from the top of an ear with your fingernail. If the fluid is watery, wait a few more days; if the fluid is milky, pick the corn immediately. If the fluid is gummy or starchy, you've waited too long.

Plant in Blocks

Corn doesn't produce well in single rows. The reason? Corn is wind pollinated, and pollen must reach the silks of each kernel to fill out the ear. Knowledgeable gardeners with space for only one or two rows solve this problem by shaking the tassels over the silks of each plant. On windless days, an occasional shake of each plant will ensure almost 100 percent pollination.

Container Corn

Sometimes the only way gardeners with limited space can obtain garden-fresh corn is to grow it in containers. The secret? Start corn seeds in a small pot, moving to progressively larger pots but keeping the plants slightly root-bound. Start seedlings in 6-inch pots. Move the plants into the next larger container as soon as the roots start to crowd (when the white roots poke out of the holes again, it's time to move on). Finally, plant in 5-, 10-, and 15-gallon plastic containers. To keep the plants growing steadily, water twice a day and fertilize often. When the tassels mature, encourage the ears' development by hand pollinating. Run the tassels through your hand to strip them of pollen, then pour this fine dust over the silks at the end of each ear.

Sunflower Solution

If cornstalk borers are a problem, try planting giant sunflowers on an outside row. The sunflowers will be infested, but the corn will be left almost worm-free.

Bird Barrage

When birds raid your corn patch to devour the kernels at the ear tips, stop them by slipping a paper bag over each ear. Hold the bags in place with string or rubber bands.

Sweet Corn Varieties

The following definitions of the types of sweet corn listed in seed catalogs will help you choose what's best for your needs.

Homozygous "shrunken" 2 gene type (sh_2). Full homozygous (100 percent of the kernels are super sweet), with two to three times the sugars of normal sugary types at peak harvest. Kernels are characterized by high sugar content, low water-soluble polysaccharides, and crisp texture. Conversion of the sugars to starch is much slower than for normal sugary types, allowing longer storage. Isolation is required.

Homozygous sugary enhancer gene type (se). Full homozygous (100 percent of the kernels are sugary enhanced). Each tasty kernel has a higher sugar content than normal surgary types, but comparable levels of starch contribute to its creamy texture and corn flavor. Kernels also have very tender pericarps. Best used within two days of picking. Isolation is suggested but not required.

Heterozygous "shrunken" 2 gene type. Several sweet corn varieties have some super sweet parentage, so approximately 25 percent of the kernels on each ear have the extra-high sugars of sh_2. Use immediately after picking because the sugar converts to starch rapidly. Isolation is suggested but not required.

Heterozygous sugary enhancer gene type. Many so-called "se" types fall into this category, with approximately 25 percent of the kernels on each ear being sugary enhanced. This gene provides about 15 percent more sugars at peak harvest than normal sugary types. Use immediately after picking because the sugar converts to starch rapidly. Isolation is suggested but not required.

Normal sugary gene type (su). This type produces sweet, creamy kernels with tender skin and is best used immediately after picking; conversion of sugar to starch is rapid. Isolation is not required.

Isolation

Just as gardeners isolate white corn from yellow corn, they should isolate super sweet (**sh₂**) types to prevent cross-pollination with normal sugary sweet corn or field corn. Do this in one of three ways: by maturity (10 days to two weeks), by distance (100–150 feet upwind), or barrier planting.

VARIETY	DAYS	DESCRIPTION	SOURCES (p. 385)
CORN (YELLOW, STANDARD—NORMAL "SU" GENE) EARLY SEASON			
ASHWORTH (OP)	69	5-foot stalk, 6-inch ears, 12 rows of bright yellow kernels; widely adapted.	JOH SOU
AZTEC (hybrid)	69	6½-foot stalk, 7½-inch ears, 14–16 rows of deep golden kernels.	STO
BUTTERVEE (hybrid)	58–73	8–12-inch ears, 12–14 rows of butter yellow kernels.	GAR STO
DEBUT (hybrid)	71–73	7-foot stalk, 8-inch ears, 16–18 rows of yellow kernels; vigorous seedlings in early spring.	JUN WIL
EARLIKING (hybrid)	63–66	5½-foot stalk, 8-inch ears, 12 rows of yellow kernels; excellent variety for short season areas.	HEN JUN TWI
EARLIVEE (hybrid)	63–69	5-foot stalk, 7-inch ears, 12–14 rows of bright yellow kernels.	FAR GAR JOH LIB PIN STO TIL
EARLIVEE II	57	This variety, with 7½-inch ears, tolerates weather stress well. Ears grow at acute angles, which discourages bird damage.	STO
EARLY SUNGLOW (hybrid) (American Early Yellow)	63	4½-foot stalk, 7-inch ears, 12 rows of yellow kernels; young vigor in cold weather; tolerant to bacterial wilt.	BURP BURR FAR FIS GUR HEN MEY NIC PAR POR SHE SOU TIL VER WIL
EXTRA EARLY GOLDEN BANTAM	69–80	5-foot stalk, 5–6-inch ears; can be planted close together without affecting ear size.	ALL GAR HIG WILL
FISHER'S EARLIEST (OP)	60	5–6-inch ears, 10–12 rows of golden yellow kernels; good cool climate variety.	FIS
GOLDEN BEAUTY (hybrid)	58–73	5½–6-foot stalk, 7–8-inch ears, golden kernels; good short season variety; All-American winner.	BURR FAR FIS GUR HEN
MONTANA BANTAM	65	6–7-inch ears, 8 rows of yellow kernels; short season variety.	FIS
NORGOLD	75	7¾-inch ears, 16 rows of yellow kernels; vigorous in cold soil.	STO
NORSWEET	69	7¾-inch ears, 16 rows of yellow kernels.	STO
NORTHERN SWEET (hybrid)	65–68	8-inch ears, 12–14 rows of yellow kernels.	FAR
NORTHERNVEE (hybrid)	62	7¾-inch ears, 12–14 rows of yellow kernels; excellent early vigor in cold soils.	STO

VARIETY	DAYS	DESCRIPTION	SOURCES (p. 385)

CORN (YELLOW, STANDARD—NORMAL "SU" GENE) EARLY SEASON (continued)

VARIETY	DAYS	DESCRIPTION	SOURCES (p. 385)
POLARVEE (hybrid)	52–55	3½-foot stalk, 6–8-inch ears, 12–14 rows of yellow kernels; resistant to cold; short season variety.	GAR GUR HEN STO
SENECA 60	64	Exceptional quality.	ALL
SENECA ARROW (hybrid)	72	The 7-inch ears with yellow kernels hold for a long time on plants.	COO
SENECA HORIZON	65–75	8-inch ears, 14–18 rows of yellow kernels; vigorous in cool soils.	ALL BURR LIB MEY STO TWI WIL WILL
SENECA STAR	67	8-inch ears, 14–16 rows of yellow kernels; resistant to cold and drought.	ALL LIB STO TWI WIL
SPARTAN (hybrid)	71–75	5½-foot stalk, 8-inch ears, 14–16 rows of yellow kernels; tolerant of cold soil.	GAR STO
SPRINGDANCE	70	7¾-inch ears, 16 rows of yellow kernels; vigorous in cold soil.	STO
SPRING GOLD	67	7-inch ears, 12–16 rows of small, tight, yellow kernels.	ABU
SUNNYVEE (hybrid)	64	7-inch ears, 12 rows of yellow kernels; excellent short season variety.	STO WILL

CORN (YELLOW, STANDARD—NORMAL "SU" GENE) MIDSEASON

VARIETY	DAYS	DESCRIPTION	SOURCES (p. 385)
BONANZA	72–83	6½-foot stalk, 9-inch ears, 16–18 rows of yellow kernels.	WIL
CALUMET (hybrid)	82	The 7-foot stalk grows long, slender ears with 12–14 rows of yellow kernels. Variety is resistant to earworms.	POR WIL
EARLIGLOW	75	8-inch ear, yellow kernels.	WILL
GOLDEN BANTAM (OP)	78–83	6½-foot stalk, 7-inch ears, 8 rows of yellow kernels; 1902 heirloom variety; pick ears promptly.	ABU ALL BOU BURR BUT GAR GUR HEN JOH LED ORG SEE SOU WIL
GOLDEN BANTAM IMPROVED (OP)	84	6-inch ears, 10–14 rows of yellow kernels, 2 ears per stalk.	ABU NIC
GOLDEN CROSS BANTAM (hybrid) (Golden Cross)	80–90	7-foot stalk, 8-inch ears, 10–14 rows of yellow kernels; resistant to bacterial wilt.	BURP FAR GUR PON POR ROS VER WIL
IOCHIEF (hybrid)	86–93	2 10-inch ears per 6½-foot stalk, 14–18 rows of yellow kernels; drought resistant.	BURR FAR GUR HEN LIB VER
JUBILEE (hybrid) (Golden Jubilee)	81–85	5½-foot stalk, 8½-inch ears, 16–20 rows of deep, narrow, yellow kernels; good variety for cool climates.	ALL COM NIC STO TER TIL TWI VER WIL WILL
MERIT (hybrid)	84	8½-foot stalk, 9-inch ears, 20 rows of yellow kernels.	PAR POR WIL

VARIETY	DAYS	DESCRIPTION	SOURCES (p. 385)

CORN (YELLOW, STANDARD—NORMAL "SU" GENE) MIDSEASON (continued)

VARIETY	DAYS	DESCRIPTION	SOURCES (p. 385)
NK 199 (hybrid) (Elephant Ear)	84	8-foot stalk, 8-inch ears, 14–20 rows of yellow kernels; grows well everywhere.	BURR GUR HEN JUN LIB MEY ORN TWI
SENECA CHIEF (hybrid)	86	6½-foot stalk, 8½-inch ears, yellow kernels; highly resistant to bacterial wilt.	ALL BURR PAR STO WILL
SENECA HORIZON (hybrid)	75–78	5½-foot stalk, 10-inch ears, 16–18 rows of yellow kernels; short season variety with rapid seedling growth.	GAR JUN MEY TER TWI WIL WILL
SPIRIT (hybrid)	72–75	Full-size ears with yellow kernels; excellent tolerance to cold soil.	GAR
SWEET TENNESSEE	85	8–9-foot stalk, 7¼-inch ears with yellow kernels.	ROS
TRUE GOLD	80	6–7-foot stalk, 8½-inch ears with golden yellow kernels.	SEED

CORN (YELLOW, STANDARD—NORMAL "SU" GENE) LATE SEASON

VARIETY	DAYS	DESCRIPTION	SOURCES (p. 385)
FLAVORVEE	86	8½-inch ears, 14–18 rows of yellow kernels.	STO
GOLDEN QUEEN (hybrid)	88	9-foot stalk, 8–9-inch ears, 14–16 rows of yellow kernels; tolerant to leaf blight.	LED MEY PAR TWI WIL
REWARD (hybrid)	95	Many stalks produce 2 9-inch ears with 16–20 rows of yellow kernels. Variety has good tolerance to cold soil.	TER
STYLEPAK (hybrid)	93	8-inch ears, 18–20 rows of yellow kernels.	STO

CORN (WHITE, STANDARD—NORMAL "SU" GENE) EARLY SEASON

VARIETY	DAYS	DESCRIPTION	SOURCES (p. 385)
ART VERRELS (OP)	70	7-inch ears with white kernels; heirloom variety from southwest Oregon.	GAR
CASPER II	57	6¾-inch ears, 12 rows of white kernels.	STO
CORONATION	72	7-foot stalk, white kernels; tolerates cool weather for early planting.	LIB
GLACIER	65	White kernels; short season variety.	FIS
PLATINUM LADY (hybrid)	75–85	2 8-inch ears per 7-foot stalk, 14–16 rows of white kernels; drought resistant.	BURP BURR COM GAR GUR MEY NIC ORN PIN STO TIL TWI VER
SPRING CRYSTAL (hybrid)	66	7½-inch ears, 12–14 rows of tender kernels.	MEY PIN STO
STAR DUST	66–70	7½-inch ears, 14–16 rows of white kernels; cold tolerant.	PAR

VARIETY	DAYS	DESCRIPTION	SOURCES (p. 385)

CORN (WHITE, STANDARD—NORMAL "SU" GENE) EARLY SEASON (continued)

VARIETY	DAYS	DESCRIPTION	SOURCES (p. 385)
WHITE SUNGLOW (hybrid)	68	6-foot stalk, 6½-inch ears, 12–14 rows of snow white kernels; short season variety.	BURP MEY

CORN (WHITE, STANDARD—NORMAL "SU" GENE) MIDSEASON

VARIETY	DAYS	DESCRIPTION	SOURCES (p. 385)
ALPINE (hybrid)	79	6½-foot stalk, 8½-inch ears, 16 rows of creamy white kernels.	MEY TWI
ASPEN	82	8-foot stalk, 9-inch ears, white kernels.	LED
LUTHER HILL	82	3–4-foot stalk, 6-inch ears, white kernels; heirloom variety.	SEED
MIDNIGHT SNACK	84	This heirloom variety has 5½-foot stalks that grow 7½-inch ears with 14–16 rows. Creamy white when they're ready to eat, kernels are blue-black at full maturity.	GAR
PRISTI	80	8–10-inch ears, 12–14 rows of bright white kernels; strong yields.	HEN TWI
SIX SHOOTER	80	10 rows of white kernels; as many as 6 ears per plant.	GUR HEN
STARSHINE (hybrid)	83	7-foot stalk, 8-inch ears with white kernels.	COO
TRUCKER'S FAVORITE (OP)	78	9-inch ears with 16 rows of white kernels; hardy variety.	FAR ROS SEE WIL
TRUE PLATINUM	78–84	5–7-foot stalk, 8–9-inch ears, 10–14 rows of white kernels; tolerant to blight, rust, and drought.	SEED
WHITE SUPER SWEET (hybrid)	82	8-foot stalk, 9-inch ears, 16–18 rows of white kernels.	ALL

CORN (WHITE, STANDARD—NORMAL "SU" GENE) LATE SEASON

VARIETY	DAYS	DESCRIPTION	SOURCES (p. 385)
AUNT MARY'S	105	6-foot stalk, large ear with 8–10 rows of white kernels; heirloom variety.	SOU
COUNTRY GENTLEMAN (OP) (Shoepeg)	73–100	This 1891 heirloom variety has a 7½-foot stalk with 9-inch ears of white, tightly packed kernels. Dry grains are thin and narrow.	ABU BOU BUT HEN RED SEE SOU
HICKORY KING	85–100	This 12-foot stalk produces 9-inch ears with large, flat, white kernels. Not a sweet corn, use it for drying, flour, and hominy grits. There are 2 ears per stalk. This pre-1900 heirloom variety has some tolerance to blights.	HEN SEE SOU

VARIETY	DAYS	DESCRIPTION	SOURCES (p. 385)

CORN (WHITE, STANDARD—NORMAL "SU" GENE)
LATE SEASON *(continued)*

VARIETY	DAYS	DESCRIPTION	SOURCES (p. 385)
SILVER QUEEN (hybrid)	94	This variety—with 8-foot stalks, 9-inch ears, and 14–16 rows of snowy white kernels—germinates slowly in cool soil. It has some drought resistance and is tolerant to leaf blights as well as Stewart's wilt.	ALL BURP COM DEG FAR GOU GUR HEN JOH JUN LED LIB MEY PAR PON POR ROS SHE STO SOU TWI VER WIL
STOWELL'S EVER-GREEN (hybrid)	90–100	10-foot stalk, 9-inch ears, 14–18 rows of white kernels; 1846 heirloom variety.	GUR HEN RED SEE SOU

CORN (BICOLORED, STANDARD—NORMAL "SU" GENE)
EARLY SEASON

VARIETY	DAYS	DESCRIPTION	SOURCES (p. 385)
DOUBLE STANDARD (OP)	73	This short season variety has 7-inch ears with 12–14 rows. If you plant only white kernels, you will have an all-white corn.	JOH
EARLIEST BI-COLOR	65	6–7-inch ears, 12 rows of golden yellow and white kernels.	FIS
GOLD AND SILVER	62	8½-inch ears, 12–14 rows of yellow and white kernels.	STO
METIS HORIZON (hybrid)	65	8-inch ears, 18–20 rows of yellow and white kernels; no special disease tolerance.	STO
PEACHES AND CREAM EXTRA EARLY (hybrid)	62	4½-foot stalk, 7-inch ears with yellow and white kernels; cold-resistant for early planting.	SHE VER WILL
SWEET G–90 (hybrid)	75	2 medium to large ears per stalk; yellow and white kernels.	POR

CORN (BICOLORED, STANDARD—NORMAL "SU" GENE)
MIDSEASON

VARIETY	DAYS	DESCRIPTION	SOURCES (p. 385)
BUTTER AND SUGAR (hybrid)	73	6-foot stalk, 8-inch ears, 12–14 rows of yellow and white kernels.	ALL COM DEG FAR JUN
CALYPSO	82	8½-inch ears, 18 rows of deep, narrow, yellow and white kernels.	COM TWI
HONEY AND CREAM (hybrid)	78	7½-inch ears, 12–14 rows of tightly packed, yellow and white kernels.	ALL BURP GUR LIB PIN PON WIL
TRIPLE PLAY	70–80	6-foot stalk, tricolored white, yellow, and blue; does best in cool soil.	SEED

VARIETY	DAYS	DESCRIPTION	SOURCES (p. 385)

CORN (BICOLORED, STANDARD—NORMAL "SU" GENE) LATE SEASON

VARIETY	DAYS	DESCRIPTION	SOURCES
BI-QUEEN	92	9-foot stalk, 8½-inch ears, 14–16 rows of yellow and white kernels; disease tolerant.	LED TWI

CORN (YELLOW, SUGARY ENHANCED—"SE, SE+" GENE) EARLY SEASON

VARIETY	DAYS	DESCRIPTION	SOURCES
ADVANTAGE	64	5–5½-foot stalk, 7½–8-inch ears, 12–14 rows of yellow kernels.	LIB
BODACIOUS	75	6½-foot stalk, 8-inch ears, 16 rows of yellow kernels; holds well after harvest.	BURR COM GUR HEN LIB NIC PAR STO TER TIL VER WIL
BREEDER'S CHOICE (hybrid)	73	7-foot stalk, 8-inch ears, 16–18 rows of yellow kernels; vigorous seedlings.	BURP
CANDY MOUNTAIN (OP)	68	Midsize ears with golden yellow kernels.	FIS
CHAMP (hybrid)	64	7½-inch ears with yellow kernels; highly recommended for short season areas; moderately resistant to rust and common smut.	THO
CHIEF OURAY	70	5½-foot stalk, 8½-inch ears, 16–20 rows of yellow kernels.	LIB
CUSTER (hybrid)	56	7½-inch ears, 14–16 rows of light golden yellow kernels.	STO
EARLY XTRA-SWEET	71–85	6-foot stalk, 9-inch ears, 12–16 rows of yellow kernels; isolate from other corn; All-American winner.	BURP FAR GOU GUR HEN PON VER WILL
EXPRESS	66	The 7½-inch ears have 14–16 rows of yellow kernels. Variety does well in cool soils. Seedlings have outstanding vigor.	FAR LED
EXTRA EARLY SUPER SWEET (hybrid)	67	10–12-inch ears, 12–14 rows of bright yellow kernels; isolate from other corn; good cold tolerance.	STO
GRANT (hybrid)	53	7¾-inch ears, 12–14 rows of yellow kernels.	STO
KING ARTHUR (hybrid)	66	9-inch ears, 16–18 rows of golden kernels.	STO
LYRIC (hybrid)	57	7-inch ears, 14 rows of yellow kernels; good vigor in cold soil.	STO
MAPLE SWEET	63–70	7½-inch ears with 14–16 rows of yellow kernels.	GAR LIB STO
PATTON (hybrid)	60	7¾-inch ears with 14–16 rows of light gold kernels.	STO
PRECOCIOUS (hybrid)	56	6¾-inch ears with 12–14 rows of yellow kernels.	STO TER
SPECTRUM	70	6–6½-foot stalk, 7½–8½-inch ears, yellow kernels; not resistant to rust.	LIB
SUGAR BUNS	65–72	6-foot stalk, 8-inch ears, 14–16 rows of yellow kernels; no need to isolate.	COM FAR JOH LIB TER TIL WIL

VARIETY	DAYS	DESCRIPTION	SOURCES (p. 385)

CORN (YELLOW, SUGARY ENHANCED—"SE, SE+" GENE) EARLY SEASON *(continued)*

VARIETY	DAYS	DESCRIPTION	SOURCES
SUMMER FLAVOR BRAND VARIETY 62 Y (hybrid)	62	6-foot stalk, 7½-inch ears, 16 rows of yellow kernels.	TWI
SUMMER FLAVOR BRAND VARIETY 64 Y (hybrid)	64	5-foot stalk, 6½–7-inch ears, 14 rows of yellow kernels; tolerant to Stewart's wilt.	TWI
SUMMER FLAVOR BRAND VARIETY 72 Y (hybrid)	72	5½-foot stalk, 7½-inch ears, 16 rows of yellow kernels.	TWI
SUMMER FLAVOR BRAND VARIETY 73 Y (hybrid)	73	6-foot stalk, 8-inch ears, 18–20 rows of yellow kernels.	TWI
TUXEDO (hybrid)	67–74	7½-inch ears, 16 rows of yellow kernels; good choice for drier soils and areas with disease problems.	JOH LIB STO

CORN (YELLOW, SUGARY ENHANCED—"SE, SE+" GENE) MIDSEASON

VARIETY	DAYS	DESCRIPTION	SOURCES
DOUBLE DELICIOUS (hybrid)	83	9-inch ears with yellow kernels; good seed germination.	GUR
FLAVOR KING (hybrid)	85	8½-inch ears with 16 rows of golden kernels.	STO
FLAVOR QUEEN (hybrid)	84	8-inch ears with 16 rows of yellow kernels; some tolerance to Stewart's wilt and rust.	STO
HONEYCOMB (hybrid)	79	6-foot stalk, 8-inch ears, 16–18 rows of yellow kernels.	BURR
ILLINICHIEF XTRA SWEET (hybrid)	85	Each stalk develops 2 medium to large ears. Plant after the ground is thoroughly warm.	POR
INCREDIBLE	80–85	7½-foot stalk, 9½-inch ears, 18 rows of yellow kernels.	GUR HEN LIB
KANDY TREAT (hybrid)	84	9½-inch ears with 14–16 rows of yellow kernels; no need to isolate.	BURR
MERLIN	80–84	10-inch ears with 20–22 rows of yellow kernels.	LIB STO
MIRACLE (hybrid)	78–100	6½-foot stalk, 9½-inch ears, 20–22 rows of yellow kernels; does not need isolation; usually 2 ears per stalk.	BURP BURR COM FAR GOU GUR HIG LIB NIC STO TER WILL
SUGAR LOAF	83	6-foot stalk, 8-inch ears with yellow kernels; rust-resistant and tolerant to maize dwarf mosaic virus and northern leaf blight.	LIB WIL

VARIETY	DAYS	DESCRIPTION	SOURCES (p. 385)
CORN (YELLOW, SUGARY ENHANCED—"SE, SE+" GENE) LATE SEASON			
CRISP 'N SWEET 720 (hybrid)	87	9½-inch ears with 20 rows of yellow kernels; resistance to northern leaf blight and tolerance to races of Stewart's wilt.	WIL
KANDY KORN (hybrid)	89	8½-foot stalk, 8-inch ears, 16–18 rows of yellow kernels; no required isolation.	BURP BURR DEG FAR FIS GAR GUR HEN JUN LIB MEY ORN PON POR STO TIL TWI VER WIL WILL
CORN (WHITE, SUGARY ENHANCED—"SE, SE+" GENE) EARLY SEASON			
CORONATION (hybrid)	75	8½-inch ears with 16 rows of white kernels; 90-inch plant.	VER
COTTON CANDY (hybrid)	72	7½-inch ears with 16–18 rows of white kernels.	GUR HEN VER
GUINEVERE (hybrid)	56	7¾-inch ears with 14–16 rows of white kernels.	STO
ILLUMINATION (90–37–SE70W)	68	6–6½-foot stalk, 7–7½-inch ears, white kernels; some disease tolerance.	LIB
SENECA SUNSHINE (hybrid)	71	5½–6-foot stalk, 8–8½-inch ears, 14–16 rows of white kernels.	BURP LIB TER TWI
SENECA WHITE KNIGHT (hybrid)	74	8–8½-inch ears, 14–16 rows of white kernels; partially tolerant to Stewart's wilt.	GUR JUN TWI
SNOW SWEET (hybrid)	68	7½-inch ears with 14–16 rows of white kernels; some disease tolerance.	STO
SUGAR SNOW (hybrid)	68	8-inch ears with 12–14 rows of white kernels.	LIB STO TER
SUMMER FLAVOR BRAND VARIETY 73 W (hybrid)	73	5½–6-foot stalk, 7½-inch ears, 14–16 rows of white kernels.	TWI
SWEET SILVER	74	6–6½-foot stalk, 8-inch ears, 14–16 rows of white kernels; good vigor and sprouting ability in cool soils.	LIB
WHITE 1745	71	7½-inch ears with 14 rows of white kernels.	LED
CORN (WHITE, SUGARY ENHANCED—"SE, SE+" GENE) MIDSEASON			
ALPINE	76	6½–7-foot stalk, 8-inch ears, 16 rows of white kernels; good vigor in the soil; rust-tolerant.	FAR JOH LED LIB MEY TWI
ARGENT	82	6-foot stalk, 8½-inch ears, 16 rows of white kernels.	LIB TWI
DIVINITY	75	5½–6-foot stalk, 9-inch ears, 16 rows of white kernels; fair tolerance to Stewart's wilt and good tolerance to drought.	LIB STO

VARIETY	DAYS	DESCRIPTION	SOURCES (p. 385)

CORN (WHITE, SUGARY ENHANCED—"SE, SE+" GENE) MIDSEASON (continued)

VARIETY	DAYS	DESCRIPTION	SOURCES
PRISTINE	79	7½-inch ears, 16 rows of white kernels; superior germination in cool soil.	GUR JOH
SUMMER FLAVOR BRAND VARIETY 72 W (hybrid)	76	6-foot stalk, 7½-inch ears, 14–16 rows of white kernels.	TWI
SUMMER FLAVOR BRAND VARIETY 78 W (hybrid)	78	6-foot stalk, 7½–8-inch ears, 16 rows of white kernels.	TWI
SUMMER FLAVOR BRAND VARIETY 81 W (hybrid)	81	8-foot stalk, 8½-inch ears, 16 rows of white kernels; tolerance to Stewart's wilt.	TWI
SWEET ELITE 181	83	7½-inch ears with 14–16 rows of white kernels; average cool-soil tolerance.	JOH

CORN (WHITE, SUGARY ENHANCED—"SE, SE+" GENE) LATE SEASON

VARIETY	DAYS	DESCRIPTION	SOURCES
SNOW QUEEN (hybrid)	87	7–8-foot stalk, 10-inch ears, 16–20 rows of white kernels; no need for isolation.	FAR

CORN (BICOLORED, SUGARY ENHANCED—"SE, SE+" GENE) EARLY SEASON

VARIETY	DAYS	DESCRIPTION	SOURCES
ALADDIN (hybrid)	56	7¾-inch ears with 14 rows of yellow and white kernels; bicolored version of Custer.	STO
AMBROSIA (hybrid)	75	8-inch ears, 16 rows of yellow and white kernels; bicolored Bodacious.	STO VER
ATHOS (hybrid)	67	7¾-inch ears with yellow and white kernels; tolerance to Stewart's wilt and rust.	STO
BREEDER'S BICOLOR (hybrid)	73	6-foot stalk, 8-inch ears, 16–18 rows of yellow and white kernels.	BURP
CLASSIC TOUCH	61–66	8-inch ears, 12–14 rows of yellow and white kernels.	COM STO
D'ARTAGNAN	66	5–5½-foot stalk, 7½–8-inch ears, 14–16 rows of yellow and white kernels.	GAR LIB TER
DOUBLE GEM (hybrid)	75	The 7½-inch ears have 16–18 rows of yellow and white kernels. Seeds germinate in cool soil.	JOH
DUET (hybrid)	74	6-foot stalk, 8–9-inch ears, 12–14 rows of yellow and white kernels.	JOH
GEMINI (hybrid)	68	9-inch ears with 16 rows of yellow and white kernels; some tolerance to rust, Stewart's wilt, and birds.	STO

VARIETY	DAYS	DESCRIPTION	SOURCES (p. 385)

CORN (BICOLORED, SUGARY ENHANCED—"SE, SE+" GENE)
EARLY SEASON (continued)

VARIETY	DAYS	DESCRIPTION	SOURCES (p. 385)
GERONIMO (hybrid)	63	1 ear per stalk; 8½-inch ears with 16–18 rows of yellow and white kernels; bicolored King Arthur.	STO
GOLD 'N PEARLS	68	7½-inch ears, 12 rows of yellow and white kernels; not resistant to Stewart's wilt.	TIL VER
IVANHOE (hybrid)	66	8¾-inch ears with 16–18 rows of yellow and white kernels.	STO
JESTER (hybrid)	60	7½-inch ears with 14 rows of yellow and white kernels; bicolored Patton.	STO
KISS AND TELL (hybrid)	64	7½-inch ears with 16 rows of yellow and white kernels; bicolored Sugar Buns.	STO
NATIVE GEM (hybrid)	58	8-inch ears with 14 rows of yellow and white kernels; bicolored Patton.	STO
QUICKIE (hybrid)	65	5-foot stalk, 7-inch ears, 14 rows of yellow and white kernels; recommended for all cooler bicolored corn areas.	COM GAR GUR JOH LIB
SENECA BRAVE (hybrid)	72	8-inch ears with 18–20 rows of yellow and white kernels.	TWI
SENECA DAWN (hybrid)	69	7–7½-inch ears, 14–16 rows of yellow and white kernels.	LIB TER TWI
SPEEDY SWEET (hybrid)	57	7½-inch ears with 12–14 rows of yellow and white kernels; bicolored Maple Sweet.	STO
SUGAR AND GOLD	55–67	7-foot stalk, 8½-inch ears, 16–18 rows of yellow and white kernels.	COM FAR GUR
TRI SWEET (hybrid)	65	8-inch ears with 16 rows of yellow and white kernels.	STO

CORN (BICOLORED, SUGARY ENHANCED—"SE, SE+" GENE)
MIDSEASON

VARIETY	DAYS	DESCRIPTION	SOURCES (p. 385)
BURGUNDY DELIGHT (hybrid)	73–84	9-foot stalk, 8-inch ears, 12–14 rows of yellow and white kernels.	JOH ORN PIN STO
CLOCKWORK (hybrid)	78	6–7-foot stalk, 8-inch ears, 16 rows of yellow and white kernels; good emergence in cold soil.	JOH
COMSTOCK'S PRIDE AND JOY (hybrid)	76	Large ear with yellow and white kernels.	COM
DOUBLE DELIGHT	77–85	7½-foot stalk, 8-inch ears, 16–18 rows of yellow and white kernels; no isolation required.	COM HEN
DOUBLE TREAT (hybrid)	84	9-inch ears, 20 rows of yellow and white kernels; no disease tolerance.	STO
LANCELOT (hybrid)	80	Yellow and white kernels; good tolerance to Stewart's wilt and rust.	STO

VARIETY	DAYS	DESCRIPTION	SOURCES (p. 385)

CORN (BICOLORED, SUGARY ENHANCED—"SE, SE+" GENE) MIDSEASON (continued)

VARIETY	DAYS	DESCRIPTION	SOURCES
PEACHES AND CREAM	78	6½-foot stalk, 8-inch ears, 8 rows of yellow and white kernels; cold-resistant for early planting.	SHE WILL
SIR GALAHAD (hybrid)	85	8½-inch ears with 18 rows of yellow and white kernels; bicolored Flavorvee.	STO
SUMMER FLAVOR BRAND VARIETY 76 (hybrid)	76	5-foot stalk, 7-inch ears, 14 rows of yellow and white kernels; tolerance to Stewart's wilt.	TWI
SUMMER FLAVOR BRAND VARIETY 77 (hybrid)	77	6-foot stalk, 7½-inch ears, 14–16 rows of yellow and white kernels.	TWI
SUMMER FLAVOR BRAND VARIETY 79 (hybrid)	79	6½-foot stalk, 8-inch ears, 16–20 rows of yellow and white kernels.	TWI

CORN (BICOLORED, SUGARY ENHANCED—"SE, SE+" GENE) LATE SEASON

VARIETY	DAYS	DESCRIPTION	SOURCES
PILOT (hybrid)	90	7-foot stalk, 8–8½-inch ears, 16–18 rows of yellow and white kernels.	JOH

CORN (YELLOW, SUPERSWEET—SH$_2$ "SHRUNKEN" GENE) EARLY SEASON

VARIETY	DAYS	DESCRIPTION	SOURCES
EARLY XTRA-SWEET	71	6-foot stalk, 9-inch ears, 12–16 rows of yellow kernels; isolate; All-American winner.	BURP FAR GOU GUR HEN PON WILL
EXTRA EARLY SUPER SWEET (hybrid)	67	10–12-inch ears with 12–14 rows of yellow kernels; isolate; good tolerance to cold stress.	STO
ILLINICHIEF X-TRA SWEET (hybrid)	75	Each stalk has 2 medium to large ears with yellow kernels. Plant after the ground is thoroughly warm.	POR
NORTHERN XTRA-SWEET (hybrid)	71	5-foot stalk, 8–9-inch ears, yellow kernels; good germination in cool soil; isolate from other corn.	FAR JOH JUN VER WILL
POLAR SUPER SWEET (hybrid)	59	8-inch ears, 12–14 rows of yellow kernels; best cold-soil tolerance in a shrunken type; good yield in shorter season areas; isolate.	STO
SWEET DESIRE (hybrid)	69	8½-inch ears with 14–16 rows of yellow kernels; needs isolation.	STO
SWEET DREAMS (hybrid)	75–77	9-inch ears with 16 rows of yellow kernels; isolate from other corn.	STO
SWEET TREAT	70–80	6-foot stalk, 8-inch ears, 14 rows of dark yellow kernels.	TER

VARIETY	DAYS	DESCRIPTION	SOURCES (p. 385)

CORN (YELLOW, SUPERSWEET—SH_2 "SHRUNKEN" GENE) MIDSEASON

VARIETY	DAYS	DESCRIPTION	SOURCES (p. 385)
CRISP 'N SWEET 711 (hybrid)	85	6½-foot stalk, 9-inch ears, 18 rows of yellow kernels; resistance to northern leaf blight and tolerance to Stewart's wilt; isolate from other corn.	BURR PIN
EXCEL	82	7-foot stalk, 8½-inch ears, 16 rows of yellow corn.	LED
ILLINI GOLD (hybrid)	79–85	5-foot stalk, 8½-inch ears, 16 rows of yellow kernels; widely adapted; good emergence in cool soils.	BURP MEY
ILLINI GOLD EXTRA SWEET	85	6½-foot stalk, 8-inch ears, 14–18 rows of yellow kernels.	BURP DEG FAR GUR HEN JUN MEY VER WIL
SPRINGSWEET SUPER SWEET (hybrid)	82	9-inch ears with 16–18 rows of yellow kernels; needs isolation.	STO
SUMMER SWEET BRAND VARIETY 7210 (hybrid)	78	6-foot stalk, 8-inch ears, 14–16 rows of yellow kernels; multiple-disease tolerance; isolate.	TWI
SUMMER SWEET BRAND VARIETY 7410 (hybrid)	81	6-foot stalk, 7½–8-inch ears, 16–18 rows of yellow kernels; tolerance of northern leaf blight; isolate.	TWI
SUMMER SWEET BRAND VARIETY 7500 (hybrid)	80	5½-foot stalk, 7–7½-inch ears, 16–20 rows of yellow kernels; multiple-disease tolerance.	TWI
SUMMER SWEET BRAND VARIETY 7620 (hybrid)	82	6½-foot stalk, 7¾-inch ears, 14–16 rows of yellow kernels; tolerance to many diseases.	TWI
SUMMER SWEET BRAND VARIETY 7630 (hybrid)	84	6½-foot stalk, 7½–8-inch ears, 16–20 rows of yellow kernels; tolerance to northern leaf blight; isolate from other corn.	TWI
SUMMER SWEET BRAND VARIETY 7710 (hybrid)	83	6½-foot stalk, 7½-inch ears, 20 rows of yellow kernels; multiple-disease tolerance; isolate.	TWI
SUMMER SWEET BRAND VARIETY 7720 (hybrid)	84	6-foot stalk, 8-inch ears, 16–20 rows of yellow kernels; tolerance to northern leaf blight; isolate.	TWI
SUMMER SWEET BRAND VARIETY 7910 IMPROVED (hybrid)	85	6½-foot stalk, 7½-inch ears, 20–22 rows of yellow kernels; tolerance to Stewart's wilt and leaf blight; isolate from other corn.	TWI
SUPERSWEET JUBILEE (hybrid)	82	7–9-foot stalk, 8½–9-inch ears, 18 rows of yellow kernels; widely adapted; needs isolation.	JUN NIC TIL TWI
SWEET DREAMS (hybrid)	77	9-inch ears with 16 rows of yellow kernels; bred for short season areas.	STO
SWEETIE 82 (hybrid)	82	8-inch ears with 16–18 rows of yellow kernels; tolerant to common rust; isolate.	FAR JUN TWI

VARIETY	DAYS	DESCRIPTION	SOURCES (p. 385)
CORN (YELLOW, SUPERSWEET—SH$_2$ "SHRUNKEN" GENE) **LATE SEASON**			
BUNKER HILL (hybrid)	87	9-inch ears with 20 rows of yellow kernels; tolerant to Stewart's wilt, northern leaf blight, and downy mildew; isolate from other corn.	STO
STAY SWEET	87–89	All the qualities of Illini Extra Sweet; good insect resistance; needs isolation.	VER
TENDERTREAT (hybrid)	95	9–10-foot stalk, 9-inch ears, 16–18 rows of yellow kernels; isolate.	TWI
CORN (WHITE, SUPERSWEET—SH$_2$ "SHRUNKEN" GENE) **EARLY SEASON**			
SUMMER SWEET BRAND VARIETY 7301 (hybrid)	73	5¼-foot stalk, 7-inch ears, 14–16 rows of glossy, white kernels; isolate.	TWI
CORN (WHITE, SUPERSWEET—SH$_2$ "SHRUNKEN" GENE) **MIDSEASON**			
BLIZZARD SUPER SWEET (hybrid)	83	8½-inch ears with white kernels; needs isolation.	STO
CORN (WHITE, SUPERSWEET—SH$_2$ "SHRUNKEN" GENE) **LATE SEASON**			
HOW SWEET IT IS	87	7-foot stalk, 8-inch ears, 16 rows of white kernels; All-American winner; isolate.	GUR HEN JUN LED MEY NIC ORN PAR PIN POR TIL TWI VER WIL
PEGASUS (hybrid)	90	7-foot stalk, 8-inch ears, 16–18 rows of white kernels; good seedling vigor; isolate.	MEY TWI
CORN (BICOLORED, SUPERSWEET—SH$_2$ "SHRUNKEN" GENE) **EARLY SEASON**			
BSS4011 (hybrid)	69	8-inch ears with yellow and white kernels; isolate from other corn.	LED
IVORY AND GOLD (hybrid)	75	6-foot stalk, 9-inch ears, 16 rows of yellow and white kernels; needs isolation.	STO VER
MEDLEY (hybrid)	68	Yellow and white kernels; resistance to Stewart's wilt; isolate.	LED
MILK N' HONEY II (hybrid)	71	8½-inch ears with 14–16 rows of yellow and white kernels; isolate.	STO
SKYLINE (hybrid)	73	6-foot stalk, 8-inch ears, 14 rows of yellow and white kernels; good ability to germinate in cool soil; isolate.	JOH

VARIETY	DAYS	DESCRIPTION	SOURCES (p. 385)

CORN (BICOLORED, SUPERSWEET—SH$_2$ "SHRUNKEN" GENE) EARLY SEASON (continued)

VARIETY	DAYS	DESCRIPTION	SOURCES
SWEET HEART (hybrid)	65	8-inch ears with yellow and white kernels; for cooler soils and shorter season areas; requires isolation.	STO

CORN (BICOLORED, SUPERSWEET—SH$_2$ "SHRUNKEN" GENE) MIDSEASON

VARIETY	DAYS	DESCRIPTION	SOURCES
ALOHA (hybrid)	82	9-inch ears with 16 rows of yellow and white kernels; isolate from other corn.	STO
DIABOLO (hybrid)	77	6-foot stalk, 8–9-inch ears, 16–18 rows of yellow and white kernels; vigorous in cool soil; isolate.	JOH
DIAMONDS & GOLD (hybrid)	79	8-inch ears with 18 rows of yellow and white kernels; isolate.	LED
HONEY & PEARL	78	7-foot stalk, 9-inch ears, 16–18 rows of yellow and white kernels; All-American winner; needs isolation.	BURP JOH JUN PAR TWI VER
HUDSON (hybrid)	86	The 8-inch ears have 16–20 rows of yellow and white kernels. Variety requires isolation and warm soil to germinate properly.	JOH
PHENOMENAL (hybrid)	85	8½-inch ears with 16 rows of yellow and white kernels; isolate.	STO
RADIANCE (hybrid)	80	8-inch ears with 16–20 rows of yellow and white kernels; suitable for planting in cool soil; isolate.	JOH
STARSTRUCK (hybrid)	78	6-foot stalk, 8–9-inch ears, 14–16 rows of yellow and white kernels; not for windy areas; isolate.	JOH
SUMMER SWEET BRAND VARIETY 7702 (hybrid)	82	6½-foot stalk, 7½-inch ears, 16–18 rows of yellow and white kernels; tolerant to disease; needs isolation.	TWI
SUMMER SWEET BRAND VARIETY 8102 (hybrid)	81	6-foot stalk, 8–8½-inch ears, 16–18 rows of yellow and white kernels; tolerant to disease; isolate.	TWI

CORN (SPACE SAVERS)

VARIETY	DAYS	DESCRIPTION	SOURCES
BABY CORN	65	Harvest within 5 days of silk appearance. Not a sweet corn, it is used for hors d'oeuvres, fries, and pickles.	NIC
GOLDEN MIDGET (OP)	58–65	3-foot stalk, 4-inch ears, 10 rows of yellow kernels.	ABU GAR SEED VER

CORN (POPCORN, WHITE)

VARIETY	DAYS	DESCRIPTION	SOURCES
A265 (hybrid)	108	Hull-less Japanese type with small, white kernels.	WIL

VARIETY	DAYS	DESCRIPTION	SOURCES (p. 385)

CORN (POPCORN, WHITE) *(continued)*

VARIETY	DAYS	DESCRIPTION	SOURCES (p. 385)
BURPEE'S PEPPY (hybrid)	90	The 6-foot stalk has 4-inch ears with deep, pointed, hull-less, white kernels. There are 2–3 ears per stalk. It's a good variety for short season areas.	BURP
JAPANESE WHITE HULL-LESS (hybrid)	83–95	7-foot stalk, 4¾-inch ears with deep, narrow, white kernels.	GUR LED SEE SEED
PENNSYLVANIA BUTTER-FLAVORED	102	8-foot stalk, 4–6-inch ears, 26–28 rows of white kernels; 2 ears per stalk; pre-1885 heirloom variety.	SOU
ROBUST 20–82W (hybrid)	100	Medium-size, white kernels.	COM VER
TOM THUMB (OP) (Dwarf Rice, Hull-less, Squirrel Tooth, Australian Hull-less, Bumble Bee)	85	The 3½-foot stalk has 2 3½-inch ears with long, narrow, pointed, white kernels. Variety matures even in short season areas.	ALL BOU FIS JOH TIL
WHITE CLOUD (hybrid)	110	Short stalk and small, white kernels; hull-less, almost no waste.	BURR DEG LIB PIN PON STO TWI WILL
WHITE HULL-LESS (hybrid)	85–108	6-foot stalk, 5-inch ears with white kernels.	DEG RED
WHITE RICE	110	Standard white variety; 2–3 ears per stalk.	MEY
WHITE SNOW PUFF (hybrid)	90	Completely hull-less; small, white kernels.	VER

CORN (POPCORN, YELLOW)

VARIETY	DAYS	DESCRIPTION	SOURCES (p. 385)
A-222 YELLOW (hybrid)	110	Short, strong stalk; small, tender, hull-less, yellow corn.	WIL
A-332 YELLOW (hybrid)	114	Medium-large kernels; widely adapted.	WIL
GIANT YELLOW (hybrid)	105	Giant yellow variety turns fluffy white when popped.	GUR
IOPOP 12 (hybrid)	98	7-inch, hull-less ears; widely adapted.	LIB
JAPANESE HULL-LESS YELLOW	110	This corn pops fluffy white.	GUR
PURDUE 410 (hybrid)	90–105	Heavy yielder.	BURR DEG PAR TWI
ROBUST (hybrid)	100	Variety does well under adverse conditions.	COM LIB NIC
ROBUST 10–84 (hybrid)	98	For short season areas; requires isolation.	STO
ROBUST 20–70 (hybrid)	98	16 rows of yellow kernels; expands greatly with popping.	JOH TWI
SOUTH AMERICAN YELLOW GIANT	105–115	7-foot stalk, 8-inch ears with butter yellow kernels.	GUR LED MEY SEE

VARIETY	DAYS	DESCRIPTION	SOURCES (p. 385)
CORN (POPCORN, OTHER COLORS)			
BLACK	90	7-inch cobs; Southern variety.	SEED
CALICO	100	Easy-to-grow heirloom variety produces 5–7-foot stalks with 6–8-inch brilliantly colored ears.	HEN SHE TWI
CAROUSEL	104	3–5-inch ears with multicolored kernels; 4–6 ears per stalk.	COM GOU MEY NIC PON TWI VER
CHAPALOTE POPCORN	100	This ancient variety has brown kernels on slender ears and is best suited to low desert areas.	PLA
CHOCOLATE POP	135	5½–6-foot stalk, 6-inch ears, 16–18 rows of brown kernels; 2 ears per stalk; good resistance to drought and earworms.	SOU
CUTIE POPS	100	4-inch ears of multicolored kernels.	STO
MINIATURE INDIAN ORNAMENTAL	100	5-foot stalk, 4-inch ears, red and yellow kernels.	LED MEY PAR PLA SEE STO
MINI BLUE	110–115	2–4-inch, deep blue ears with 12 rows of kernels that pop white.	GUR
PRETTY POPS	95	6-foot stalk, 5-inch ears with multicolored kernels.	PAR
SENECA MINI INDIAN	100	4–6-inch ears with bright red, blue, white, yellow, black, and purple kernels; 2–3 ears per stalk.	JLH
STRAWBERRY ORNA-MENTAL POPCORN (OP)	98–110	4-foot stalk, 2-inch ears with mahogany kernels.	ALL COM COO GOU GUR HEN JLH JOH LED LIB MEY NIC PAR PLA SEE SHE SOU STO TIL TWI VER WIL
WISCONSIN BLACK POPCORN	100	This heirloom variety's 3–5-inch ears are filled with shiny, black, pointed kernels.	ORG
CORN (DRY, FIELD CORN)			
ALAMO-NAVAJO BLUE CORN	90	Large, full ears of dark blue-purple to almost black kernels; drought-tolerant, disease-resistant plant.	PLA
ANASAI	100	6–9-foot, multieared stalk; multicolored, ancient variety.	SEED
APACHE RED	110	6-foot stalk, black to reddish seed; Apache heirloom variety.	SEED
AZTEC RED	160	The 10-foot stalk's ears have 10–12 rows of huge, red kernels.	RED
BLACK AZTEC (Black Mexican, Mexican, Black Iroquois, Black Sweet, Mexican Sweet)	90	6½–7½-foot stalk, 6-inch ears, 8–10 rows of black kernels; pre-1860 heirloom variety.	ABU BOU JLH NIC RED SEED SOU
BLOODY BUTCHER	120	There are 2–6 ears on each 8–10-foot stalk of this 1700s heirloom variety. Red kernels are striped with darker red.	JLH SEE

VARIETY	DAYS	DESCRIPTION	SOURCES (p. 385)

CORN (DRY, FIELD CORN) (continued)

VARIETY	DAYS	DESCRIPTION	SOURCES
BLUE CLAREDGE	108	7-foot stalk, 7–8-inch ears, 14–16 rows of purple and white kernels; heirloom variety.	JLH
BLUE TORTILLA (Blue Corn)	100	This heirloom variety has 4–6-inch ears with dark blue kernels. Plant tolerates drought and resists disease. Kernels turn from white to lavender to deep blue.	GUR HEN PLA
CHEROKEE RED	80–95	Red-brown, flinty corn for flour; good short season variety.	RED
GARLAND FLINT	98	7–8-foot stalk, 7–8-inch ears with bright yellow and deep red kernels; heirloom variety.	JOH
GIANT CORN (Redwood)	100	13–15-foot stalk, superlong ears with pure white kernels.	GUR HEN
HOOKER'S SWEET INDIAN (OP)	75–100	The 4½-foot stalk of this heirloom variety develops 5–7-inch, thin ears. White kernels dry to blue-black when mature.	ABU ORG TER
HOPI BLUE	80–95	4–5-foot stalk, 7–9-inch ears, 12–14 rows of kernels.	JLH ORN RED SEE
HOPI ORANGE RED	96–115	Similar to Hopi Red, but with orange kernels.	RED
HOPI PINK	70	Drought-tolerant, 4–4½-foot plant; 8-inch ears with 12–14 rows of pastel pink kernels.	SEED
HOPI PURPLE	96–115	3–5-foot stalk, 8-inch ears, 10 rows of purple kernels.	RED SEED
HOPI RED	80–95	3–5-foot stalk, 6–8-inch ears, 12–14 rows of kernels; extremely rare variety.	RED SEED
HOPI TALL BLUE	110	8–15-foot stalk, 7–10-inch ears with small, deep blue-purple kernels; ancient variety, adapted to a semiarid climate and sandy soil.	JLH
HOPI TURQUOISE	80–95	3–5-foot stalk, 8-inch ears, 12 rows of dark blue to turquoise kernels.	ORN RED SEED
HOPI WHITE	80–95	3–5-foot stalk, 8-inch ears, 10 rows of soft white kernels.	RED SEED
HOPI YELLOW	89–95	4-foot stalk, 8-inch ears, 10 rows of yellow kernels.	RED
INDIAN FLINT	105	These multicolored kernels are good for cornmeal.	NIC
ISLETA BLUE CORN	120	12-foot stalk, purple-blue kernels with a sprinkling of white and red kernels.	PLA
JICARILLA APACHE WHITE	89–95	4-foot stalk, 6-inch ears, 12 rows of white kernels.	RED
LEAMING'S YELLOW	95	7–8-foot stalk, 8½–10-inch ears, 14–22 rows of deep yellow kernels on red cobs; 1826 heirloom variety.	SOU
MAIZ BLANCO	95	Soft, large, flat, white kernels, good for flour.	JLH

VARIETY	DAYS	DESCRIPTION	SOURCES (p. 385)

CORN (DRY, FIELD CORN) *(continued)*

VARIETY	DAYS	DESCRIPTION	SOURCES
MAIZ MORADO	95	Tall stalk, 8 rows of deep purple-red kernels for flour.	JLH
MAIZ NEGRO	95	Large, flat, black kernels; flour-type corn.	JLH
MANDAN BRIDE	98	7-foot stalk, 6-inch ears, 8–12 rows of multicolored kernels.	GAR JLH JOH ORN
MANDAN RED (Mandan Rednuetta)	89–98	5–6-inch ears, 8–12 rows of rich burgundy kernels with scattered blue kernels; excellent flour corn.	GAR ORN SEED
MC CORMACK'S BLUE GIANT	85–100	10–12-foot stalk, 7–9-inch ears with large, wide, smoky blue kernels; suited for clay soils and drought-prone areas; good tolerance to leaf blights.	SOU
NAVAJO BLUE FLOUR	100	Slender ears with small, dark blue kernels; good for grinding, roasting, hominy, or fresh preparations.	JLH
NAVAJO BLUE MIXED FLOUR	100	Small blue kernels with scattered white and yellow kernels; tolerant to drought; for cornmeal or flour.	JLH
NAVAJO MIXED FLOUR	100	A mix of small, white, blue, and yellow kernels; drought-resistant corn for grinding.	JLH
NAVAJO WHITE FLOUR	100	Slender, white ears with small, soft kernels; for grinding, roasting, hominy, or fresh preparations.	JLH
NAVAJO WHITISH FLOUR	100	Dusky white, small kernels; for flour or cornmeal.	JLH
NAVAJO YELLOW FLOUR	100	These slender ears' small, soft, bright yellow kernels can be ground, roasted, made into hominy, or eaten fresh.	JLH
NORTHSTINE DENT	100	7-foot stalk, 8-inch ears, glossy yellow kernels with white caps; short season dent corn; heirloom variety.	JOH
OAXACAN GREEN	70	Dent corn; 5–6-foot stalk, 6-inch ears with emerald green kernels; Zapotec Indian heirloom variety.	SEED
PAPAGO CORN	80	Slender, small, cream-colored kernels; drought-tolerant corn for cornmeal.	PLA
POSOLE	100	Large, plump ears; drought-tolerant corn for hominy.	JLH PLA
REID'S YELLOW DENT	85–110	7-foot stalk, 9-inch ears with 16 rows of yellow kernels; 1840 heirloom variety; for cornmeal.	POR SOU WIL
ROTTEN CLARAGE	115	9–10-inch ears with 14–18 rows of dark blue, yellow, maroon, and yellow-orange striped kernels; flour corn; 1855 heirloom variety.	SOU
SEIBEL'S RED	100–105	Each 8-foot plant has 1–2 ears of red corn.	SEED
SILVER MINE	85–105	11–12-inch ears with 12–14 rows of white kernels; 1920s heirloom variety; tolerates drought and poor soil.	JLH

VARIETY	DAYS	DESCRIPTION	SOURCES (p. 385)

CORN (DRY, FIELD CORN) *(continued)*

VARIETY	DAYS	DESCRIPTION	SOURCES
TAOS BLUE	80–95	8-foot stalk, 10-inch ears, 14–16 rows of kernels.	RED
TEXAS GOURDSEED	120	This flour corn's 8-foot stalks produce ears with 18–22 rows of cream-colored kernels. It's susceptible to smut but does well in clay soils and withstands drought.	SOU
WHITE HYBRID SG 2325–W (hybrid)	100	Large kernels; good corn for flour, hominy, or roasting.	ROS

CORN (ORNAMENTAL, PARCHING)

VARIETY	DAYS	DESCRIPTION	SOURCES
BLUE SQUAW	95	Large ears with dark blue kernels; flour or ornamental corn.	ROS
CHINOOK	90–95	The 5–7-foot plant produces 5–6-inch ears. Kernel color ranges from dark maroon to tan with an occasional yellow ear.	COO
CUTIE BLUES	100	4-inch ears with dark blue kernels.	STO
FEATHER MIXED	110	5½-inch ears with tan, brown, purple, red, and copper kernels.	STO
FIESTA (hybrid)	102	7-foot stalk, 10-inch ears with a wide range of kernel colors.	HEN JOH STO TWI
INDIAN ORNAMENTAL (Indian Squaw, Calico)	110	Large, decorative ears in an array of color combinations.	ALL BURR COM HEN LED LIB POR SEE STO TWI VER WIL
LITTLE INDIAN	95	2–3-inch ears with multicolored kernels.	BURR GUR
LITTLE JEWELS	95	5–6-foot stalk, 4-inch ears in a wide range of colors.	JOH
MINI BLUE	100	The 4–6-inch ears have blue kernels for popping or decoration.	LIB
MINI PINK	100	The tiny, pink ears are shaded with blue.	LIB
PAPOOSE MINI INDIAN CORN	85	The 4–5-inch ears are brightly colored with variegated kernels. There is more than one ear per stalk.	LIB
PENCIL COB	95	Pencil-size cob with very deep yellow kernels.	JOH SEE WIL
PODCORN	110	Each kernel has its own husk. Husk colors range from red and copper through brown shades.	LIB
RAINBOW	100–112	Full-size ears with richly colored kernels.	GUR NIC PLA ROS TIL
RED STALKER	110	All-red selection of Indian ornamental corn.	COO GUR LIB
SENECA MINI INDIAN CORN	103	3–5-inch ears, dark and light colors.	BURR NIC TIL WIL
WAMPUM ORNAMENTAL	95	6–7-foot stalk, 4–5-inch ears, 16–20 rows of variegated kernels; rainbow shaded tassels.	COO JOH NIC

CORN SALAD

CORN SALAD

BOTANICAL NAME: *Valerianella locusta*

DAYS TO MATURITY: 45–80.

PLANTING TIME: In cooler climates, sowing can begin in midsummer. Elsewhere, sow in late summer.

SOIL: Sandy, well-cultivated.

NUTRIENTS: Feed plants at least once during the growing season with fish emulsion.

WATER: Since this is a hardy annual that grows during the winter, don't worry about water. A light mulching with straw or hay will keep the plants moist and protected from harsh winter weather.

LIGHT: Full sun.

SPACING: Sow seeds ½ inch deep; thin seedlings until they're 6 inches apart. Rows should be 6 inches apart.

HARVEST: Harvest either the entire plant or only the leaves.

STORAGE: Use corn salad fresh.

VARIETY	DAYS	DESCRIPTION	SOURCES (p. 385)
CORN SALAD (MACHE, LAMB'S LETTUCE)			
A GROSSE GRAINES (Large Seeded)	45	Round, smooth, bright green leaves.	GOU ORN RED SEE
BIG SEED (Large Seeded Dutch)	45	Large leaves.	JLH NIC PIN TWI
BLONDE SHELL LEAVES	50	Small plant is extremely hardy.	NIC
COQUILLE DE LOUVIERS (Scallop of Louviers, Coquille)	40–45	Spoon-shaped, shiny, green leaves with minty taste; resistant to cold.	COO GOU
D'ESTAMPES	50	Large, round leaves with mild flavor; cold-tolerant, compact plant.	COO
ELAN	50	Small, smooth leaves with mild flavor; resistant to mildew; good choice for baby mache.	COO
GAYLA MACHE	70–80	This French variety's 4–5-inch, tender, oval leaves grow in upright rosettes. Their flavor is subtle.	SHE
GREEN CAMBRAI	40–45	Large, round, dark green leaves; resistant to cold.	ABU SEE
LARGE ROUND LEAVED	60	Mild flavor.	MEY WILL
MACHE (Corn Salad, Lamb's Lettuce)	45–65	These 3-inch-long, green, spoon-shaped leaves have a nutty flavor and grow best in cool weather.	BOU FIS GAR STO TWI

VARIETY	DAYS	DESCRIPTION	SOURCES (p. 385)
CORN SALAD (MACHE, LAMB'S LETTUCE) *(continued)*			
PIEDMONT	65	Large, long, pale, spoon-shaped leaves with good heat resistance; big seeded type; mild flavor.	COO
VALERIANELLA OLITORIA	45	Broad, thick leaved winter plant.	COM
VALGROS	65	Dutch type with elongated, dark green leaves.	TER
VERTE A COEUR PLEIN	65	Compact variety; superior cold resistance.	ORN
VERTE DE CAMBRAI	50–80	3–4-inch, flat, teardrop-shaped leaves; very cold tolerant; French variety.	DEG GOU HIG NIC ORN PIN STO
VIT	50	Long, glossy, green leaves with minty flavor; mildew-tolerant.	JOH ORN

CUCUMBERS

BOTANICAL NAME: *Cucumis sativus*

DAYS TO MATURITY: 50–75.

PLANTING TIME: Plant seeds directly in the ground after the soil temperature has warmed to 60°F. To get a jump on the growing process, sow seeds indoors in peat pots three weeks before the regular planting season.

SOIL: Sandy to loam, with well-rotted manure or compost mixed in; pH 5.5–7.0.

NUTRIENTS: Fertilize with nitrogen (blood meal) only during the growth period before blooming.

WATER: Water these plants deeply.

LIGHT: Full sun.

SPACING: Sow seeds ½ inch deep; space them 10–12 inches apart for the trailing variety.

HARVEST: Cut cucumbers from the vine when they are dark green.

STORAGE: Use fresh or for pickles.

Cucumber Growing Tips

Bitter Cucumber Cure

To salvage bitter cucumbers for eating, first remove the stem end. Peel off the skin and the thin layer of flesh just beneath the skin where the bitterness is concentrated. The remainder of the cucumber will taste just fine.

CUCUMBERS

Compost Ring

For cucumber salads all summer long, try planting a few cucumbers in a "compost ring." Bend a section of wire into a cylinder 4 feet wide and 10 feet long, and fasten the wire together. Locate the ring where it will receive full sun and fill with leaves, grass clippings, wood chips, sawdust, and other organic matter, alternating these materials with a few shovelfuls of soil and a handful of blood meal. Mound the earth into two small hills opposite each other just outside the ring, and plant 2–4 seeds in each hill. As the plants come up, remove all but the two healthiest ones from each hill. Train these plants to climb the wire. Add grass clippings and other plant waste to the ring during the growing season.

Pickle Pole

Organize your garden space by building a pickle pole from a 6 foot, 6x6-inch pole or an 8x8-inch post with foot-long, ½-inch dowels stair-stepped around the sides of the post 18 inches apart. Plant eight cucumber vines spaced 6 inches apart around the post. Pickle poles produce all the cucumbers you can eat while taking up little space (Figure 9-1).

Hanging Baskets

Amaze your friends with hanging baskets of acrobatic dwarf cucumbers. Line wire baskets with moss to hold planter mix. Fill each container with 2–3 gallons of lightweight mix and two or three plants. Cut out all but one of the plants with a pair of scissors. When the plants have grown to be about a foot long, pinch off the growing tip. This will encourage your cucumbers to grow out, over the edge, and down.

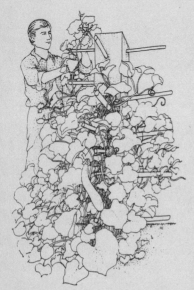

figure 9-1

VARIETY	DAYS	DESCRIPTION	SOURCES (p. 385)
CUCUMBERS (EXTRALONG) **OPEN POLLINATED (OP), GYNOECIOUS (GYN)**			
ARMENIAN YARD LONG (Serpent Cucumber, The Duke)	65–75	3-foot-long, gray-green cucumber with unique fluting.	ABU BURR DEG GOU NIC PLA POR RED ROS SEE TER
CHINA LONG GREEN (Japanese Climbing)	75	20–24 inches, light green with black spines.	COM FAR
CHINESE SNAKE	75	Dark green, smooth, long, and curved.	SEE
EARLY PERFECTION (hybrid)	62	Burpless. This 15–18-inch, slender, straight, Japanese variety has no bitterness and doesn't need to be peeled. Fruit sets on almost every node.	SHE
ENGLISH TELEGRAPH (OP)	66	18-inch, straight, dark green, nonbitter European variety.	STO

VARIETY	DAYS	DESCRIPTION	SOURCES (p. 385)

CUCUMBERS (EXTRALONG) (continued)

VARIETY	DAYS	DESCRIPTION	SOURCES (p. 385)
EUROAMERICAN (hybrid)	60	Indoor/outdoor type; 10 inches long, slightly tapered, thin skin; tolerant to disease.	GAR
HOLLAND (hybrid)	60	12–15 inches, dark green with slight ribbing; no need to peel; self-pollinating; no bitterness.	SHE
KYOTO	60	19 inches to 3 feet long, light green.	GLE SEE SUN THO
ORIENT EXPRESS (hybrid) (gyn)	64	Burpless. 12–14 inches long, 1½ inches thick, dark green.	BURP COO FAR JUN STO
PALACE KING (hybrid)	62	This Oriental type is more than 1 foot long, 2 inches in diameter, with thin skin. It's tolerant to powdery mildew.	BURP
SUYO LONG (Soo-Yoh)	61	12–15 inches, dark green with white spines; burpless; tolerant to powdery mildew.	GAR JOH RED SEE SEED SOU SUN
YAMOTO EXTRA LONG	65–75	24 inches long, straight with dark green, smooth skin.	NIC

CUCUMBERS (SLICING, LONG)

VARIETY	DAYS	DESCRIPTION	SOURCES (p. 385)
GREEN KNIGHT (hybrid)	48	9–11 inches long with smooth skin; no bitterness; small seed cavity.	FAR
LONG GREEN	70	10 inches, dark green; poor appearance but good flavor.	ALL
LONG GREEN IMPROVED (OP)	60–70	14 inches long, 2 inches thick, dark green with black spines.	DEG RED
SOOYOW (Suyo Long)	61	12–15 inches long, dark green, ribbed, and high spined.	ALL
STREAMLINER (hybrid) (gyn)	60	10½ inches long, medium green; small seed cavity; resistant to mosaic and mildew.	BURP
SUYO CROSS (hybrid)	62	11-inch-long Japanese variety; highly tolerant to powdery mildew, downy mildew, and cucumber mosaic virus.	NIC
SWEET SALAD (hybrid)	60	12–14-inch, slender, straight cucumber; tolerant to mosaic virus.	POR
SWEET SUCCESS (hybrid) (gyn)	54–58	14-inch, thin, smooth-skinned cucumber with no bitterness; disease-resistant All-American winner.	BURP DEG GUR HEN LED NIC PAR PIN TIL TWI VER

CUCUMBERS (SLICING, MEDIUM)

VARIETY	DAYS	DESCRIPTION	SOURCES (p. 385)
AMIRA (hybrid)	55–62	3–6-inch-long, thin-skinned cucumber; tolerant to downy mildew, mosaic, and powdery mildew.	BURR COO FAR LED NIC PIN TER WILL
ASHLEY (OP)	66	8 inches long, 2¼ inches thick, dark green with white spines; resistant to downy mildew; recommended for hot, humid areas.	JUN LED SOU WIL

VARIETY	DAYS	DESCRIPTION	SOURCES (p. 385)

CUCUMBERS (SLICING, MEDIUM) *(continued)*

VARIETY	DAYS	DESCRIPTION	SOURCES (p. 385)
BURPEE HYBRID II (gyn)	55	8½x2½ inches, straight; medium seed cavity; resistant to downy mildew and mosaic.	BURP
DANIMAS (hybrid) (gyn)	58	7–8 inches long, dark green, almost seedless.	THO
DASHER (hybrid)	58	8-inch, straight, slim, dark green cucumber with white spines.	MEY
DASHER II (hybrid) (gyn)	55–60	8½x2¼-inch, slim, dark green cucumber; resistance to anthracnose, angular leaf spot, downy and powdery mildews, scab, and mosaic.	LIB POR STO TWI WIL
EARLY PRIDE (hybrid) (gyn)	55	8½x2-inch, straight, dark green cucumber; resistance to mosaic and mildew.	BURP
EARLY TRIUMPH	56–62	8 inches, straight, dark green; disease-resistant.	JUN PIN TWI
GENERAL LEE (hybrid) (gyn)	55	7½–8 inches, dark green with white spines; tolerant to mosaic, downy and powdery mildews, and scab.	STO
HARVESTMORE	63	8–9-inch, straight, medium green cucumber; disease-resistant plant.	GUR
HYBRID 1811	63	9x2½ inches, very dark green, smooth and straight; monoecious, disease-tolerant plant.	TWI
KIDMA (hybrid)	68	5–8-inch, smooth, glossy, medium green cucumber; Beit Alpha type.	SHE
LONG GREEN WHITE SPINE	60	8–9-inch, smooth, dark green, straight cucumber.	DEG
MARKETER (OP) (Early Green Market)	60–68	10x2¼-inch, dark green cucumber with white spines.	COM FAR LED LEJ WILL
MARKETMORE	76	8 inches long, dark green; resistant to scab and downy and powdery mildews.	DEG PON SEED TIL
MARKETMORE 76 (OP)	58–68•	8 inches long, glossy, dark green with white spines; resistant to disease.	ABU BURR COM DEG FAR GAR GUR HEN LIB MEY ROS STO TER TWI VER WIL WILL
MARKETMORE 80 (OP)	60	8–9 inches, dark green; no bitter taste; resistant to disease.	LED LIB SOU STO
MARKETMORE 86 (OP)	62	Disease-tolerant semibush yields 9-inch, dark green, bitter-free cucumbers. Also burpless.	FAR HIG JOH JUN PAR STO
MAXIMORE BRAND HYBRID BLEND 103	58	8½–9x2¼ inches; blended gynoecious hybrid and hybrid monoecious pollenizer; widely adapted; tolerant to disease.	TWI
MAXIMORE BRAND HYBRID BLEND 104	58	9x2¼ inches; very similar to Maximore 103.	TWI
MIDEAST PROLIFIC	70–85	Nonbitter; 3–5-foot vine; heavy bearer; widely adapted.	SEED

VARIETY	DAYS	DESCRIPTION	SOURCES (p. 385)

CUCUMBERS (SLICING, MEDIUM) *(continued)*

VARIETY	DAYS	DESCRIPTION	SOURCES (p. 385)
OLYMPIAN (hybrid) (gyn)	59	7½x1¾-inch, dark green cucumber; disease-resistant plant.	GUR WIL
POINSETT	65	8 inches; resistant to mosaic and powdery mildew.	POR
POINSETT 76 (OP)	67	7–8-inch, straight, glossy, deep green cucumber with white spines; multiple disease resistance.	BURR DEG MEY ORN ROS SOU TWI WIL
REVENUE (hybrid) (gyn)	48	Dark green cucumbers are 6¾–7 inches long. Plant has multiple disease tolerance. Fruit sets under cool conditions.	STO
SARIA BEIT ALPHA	56	Dark green cucumber with small seed cavity; Middle Eastern type; tolerant to scab and powdery and downy mildews.	GOU
SENECA COMET	60	Bitter-free, long, dark green, straight cucumber; disease-tolerant plant.	LIB
SENECA TRAILBLAZER (hybrid)	62	8–9-inch, glossy, dark green cucumber; monoecious, disease-tolerant plant.	LIB STO
SLICE KING (hybrid)	49	This disease-tolerant variety produces its 8½-inch, dark green, slim cucumbers well during cool weather. It's a good bitter-free type for short season areas.	STO
SLICEMASTER (hybrid) (gyn)	55	Slim, dark green cucumber; resistant to disease.	BURR COM GUR LED MEY PIN POR VER WIL
SLICEMASTER SELECT (hybrid) (gyn)	61	Improved Slicemaster; tolerant to disease.	TER TWI
SLICE NICE (hybrid) (gyn)	62–70	8½x2½ inches, dark green; resistant to disease.	BURR TWI
SPEEDWAY (hybrid) (gyn)	56	8 inches long, dark green, straight; tolerant to disease.	STO TWI
STOKES EARLY HYBRID	55	9 inches, dark green; monoecious, disease-tolerant plant.	STO
STRAIGHT 8 (OP)	60–67	8-inch, white spined cucumber with small seed cavity; All-American winner.	ABU ALL BURP COM DEG FAR FIS GUR HEN MEY POR SEE VER WIL WILL
STRAIGHT 9	65	9x1½ inches, dark green; resistant to downy and powdery mildews.	BOU PIN PON WIL
SUPERSETT (hybrid)	53	8½x2¼ inches, smooth, tapered; resistant to disease.	ALL JOH STO TWI
SURE CROP (hybrid)	85	8½x2½ inches, dark green, straight; All-American winner.	DEG
SWEET ALPHEE (hybrid)	55	Extra-dark-green Beit Alpha type; no bitterness; mostly female but requires no added pollinator; tolerant to disease.	JOH

VARIETY	DAYS	DESCRIPTION	SOURCES (p. 385)
CUCUMBERS (SLICING, MEDIUM) *(continued)*			
SWEET CRUNCH (hybrid)	57	6 inches, glossy green, smooth; Beit Alpha type; mostly female.	GAR
TIMUN HIJAN (Tempatan Jenis)	60	4–6x1–2 inches, thin skin.	RED
TRIUMPH (hybrid)	62	8 inches long; resistant to mosaic and downy mildew; All-American winner.	FAR
TURBO (hybrid)	65	7½ inches, dark green, straight; gynoecious with a monoecious pollinator; disease-tolerant.	LIB STO TWI
ULTRA-SLICE EARLY (hybrid)	56	8½x2⅜ inches, smooth, dark green; good results during stressful weather conditions; disease-resistant.	STO
VAL-U-MORE BRAND HYBRID VARIETY 110	60	8x1⅝ inches, dark green, straight; disease-tolerant.	TWI
WHITE SPINE IMPROVED	62	9x2½ inches, deep green.	ALL
WINDERMOOR WONDER	60	Heirloom variety.	SEE

CUCUMBERS (SLICING, SPACE SAVERS/BUSH)

VARIETY	DAYS	DESCRIPTION	SOURCES
BOUNTIFUL BUSH	70–80	10x2-inch fruit.	SEED
BURPLESS BUSH	42	12-inch-long, dark green, spineless cucumber; dwarf plant.	COM LIB
BUSH CHAMPION	55	11-inch-long, straight, bright green cucumber; short, compact vines.	BURP PON THO
BUSH CROP (hybrid)	55	8-inch-long cucumber; dwarf bush.	GUR JUN MEY PIN VER
FANFARE (hybrid)	52	8–9-inch-long, smooth, green cucumber; disease-tolerant All-American winner.	GUR LIB POR STO TWI VER WILL
PATIO PIC (hybrid) (Patio Pik)	50–55	6½-inch, straight, blocky cucumber; resistant to scab and downy and powdery mildews.	GLE
POT LUCK (hybrid)	50–55	7 inches, straight, green with white spines; resistant to mosaic.	COM DEG MEY ORN WIL
SALAD BUSH (hybrid)	57	8-inch-long cucumber; compact, disease-tolerant plant; All-American winner.	BURP COM DEG HEN JUN LED LIB NIC PAR PIN POR SHE TIL TWI VER WILL
SPACEMASTER	60	7½–8-inch, slender cucumber; 18–24-inch bush; widely adapted and resistant to disease.	ALL COM DEG FIS GAR GUR LIB ORN PIN PLA POR SEE SOU VER WILL

VARIETY	DAYS	DESCRIPTION	SOURCES (p. 385)
CUCUMBERS (PICKLING)			
ANKA PICKLING (hybrid)	50	Small, bright green, smooth; no bitterness; resistant to disease.	NIC
ARMADA (hybrid) (gyn)	50	Medium-long, dark green with white spine; resistant to disease.	ORN
BEIT ALPHA MR	56	6 inches, straight, medium green with black spines; resistant to mosaic.	BOU
BOSTON PICKLING	52–58	6 inches, rich green.	ABU ALL COM SEE TIL
BURPEE PICKLER	53	Medium green, black spines, warted; tolerant to mosaic.	BURP PON
CALYPSO (hybrid) (gyn)	56	6 inches, dark green; resistant to disease.	ALL DEG LIB STO TWI VER WIL
CAROLINA (hybrid)	49	Straight, blocky cucumber; resistant to disease.	BURR JUN WIL
CHICAGO PICKLING	59	6½x2½ inches.	BURG DEG FAR SEE
CHINA-SCHLANGEN	75	Up to 20 inches, crooked; will withstand adverse conditions and resist disease.	STO
CONQUEST (hybrid) (gyn)	50	Medium-long, well-colored, white spine; pollinator added; disease-tolerant.	JOH
CORNICHON DE BOURBONNE	53	This disease-resistant French variety's slightly curved cucumbers need frequent harvesting.	ORN SHE
CORNICHON VERT DU MASSY	53	Harvest fruit at 2–3 inches.	COM NIC
DOUBLE YIELD PICKLING (OP)	50	These dark green cucumbers are good for gherkins or dill pickles.	STO
EARLIPIK 14 (hybrid) (gyn)	53	5x1½ inches, dark green, warted; resistant to disease.	STO
EARLY RUSSIAN	50	4–5x2 inches, small, uniform.	ABU ALL JLH SEE
EDMONSON	70	4 inches, whitish green; 1913 heirloom variety with resistance to disease, insects, and drought.	SOU
EVERBEARING	55	Blocky cucumbers are 5 inches long. Variety keeps producing as long as vines are picked.	HEN GUR
EXPLORER (hybrid) (gyn)	50–55	Straight with white spines; adapted to moist climates; resistant to disease.	DEG
EXPRESS (hybrid) (gyn)	50	6x2 inches, medium green; no bitterness; resistant to disease.	WILL
FANCIPAK (hybrid)	55	Medium to dark green, blocky; endures adverse conditions; resistant to disease.	PAR POR
FREMONT (hybrid)	60	Medium green; resistant to disease.	BURG
GHERKIN	60	2 inches long, chunky, covered with tender spines.	GUR RED TIL

VARIETY	DAYS	DESCRIPTION	SOURCES (p. 385)
CUCUMBERS (PICKLING) *(continued)*			
GREEN SPEAR 14 (gyn)	55	Long, medium green with white spines; resistant to disease.	STO
H–19 LITTLE LEAF	55	Blocky, medium length, white spines; disease-tolerant.	BURR HEN JOH JUN LED PAR TER
HOKUS ORIGINAL	59	No ridges, white spines.	WILL
HOMEMADE PICKLES	55	Can be picked at 1½–6 inches; white spines, solid interior.	FAR GAR HEN POR
JAPANESE LONG PICKLING	60	18x1½ inches, dark green pickler with small seeds.	STO
KATSURA GIANT PICKLING	60	This 12½x4½-inch Japanese variety's light green skin turns almost white.	GLE
LUCKY STRIKE (hybrid) (gyn)	52	Blocky, medium green, warted; resistant to blight.	LIB PIN POR VER
MASTERPIECE	60	English heirloom variety.	BOU
MINCU	50	4x1¾ inches, white spines.	FIS HIG
MISS PICKLER (hybrid) (gyn)	50	6 inches long, blocky, white spines, warty; small seed cavity.	GUR HEN
NATIONAL PICKLING (OP)	53	5x2½ inches, dark green; resistant to mosaic and scab.	DEG FIS GUR JUN LEJ PIN STO TIL WIL WILL
NORTHERN PICKLING	48–50	Medium green; resistant to scab, but not recommended in areas troubled by mosaic.	GAR HIG JOH SEE
PICCADILLY (OP) (hybrid)	56	4½–6 inches long, blocky; small vines.	PAR
PIK-RITE (gyn)	63	Blocky, dark green, white spines; short season variety; resistant to disease.	STO
PIONEER (hybrid) (gyn) (Mrs. Pickler)	48–55	Medium green with black spines; short season variety; resistant to disease.	BURR COM JUN STO TIL WILL
POONA KEERA	60	Light green, smooth, small cucumber.	SEE
SALADIN (hybrid) (gyn)	55	5x1¾ inches, curved, bright green; disease-resistant Dutch variety.	PAR PIN SHE
SALTY (hybrid)	53	5 inches, dark green with white spines; doesn't hollow; resistant to disease.	STO
SENA	60	Bright green gherkin type; scab-tolerant.	WILL
SIBERIAN PICKLING	50	Heavy yields for short season gardens.	SEED
SLENDERSWEET	50	Pickle this cucumber at 4 inches or let it grow for slicing.	SEED
SMALL PARIS (Verte Petite de Paris)	50–60	Harvest the short, spiny fruit at 2 inches.	GOU SEE

VARIETY	DAYS	DESCRIPTION	SOURCES (p. 385)

CUCUMBERS (PICKLING) *(continued)*

VARIETY	DAYS	DESCRIPTION	SOURCES
SMART PICKLE	55	Best pickled young; disease-tolerant.	SEED
SMR 58 (Wisconsin SMR 58)	56	6½x2½ inches, medium green with black spines; resistant to disease.	ALL BURG BURR GUR HEN JUN MEY NIC PON POR ROS STO TER WILL
SPEAR IT (gyn)	52	White spines; resistant to disease and widely adapted.	STO
SUMTER	56	Slightly tapered, blocky, dark green with white spines; no bitterness; resistant to disease.	SOU
TRIPLE MECH (hybrid) (gyn)	52	White spines; resistant to disease.	TWI
VERT DE MASSY	53	French Cornichon type; 4 inches long, black spines.	COO GOU HIG JOH NIC SEE
WEST INDIA GHERKIN (Burr)	60–65	3x1½ inches, light green.	BURG ORG PIN TER
WHITE WONDER	58	This 6-inch, Southern heirloom cucumber turns ivory when mature.	BURG SOU

CUCUMBERS (PICKLING/BUSH)

VARIETY	DAYS	DESCRIPTION	SOURCES
BABY BUSH (hybrid)	51	Dark green, white spines; 18–24-inch vine; resistant to disease.	ORN STO
BUSH PICKLE (Pickle Bush)	52	4½x1½ inches; 20–24-inch vine; resistant to disease.	BURP GUR HEN JUN LED LIB MEY PAR STO
CASCADE (hybrid)	55	White spines.	TER
CROSS COUNTRY (hybrid)	51	Dark green cucumber with white spines; disease-tolerant semibush type.	STO
PICKALOT (hybrid)	54	5¼x1¾-inch dark green cucumber; 4-foot plant; tolerant to powdery mildew.	BURP

CUCUMBERS (BURPLESS)

VARIETY	DAYS	DESCRIPTION	SOURCES
BURPLESS HYBRID	62	This 10-inch-long, curved, nonbitter, Japanese variety makes a good bread and butter pickle. Plant is resistant to downy and powdery mildews.	BURP DEG FAR FIS LED LEJ PIN PON POR TIL
BURPLESS HYBRID NO. 26	50–70	9x1½ inches, straight, dark green, white spines; resistant to downy and powdery mildews.	LIB
BURPLESS MUNCHER (OP)	65	7x2½ inches, medium green.	ALL
COMET II (hybrid) (gyn)	60	7½ inches long, dark green, straight; no bitterness; disease-tolerant.	STO
CRISPY SALAD (hybrid)	55	5 inches, chunky, deep green, thin skin; mosaic-tolerant.	THO

VARIETY	DAYS	DESCRIPTION	SOURCES (p. 385)

CUCUMBERS (BURPLESS) *(continued)*

VARIETY	DAYS	DESCRIPTION	SOURCES
EARLY SPRING	52	12–15 inches, dark green, white spines; no bitterness.	GUR HEN
EURO-AMERICAN (hybrid)	45	1-foot, bright green cucumber with a small seed cavity.	PAR
GREEN KNIGHT (hybrid)	60	8 inches, dark green, thin skin; resistant to heat and scab.	BURP
GY 200 (hybrid)	65	12 inches, dark green, tapered at both ends.	TER
HEIWA PROLIFIC	60	18 inches long.	ORG
JAZZER (hybrid)	48	8 inches, dark green, smooth; no bitterness; tolerant to disease.	JOH PIN STO
PERFECTION	60	8–12 inches, dark green.	ORG
ROLLINSON'S TELEGRAPH	60–63	18 inches, slim, straight, dark green; nonbitter British variety.	SHE
SO LONG BURPLESS	60	2 feet or longer, ribbed; no bitter taste.	ORG
SOUTHERN DELIGHT (hybrid)	60	7½ inches, brilliant deep green; resistant to heat and disease.	DEG
SWEET DELIGHT (hybrid)	65	10x2 inches, medium green, no bitterness; resistant to mosaic and scab.	BURR ROS WIL
SWEET SLICE (hybrid)	62	12 inches, dark green; bitter-free; resistant to disease.	ALL BURR COM GLE GOU GUR HEN LIB MEY ORN PAR POR STO TWI VER WIL
SWEET SUCCESS (hybrid) (gyn)	65	12 inches, dark green; bitter-free; All-American winner.	BURP HEN JUN LED LIB MEY NIC PIN POR TWI VER WILL
TASTY GREEN (hybrid)	52–60	9x1 inches, dark green; tolerant to cool soil and resistant to disease.	COM JUN NIC SUN THO TWI VER WILL
TASTY GREEN NO. 26 (hybrid)	62	2 feet long; productive in all climates.	GUR HEN NIC PAR

CUCUMBERS (GREENHOUSE)

VARIETY	DAYS	DESCRIPTION	SOURCES
AFICIA (hybrid) (gyn)	65	This variety sets its dark green fruit in cool temperatures.	STO
AIDAS (hybrid) (gyn)	65	Long, smooth, dark green; no bitterness; resistant to scab and leaf spot.	THO
BEAUTY (hybrid) (gyn)	65	14 inches long; straight.	LIB NIC
CARMEN (hybrid) (gyn)	65	Dark green; tolerant to mildew.	STO THO
CORONA (hybrid) (gyn)	65	16 inches; good performer in hot or cold weather.	STO
ENGLISH TELEGRAPH	65	18 inches, slim, straight, dark green; bitter-free English variety.	STO

VARIETY	DAYS	DESCRIPTION	SOURCES (p. 385)

CUCUMBERS (GREENHOUSE) *(continued)*

VARIETY	DAYS	DESCRIPTION	SOURCES
FEMBABY (hybrid) (gyn)	60	8 inches long; tolerant to cold and resistant to disease.	THO
FLAMINGO (hybrid) (gyn)	65	Very dark green; tolerant to mildew.	STO
HAYAT (hybrid) (gyn)	65	7–8 inches, dark green; tolerant to disease.	STO
HOLLAND (hybrid)	65	This 15-inch-long, nonbitter English seedless variety is resistant to scab and leaf spot. Seed needs heat for germination.	WILL
NIAGARA (hybrid) (gyn)	65	12 inches, dark green, slender; tolerant to mildew.	STO
RADJA (hybrid) (gyn)	65	Dark green.	STO
ROLLINSON'S TELEGRAPH	65	Long, dark green; non-hybrid and not as high yielding or disease-resistant as a hybrid.	SHE
SANDRA (hybrid) (gyn)	65	15–16 inches, dark green; no male flowers.	STO WILL
SUPERATOR (hybrid) (gyn)	65	15 inches; no male blossoms; resistant to downy and powdery mildews.	STO
SUPER SANDRA (hybrid) (gyn)	65	16 inches; not for winter harvest; resistant to powdery mildew.	STO
TELEGRAPH IMPROVED	62	Smooth-skinned, long, 19th-century variety; non-hybrid.	ABU WILL
TOSKA 70 (hybrid) (gyn)	65	14 inches, deep green; no bitterness; remove the male blossoms.	WILL

CUCUMBERS (OTHER TYPES/COLORS)

VARIETY	DAYS	DESCRIPTION	SOURCES
BIANCO LUNGO DI PARIGI	60	Creamy white, very knobby.	PIN
CRYSTAL APPLE	65	Apple-shaped, creamy white New Zealand variety.	GLE JLH ORN ROS
DE BOUENIL	60	Standard size, white.	COO
LEMON	64	3 inches in diameter, round, yellow, flat on the stem end; American heirloom variety.	ABU BOU COM COU DEG FIS GAR GUR JUN LIB NIC ORG ORN PLA POR SEE SEED SHE STO TER
LONG WHITE	65	This European variety is white inside and out.	ORN
POONA KHEERA	60	Small, smooth, greenish white Indian variety.	GLE
PRECOCE GROSSO BIANCO CREAMA	65	5x2 inches, creamy white Italian variety; no bitter taste.	RED
WHITE WONDER	58–65	5–10 inches long, ivory when mature.	DEG FAR GLE GUR SEE

EGGPLANT

EGGPLANT

BOTANICAL NAME: *Solanum melongena esculentum*

DAYS TO MATURITY: 53–125.

PLANTING TIME: Eggplant likes night temperatures to remain above 55°F. Sow seeds or seedlings in the spring.

SOIL: Fertile and well-drained, with decomposed manure added; pH 5.5–6.5.

NUTRIENTS: Feed every three to four weeks with fish emulsion. Excess nitrogen results in all foliage and little fruit.

WATER: Soak the soil deeply, but never keep it saturated. Water in basins around the individual plants.

LIGHT: Full sun.

SPACING: Sow seeds ½ inch deep; space seedlings 2½ feet apart. For row gardens, space rows 3 feet apart.

HARVEST: Eggplant is ready when it is shiny purple. If the color is dull, it is overripe.

STORAGE: Use this vegetable fresh.

Eggplant Growing Tips

Large Fruit

For replete, bushy plants that produce a number of large fruits, pinch off the growing tips when the plants are 6 inches high. This encourages several branches to form. After some fruits have started to form, clip several branches. This encourages the plants to produce fewer and bigger fruits.

Planting-Mix Culture

Produce eggplants on the front porch, in a child's wagon, or up against the corner of the garden. Just buy a 10-pound (or larger) plastic bag of planting mix. Cut a hole in each side (on top), and pop in a couple of eggplant seedlings. With full sun exposure, they will grow quickly and produce fully formed fruits.

VARIETY	DAYS	DESCRIPTION	SOURCES (p. 385)
EGGPLANT (BELL-SHAPED)			
BEAUTY (hybrid)	65–70	7 inches long, 6 inches thick, glossy black; tolerant to fusarium wilt.	PAR
BLACK BEAUTY	73–80	Dark purple with a small seed cavity; 24–28-inch plant.	ABU ALL BURP BURR BUT COM DEG GUR HEN LED LEJ MEY ORN PON POR RED ROS SEE SOU VER WIL WILL

VARIETY	DAYS	DESCRIPTION	SOURCES (p. 385)

EGGPLANT (BELL-SHAPED) *(continued)*

VARIETY	DAYS	DESCRIPTION	SOURCES (p. 385)
BLACK BELL (hybrid)	68–70	6-inch-long, oval, glossy, dark purple fruit; 28–30-inch plant.	LED STO TWI VER WIL
BLACKNITE (hybrid)	61	8x3½ inches, deep purple; tolerant to tobacco mosaic virus.	STO
BURPEE HYBRID	70	Oval, glossy purple; resistant to drought and disease.	BURP
EARLY BIRD (hybrid)	67	7 inches long, 6 inches thick, glossy purple; Black Beauty type.	ORN
EPIC (hybrid)	64	8¾x4-inch, deep purple-black fruit; 36-inch plant; widely adapted and resistant to tobacco mosaic virus.	TWI
FLORIDA HIGHBUSH (Hybush, Fort Meyers Market, Florida Special)	87	Dark purple fruit; tall plant.	LED
IMPERIAL BLACK BEAUTY (OP)	80	Dark purple, egg-shaped fruit.	SEED STO
MIDNITE (hybrid)	68	Pear-shaped, deep purple fruit; 28–30-inch plant.	COM POR

EGGPLANT (LONG, CYLINDRICAL)

VARIETY	DAYS	DESCRIPTION	SOURCES (p. 385)
AGORA (hybrid)	68	This long, bitter-free, Italian variety develops as an upright bush with strong stems.	SHE
CHINESE LONG	125	10 inches long, 1¾ inches thick, purple; late Japanese variety; heavy cropper; tolerant to disease.	GLE THE
CLASSY CHASSIS (hybrid)	68	8½x4-inch, deep purple to glossy black fruit; 36-inch plant; tolerant to tobacco mosaic virus.	STO
DEBARENTANE	65	This variety with very elongated fruit is named for a town in France.	SEE
DUSKY (hybrid)	56–68	8x3½-inch, dark purple fruit; 36-inch plant; resistant to tobacco mosaic virus.	BURR COM FIS HEN JUN LED LIB MEY NIC PIN STO TER TIL TWI VER
EARLY BIRD (hybrid)	65–70	Fruit is best picked when 5–6 inches long.	TER
EARLY LONG PURPLE	78–80	12x4 inches, dark violet.	COM SEE
ELONDO (hybrid)	68	Elongated teardrop, glossy, dark purple; good potential in stress from heat and cold.	JOH
EXTRA LONG	80	12x1½ inches, purple.	SUN
FLORIDA MARKET (Cook's Strain)	82	Long, narrow, glossy, blackish purple fruit; 20–36-inch plant.	BURR LED MEY SEE
FRENCH IMPERIAL (Imperial)	63	10-inch-long, slender, purple-black fruit; 36–40-inch plant; tolerant to tobacco mosaic virus.	ORN STO

VARIETY	DAYS	DESCRIPTION	SOURCES (p. 385)

EGGPLANT (LONG, CYLINDRICAL) *(continued)*

VARIETY	DAYS	DESCRIPTION	SOURCES (p. 385)
ICHIBAN (hybrid)	58–65	Up to 12 inches long, purple; 36–40-inch plant.	BURR COM DEG GUR LED PAR PIN POR TWI VER
KURUME LONG PURPLE	65	This 8–10-inch, black-purple Japanese variety grows well in warm areas.	GLE THE
LONG BLACK (hybrid)	65	8x2½ inches, purplish black Japanese variety with tender skin.	GLE
LONG DARK PURPLE	80	10x2-inch, shiny, violet fruit; 22–26-inch plant.	BOU DEG SOU
LONG JOHN	75	8 inches long; tolerates heat and water stress.	DEG
MEGAL (hybrid)	60	7–9 inches long, purple-black; tolerant to disease.	TWI
MILLIONAIRE (hybrid)	55	12x2-inch fruit; upright plant.	BURP DEG
MONEYMAKER (hybrid)	60	Plant bears its blackish-purple fruit until frost.	WILL
ORIENTAL EXPRESS (hybrid)	58	This variety sets its 10-inch-long, glossy, black fruit in cool weather as well as when under heat stress.	JOH
OSAKA HONNOGA (Burgundy)	65	7½-inch fruit; 4-foot plant; withstands light frost.	SOU
PINGTUNG LONG	65	Fruit is 10–11x1½ inches. Plants are resistant to extreme heat and wetness.	LEJ PAR
PRELANE (hybrid)	60	7–9-inch-long, violet-black French variety; some tolerance of verticillium wilt.	NIC SHE
SHORT TOM (hybrid)	60	3–5x1-inch, shiny, black fruit; Japanese variety; 2½-foot plant.	TER
SLICE RITE (hybrid)	74	1-pound, shiny, black fruit; disease-resistant plant.	DEG
SLIM JIM	65	Lavender to purple eggplants can be grown in pots.	COO
SWALLOW (hybrid)	51	7x1¾ inches; Oriental type.	PIN
TAIWAN LONG (hybrid)	65	Plant produces about 45 purple-black, 7x½-inch fruits.	SUN
TAIWAN PINTONG LONG IMPROVED	65	This variety produces up to 20 fruits (8–10x1–2 inches) per plant.	RED
TYCOON (hybrid)	54–61	8x1¼ inches, shiny, purple-black; Oriental type; 36-inch plant.	NIC
VERNAL (hybrid)	70	This French variety produces elongated teardrop, 10-ounce, shiny, black fruit.	GOU
VIOLETTA DI FIRENZE	65	Oblong, very large fruit have fluted grooves that are pale violet. This Italian heirloom variety needs plenty of heat to grow.	COO ORN PIN
VIOLETTA LUNGA	65	8 inches, deep purple; Italian variety.	COO
VITTORIA (hybrid)	61	9½x2½-inch fruit; 8-foot plant; resistant to tobacco mosaic virus.	BURP LED STO

VARIETY	DAYS	DESCRIPTION	SOURCES (p. 385)
EGGPLANT (SMALL)			
BABY WHITE TIGER	45	1½ inches long, bite size.	SEE
BAMBINO (Baby Bell)	45	Plant is ornamental and grows only 12 inches tall. This baby eggplant variety is ideal for containers.	BURP GUR LIB SHE STO TER
EARLY BLACK EGG (OP)	65–75	4x2-inch, shiny, black fruit; Japanese variety; bushy plant.	GAR GLE SOU
EMERALD PEARL	60	This ¼-inch-long, bitter eggplant is used in Asian dishes.	SEE
JAPANESE EARLY PURPLE	60	Small, European variety.	ABU
JAPANESE PURPLE PICKLING	75	Small.	NIC SEED
LITTLE FINGERS (OP) (Mini Fingers)	68	An Oriental type, the 3–7x¾-inch, glossy, dark purple fruit grows in clusters on a spreading plant.	SHE
PIROUETTE (hybrid)	50	2½–4-inch-long, dark purple fruit; fertile soil recommended.	JOH
SMALL RUFFLED RED	60	2 inches in diameter; bitter; used in Asian cuisine.	SEE
EGGPLANT (NON-PURPLE)			
ALBA	60	Full-size, pure white fruit.	BOU
ASIAN BRIDE (hybrid) (Bride Asian)	75	5–7 inches long, white skin streaked with lavender.	COO SHE
BIANCA OVALE	60	Try growing these egg-size, pure white fruit in containers.	ORN
BUSH WHITE (Bush-L-Full-O'Egg, Egg Tree)	90	This egg-shaped Asian variety needs warmth and well-drained soil.	GLE
CASPER (OP)	70	6x2¾-inches, shiny, ivory skinned.	SEE SEED STO
DARK LONG RED	65	Long, red-purple fruit; Malaysian variety.	RED
DOURGA (OP)	70	8x2-inch, white fruit; well-adapted plant.	ORN PAR TWI
EASTER EGG (hybrid)	52–65	Pick the 2–3-inch, egg-shaped, white eggplants before they turn yellow. Plants grow to 23 inches tall.	COM LED ORN VER
ITALIAN PINK BICOLOR (OP)	75	8 inches, bell-shaped, creamy and rosy pink.	SEED STO
ITALIAN WHITE	72–78	Plump, round fruit tastes like mushrooms and is never bitter.	SEED
LISTADA DE GANDIA	75	6–10 inches long, white with purple stripes; Italian heirloom variety.	ORN SEE SEED SOU

VARIETY	DAYS	DESCRIPTION	SOURCES (p. 385)

EGGPLANT (NON-PURPLE) *(continued)*

VARIETY	DAYS	DESCRIPTION	SOURCES (p. 385)
LONG WHITE SWORD (White Sword)	100	Elongated, 2x9 inches.	SOU
LOUISIANA GREEN OVAL (Green Banana)	100	7 inches long, banana-shaped, glossy light green with creamy green stripes; 3½-foot plant.	GLE SOU
LOUISIANA LONG GREEN	100	Long, green type.	GLE
NEON (hybrid)	65	Deep pink, midsize, somewhat cylindrical, with nonbitter, white flesh.	JOH
OSTEREI (hybrid)	80	White, oval fruit; great container variety.	COO
PINK BRIDE (hybrid)	80	8½x2½ inches, pink-violet with white stripes.	GLE
PINKY	80	8–10-inch-long, pink-violet fruit; 20–24-inch plant.	GLE
ROMANESCA (Tonda Sumata Di Rosa)	80	Large, oval, white with pink-purple blush; Italian variety.	JLH
ROSA BIANCO	75	This meaty, globular, lavender and white, Italian heirloom variety is hard to pick.	ORN SEE SHE
ROSITA (hybrid)	68	8 inches long, cylindrical, rosy pink.	STO
SWEET RED	80	Use fruit in cooking when green, as decoration when red.	SEE
THAI GREEN (Thai Long Green)	80	10x1½ inches, light green; Thai heirloom variety; 2-foot plant; endures light frost.	JLH LEJ SEE SOU
THAILAND WHITE	65	White, flat, deeply lobed, 6–7 inches across.	DEG
THAI ROUND GREEN	65	The 2–3-inch-thick, round, apple-green fruit is used in southeast Asian cuisine.	JLH LEJ
TURKISH ITALIAN ORANGE	85	This heirloom variety from Turkey and Italy yields 2-ounce, orange-red fruits that look like tomatoes.	ABU DEG SEED SOU
WHITE BEAUTY	70	Slightly oval, 5–6 inches in diameter; does well in hot, humid areas.	SOU
WHITE EGG	65	Size of a hen's egg.	SEE
WHITE KNIGHT	75	6x3 inches, ivory.	GLE

KALE

BOTANICAL NAME: *Brassica oleracea acephala*

DAYS TO MATURITY: 47–75.

PLANTING TIME: In mild climates, sow seed from mid to late spring. Wait until midsummer in cooler climates.

SOIL: Use rich soil that was manured for a previous crop.

NUTRIENTS: Feed every three to four weeks with fish emulsion or use 1 tablespoon of blood meal mixed with 1 gallon of water.

WATER: Water kale well in dry weather.

LIGHT: Full sun to partial shade.

SPACING: Sow seeds ½ inch deep; thin seedlings until they're 1½ feet apart.

HARVEST: The inside leaves are generally tastier than the outer leaves. You can harvest the outer leaves or cut the entire plant.

STORAGE: Use fresh.

Kale Growing Tip

More Kale

To make the leaf and spear varieties produce a bounty of kale, harvest the loose crowns in the spring. Then remove the leaves from the top down. Without crowns or leaves, side shoots will develop; pick these just as you would broccoli.

VARIETY	DAYS	DESCRIPTION	SOURCES (p. 385)
KALE (CURLED)			
BLACK	70	Long, savoyed, dark green leaves.	ORG
BLUE ARMOR (hybrid)	45–75	Deep blue-green leaves; vigorous plant.	TWI
BLUE CURLED SCOTCH	65	Finely curled, bluish green leaves; low, compact plant.	WIL
BLUE KNIGHT (hybrid)	55	The curly, deep blue leaves have a reduced tendency to yellow. The plant grows to 7–8 inches tall in 45 days.	TWI
DWARF BLUE CURLED VATES (OP) (Gem)	55–70	Leaves are finely curled and bluish green. This low, compact, short-stemmed plant can withstand below-freezing temperatures.	ABU BURP BUT COM DEG GAR GUR HEN JUN LED LIB MEY NIC ROS SEE SOU STO TIL TWI WIL
DWARF GREEN CURLED SCOTCH (Bloomsdale, Jamaica)	50–65	Large, finely curled leaves; extremely hardy, can withstand severe frost.	ABU ALL BOU STO VER WILL
KONSERVA	60	Broad, tall, dark green leaves; Danish variety; 24–30-inch plant.	JOH ORN
SEMI-DWARF WESTLANDSE	65	Frilly leaves.	WILL
SQUIRE	60	Curly leaves and short stems; slow to bolt in spring.	SOU STO
VERDURA	60	Dark blue-green leaves; vigorous Dutch variety.	SHE

VARIETY	DAYS	DESCRIPTION	SOURCES (p. 385)

KALE (CURLED) *(continued)*

VARIETY	DAYS	DESCRIPTION	SOURCES
WESTLAND WINTER	60	With extremely curled and frilled, dark green leaves, the 24-inch plant forms a pale, yellow rosette. It's a Dutch variety.	TER
WINTERBOR (hybrid)	60–65	Well-curled, blue-green leaves; hybrid Vates type.	COO JOH ORN PAR TER

KALE (SIBERIAN)

VARIETY	DAYS	DESCRIPTION	SOURCES
BLUE SIBERIAN (Sprouts)	65	Frilled, bluish green, large, coarse leaves; 12–16-inch-tall plant with a 24–36-inch spread.	SEE
CURLED SIBERIAN	60	Curled, bluish green leaves; hardy.	MEY
DWARF ESSEX RAPE	30	Smooth, light green leaves; 16-inch plant.	MEY
DWARF SIBERIAN IMPROVED	65	Plumed, grayish green leaves; 12–16-inch-tall plant with a 24–36-inch spread; endures cold well.	TIL
GREENPEACE	65	Large, fringed, red-purple leaves; 2½–4-foot-tall plant.	JLH
HANOVER LATE SEEDLING (Long Seasons)	68	Smooth, dark green leaves; 14-inch-tall plant.	ABU
KONSERVA	60	Moderately curly, moss green leaves; 24–30-inch-tall plant.	GAR HIG
RUSSIAN RED (Rugged Jack)	40–60	Wavy, red-purple leaves; American heirloom variety; 2-foot-tall plant.	ABU BOU GAR JLH JOH NIC ORG ORN PIN SEED SHE SOU
SIBERIAN (Dwarf German)	65	Frilled, dark blue-green leaves; 14-inch-tall plant with sprawling growth.	ABU DEG FIS HIG TER VER
SIBERIAN IMPROVED	60–70	Frilled, bluish green leaves; 12–15-inch-tall plant with a 36-inch spread; extremely hardy.	POR WIL
SPRING (Hanover, Smooth)	30	Large, smooth, light green leaves; 16-inch-tall, hardy plant.	ABU RED SOU
WINTER RED	50	Red and purple huge leaves; highly resistant to disease.	TER

KALE (ORIENTAL)

VARIETY	DAYS	DESCRIPTION	SOURCES
CHINESE KALE (Gai Lohn)	70	A dark green, broccolilike kale, the 12–14-inch plant grows best in cool weather.	NIC ORN THE
GREEN LANCE (hybrid)	45–60	This Oriental type produces edible young leaves, buds, and stalks even in hot weather. It resists heat and drought.	THE TWI
KAILAAN	65	The deep green leaves are smooth and tender, with a mild flavor.	VER

VARIETY	DAYS	DESCRIPTION	SOURCES (p. 385)

KALE (ORIENTAL) *(continued)*

VARIETY	DAYS	DESCRIPTION	SOURCES
SEKITO	60	This Japanese, loose-leaf head variety yields carmine-rose, fringed leaves.	GLE
THOUSAND HEADED	70	Large, green leaves; English heirloom variety; 2–3-foot-high plant.	ABU ORG SEED
WHITE FLOWER	70	Smooth, pointed leaves, white flowers; hardy variety.	SUN
YELLOW FLOWER	70	This dwarf plant with yellow flowers and light green leaves may bolt in cold weather.	SUN

KALE (OTHER TYPES)

VARIETY	DAYS	DESCRIPTION	SOURCES
CHRISTMAS FRINGED WHITE FLOWERING	70	Ruffled, green leaves with a white center; Japanese variety.	GLE
LACINATO ITALIAN	62	10-inch-long, 3-inch-wide, blue-green leaves; Italian heirloom variety; ornamental and hardy in winter weather.	SHE
MARROW STEM GREEN (Chou Moellir)	70	Very thick stems; 5-foot-tall plant.	SEE WILL
NAGOYA GARNISH RED HYBRID	70	Frilled, burgundy leaves, deep rose center; ornamental.	THE TWI
NAGOYA GARNISH WHITE HYBRID	70	Blue-green leaves, ivory center; ornamental.	THE TWI
ORNAMENTAL FLOWERING (hybrid)	70	Early season leaves are green, but change to cream and red shades in the fall.	COM COO GAR GUR NIC ORN SEE SHE THE
PALM TREE CABBAGE	90	This variety can grow to 6 feet, with finely crimped, 3-foot leaves. (The name comes from the way its leaves spread out from the top of the plant.)	RED
PEACOCK RED (hybrid)	80	A good garnish, the deeply notched, serrated foliage resembles feathers. Variety has a large head and withstands severe cold.	TWI
PEACOCK WHITE (hybrid)	80	Similar to Peacock Red; ornamental type.	TWI
PENTLAND BRIG	75	Broccolilike, curled leaves; very hardy.	BOU
RAGGED JACK	80	Red, oak-type leaves.	SEE
RED KAMOME (hybrid)	60	The frilly, fan-shaped leaves with red centers and green edges make a fine garnish.	JOH
WHITE KAMOME (hybrid)	60	A garnishing kale, the leaves have white centers and green edges.	JOH

KOHLRABI

KOHLRABI

BOTANICAL NAME: *Brassica oleracea*

DAYS TO MATURITY: 44–70.

PLANTING TIME: In areas where frost is expected during the winter, sow seeds in early spring as soon as the soil can be worked. Where winter temperatures rarely fall below 30°F, sow seeds at two-week intervals beginning in late summer.

SOIL: Fertile and loamy; pH 6.0–7.5.

NUTRIENTS: Feed every three weeks with fish emulsion or use 1 tablespoon of blood meal to 1 gallon of water.

WATER: Keep well watered.

LIGHT: Full sun.

SPACING: Sow seeds ½ inch deep, 6 inches apart. In row gardening, plant the rows 18–24 inches apart.

HARVEST: Cut the stems at soil level when they are about the size of an apple (2–2½ inches in diameter).

STORAGE: Use fresh.

Kohlrabi Growing Tips

Prime Eating Size

Kohlrabi connoisseurs say that a kohlrabi is just right when it's about 2½ inches wide. After that it matures into a tough, elongated root. To salvage an overdeveloped kohlrabi, peel off the tough skin and discard it. Slice the center thinly, then steam or sauté.

More Kohlrabi

To double your pleasure with kohlrabi, plant in rows about 2 inches apart, then thin to 4 inches apart when the swollen stems reach 2 inches in diameter. Lift every other plant to let the remaining kohlrabies grow larger. You'll have almost twice the yield.

VARIETY	DAYS	DESCRIPTION	SOURCES (p. 385)
KOHLRABI (PURPLE)			
BLARO	43	Purple skin and pale green, crisp, nonfibrous flesh.	JOH
EARLY PURPLE VIENNA	60	3-inch-thick globe with purplish skin and green-white flesh.	ABU COM COO DEG GAR GUR HEN JLH JUN LED LEJ LIB ORN PON SEE SOU STO SUN TIL VER WILL

VARIETY	DAYS	DESCRIPTION	SOURCES (p. 385)

KOHLRABI (PURPLE) *(continued)*

VARIETY	DAYS	DESCRIPTION	SOURCES
KOLIBRI (hybrid)	43	Medium purple skin, white interior; Dutch variety.	PIN
PURPLE DANUBE (hybrid)	46	This round kohlrabi's color fades when cooked.	ORN
RAPID	45–60	3-inch-thick, red-purple globe with white flesh; 15–18-inch-tall plant.	PAR TER

KOHLRABI (GREEN/WHITE)

VARIETY	DAYS	DESCRIPTION	SOURCES
EARLY WHITE VIENNA	55–60	10x2-inch globe, light green skin with creamy white flesh; dwarf plant.	ABU ALL BOU BURP BURR COO DEG FIS GAR GUR HEN JUN LED LIB MEY NIC ORN PIN PON SEE STO SUN TIL VER WIL WILL
EXPRESS FORCER	42	This plant with 4-inch bulbs holds up well even in warm spring temperatures.	PAR
GIANT WINTER	62	An average bulb weighs 27 pounds and measures 8–10 inches. Plant is resistant to root maggots.	NIC SOU
GRAND DUKE (hybrid)	45–60	4-inch semiglobe with white skin.	COM GUR HEN JUN LED PIN POR STO TWI VER
GREEN WALDEMAR (hybrid)	60	Light green skin; Austrian variety.	SHE
KOLPAK (hybrid)	38–50	Round, nonpithy, white flesh.	JOH PIN TER
PEKING	55	Pale green bulbs, pure white flesh.	SUN
SUPERSCHMELZ	60	This giant Swiss variety remains tender. Large root system lends itself to dry gardening.	TER
TRIUMPH	55	Tolerant to yellows.	STO
WINNER (hybrid)	53–60	Round, light green skin; Japanese variety.	LIB

LEEKS

BOTANICAL NAME: *Allium ampeloprasum porrum*

DAYS TO MATURITY: 70–150.

PLANTING TIME: Plant leeks outside about four weeks before the last frost. In frost-free regions, plant directly into the garden in late summer.

SOIL: Light, sandy to loam, and well-manured; pH 6.0–8.0.

NUTRIENTS: Feed every four weeks with fish emulsion.

WATER: These plants need steady watering.

LIGHT: Full sun.

LEEKS

LEEKS

SPACING: Sow groups of 3–4 seeds together, ⅛ inch deep. Space the groups 6 inches apart in trenches or rows, which should be 15–18 inches apart.

HARVEST: Be sure to blanch the vegetables first by pushing soil up around the stems. Blanching will keep the leeks white and tender. Leeks are edible from the baby stage through full maturity. Lift leeks with a spading fork.

STORAGE: Use fresh.

Leek Growing Tip

Blanching Leeks

To blanch leeks easily, tie black plastic around the individual plants, then hoe some soil up between the rows. An alternate method is to place a 6-inch paper collar around each plant shortly after putting them into your garden bed.

VARIETY	DAYS	DESCRIPTION	SOURCES (p. 385)
LEEKS			
ALASKA	105	8-inch shaft, dark blue-green foliage; tolerant to freezing temperatures.	GOU STO WILL
ALBERTA	120	Hardy in cold weather; won't bolt.	NIC
AMERICAN BROAD FLAG (Giant Mussel-burgh, Broad London, Large American Flag, London Flag, Broad Scotch)	90–130	7½–9½ inches, medium green leaves.	ABU ALL BOU BURP DEG FAR HEN JLH JUN LED LEJ LIB MEY NIC PAR PIN ROS SEED SOU TIL
ARCONA	100	Dark blue-green leaves, 8-inch shafts; hardy in winter; doesn't form bulbs.	STO
ARGENTA	90	Thick, heavy stems.	THO
ARKANSAS	108	Bulbless, winter-hardy strain; 6-inch, white shafts; storable.	STO
ARTABAN	110	Extrathick, white shaft; Dutch variety.	ORN
AUTUMN GIANT	120	Thick shaft, gray-green leaves; no bulbs.	JLH
BLUE SOLAIZE	145	This cold-resistant 19th-century French heirloom variety turns violet during autumn.	COO ORN SEE
CARENTAN WINTER (Giant Carentan, Winter Giant)	95–150	8-inch-long, 2-inch-thick stalks; resistant to cold.	ABU GAR SEE SEED WILL
CARINA	150	Heavy, thick, long, white shanks; broad, dark blue-green leaves.	SHE TWI

VARIETY	DAYS	DESCRIPTION	SOURCES (p. 385)
LEEKS (*continued*)			
CHINESE LEEKS	110	Strong flavor.	SUN
DURABEL	125	5-inch shaft; slow growing Danish variety.	TER
ELEPHANT LEEK (**Elefant**)	85–150	Large, vigorous variety.	SEE WILL
FRENCH SUMMER-KILMA	75	Long shaft; rapid growth.	SEE WILL
FUROR	100	Long, thin, white shafts; French variety.	ORN
GABILIAN	125	Long, white shaft; dark green leaves.	LIB
KALEM KARTAL	120	Turkish variety with thin stalks.	RED
KING RICHARD	75	12-inch-tall shaft with light green leaves; not frost hardy.	COO FIS GAR GUR HIG JOH PIN
LONG FALL	80–90	Long, tender shaft; a summer leek, it doesn't survive winter well in freezing climates.	SEED
LONGINA	102	8 inches long.	STO
LUNGO D'INVERNO	120	10x1-inch stalks; Italian variety.	RED
OTINA	120	This French variety with long, thick stems is also good as a baby leek.	SHE
PANCHO (Poncho)	80–100	Heavy, thick, white stalks; resists bulbing; tolerant to foliage diseases and cold.	JOH SEED
PRIMOR	135	Long, straight, bulbless shanks; well suited for short season areas.	TWI
PRIZETAKER (**The Lyon**)	135	Solid white stems; highly cold-tolerant 1886 English heirloom variety.	BOU
SCOTLAND	85–90	Short shank; overwinters well; hardy Scottish heirloom variety.	SEED
SHERWOOD	75	This excellent summer and fall leek doesn't overwinter.	SEED
SPLENDID	95–105	8–10-inch-long stems; some frost tolerance; Danish variety.	STO TER
ST. VICTOR	145	Widely adapted, newly selected strain of Blue Solaize.	SHE
TENOR	90–100	Deep blue-green leaves; 2-foot-tall French variety.	ORN SEED WILL
TITAN	70–110	8x2-inch shanks.	BURP SEE STO
UNIQUE	100	8x2-inch shanks.	SEE STO
VARNA	50–105	14–24-inch-long shafts; bunching leek.	JOH NIC TER
VERNOR	110	Improved Blue Solaize; French variety.	ORN

LETTUCE

BOTANICAL NAME: *Lactuca sativa*

DAYS TO MATURITY: 45–100.

PLANTING TIME: Lettuce can be planted four to six weeks before the average frost-free date in your area. Where summers are hot, plant in early spring and again in the late summer for a fall crop. To get a jump on the season, plant lettuce in simple protective devices such as cloches or cold frames.

SOIL: Moist but well-drained, mixed with well-rotted manure; pH 6.0–7.0.

NUTRIENTS: Because lettuce grows so fast, it's best for the nutrients to be in the soil at planting time. Otherwise, nourish with fish emulsion every three weeks.

WATER: Keep moist.

LIGHT: Full sun.

SPACING: Sow seeds ½ inch deep, 6–12 inches apart (depending on the variety). For row gardening, plant in rows 1½ feet apart.

HARVEST: Lettuce leaves are edible at all stages of growth. To harvest the whole head, cut just above the lower leaves.

STORAGE: Use fresh.

Lettuce Growing Tips

Summer Lettuce

In the summertime, try planting lettuce in shaded ground beneath a bean or cucumber A-frame tepee. As soon as the sprouts poke through the warm soil, tuck mulch around them to keep the roots cool. Keep the growing plants well watered.

Bigger Heads

As your head lettuce starts to grow, pick the outer leaves a few at a time just as you would leaf lettuce. This doesn't affect the heading since the heads grow from the center out. What it does is make the plant smaller in comparison to the root structure, which gives the roots time to gain the strength to produce larger tops.

Season Extension

When the weather turns hot and sunny, many cool season leaf vegetables, such as lettuce and chard, flower and set seed (referred to as bolting). To extend your harvest by about a month, place a light lattice over the garden supported by 4-foot-high, 1–2-inch-square cedar or redwood stakes. This slows the bolting process.

LETTUCE

Hanging Salad

You can grow a big, leafy salad bar in a standard size, moss-lined, hanging wire basket. Soak the moss in water, then line the basket with it, starting at the bottom and packing it tightly between the wires. Make planting holes by pushing your fingers through the basket's sides. Plant about 15 lettuce seedlings in these openings, starting at the bottom. Fill the basket with potting soil, and plant four or five seedlings on top. (The basket will look especially nice displaying various colors of lettuce.) Finally, bend a wire hanger around the basket top and hang it in partial sun.

Pot Lettuce

Apartment dwellers can easily grow leaf lettuce in a pot on a windowsill or outdoors on a patio. Keep the plant watered and protected from direct sunlight.

Baby Lettuce

These days, everybody's raving about baby lettuce. At maturity, its heads are only 5–6 inches in diameter. The bite-size leaves are more tender than standard varieties. Just toss them whole into a mix of greens. These babies fit beautifully on a salad plate.

VARIETY	DAYS	DESCRIPTION	SOURCES (p. 385)
LETTUCE (CRISP HEAD/ICEBERG—LARGE)			
BURPEE'S ICEBERG	85	Light green, savoyed leaves; vigorous and hardy.	BURP
CANASTA	50	The bright green, puckered leaves are red tinged. This French variety is resistant to tip burn, bottom rot, and bolting.	ORN
CENTENNIAL	52	Harvest at any stage. Variety is slow to bolt, adapted to both hot and cold, and tolerant to lettuce mosaic virus.	JOH
CRISPINO	57	With a glossy, green, large, firm head, this plant does well in imperfect conditions.	JOH
CYBELE BATAVIAN	60	Red, ruffled leaves; for fall or spring planting; fades in summer heat.	ORN
EARLY GREAT LAKES	70	Dark green leaves; resistant to tip burn and heat.	FIS
FORMDINA	60	Fine head.	SEED
FROSTY	98	Dark green leaves; tolerant of light frost.	STO
GEMINI	85	Deep green leaves.	STO
GREAT LAKES	90–100	Bright green, large, dense head; resistant to tip burn, sunburn, and heavy rain; slow to bolt.	ALL BURP COM DEG HEN MEY NIC PIN SEE TIL

VARIETY	DAYS	DESCRIPTION	SOURCES (p. 385)

LETTUCE (CRISP HEAD/ICEBERG—LARGE) *(continued)*

VARIETY	DAYS	DESCRIPTION	SOURCES (p. 385)
GREAT LAKES 118A	78	This variety thrives under the most adverse conditions.	BURG
GREAT LAKES SELECT	60	Green, thick leaves..	SEED
GREAT LAKES 659–G (Mesa)	80	Deep green, extra-fringed leaves; good tip burn tolerance.	BURR LED LIB ROS TWI WIL WILL
GREEN LAKE	88	Light green leaves; tolerance to bolting, root rot, and tip burn.	STO
ICEBERG (Giant Crystal Head)	85	The wavy, light green leaves are tinged with brown. Plant is slow to bolt in summer.	ALL DEG GUR LED LEJ MEY POR ROS SUN WIL WILL
IMPERIAL NO. 847	83	Dark green leaves; heads well even in midsummer.	COM
ITHACA (Improved Iceberg)	60–80	Head is 5–6 inches across with glossy, green, frilled leaves. Resistant to tip burn; slow to bolt.	ALL GUR HEN HIG STO TIL TWI WILL
KING CROWN	70	Drought-tolerant and resistant to bottom rot; large head with thick, green leaves.	GAR
LONG STANDING BATAVIAN	50–60	The large, upright head's thick leaves store water during hot weather. Plant resists bolting.	SEED
MISSION	74	6–8-inch-diameter head protected by long, thick outer leaves.	PAR
MONTELLO	88	Glossy, green leaves; good resistance to tip burn and tolerance to bolting.	STO TWI
NEW YORK (Wonderful)	70–80	3–4 pounds of solid head.	ORG SEE
NEW YORK NO. 12	75	Bright green leaves and solid heads; grows in well-drained soil almost anywhere.	VER
ROSA	75–80	Red leaves, 5–6-inch-diameter head.	ORN PIN
SALAD CRISP	86	Strain from Ithaca; tolerant to common mosaic virus.	STO
SALINAS (Saladin)	70–85	Head has dark green leaves and is slow to develop. Variety resists tip burn and downy mildew.	BOU TER
SIERRA	56	Wavy, bright green, red-tinged leaves; resistant to tip burn, bottom rot, and bolting; summer variety.	COO HIG JOH NIC ORN SOU TER
SUMMERTIME	70	Dark green, compact head; resistant to tip burn.	BURP COO FAR JUN LED LIB NIC PIN PON SHE SOU TER WILL
VICTORIA	55	Dark green, upright head; combines iceberg, leaf, and romaine tendencies; can produce in hot weather; summer variety.	JOH
WARPATH	75	This lettuce is a cross between a crisp head and a cos. Compact plant is ideal for containers or small gardens.	BURP

VARIETY	DAYS	DESCRIPTION	SOURCES (p. 385)

LETTUCE (CRISP HEAD/ICEBERG—LARGE) *(continued)*

VARIETY	DAYS	DESCRIPTION	SOURCES
WEBB'S WONDERFUL	85	Wrinkled leaves on a tight, crisp head; good in both wet and dry summers; slow to bolt.	BOU
WINTER MARVEL	60–75	Clear green, slightly wavy leaves; hardy to 18°F.	COO

LETTUCE (CRISP HEAD/ICEBERG—MEDIUM)

VARIETY	DAYS	DESCRIPTION	SOURCES
ALL-YEAR-ROUND	72	Pale green leaves; for spring or late summer sowing.	ABU FAR ORN POR SEE
BATAVIA BORD ROUGE	59	The crumpled, dark green leaves are tinged deep red. This bitter variety stands about 45 days before bolting.	PIN
BATAVIA LAURA	60	French variety; crisp, green, savoyed leaves.	ORG
BEATRICE	75	For organic gardeners, the fast-growing plant has excellent mildew and root aphid resistance. It yields medium-large, bright green heads.	THO
CERISE	64	The medium green outer leaves are overlaid with shiny red. Variety gives a medium size, round head.	JOH
CHOU DE NAPLES	70	Bright green, crisp head; Dutch variety.	ORN
EMPIRE	72	Medium green leaves; slow to bolt; fair tip burn resistance.	MEY
ETNA	72	Red French variety.	ORN
HANSON (Hanson Head)	80	Yellow-green, frilled leaves; white seeds; tolerant to tip burn; pre-1855 heirloom variety.	SEE SOU
LA BRILLIANTE	75	This French cross of a crisp head type with butter-head tenderness yields toothed, vibrantly green leaves.	COO
MINILAKE	80	Dark green leaves; solid head.	STO
RED GRENOBLE (Red Grenobloise, Rouge Grenobloise)	55	Light green leaves are tinted red. This French variety does well in warm or cool weather.	COO GOU SHE
REINE DES GLACES (Ice Queen)	75	Deeply cut, lacy, green leaves; good variety for spring planting.	COO ORN SEE

LETTUCE (CRISP HEAD/ICEBERG—SMALL)

VARIETY	DAYS	DESCRIPTION	SOURCES
AVENUE	50	Bright, glossy, green leaves; tolerant to heat.	JOH SOU
EMPIRE	80	Yellow-green leaves; black seeds; round, compact head; suitable for warm weather.	MEY
ROSY	75	Red to burgundy coloring; tolerant of bad weather conditions and slow to bolt.	COO

VARIETY	DAYS	DESCRIPTION	SOURCES (p. 385)
LETTUCE (BUTTERHEAD/BIBB—LARGE)			
AVON DEFIANCE	70	Dark green leaves; solid hearts; resistant to mildew; sow in summer.	BOU
BELLA GREEN	68	A large dark green Boston with glossy leaves and an 11–12-inch head.	STO
BEN SEMEN	70	Deep green leaves on a large, compact head; resistant to heat and bolting.	GLE
BIG BOSTON	55–79	Wavy leaves with slightly brown edges; yellow center.	COM LED POR
BRUNE D' HIVER	56	Smooth, fan-shaped, green leaves with bronzy red edges; French heirloom variety for cool season cultivation; a combination of Bibb and romaine in shape.	ABU COO HIG ORN SEE SOU
BUTTERCRUNCH	49–75	Smooth, dark green leaves; 6-inch-wide rosette center; black seeds; tolerant to heat, slow to bolt; All-American winner.	ABU ALL BOU BURP BURR BUT COM COO DEG FAR FIS GUR HEN HIG JOH JUN LED LIB MEY NIC PAR PIN PON POR ROS SEE SOU STO TER TIL VER WIL WILL
BUTTER KING	60–85	Wavy green leaves on a 12–13-ounce head; Israeli variety; resistant to heat.	ORG SEED
CANASTA	74	Bright green leaves are tinged red. Plant resists bolting.	TER
CAPITANE	62	Loosely folded, light green leaves; Dutch variety; resistant to bolting.	SHE SOU
CARMONA	55	Brilliant red butterhead; tolerant to disease and stress.	JOH
CINDY	57–74	Light green leaves; 12–14-inch-thick head.	PAR TER
CITATION	62–74	Frilly, light green leaves; conical, blanched heart; slow to bolt; Dutch variety.	SHE
DIVINA	70	Thick, dark green, shiny leaves; resistant to tip burn; French variety.	GOU
ERMOSA	52	Deep green leaves; resistant to disease; tolerant to summer conditions.	JOH
HILDE	65	Yellowish green leaves.	WILL
JULIET	61	Thick, green leaves overlaid with a burgundy blush; medium-size rosette; French variety.	SHE
KAGRANER SUMMER (Kagraner)	54	Light green leaves; resistant to heat; no tip burn; German variety.	PIN WILL
MANTILLA	60	Apple-green leaves; disease-resistant, heat-tolerant, and slow to bolt; French variety.	ORN SHE

VARIETY	DAYS	DESCRIPTION	SOURCES (p. 385)

LETTUCE (BUTTERHEAD/BIBB—LARGE) *(continued)*

VARIETY	DAYS	DESCRIPTION	SOURCES (p. 385)
MERVEILLE DES QUATRES SAISONS (Marvel of 4 Seasons, 4 Seasons)	50–72	Wavy green leaves with ruby tips; radiantly colored rosettes; slow to bolt; heirloom variety.	COO GOU HIG JLH ORG ORN PIN RED SEE SEED SHE TER
NANCY	58	Glossy, medium green leaves; resistant to disease; for spring or fall.	JOH
NEVADA	60	Shiny, bright, medium green leaves; heat-tolerant; French variety.	GOU SHE
PRADO	60–75	Heavy, green head; resists bolting.	COO
RED BOSTON	65–68	Red tinged leaves; green heart; slow to bolt.	JLH PIN STO
REDCAP	60	Red-bronze leaves on a 6-inch-wide head.	PAR
RED RIDING HOOD	60–75	A red Boston type; tolerant to heat and drought.	COO
SANDRINA	60	Large, yellow-green butterhead; good cold tolerance.	SEED
SELMA-WISA	75	Tolerates freezing; for fall or spring planting; Swiss variety.	NIC
SUDIA	66	Dark green, thick, dimpled leaves; 14-ounce head; resists bottom rot and tip burn; slow to bolt.	GOU
SUMMER BOSTON	70	Light yellow-green leaves; slow to bolt; harvest in summer.	STO TWI
VERANO	58	Wavy green leaves with rosy tones; heat-resistant Dutch variety.	SHE
WHITE BOSTON (Summer Unrivalled)	66–76	Smooth, wavy, bright green leaves; free from tip burn and bottom rot.	DEG SEE STO WILL
WINTER DENSITY	75	Green leaves; semi-cos, tall buttercrunch type; hardy.	ABU COO
WINTER MARVEL	75	Pale green leaves; hardy in winter.	ABU

LETTUCE (BUTTERHEAD/BIBB—MEDIUM)

VARIETY	DAYS	DESCRIPTION	SOURCES (p. 385)
BURPEE BIBB	75	Dark green outer leaves, tinged with brown; slow to bolt.	BURP
COBHAM GREEN	75	Dark green leaves; solid hearts that stand well.	BOU
CONTINUITY (Crisp As Ice, Hartford Bronzehead)	65–70	Wavy, dark green leaves overlaid with red-brown; tolerates hot weather well.	BOU GUR HEN SEED TER
DARK GREEN BOSTON	68–80	Smooth, dark green leaves; dependable under various conditions; resistant to tip burn.	DEG LIB MEY TWI
DEER TONGUE (Matchless, Rodine)	48–90	Triangular, green leaves with rounded tips; withstands heat well; slow to bolt; heirloom variety.	ABU GAR SHE

VARIETY	DAYS	DESCRIPTION	SOURCES (p. 385)

LETTUCE (BUTTERHEAD/BIBB—MEDIUM) *(continued)*

VARIETY	DAYS	DESCRIPTION	SOURCES
ESMERALDA	68	Medium green leaves; slow to bolt; tolerant to tip burn; Plant Variety Patented (PVP).	COO STO
KINEMONTPAS	60–75	Pale green leaves; French variety; slow to bolt.	COO
NORTH POLE	50	Compact head with light green leaves is cold-resistant. This winter variety bolts during summer.	COO
PIRAT (Brauner Trotz Kope)	55	Savoyed, medium green leaves are overlaid with soft brick red. This German variety resists bolting.	COO JOH ORG
RAINHA DE MAI (May Queen)	75	Medium-size, blond head.	RED
RED VOGUE	65	Leaves are light green with rosy red shades.	STO
SANGRIA	55	Medium green leaves are tinted rosy red. Variety resists bolting and tip burn.	JOH ORN STO
ST. ANNE'S SLOW BOLTING	75	Slow to bolt; butterhead type.	RED
SUDIA	66	Dark green leaves; slow to bolt; tolerant to tip burn; improved Little Gem type.	HIG STO
SUSAN'S RED BIBB	60	Ruffled leaves with rose margins; great color; heirloom variety.	SOU
TENNIS BALL	55	This pre-1804 heirloom variety was grown by Thomas Jefferson at Monticello. Light green leaves are yellow-green at the base. Seeds are black.	SOU
VISTA	50	With curled, bright green leaves, this French variety was developed for hot, dry areas where summer lettuce is difficult to grow. Plant resists disease and tip burn.	NIC ORN
YUGOSLAVIAN RED BUTTERHEAD	58	Red, 10-inch-thick head with yellow interior; Yugoslavian heirloom variety.	SOU

LETTUCE (BUTTERHEAD/BIBB—SMALL)

VARIETY	DAYS	DESCRIPTION	SOURCES
ATTRACTIVE (Unrivalled)	70	The 6-ounce head has a brittle, golden yellow heart. These white seeds can be sown anytime.	BOU
BIBB (Limestone, Kentucky)	60–70	Smooth, waxy, green leaves; black seeds; bolts in hot weather; 1880 Kentucky heirloom variety.	ALL COO DEG LED MEY NIC POR WIL
MAY QUEEN	70	Pale green leaves blushed with bronze; early butterhead type for spring sowing.	JLH
MIGNONETTE BRONZE	65	Frilled, medium brown leaves with dark green tinge; black seeds; slow to bolt.	ORN SEE SEED
MIGNONETTE GREEN	65	Deep green leaves; black seeds; grown mostly in tropical climates.	NIC ORN SEE

VARIETY	DAYS	DESCRIPTION	SOURCES (p. 385)

LETTUCE (BUTTERHEAD/BIBB—SMALL) *(continued)*

VARIETY	DAYS	DESCRIPTION	SOURCES
PARELLA ROSSA (Red Parella, Italian Red Parella)	70	Dark green leaves with dark ruby edges; Italian small butterhead variety.	ORN SHE
REINE DE MAI	70	Misty green leaves burnished bronze; Dutch butterhead variety.	ORN
ROUGETTE DU MIDI (Red Montpelier)	60–75	This French variety with bronze-red leaves needs lots of water. It's not for summer planting.	COO ORN
SCHWEITZER'S MESCHER BIBB	50	Green leaves ringed with red on a small, tight, crisp head; 1700s heirloom variety from Austria.	SOU
SUMMER BIBB (Bibb Slow Bolting)	60–70	Wavy, thick, dark green leaves; black seeds; slow to bolt; grows well on upland or muck soils.	COM LIB TWI

LETTUCE (SPACE SAVERS)

VARIETY	DAYS	DESCRIPTION	SOURCES
BUBBLES	65	Little Gem type; very crinkly leaves; small head.	THO
DIAMOND GEM	60	Small, robust, green heads.	COO
LITTLE GEM (Sucrine)	50	Miniature romaine with bright green, slightly wavy leaves; 5–6 inches tall; moderately tolerant of frost.	BOU GAR ORN PAR SEED TER
TOM THUMB	52–65	Tennis-ball-size buttercrunch with medium green, crumpled leaves; English heirloom variety.	GUR HEN HIG LED NIC ORG ORN PIN POR SEE SEED SHE SOU TIL VER

LETTUCE (GREENHOUSE/HYDROPONIC)

VARIETY	DAYS	DESCRIPTION	SOURCES
AKCEL	60	French forcing lettuce with deep green, compact, heavy heads.	COO
KWIEK	60	Small-headed variety.	ABU
LUXOR	60	Well-filled, medium green head; tolerances to multiple diseases and mildew; slow to bolt.	STO
MAY KING	65	Light green leaves, fringed brown; hardy.	BOU COO
MUSCA	60	Red Batavian type; improved Rouge Grenobloise.	COM ORN
OSTINATA	60	The best Boston type for summer greenhouse or hydroponic culture, it has a medium green head. It tolerates tip burn and is slow to bolt.	STO
SALINA	60	Dark green, compact head; resistant to bolting; sow January through August.	STO
TITANIA	60	Medium green heads with tip burn tolerance; slow to bolt.	STO
VALDOR	60	Green leaves; very hardy in cold and wet; good resistance to botrytis (gray mold).	BOU

VARIETY	DAYS	DESCRIPTION	SOURCES (p. 385)

LETTUCE (LOOSE-LEAF)

VARIETY	DAYS	DESCRIPTION	SOURCES (p. 385)
AUSTRALIAN YELLOW	54	Crinkled, light yellow-green leaves; 12–16 inches in diameter. Variety is moderately bolt resistant.	SEE SOU
BIONDO A FOGLIE LISCE (Biondo Lisce)	45–60	Smooth leaves; quick growing.	COO
BLACK SEEDED SIMPSON	45	Light green, frilled outer leaves; 1850 heirloom variety.	ABU ALL BURG BURP BURR BUT COM COO DEG FAR FIS GAR GUR HEN HIG JOH JUN LED LEJ LIB MEY NIC ORG PAR PIN PON POR ROS SEE SEED SOU STO TIL VER WIL WILL
BRONZE ARROW-HEAD	60	Arrow-shaped, green leaves overlaid with magenta; rare heirloom variety.	BOU SEE
BRUNIA	62	Oak Leaf type; deeply cut leaves are reddish brown.	COO GOU NIC SEE STO
CORCARDE	49	Trumpet-shaped head; lobed, dark green leaves with rusty red hues; Oak Leaf type; slow-bolting.	JOH SEED
CURLY OAKLEAF (Feuille De Chene, Foglie Di Quercia)	45–60	A cutting lettuce; will form a head if thinned.	COO
DEEP RED	50	Savoyed, dark green leaves with bronze-red tinge; does not stand up under hot weather; Plant Variety Patented (PVP).	ORN
DUNSEL	35	Round, yellow-green leaves; European variety.	WILL
EARLY CURLED SIMP-SON (Silica Curled)	45	Crinkly, light green leaves; white seeds; slow to bolt.	HEN LED
FANFARE	48	14–16-inch-wide frame; tolerant to tip burn.	STO
FLAME	50	Frilled, deep red leaves; slow to bolt.	ORN
GRAND RAPIDS (Burpee's Greenhart)	45	Frilled, light green leaves; resistant to mildew and tip burn; slow to bolt.	BURP FAR HEN JUN LED LIB MEY PIN SEE STO TWI WILL
GRAND RAPIDS SPECIAL	43	Compact head and leaves.	DEG
GREEN ICE	45	Savoyed, dark green leaves with fringed margins.	ALL BURP COM COO JUN LED ORN PAR PIN PON
GREEN WAVE	45	Resistant to heat and diseases; Grand Rapids type.	VER
LOLLO BIONDO	45–60	Ruffled, bright green leaves.	COO ORN
LOLLO ROSSA (Lollo Rosso)	56–75	Very frilly magenta leaves with light green edges; Italian variety for cutting.	COO JOH SEE SHE SOU THO TWI VER
MASCARA	65	Dark red, Oak Leaf type; bolt-resistant Dutch variety.	TER
OAK LEAF	38–50	These medium green leaves look like oak leaves.	ABU ALL BURG BUT COM DEG FAR FIS GAR GOU GUR HEN HIG JLH JOH LED LIB MEY NIC ORN PIN PON POR RED SEE SOU VER

VARIETY	DAYS	DESCRIPTION	SOURCES (p. 385)

LETTUCE (LOOSE-LEAF) (continued)

VARIETY	DAYS	DESCRIPTION	SOURCES (p. 385)
PARELLA GREEN	50	Fairly thick, triangular, flat leaves; Italian variety.	RED
PARELLA RED	50	This is like the green variety, but its leaves are tinged red.	RED
PRIZEHEAD (Jung's All Cream, Red Leaf)	47	The wrinkled leaves are medium green with a reddish tinge to the edges.	ABU ALL BURR DEG FAR FIS GAR GUR JUN LIB ORG RED SEE SEED TIL
RED FIRE (New Red Fire)	43–45	Savoyed and frilled, intensely red leaves.	GAR JOH LIB PIN STO VER
RED GRENOBLE	45	Green leaves with magenta tinge; hardy in cold weather.	SEE
RED OAK LEAF	50	Deeply indented crimson, cranberry, or burgundy leaves; gourmet type.	ORN SEED SHE
RED SAILS	45	Heavy, ruffled, deep red-bronze leaves; slow to bolt; Plant Variety Patented (PVP); All-American winner.	ALL BOU BURR COM COO DEG GUR HEN JUN LIB MEY NIC ORN PAR PIN POR SOU STO TER TIL TWI VER WILL
RED SALAD BOWL	50	Maroon, deeply lobed leaves; slow to bolt.	BURP BUT HIG JOH ORN PIN
ROSSA D'AMERIQUE	45–60	Use this as a cutting lettuce, or thin to let it form a head. This Italian variety's pale green leaves are tipped with sparkling rosy red.	COO
ROSSA DI TRENTO	45–60	Savoyed leaves have wine red margins. This Italian cutting lettuce can be grown year-round in mild climates.	COO
ROYAL GREEN	45	Darker green version of Grand Rapids; tolerant to tip burn.	STO
ROYAL OAK LEAF	50	Dark green, oak-leaf-shape leaves; tolerant to heat; Plant Variety Patented (PVP).	BUR COO JUN ORN WILL
ROYAL RED	45	Red version of Royal Green; tolerant to tip burn.	STO
RUBY	47–65	Frilled, bright green leaves with intensely red edges; All-American winner.	BURP COM JLH LED LEJ LIB ORN PIN PON ROS SEE STO WIL WILL
SALAD BOWL	45	Wavy, light green, deeply lobed leaves; slow to bolt; endures heat well; All-American winner.	ABU ALL BOU BURP BURR BUT COM COO DEG FAR FIS GAR GUR HEN HIG JOH JUN LED LIB MEY NIC ORN PAR PIN SEE SOU TER TIL WIL WILL
SALAD BOWL RED	46	Brilliant, burgundy version of Salad Bowl; stands well in heat; slow to bolt.	COO DEG FIS GAR
SALAD TRIM	55	Red, leafy lettuce; slow to bolt.	ORG
SELMA LOLLO	45	Head has soft, green leaves with dark pink, frilly edges and measures 12 inches across.	PAR

VARIETY	DAYS	DESCRIPTION	SOURCES (p. 385)

LETTUCE (LOOSE-LEAF) *(continued)*

VARIETY	DAYS	DESCRIPTION	SOURCES
SIMPSON ELITE	41	Improved, black-seeded Simpson; Plant Variety Patented (PVP).	FAR POR SOU STO
SLOBOLT	45–53	Purplish red, crumpled, frilled leaves; black seeds; no bolting in summer.	FAR JOH SOU STO TER
SUPER PRIZE	45	Red tinged leaves; good tolerance to bolting.	STO
TANGO	45	This head, with dark green, deeply cut, pointed leaves, forms tight, erect rosettes. Plant bolts easily.	COO ORN
THAI OAKLEAF 88 (Thai 88)	88	Larger than Oak Leaf, this Thai variety withstands hot temperatures and is moderately slow to bolt.	SOU
VULCAN	44	Slightly frilled, bright red leaves; slow to bolt.	JOH STO
WALDMAN'S DARK GREEN GRAND RAPIDS	45–60	Deep green, wavy leaves; resistant to tip burn.	GAR JOH ORG ORN STO

LETTUCE (ROMAINE)

VARIETY	DAYS	DESCRIPTION	SOURCES
APOLLO	75	Short day lettuce for winter culture.	COO WILL
AUGUSTUS	70	This variety has an open top for better air circulation in heat. It tolerates corky root rot and is Plant Variety Patented (PVP).	STO
BALLOON	75	Tall, heat-tolerant French variety; late bolting.	COO SEE
BROAD SWORD	66	Leaves are separated and each stands erect. Variety is slow to bolt.	PIN
BROWN GOLDING	65	Golden amber leaves; heirloom variety.	ORG
CIMMARON	60	Broad, flat leaves range from greenish to deep red to bronze. Variety tolerates cold and hot weather.	COM GAR HIG PIN
COSMO	65	11-inch-thick head with savoyed, bright green leaves; for spring or fall.	ORG SEED SHE SOU
CRAQUANTE D'AVIGNON (Craquerelle Du Midi)	65	Deep green leaves; semiromaine type; resistant to cold and slow to bolt in summer.	COO
FRECKLES	65	Green leaves splashed with red; stands a long time.	SEE
JERICHO	60	Sword-shaped leaves; Israeli variety; adapted to many climates.	SHE
LITTLE GEM (Sugar Cos)	70	6-inch-tall, 4-inch-wide, glossy green leaves; English heirloom variety.	BURP ORG SHE SOU TER
LOBJOIT'S GREEN COS (Dark Green Cos)	55–70	12-inch-tall, dark green leaves; white seeds; does well in summer.	BOU ORG
MAJESTIC RED	75	Tall, green leaves overlaid with deep burgundy; loose-leaf romaine.	TER WILL

VARIETY	DAYS	DESCRIPTION	SOURCES (p. 385)

LETTUCE (ROMAINE) (continued)

VARIETY	DAYS	DESCRIPTION	SOURCES (p. 385)
PARIS WHITE COS (Trianon, Valmaine, Romaine)	70–83	10–12-inch-tall head; tolerant to mildew and heat; resistant to disease; widely grown in the cooler climates.	ABU BOU BURR BUT DEG FAR FIS GUR JUN ORN PAR SEE TER VER WILL
PARRIS ISLAND COS (Paris Island)	70–75	8–9-inch-tall, dark green leaves.	BURP COM GAR HEN JOH LIB MEY PIN POR RED SEE SEED SOU STO TIL VER WIL WILL
PARRIS ISLAND 318	71	Special selection of Parris Island; tall, narrow heads; widely adapted; Plant Variety Patented (PVP).	JOH TWI
PLATO	80	Upright heads; resistant to disease and slow to bolt.	NIC
RED LEPRECHAUN	65	Very dark red leaves; large plant.	ORG
ROMANCE	50–75	Large head; virus- and mildew-resistant.	SHE
ROMULUS	59	Broad, heavy, dark green, 11–12-inch-tall head; slow bolting and tolerant to tip burn.	JOH
ROSALITA	55	Midsize, emerald green leaf with deep purple-red overlay; widely adapted.	COO JOH PAR
ROUGE D'HIVER (Red Winter)	60	Bronze to deep red, broad, flat leaves; French heirloom variety; resistant to cold and heat; requires plenty of water.	COO JLH ORN SEE SEED SHE
RUBENS	56	The 12-inch-tall, deep cranberry head tapers down to a contrasting lime-green heart.	SEED SHE
ST. BLAISE	75	Small, upright, bright green heads with few outer leaves.	COO
SWEET VALENTINE	65	Garnet red on both sides of slightly savoyed leaf edges.	ORN SEED
TALL GUZMAINE	65	Very dark green, smooth leaves; Plant Variety Patented (PVP).	STO
VERTE MARICHERE (Verte Mar)	64	Dark green leaves; French variety.	GAR GOU HIG ORN
WINTER DENSITY	54–65	10-inch-tall, dark green leaves; white seeds; resistant to cold and bolting.	ABU BOU JOH SEE SOU TER

MELONS

MELONS

BOTANICAL NAME: *Cucumis melo*

DAYS TO MATURITY: 70–120.

PLANTING TIME: Plant melons outdoors around the date of the last frost. They grow best when nighttime temperatures are above 55°F and daytime temperatures are no lower than 80°F.

SOIL: Light, sandy; pH 6.0–7.5.

NUTRIENTS: Feed melons every six weeks with fish emulsion.

WATER: Water thoroughly in dry weather. Keep a 6-inch-deep trench around each plant and fill when needed. Do not keep the soil soaked; and do not overhead water.

LIGHT: Full sun.

SPACING: All melons spread (unless they are the bush variety) and need plenty of space. Plant them at least 4–6 feet apart.

HARVEST: Cantaloupes can be picked at what is called the "slip" stage: they slip easily from the stem and have a fresh melon aroma. Casaba and honeydew melons are ripe when the skins turn yellow and feel slightly sticky. Crenshaw and Persian melons are ripe when they develop a fruity scent.

STORAGE: Eat melons fresh or pickle them.

Melon Growing Tips

More Melons

To turn your vines into a melon factory, pinch off each vine's growing tip when the main stem has produced five large leaves. Nip subsequent side shoots when the tip develops three leaves. This halts leafy growth and forces more fruit production. When the plants are growing vigorously, keep them well watered and give them a liquid organic feeding as the first fruits reach walnut size.

Bitter Melons

Uneven watering leads to bitter melons. Therefore never let the soil dry out completely. Ideally you should water deeply, then don't water again until the soil has dried to about 8 inches down.

Cantaloupe Tree

To create a cantaloupe tree, plant three midget cantaloupe vines about 12 inches apart in a wire mesh cage (3 feet high, 18 inches in diameter) set over a container filled with planter mix or soil fortified with manure. The cantaloupes will grow upward both inside and outside the cage.

Better Tasting

For delicious cantaloupes, rototill a 10x10-foot area with rotted horse manure. Three to four weeks later, rototill the plot again, adding 10 more bushels of horse manure. Plant your cantaloupe in hills, three to a hill, 5 feet apart. In about 100 days, you'll have all the toothsome cantaloupes you can eat.

Rotting Cantaloupes

Don't let your cantaloupes rot. Save those plastic foam trays that come with supermarket meats. Place one upside-down tray under each cantaloupe. They're waterproof and will keep the fruit from spoiling. At the end of the season, pick up the trays and throw them away.

Early Female Flowers

Melons have a lazy streak: they sometimes produce too many male flowers before they start growing the female flowers that bear fruit. But you can give them a push in the right direction. Count four adult leaves from the base, then pinch off the growing tip. This hastens side growth and the formation of female flowers. If none appear, again remove the growing point beyond the fourth or fifth leaf.

Increased Melon Production

Although bees are great at pollinating melons, you can increase production by taking on the job yourself. To pollinate artificially, remove the male flowers, which grow in clusters and have a prominent central core. Shake this powdery core into the center of the open female flower—the one with a flattish center and a swelling behind the flower.

MELONS

VARIETY	DAYS	DESCRIPTION	SOURCES (p. 385)
CANTALOUPE (LARGE)			
BIG DADDY (OP)	88	14-pound melon with bright orange, firm flesh; lightly netted; vigorous vine growth.	GUR HEN
GIANT HYBRID	80	Melon is up to 18 pounds, with firm, sweet, orange flesh. Compact vine has heavy fruit set.	GUR HEN
GIANT PERFECTION (OP)	97	14 pounds, 8 inches in diameter; large seed cavity, firm flesh; productive plant.	SEE
IMPROVED MILWAU-KEE MARKET (Schoon's Hardshell, New Yorker)	90	5–8-pound melon with extrahard yellow shell and salmon red flesh.	BURR DEG LED WIL

VARIETY	DAYS	DESCRIPTION	SOURCES (p. 385)

CANTALOUPE (LARGE) *(continued)*

VARIETY	DAYS	DESCRIPTION	SOURCES (p. 385)
JUMBO	100	Up to 25 pounds; sweet, orange flesh.	GLE
OLD TIME TENNESSEE MUSKMELON	90–100	12-pound, elliptic melon with deep creases and salmon flesh.	SOU WIL
STUTZ SUPREME	100	The 5–10-pound melon has a smooth, tan rind and orange flesh. Plant requires heat to develop full flavor and will bear until frosts begin.	ABU
TURKEY	100	7–17-pound, 12–16-inch oval melon, slightly netted, with light green sutures; thick, firm, salmon flesh.	SOU

CANTALOUPE (EARLY SEASON)

VARIETY	DAYS	DESCRIPTION	SOURCES (p. 385)
ACOR	80	Charentais type with aromatic, deep orange flesh; concentrated fruit set.	ORN
ALASKA (hybrid)	65–80	This short season variety produces 4½-pound, football-shaped melons with medium netting and salmon flesh. Pick when netting turns light reddish brown.	COM FAR GAR GUR HEN LIB NIC PIN VER WILL
BURPEE HYBRID	72	4½ pounds, oval, heavily netted and ribbed; small seed cavity; deep orange flesh.	MEY STO TWI WILL
CANADA GEM (hybrid)	78	Oval, heavily netted melon with deep orange flesh; resistant to powdery mildew and fusarium.	STO
CARAVELLE (hybrid)	77–80	3½-pound melon with small seed cavity and orange flesh; good tolerance to powdery mildew Race 1.	WIL
CAROLE (hybrid)	80	Round to slightly oval melon with thick, dark salmon flesh; tolerant to powdery mildew.	WIL
CHACA (hybrid) (Early Chaca)	67–75	3–3½ pounds; French variety; salmon flesh; resistant to powdery mildew and fusarium wilt.	NIC PIN POR
CHARENTAIS	74–90	3½-pound melon; French variety.	NIC ORG SEE
CHARMEL	78	The 2-pound melon has a smooth, gray-green exterior, small seed cavity, and deep orange flesh. Plant resists fusarium and powdery mildew.	SHE
DALLAS (hybrid)	75–80	The 4-pound, slightly ribbed, netted melon turns yellow-gold when ripe. Its flesh is deep salmon. Plant has disease tolerance.	WIL
DIXIE JUMBO (hybrid)	74–84	6 inches thick, 7 inches long; heavy netting; high sugar content in salmon flesh; tolerant to powdery mildew and downy mildew.	BURR LIB POR TWI
EARLIGOLD (hybrid)	73	3½–4 pounds; round with fine, dense netting; tolerant of cool weather.	ALL JOH TER
EARLIQUEEN (hybrid)	73	3½-pound, well-ribbed, heavily netted, oval to round melon with thick, orange flesh.	HEN JOH LIB STO

VARIETY	DAYS	DESCRIPTION	SOURCES (p. 385)

CANTALOUPE (EARLY SEASON) *(continued)*

VARIETY	DAYS	DESCRIPTION	SOURCES (p. 385)
EARLISWEET (hybrid)	73–75	Melon is 5½x5½ inches with medium netting and salmon flesh. Resistant to fusarium wilt, this variety produces where others fail.	BURR FAR NIC STO TWI WILL
EARLY ATHENA (hybrid)	75	5–6 pounds with small seed cavity and firm flesh; resistant to fusariums 1 and 2, also powdery mildew.	TWI
EARLY DELICIOUS	75	4–5 pounds with orange flesh.	SEE
EARLY HANOVER	80	Globe-shaped melon; heirloom seed.	ABU SEED
FAR NORTH	64–70	Heavily netted melon is 4–5 inches long with a large seed cavity and salmon flesh. A good short season variety, each vine produces 6–8 melons.	GLE
FLYER (hybrid)	75	Very productive, grapefruit-size European variety is Charentais type. Melon has netting with dark green sutures.	JOH
KANGOLD	80	4–5 pounds; sweet, thick flesh.	SEE
LAGUNA (hybrid)	77	3 pounds; heavily netted with no sutures; deep salmon flesh.	WIL
LUSCIOUS (hybrid)	85	4-pound melon with orange flesh; resistant to powdery mildew and fusarium wilt.	PAR
MAGNUM 45 (hybrid)	80	Deep orange flesh; small seed cavity; disease-resistant.	FAR JUN POR TWI WIL
MAINROCK (hybrid)	75	6 inches long, 4 inches thick; medium netting; salmon flesh; tolerant to fusarium wilt.	FAR
MISSION (hybrid)	80	4-pound, well-netted melon with no sutures; deep salmon flesh; stands up to weather stress.	POR WIL
MONTANA GOLD	60	Short season variety starts to set with first blossoms.	FIS
PANCHA (hybrid)	80	2-pound, 6-inch-long melon with deep orange flesh; French variety; resistant to powdery mildew and fusarium wilt.	SHE
PENNSWEET	80	Midsize melon with thick, salmon flesh; heavy yielding.	ABU
PERFECTION (hybrid)	75	4½-pound, round, well-netted melon with salmon flesh; heavy cropper.	STO
PERFORMER (hybrid)	75	5¼x6 inches; light netting with light sutures; thick, solid, deep orange flesh; tolerant to disease.	TWI
PERLITA	80	Round to oval, well-netted melon with yellow-orange flesh; tolerant to downy and powdery mildews.	WIL
PRIMO (hybrid)	79	5–7 pounds and 7x7½ inches; sugar-rich, dark orange flesh; heavily netted, almost no suture; small, dry seed cavity; tolerance to powdery mildew.	POR STO TWI

VARIETY	DAYS	DESCRIPTION	SOURCES (p. 385)

CANTALOUPE (EARLY SEASON) *(continued)*

VARIETY	DAYS	DESCRIPTION	SOURCES
PRONTO (hybrid)	80	4½–5 pounds and 6x6 inches; round; almost sutureless with good netting; thick, orange flesh; tolerant to fusarium and powdery mildew.	TWI
PULSAR (hybrid)	80	Round fruit with thick, firm, orange flesh; heavily netted, lightly sutured; tolerant to powdery mildew and fusarium.	STO
QUICK SWEET (hybrid)	73	6-inch, oval melon with thick, deep orange flesh; tolerance to fusarium, powdery mildew, and downy mildew.	STO
SAVOR (hybrid)	75	French Charentais type produces a 2-pound melon with deep orange flesh. Melon does not slip. Harvest when skin between sutures turns straw colored and aroma is strong. Plant is resistant to fusarium wilt.	JOH NIC ORN TWI
SOLID GOLD (hybrid)	80	Melon is 6½x5½ inches, heavily netted, nearly sutureless, with a high sugar concentration, a small seed cavity, and thick, dark orange flesh. A good short season variety, it's resistant to some powdery mildews and fusariums.	SHE
SUMMET (hybrid)	75	6 inches long with heavy netting; tolerant to fusarium wilt, downy mildew, and some races of powdery mildew.	STO
SUPER 45 (hybrid)	45	3-pound, oval, well-netted, sutureless melon with dark salmon orange flesh; tolerant to powdery mildew.	WIL
SWEET GRANITE	70–80	2–3½ pounds, lightly netted, with orange flesh; good short season variety.	ABU ALL JOH ORG SEE
SWEETHEART	65	Globe-shaped melon has no netting but smooth, green-white skin. Flesh is salmon red.	VER
SWEETIE (hybrid)	65	Salmon flesh; highly resistant to melon diseases caused by high humidity.	HEN
SWEET 'N EARLY (hybrid)	75	4½-inch-long melon with corky netting, bright salmon flesh, and a small seed cavity; 6–8 fruit per plant; resistant to powdery mildew.	BURP JUN
TASTY SWEET (hybrid)	80	5½x5 inches; light netting, sutureless; deep salmon flesh; tolerant to some powdery mildew and fusarium.	BURR
TEKOS (hybrid)	75–80	3–4 pounds; salmon flesh; good disease tolerance.	WIL
VEDRANTAIS	80	Charentais type with smooth skin.	SEE

VARIETY	DAYS	DESCRIPTION	SOURCES (p. 385)

CANTALOUPE (MIDSEASON)

VARIETY	DAYS	DESCRIPTION	SOURCES (p. 385)
ALIENOR (hybrid)	80	French, 2-pound, round to oblong melon with medium netting, slightly ribbed; light green-gray rind; vivid orange flesh; resistant to fusarium.	TER
AMBER NECTAR	86	3–3½ pounds; ideal for cool climates; sugar-rich, orange flesh.	THO
AMBROSIA (hybrid)	83–86	4–5-pound, 6½-inch, heavily netted melon with very sweet, thick, deep orange flesh and a small seed cavity; resistant to powdery mildew.	BURP LED LIB ORN PAR PIN POR TWI VER
BURPEE'S HYBRID	82	4½-pound, 6–7-inch, oval, well-netted melon with sweet, firm, deep orange flesh; resistant to powdery mildew.	BURP LED LIB MEY TWI
CLASSIC (hybrid)	85–87	4–4½ pounds; netted with slight ribbing; salmon flesh; resistant to powdery mildew and fusarium wilt.	BURR FAR JUN LED LIB MEY POR TWI WIL
DELICIOUS (OP)	83	3–4 pounds, 7 inches; very sweet; heavy yields on strong vine.	PIN
DELICIOUS 51 (OP)	83–85	Good short season variety; 6–6½ pounds with light to medium netting and thick, sweet, crispy, salmon flesh; will grow in infected soil; resistant to fusarium wilt.	ALL BURR COM GAR JUN LED LIB PON SOU WILL
DURANGO (hybrid)	85	Oval fruit fully covered with coarse netting; sugary, firm, orange flesh; strong, vigorous plant with tolerance to powdery mildew and some fusarium.	TWI
EDISTO	88	Hard rind outside, rich, salmon flesh inside; resistance to alternaria and powdery mildew; tolerance to downy mildew.	BURR
EDISTO 47	88	6½-inch-long, oval, heavily netted melon with salmon flesh; resistant to downy and powdery mildew.	MEY SOU
FOUR-FIFTY	90	Blocky, oval melon with heavy netting and moderate ribbing; sweet, firm, thick, salmon flesh; tolerant to several strains of powdery mildew.	BURR
GRANDE GOLD (hybrid)	88	6½x6 inches; medium strong netting, shallow sutures, small seed cavity with deep salmon, sugary flesh; tolerance to downy and some powdery mildews.	BURR
HALE'S BEST	86	6½-inch oval melon with heavy netting, a small seed cavity, and thick, sweet, orange flesh.	ALL BOU GUR HEN LEJ
HALE'S BEST JUMBO	85	4½ pounds, 7½x6 inches; deep salmon flesh.	BURR BUT DEG LED PON POR ROS SEE SOU VER WIL
HALE'S BEST NO. 936	82–87	5–5½ inches; heavy netting; small seed cavity with thick, salmon flesh.	MEY

VARIETY	DAYS	DESCRIPTION	SOURCES (p. 385)

CANTALOUPE (MIDSEASON) *(continued)*

VARIETY	DAYS	DESCRIPTION	SOURCES (p. 385)
HALE'S BEST NO. 36	86	5½–6 inches; medium netting; sweet, salmon flesh.	DEG POR WIL
HARPER (hybrid)	85	3½–4 pounds; fine netting; deep salmon flesh; tolerant to fusarium wilt.	TIL
HONEY ROCK (Sugar Rock)	74–85	5½ inches; heavy netting; sweet, salmon flesh; tolerant to fusarium wilt.	HEN PON
IMPERIAL	90	3–4-pound, oval, heavily netted melon with small seed cavity.	SEED
IMPERIAL 45 (Hale's Best No. 45)	87	3½ pounds, 6½x5½ inches; solid ribbing; small seed cavity with sweet, firm, bright orange flesh.	BURR DEG WILL
MAINSTREAM	85	2¾-pound, round melon with medium netting, a small seed cavity, and orange flesh; resistance to powdery and downy mildews.	BURR
MARKET PRIDE (OP)	83	Strong vines set 4–4½-pound, 7x5½-inch, well-netted melons with thick, deep orange flesh.	TWI
MARKET STAR (hybrid)	84	5½–6 inches long; medium netting and light ribbing; thick, sweet, salmon flesh; tolerant to powdery mildew.	TWI
OTERO (hybrid)	87	Large, oval, sweet melon; sutureless and heavily netted; thick, orange flesh; resistant to powdery mildew and watermelon mosaic virus.	BURR
PERLITA	80–88	Well-netted melon with salmon flesh; mildew-resistant.	WIL
PIKE (OP)	85	This hardy heirloom variety, originally bred for unirrigated clay soil, sets 3–7-pound, heavily netted melons.	SOU
PLANTERS JUMBO	85	4-pound, oval, well-netted melon with orange flesh and a small seed cavity; resistant to downy and powdery mildews.	BURR WIL
PM RESISTANT NO. 45	85	5¼x6 inches; well-netted; firm, salmon flesh.	BURR ROS SOU WIL
PRIOR (hybrid)	85	Charentais melon; vigorous vines; round melon with light grayish green rind and vivid orange flesh.	PIN
PUSLAR (hybrid)	72–86	5–5½-pound melon with coarse netting and deep sutures; resistance to one type of fusarium and powdery mildew.	BURR LED LIB PIN TER TWI
RESISTANT 4–50	50	Heavy netting and medium sutures; firm, sweet, thick, orange flesh; resistance to powdery mildew.	POR
ROAD RUNNER (hybrid)	87	4–4½-pound, 6½x6½-inch melon with coarse netting, deep sutures, and deep salmon flesh; resistance to one type of powdery mildew.	TWI

VARIETY	DAYS	DESCRIPTION	SOURCES (p. 385)

CANTALOUPE (MIDSEASON) *(continued)*

VARIETY	DAYS	DESCRIPTION	SOURCES (p. 385)
ROADSIDE (hybrid)	85–90	7x6 inches; well-netted; sweet, thick, orange flesh; resistance to powdery mildew and fusarium wilt.	HEN JUN LIB VER WIL
SIERRA GOLD	80–85	3½-pound, well-netted, nearly round melon with a small seed cavity and orange flesh.	DEG WIL
STAR HEADLINER	84	4–4½ pounds; solid, deep orange flesh; widely adapted.	TWI
SUGAR QUEEN (hybrid)	85	Vigorous, large vines are high yielders of 6-pound melons. Sparse netting turns coppery orange when fully mature.	WIL
SUPER MARKET (hybrid)	82–90	4½-pound, 7x6-inch, well-netted melon with deep orange flesh; resistance to fusarium wilt and downy mildew.	BURR GUR HEN JUN
SUPERSTAR (hybrid)	86	6–8-pound, round to flattened, deeply ribbed and thickly netted melon with salmon flesh.	LED WIL
SWEET GEM (hybrid)	90	2½-pound, round, finely netted melon with green skin and salmon orange flesh; productive variety.	GLE
TAM PERLITA	90	2–3-pound, round melon with light netting, light sutures, and salmon flesh; resistant to powdery and downy mildews.	POR
TAM UVALDE	85–90	Well-netted, hard rind; deep orange flesh; small seed cavity; tolerant to downy and powdery mildews.	POR WIL
TANGIERS (hybrid)	82	The 6-inch, round melon has a pale lime rind and deep orange flesh. The French variety makes a good dessert melon. It's resistant to powdery mildew and fusarium wilt.	SHE
TESORO (hybrid) (Treasure)	87	4–5½ pounds; strong netting, slightly sutured; tolerant to downy and powdery mildews as well as one kind of fusarium.	BURR

CANTALOUPE (LATE SEASON)

VARIETY	DAYS	DESCRIPTION	SOURCES (p. 385)
EDISTO	90–95	5 pounds; heavy netting; firm, rich salmon flesh; resistance to alternaria and powdery and downy mildews.	DEG WIL
HARVEST PRIDE (Pride of Wisconsin, Queen of Colorado)	80–92	6½x5½ inches; well-netted; deep orange flesh; resistance to fusarium wilt.	DEG LED MEY RED SEE VER WIL
HARVEST QUEEN	92	3–4-pound, heavily netted, lightly ribbed melon with deep orange flesh; disease-resistant.	SEED
HEARTS OF GOLD (Hoodoo)	90–95	3-pound, well-netted melon with deep orange, finely grained flesh.	BURR DEG GAR MEY SEE

VARIETY	DAYS	DESCRIPTION	SOURCES (p. 385)

CANTALOUPE (LATE SEASON) *(continued)*

VARIETY	DAYS	DESCRIPTION	SOURCES (p. 385)
IMPERIAL NO. 4–50	90	Oval, heavily netted melon with small seed cavity and salmon flesh.	WIL
IROQUOIS (OP) (Giant Early Wonder)	90	7x8 inches; coarse netting; small seed cavity; salmon flesh; resistance to powdery mildew.	COM DEG FAR GUR HEN JUN LIB PON STO TER TWI VER WIL
ISRAELI (hybrid) (Old Original)	90–95	The 7–8-pound, oval melon has creamy orange flesh. Its yellow-orange rind has sparse netting and no ribs or sutures. Variety is resistant to powdery mildew.	POR
KANSAS	90	Heirloom variety; 4-pound, oval melon, moderately netted and ribbed with orange flesh.	POR
MAINSTREAM	90	3–4 pounds; slight sutures and netting; bright orange flesh; tolerant to downy and powdery mildews.	WIL
RED QUEEN (hybrid)	90	2¼-pound, round melon with beige-pink rind and orange, sugary flesh; Chinese variety.	GLE
SATICOY (hybrid)	84–90	4-pound melon with medium netting and deep orange flesh; tolerance to fusarium wilt and powdery mildew.	BURR COM JUN LED LIB MEY TWI WIL
SUPER STAR (hybrid)	86–90	8–10 pounds, 6½x6–8 inches; heavy netting; salmon flesh.	MEY
TEXAS SWEET	92	Heirloom Texas variety; 8–10 pounds; lightly netted, yellow rind; orange flesh.	SOU
TOPMARK	85–90	6–7 inch, well-netted melon with small seed cavity and salmon flesh.	BURR DEG GUR ROS WIL

CANTALOUPE (SPACE SAVERS)

VARIETY	DAYS	DESCRIPTION	SOURCES (p. 385)
BUSH MUSKETEER	90	This 3–4-pound, 5½–6-inch, heavily netted melon with orange flesh can be grown in pots and containers.	HEN JUN MEY PAR STO
BUSH STAR (hybrid)	75–88	2–2½ pounds, 4x5 inches; medium netting.	LED LIB PON POR
ITSY BITSY SWEETHEART	70	2½-pound, round melon with heavily netted golden rind and salmon flesh; very sweet.	GUR
JENNY LIND	75	The 1–2-pound baby melon has sweet, green flesh. This 1846 heirloom variety is a 5-foot vine. Many melons have knobs on the ends.	ABU LED PIN SEE SOU
SWEET BUSH (hybrid)	74	Each plant bears 3–4 round, well-netted, 2-pound melons with deep orange, fragrant flesh.	BURP

VARIETY	DAYS	DESCRIPTION	SOURCES (p. 385)

CANTALOUPE (GREEN FLESH)

VARIETY	DAYS	DESCRIPTION	SOURCES (p. 385)
CAVAILLON ESPANOL	90	1850s heirloom variety; large, oblong, heavily netted fruit; salmon center.	SOU
GALLICUM (hybrid)	80	2–2½-pound, round, greenish yellow Mediterranean melon with light sutures; resistance to powdery mildew.	NIC VER
GREEN NUTMEG (Eden Gem)	63–89	2–3-pound, oval, heavily netted melon; 1880 heirloom variety.	SEE SOU VER
HA OGEN	82–85	This round Israeli melon weighs 3–5 pounds and has medium green flesh. Green rind turns yellow when ripe.	SEED
ISRAEL (Ogen, Galia)	80	Pale yellow rind with wide sutures; small seed cavity.	ABU BOU ORG SHE
MUSKOTALY	90	2 pounds; pale green flesh.	RED
PASSPORT (hybrid)	75	6-pound, 7x7-inch, round melon with fine, full netting, no sutures, and aromatic, light green flesh.	GUR JOH TER TWI
ROCKY FORD GREEN FLESH	84–92	2½-pound, 5-inch, oblong melon with solid netting; fine grain; rust-resistant.	BURR DEG ROS SOU WIL
ROCKY SWEET (hybrid)	85	2½–3½-pound, globular melon with sparse netting and sweet flesh; high yields.	LED WIL
SWEET DREAM	79	5 pounds, 7 inches; small seed cavity with thick flesh; mildew resistant.	BURP

CANTALOUPE (ODDLY SHAPED/OTHER TYPES)

VARIETY	DAYS	DESCRIPTION	SOURCES (p. 385)
AMARELO AURO DE VALENCIA (Gold-Yellow Melon of Valencia)	100	This 1870s heirloom variety has pale green flesh. Medium-size melon turns golden-yellow when ripe.	RED
ANANAS (Israeli, Sharlyn)	100–110	The 5-pound, oblong, slightly netted melon has whitish yellow flesh. Green rind turns orange when ripe.	ORG POR RED SEE SEED WIL
BANANA	90–95	The 7-pound, 18x24-inch melon resembles a giant banana. It has little or no netting, yellow rind, and sweet, spicy salmon pink flesh.	DEG JUN LIB MEY POR SEE VER WIL
BALSAM PEAR (OP) (Balsam Apple, Bitter Melon, Foo Gwa)	75–80	This 2x8-inch melon with light green flesh looks like a warty cucumber. Soak fruit in salt water to help leach out bitterness before cooking. Plant does best in hot, moist soil in summertime.	SUN
EARLY SILVER LINE	76	Elongated, Oriental melon has white, crisp, fragrant flesh. Yellow rind is lined with silvery furrows and is so thin it can be peeled.	BURP
EMPEROR	90	20 pounds; smooth, thick, orange flesh; good winter storage melon.	GUR

VARIETY	DAYS	DESCRIPTION	SOURCES (p. 385)

CANTALOUPE (ODDLY SHAPED/OTHER TYPES) *(continued)*

VARIETY	DAYS	DESCRIPTION	SOURCES
HONEY GOLD SWEET	90	10-ounce, egg-shaped, golden yellow fruit with aromatic, crisp flesh.	SUN
HONG KING BITTER MELON	80	5 inches long; similar to Balsam Pear, but shorter and dark green.	SUN
MR. UGLY MUSKMELON	100	Italian melon with deep ribs, big warts, and rough rind; sweet salmon flesh.	GLE
PEACH VINE	90	Small melon has light-colored flesh. Harden off plants one week before harvesting by withholding water.	DEG
PINYONET DE VALENCIA (Pele de Sapo, Toad Skin)	90	Green skin with yellow tint; white flesh.	RED
ROCKET DE VALENCIA	90	Medium-large fruit with green, slightly wrinkled skin; very sweet, nearly white flesh.	RED
SPANISH ESPANHOL (Valencia Espanhol)	90	Dark green, wrinkled skin; sweet, clear green flesh.	GLE RED
SUNRISE	90	Melon weighs 3½–4 pounds and has sweet, creamy white flesh. Canary yellow skin is slightly rough.	BURP
SWAN LAKE (OP)	85	Each vine sets 10 1–2-pound melons. Flesh is white to orange-swirled.	SEED
SWEET SURPRISE	75	Round, striped; 2 pounds.	DEG

CANTALOUPE (OTHER COLORS)

VARIETY	DAYS	DESCRIPTION	SOURCES
BLANCO (White)	85	White skin; sweet flesh.	RED
COB MELON	85	Large, old-time melon with lightly mottled, green and white flesh.	GLE POR
GOLDEN CRISPY (hybrid)	85	Golden yellow melon weighs 12 ounces. Eat this Japanese variety like a pear, skin and all.	DEG GLE NIC THE VER
MARBLE WHITE (hybrid)	95	2-pound melon with a white, smooth rind and creamy white flesh; Japanese variety; withstands heat and drought conditions.	ORN VER
SPEAR	85	Heavily netted; yellow flesh; popular in maritime Northwest.	ABU
SPRITE (hybrid)	69	This 1-pound melon's skin and flesh are white. When skin takes on a yellow tinge, melon is mature.	PIN
TIGER	85	Oval, green rind splashed with yellow; pink flesh.	BOU
YUKI LARGE	90	½-pound Japanese variety; pure white rind, distinctly ribbed; thick, sweet, white flesh with fine aroma.	GLE

VARIETY	DAYS	DESCRIPTION	SOURCES (p. 385)
CANTALOUPE (HONEYDEW—GREEN FLESH)			
A-ONE (hybrid)	85	An Ogen-type melon with the sweet flavor of Anjou pears; resistant to fusarium and powdery mildew.	PAR
CRETE (hybrid)	88	A Galia type; 2½ pounds; good netting; high sugar content; pale green flesh; tolerance to powdery and downy mildews and fusarium; for greenhouse or field culture.	STO
EARLI-DEW (hybrid)	70–86	2¼–3 pounds, 5–6 inches; smooth skin; sugar-rich flesh; short season variety.	COM FAR HEN JOH JUN LIB NIC PIN PON STO TER TWI VER WIL WILL
FRUIT PUNCH (hybrid)	80	6 inches; heavily netted; gourmet flavor.	PAR
GOLDEN HONEY-MOON (Golden Rind Honeymoon)	92	Melon has emerald green flesh. Leave fruit on vine until fully ripe.	ABU BURR WIL
HONEY BREW (hybrid)	90	3–4 pounds, 6x6 inches; smooth rind; pale green flesh; resistance to fusarium and powdery mildew.	TWI
HONEYCREAM (hybrid)	95	6–8 pounds; creamy white rind; good producer even under less than perfect conditions.	LED
HONEYDEW (Green Flesh)	110–112	6–8 pounds, 7–7½ inches; smooth, ivory rind; emerald green flesh; prefers a warm, dry climate.	BURR DEG LEJ MEY NIC ORG SEE
LIMELIGHT (hybrid)	96	7–7½ pounds; sweet, thick flesh.	BURP
MAGIC-TO DEW (hybrid)	92	4 pounds; smooth, thick rind; sweet, light green flesh; tolerance to fusarium and powdery mildew.	TWI
MILKY WAY (hybrid)	80	Short season variety; pale green flesh; wilt-resistant vines.	GUR
MONTANA	75	3 pounds; thick flesh; excellent short season variety.	FIS
OGEN (hybrid) (Israel)	80	5½–6 inches long; flavor of Anjou pears.	WIL
PASSPORT (hybrid)	73–78	5–8 pounds, 6–7 inches; bananalike aroma; disease tolerant.	PAR STO VER
PINEAPPLE	80	5 pounds; netted rind; pineapple flavor.	PAR
ROCKY SWEET (hybrid)	77	2½–3½-pound melon has a high sugar content. Rind turns yellow-orange when ripe.	JUN LED
SILVER WORLD (hybrid)	85–90	3 pounds; round, smooth, ivory rind; thick, light green flesh; high sugar content.	TWI
TAM DEW	90–100	6½-pound, 8x6-inch melon; rind turns ivory when ripe. Plant resists downy and powdery mildews.	WIL

VARIETY	DAYS	DESCRIPTION	SOURCES (p. 385)

CANTALOUPE (HONEYDEW—GREEN FLESH) (continued)

VARIETY	DAYS	DESCRIPTION	SOURCES
TAM DEW IMPROVED	110	3–4 pounds, 5x5 inches; smooth, whitish rind; lime green flesh; tolerant to downy and powdery mildews.	ROS
TUTTI FRUTTI TRIO	80	5½–6 inches long; a selection of honeydews, each uniquely flavored.	PAR
VENUS (hybrid)	88	The 5¼x5¾-inch melon has light netting on a golden rind and very sweet, green flesh. Fruit slips from vine when ripe.	BURP

CANTALOUPE (HONEYDEW—ORANGE FLESH)

VARIETY	DAYS	DESCRIPTION	SOURCES
HONEYDEW (Orange Flesh)	110	5–6 pounds; smooth, creamy white rind when ripe; small seed cavity; salmon flesh.	ROS
HONEYLOUPE	75	Honeydew and cantaloupe combination; 4-pound melon; tolerant to verticillium wilt.	SEED STO
KAZAKH	70	2–3 pounds; slightly netted, orange rind; cream colored flesh; distinctive flavor.	ABU
ORANGE FLESH	90	The 3-pound melon has a gold rind and very sweet flesh. Vines are sulfur-tolerant. Plant has resistance to verticillium wilt and crown blight.	BURR
TEMPTATION (hybrid)	85	3–4 pounds; nearly round; smooth rind; honeydew flavor; resistance to powdery mildew and fusarium wilt.	TWI

CANTALOUPE (CASABA, CRENSHAW, AND PERSIAN)

VARIETY	DAYS	DESCRIPTION	SOURCES
BURPEE EARLY (hybrid) (Crenshaw)	90	Melons weigh up to 14 pounds and have salmon flesh. Rind has no netting and turns yellowish when ripe.	BURP TWI
CASABA	120	6–8 inches long; golden rind; very sweet, white flesh; will keep a long time.	SEE
CRENSHAW	90–110	5 pounds, 6x8 inches; rough, dark green rind that turns yellow when ripe; salmon flesh.	BURR DEG HEN GLE ROS SEE
EARLY HYBRID (Crenshaw)	88–90	Up to 14 pounds, 8x7½ inches; round with salmon flesh; grows almost anywhere.	TWI
EARLY SUGAR SHAW CRENSHAW (hybrid)	80	Free of netting and sutures; pale orange flesh.	VER
GOLDEN BEAUTY (Casaba)	110–120	6–8 inches long; wrinkled, golden rind; nearly white flesh; good keeper.	BURR DEG POR ROS VER
GOLD KING (hybrid)	90	4 pounds; oval; thick, yellow rind; nearly white flesh; storable.	PIN
HONEYSHAW (hybrid) (Crenshaw)	75–85	Rind is free of netting. Flesh is salmon. This short season variety does not slip when ripe.	LIB ORN NIC

VARIETY	DAYS	DESCRIPTION	SOURCES (p. 385)

CANTALOUPE (CASABA, CRENSHAW, AND PERSIAN) (*continued*)

VARIETY	DAYS	DESCRIPTION	SOURCES
JAUNE DES CANARIES (Yellow Canary, Juan Canary)	105	This casaba melon is 8–9 pounds, 8x6 inches, and egg shaped, with a yellow rind. Its very sweet flesh varies in color from pale green to whitish yellow.	BURR SEED WIL
MARYGOLD	80–88	3½–4 pounds; 6 inches; bright yellow wrinkled rind; very sweet white flesh; resistance to powdery mildew and one strain of fusarium.	STO TER
PERSIAN MEDIUM	95–110	7–8 pounds, 7x7½ inches; heavily netted; small seed cavity; thick, sweet, deep orange flesh; grows well in arid areas.	ROS
SANTA CLAUS (Christmas, Casaba)	108	6–9 pounds, 12x6 inches; faint netting on wrinkled gold rind with dark green mottling; white to pale green flesh.	GLE ORN
SUNGOLD	85–95	5–7 pounds; golden yellow, ribbed rind; greenish white flesh; good for storing.	SEED

CANTALOUPE (PRESERVING MELON)

VARIETY	DAYS	DESCRIPTION	SOURCES
PICKLING MELON	73	12x3 inches; dark green rind with slender stripes; good for pickling or cooking.	SUN

MUSTARD

BOTANICAL NAME: *Brassica juncea*

DAYS TO MATURITY: 34–85.

PLANTING TIME: Plant mustard in the spring as soon as the soil can be worked, two to four weeks before the last frost.

SOIL: Rich, mixed with rotted manure; pH 6.0–7.5.

NUTRIENTS: If the soil has been prepared with plenty of organic matter, no fertilizing should be necessary.

WATER: Regularly.

LIGHT: Full sun.

SPACING: Sow seeds ½ inch deep; thin seedlings to 4–6 inches apart. Separate rows by 18 inches.

HARVEST: Cut individual leaves as needed, or harvest the entire plant.

STORAGE: Use fresh.

MUSTARD

Mustard Growing Tip

The Right Temperature

As the daily temperatures begin to rise above 85°F, mustard leaves become inedible. In hot areas, grow mustard only in the cool weather (under 65°F) of early spring and fall.

VARIETY	DAYS	DESCRIPTION	SOURCES (p. 385)
MUSTARD (CURLED)			
FORDHOOK FANCY	40	Deeply curled, fringed, dark green leaves with a tangy flavor; slow to bolt.	COO SEE
GIANT RED (Red Giant)	23	Large, savoyed leaves are maroon with chartreuse undersides. This Japanese variety is hardy in winter and slow to bolt.	COO JOH ORN PAR SEED VER
GREEN WAVE	45–55	Edges are finely ruffled and dark green.	COM DEG JOH LIB MEY ORG SEED STO VER
KYONA (*Brassica japonica*, Mizuna)	40–45	Deeply cut, frilled leaves; narrow, white stalk; Japanese variety.	COO GAR JOH ORG SEE SEED TER THE VER
MIIKI GIANT	50	Large, wavy, green leaves with thick midribs; Japanese variety; good for warm areas.	GLE
OSAKA PURPLE	80	Fringed, purplish red leaves have a tangy flavor. This Japanese variety grows to 26 inches. Harvest leaves at 4–6 inches.	COO GLE JOH ORG RED SEED
SOUTHERN GIANT CURLED (OP) (Mustard India)	40–60	Wide, crumpled, bright green leaves with an 18–24-inch spread; slow to bolt.	BOU BURR DEG JUN LED MEY PAR POR ROS SEE SUN TIL TWI WIL
MUSTARD (PLAIN)			
BAU SIN	50	Short, thick, flat, wide petals.	GLE
FLORIDA BROAD LEAF	43–50	Broad, smooth leaves with flattened, greenish white ribs; 16–22-inch spread.	BURR COM DEG MEY POR RED ROS SEE STO SUN TWI VER WIL
KOMATSUNA LATE	30	Round, broad, dark green leaves; Japanese variety; bolts in mid-May.	GLE RED VER
SAVANNAH (hybrid) (Tendergreen Improved)	25–40	Smooth, thick, dark green leaves with narrow, creamcolored ribs; large plant.	LED PAR TWI VER
TENDERGREEN (Mustard Spinach, Komatsuma)	34–40	Large, broad, thick, dark green leaves; 16–22-inch spread; suited to warm areas.	ALL BURG COM DEG FAR GUR HIG MEY PAR ROS SEE SUN VER WIL

VARIETY	DAYS	DESCRIPTION	SOURCES (p. 385)

ORIENTAL MUSTARD CABBAGE (GREEN STALKS)

VARIETY	DAYS	DESCRIPTION	SOURCES
AUTUMN POEM	38	This bright green broccolilike plant bolts easily but produces edible flowers, stalks, young buds, and leaves. If cut back, it will produce all summer.	PIN
CANTON DWARF PAK CHOY	42	This variety resembles an immense head of lettuce.	DEG
CHINESE STEM MUSTARD (Chinese Pac Choi)	60	Light green serrated leaves are 8 inches long, 2 inches wide.	STO
CHINESE TSI SHIM (Choi Sum, *Brassica chinensis var parachinensis*)	60	Light green leaves and flowering stalks; resistant to heat; harvest when flowers begin to open.	GAR SUN
DAI GAI CHOY (India Mustard, Broadleaf Mustard Cabbage, *Brassica juncea var rugosa*)	65	With broad, thick stems and leaves, it grows best in humid climates and abundant moisture.	SUN THE
GAI CHOY (India Mustard, Chinese Mustard Greens, *Brassica juncea var foliosa*)	45	This pungent mustard-flavored plant grows fast in cool, moist areas.	THE
MEI QUING CHOI (hybrid)	45	This vase-shaped plant with pale green stems and oval, green leaves is widely adapted, tolerant to heat and cold, and slow to bolt.	BOU DEG JOH NIC ORN PAR PIN SHE STO TWI VER

ORIENTAL MUSTARD CABBAGE (SPOON-SHAPED LEAVES, WHITE STALKS)

VARIETY	DAYS	DESCRIPTION	SOURCES
BOK CHOI (Bok Choy)	45–60	Thick, green leaves and broad, white stalks.	GUR HEN LIB NIC SEED STO SUN THE
CHINA CHOY	70	Similar to Bok Choy, this variety has more loosely heading rosette leaves.	SEED
CHINESE FLAT CABBAGE	40	Deep green leaves; midsize plant.	SUN
FLOWERING PURPLE PAK-CHOI (Hon Tsai Tai Greens, Chinese Tsaishim)	40–60	Harvest the yellow-flowering stalks like broccoli. Variety doesn't form heads.	ABU NIC SUN THE
GREEN-IN-SNOW	45	Plain leaves; 20-inch-tall plant; withstands cold.	NIC ORN SEE TER THE
JAPANESE WHITE CELERY MUSTARD	50–60	Thick, light green leaves with sharp flavor; resistant to cold; slow to bolt.	TWI WILL
JOI-CHOI (hybrid)	45–50	Dark green leaves and white stalks on a 12–15-inch-tall plant; tolerant to cold and heat; slow to bolt.	JOH JUN NIC PAR STO TER VER
LEI-CHOI	47	Each plant has green leaves and 10–14 white, celerylike stalks that are 8–10 inches long. Variety is slow to bolt and Plant Variety Patented (PVP).	BURP LIB SEE STO TWI

VARIETY	DAYS	DESCRIPTION	SOURCES (p. 385)

ORIENTAL MUSTARD CABBAGE (SPOON-SHAPED LEAVES, WHITE STALKS)
(continued)

VARIETY	DAYS	DESCRIPTION	SOURCES (p. 385)
MITSUBA	60	Plain, parsleylike leaves on long, slender, white stems; Japanese variety.	GLE VER
MIZUNA (Kyona, Toyoko Beau)	36–65	Deeply indented leaves and white stalks; Japanese variety; high resistance to cold.	ABU JOH NIC ORN PIN RED SEE SEED STO SUN TER THE
OSAKA PURPLE LEAVED	80–150	20-inch-long, round, purplish red leaves with white ribs.	RED
PAK CHOI (OP) (Shakushina)	65	Smooth, rounded, green leaves and white stems; bolts easily on exposure to cold.	ABU HIG JOH SUN TIL
PAK CHOI, BOK CHOI (Chinese Pac Choi, *Brassica chinensis var chinensis*)	50–65	With tangy leaves and stalks, this plant grows best in cool, moist soil.	COM GAR HIG JOH NIC TER TIL
PRIZE CHOY	50–60	Large, dark green, spoon-shaped leaves and a white, celerylike base; 18-inch-tall plant; slow to bolt.	HIG JOH
ROUND LEAVED SANTUNG	35	Deep green leaves; large, erect plant.	SUN VER
RYOKUSAI	47	Hybrid version of Tah Tsai; glossy, deep green leaves.	VER
SHANGHAI PAC CHOI	40–50	Light green leaves; dwarf plant; highly heat resistant.	GAR HIG NIC SUN
SPOON CABBAGE	45	Green leaves on a large, erect plant.	SEE SUN
TATSOI (Tah Tsai, Taisai)	45–50	Deep green leaves; 12-inch spread; thick rosettes; slow to bolt.	ABU BOU DEG JOH NIC ORN PIN SEED SHE STO VER
TOKYO BEAU	40	This hybrid version of Mizuna produces 4 pounds of stalks per head. These sweet yields are extensively used in Japanese cooking.	VER

OKRA

BOTANICAL NAME: *Hibiscus esculentus*

DAYS TO MATURITY: 48–90.

PLANTING TIME: Plant the seeds outside when the soil temperature has reached 75°F. You can also sow seeds indoors or in a hotbed about a month before the last frost. Soak the seeds in water 24 hours before planting.

SOIL: Rich, loamy; pH 6.0–8.0.

NUTRIENTS: Fertilize twice during the growing season with fish emulsion.

OKRA

WATER: Keep moist but don't overwater.

LIGHT: Full sun.

SPACING: Sow seeds ½ inch deep, 18 inches apart. Space rows 3 feet apart.

HARVEST: The pods produce rapidly and should be picked daily, beginning a few days after the flower petals have fallen, whether or not the pods are to be used. If the pods ripen, the plant stops producing.

STORAGE: Use fresh or as pickles.

Okra Growing Tip

Cut, Don't Pull

Instead of straining to pluck okra pods, cut them off with scissors. Do this when they are young and tender, with half-grown, immature seeds. If left on the plant, the pods become hard and unpalatable.

VARIETY	DAYS	DESCRIPTION	SOURCES (p. 385)
OKRA (GREEN, FULL SIZE)			
ANNIE OAKLEY (hybrid)	48–57	Long, slender, spineless pods; 3–4-foot plant.	BURP BURR GOU GUR HEN JOH LED MEY PAR PIN POR TER WIL WILL
ANNIE OAKLEY II (hybrid)	57	Improved Annie Oakley; medium green, spineless pods; compact plant.	NIC STO TWI
CLEMSON SPINELESS (Gumbo)	55–60	An All-American winner, the 4–5-foot plant develops 6–9-inch-long, rich green, slightly grooved pods. Pick pods when they are 3 inches or shorter.	BOU BURP BURR COM DEG GUR JLH JUN LED LEJ MEY PAR PIN POR RED ROS SEE SOU VER
CLEMSON SPINELESS 80 (OP)	55	Medium green, spineless pods; 4–5-foot plant.	HEN TWI
COWHORN	30–45	Extralong, slender pods.	POR
EMERALD GREEN (Emerald Green Velvet)	50	7–9-inch-long, medium green, smooth pods with some ridging; 6–9-foot plant.	POR TWI
EVERTENDER	50	5–7-inch-long, green pods; 5½-foot plant; unbranched India variety; resistant to disease.	GLE SOU
GOLD COAST	75	The light green, 6x1⅛-inch pods are smooth and spineless with almost no fluting. The well-branched 5-foot plant tolerates drought and heat.	SOU
GREEN VELVET SPINELESS	60	7-inch-long, light green pods; 5-foot-tall plant.	JLH POR
JADE	55	Dark green pods remain tender to a length of 6 inches. Plant grows to 4½ feet.	SOU

VARIETY	DAYS	DESCRIPTION	SOURCES (p. 385)

OKRA (GREEN, FULL SIZE) *(continued)*

VARIETY	DAYS	DESCRIPTION	SOURCES (p. 385)
LOUISIANA GREEN VELVET	60	6–7-inch-long, velvety green pods; 6-foot-tall, branching plant.	ORN
PARK'S CANDELABRA BRANCHING	50–60	4–6 spikes per plant; open habit.	PAR
PERKINS LONG POD	60	7–8-inch-long, dark green, ribbed pods; medium tall plant.	POR
PERKINS MAMMOTH	60	6–9-inch, brown-green, ribbed pods; 6–12-foot-tall plant.	MEY SEE SEED STO
PERKINS SPINELESS	53	6–9-inch, ribbed pods; 4½–7-foot plant.	DEG MEY
SPIKE	48	4–5-inch, green pods; open habit; tolerant to yellow vein mosaic virus.	WIL

OKRA (SPACE SAVERS)

VARIETY	DAYS	DESCRIPTION	SOURCES (p. 385)
DWARF GREEN LONG POD	50	7-inch-long, dark green, ribbed pods; 2½–3-foot tall plant.	ALL DEG LED MEY POR SEE
EMERALD	56–58	Round, dark green, spineless pods; 6–7-foot plant.	LED POR
LEE	50	6–7-inch-long, bright green, spineless pods; 3-foot-tall plant; open habit.	HEN PAR POR
PERKINS DWARF SPINELESS	53	7-inch-long, dark green pods; 3½-foot-tall plant.	BURR COM
SUN PERKINS DWARF	50	Dark green, 7-inch-tall, ridged pods; 2½–3-foot, well-branched plant.	ROS

OKRA (OTHER COLORS)

VARIETY	DAYS	DESCRIPTION	SOURCES (p. 385)
BLONDY	50	Harvest before the spineless pods are 3 inches long. This 3–4-foot-tall plant is a short season variety.	GUR HEN ORN POR
BURGUNDY (hybrid)	60	6–8-inch-long, deep burgundy pods; 5-foot plant; All-American winner.	BOU COM HEN JOH LED NIC ORN POR SOU VER
RED OKRA	60	Red pods; 5–6-foot plant.	DEG SEE
RED VELVET	56	Red, slightly ribbed pods; tall, red stalks with red ribbed leaves.	ORN SEED
RED WONDER	60	This India variety's long pods stay tender to maturity.	GLE
ROSELLE	60	Imported from India, this variety's scarlet flower buds and leaves make clear wines and jelly.	GLE
STAR OF DAVID	61	Harvest the pods before they reach a mature 5–9 inches. This Israeli variety has an unbranched, 8–10-foot stalk.	SEED SOU

VARIETY	DAYS	DESCRIPTION	SOURCES (p. 385)

OKRA (OTHER COLORS) *(continued)*

WHITE VELVET	60	6–7-inch-long, smooth, velvety white pods; 5-foot plant.	DEG

ONIONS

BOTANICAL NAME: *Allium cepa*

DAYS TO MATURITY: 95–150.

PLANTING TIME: Plant sets, seeds, or plants outside four to six weeks before the last frost.

SOIL: Firm, sandy to loam, fertile; add generous amounts of organic matter, rock potash, and bonemeal before planting; pH 5.5–7.0.

NUTRIENTS: Fertilize twice. Use fish emulsion.

WATER: Water steadily, never letting the soil dry out.

LIGHT: Full sun.

SPACING: It is best to plant seedlings or sets. Set 2 inches deep, 2–4 inches apart. If you sow seeds, plant them ½ inch deep and 2 inches apart. For row planting, space rows 12–18 inches apart.

HARVEST: Bunching onions should be harvested as needed. Storage onions are ready when the tops bend over. Discontinue watering for at least a week before harvesting. Lift onions with a spading fork, and allow the bulbs to dry on the ground.

STORAGE: Bulb onions can be stored on trays of wire netting, tied with string and braided or placed on wooden shelves. Store them in a dry, frost-proof area where air circulates freely.

Onion Growing Tips

When Onions Flower

Onions planted from sets sometimes form flowers and fail to produce mature bulbs. Avoid this by selecting and planting smaller size onion sets. When flowers appear, break off the flower buds and use these poorer onions first.

Drying Onions

To dry onions, hang them from string. Knot a loop of string around a bottom shoot and twist the string around upper shoots. Hang onions outside in dry, warm weather.

ONIONS

VARIETY	DAYS	DESCRIPTION	SOURCES (p. 385)

ONIONS (GLOBE, RED)

VARIETY	DAYS	DESCRIPTION	SOURCES
APACHE (hybrid)	115	Red scales, red interior.	BURR
BENNY'S RED (Bennie's Red)	112	Bright red scales, pink to white flesh; large and pungent; stores 4–5 months.	JOH LIB STO
BIG RED (hybrid)	110	Dark red scales, white flesh; long day onion; stores well.	TWI
CALIFORNIA WONDER RED	80–85	Deep burgundy scales, red ringed slices; medium pungency; for long-term storage.	SHE
CARMEN (hybrid)	108–155	Deep bloodred scales, bright pink flesh; stores well.	THO
LUCIFER (hybrid)	106	Bloodred scales; large.	STO
MOUNTAIN RED	100	Deep red scales, white flesh; mild flavor.	FIS
REDMAN	105	Deep burgundy scales, red interior rings; Bennie's Red type; medium pungency; stores 4–5 months.	JOH STO TER WILL
SOUTHPORT RED GLOBE	100–120	Deep red scales, pink tinged, white rings; pungent flavor; long day onion for short storage.	JLH LIB PIN THO
TANGO (hybrid)	112	Glossy, dark red scales; medium-length storage.	BURR

ONIONS (GLOBE, WHITE)

VARIETY	DAYS	DESCRIPTION	SOURCES
ALBION (hybrid)	110	White scales, white flesh.	THO
BLANCO DURO	120	White scales, white flesh; resistant to pink root.	BURR
KELSAE SWEET GIANT	110	This long-keeping, white onion weighs up to 7 pounds, 8 ounces.	PIN STO
LANCASTRIAN (Football Onion)	120	Yellowish white scales, white flesh; up to 7 pounds; stores well.	THO
SOUTHPORT WHITE GLOBE	100–110	Clear, white scales; long day type; mild flavor.	BOU DEG LED MEY PIN
WHITE SWEET SLICER	110	This long day, mildly flavored onion weighs up to 1 pound and stores well.	GUR

ONIONS (GLOBE, YELLOW/BRONZE)

VARIETY	DAYS	DESCRIPTION	SOURCES
ALISA CRAIG (Exhibition)	110	Golden straw-colored scales; mild flavor; long-keeping.	BOU JOH PIN VER
BEDFORDSHIRE CHAMPION	110	Brownish scales, white flesh; old variety.	BOU
BINGO	100	Bronze scales; extrahard flesh; will store long.	STO
CANADA MAPLE (hybrid)	110	Extrahard flesh; will store long; excellent yields in deep muck.	STO

VARIETY	DAYS	DESCRIPTION	SOURCES (p. 385)
ONIONS (GLOBE, YELLOW/BRONZE) *(continued)*			
COPPER KING (hybrid)	95	Jumbo size with dark copper scales; will store long; tolerance of pink root.	STO
COPRA (hybrid)	105–111	Dark, heavy yellow scales; Dutch variety for long storage.	GAR JOH STO
DANVERS YELLOW GLOBE	100	Coppery yellow scales, white flesh; medium-large and solid.	ALL MEY
DOWNING YELLOW GLOBE (Trapp's)	90–112	Dark yellow scales; long day type; medium size; pungent flavor; for long storage.	COM TIL
DURATION (hybrid)	110	Coppery bronze scales; long-term storage; tolerance to fusarium and pink root; good variety for deep muck.	STO
EARLY YELLOW GLOBE (OP)	98–114	Deep yellow scales, clear white flesh; long day type; mild flavor; keeps well.	ABU DEG FAR JUN PIN SOU STO TER VER WILL
ESKIMO (hybrid)	85	Light bronze scales; long day type for short-term storage; resistance to botrytis and tolerance to basal rot.	STO TWI
FIRST EDITION	105	For long-term storage; widely adapted; long day type; tolerant to root rot.	GUR HEN LIB WILL
GOLDEN CASCADE (hybrid)	120	Firm flesh; good for storing.	NIC
HI-BALL (hybrid)	110	10–12-ounce bulb with firm, yellowish white flesh and yellowish tan scales; medium pungency.	TER
LEGACY (hybrid)	108	Good for storing; tolerance to pink root and fusarium; recommended for shallow muck.	STO
MAGNA SWEET (hybrid)	110	Tan to medium brown scales and firm flesh; long day type that keeps well; tolerant to pink root.	TWI
NEW YORK EARLY	98	Medium-large, yellow onion for medium-length storage.	JOH
NORSEMAN (hybrid)	98	Golden yellow scales; stores well; tolerant to pink root.	STO
NORSTAR (hybrid)	80–85	Light bronze scales; short season, long day variety for short-term storage; resistance to botrytis and tolerance to basal rot.	LIB STO TWI
NORTHERN OAK (hybrid)	108	Large storage onion has rich oak-colored scales. Variety has tolerance to fusarium and some strains of pink root.	STO
PRINCE (hybrid)	106	Large onion with yellow scales.	JOH
SIMCOE (hybrid)	110	Golden bronze scales; long day type for storage; pungent flavor; good for muck soil.	TER
SPARTAN BANNER (hybrid)	110	Bright yellow scales; long day type; will keep.	FAR

VARIETY	DAYS	DESCRIPTION	SOURCES (p. 385)

ONIONS (GLOBE, YELLOW/BRONZE) *(continued)*

VARIETY	DAYS	DESCRIPTION	SOURCES
SPARTAN BANNER '80 (hybrid)	107–114	Bronze scales; long day type; good storage onion.	LIB PAR
STOKES EXPORTER II (hybrid)	100	Long storage type; tolerant to fusarium.	STO
TARMAGON (hybrid)	76	Short storage.	STO
X-201 (hybrid)	115	Bronze scales, white flesh; stores well.	BURR

ONIONS (SPANISH, WHITE/RED)

VARIETY	DAYS	DESCRIPTION	SOURCES
SWEET SPANISH UTAH (Jumbo White)	110	White scales; 4-inch diameter; resistant to thrips; not for storing.	TER
WHITE SWEET SPAN-ISH (hybrid) (Valencia)	110	White scales and flesh, large and firm; limited storage.	DEG FIS GUR HEN JUN LED NIC PIN PON ROS STO TIL WIL WILL
ZAPOTEC (hybrid)	120	3–4-inch diameter; stores well; tolerance to pink root and fusarium.	BURR
ZUNI (hybrid)	129	4–5-inch diameter; for medium-length storage; tolerant to pink root.	BURR

ONIONS (FLAT, RED)

VARIETY	DAYS	DESCRIPTION	SOURCES
CARDINAL (hybrid)	110	This medium to large red onion can be stored for several months.	TER
FLAT RED	110	Red scales, white flesh; 3–4-inch diameter; mild taste; does not store.	JUN
RED CREOLE	190	Reddish buff scales on firm, small bulbs; short day type; very pungent; keeps well.	GUR
RED WETHERFIELD	103	Deep red scales, white flesh; long day type; mild flavor.	ALL COM DEG SEE VER
STOCKTON EARLY RED (OP)	110	This large onion with bright red scales and thick, pinkish white flesh is recommended for Northern California, coastal areas, and southern Oregon.	COO TER

ONIONS (FLAT, YELLOW)

VARIETY	DAYS	DESCRIPTION	SOURCES
BUFFALO (hybrid)	88	Yellow scales; short-term storage.	JOH TER THO
EBENEZER	105	Yellow-brown scales, yellowish white flesh; 3-inch diameter; mild flavor.	NIC PAR SOU THO
EQUANEX	170	Bronze scales; short day variety; tolerant to pink root.	GUR
GIALLO DI MILANO	110	Golden yellow scales; stores well.	COO

VARIETY	DAYS	DESCRIPTION	SOURCES (p. 385)

ONIONS (FLAT, YELLOW) *(continued)*

VARIETY	DAYS	DESCRIPTION	SOURCES (p. 385)
GIANT ZITTAU	110	Golden brown scales; long-keeping.	BOU
RELIANCE	110	Yellow scales; hardy in winter.	BOU
STUTTGARTER	120	Large onion with dark yellow scales; keeps well.	JUN THO WILL
WALLA WALLA	110–300	Large and sweet; not for storing.	BURP COO FIS GAR GOU GUR HEN JOH JUN LIB NIC ORG ORN PIN SEE TER TIL

ONIONS (FLAT, WHITE)

VARIETY	DAYS	DESCRIPTION	SOURCES
WHITE EBENEZER	100	White scales; long day type.	PAR

ONIONS (GRANEX—THICK, FLAT)

VARIETY	DAYS	DESCRIPTION	SOURCES
GRANEX RED	82	Large, dark red onion; short day type.	PAR
GRANEX WHITE (hybrid)	105–175	Clear, white flesh; short day type; mild flavor.	PAR POR SOU
GRANEX YELLOW (hybrid)	110	Yellow scales; mild flavor; short storage life.	HEN PAR POR
VIDALIA	110	Extremely sweet and mild; short day variety; widely adapted.	GUR HEN PAR POR

ONIONS (GRANO—TOP-SHAPED)

VARIETY	DAYS	DESCRIPTION	SOURCES
EARLY WHITE GRANO	185	Snow white onion with mild flavor; short day type; not for storage.	GUR ROS
NEW MEXICO YELLOW	150	Light yellow scales and soft flesh with mild flavor.	ABU WIL
RED GRANO	90	This midsize onion with dark red scales stores up to 3 months and is resistant to pink root rot.	ROS
TEXAS EARLY YELLOW GRANO 502	168	Yellow scales and soft, mild flesh; short-term storage; resistant to thrips and pink root.	POR SEE SEED
TEXAS GRANO 1015Y	175	Light yellow scales; tolerant to heat and drought; Plant Variety Patented (PVP).	GUR HEN JUN LIB POR WIL
YELLOW GRANO	90	A large, mild onion with straw-colored scales and white flesh.	ROS

ONIONS (SPINDLE-SHAPED)

VARIETY	DAYS	DESCRIPTION	SOURCES
ITALIAN BLOOD RED BOTTLE	120	Large onion with spicy, tangy flavor.	NIC

VARIETY	DAYS	DESCRIPTION	SOURCES (p. 385)

ONIONS (SPINDLE-SHAPED) *(continued)*

VARIETY	DAYS	DESCRIPTION	SOURCES (p. 385)
ITALIAN RED (Torpedo)	95–115	Purplish red scales, red flesh; short-term storage; good variety for central California; will not bolt.	GUR HEN SEED
RED FLORENCE	95	6 inches long, bronzy pink-red; for storing; mild flavor.	COO
SIMIONE RED BOTTLE (Red Simione)	120	Intense carime color; French variety.	GAR GOU

ONIONS (BERMUDA, FLATTENED)

VARIETY	DAYS	DESCRIPTION	SOURCES (p. 385)
CALIFORNIA EARLY RED	110	Large, sweet onion with red scales and white flesh; stores well.	POR
CRYSTAL WHITE WAX (Eclipse, 1–303)	95	Midsize onion with white scales and flesh; short day variety.	DEG HEN PAR POR ROS WIL
RED BURGUNDY (Hamburger Onion)	95	Soft, mild onion; short storage life.	BURP DEG FAR GUR HEN NIC POR ROS SEE WIL
ROSSA DI MILANO	110	Pungent Italian red onion for storage.	COO
WHITE BERMUDA	92–185	White scales, white flesh; mild flavor; unharmed by frost.	BURP GUR HEN PAR
YELLOW BERMUDA	92–185	Midsize, mildly flavored onion with straw-colored scales; short day type.	BURP DEG POR

ONIONS (BUNCHING, SCALLIONS)

VARIETY	DAYS	DESCRIPTION	SOURCES (p. 385)
ASAGI BUNCHING	65	High yielding; mild flavor.	DEG
BELTSVILLE BUNCHING	65	Slight bulbs; hardy in winter.	SEE STO
BENIZOME RED BUNCHING	65	Shafts are red only in cool seasons.	ORN
EMERALD ISLE	64	Medium green, strong, straight tops; long, white, bulbless shanks; tolerant to heat.	STO
EVERGREEN HARDY WHITE	60–65	Small or no bulbs; hardy in winter.	GAR HIG JOH NIC SOU
EVERGREEN LONG WHITE BUNCHING	65–120	With long, silvery white stems, these pungent stalks form no bulbs and are slow to bolt.	ABU BURP DEG FIS JLH PAR PON SEE SUN TWI WILL
GET SET RED	70	This variety forms large bulbs in its second year.	SEE
HE SKI KO EVER-GREEN (Long White Bunching Welsh, Nebuka, Japanese Bunching, Hardy White Bunching, White Spanish)	60–80	Winter-hardy perennial; white, pungent flesh without bulbs.	ALL BOU COM FAR GUR HEN JLH JUN NIC PIN SEE STO THE VER

VARIETY	DAYS	DESCRIPTION	SOURCES (p. 385)
ONIONS (BUNCHING, SCALLIONS) *(continued)*			
ISHIKURA LONG (Ishikuro)	65	Thick, cylindrical, bulbless stalks; winter-hardy Japanese type.	GLE SEE STO THO
KINCHO	75	Long, slim, pure white stems without bulbs.	MEY STO
LONG WHITE SUMMER BUNCHING	60–75	6–7-inch-long, white shafts without bulbs; tolerant to fusarium and pink root.	COO STO
MULTI-STALK 9 (Watsuki)	80	7-inch-long, white stalks.	SUN
RED BEARD	60	Red Japanese variety with mild flavor.	GOU SUN
RED WELCH BUNCHING	65	The 14-inch-long, red, bulbless onions grow in clusters.	VER
SANTA CLAUSE	56	This Ishikuro type is rose colored at the base and can grow to be the size of a leek.	THO
SOUTHPORT WHITE GLOBE	65	Strain of Southport White Globe; mild flavor.	STO
WHITE BUNCHING	40	14–18-inch-long, white stalks; endures heat well.	DEG HEN
WHITE LISBON (Improved Green Bunching)	60–70	Resistant to heat and cold.	BOU DEG FAR ROS SEE SHE STO TER THO WILL
WHITE SPEAR BUNCHING	60–65	These long, slender, pure white stalks are slow to form bulbs even in hot weather.	JOH LIB SOU
WHITE SWEET SPANISH BUNCHING	65	Slow to form bulbs; mild flavor.	BURR LIB STO TIL
WINTER WHITE BUNCHING	60	Excellent overwintering qualities.	THO
YAKKO SUMMER	100	Stands summer heat well.	RED
ZIPPY (hybrid)	65	Resistant to pink root.	LIB
ONIONS (EGYPTIAN/MULTIPLYING)			
EGYPTIAN TREE TOP (Pickle Onion, Salad Onion, Winter Onion)	120	Top sets are ½ inch in diameter, while bottom onions are 1 inch in diameter. This hardy 24–36-inch-tall plant multiplies at the top and divides at the bottom.	ABU KAL SEE
MORITZ EGYPTIAN	120	Top set onion with red-purple bulbs; Missouri heirloom variety.	KAL SOU
OLD FASHIONED (Hill Onion, Potato Onion, Mother Onion, Pregnant Onion)	120	The best multiplying onion propagates in soil only. It doesn't go to seed. There are yellow, red, and white varieties.	SOU

VARIETY	DAYS	DESCRIPTION	SOURCES (p. 385)

ONIONS (EGYPTIAN/MULTIPLYING) *(continued)*

VARIETY	DAYS	DESCRIPTION	SOURCES
PAPAGO	120	Grown by Arizona's Papago Indians for years. With a flavor like shallots, this variety spreads rapidly to form clumps of small bulbs.	PLA

ONIONS (OTHER TYPES)

VARIETY	DAYS	DESCRIPTION	SOURCES
RED BEARD	75	Red-stalked, bunching onions with dark green leaves and bulbless white tips and roots.	STO

ONIONS (PICKLING)

VARIETY	DAYS	DESCRIPTION	SOURCES
BARLETTA (White Pearl)	70	Small, round bulbs.	FIS ORN STO WILL
BORETTANA (Cipollini, Italian Button)	120	This Italian heirloom variety is 1½–2 inches in diameter and ¾ inch thick with rosy bronze skin.	SHE
CRYSTAL WAX	60	Small, pearly white bulbs; resistant to pink root; Plant Variety Patented (PVP).	HEN PAR PON SEE STO TER
EARLY AVIV	68	This Israeli variety is ¾–2 inches in diameter with a flattened shape and silvery white color.	SHE
GOLDEN MOSQUE	105	This variety for yellow sets has the nonsprouting features of Stuttgarter.	STO
PURPLETTE	60	Purple-red onion turns pastel pink when cooked. Bulbs have purple-pearl ends.	COO HIG JOH ORN SEE
SNOW BABY (hybrid)	57	Round, waxy, white, 1–2 inches in diameter.	JOH
WHITE PORTUGAL (Silverskin)	60	Flat, white, mild onion.	STO TIL
WONDER OF POMPEII (Pompeii Perla Prima)	60–100	Very small, round onion.	COO GAR HIG NIC SEE STO

SHALLOTS

VARIETY	DAYS	DESCRIPTION	SOURCES
ATLANTIC	90	Plump, round, yellow-tan shallots; high-yielding Dutch variety; mild flavor.	COO
ATLAS	90	Grown from true seed in Holland, this French-style shallot with brown-red skin and pinkish red flesh will grow almost anywhere.	JOH
DUTCH YELLOW	90	Mild flavor; often keeps up to 12 months.	NIC
FRENCH SHALLOTS	90	Multiplies in soil; plant in spring or fall.	GAR JOH NIC SOU VER WILL
FROG LEGS SHALLOTS	90	One shallot multiplies into a cluster of more than 15.	LEJ

VARIETY	DAYS	DESCRIPTION	SOURCES (p. 385)
SHALLOTS (*continued*)			
GIANT RED	70	Mild, spicy; stores through winter.	THO
GOLDEN GOURMET	77	Firm, crisp, golden brown-skinned shallots with good storing ability.	THO
GREY SHALLOT	90	Considered the true shallot in France; for fall planting.	LEJ
ODETTA'S WHITE SHALLOT	90	Bulb is ¾–1¼ inches in diameter. This pre-season 1900 heirloom variety is widely adapted.	SOU
PINK SHALLOT	90	Large French variety; vivid reddish pink skin and flesh.	SEE
SHALLOTS (Yellow Multiplier Sets)	90	Mild flavor; widely adapted; keeps well.	BURP FAR HEN JUN LEJ MEY RED WILL
SUCCESS	90	Auburn-skinned shallots.	COO

PARSNIPS

BOTANICAL NAME: *Pastinaca sativa*

DAYS TO MATURITY: 94–145.

PLANTING TIME: Sow seeds as soon as the ground can be worked in early spring. In areas where winter temperatures rarely fall below 25°F, sow seeds in early fall for harvesting the following spring.

SOIL: Parsnips need rich, recently manured soil. Cultivate the bed to a depth of at least 18 inches and remove all rocks.

NUTRIENTS: Fertilize once a month during the growing season. Use fish emulsion.

WATER: Some watering is necessary, especially in the early stages while the roots are small.

LIGHT: Full sun to partial shade.

SPACING: Sow seeds ½ inch deep. For row gardening, space rows 2–2½ feet apart. Thin seedlings to 6 inches apart.

HARVEST: Parsnips' flavor is enhanced if the roots are left in the ground all winter.

STORAGE: Pull them as needed, and keep the rest stored in the ground.

PARSNIPS

Parsnip Growing Tips

Top Flavor

For the best flavor, lift a few roots in early fall and leave them on the surface of the soil through several hard frosts. This brings them to top flavor long before the roots in the ground reach the same stage. Others can be stored in peat or sand.

Germinating Parsnip Seed

Enticing parsnips to peek through the soil can be tricky. The seed won't stay moist and is slow to germinate. Try sowing 8–12 (or more) seeds per foot, ½ inch deep, and laying down a clear plastic covering. Remove this plastic when the seeds germinate. Later, thin the plants so they are 3–4 inches apart.

VARIETY	DAYS	DESCRIPTION	SOURCES (p. 385)
PARSNIPS			
ALL AMERICAN (Harris Model)	95–145	Smooth, wedge-shaped, white root is 12 inches long and 1½–3 inches thick.	ABU DEG FIS GAR GUR HEN HIG LIB NIC STO TER TWI
COBHAM IMPROVED MARROW	120	Half-long, tapered, smooth, white roots with a high sugar content; resistant to canker; English variety.	JOH ORN
GLADIATOR (hybrid)	110	Smooth, white skin; resistant to canker; English variety.	TER
HARRIS EARLY MODEL	100–120	10x3½ inches, white skin.	BURR DEG JUN SEE STO
HOLLOW CROWN (Sugar)	95–135	12x2¾-inch, white, smooth roots; 1850 heirloom variety.	ABU ALL BURP BURR BUT COM DEG FAR PAR SEE SEED SOU VER
IMPROVED HOLLOW CROWN	95–120	10-inch-long, 3-inch-thick, smooth, white roots.	LED MEY STO WILL
IMPROVED STUMP ROOTED	95	5–8x3 inches, white skin.	JUN
JUNG'S WHITE SUGAR	120	White skin, half-long, stocky, heavy at the shoulders.	JUN
LANCER	120	Refined Harris Model type; long, slender, smooth roots; tolerance to canker.	JOH
LONG WHITE	120	Large, smooth, and sweet.	TIL
TENDER AND TRUE	102	Reputed to be the longest and best flavored, this parsnip has no hard core and is resistant to canker.	BOU
THE STUDENT	110	15–30-inch-long, tapering roots with a 3-inch diameter; 1860 heirloom variety.	BOU
WHITE MODEL	100	Pure white, smooth skin; good variety for short season areas.	FAR PIN

PEAS

BOTANICAL NAME: *Pisum sativum*

DAYS TO MATURITY: 57–100.

PLANTING TIME: Start your peas in the spring as soon as the soil can be worked, and continue to sow seeds every 10 days until 60 days remain before the average daytime temperatures are expected to be about 75°F. In milder regions, start successive planting in the fall.

SOIL: Rich and recently manured; pH 6.0–7.5.

NUTRIENTS: Peas supply their own nitrogen. Fertilize them with fish emulsion only while the plants are developing. Too much nitrogen encourages bushy growth and little yield.

WATER: Peas need plenty of water.

LIGHT: Full sun.

SPACING: Sow these seeds 2 inches deep, 2 inches apart. If you plant rows, space them 18–30 inches apart.

HARVEST: Edible podded peas should be picked when the pods are still flat and the peas barely there. Pick regular peas while they are firm but still succulent. Hold the vine in one hand while picking peas with the other to prevent pulling the vine from the ground.

STORAGE: Some varieties of peas are eaten fresh, some dried, others frozen.

Pea Growing Tips

Pollinating Peas

When peas yield a profusion of blossoms but no pods, the pollen isn't being transferred from the male parts to the female parts of the flower. Peas are self-pollinating, but once in a while they need a little help. Shake them a couple of times a day for about a week. Then get ready for a bumper crop.

Presprouting Peas

To ensure that peas will come up fast, sprout the seeds ahead of time. Spread a paper towel on a waterproof surface, scatter the pea seeds evenly over it, and cover this with another paper towel. Dampen your pea sandwich, roll it up, and put it in a plastic bag in a warm room. A few days later, unroll the towels, and remove the germinated seeds. Plant them outdoors. They'll even grow in cold soil.

PEAS

Pea Sticks

You can use what the English call "pea sticks" to support your growing peas. These are long branch cuttings from deciduous shrubs and trees that gardeners simply push into the ground. An alternative method is to construct a short bamboo fence, with pea-stick supports. As the peas spread, both the fence and the pea sticks disappear.

VARIETY	DAYS	DESCRIPTION	SOURCES (p. 385)
PEAS (BUSH, UP TO 24 INCHES)			
BLUE BANTAM	60–64	18-inch-long vine, 4-inch-long pods; long bearing.	ALL VER
BURPEEANA EARLY	63	18–24-inch-long vine, 3-inch-long pods, 8–10 peas per pod; all-purpose pea.	BURP
CURLY	60	Nearly leafless; shelling pea; mildew resistant.	ORN
DAYBREAK	52	2-foot vine, 3-inch, blunt ended pods with 6–8 peas per pod; resistant to fusarium wilt.	GAR HEN JOH LED PAR PIN THO
DWARF TELEPHONE (Daisy)	70–76	20-inch vine, 2-inch pods, 9 peas per pod; does well in cooler climates.	ALL
FROSTY	62	The 24–28-inch vine has 3⅓-inch pods with 6–8 peas per pod. This wilt-resistant variety sets double pods.	FAR FIS MEY
HOLLAND CAPUCIJNERS	85	Large, wrinkled, brown-gray shelling peas; compact plant with violet, red, white, or pink flowers; Dutch variety.	ORN
KELVEDON WONDER	65	18-inch vine, 3-inch pods with wrinkled peas; cold-tolerant vines.	BOU
KNIGHT	56–61	18-inch vine, 3½–4-inch pods, 7–9 peas per pod; sets double pods; resistant to mosaic virus, powdery mildew, and common wilt.	COM GAR JOH LED MEY PIN SHE STO TWI
LACY LADY	55	18-inch vine, 3-inch pods; sets double pods; semileafless variety.	FAR VER
LAXTONIAN	62	16–18-inch vine, 8–10 peas per pod.	DEG
LAXTON'S PROGRESS (Morse's Progress No. 9, Progress No. 9, Big Dakota, Early Giant, Jung's Blue Bantam)	60	15–20-inch vine, 4½-inch pods, 7–9 peas per pod; high resistance to fusarium wilt.	ALL BURR FAR FIS GUR HEN JUN LED MEY TIL TWI VER WIL WILL
LAXTON'S PROGRESS IMPROVED	55	16–18-inch vine, 3½-inch pods, 7–9 peas per pod.	SEE STO
LAXTON'S SUPERB (Early Bird)	60	24-inch vine, 3½-inch pods, 7–9 peas per pod; semiwrinkled pea.	MEY
LITTLE MARVEL (Improved American Wonder)	58–64	18-inch vine, 3-inch pods, 7–9 peas per pod.	ABU ALL BURP BURR DEG FAR GUR HEN JUN LED MEY PON POR SEE SOU STO TIL WIL WILL

VARIETY	DAYS	DESCRIPTION	SOURCES (p. 385)

PEAS (BUSH, UP TO 24 INCHES) *(continued)*

VARIETY	DAYS	DESCRIPTION	SOURCES (p. 385)
MAESTRO	57–61	24-inch vine, 4-inch pods, 9–10 peas per pod; shelling pea; multiple disease resistance.	BURP GAR GUR HEN HIG JOH JUN ORN PAR TER
MONTANA MARVEL	64	18-inch vine, 3½-inch pods, 8–9 peas per pod; well adapted to mountain climates.	HIG
NOVELLA	57	This semileafless variety's 3-inch pods form at the top of the 20–25-inch vine.	COM COO GUR JUN PAR POR WILL
NOVELLA II	64	2-foot vine, 3-inch pods; semileafless; easy to shell; resistant to powdery mildew.	GAR JOH NIC PIN
OLYMPIA	60–62	16–18-inch vine, 4½-inch pods, 8–9 peas per pod; high percentage of double pods; resistant to mosaic viruses and powdery mildew.	FAR STO WILL
PATRIOT	65	18–22-inch-long vine, 4-inch-long pods, 9–10 peas per pod.	PAR STO VER
PETIT PROVENCAL (Petit Pois)	58	18–20-inch vine; French variety; best when young.	BURP
PRECOVELLE	60	2½-inch pods with tiny peas; French variety; resistant to fusarium wilt and top yellow.	SHE
RAISIN CAPUCIJNERS	60	24-inch vine; large, brownish peas for shelling.	WILL
ROUND GREEN	55	24-inch-long vine; round, green shelling pea.	WILL
SPARKLE	55–60	15–24-inch vine, 2½–3½-inch pods, 7–9 peas per pod; resistant to common wilt.	ALL COM FAR LED
SPRING	52	22-inch vine, 3-inch pods, 6–7 peas per pod.	STO
TOP POD	70	2-foot vine, 5–6-inch pods, 8–10 peas per pod; does well in high temperatures and dry weather.	PIN
TWIGGY	68	24-inch vine with lots of tendrils, 3½-inch pods.	FIS
WAVEREX	55–65	20-inch vine, 2–3-inch, blunt pods, 7–8 small peas per pod; German Petit Pois variety; grows well in cool climates.	BOU COO

PEAS (25 INCHES OR MORE)

VARIETY	DAYS	DESCRIPTION	SOURCES (p. 385)
ALASKA (Earliest of All)	52–58	The main variety used to make split pea soup, it has a 29-inch vine and 2½-inch pods with 6–8 peas per pod. Variety is resistant to fusarium wilt.	ABU BURR BUT DEG FAR MEY PIN SEE TIL VER WIL
ALMOTA	60	34-inch-tall plant; hardy, disease-resistant pea.	VER
ARGONA	60	Petit Pois pea; 3-foot-long vine, 2½-inch-long pods with 8 tiny, round peas; resistant to common wilt.	JOH
BLUE POD CAPUCIJNERS	60	4-foot vine; grayish shelling pea.	ORN WILL

VARIETY	DAYS	DESCRIPTION	SOURCES (p. 385)

PEAS (25 INCHES OR MORE) *(continued)*

VARIETY	DAYS	DESCRIPTION	SOURCES
BOUNTY	61	The 2–2½-foot vine has 3½-inch, blunt ended pods with 8 peas per pod. Variety resists powdery mildew and wilt.	JOH SHE
EARLY FROSTY	64	28-inch vine, 4-inch pods, 7–8 peas per pod.	ALL BUT COM TWI VER
EARLY MAY	55	This 3-foot vine does well in adverse weather. Its yellow, round seed is used as a dry pea.	WILL
EXTRA EARLY ALASKA	51	30-inch vine; use peas fresh or dried.	GUR HEN
GIROY	65	36-inch vine, 3-inch pods, 9–10 tiny Petit Pois-type peas per pod; resistant to fusarium wilt and top yellows.	PAR
GREEN ARROW (Greenshaft, Hurst Green Arrow)	62–100	Dwarf shelling pea with a 28-inch vine, 4-inch pods, 8–12 peas per pod; resistant to mildews.	ABU ALL BOU BURP BURR COM COO DEG FAR FIS GAR GUR HEN JOH JUN MEY NIC PAR PIN PON POR STO THO TWI VER WILL
HYALITE	68	30-inch vine, 3½-inch pods.	FIS
ICER NO. 95 (Improved Dwarf Telephone)	74	Very large pods filled with immense peas.	TIL
LINCOLN	66	3-foot vine, 3-inch pods, 9 peas per pod; heirloom variety; not resistant to disease.	ALL BURR COO DEG FAR FIS GAR GUR PIN SEE STO VER WILL
MEXICAN SOUP PEA	80	The round, yellow peas are used for soup. This Mexican variety is heat tolerant.	PLA
MIRAGREEN	70	48-inch vine, 8–10 peas per pod; very hardy.	JUN
MULTISTAR	70	4–5-foot vine, 3-inch pods; tolerant to heat.	JOH
OREGON PIONEER (OSU 700)	61	24–30-inch vine with long pods; resistant to mosaic virus and fusarium.	NIC TER
OREGON TRAIL (OSU 695)	69	24–30-inch vine with double pods; multiple disease resistance.	NIC TER
PRIM D'OR	60	Tiny, French, Petit Pois shell pea.	GOU ORN
REMBRANDT	60	4-foot vine, 4–5-inch pods.	ORN
SNOW FLAKE	58–72	The 2–3-foot vine produces straight, flat pods that are 4 inches long and 1 inch wide. Pick as pods begin to swell.	LED PLA
SOMERSET	63	8–10 wrinkled, dark green peas per pod; resistant to disease.	HEN
THE PILOT	70	Hardy 4-foot vine with large, deep green, pointed pods.	BOU
THOMAS LAXTON	65	3-foot vine, 3½-inch pods, 7–9 peas per pod; grows well under a wide variety of conditions.	ALL MEY POR VER WIL

VARIETY	DAYS	DESCRIPTION	SOURCES (p. 385)

PEAS (25 INCHES OR MORE) *(continued)*

VARIETY	DAYS	DESCRIPTION	SOURCES
UTRILLO	71	30-inch vine, 5-inch pods, 8–10 peas per pod; tolerant to powdery mildew; Plant Variety Patented (PVP).	STO
VICTORY FREEZER	65	30-inch vine, 3½-inch pods; resistant to fusarium wilt.	GUR HEN
WANDO (Main Crop)	68	2½-foot vine, 2½-inch pods, 7–8 peas per pod; tolerant to cold, dry, and hot weather.	ALL BURG BURP COM FAR GAR GUR HEN JUN LED LEJ MEY PLA PON POR ROS SEE SOU TWI VER WIL
WORLD'S RECORD	58	28-inch vine, 4-inch pods, 7–9 peas per pod.	ALL

PEAS (EXTRA TALL)

VARIETY	DAYS	DESCRIPTION	SOURCES
ALDERMAN (Tall Telephone)	75	4–6-foot-long vine, 5-inch-long pods, 8–9 peas per pod; heirloom shelling pea; resistant to common wilt.	ABU ALL BOU COM FAR GAR LED ORN PIN SEE STO TER TIL VER WILL
FREEZONIAN	60	2½-foot vine, 3½-inch pods, 7–9 peas per pod; wilt-resistant vines.	ALL BURG BURR DEG FAR LED TIL VER

PEAS (EDIBLE PODS)

VARIETY	DAYS	DESCRIPTION	SOURCES
BUSH SNAPPER	58	3¾-inch pods; highly productive.	DEG
CAROUBY DE MAUSSANE	55–65	Tall vine.	COO ORN
CASCADIA	58	Short vines, 3-inch-long, deep green pods; resistant to powdery mildew and pea enation virus.	JOH NIC
CHINESE SNOW	65	9-foot vine with purple flowers.	ABU
DWARF GREY SUGAR	65–70	2½-foot vine, 3-inch pods.	ABU BOU COM FIS GUR HEN JLH LEJ POR RED SEE SUN WILL
DWARF WHITE SUGAR (China Snow)	50–65	30-inch vine, 2½–3-inch pods.	TER VER
EARLY SNAP	58	24-inch vine, 3-inch pods; resistant to mosaic.	COM
EDIBLE POD	65	Bush type, with 3-inch, light green, curved pods.	ALL
HENDRIKS	60	This 3-foot vine with 2½-inch pods and white flowers does well in summer.	WILL
LITTLE SWEETIE	60	16-inch vine, 2½-inch pods.	STO
MAMMOTH MELTING SUGAR	70–75	4–5-foot vine, 4–5x⅞-inch pods; resistant to disease.	ABU BURP COM DEG GOU HEN HIG RED SEE VER
MEGA	60	2½–3-foot plant with 4-inch, light green pods; resistant to enation.	TER

VARIETY	DAYS	DESCRIPTION	SOURCES (p. 385)

PEAS (EDIBLE PODS) *(continued)*

VARIETY	DAYS	DESCRIPTION	SOURCES (p. 385)
NORLI	50–58	1½-foot vine, 2½-inch pods; white flowers; Dutch variety.	SHE WILL
OREGON GIANT	60	2½-foot vine with 4½x1-inch, medium green pods; resistant to disease.	GAR JOH NIC SHE STO TER
OREGON SUGAR POD	68	28-inch vine; resistant to pea enation virus.	LED MEY ROS SEE SUN TIL
OREGON SUGAR POD II	68	24–30-inch vine, 4-inch pods; multiple disease resistance.	ABU BOU BURP DEG GUR HEN HIG JUN NIC TER THO TWI VER WILL
SAPPORO EXPRESS	40	Oriental variety; medium-tall vine.	RED
SEEDLING SUGAR PEA	60	This Chinese variety is grown for seedlings. Pick them when 4–5 inches tall to use in chow mein noodles.	SUN
SNAPPY	106	6-foot vine, 1½–2-inch pods; resistant to powdery mildew; Plant Variety Patented (PVP).	TER
SNOWBIRD	58	This short season variety's 18-inch vine produces 3-inch pods in double and triple clusters.	BURP
SNOW PEA (Ho Lohn Dow, Sugar Pea)	60	2½-foot plant; rich green, large pods.	BOU
SUGAR ANN	56	18-inch vine; space-saving All-American winner; Plant Variety Patented (PVP).	ABU BURG GAR GOU HEN HIG JOH JUN LED MEY NIC PIN PON POR STO SUN TER TWI WILL
SUGAR BON	57	24-inch vine, 3-inch pods; Plant Variety Patented (PVP).	ALL BURP COO HEN PAR TWI WIL
SUGAR DADDY	74	30-inch vine; Plant Variety Patented (PVP).	BOU COO GUR HEN JUN LED PAR STO TER TWI VER
SUGAR MEL	60–70	24-inch vine, 3–4-inch pods; heat-tolerant and resistant to powdery mildew; Plant Variety Patented (PVP).	BURR FIS GAR ORN PAR PIN SHE SOU
SUGAR POP	60	18-inch vine, 3-inch pods; resistant to powdery mildew.	PAR
SUGAR SNAP	62–70	6-foot vine, 3-inch pods; high yielding All-American winner; Plant Variety Patented (PVP).	ABU ALL BOU BURG BURP BURR BUT COM DEG GAR GUR HEN HIG JOH JUN LED MEY NIC PAR PLA POR RED ROS SEE SOU SUN TIL TWI VER WIL WILL
SUPER SNAPPY	65	28–32-inch vine, 5–5¾x¾-inch pods, 8–10 peas per pod; tolerant to powdery mildew.	BURP DEG
SUPER SUGAR POD	70	The 5-foot vine sets 4-inch pods. Grown in California for Chinese restaurants in San Francisco, this variety resists wilt but has no tolerance to powdery mildew.	STO
SWEET SNAP	66	34-inch vine, 3-inch pods; resistant to disease.	DEG VER

VARIETY	DAYS	DESCRIPTION	SOURCES (p. 385)

COWPEAS (BLACKEYED PEAS)

VARIETY	DAYS	DESCRIPTION	SOURCES (p. 385)
BIG BOY	60–65	The 10½-inch pods with light green peas are easy to shell.	POR WIL
BLACKEYED SOUTHERN PEAS (Cowpeas)	60–85	24-inch vine, 6–8-inch pods.	COM LEJ MEY ROS SEE VER
CALIFORNIA BLACKEYE	75	7–8-inch pods; resistant to pea diseases.	GUR HEN PAR
CALIFORNIA BLACKEYE NO. 5	95	Semispreading vine with 6–8-inch pods; tolerant to drought and resistant to pea diseases.	BURR LED POR WIL
QUEEN ANNE (Black Eye Bean)	56–68	Bushy, compact plant with 7–9-inch pods; resistant to disease.	SOU

COWPEAS (CROWDER)

VARIETY	DAYS	DESCRIPTION	SOURCES (p. 385)
BLACK CROWDER	70	Bush type with 12–15 peas per pod.	WIL
BLACKEYE WHITE CROWDER	70	The 6-inch pods' small seeds are white with small black eyes.	WIL
BLUE GOOSE (Gray Crowder, Taylor)	80	3-foot vine.	MEY
BROWN CROWDER	74–85	This vining variety's cream-colored seed turns brown when cooked.	HEN WIL
BROWN SUGAR CROWDER	85–90	30-inch plant with 9-inch pods, 8–12 peas per pod.	SOU
CALICO (Hereford, Polecat)	79	Seed is maroon, red, and white.	POR SOU
CLEMSON PURPLE	66	21-inch plant, 6½-inch pods, 16 peas per pod; resistant to disease; Plant Variety Patented (PVP).	WIL
COLOSSUS	75–80	Good producer.	POR
KNUCKLE PURPLE HULL	75	Semivining type.	SEE WIL
MISSISSIPPI CREAM	75	Large, plump, off-white seed with a dark eye; tolerant to disease; Plant Variety Patented (PVP).	WIL
MISSISSIPPI PURPLE HULL	70	Pods are green when young, bright purple when mature.	PAR WIL
MISSISSIPPI SILVER	64–70	Low, bushy plant with 6½-inch pods, 8–12 peas per pod.	LED MEY PAR POR SEE SOU VER WIL
PINKEYE PURPLE HULL	50–85	The 18–24-inch plant with 6–7-inch pods often produces two crops.	GOU GUR HEN VER WIL
PINKEYE PURPLE HULL BVR	63–65	Similar to Pinkeye Purple Hull; resistant to disease.	WIL
PURPLE HULL 49	75	Large pods are purple when mature.	POR

VARIETY	DAYS	DESCRIPTION	SOURCES (p. 385)

COWPEAS (CROWDER) *(continued)*

VARIETY	DAYS	DESCRIPTION	SOURCES
TENNESSEE WHITE CROWDER	65	This vining type has round seed with a light brown eye. Pods are dark green at maturity.	WIL

COWPEAS (CREAM)

VARIETY	DAYS	DESCRIPTION	SOURCES
BANQUET	52	Creamy colored peas with brown eyes.	PAR
CREAM	70	Very sweet.	POR
CREAM 8	70	Kidney-shaped peas; bush type plant.	WIL
CREAM 40	70	6–8-inch, kidney-shaped, white peas with orange eyes; semibush variety.	WIL
ELITE	75	Bush type with 7-inch pods.	WIL
RUNNING CONCH	90	The vines of this insect-resistant 1800s heirloom variety need wide spacing. The 7-inch pods, with 12–14 peas per pod, are harder to shell than modern varieties.	SOU
SUZANNE	90	Vigorous climbing vines with 12-inch pods, 14–16 peas per pod; Alabama heirloom variety.	SOU
ZIPPER CREAM	70	Off-white seed with small darker eye; an old favorite.	HEN POR WIL

COWPEAS (OTHER TYPES)

VARIETY	DAYS	DESCRIPTION	SOURCES
LADY	60	This bush type's small, white pea turns cream when mature.	WIL
QUEEN ANNE	60	26-inch-tall plant, 9-inch pods, 8–12 peas per pod.	MEY
WHIPPOORWILL	75–82	Old standard variety; tall plant.	POR WIL

PEPPERS

BOTANICAL NAME: *Capsicum frutescens* (sweet peppers) and *C. annuum* (hot or chili peppers)

DAYS TO MATURITY: 45–86.

PLANTING TIME: Start these indoors in the spring, six to eight weeks before average nighttime lows are expected to stay above 55°F. Set the plants out in the garden around the date of the last frost.

SOIL: Rich, well-drained loam; pH 5.5–7.0.

NUTRIENTS: Fertilize every four weeks with fish emulsion. Excess nitrogen produces a bushy plant with little fruit.

WATER: Never let these plants droop. Provide an even water supply.

LIGHT: Full sun.

SPACING: Space pepper plants 18–24 inches apart. Leave 24–36 inches between rows.

HARVEST: Cut the peppers from the plant with a sharp knife. The flesh is much sweeter when left on the vine to turn red. Hot peppers should ripen on the vine to obtain full pungency.

STORAGE: Peppers can be used fresh, frozen, or pickled. When handling hot peppers, never put your hands near your eyes or mouth.

Pepper Growing Tips

Increasing Pepper Production

To double and triple production, plant only stocky seedlings that show well-developed root systems. Leggy seedlings that are already blossoming will not produce like younger, fuller plants. When the first pepper appears, pick off the first "crown set" to encourage the development of additional big fruit throughout the season.

Night Temperatures

When nighttime temperatures are below 55°F, spring-planted peppers may just sit passively with their leaves turning yellow. Wait until the weather turns warm before popping your peppers into the ground.

Helping Hand

If your peppers are slow to set fruit in hot weather, spray the plants with water. Then, when the first fruits start to swell, dose the plants with liquid fish fertilizer every seven to 10 days. They will produce larger, heavier crops.

Adding Sulfur

Some old-time gardeners swear that peppers and sulfur are bosom buddies. They put about half a teaspoon of garden sulfur in the bottom of the planting hole before setting out their transplants. Sulfur lowers the soil's pH, which leads to an abundance of peppers.

Cool Climate Peppers

Growing good pepper crops in cool climates takes some know-how. The problem is that when night temperatures dip

PEPPERS

PEPPERS

below 50°F peppers usually won't set fruit. In addition, several 40° nights in a row can stunt growth. To ease such difficulties, use the short season varieties, and set them out when the soil is above 55°F. Plant them through black plastic, and cover them with hot caps.

Early Peppers

You can force peppers by spreading aluminum foil, shiny side up, for 12 inches on each side of the plants, leaving a little space for moisture penetration. The foil reflects sunlight upward, warming the plants, which then give earlier peppers.

Greener Peppers

Green your peppers by spraying them with a dilute solution of one tablespoon Epsom salts in a quart of water. Start at blossom time. This also aids fruit production.

VARIETY	DAYS	DESCRIPTION	SOURCES (p. 385)
HOT PEPPERS (LONG, TAPERING)			
ACI SIVRI	55–150	7 inches long, ¾ inch thick; from mild to very hot; Turkish variety.	RED
ANAHEIM CHILI (California Chili, California Long Green)	80–90	Mildly pungent, 8x1 inches, turns from green to red when ripe; 2–3-foot-tall plant; used extensively in California.	ABU COO DEG HOR JLH PIN POR RED SEE SEED SHE SOU WIL
ANAHEIM COLLEGE 64	74	6–8 inches long with thick walls; moderately hot.	TER
ANAHEIM M	80	8 inches long, 1¾ inches thick, changes from green to red when ripe; 28–34-inch plant; hot variety.	LIB PLA VER
ANAHEIM TMR	70–80	Mildly pungent peppers go from green to red when ripe.	GAR GUR HEN PAR TOMA
ANAHEIM 23 (OP)	74–77	7½–8x2 inches, turns from green to red when ripe, pungent; resistant to tobacco mosaic virus.	BURP BURR NIC ORN PAR TWI
BARKER	80	Native to New Mexico; extremely hot.	ROS
CALIENTE	65	6x¾ inches with thin walls, changes from green to red when ripe, medium hot.	JOH
CAYENNE LONG RED SLIM	70–75	This very hot pepper is 6x¾ inches, pointed, wrinkled, and goes from green to red when ripe. The plant is 20–24 inches tall.	ALL BURG BURP COM COO DEG FAR GAR HEN HOR JUN LEJ LIB MEY ORG PAR PLA PON POR ROS SEE SEED SHE SOU TER TIL VER WIL WILL
CAYENNE LONG THICK RED	70–74	7x2¼ inches, bright red when ripe, very hot; 24-inch plant.	LIB NIC PAR SEE TWI
CHILICATE	65	This 2½-foot, Bolivian plant has medium hot, 4–7x½-inch, smooth peppers with thin walls.	SEED

VARIETY	DAYS	DESCRIPTION	SOURCES (p. 385)

HOT PEPPERS (LONG, TAPERING) *(continued)*

VARIETY	DAYS	DESCRIPTION	SOURCES (p. 385)
CHIMAYO	80–95	Thin, curved peppers, from green to red when ripe; 24–30-inch plant; very hot New Mexican variety.	PLA RED
CRIMSON HOT	60	The medium hot, 6–6½x½-inch, thick-walled peppers are waxy crimson when ripe.	STO
DIABLO GRANDE (hybrid)	65	7x2-inch, fiery hot peppers, dark red when ripe; 24-inch plant.	STO
EARLY CAYENNE	65	The long, thin, fiery hot pepper turns bright red when ripe.	GAR
ECLIPSE (New Mex Eclipse)	90–150	5–7x1–1½-inch, dark brown (nearly black) pods.	PLA RED
ESPANOLA IMPROVED	60–70	Small, pointed, and bright red when ripe; very hot short season variety.	HOR PLA ROS SEED TOMA
ESPANOLA RISTRA	65	6–7 inches long, fire-engine red when ripe; 2-foot plant; medium hot short season variety.	SHE
GOAT HORN	70	The 5x1-inch peppers turn from green to cherry red when ripe and are often curled and twisted.	SUN THE
GOLDEN CAYENNE	70	6-inch-long, pencil-thin, very hot peppers.	STO
GOLDEN PROLIFIC (hybrid)	65	5–6 inches long, clear yellow when ripe; Hungarian Wax type.	LIB
GUAJILLO	125	Very hot, 4½–6x1¼-inch Mexican variety.	PLA RED
HOT PORTUGAL	64	6 inches long, pointed, ripens to bright red; fiery hot short season variety.	GAR
HUNGARIAN WAX SHORT (OP) (Rainbow Waxed)	60	Blocky and long, with thick walls, goes from yellow to red when ripe; medium hot.	LIB
HUNGARIAN YELLOW WAX (OP) (Cayenne Long Thick Yellow, Bulgarian Banana, Hot Banana)	60–68	6x1¼ inches, goes from light yellow to red when ripe; 14–22-inch plant; medium hot short season variety.	BOU BURG BURP BURR COM DEG GAR GUR HEN HIG HOR JOH LED LEJ LIB MEY NIC PAR PIN POR ROS SEE SEED SOU STO TER TIL TWI WIL WILL
IBERIAN LONG CAYENNE	75	6–8 inches long, mild flavor.	SEED
INFERNO (hybrid)	65	Hot Anaheim type; slim tapered, smooth pepper with medium-thick walls.	STO
LONG RED CAYENNE	70–75	This very hot, 5x½-inch, pointed pepper changes from waxy yellow to bright red when ripe.	ABU ALL BURG STO TOMA
LONG THICK RED CAYENNE	60–76	4–6x1¼ inches, very hot.	STO TOMA
MEXICAN NEGRO (Pasilla)	100	6x1½ inches, hot.	PLA RED

VARIETY	DAYS	DESCRIPTION	SOURCES (p. 385)

HOT PEPPERS (LONG, TAPERING) *(continued)*

VARIETY	DAYS	DESCRIPTION	SOURCES (p. 385)
MIRASOL (New Mexico Chili Improved)	75	This very hot, 5x1-inch pepper turns from green to red when ripe. The 27-inch plant's name means "it follows the sun."	BURR HOR PLA
MULATO ISLENO	85–95	6x3 inches, turns chocolate brown; virus-resistant variety.	PLA RED SEE TOMA
NEW MEX BIG JIM (Nu Mex Big Jim, Slim Jim)	83	This medium hot pepper is 8–12 inches long and 4–6 ounces or more. The 16–24-inch plant sets fruit under hot, dry conditions.	BURR GUR HEN HOR PLA POR ROS TOMA
NEW MEXICO HATCH	90–150	Anaheim type; New Mexican variety.	RED
NEW MEXICO NO. 6 (Numex 6)	75	This mildly pungent, 6–8x2½-inch, bluntly pointed pepper turns from green to red when ripe. It dries to dark red or maroon.	PLA ROS
NEW MEXICO R NAKY	80	Mild, medium-size chili.	HOR PLA POR
NEW MEXICO 64	72–75	4½–5½x2½ inches, thin walls, from dark green to red when ripe.	WIL
NEW MEX JOE PARKER (Nu Mex Joe E. Parker)	65	6–7 inches long, tapering, with thick walls, turns from bright green to red when ripe; mild but full flavored.	SHE TOMA
NU MEX SUNRISE	80	This medium hot, tapered chili is bright yellow when ripe.	PLA
NU MEX SUNSET	80	Tapered, medium hot chili is bright orange when ripe.	PLA
PEPPERONCINI	65–75	5 inches, red when ripe; mildly hot variety from Southern Italy.	ABU HOR NIC ORN SHE
RING OF FIRE	60	This short plant produces extremely hot, 4-inch-long, pencil-thin peppers. It's a short season variety.	SEE SEED STO TOMA
SANDIA (New Mexico Sandia, New Mex Sandia)	80	4–6 inches long, from green to red when ripe, very hot.	PLA RED TOMA
SMALL RED CHILI	75	5½x2½-inch, pointed peppers with medium-thick walls.	MEY
SONORA	77	8x1½ inches, from green to red when ripe; mildly pungent Anaheim type; midsize plant; resistant to tobacco mosaic virus.	TOMA
SUAVE ROJO	90–150	5x1 inches, very dark red when ripe, mildly hot.	RED
SUPER CAYENNE (hybrid)	72	Very hot cayenne type; turns from green to red when ripe; All-American winner.	LED NIC TWI WIL
SUREFIRE (hybrid)	65	5½x1½ inches, thick walls, from green to red when ripe, hot.	TER TWI
YELLOW CAYENNE (hybrid)	68–70	The 8x¾-inch peppers change from yellowish green to dark red when ripe, but harvest them at the yellow stage. The 28-inch plant is a Goat Horn type.	BURP

VARIETY	DAYS	DESCRIPTION	SOURCES (p. 385)

HOT PEPPERS (LONG, TAPERING) (continued)

VARIETY	DAYS	DESCRIPTION	SOURCES (p. 385)
YUNG KO	70	Long, curved, from dark green to red when ripe; hot Taiwanese variety.	HOR
ZIPPY (hybrid)	57	The plant bears these fiery, 6x⅜-inch peppers until frost.	BURP

HOT PEPPERS (CYLINDRICAL)

VARIETY	DAYS	DESCRIPTION	SOURCES (p. 385)
AJI ROJO (Puca-uchu)	90–150	The very hot, 4x¾-inch peppers turn from green to red when ripe. Grown at the base of the eastern Sierra but originally from Peru, this perennial is somewhat frost tolerant.	RED
ANCHO (Poblano)	65–100	4 inches long, goes from dark green to brownish red when ripe; 36-inch plant.	BURP HEN HOR NIC PIN PLA RED SEE SEED SHE
ANCHO 101	76–80	4 inches long, goes from black-green to brown-red when ripe, medium hot.	DEG GOU JOH POR ROS TOMA
ANCHO SAN LUIS	76–80	6 inches long, 3 inches thick, turns from dark green to red when ripe, mildly pungent.	JLH TOMA
ARLEDGE	75	4 inches long; very hot Louisiana heirloom variety; widely adapted.	SEED
AURORA	75	1½x¾ inches, from green to red when ripe, very hot; 18-inch plant.	SOU
COLORADO	80	There are two varieties of this large pepper—one mild, one hot.	HOR
CZECHOSLOVAKIAN BLACK (Czech Black)	65	This 2-inch-long pepper has the shape of a jalapeño, conical with a blunt end. It changes from dark green to red when ripe. The plant grows to 2½ feet.	ABU SEED SOU
CZECHOSLOVAKIAN BLACK SWEET (Czech Black Sweet)	70	2–3 inches long, conical, goes from dark purple to red when ripe, mildly hot; 3-foot plant.	SEED
DE ARBOL	90	Known as a "Tree Chili," this 2½–4x⅜-inch pepper doesn't upset the stomach, although it's very hot.	PLA RED SEE SEED TOMA
EARLY JALAPENO	60–68	3x1½ inches, from deep green to red when ripe, very hot; 2-foot plant.	ABU BURR DEG GAR HIG JOH JUN PIN SHE TER TIL WILL
EAST INDIAN SMALL	90–150	2x½ inches, dark red when ripe, 33 times hotter than a jalapeño.	RED
GARDEN SALSA (hybrid)	73	8–9x1 inches, turns from green to red when ripe, medium hot; large plant; resistant to tobacco mosaic virus.	LIB POR TOMA WIL
GUAJILLO CASTENO	70–75	3 inches long, tapered, with thin walls, quite hot, translucent red when ripe.	SEED
HOT STUFF (hybrid)	60	6½ inches long, goes from green to red when ripe, medium hot.	STO

VARIETY	DAYS	DESCRIPTION	SOURCES (p. 385)

HOT PEPPERS (CYLINDRICAL) *(continued)*

VARIETY	DAYS	DESCRIPTION	SOURCES (p. 385)
JALAPA (hybrid)	65–68	3½x1½ inches, blunt tip, from green to red when ripe; short season variety.	DEG LED PAR POR TOMA TWI VER
JALAPENO	72–80	3½x1½ inches with thick walls, from green to red when ripe, hot; 26–36-inch plant.	BURR BUT COM COO DEG FIS GLE GUR HEN HOR NIC PLA PON POR RED ROS SEE SEED SOU STO SUN
JALAPENO M	75	3x1½ inches, turns from dark green to red when ripe, very pungent; 26-inch plant.	BURP DEG LIB ORN PAR TOMA TWI VER WIL
JALORO (Yellow Jalapeño)	80	This pungent, bright yellow jalapeño turns red at maturity. Variety has resistance to multiple viruses.	POR
JUMBO HUNGARIAN HOT (hybrid)	65	8 inches long, tapers to a point, changes from lime green to red when ripe, medium hot.	STO
LOUISIANA HOTS	69	3x1½ inches, conical, goes from yellow to deep red when ripe; hot Southern heirloom variety.	JLH SOU
MAURITIUS	90–150	This variety from the island of Mauritius produces 4x½-inch, slender peppers that turn red when ripe.	RED
MERAH (Temptation)	90–150	2½x¾ inches, very hot; grown in China and Malaysia.	RED
MISSISSIPPI SPORT	82	These very hot, 2x½-inch, conical peppers go from green to deep red when ripe.	BURG
OLE!	60	3½–4 inches long, very hot; giant jalapeño type.	NIC
PEQUIN	80–120	3 inches long, very hot.	PLA TOMA
PRETTY HOT PURPLE	80	1½ inches long, ¾ inch thick, from green to red when ripe, quite hot; 30-inch plant.	SOU
PUYA (Rooster Spur, Spur)	60–70	These tapering peppers measure 3½x1 inches. The 2-foot plant grows upward.	JLH JOH SUN
RELLENO	75	6½x2½ inches, turns from green to red when ripe, mildly hot.	HEN NIC SEED
RIO GRANDE HOT	85	This medium hot pepper is slightly larger than a jalapeño.	SEED
SANTO DOMINGO PUEBLO	90–150	3x1 inches, conical, hot; New Mexican variety.	RED
SERRANO	70–80	These 2x2½-inch, dark green peppers are tinged orange and burning hot. The plant grows to be 30–36 inches.	BURP COO DEG GUR HEN HOR PIN PLA POR RED ROS SEE SEED SHE TER WIL
SPANISH SPICE (hybrid)	70	5–6 inches long and tapered, red when ripe; variety for frying.	DEG JUN LIB
SUPER CAYENNE (hybrid)	72	3–4 inches long, from green to red when ripe, fiery hot; 2-foot plant.	PAR TOMA

VARIETY	DAYS	DESCRIPTION	SOURCES (p. 385)

HOT PEPPERS (CYLINDRICAL) *(continued)*

VARIETY	DAYS	DESCRIPTION	SOURCES (p. 385)
SUPER CHILI (hybrid)	75	The 2½x½-inch, conical pepper is quite hot. This All-American winning, 15-inch plant is ideal for small gardens or containers.	COM GUR HEN LIB ORN PAR SHE TOMA TWI VER WILL
TAM HIDALGO	80	Serrano type but not as hot; resistant to pepper diseases; Plant Variety Patented (PVP).	HOR POR
TAM JALAPENO	65–70	3½x1½ inches, blunt ends, medium-thick walls, mildly pungent, goes from dark green to red when ripe; 22–24-inch plant; resistant to potato yellow virus.	GAR GUR HEN HOR ORN ROS TER TOMA WIL
TAM JALAPENO 1 (OP)	73	2½x1½ inches, dark green, thick walls, mildly pungent; resistant to viruses.	NIC POR TWI
TAM VERA CRUZ JALAPENO	80	Very hot pepper; virus-resistant plant.	HOR
YATSAFUSA	80–95	3–4x¼ inches, tapered, red at maturity; 20-inch plant; Japanese variety.	NIC RED SEED

HOT PEPPERS (MEDIUM AND SMALL, TAPERING)

VARIETY	DAYS	DESCRIPTION	SOURCES (p. 385)
COCHITI	100	This chili was developed centuries ago by the Cochiti Pueblo people along the Rio Grande in New Mexico. The pods are medium length.	PLA
FIRE!	75	2x½ inches, turns from bright green to red when ripe, especially hot.	TOMA
FRESNO	78	2½–4x1 inches, green with a trace of red, very pungent; 24-inch plant.	HOR SEED
PETER PEPPER	80	4 inches long, from green to red when ripe.	GLE
RED CHILI	70–85	3 inches long, ½-inch thick, very pungent; ripens from green to red; 18–20-inch plant.	DEG FAR LED RED
TABASCO	80–120	This fiery, greenish yellow pepper turns scarlet when ripe.	PLA POR RED SEE SHE TOMA
THAI HOT (Tai Hot)	40–90	1½ inches long, goes from green to red when ripe; 18-inch plant; extremely hot Asian pepper.	COO DEG HIG PAR RED SEE SUN THE TOMA

HOT PEPPERS (YELLOW)

VARIETY	DAYS	DESCRIPTION	SOURCES (p. 385)
AJI YELLOW	90–150	A favorite of the Incan Empire, the plant is perennial. Pick the chilies when green for mild flavor. When yellow, they are very hot.	RED
CALORO	75–80	2½–3½ inches long, 1¼ inches thick, conical, waxy yellow-orange when mature, medium hot; 25-inch plant; resistant to tobacco mosaic virus.	HOR PIN ROS TOMA
CASABELLA	75–80	The 1¼-inch-thick, round pepper goes from yellow to orange. The plant grows to 28 inches.	NIC ORN ROS TOMA

VARIETY	DAYS	DESCRIPTION	SOURCES (p. 385)

HOT PEPPERS (YELLOW) *(continued)*

VARIETY	DAYS	DESCRIPTION	SOURCES (p. 385)
FLORAL GEM GRANDE	75	2½x1 inches, from yellow to red when ripe; 20–24-inch plant.	HOR
GOLDSPIKE (hybrid)	75	2½x1½-inch pepper; 32–36-inch plant.	HOR POR
ROUMANIA	65	The 4x2½-inch, stubby, medium hot pepper goes from yellow to red when ripe. The plant reaches 22–24 inches.	HOR LIB ORN
SANTA FE GRANDE	75	The hot, 3–3½x1½-inch pepper turns from yellow to orange-red at maturity. The 25-inch plant is resistant to tobacco mosaic virus.	BURR DEG HOR ORN PLA RED ROS WIL
SYLVAN'S SELECT	70	Medium hot, light yellow pepper turns orange-red at maturity. The plant is 16–18 inches.	LIB
SZENTESI SEMI-HOT	60	4½ inches long, goes from lime green to yellow-orange when ripe, medium hot.	STO
YELLOW CAYENNE (hybrid)	70	This pungent, 8x¾-inch, tapering pepper goes from yellowish green to golden yellow to dark red. Harvest peppers at any stage. The 28-inch plant is a Goat Horn type.	TOMA
YELLOW MUSHROOM (Squash Pepper)	70	The very hot pepper turns from green to yellow when ripe.	GLE POR

HOT PEPPERS (SQUARE, ROUND, CLAWLIKE, TINY)

VARIETY	DAYS	DESCRIPTION	SOURCES (p. 385)
ALMAPAPRIKA	90–150	This hot, mushroom-shaped (2 inches tall, 1 inch wide) pepper turns red when ripe and has medium-thick walls.	RED
BOLIVIAN RAINBOW	75	Very hot, tiny, pointed peppers turn from rainbow colored to purple when ripe. The plant grows to 2–3 feet.	SEED
CENTENNIAL	125	This very hot pepper measures ½ inch in diameter and goes from purple to white to bright red when ripe. Pods are edible at any stage.	PLA
GRANDPA'S HOME PEPPER	70	Small, fairly hot, brilliant red peppers; 12-inch plant.	HIG
HABANERO (Scotch Bonnet, Of Havana)	85–100	1½x1 inches, ripens from green to golden orange; very hot Mexican variety; must handle carefully; 36-inch plant.	BURP BURR COO DEG GLE HOR JLH JOH LIB NIC PAR PIN PLA POR RED ROS SEE SHE STO TOMA VER
HOT APPLE	70	2½x1½ inches, butter yellow, moderately hot.	ORN
HOT CLAW	80	3 inches long; Japanese variety.	GLE
LARGE RED CHERRY	75–80	1¼ inches long, goes from green to red when ripe, medium hot.	BURP BURR COM DEG HOR LED LIB MEY NIC ORN PLA POR ROS STO TWI
MANZANO (Rocoto)	90–150	This very hot, 2-inch-square pepper turns yellow or red when ripe. Variety tolerates cold.	RED

VARIETY	DAYS	DESCRIPTION	SOURCES (p. 385)

HOT PEPPERS (SQUARE, ROUND, CLAWLIKE, TINY) *(continued)*

VARIETY	DAYS	DESCRIPTION	SOURCES
PEQUIN	90–150	½x¼-inch pepper; 4-foot bush.	RED SHE
PERUVIAN PURPLE	90	The mild, 1-inch-long, stubby pepper goes from deep purple to red when ripe. Perennial in warmer climates, the plant grows to 2 feet.	SEED
PRETTY IN PURPLE (NO. 1066)	60	Pungent, deep purple, ¾-inch, rounded, glossy peppers ripen to scarlet.	JOH
SMALL RED CHERRY	80	Very pungent, 1x¼-inch pepper changes from green to red when ripe. This variety is an 18–20-inch plant.	COM
TEPIN	85	This ¼-inch, round Southwest variety is the hottest pepper known.	RED SEE
TINY SAMOA	85	The hot, ½x⅛-inch pepper turns from green to red when ripe.	GLE
TOKANTOTSUME	85	This old-fashioned Japanese variety produces extremely hot, 2x¼-inch peppers.	HOR
TURKEY CLAW (Una De Pavo)	85	½–1-inch-long, conical peppers; very hot Ecuadoran variety.	JLH
ZIMBABWE BIRD	85	Tiny, triangular pod is exceedingly hot.	RED

SWEET PEPPERS (BLOCKY)

VARIETY	DAYS	DESCRIPTION	SOURCES
ACE (hybrid)	55–60	4 inches long, 3½ inches thick, with 2–4 lobes, glossy deep green; short season variety.	ALL GAR HIG JOH STO
BELL BOY (hybrid)	63–70	The 3¼x3½-inch glossy green pepper turns red at maturity. This All-American winning, 24-inch plant is tolerant to tobacco mosaic virus.	COM DEG FAR GUR HEN JUN LED MEY PIN STO TOMA VER WIL WILL
BELL CAPTAIN	72	The 4½x4-inch, dark green pepper has 4 lobes. The 19–22-inch plant is resistant to mosaic virus.	LED MEY TOMA TWI
BELL STAR	74	4½x4 inches, 4 lobes; tolerant to disease.	LIB
BELL TOWER (hybrid)	70	Large, blocky, deep green pepper turns red when mature. This disease-resistant variety has 3–4 lobes.	JOH LIB STO
BETTER BELL HYBRID IMPROVED	65	4 lobes, ripens from green to red; resistant to tobacco mosaic virus.	TOMA
BIG BELLE (hybrid)	72	The 4½x3¼-inch, blocky, green pepper has 4 lobes.	HEN
BIG BERTHA	70	Thick-walled, 6½x4-inch pepper with 3 lobes goes from green to red at maturity. Variety tolerates tobacco mosaic virus.	GUR HEN JUN LED LIB MEY POR STO THO TOMA VER WIL
BIG DIPPER	73	4½x4½ inches, 4 lobes; 20–24-inch-tall plant; California Wonder strain.	BURP

VARIETY	DAYS	DESCRIPTION	SOURCES (p. 385)

SWEET PEPPERS (BLOCKY) *(continued)*

VARIETY	DAYS	DESCRIPTION	SOURCES
BULL NOSE (Large Bell, Sweet Mountain)	55–70	3½x4 inches, matures from deep green to red, 4 lobes.	ABU SOU
CADICE	55	Large pepper ripens from green to crimson. This French variety does well in cool areas.	SHE
CALIFORNIA WONDER	75	4½x4 inches, thick walls.	ALL BURG COM DEG FAR GUR HEN LEJ MEY NIC ORG PIN PON POR RED ROS SOU STO TIL VER WIL WILL
CALIFORNIA WONDER 300 (OP)	71–74	4x4-inch, emerald green pepper; 24–28-inch plant; resistant to tobacco mosaic.	BURR GAR TWI
CAMELOT (hybrid)	74	Large pepper with thick walls and 3–4 lobes goes from green to red when ripe; resistant to tobacco mosaic.	LIB TWI
CAPISTRANO	70	4x3½ inches, from dark green to red when ripe; resistant to tobacco mosaic.	LIB STO
CRISPY (hybrid)	70	With thick walls and 3–4 lobes, this 2½x3½-inch pepper changes from green to red when ripe.	BURP GUR
EARLY BOUNTIFUL (hybrid)	58–65	3x2¾ inches, ripens from dark green to red; tolerant of mosaic.	WILL
EARLY CALIFORNIA	65	Sweet and mild.	SEE
EARLY CALWONDER	70	4x4 inches, goes from green to red.	ALL COM LIB TER
EARLY NIAGARA GIANT	65	With 3–4 lobes and thick walls, this 4½-inch-square pepper ripens from green to red. The 24-inch plant sets well during cool summers and is tolerant to mosaic.	STO
ELISA (hybrid)	72	With 3–4 lobes and thick walls, the 6x5½-inch pepper ripens from medium green to bright red. The disease-tolerant plant sets well in cool temperatures.	LIB STO TOMA
EMERALD GIANT	74	4½x3¾ inches, 4 lobes, thick walls; tolerant to mosaic.	BURR DEG ORN SEE TIL TWI
FOUR CORNERS	72	The 4½x4½-inch pepper has thick walls and 4 lobes. Mosaic-tolerant variety sets well in high temperatures.	LIB
GALAXY	72	Peppers measure 4¾x4½ inches, with 4 lobes. Disease-resistant variety sets fruit in cool weather.	STO
GATOR BELLE (hybrid)	75	Large, with 3–4 lobes and thick, green walls; resistant to tobacco mosaic virus.	TOMA
GEDEON (hybrid)	78	Extralarge pepper with thick walls.	BURP
GREAT STUFF	75	The 6–8x5-inch pepper with firm walls ripens from green to dark red. The 28-inch plant is resistant to mosaic.	BURP
JUPITER ELITE (OP)	66–70	4½ inches long, with very thick walls, ripens from dark green to red; Plant Variety Patented (PVP).	HOR JUN LIB MEY POR STO TOMA TWI

VARIETY	DAYS	DESCRIPTION	SOURCES (p. 385)
SWEET PEPPERS (BLOCKY) *(continued)*			
JUPITER STERLING	70	4½-inch square.	STO
KEYSTONE RESISTANT GIANT	70–80	4½ inches long, 4½ inches thick, ripens from green to red, 4 lobes and thick walls; tolerant to mosaic.	DEG POR SOU
KEYSTONE RESISTANT GIANT NO. 3	57–65	4 lobes, very thick walls; 28-inch plant.	BURR LIB
KING ARTHUR (hybrid)	72	5 inches square; tolerant to mosaic.	STO
KING OF THE NORTH (King, Ruby King)	57–65	6x3½ inches, 3 lobes.	ABU GUR HEN
LITTLE DIPPER	66	This 2x1¾-inch, miniature bell pepper ripens from green to red. The 26-inch plant is resistant to mosaic.	BURP
MA BELLE (hybrid)	62	4 inches long, 4 lobes, thick walls; 20-inch plant; tolerant to mosaic.	DEG FAR
MAYATA (hybrid)	71	The 5x4-inch, dark green pepper turns bright red when ripe. It has 3–4 lobes and thick walls. Variety is tolerant to mosaic.	STO
MERLIN (hybrid)	68	4½x3¾ inches, 4 lobes, thick walls, ripens from dark green to dark red; tolerant to mosaic.	LIB STO
MEXI BELL (hybrid)	70–75	This sweet variety has a mild chili flavor and 3–4 lobes. The 26-inch plant is tolerant to mosaic.	COM PLA POR TOMA
MIDWAY	70	4½x4½ inches, ripens from green to red, 3–4 lobes and thick walls; 18–24-inch plant; tolerant to mosaic.	COM DEG STO
MINI BELL	70	The full-size plant is loaded with tiny bell peppers.	GLE
NEW ACE (hybrid)	62–68	3½x4 inches, 3–4 lobes and medium-thick walls; short season variety.	PIN VER
NORTH STAR (hybrid)	66	Bright red and green peppers measure 4½x3½ inches and have thick walls. Mosaic-tolerant plant sets in cool temperatures.	BURG BURP BURR JUN LED LIB NIC STO TER TOMA TWI WILL
PARK'S EARLY THICK-SET IMPROVED (hybrid)	45	4½x3½ inches, thick walls and 3–4 lobes, ripens from green to bright scarlet.	PAR
PARK'S WHOPPER IMPROVED	71	4x4 inches, 4 lobes and thick walls.	PAR
PERMAGREEN	73	This 3-lobed pepper stays green even when mature.	SOU
PETO WONDER (hybrid)	78	4½x7½ inches, 4 lobes and thick walls; resistant to mosaic.	DEG PAR TER TOMA
PRIMA BELLE	75	This 4-lobed pepper ripens to red if left. Variety sets under many weather conditions and is resistant to tobacco mosaic virus.	TOMA

VARIETY	DAYS	DESCRIPTION	SOURCES (p. 385)

SWEET PEPPERS (BLOCKY) *(continued)*

VARIETY	DAYS	DESCRIPTION	SOURCES
RESISTANT GIANT 4 (OP)	75	4x3¾ inches, 4 lobes, thick walls; widely adapted.	TWI
RUBY GIANT	72	5x3½ inches, ripens from green to red.	DEG SOU
SECRET (hybrid)	60	Blocky, matures from purple-black to dark red; resistant to mosaic.	JOH
SHAMROCK (hybrid)	70	Medium-large, glossy green pepper with 4 lobes; resistant to mosaic.	POR
SOVEREIGN	68	Midsize, thick walls, 3–4 lobes.	JOH
STADDON'S SELECT (Missile)	64–72	4x4 inches, 3–4 lobes, thick walls; 26-inch plant.	FIS HIG JLH LIB PLA TER
ULTRA SET	65	3¾–4 inches long, apple bell shaped, extrathick walls, ripens from green to red; mosaic-tolerant variety.	STO
VANGUARD (hybrid)	59	Medium-large pepper has 3–4 lobes and changes from green to red when mature. This mosaic-resistant variety sets fruit even when stressed by cold or heat.	JOH
VERDEL (hybrid)	78	4x3½ inches, dark green, blocky.	TWI
WORLD BEATER	74	5x3½ inches, ripens from green to red.	DEG SEE
YANKEE BELL (OP)	60	Blocky, 3–4-lobed, midsize pepper matures from green to red. Variety was developed for all short season gardens.	JOH
YOLO WONDER	77	4x4¾ inches, 4 lobes, thick walls; tolerant to mosaic.	BOU DEG LEJ STO
YOLO WONDER B	77	4x4 inches, 4 lobes, thick walls, dark green; resistant to mosaic.	WIL
YOLO WONDER L	75	4x3¾ inches; resistant to mosaic.	BURR TWI

SWEET PEPPERS (RED)

VARIETY	DAYS	DESCRIPTION	SOURCES
CARDINAL (hybrid)	70	Blocky, 4½-inch, thick-walled pepper changes from dark green to dark red when ripe. Variety is tolerant to cold and mosaic.	STO
CORBACI (Sari Tatli Sivri)	75	Long, bright red pepper is shaped like a Turkish scimitar.	RED
EARLIEST RED SWEET	55–60	3x4 inches, 2–3 lobes; not uniform in shape, bright red when ripe; no disease tolerance.	HIG PIN STO
EARLIRED	70	Small bell pepper; short season variety.	SEE
GAMBRO	62	This thick and meaty, flattened, rich red bell measures 3–3½x1½–2 inches.	SOU

VARIETY	DAYS	DESCRIPTION	SOURCES (p. 385)
SWEET PEPPERS (RED) *(continued)*			
ITALIAN RED MACARONI	75	12x3 inches, 3 lobes, bright red.	ABU COO
RAMPAGE (hybrid)	66	4½x3½ inches, 3–4 lobes, medium-thick walls, ripens to bright red.	PIN TOMA
RED BOY	75	Large, with 4 lobes and thick walls, bright red when mature.	LIB
REDWING	72	6x5½ inches, 3–4 lobes, thick walls; tolerant to disease.	STO
SCARLET KING (hybrid)	72	Economical Stokes pepper.	STO
SUMMER SWEET BRAND 862 R (hybrid)	76–86	3½x3¼ inches, thick walls, 4 lobes; tolerant to disease.	TWI
SUPER SET	64	4x5 inches, medium-thick walls.	STO
SWEET RED CHERRY (OP) (Cherry Sweet)	73	1-inch-long, flattened globe, bright red when ripe; 18-inch plant.	LIB NIC VER

SWEET PEPPERS (LONG)

VARIETY	DAYS	DESCRIPTION	SOURCES (p. 385)
ANDEAN	75	8–11 inches long, 2½ inches thick, turns from yellow-green to red when ripe, shaped like the Cubanelle variety; Argentine variety.	SEED
BANANA SUPREME (hybrid)	65–70	6¾ inches long, matures from light yellow to red.	POR STO TER TOMA TWI
BELCONI	77	7–8x2¼–3 inches, from intense green to shiny red at maturity; French variety; Italian type pepper.	GOU
BISCAYNE (hybrid)	63	6-inch-long, blunt ended, light green pepper; 26-inch plant.	LED LIB NIC PAR STO TOMA
CALISTAN	70	7x1½ inches; Turkish variety.	RED
CANAPE (hybrid)	51	2x2½-inch, elongated, dark green pepper; short season variety; mosaic-resistant 25–30-inch plant.	VER
CETINEL	70	5x½–¾ inches, very sweet.	RED
CORNO DI TORO RED	70–100	6–12 inches long; red version of yellow variety; Italian heirloom variety.	COO GLE PIN SEED SHE TOMA
CORNO DI TORO YELLOW	90–100	8–12x1½ inches; same as red Corno di Toro. Limited sweetness.	GLE SHE TOMA
FLAVOR FRY (hybrid)	67	Cubanelle type; 6x2¼ inches, yellow-green, medium-thick walls; tolerant to mosaic.	TWI
GIANT YELLOW BANANA	60	7 inches long, thick flesh; Hungarian variety; 26-inch plant.	STO

VARIETY	DAYS	DESCRIPTION	SOURCES (p. 385)

SWEET PEPPERS (LONG) *(continued)*

VARIETY	DAYS	DESCRIPTION	SOURCES (p. 385)
HUNGARIAN YELLOW WAX	65	6x1½ inches, tapered, waxy yellow; 18–20-inch plant.	DEG JLH STO TOMA
ITALIA	55	8x2½ inches, goes from green to dark crimson; similar to Corno di Toro.	JOH
ITALIAN SWEET (Italian Sweet Relleno)	60	The 6x2½-inch pepper tapers to a blunt end and ripens from deep green to bright red. This dwarf plant saves on space.	DEG HOR ORN SEED
JIMMY NARDELLO (Nardello)	70	8 inches long; heirloom variety.	JLH SEED
LAPARIE (hybrid)	72	8-inch, tapered pendant, dark red when ripe.	STO
LONG SWEET BANANA (Sweet Hungarian, Sweet Banana)	58–70	6x1½ inches, turns from yellow to red when ripe, medium-thick walls.	ABU BURP COM DEG GUR HEN JUN LIB MEY NIC ORN PAR PIN PON POR ROS SOU STO TOMA TWI VER WIL WILL
MARCONI YELLOW	70	12x3 inches, 3 lobes; Italian variety.	COO
MATADOR (hybrid)	78	5½x4 inches, medium-thick walls, goes from green to yellow; tolerant to disease.	TWI
MAYATA (hybrid)	75	6 inches long, 3–4 lobes, red at maturity.	TOMA
MIDAL (hybrid)	73	This 8-inch-long, oval, cream-colored pepper turns reddish orange when ripe.	ORN
MONTEGO	60	7–9x2–3 inches, pale yellow-white ripens to red; short, compact plant; Cubanelle type.	JOH
ORI (hybrid)	70	This French variety sets its 7x3½-inch peppers under stressful conditions.	TOMA
PAPRIKA	80–120	6-inch-long, flat pepper with thin walls; red when ripe.	ABU DEG NIC POR RED SEE SEED SOU
PAPRI MILD II	78	This nonpungent 5–7x1½-inch pepper was developed to make paprika.	TOMA
PARK'S SWEET BANANA WHOPPER (hybrid)	65	Large fruit with thick walls.	PAR
PETO WONDER (hybrid)	70	6½x4½ inches; 2-foot, mosaic-tolerant plant.	GAR
SPANISH SPICE (hybrid)	65	Long, frying type, nonpungent pepper ripens from green to red.	POR TOMA WILL
TA TONG	70	Elongated, ripens from green to red; Taiwanese variety.	HOR
ULTRA GOLD	71	6½x3½ inches, 2 lobes, matures from gold to orange to red.	STO
VIDI (hybrid)	64	Elongated, 6–7-inch, lobed bell pepper with thick walls turns from glossy green to deep red at maturity. This French variety is disease tolerant.	COO GOU PIN SHE TOMA

VARIETY	DAYS	DESCRIPTION	SOURCES (p. 385)
SWEET PEPPERS (SPACE SAVERS)			
BABY BELL	55	3-inch-long, tiny bell pepper.	SEE
JINGLE BELLS (hybrid)	55–60	1½–2 inches long, goes from green to red when ripe; 14-inch plant; short season variety.	DEG GAR NIC PIN POR TER TOMA TWI WILL
PARK'S POT (hybrid)	45	This 10–12-inch plant bears a heavy crop of medium-size peppers.	PAR
PARK'S TEQUILA SUNRISE	77	4–5 inches long, ripens from green to warm golden orange; 12-inch plant.	SOU
SWEET PEPPERS (YELLOW/ORANGE)			
ARIANE	68	Big, blocky peppers are rich orange when ripe. This Dutch variety is tolerant to mosaic.	NIC ORN SHE
BUTTER BELLE	70	2½x2¾ inches, 3–4 lobes, extrathick walls, butter yellow.	SEE
CAL WONDER GOLDEN	75	3½x3½ inches, medium-thick walls.	ORN SOU
CANARY (hybrid)	72	5 inches long, blocky, very thick walls, 4 lobes, ripens to yellow; tolerant to mosaic.	STO
CORONA	66	Blocky, midsize pepper turns glowing orange when ripe. This Dutch variety resists mosaic.	GOU JOH SOU
CUNEO (OP) (Carnosissimo di Cuneo)	70	Softball-size and pointed; bright yellow Italian variety.	PIN
GARDEN SUNSHINE	70	Large bell type, yellowish green.	GLE ORN
GIANT SZEGEDI	60–70	5x3 inches, conical; similar to Yellow Romanian; tolerant to verticillium.	GAR SEE SEED STO
GOLD CREST (hybrid)	62	Medium-large pepper with 3–4 lobes changes from dark glossy green to golden yellow when ripe.	JOH ORN
GOLDEN BELL (hybrid)	65	4x3½ inches, 3–4 lobes, golden color when mature.	COM MEY PIN TER VER WIL
GOLDEN GIANT	75	Hefty, golden pepper with thick walls; 26-inch plant; resistant to disease.	BURP TOMA
GOLDEN PEPPER P–324 (hybrid)	70	A short season variety, the midsize pepper with 3–4 lobes ripens to golden yellow.	WIL
GOLDEN SUMMER (hybrid)	67	4x3½ inches, 4 lobes, ripens from lime green to golden yellow; resistant to mosaic.	COO GUR HEN LIB PAR POR TOMA
GOLD FINCH	72	4¾ inches, blocky, 4 lobes, goes from pale lemon yellow to red.	STO
GYPSY (hybrid)	65	This sweet Italian type with thick, pale yellow walls measures 4½x2¼ inches. The 16–20-inch plant is an All-American winner and a short season variety.	BURP COM FAR GUR HEN JUN LED LIB NIC ORN PAR PIN POR TER TOMA VER WILL

VARIETY	DAYS	DESCRIPTION	SOURCES (p. 385)
SWEET PEPPERS (YELLOW/ORANGE) *(continued)*			
KARLO	60–80	This Yellow Romanian type sets its 4x2½-inch fruit even in cool weather.	SEED
KLONDIKE BELL	72	4½ inches square, turns gold when ripe; tolerant to mosaic.	STO
LEMON BELLE (hybrid)	70	4x3¼ inches, thick walls, 3 lobes, lemon yellow; resistant to mosaic.	BURP
LEMON KING (hybrid)	72	Stokes economical pepper.	STO
ORANGE GRANDE (hybrid)	76	5½ inches, ripens from dark green to orange; tolerant to mosaic.	STO
ORANGE KING (hybrid)	72	Stokes economical pepper.	STO
ORI (hybrid)	70	Yellow, elongated bell with thick walls; French variety; sets fruit under stressful conditions.	GOU
ORIOLE (hybrid)	74	4¾ inches, blocky, 4 lobes, ripens to tangerine color; some mosaic tolerance.	STO
OROBELLE (hybrid)	70	Medium-large pepper with thick walls and 3–4 lobes turns from dark green to yellow when ripe. Variety is resistant to disease.	JOH LED LIB TOMA
PEPPOURRI ORANGE (hybrid)	75	3½x3¼ inches, thick walls, ripens from dark green to orange.	TWI
QUADRATO D' ORO (hybrid)	70	Golden yellow when ripe; Dutch variety.	SHE
SUMMER SWEET BRAND 860	86	4½x4½ inches, 4 lobes, matures from medium green to yellow.	TWI
SUNRISE ORANGE SWEET	75	4½x4 inches, medium-thick walls, 4 lobes. Turns from yellow-orange to deep red.	SEED
SUPER STUFF	67	6x3¾ inches, thick walls, 3–4 lobes; Butter Belle type.	STO
SWEET PICKLE	65	2 inches long, oval, thick walls, turns from yellow to orange to purple; 12–15-inch plant.	ORN PAR SEE
SWEET ROMANIAN YELLOW	67–80	4x2½ inches, waxy yellow; 22–24-inch plant.	HOR LIB POR
TANGERINE PIMENTO	80	This thick-walled pepper looks like a tangerine.	SEED
YELLOW BELLE	65	3½x3 inches, medium-thick walls, 4 lobes, turns bright red if left to mature.	JUN SOU STO

SWEET PEPPERS (HEART- OR TOMATO-SHAPED)

VARIETY	DAYS	DESCRIPTION	SOURCES
ANTOHI ROMANIAN	53	4x2 inches, tapered, pointed, pale yellow ripening to red.	JOH

VARIETY	DAYS	DESCRIPTION	SOURCES (p. 385)

SWEET PEPPERS (HEART- OR TOMATO-SHAPED) *(continued)*

VARIETY	DAYS	DESCRIPTION	SOURCES (p. 385)
CANADA–CHEESE	75	2x1¼ inches, ripens from green to red; miniature red pimento.	STO
CHERRY	78	1½x1¼-inch, round, red pepper; 20-inch plant.	GAR GLE HOR TWI
EARLY SWEET PIMENTO	73	2½x3-inch, flat, tomato-shaped pepper.	SEE
GAMBO	90	This 2½x4-inch, rich red pimento type has a flat-globe shape and 4 lobes.	GLE
GRANDE	80	Midsize pimento with thick walls goes from green to red-orange when ripe.	HOR
LIPSTICK	53	5 inches long, tapered to a blunt point, thick walls, ripens from dark green to red.	JOH ORN
PIMENTO (Perfection, True Heart)	65–80	This heart-shaped, 3x2½-inch pepper with thick walls ripens from dark green to red.	ABU BURG COM NIC ORN PIN POR ROS SOU TIL
PIMENTO L	75	Heart-shaped, 3½-inch-long pepper goes from dark green to deep red when ripe.	DEG TOMA WIL
PIMENTO SELECT	73–75	These heart-shaped, dark green peppers with thick walls set on a 33-inch plant.	HEN JLH LIB
RED HEART	90	Large, thick, heart-shaped pimento.	SEED
RED RUFFLED	85	Pimento with thick walls, dark red when ripe.	SEED
SUPER GREYGO (hybrid)	68	6 inches wide, 4½ inches deep, ½-inch-thick walls; mosaic tolerant; Cheese type.	STO
SUPER RED PIMENTO	70	The 5x3¼-inch, flat pimento ripens from green to red. Variety is tolerant of mosaic.	ORN STO TOMA
YELLOW CHEESE PIMENTO	73	This large, squash-shaped fruit turns from green to orange when ripe.	ORN SEE STO

SWEET PEPPERS (OTHER TYPES/COLORS)

VARIETY	DAYS	DESCRIPTION	SOURCES (p. 385)
ACONCAGUA	75	This frying pepper turns from yellow to red when ripe.	GLE TOMA
ALBINO PEPPER	75	Bell-shaped, ripens from white to red; especially dwarf-size bush.	GLE
BLACKBIRD (hybrid)	73	This 3½x3¾-inch, purple and brown crossbreed turns dark red when ripe. Variety is tolerant to mosaic.	STO
BLUE JAY (hybrid)	73	4½x4 inches, ripens from green to dark red; mosaic-tolerant variety.	STO
BRUPA DUTCH CHOCOLATE	75	This thick-walled bell is chocolate colored all the way through.	ORN

VARIETY	DAYS	DESCRIPTION	SOURCES (p. 385)
SWEET PEPPERS (OTHER TYPES/COLORS) *(continued)*			
CHERRY SWEET (Red Cherry Sweet, Red Cherry)	78	The rounded, 1x1½-inch pepper is dark crimson when ripe. The 20-inch plant is an 1860 heirloom variety.	BURG BURP BURR DEG HOR ORN POR ROS SEE SEED SOU STO
CHINESE GIANT	80	6x4–5 inches, goes from dark green to brilliant cherry red when ripe.	GLE
CHOCO	75	Chocolate-colored pimento type.	GLE JLH TOMA
CHOCOLATE BEAUTY	75–88	Medium-large bell type with thick walls ripens from deep green to warm chocolate. Variety tolerates mosaic.	SHE TER TOMA
CHOCOLATE BELL (hybrid) (Sweet Chocolate)	58–86	4½ inches long, 3–4 lobes, turns from tan to red when ripe; Dutch variety.	BOU BURP COO HIG JOH PAR SEE SOU STO TOMA
CUBANELLE	62–70	5–6x2½ inches, blunt ended, medium-thick walls, goes from yellow-green to red when ripe; Italian type.	ABU BURR COM DEG GLE HOR JLH LIB PIN POR RED SEE SEED SHE STO TOMA WIL
DOVE (hybrid)	71	Pick this 5x4¾-inch pepper when immature for near white color. Fruit ripens to red if left on the vine.	STO
ELEPHANT'S TRUNK	80	8–10 inches long, ripens from dark green to brilliant scarlet.	GLE
FEHEROZON	75	Triangular, 4x2¼ inches; Hungarian white pepper.	RED
IVORY CHARM	67	Blocky, 4 lobes, from creamy white to pastel yellow when ripe; resistant to disease.	SHE
LILAC BELLE (hybrid)	68–70	4½x3¼ inches, 3–4 lobes, ripens from ivory to crimson red.	BURP GAR PAR SHE
MOLE SWEET	90	4–5x2-inch, brown pepper with thin walls.	SEED
PARADICSOM ALAKU SARGA SZENTESI	75	2 inches across, golden yellow when ripe.	RED
PARADICSOM ALAKU ZOLD SZENTESI	75	Muffin-shaped pepper with a 2-inch diameter; paprika type; Hungarian variety.	RED
PEPPOURRI LILAC (hybrid)	75	3¼x3-inch bell type with medium-thick walls, light purple ripens to red.	TWI
PURPLE BEAUTY	70	Midsize, blocky bell with thick walls turns from green to deep purple to red.	COM COO DEG GAR GUR HEN LED LIB NIC PAR PIN POR SEE SOU TOMA WILL
PURPLE BELL (Purple Belle)	68	Blocky, 4½-inch bell with 4 lobes, matures from green to bloodred. Plant is tolerant to mosaic.	GOU TOMA
PURPLE KING (hybrid)	72	Stokes economical pepper; mosaic-tolerant variety.	STO
ROBIN (hybrid)	72	4¾x4½ inches, 3–4 lobes, thick walls.	STO
SUPER SWEET CHERRY	75	1¾-inch diameter, round, ripens from green to red; mosaic-tolerant variety.	STO

VARIETY	DAYS	DESCRIPTION	SOURCES (p. 385)
SWEET PEPPERS (OTHER TYPES/COLORS) *(continued)*			
TURKISH 11–B–14	75	3½–4 inches long, 3 inches wide, light greenish yellow, triangular bell shape with pointed ends.	RED
VIEJO ARRUGA DULCE (Wrinkled Sweet Old Man)	75	3x1 inches.	RED
WHITE KING	72	Stokes economical pepper; mosaic-tolerant variety.	STO

POTATOES

BOTANICAL NAME: *Solanum tuberosum*

DAYS TO MATURITY: 70–120.

PLANTING TIME: Plant as soon as the soil can be worked thoroughly. You can start sooner in a raised wooden bed covered with polyethylene.

SOIL: Light and sandy to loam will serve potatoes. Add generous amounts of manure or other organic materials, plus phosphorus and potash. Spade thoroughly; pH 4.8–6.5.

NUTRIENTS: The only fertilizing the plants should need is a light application of organic nitrogen when they are about 6 inches high. Seaweed dug into the soil the previous autumn is an excellent conditioner.

WATER: Potatoes need continuous moisture. Never saturate the soil, however.

LIGHT: Full sun.

SPACING: You can buy potato seed or certified seed potatoes. Cut pieces about 1½ inches square with one good eye per piece. Sow the pieces with the cut side down, 4 inches deep, 12 inches apart. For row gardening, align rows 24–36 inches apart. When the plants are 5–7 inches high, work the soil up around the plant and cover the stems. This keeps the sun from turning the potatoes green.

HARVEST: Dig up early varieties when flowers form on the plants. For later varieties, wait until the vines yellow and die.

STORAGE: Store in a cool, dark place.

Potato Growing Tips

Windowsill Potatoes

To grow potatoes on your windowsill, cut seed potatoes into pieces, one eye per piece. Plant 1–3 pieces in an 8-inch pot filled

POTATOES

with planting mix. Set this in a sunny window. You'll have a slew of small potatoes within a few months.

Potato Ring

Plant potatoes 6 inches apart in a 2-foot-diameter circle. When the plants are about 6 inches high, place an old tire around them and fill it with compost or rotted manure up to the top few leaves. Keep adding tires as the plants grow and compost until the structure is 2–3 feet high. To harvest, pick out the potatoes in the top tire, then remove the compost and the tire. Repeat this until you reach ground level. Fork up any remaining potatoes.

Plastic Cylinders

You can grow five potato plants in an 18-inch plastic cylinder (available as a compost bin from mail-order nurseries). Fill the cylinder with 12 inches of planting mix. Cut seed potatoes into sections with at least one eye each; plant with the eye up. When the plants are about 10 inches high, fill the cylinder with more planting mix. Continue this process until the cylinder is full. You can start harvesting the small potatoes; remove one of the slats of the cylinder so the rest of the slats fall away, exposing the potatoes.

VARIETY	DAYS	DESCRIPTION	SOURCES (p. 385)
POTATOES (RED SKIN)			
DESIREE	80+	Large, round to oblong potato with pinkish red skin and golden flesh; highly resistant to common diseases.	GAR PAR SHE TER
FISHER'S EARLY RED	80+	Shallow eyes and good red color.	FIS
NORLAND	80+	Oblong, with shallow eyes; moderately resistant to scab.	FAR FIS GAR GUR HEN JUN MEY TIL
RED DALE	80+	Mid-early red skin potato; medium to large, blocky-round shape; resistant to scab, verticillium, and late blight; best planted about 8 inches apart.	COO JOH
RED GOLD	80+	Midsize potato with golden flesh; resistant to disease.	GAR
RED PONTINAC	80+	This early to midseason, round potato with shallow eyes does well in heavy soils.	BURP FAR GUR HEN JUN LED MEY
REDSEN	80+	Bright red skin and white flesh, round to oval shape; early to midseason variety; exceptionally long-keeping.	PAR TER
RUBY CRESCENT	80+	Deep pink skin, yellow flesh; fingerling type.	ORG SEE

VARIETY	DAYS	DESCRIPTION	SOURCES (p. 385)

POTATOES (RED SKIN) *(continued)*

VARIETY	DAYS	DESCRIPTION	SOURCES
SANGRE	80+	Slightly elongated, 4–10-ounce potato with dark red, shallow eyes; keeps well.	GAR
VIKING (hybrid)	70	Red skin, jumbo size; drought-resistant variety.	GUR

POTATOES (WHITE SKIN)

VARIETY	DAYS	DESCRIPTION	SOURCES
ANOKA	65+	Tan skin and white flesh, medium-size, oval; bred in Minnesota.	GAR
BELTSVILLE	80+	This big, round, white, midseason potato withstands golden nematodes, potato scab, and verticillium wilt. It stores well.	GUR HEN
GREEN MOUNTAIN	80+	White skin, white flesh; an old-timer variety that's as disease resistant as others.	LED SEE
IRISH COBBLER	100	Round, with deeply set eyes.	GAR GUR LED MEY
KATAHDIN	110	Glossy white skin, shallow eyes.	LED MEY
KENNEBEC	115	These large, oval potatoes with buff-colored skin are best planted closer than 8–10 inches. For fall harvest and winter storage, this drought-tolerant variety is resistant to late blight, viruses, and wart.	BURP FAR GUR HEN JOH JUN LED MEY TIL
ONAWAY	80+	This large, blocky potato has white flesh and buff-colored skin. An early variety, it's resistant to scab, late blight, and potato virus. These tubers store well through the winter.	JOH
SUPERIOR	80+	Smooth, oval potato with shallow eyes.	JUN LED MEY
WHITE COBBLER	80+	Smooth, oval potato has light buff-colored skin and white flesh. This early variety adapts to almost any growing condition.	BURP HEN
WHITE ROSE	80+	Long, flattened potato; early variety; does not store well.	TIL

POTATOES (RUSSET)

VARIETY	DAYS	DESCRIPTION	SOURCES
ACADIA	80+	Long, oval, lightly russeted, reddish brown.	BURP
BUTTE	80+	Long potato with brownish skin and white flesh; late variety; good disease resistance.	COO GAR GUR JOH
FRONTIER	80+	Midseason variety; oblong or cylindrical, with white flesh; stores well; resistant to scab, fusarium dry rot, verticillium, bruising, knobby development, and growth cracks.	HEN JOH
GOLD RUSH	80+	Smooth texture; early to midseason; Plant Variety Patented (PVP).	PAR SHE

VARIETY	DAYS	DESCRIPTION	SOURCES (p. 385)

POTATOES (RUSSET) *(continued)*

VARIETY	DAYS	DESCRIPTION	SOURCES
NETTED GEM	80+	Late variety; keeps very well.	TIL
NORGOLD RUSSET	80+	Golden netting, white flesh; resistant to scab.	FAR GUR HEN
NORKOTAH	80+	Matures early; smooth, russet skin with shallow eyes and white flesh.	FIS JUN
RUSSET BURBANK	80+	The potato is long with russet-brown skin and white flesh. This late season, 1874 heirloom variety is resistant to scab, blackleg, and fusarium storage rot. Plant 14–16 inches apart and irrigate to prevent dryness.	FIS GAR HEN JOH JUN

POTATOES (OTHER COLORS)

VARIETY	DAYS	DESCRIPTION	SOURCES
ALL BLUE POTATO	80+	Blue skin, blue flesh; good flavor.	GUR HEN PAR SHE TER
BENTJI	80+	Waxy yellow skin, yellow flesh, early to midseason variety; 1911 heirloom variety; virus-free and widely adapted; keeps well.	GAR SEE
BLOSSOM	80+	Pink skin, pink flesh; oblong, somewhat flat shape that tapers at ends; stands up to summer heat.	SEE
CARIBE	80+	Early variety; large, oblong potato with purple skin and white flesh; resistant to scab and virus.	GAR JOH LED
CAROLA	80+	Midseason variety; medium-large, oval potatoes with buff-colored skin and yellow flesh; storable.	JOH
CHERRIES JUBILEE	80+	Small, rounded, with bright cherry pink skin and pale pink flesh; keeps well.	SHE
FINGERLINGS	80+	1 inch long, yellow skin, yellow flesh.	JUN SEE
FLAVA	80+	Flattened and round, with shallow eyes and yellow flesh; late to mature.	SEE
GERMAN YELLOW	80+	4 inches long, 1 inch wide, yellow skin, yellow flesh.	GAR ORG
GOLD RAE	80+	Very round potato with pink rays radiating through bright yellow flesh; late variety.	SEE
LADY FINGER	80+	5x1 inches; golden brown skin, yellow flesh; fingerling type.	GUR
LAVENDER	80+	Lavender skin and flesh; medium to late maturity.	SEE
PERUVIAN BLUE	80+	A two-bite potato; purple flesh.	SEE
PINK CHAMPAIGN	80+	Rounded, somewhat irregular, with light pink flesh.	SEE
POTATO BLUSHING	80+	Large, round potato with deep eyes and bright pink flesh; medium maturity.	SEE
PURPLE MARKER	80+	Dark purple skin, purple flesh with white veins; lightens when cooked.	GAR

VARIETY	DAYS	DESCRIPTION	SOURCES (p. 385)
POTATOES (OTHER COLORS) *(continued)*			
PURPLE PERUVIAN	80+	Purple skin, purple flesh; very hardy and storable.	ORG
RUSSIAN BANANA	80+	This long, slender fingerling type is banana shaped, with smooth, buff-yellow skin and light yellow flesh. It's a summer potato when harvested young. Variety is resistant to scab.	COO JOH ORG
URGENTA	80+	Red skin, yellow flesh; sold as "new potatoes" in markets.	SEE
YELLOW FINN	80+	Yellow flesh.	GAR PAR SEE SHE TIL
YUKON GOLD	80+	Yellow flesh; early to midseason variety; keeps well.	BURP COO FIS GAR GUR HEN JOH LED SEE TIL
POTATOES (TRUE POTATO SEEDS)			
HOMESTEAD (hybrid)	90	4-inch-long tuber; large potatoes that grow larger into the summer.	PAR

PUMPKINS

BOTANICAL NAME: *Cucurbita pepo*

DAYS TO MATURITY: 75–120.

PLANTING TIME: Plant pumpkin seeds outdoors around the time of the last frost or when the weather warms up and night temperatures are expected to stay above 55°F.

SOIL: Rich, well-manured; pH 5.5–7.5.

NUTRIENTS: Nourish plants with fish emulsion or another organic fertilizer only during the growth period before blooming.

WATER: Do not cover the crowns with water or keep the soil continuously moist. Mulch to conserve moisture.

LIGHT: Full sun to partial shade.

SPACING: Sow seeds 1 inch deep; thin the seedlings of vining pumpkins to 8–10 feet apart, 4 feet apart for bush pumpkins.

HARVEST: Harvest when the leaves die and the pumpkins are a bright, rich orange. Cut the stems because pumpkins will rot faster if they're pulled from the stem. Leave the picked pumpkins in the sun for a week before storing.

STORAGE: Store in a cool, dry place.

PUMPKINS

Pumpkin Growing Tip

Prize Winners

To grow a blue-ribbon pumpkin, first select one of the large varieties from a seed catalog. When it's time to plant, dig a big hole and put in about a bushel of aged manure and a cup of organic fertilizer (equal parts bonemeal, blood meal, and rock phosphate). Spread a layer of dirt over the manure, and plant three seeds.

When the seedlings have two or three leaves, choose the healthiest plant and pull up the other two. As soon as the vine has three small pumpkins, break off the fuzzy end so it won't grow any farther. If new female blossoms form, pluck them off. When the pumpkins get to be about the size of a man's fist, select the one with the best shape and pick the other two; all the growing energy will go into the remaining pumpkin. Roll it a little now and then to maintain round contours. This pumpkin will be the biggest one you've ever grown.

VARIETY	DAYS	DESCRIPTION	SOURCES (p. 385)
PUMPKINS (EXTRA LARGE)			
ATLANTIC GIANT (OP) (Dill's Atlantic Giant)	115–125	400 pounds or more; round, flattened shape; bright orange rind; thick and meaty, with a small seed cavity; Plant Variety Patented (PVP).	COM FAR GLE GUR HEN JUN LED LIB NIC PIN SEE SOU STO THO TIL VER WIL
BIG MAX	120	100 pounds, 70 inches in diameter; pink-orange rind; flattened, round shape; yellowish orange flesh.	ALL BURG BURP BURR COM GUR HEN LED MEY PLA POR SEE SOU TWI WIL WILL
BIG MOON (OP)	120	Over 200 pounds; medium orange rind with slightly rough texture; light orange flesh; Plant Variety Patented (PVP).	JUN LIB PAR PON POR TWI VER
JUMBO (Mammoth Gold)	110	75–100 pounds.	BURG MEY WIL
MAMMOTH KING (Potiron)	120	100 pounds or more; orange-salmon rind, orange flesh.	BOU
PRIZEWINNER (hybrid)	120	Twice the size of Big Max; smooth, round, bright reddish orange, glossy rind.	BURP JUN LIB STO WILL
THE GREAT PUMPKIN	120	100 pounds, 35-inch diameter; pinkish orange rind, orange meat.	SHE
PUMPKINS (MEDIUM-LARGE)			
ASPEN (hybrid)	93	This semibush grows 13 inches tall by 12 inches wide. Its rich orange pumpkin weighs 20 pounds.	COM

VARIETY	DAYS	DESCRIPTION	SOURCES (p. 385)

PUMPKINS (MEDIUM-LARGE) (continued)

VARIETY	DAYS	DESCRIPTION	SOURCES (p. 385)
CONNECTICUT FIELD (Yankee Cow Pumpkin, Southern Field, Large Yellow, Big Tom)	120	This pre-1700 heirloom variety produces a 25-pound, 10-inch-tall, 14-inch-wide pumpkin, flattened at the ends, with a deep orange rind and orange-yellow flesh.	ALL BURR BUT COM DEG GAR GUR HEN JOH LED LIB MEY PON POR ROS SEE SOU STO TWI WIL WILL
GHOST RIDER	115	Up to 20 pounds and 16 inches across; yellow-orange flesh, dark orange rind; Plant Variety Patented (PVP).	ALL BURP JOH JUN LIB MEY STO
HALF MOON	115	Connecticut Field-class pumpkin.	TWI
HAPPY JACK	110	15–20 pounds, 12 inches tall; dark orange rind, slightly ribbed; Plant Variety Patented (PVP).	COM LED LIB PIN STO TWI WILL
HOWDEN	115	20–30-pound, rounded pumpkin with a rich orange rind; Plant Variety Patented (PVP).	BURR
HOWDEN'S FIELD	115	10–15-pound, round, ridged pumpkin with extrathick flesh.	TER WIL
JACK–O–LITE	90	12–15-pound, classic orange jack-o'-lantern.	SEED
PANKOW'S FIELD	120	20–30 pounds, 13–16 inches tall; orange rind and yellow-orange meat; large, sturdy stems to use as handles.	WIL
PRO GOLD BRAND VARIETY 500 (hybrid)	95	18–22 pounds, 12–14 inches in diameter; round, with bright orange rind.	TWI
PRO GOLD BRAND VARIETY 510 (hybrid)	95	22–26 pounds, 14–16 inches across; round, with deep orange rind; Howden type.	TWI
TALLMAN	110	15–30 pounds, 16 inches tall; deep orange rind; some tolerance to powdery mildew.	STO
WHITE RIND SUGAR	120	Solid flesh.	SEE
WINTER QUEEN (Luxury)	110	10-inch diameter, globe-shaped pumpkin with closely netted, yellow rind.	SEE
WIZARD	115	10–12 pounds, 10–12 inches in diameter; semibush plant; yellow to orange rind.	WIL
WORCESTER INDIAN	120	15–20-pound pumpkin with red-orange rind; old heirloom variety.	JLH

PUMPKINS (SMALL)

VARIETY	DAYS	DESCRIPTION	SOURCES (p. 385)
AUTUMN GOLD (hybrid)	90	10 pounds; short season variety; medium-size vine; bright orange rind even when immature; All-American winner.	BURP BURR COM GUR HEN LED LIB MEY NIC PAR POR STO TIL TWI VER WILL
BIG AUTUMN (hybrid)	100	16-pound pumpkin with slightly ribbed, dark orange rind; semibush plant.	BURR LIB STO TWI
EARLY SWEET (Sugar Pie)	90	6–8 pounds, 9x8 inches; dark orange rind, orange flesh.	DEG GUR

VARIETY	DAYS	DESCRIPTION	SOURCES (p. 385)

PUMPKINS (SMALL) *(continued)*

VARIETY	DAYS	DESCRIPTION	SOURCES (p. 385)
JACK O' LANTERN (Halloween)	115	10 pounds, 9x8 inches; medium orange rind.	ABU ALL BURP BURR COM DEG FIS GUR LED LEJ LIB MEY PON ROS TIL TWI VER WIL
OMAHA	79	4-inch diameter.	SEE
OZ	105	Round, 4–5 pounds, 6 inches in diameter; matures from yellow to bright orange; semibush type.	WIL
SENECA HARVEST MOON (hybrid)	90	8–12 pounds, 6–14 inches in diameter; solid orange color; short season variety.	PIN
SMALL SUGAR PIE (Boston Pie, New England Pie)	100–110	5–7 pounds, 8–10 inches; round and ribbed; pre-1860 heirloom variety.	ABU ALL BURP BURR COM COO GAR GOU HEN JOH LED LEJ LIB MEY NIC ORN PIN PON POR RED ROS SEE SEED SOU STO TER TIL VER WIL WILL
SPOOKTACULAR (hybrid)	85	3–4 pounds, 5–6 inches in diameter; rounded, deep orange rind.	SHE
SUGAR BABY (Honey Pumpkin)	95	8x3½ inches; distinct ribbing; long, disease-resistant vine; 1880s heirloom variety.	SOU
TOM FOX	110	Ribbed, medium-large, deep orange pumpkin.	JOH
TRICK OR TREAT (hybrid)	105	This medium ribbed pumpkin with thick orange meat measures 10–12 pounds and 11 inches in diameter. Hull-less seeds can be eaten raw or roasted.	BURG LED PIN TWI
TRIPLE TREAT	110	6–8 pounds, 8–10 inches in diameter; deep orange flesh; hull-less seeds.	BURP PLA PON
YOUNG'S BEAUTY	108–112	8–15 pounds, 7½x8 inches; orange-yellow flesh, deep orange, moderately ribbed rind.	GAR JLH MEY

PUMPKINS (SPACE SAVERS)

VARIETY	DAYS	DESCRIPTION	SOURCES (p. 385)
ASPEN (hybrid)	95	This semibush plant produces 15-pound, 12-inch-deep, dark orange, globe-shaped pumpkins that store well.	STO
BUSH FUNNY FACE (hybrid)	90–95	10–15-pound pumpkins; semibush with 5-foot vine.	DEG LED PIN POR TWI WIL
BUSHKIN	95	The 6-foot vine sets 1–3 fruits. These weigh 10 pounds and have yellow flesh.	BURP
BUSH SPIRIT	90–100	10–15 pounds, 12 inches in diameter; golden yellow meat; 4-foot semibush; All-American winner.	BURG COM DEG GUR HEN JUN LED LIB NIC ORN POR STO TER TWI
FROSTY (hybrid)	95	10 inches in diameter; bright orange rind; bush type; stores well.	BURR FAR LIB STO TWI
NORTHERN BUSH	90	5–8 pounds, 6–8 inches in diameter; bright orange rind; fairly compact vine; short season variety.	FIS HIG

VARIETY	DAYS	DESCRIPTION	SOURCES (p. 385)
PUMPKINS (SPECIAL TYPES)			
BABY BEAR (OP)	105	Baby pumpkins: 4–6x3–4 inches, 1½–2 pounds each; seminaked seed; some disease tolerance; All-American winner.	ALL BURP COM COO FAR HIG JOH LED LIB NIC PAR POR SOU TWI
BABY BOO	95	A creamy white version of Sweetie Pie; 2–3-inch-wide pumpkin with white flesh; Plant Variety Patented (PVP).	LIB PAR SEE SHE STO WIL
BUCKSKIN (hybrid)	110	12 pounds, 8 inches across; dark orange flesh, buff-colored rind; large vine type.	DEG STO
CUSHAW, GREEN STRIPED	110	This 10–15-pound, 18x10-inch crookneck has whitish green rind with darker green stripes and thick, cream-colored flesh.	LED MEY ROS SEE TER VER
DICKINSON	115	To 40 pounds, 18x14 inches; buff-colored, slightly furrowed rind and orange meat; oval shape.	JLH
FLAT WHITE BOER NIEKERK	115	Large, flattened fruit with pure white rind and deep orange flesh; high sugar content; good for storing.	JLH
GREMLIN	100	5x5½-inch pumpkin; compact vine.	LIB
HOPI PALE GREY	110	5–10-pound pumpkin with pale gray, nearly white rind and yellow flesh.	JLH
HOPI WHITE	110	15 pounds, white rind.	SEE
JACK BE LITTLE	85–110	2x3 inches with deep orange rind and flesh; about 10 fruits per vine; pick when stem is dry; storable.	ABU ALL BURP BURR COM COO DEG FIS GUR HEN JOH JUN LED LIB MEY NIC PAR PIN POR ROS SEE TER TIL TWI VER WIL WILL
JAPANESE PUMPKIN (Golden Debut)	110	3–4 pounds, flat, orange rind; keeps well.	THE
JARRAHDALE	110	Australian variety; silvery rind, orange-yellow, stringless flesh; adapts well to climatic conditions.	BOU
KENTUCKY FIELD LONG	120	35–40-pounds; large, oblong, and blocky; smooth, tan rind, deep orange flesh.	JLH VER
LADY GODIVA (Streaker)	110	6 pounds, 8 inches in diameter; green-and-yellow striped rind.	GLE
LITTLE GEM	110	The small, apple-size, green pumpkin turns orange when mature. This African heirloom variety is a vining type.	ABU
LITTLE LANTERN	100	5x5½ inches; slightly ribbed rind, deep orange flesh; 10-foot vine.	STO
LONG CHEESE	120	20–30 pounds; tan rind, dark orange flesh; flattened cheese-box shape.	JLH
LUMINA	110	10–15 pounds, 8–10 inches; globe or flat globe shape; white rind, bright orange flesh; Plant Variety Patented (PVP).	BURP BURR COM COO FAR HEN LIB PAR PIN SHE STO TER VER WIL

VARIETY	DAYS	DESCRIPTION	SOURCES (p. 385)

PUMPKINS (SPECIAL TYPES) *(continued)*

VARIETY	DAYS	DESCRIPTION	SOURCES
MANTECA LARGE WHITE	110	Smooth, creamy white rind.	RED
MINI JACK	100	3–6-inch diameter; round; bright orange rind.	SEE
MUNCHKIN	90–110	3–4-inch diameter; hard ridged, deep orange rind, orange-yellow flesh.	ORN SHE WIL
OLD-FASHIONED TENNESSEE VINING PUMPKIN	120	Oval shape; 12–15 pounds; ripens to a tan color, with deep orange flesh; resistant to squash vine borer.	SOU
ORANGE HOKKAIDO (Uchiki Kuri)	120	10 pounds; orange-red rind, clear yellow meat.	BOU
ROUGE D' ETAMPES (Rouge Vif d'Etampes, Cinderella)	95–160	5–40 pounds; deeply ridged, flattened, red rind with rough, pebbled texture; antique French heirloom variety.	BOU COM COO GOU SEE SEED SHE
STYRIAN HULL-LESS	110	Up to 20 pounds; hull-less seeds; green variety from Styria, Austria.	JLH
SWEETIE PIE	110	5 ounces, 3x1¾ inches; deeply ribbed.	STO
TRIAMBLE	120	15 pounds; 3-cornered shape; slate gray, thick, tough rind, deep orange flesh; keeps well.	GLE
WHANGAPAROA CROWN	120	Hard gray rind, solid, deep orange flesh; small seed cavity; stores well.	GLE

RADISHES

BOTANICAL NAME: *Raphanus sativus*

DAYS TO MATURITY: 21–150.

PLANTING TIME: Sow radish seeds when the soil can be worked; then plant every 10 days for a continual crop. Start sowing in late summer for a fall crop. In areas with mild winters, you can also sow in the early fall.

SOIL: Mix in ample well-rotted manure; pH 6.0–7.0.

NUTRIENTS: All organic material should be added to the soil before planting.

WATER: Keep the soil moist.

LIGHT: Full sun.

SPACING: Sow seeds ½ inch deep, ½ inch apart. Arrange rows 4–6 inches apart.

HARVEST: Harvest each variety when the roots reach the size listed on the package.

STORAGE: Use as needed by picking from garden.

Radish Growing Tip

Plant Radishes with Carrots

Mix carrot and radish seeds together and scatter them across a bed or down a row at the approximate spacing for carrots. The radishes will come up quickly and mark the bed. Harvest the radishes shortly before the baby carrots need thinning.

VARIETY	DAYS	DESCRIPTION	SOURCES (p. 385)
RADISHES (RED, ROUND)			
CHAMPION	25–28	Bright scarlet, seldom pithy; does well in hot weather; heirloom variety.	BURG BURP COM DEG FAR FIS GAR GUR HEN HIG JUN LED LIB MEY POR SEE STO VER WIL
CHERRIETTE (hybrid)	24	Fire-engine-red roots grow to be 2 inches.	MEY PAR
CHERRY BELLE (OP)	20–24	The ¾-inch radish resembles a cherry. This All-American winner is widely used in muck soils or for greenhouse forcing.	ABU ALL BOU BURP BURR COM DEG FAR FIS GUR HEN JUN LED LEJ LIB MEY NIC PIN PON POR SEE SEED SOU STO TIL TWI VER WIL WILL
CHERRY BOMB	25	Red, round, not pithy; heat-resistant variety.	BURP
COMET	25	1-inch diameter, cherry red, with short tops and white flesh; good forcing variety.	DEG HEN SEE STO
CRIMSON GIANT (Butter, Silver Dollar)	29	1½-inch diameter, crimson; solid, white, mild flesh; grows large without becoming pithy and hollow.	ALL BURP DEG FAR HEN LED LEJ PON POR ROS SEE TIL
DANDY	23	Round, deep scarlet; resistant to cracking and yellows.	BURR
EARLY SCARLET GLOBE MEDIUM TOP (Vicks)	24–30	Bright scarlet; crisp, white flesh.	ALL BURG BURR BUT FAR HEN JUN LED LEJ MEY SEE VER WIL WILL
EARLY SCARLET GLOBE SHORT TOP	24	Round, bright, and attractive.	COM PLA ROS
EASY RED	21–24	Fast growing; short tops; requires prompt harvest during heat.	SEE
FUEGO	22–24	2¾ inches in diameter, deep scarlet; disease-tolerant variety.	LIB STO
GALA	26	Round, scarlet; Dutch variety; resistant to splitting and sponginess.	SHE
GALAHAD	20	Tolerant to club root.	STO
GERMAN GIANT (Parat)	29	This slightly pungent German variety grows to be the size of a baseball.	GLE GUR HEN JUN ORG PIN VER
JULIETTE (hybrid) (Crunchy Red)	22	Harvest these radishes anywhere from marble- to very large size without spoilage.	THO

VARIETY	DAYS	DESCRIPTION	SOURCES (p. 385)
RADISHES (RED, ROUND) *(continued)*			
JUMBO	24	This European variety's bright red root is the size of a cue ball and does not get pithy during hot weather.	STO
MARABELLE	23	Medium size; short tops; for outside or greenhouse growing.	JOH ORN
MEXICAN BARTENDER	24	Round to olive shaped, bright red.	DEG
NOVIRED	21	Bright red, round; medium tops; Dutch variety with some disease tolerance; Plant Variety Patented (PVP).	GOU STO
POKER	25–70	This bright red, round, mild radish was bred for the greenhouse but does well in gardens.	TER
RAVE BRAND VARIETY 2300 (hybrid)	23	Uniform, round, red; fusarium-resistant variety.	TWI
RED BALL (Roodbol)	24	Widely adapted; does not become woody or pithy; Dutch variety.	SHE
RED BOY	25	Sparkling red; short tops.	STO
RED BOY II	23	Blazing scarlet, solid, round; short tops; spicy.	FAR
RED KING	25–30	Bright red; resistant to fusarium yellows and club-root; Plant Variety Patented (PVP).	TER
RED PAK	25	Intensely red; large to medium tops; tolerance to disease but none to clubroot; Plant Variety Patented (PVP).	JOH STO
RED PRINCE (Prinz Rotin)	25	Globe-shaped radish.	DEG JUN
REVOSA	26	Red, round radish with white flesh.	PIN
RIBELLA	25	Round, refined Cherry Belle; medium tops; resists pithiness.	SOU TER
SAXA	18	Bright scarlet; short tops; adapted to garden or greenhouse growing.	GUR HEN
SCARLET GLOBE	24	1-inch diameter, scarlet; medium tops; grows out-doors or in a greenhouse.	DEG
SCARLET GLOBE SPECIAL	23	Strain of Scarlet Globe; no disease resistance.	STO
SORA	26	Bright red, large, smooth; medium-tall tops; good tolerance to hot weather.	JOH

VARIETY	DAYS	DESCRIPTION	SOURCES (p. 385)
RADISHES (RED, LONG)			
BARTENDER RED MAMMOTH (Red Mammoth Bartender)	40	7–9 inches long, slender, red, with pink flesh.	JLH SEE
LONG RED ITALIAN	35–45	12 inches long, bright crimson.	ORN
LONG SCARLET (Long Brightest)	40	Long, red, old-time radish.	POR SEE
RADISHES (WHITE TIP)			
D'AVIGNON	21–25	3–4 inches long, ½–¾ inches thick; red tapering to a white point; French variety.	GAR JOH
EARLY SCARLET WHITE TIP	24	Round, crisp; short tops.	ALL
FLAMBOYANT	28	3 inches long, cylindrical; short tops; French variety.	SHE
FLAMIVIL	25–27	3 inches long, cylindrical; intensely red French variety.	HIG JOH
FLUO (hybrid)	24	Red, cylindrical radish with white tip; French variety.	COO GOU HIG ORN PIN
FRENCH BREAKFAST	20–30	Pull the 1¾-inch, oblong, rose-scarlet, white-tipped radish when young. This 1885 heirloom variety has short tops.	ABU ALL BOU BURP COM DEG FAR FIS GUR HEN JUN LED MEY NIC ORG ORN PIN PON POR ROS SEE STO TER TIL WILL
GAUDO	30	Scarlet with a sparkling white tip.	ORN
SPARKLER (Early Scarlet Turnip, Brightest White Tip)	25	1¾-inch-long, scarlet radish with a white tip.	BURR DEG FAR FIS GAR HEN JUN LEJ LIB MEY NIC PON POR ROS SEE STO WIL WILL
WHITE TIPPED SCARLET TURNIP	30	Round, slightly flattened, rose-crimson with white tips; 1880s heirloom variety.	JLH
RADISHES (ALL WHITE)			
BURPEE WHITE	22	3x1 inches, round, mild, and crisp.	BURP JUN
HAILSTONE	28–30	1¼ inch long, round, crisp, and sweet.	FAR FIS GAR NIC
SNOW BELLE (OP)	26–30	1¾ inch long, round; smooth, white skin; tangy flavor; Plant Variety Patented (PVP).	HEN ORN PAR STO TIL TWI
WHITE FINGER	30	3–5 inches long, mild.	ORG
WHITE GLOBE (Giant White Globe, Giant Hailstone, Mammoth)	25–28	6-inch diameter, round, white; will grow in any climate.	DEG GUR SEE

VARIETY	DAYS	DESCRIPTION	SOURCES (p. 385)

RADISHES (ALL WHITE) (continued)

VARIETY	DAYS	DESCRIPTION	SOURCES (p. 385)
WHITE ICE	27–32	The 3–6-inch white roots are mildly spicy. The 5–6-inch tops are also good to eat.	SEED
WHITE ICICLE (OP) (Icicle, Lady Finger)	27–30	4–5 inches long, white; stands heat well.	ALL BURG BURP BURR COM DEG FAR FIS GAR GUR HEN JLH JUN LED LIB MEY NIC ORN PIN PON POR SEE SOU STO TER TWI VER WIL WILL
WHITE ROUND	30	Crisp, white.	POR

RADISHES (OTHER COLORS/TYPES)

VARIETY	DAYS	DESCRIPTION	SOURCES (p. 385)
EASTER EGG (hybrid) (Easter Egg II)	25	These crisp, firm, round radishes are red, pink, white, purple, and violet.	BURP COM COO GAR GUR HEN JOH JUN LIB NIC ORN PAR PIN POR SHE TER TIL VER WILL
LONG PURPLE PODDED	45–60	The 10–23-inch-long, edible seed pods have a slightly hot taste. Pick them before they develop fiber.	SEED
MUCHEN BIER	67	Long, tapered roots; pungent German variety; grown for seed pods.	BOU COO
PINK BEAUTY	27	Large; white flesh; short tops.	GLE GUR
PLUMB PURPLE	25	Round with a 2 inch diameter; purple skin, bright white flesh; mild flavor.	COO GUR HEN ORN PAR POR
VALENTINE	25	Round radish with green and white skin; interior turns red at maturity.	SEE STO
VIOLET DE GAURNAY	67	Long; dark violet skin, pure white flesh; French heirloom variety; pungent.	ORN

RADISHES (ORIENTAL, SPRING)

VARIETY	DAYS	DESCRIPTION	SOURCES (p. 385)
APRIL CROSS (hybrid) (Daikon, Minowase, Summer Cross Hybrid)	45–63	Tapered, 14–18 inches long, 2 inches thick; pungent and white; slow to bolt; doesn't become pithy.	BURP BUT COM GAR GUR HEN NIC SUN THE TIL TWI VER
H.N. CROSS	75	Short, blunt, 1½-pound, white roots with green tinge.	TWI
LITTLE TOKYO ROUND (hybrid)	35–40	2–2½x3 inches, turnip-shaped; mild and crisp.	TER
MINO EARLY (OP)	58	16x2 inches, white.	SUN TIL
MINO SPRING CROSS (hybrid)	55	16 inches long; mildly pungent, white flesh; resistant to bolting.	SUN WILL
SHORT RED RADISH (OP)	40	8x2 inches; red skin, white flesh.	SUN
SPRING LEADER (hybrid)	60	Long, tapered, white roots; bolt resistance.	JOH

VARIETY	DAYS	DESCRIPTION	SOURCES (p. 385)

RADISHES (ORIENTAL, SPRING) *(continued)*

VARIETY	DAYS	DESCRIPTION	SOURCES
TOKINASKI (OP) (All Seasons)	45–80	Radish measures 15x2 inches and weighs 2 pounds. Seeds of these very pungent radishes can be sown anytime except where daytime temperatures drop to freezing. Variety is resistant to cold and heat.	ABU DEG NIC POR SEE SUN TER
WHITE AND LONG (OP)	55	White skin, white flesh.	SUN

RADISHES (ORIENTAL, SUMMER/FALL)

VARIETY	DAYS	DESCRIPTION	SOURCES
GREEN LONG (OP)	50	15x2 inches, green skin and flesh; sow in fall.	SUN
JAPANESE BALL (OP)	65	7x6 inches, white; for fall sowing.	SUN
LO BOK (Green Flesh)	60	The top two-thirds of the radish is green inside and out, the bottom is white. This Chinese variety grows to 10 inches and weighs 1–2 pounds.	THE
MINO SUMMER CROSS (hybrid)	45	Sow in spring for a summer crop of these 18x2½-inch, white, mildly pungent radishes.	SUN
MINOWASE SUMMER CROSS NO. 1	50	2 feet long, 1½ inches thick, white; grows vigorously during summer.	GLE
RAT'S TAIL	40	With no edible root, this pre-1860 heirloom variety is grown strictly for the 10–12-inch-long, slender, dark purple pods. Variety stands summer heat and has a moderate radish taste.	BOU
SUMMER CROSS (hybrid)	45	18x2 inches, white; disease-resistant Japanese type; tolerates heat.	LED
SUMMER CROSS NO. 3 (hybrid) (Minowase Summer Cross 3)	50–55	16x2½ inches, white; tolerant to heat; resistant to fusarium wilt.	JOH MEY TER TWI
TAE-BAEK (hybrid)	70	Sow seeds in late summer. These short, blunt, white, green-tinged roots weigh 2 pounds each. Disease-tolerant variety keeps 4–5 months in storage.	TWI
WHITE RAT (hybrid)	45	Blunt, 1¾ ounces, white, pungent; for fall planting.	TWI

RADISHES (ORIENTAL, WINTER)

VARIETY	DAYS	DESCRIPTION	SOURCES
BLACK SPANISH ROUND	53–80	Globe with 3½-inch diameter; black skin, white, pungent flesh; 1824 heirloom variety.	BOU COM DEG FAR GUR JLH JUN LED LIB MEY SEE SOU STO VER WILL
BLACK WINTER ROUND	55	Black skin, white, pungent flesh; Italian variety; sow in late summer for winter harvest.	GLE
CALIFORNIA WHITE MAMMOTH	60	8x2 inches, white.	FAR SEE

VARIETY	DAYS	DESCRIPTION	SOURCES (p. 385)

RADISHES (ORIENTAL, WINTER) *(continued)*

VARIETY	DAYS	DESCRIPTION	SOURCES (p. 385)
CELESTIAL WHITE WONDER	60	8x3 inches, white, mild.	LED MEY NIC RED
CHINESE ROSE (OP) (China Rose, Scarlet China Winter, Rose Colored Chinese)	52	6–7x2 inches; rose to light pink skin, white, pungent flesh; old variety.	DEG HEN JLH JUN LED MEY NIC PIN POR SEE SOU STO SUN VER
CHINESE WHITE	55	Long, white radish.	DEG ROS STO SUN WIL
GREEN SKIN, RED FLESH (OP)	55	5x4 inches; green skin, red flesh; sow in fall for winter harvest; keeps well.	HEN JLH SUN
KOREA GREEN	55	10x3 inches; green skin, green flesh; sow in fall for winter harvest.	JLH SUN
LONG BLACK SPANISH	55–60	Cylindrical, 8–10x2½ inches; black skin, white flesh; pre-1828 heirloom variety.	FIS NIC PIN SOU
MISATO ROSE-FLESH (hybrid)	65	4-inch diameter; white skin with green shoulders, red flesh; Chinese variety; stores well.	HEN PAR VER
MIYASHIGE	50–78	17x2½ inches, white, pungent; Japanese variety.	HIG JOH NIC SEED
NERIMA LONGEST	90	30x3 inches, white.	WILL
SAKURAJIMA (Giant Sakurajima, Mammoth White Globe)	150	25–100 pounds, globe-shaped, white flesh; keeps well in storage; Japanese variety.	BURG GLE NIC
SHOGOIN LARGE ROUND (Mammoth Shogoin Globe, Shogoin Round Giant)	65–85	5½-inch diameter; round, white.	DEG NIC
SLOW BOLT (hybrid)	60	Daikon type; 12x3 inches, white; slow to bolt.	JUN
TAMA (hybrid)	65	16x3-inch, white root; Japanese variety; tolerance to common radish diseases.	VER

RHUBARB

BOTANICAL NAME: *Rheum rhaponticum*

DAYS TO MATURITY: Rhubarb should not be harvested until the second year.

PLANTING TIME: Buy and plant the crowns in early spring as soon as the soil can be worked. Rhubarb does not fare well in areas with warm winters.

SOIL: Deep, rich, and slightly acid; pH 5.5–7.0.

NUTRIENTS: Work bonemeal and rock potash into the root-zone area. Administer a liberal dose of organic nitrogen in early spring and again in midsummer, especially when you have cut a number of stalks.

WATER: Give the plants plenty of water, but never waterlog the soil.

LIGHT: Full sun.

SPACING: Plant the crowns 1–3 feet apart.

HARVEST: Grasp each stalk near the base and twist sideways. Harvest rhubarb in the spring when the leaf stalks are 1 inch or more in diameter.

STORAGE: Use fresh as needed.

Rhubarb Growing Tips

Early Rhubarb

Those who live in one of California's cooler climates can force rhubarb during the winter months. Place a 2-foot-high barrel, wooden box, or large pot over the plant, and cover this with a lid to keep out the light. Cover the whole thing with grass clippings, straw, dead leaves, or garden compost.

Rhubarb Incubator

In cooler climates you can also try incubating rhubarb. In springtime, dig a 1-foot hole and add 6 inches of manure or decomposed organic matter; plant the root in the hole and cover it with 1 inch of soil. During the first year, give it plenty of organic fertilizer. The second year, the plant will start to put out seed pods. If you keep cutting these, the roots will produce tasty stalks all season long. The more leaves and stalks you harvest, the more the plant will produce.

RHUBARB

VARIETY	DAYS	DESCRIPTION	SOURCES (p. 385)
RHUBARB			
CANADA RED (Chipman's Canada Red)	90	Stalks are deep red and especially heavy.	FAR GUR HEN JUN
CHERRY RED	90	Stalks are large, cherry red outside, and green inside.	BURG GUR HEN PAR
CRIMSON RED	90	Large, crimson stalks are always tender and tart.	PON
McDONALD'S	90	Stalks are brilliant red and tender. No peeling is necessary.	BURP
VALENTINE	90	Stalks are deep red and measure 22x1½ inches.	BURP GUR HEN JUN
VICTORIA	90	These tart stalks are broad, with more green shading than Valentine.	DEG LED PAR PIN ROS VER WILL

RUTABAGA (SWEDE)

BOTANICAL NAME: *Brassica napobrassica*

DAYS TO MATURITY: 88–92.

PLANTING TIME: Plant rutabagas in the garden four to six weeks before the last frost. Plant again in late July or August for a fall crop.

SOIL: Light, sandy to loam; pH 5.5–7.0.

NUTRIENTS: Feed the plants with a light application of organic nitrogen when they are about 5 inches high.

WATER: Steady moisture is required. Mulch to prevent drying out.

LIGHT: Full sun.

SPACING: Sow seed ½ inch deep, 1–4 inches apart. For row gardening, space rows 12–15 inches apart.

HARVEST: Grasp the tops and pull up.

STORAGE: Rutabagas can be left in the ground and pulled as needed. If you decide to dig the roots up, cut off any top growth and keep them in a box or barrel filled with moist soil or peat; they need darkness and moderate warmth.

VARIETY	DAYS	DESCRIPTION	SOURCES (p. 385)
RUTABAGA (SWEDE)			
ALTASWEET	92	7-inch diameter, deep yellow flesh; Canadian variety; cross between Laurentian and McComber.	ORN
AMERICAN PURPLE TOP	88–90	Purple topped, buttery yellow, 4–6-inch globes; 1920 heirloom variety; good for winter storage.	ALL BURR DEG FIS GUR HEN JUN LIB MEY PAR PON POR SEE SOU TIL TWI VER
BURPEE'S PURPLE TOP YELLOW	90	This fine-grained, yellow globe with a deep purplish top cooks to bright orange. It keeps well in winter.	BURP NIC
IMPROVED AMERICAN PURPLE TOP YELLOW	90	4–5-inch diameter, yellow flesh; short-neck strain.	COM FAR LED WILL
LAURENTIAN CERTIFIED	90	This variety is recommended for commercial growers.	STO
LAURENTIAN NECKLESS (Laurentian)	90–122	Purple top, yellow globe below; free of excess roots; good for winter storage.	ABU FAR GAR LIB PIN SEE STO WILL
MARIAN	85–95	Similar to Laurentian, with a purple top and yellow, 8-inch root; resistant to clubroot; keeps well.	TER
PIKE	100	Purple top, yellow globe below, with yellow flesh.	JOH

RUTABAGA

VARIETY	DAYS	DESCRIPTION	SOURCES (p. 385)

RUTABAGA (SWEDE) *(continued)*

VARIETY	DAYS	DESCRIPTION	SOURCES
SWEDE PURPLE TOP (Acme)	100	Sweet taste; easy to grow; will stand for a long time.	BOU
YORK	90	Laurentian type with a purple top and pale yellow flesh; resistant to clubroot.	JOH

RUTABAGA (OTHER)

VARIETY	DAYS	DESCRIPTION	SOURCES
COLBAGA	100	A cross between Chinese cabbage and rutabaga, it has purple tops and white flesh below the soil. Grow and store this tuber like a rutabaga. It keeps well.	FIS

SALSIFY (OYSTER PLANT, VEGETABLE OYSTER)

BOTANICAL NAME: *Tragopogon porrifolius*

DAYS TO MATURITY: 120–150.

PLANTING TIME: Sow salsify as soon as the ground can be worked. Harvest the roots in the fall.

SOIL: Deep, rich loam, with no manure or stones.

NUTRIENTS: Spread a layer of well-rotted garden compost around the tops.

WATER: Keep well watered.

LIGHT: Full sun.

SPACING: Sow seeds ½–1 inch deep; thin the seedlings to 3 inches apart. Space rows 10 inches apart.

HARVEST: Don't lift the roots from the ground until you need them. Lift with care so the roots don't bleed and lose flavor.

STORAGE: Use as needed. Store in the ground.

SALSIFY

VARIETY	DAYS	DESCRIPTION	SOURCES (p. 385)

SALSIFY (OYSTER PLANT, VEGETABLE OYSTER)

VARIETY	DAYS	DESCRIPTION	SOURCES
BLACKROOTED DUPLEX	140	Scorzonera, a special strain of salsify; black, 8–10-inch-long roots with creamy white flesh.	WILL
BLANC AMELIORE	140	Elegant, long, tapered root with white flesh; French variety.	ORN
LANGE JAN	120	Long, cylindrical; black skin, white flesh; European strain of Scorzonera.	JOH

VARIETY	DAYS	DESCRIPTION	SOURCES (p. 385)

SALSIFY (OYSTER PLANT, VEGETABLE OYSTER) *(continued)*

VARIETY	DAYS	DESCRIPTION	SOURCES (p. 385)
LONG BLACK (Gigantia, Black Giant Russian, Scorzonera)	120–140	Long, black; very hardy Danish variety.	NIC SEE THE
MAMMOTH LONG ISLAND	120	Popular in Europe.	COM
MAMMOTH SAND-WICH ISLAND	118–140	6–8-inch-long, 1–1½-inch-thick, dull white roots; pre-1900 heirloom variety.	ABU ALL BURR DEG FAR GUR JOH JUN LED LIB MEY NIC PIN SOU STO VER WILL
WHITE FRENCH	120	White root; good oyster flavor; easy to grow.	TIL

SPINACH

BOTANICAL NAME: *Spinacia oleracea*

DAYS TO MATURITY: 39–70.

PLANTING TIME: Plant spinach outside four to six weeks before the last frost-free date in the spring, then again in late summer for a fall crop. In warm areas, plant it during the winter.

SOIL: Light, thoroughly worked, with plenty of organic matter added; pH 6.0–7.5.

NUTRIENTS: Add nitrogenous fertilizer while the crop is actively growing. Use fish emulsion or 1 tablespoon of blood meal mixed in 1 gallon of water.

WATER: Give spinach plenty of overhead watering.

LIGHT: Full sun.

SPACING: Sow seeds ½ inch deep; thin to 6 inches apart. For row gardening, separate rows by 12 inches.

HARVEST: You can harvest just the leaves or cut the whole plant off at the soil line.

STORAGE: Use fresh; some varieties can be frozen.

Spinach Growing Tips

Flowering Spinach

Some spinach varieties bolt to flower after a few warm spring days, while others will stand quite a bit of heat. In general, longer days and higher temperatures (above 75°F) hasten flowering. If your spinach tends to bolt early, try planting three or four long standing varieties. From these, select the one that works best in your garden.

Cut Back

To stop spinach from flowering, cut the plant back to the ground when it has just four or five leaves. As soon as new leaves appear, harvest again. If you wait too long hoping the leaves will grow big, you end up with less spinach.

VARIETY	DAYS	DESCRIPTION	SOURCES (p. 385)
SPINACH (SAVOYED)			
AMERICA	50	Glossy, dark green, heavily savoyed, crumpled leaves; slow to bolt; All-American winner.	LED ORG SOU TIL
BLOOMSDALE	48–60	Thick, twisted, crumpled leaves; slow to bolt.	LEJ ORG PON POR ROS SEED TER
BLOOMSDALE LONG STANDING (OP)	39–48	Very crinkled, glossy, dark green leaves; slow to bolt; 1915 heirloom variety.	ABU ALL BURP BURR BUT DEG FAR GAR GUR HEN HIG JLH JUN LED LIB MEY NIC PAR PIN PLA RED SEE SOU STO TIL VER WIL WILL
BOUQUET	40	Crumpled, dark green leaves.	TIL
COLD RESISTANT SAVOY	45	Savoyed leaves; tolerant to heat, cold, and blight.	STO
HYBRID 612 SAVOY	40	Deeply savoyed, dark green leaves; fall variety.	MEY
ITALIAN SUMMER (hybrid)	40	Green, savoyed leaves; resistant to bolting; short season Italian variety.	SHE
KING OF DENMARK	46	Dark green, crumpled, broad, rounded leaves; hardy plant.	SEE
NORFOLK	45–55	Well-crinkled, green leaves; Canadian variety.	ABU
SASSY (hybrid)	40	Dark green, savoyed leaves; upright plant for fall planting; tolerant to disease.	BURR
TYEE (hybrid)	37–53	Dark green, savoyed leaves with bland flavor; bolt-resistant; tolerant to downy mildew.	COM GAR HEN HIG JOH LIB ORN PIN STO TER TWI VER WIL
VIENNA (hybrid)	40–45	Heavily savoyed, dark green leaves; medium-large, erect plant; tolerant to disease; for spring or fall planting.	LIB MEY PAR STO
VIRGINIA BLIGHT RESISTANT	40	This variety is resistant to blight but must be sown in fall or it bolts to seed.	COM
WINTER BLOOMSDALE	42–47	Dark green, savoyed leaves; resistant to disease; for fall planting; slow to bolt.	ABU GAR HIG SOU
SPINACH (SEMISAVOYED)			
AVON (hybrid)	39–44	Large, dark green leaves; slow to bolt.	BURP HEN MEY
CHINOOK (Hybrid No. 7 Improved)	40	Large, dark green leaves; upright habit; resistant to downy mildew; for spring planting.	TIL

VARIETY	DAYS	DESCRIPTION	SOURCES (p. 385)

SPINACH (SEMISAVOYED) *(continued)*

VARIETY	DAYS	DESCRIPTION	SOURCES (p. 385)
EARLY HYBRID NO. 7	45	Large, dark green leaves; upright habit; resistant to downy mildew.	BURG COM DEG FAR LED NIC POR WILL
GIANT WINTER	45	Medium green leaves; hardy in cold.	ABU SEE WILL
HYBRID NO. 7–R	43	Dark green, semisavoyed leaves; for fall planting.	BURR
INDIAN SUMMER (hybrid)	39	Dark green leaves with excellent flavor; upright habit; tolerant to disease; for spring or fall planting.	COO JOH
MELODY (hybrid)	42	Dark green leaves; disease-resistant, fast-growing All-American winner.	BURP FAR GOU HEN JUN LED MEY NIC PAR PIN POR STO TWI VER
OLD DOMINION	40–60	Midsize plant; for fall and winter planting.	SEED
SKOOKUM (hybrid)	41	Large, round, dark green leaves; disease-resistant variety.	TWI
SPUTNIK (hybrid)	60	Dark green leaves; resistant to mildew; for spring or fall planting.	COO

SPINACH (SMOOTH LEAVES)

VARIETY	DAYS	DESCRIPTION	SOURCES (p. 385)
ESTIVATO (OP)	35–40	Tolerant to heat; for spring planting.	COO ORG
HIVERNA	45	Strong, fleshy, broad, smooth, green leaves; resistant to blue mold; for spring or fall planting.	WILL
HYBRID 424	40	Large, dark green leaves; resistant to blue mold.	WIL
LOW ACID SPINACH	40	These round leaves contain very little oxalic acid.	BOU SEED
MAZURKA (hybrid)	45	Large, rounded, dark green leaves; slow to bolt.	TER
MEDANIA	60–70	Dark green, broad leaves; tolerant to heat and cold; resistant to blue mold; for spring planting; Plant Variety Patented (PVP).	BOU GUR
NOBEL GIANT (Long Standing Quadray, Giant Thick Leaved)	46	Huge, thick, smooth, pointed leaves with round tips; large, green plants.	BURR DEG HEN JLH SEE TIL
NORDIC (hybrid)	39–45	Vibrant, deep green leaves; Dutch variety; slow to bolt; resistant to downy mildew.	PAR SHE
OLYMPIA (hybrid)	46	Deep green leaves; for spring or summer planting; tolerant of downy mildew.	GUR STO TER
SPACE (hybrid)	39	Smooth, deep green leaves; upright plant; resistant to mildew.	JOH PIN
STEADFAST	50	Smooth, dark green leaves; resistant to bolting.	TER
ST. HELENS (hybrid)	38	Dark green leaves; bolts in hot weather; resistant to mildew.	TIL

VARIETY	DAYS	DESCRIPTION	SOURCES (p. 385)
SPINACH (SMOOTH LEAVES) *(continued)*			
VIROFLAY 90 (Resistoflay)	45	Large, erect plant; for fall planting; resistant to downy mildew.	ROS
WOLTER (hybrid)	37	Almond-shaped, medium green leaves; Dutch variety; good disease resistance.	SHE
SPINACH (ORIENTAL)			
BROADLEAVED SUMMER	45	The medium green leaves are smooth and large. Birds don't eat this prickly seed.	BOU SEE WILL
IMPERIAL EXPRESS (hybrid)	35	Medium green, smooth leaves; for fall planting; good tolerance to some strains of downy mildew.	VER
IMPERIAL STAR (hybrid)	39	Medium green leaves are thick and smooth. Plant is slow to bolt and resistant to downy mildew.	VER
IMPERIAL SUN	41	Dark green, thick, smooth leaves; slow to bolt; good for spring planting; resistant to downy mildew.	VER
ORIENT SPINACH (hybrid)	45	Smooth, dark green leaves; tolerant to heat and resistant to disease.	SUN
SPINACH SUBSTITUTES			
CLIMBING SPINACH (Hinchoy, Basella Rubra)	70	Red leaves; quick growing vine.	GLE PAR
MALABAR SPINACH (Basella Alba, Poi Sag)	70–110	Large, glossy, bright green leaves; trailing type; from India.	BOU GLE NIC PAR PIN RED
MOUNTAIN SPINACH (Orach, German Spinach)	70	This variety grows to 9 feet if it isn't clipped. Orach grows in different colors.	BOU NIC SEE
MUSTARD SPINACH (Tendergreen, Komatsuna)	35	These long, glossy, dark green leaves taste like mustard.	PAR RED
NEW ZEALAND SPINACH (Tetragonia Expansa, Tetragone cornue)	70	Small, brittle, green, triangular leaves; 1–2-foot, spreading plant; heat-resistant 1772 New Zealand heirloom variety.	ALL BOU BURP BUT COM DEG FAR GAR GOU HEN JLH JUN LED LIB MEY NIC PIN POR RED ROS SEE SOU STO VER WILL
ORACH, GREEN (Mountain Spinach)	50	This annual—sometimes mistaken for Lamb's Quarters—will grow to 6 feet if not cut.	BOU PIN
ORACH, RED (Crimson Plume)	58	Annual, red-purple variety; popular as a garnish.	COO NIC PIN SEE
PERPETUAL SPINACH	60	Biennial; heavy producer through heat and cold; refined variety of chard.	COO
RUBY ORACH MOUNTAIN	60	This magenta, 4–6-foot-tall plant is a hardy biennial that grows well in cool weather and goes to seed during hot summer months.	SEED

VARIETY	DAYS	DESCRIPTION	SOURCES (p. 385)

SPINACH SUBSTITUTES *(continued)*

VARIETY	DAYS	DESCRIPTION	SOURCES
TAMPALA SPINACH (Fordhook)	60	This variety tastes like artichoke.	BURG POR SEE

SQUASH, SUMMER

BOTANICAL NAME: *Cucurbita pepo*

DAYS TO MATURITY: 47–90.

PLANTING TIME: Plant seeds directly in the ground after the last frost, when night temperatures are staying above 50°F.

SOIL: Very rich and well-manured; pH 6.0–7.5.

NUTRIENTS: Fertilize squash with nitrogen only during the growth period before blooming.

WATER: Keep well watered.

LIGHT: Full sun.

SPACING: Sow seeds of bush varieties 1 inch deep; for row gardening, space rows 18–24 inches apart. The seeds of vine varieties should be sown 1 inch deep; for row gardening, space rows 5 feet apart. Vining squash can be grown up along a fence to save space.

HARVEST: Pick squash that's tender and easily punctured. All fruit should be picked (whether it will be eaten or not) to keep the plant producing.

STORAGE: Use fresh or pickle.

Summer Squash Growing Tips

Playing Bee

If mature squash plants produce few fruit, the problem may be a lack of bees. So collect the yellow pollen with an artist's brush, and dust the female flowers (the ones with tiny squash at the base). Put pollen on the tip of the small fruit above the flower (the stigma).

Baby Squash

You don't need any particular variety to create a baby squash. Simply pick miniature-size squash with the blossoms still on the fruit. Cook and serve them whole for a tasty delicacy.

SQUASH, SUMMER

Greater Yields

Few gardeners actually want to improve the yields of summer squash. But if you don't mind being overrun with squash, try mulching with aluminized film. Experiment-station research shows this significantly boosts yields.

VARIETY	DAYS	DESCRIPTION	SOURCES (p. 385)
SUMMER SQUASH (SCALLOP)			
BENNING'S GREEN TINT	54–63	Pale green and disk-shaped, with scalloped edges; pick when small.	GAR GUR JOH MEY RED TER
BUTTER SCALLOP (hybrid)	50	Flattened, scallop shape; buttery yellow color.	JUN PAR
EARLY WHITE BUSH (White Patty Pan)	47–54	8 inches long, 3 inches wide, scallop-shaped, pale green; pre-1722 heirloom variety.	BURP BURR DEG FIS HEN JLH LED MEY ROS SOU TIL WIL
GOLDEN BUSH	68	Although this golden yellow variety grows large, harvest when small—4–5 inches in diameter.	SEE SOU
PATTY PAN (hybrid) (Early Bush Scallop)	50	Pale green rind, pale green flesh.	BOU BURG BURR ORG SEE
PETER PAN (hybrid)	45–52	Pick this medium green squash at about 4 inches. The vigorous, weather-resistant semibush is an All-American winner.	BURP FAR LIB ORG PAR POR SHE VER WIL WILL
SCALLOPINI (hybrid)	50	Bright green fruit; a crossbreed of scallop and zucchini squash; compact bush plant.	DEG JUN LIB ORN POR STO TER
SUNBURST (hybrid)	50–53	Pick when 3 inches across; bright golden yellow; All-American winner.	COM DEG GAR JOH LIB NIC ORN PAR PIN POR SHE TER VER
WOOD'S EARLIEST PROLIFIC	50	White, scallop-shaped.	ORG SEE
YELLOW BUSH SCALLOP	49	Squash bugs don't seem to favor this flattened, lemon yellow squash.	COM GUR HEN LIB POR
YELLOW CUSTARD	50	Yellow heirloom scallop.	ORG
SUMMER SQUASH (STRAIGHTNECK)			
BUTTERSTICK (hybrid)	50	Golden yellow with white flesh, this fruit is best when picked small.	BURP TER
EARLY PROLIFIC STRAIGHTNECK	50	Harvest the creamy yellow squash at 3–4 inches long. The bushy plant is a 1938 heirloom variety and an All-American winner.	ALL BURP BURR BUT COM DEG FIS GAR GUR HEN LED MEY ROS SOU VER WIL
EARLY YELLOW	50	Creamy yellow outside, pale yellow flesh; bushy, spreading plant.	POR
GOLDBAR (hybrid)	50	Harvest the squash at about 6 inches. This variety is a compact, open bush.	COM JUN MEY PIN POR VER WIL

VARIETY	DAYS	DESCRIPTION	SOURCES (p. 385)

SUMMER SQUASH (STRAIGHTNECK) *(continued)*

VARIETY	DAYS	DESCRIPTION	SOURCES
MULTIPIK (hybrid)	50	Grows to 7 inches, tapered, glossy yellow; resists mosaic virus.	POR WIL
SENECA BUTTERBAR (hybrid)	50	Fruit with 3-inch diameter; open habit, compact bush type.	PAR POR
SENECA PROLIFIC (hybrid)	51	Creamy yellow exterior; erect, bush type plant.	BURR JOH LED STO WIL
SUNBAR	43–54	Strong, upright plant produces glossy, yellow squash that should be picked at about 6 inches.	LED LIB STO

SUMMER SQUASH (CROOKNECK)

VARIETY	DAYS	DESCRIPTION	SOURCES
CRESCENT	53	This golden fruit has a small seed cavity. Compact vines grow 2–4 feet long.	GUR
DIXIE (hybrid)	45	Pick the yellow fruit at 5–6 inches long. Plant is compact and open.	PAR WIL
DWARF SUMMER CROOKNECK	50	Harvest the orange-yellow, warted squash when it's 3x10 inches.	BURR
EARLY GOLDEN SUMMER CROOKNECK	48–53	Harvest the bright yellow squash at 3x10 inches. Variety is a bush type.	ABU ALL BOU BURP COM DEG HEN LED ORN POR ROS VER WIL WILL
GIANT CROOKNECK	55	Finely warted, golden yellow outside, salmon-yellow inside.	TIL
GOLDIE (hybrid)	53	Pick the bright yellow fruit at 3–5 inches. This partially open plant has strong disease resistance.	WIL
PIC-N-PIC (hybrid)	50	Golden yellow, wart free; harvest when small; open-habit plant.	BURP
SUMMER CROOKNECK	48	Pick the yellow fruit when it's 4–6 inches long.	MEY
SUNDANCE (hybrid)	48–52	Bright yellow outside, creamy white inside.	BURG COM LIB NIC PIN STO VER WIL
SUPERSETT (hybrid)	50	This bright yellow squash with a medium-thick neck is best picked at 3–6 inches.	SHE WIL
VALLEY GOLD (hybrid)	45	Pick the fruit at about 8 inches. It's butter yellow when ready to eat. The plant is partially open.	DEG
YELLOW CROOKNECK	42–58	Bright yellow fruit is best picked when 4–5 inches long. This is a 1900 heirloom variety.	BUT GAR HIG JOH ORG PIN SEE SEED SOU TER

SUMMER SQUASH (ZUCCHINI, GREEN)

VARIETY	DAYS	DESCRIPTION	SOURCES
AMBASSADOR (hybrid)	55	Pick the fruit when it's 7–8 inches long. Variety gives a good yield over a long season.	COM LIB MEY PIN WILL

VARIETY	DAYS	DESCRIPTION	SOURCES (p. 385)
SUMMER SQUASH (ZUCCHINI, GREEN) *(continued)*			
ARISTOCRAT (hybrid)	48	8–10 inches long, glossy green; good yields.	COM DEG LIB NIC
ARLESA (hybrid)	48	Harvest the glossy green fruit when under 5 inches. This French variety has an open habit.	ORN SHE
BELOR (hybrid)	52	Glossy green; French variety; open habit.	PIN
BLACK BEAUTY	58	Pick at 6–8 inches; high yields.	BOU COM DEG HIG LED SOU TER TIL WIL
BLACKJACK (hybrid)	55	Pick when 6x2½ inches; open bush habit.	BURG FAR STO
BLACK MAGIC (OP)	55	Glossy, black-green fruit; 1–2x3–3½-foot plant.	GUR HEN JUN VER
BLACK ZUCCHINI	52–62	Pick at 6–8 inches; Black Beauty strain; bush type.	ALL BURR DEG GUR HEN MEY ORG PIN SEE
BURPEE'S FORDHOOK	57	Pick at 6–8 inches long; vigorous, bushy plant.	BURP PON
BURPEE'S HYBRID ZUCCHINI	50	Medium green fruit; compact bush.	BURP
CHEFINI	51	Pick the fruit at 6–7 inches.	DEG FAR GLE POR
CONDOR (hybrid)	48	The glossy, deep green squash can be harvested large or small. Bush is open, nearly spineless.	GOU JOH
DARK GREEN ZUCCHINI	44–60	Pick at 6–7 inches; bushy plant.	ABU DEG GAR JLH LIB RED ROS SOU WILL
EMBASSY	49	Pick the medium green fruit at about 8 inches. Plant is open, relatively spineless.	LED LIB
GREEN MAGIC II (hybrid)	48	Glossy, deep green fruit; open habit, spineless.	ORN PAR
JACKPOT (hybrid)	48	Long, medium green fruit; open plant habit.	FIS GUR HEN WIL
MAGDA (hybrid)	45	5x3 inches, creamy green; Lebanese type, imported from France.	GOU
MILANO (hybrid) (Seneca Milano)	42	The shiny, dark green, speckled fruit grows up to 12 inches without becoming spongy.	BURR PAR WIL
PARK'S GREEN WHOPPER II	48	Dark green; good producer over long season.	PAR
PRESIDENT (hybrid)	47	Dark green; adapted to garden or greenhouse.	POR WIL
RAVEN	42	Dark green fruit with uniform shape; bush type; widely adapted.	GAR SHE
RICHGREEN (hybrid)	50	Dark green fruit; bushy plant with open habit.	BURP
ROLY POLY (hybrid)	50	Unique round zucchini, ideal for stuffing; open habit.	BURP
RONDE DE NICE (Round French)	45	Up to 6 inches in diameter; round, pale green; French heirloom variety; quick growing plant.	BOU GOU SEED SHE

VARIETY	DAYS	DESCRIPTION	SOURCES (p. 385)

SUMMER SQUASH (ZUCCHINI, GREEN) (continued)

VARIETY	DAYS	DESCRIPTION	SOURCES
ROUND GREEN ZUCCHINI	52	Medium, round, 7-inch diameter.	ABU
SAKIZ	50	Light green.	RED
SENATOR (hybrid)	47	Nearly straight squash; prolific variety.	POR WIL
SENECA (hybrid)	47	Dark green fruit; widely adapted.	LED MEY NIC STO WIL
SPINELESS BEAUTY (hybrid) (Spineless Zucchini)	48	Dark green, 8x1½ inches. Picking causes no itching or prickling; good producer.	JUN LIB MEY PAR STO
SUPER SELECT	48	7–8 inches, dark green; upright plant with good leaf cover; resistant to mildew.	STO
TIPO (hybrid)	55	Medium green fruit; does well outside or in greenhouse; Swiss variety.	TER
ZUCCHINI SELECT	47	Medium green fruit; pick at about 6 inches; resistant to downy and powdery mildews; compact plant with open habit.	STO

SUMMER SQUASH (ZUCCHINI, DARK GREEN STRIPES—COCOZELLE)

VARIETY	DAYS	DESCRIPTION	SOURCES
CASSERTA	50	Light green with dark green stripes, bush type.	DEG
COCOZELLE BUSH (Italian Vegetable Marrow, Long Green Bush)	45	14 inches long, 5 inches thick, greenish white flesh; pick young for best flavor.	ALL DEG GAR HIG JOH LED NIC ORG PLA SEE SEED STO WILL
COUSA (hybrid)	51	3–5 inches long, pale greenish white; Lebanese zucchini; compact, bushy plant.	ORN STO
CUCCUZZI (Long Cocozelle, Guinea Bean, Climbing Squash)	55	Edible gourd; pick when immature—around 6–15 inches.	LED PIN SEE
CUCUZZI CARAVASI	65	This edible Italian gourd grows to be 4–6 feet and 8–15 pounds.	COM DEG JLH
FIORENTINO (hybrid)	47	A partial bush variety from Italy, its ridged fruit is striped light and dark green, and grows to 7–9 inches long.	SHE
GOURMET GLOBE (hybrid)	55	Round, 4–6 inches in diameter; light and dark green stripes; very productive bush.	ORN PAR

SUMMER SQUASH (ZUCCHINI, OTHER COLORS)

VARIETY	DAYS	DESCRIPTION	SOURCES
AZTEC	55	Normally straight, these zucchini are sometimes S–shaped.	HEN
BURPEE GOLDEN	54	Glossy, bright, golden yellow; distinct zucchini flavor.	BURP

VARIETY	DAYS	DESCRIPTION	SOURCES (p. 385)

SUMMER SQUASH (ZUCCHINI, OTHER COLORS) *(continued)*

VARIETY	DAYS	DESCRIPTION	SOURCES (p. 385)
CEREBERUS BUSH	55	Pick the dark green squash at about 6 inches in length.	NIC
CLARIMORE LEBANESE ZUCCHINI (hybrid)	44	Fruit is pastel green and cylindrical with blunt, rounded ends. This Middle Eastern variety has a compact, bushy habit.	SHE
FRENCH WHITE BUSH	50	3–5 inches long; French variety.	NIC SEE
GOLDEN DAWN II (hybrid)	45	Golden yellow fruit; spineless partial bush with open habit.	GAR PAR
GOLDEN ZUCCHINI	45	This bright, golden-colored variety yields as well as other types of zucchini.	SEE
GOLDFINGER (hybrid)	41	Deep yellow, glossy color, creamy white flesh, 6–7 inches long; bushy plant.	DEG
GOLD RUSH (hybrid)	50–52	4–8-inch-long, glossy, golden fruit; small, open plant; All-American winner.	BURR COM DEG GOU GUR JOH JUN LED LIB MEY NIC ORN PIN PON POR ROS STO TER TIL VER WIL WILL
GREY (Slate)	61	7 inches long, gray-green with dark green mottling; medium to large plant.	GUR HEN HIG ROS SOU WIL
GREYZINI (hybrid)	55	Gray fruit; bush type.	FAR PIN STO
LONG WHITE VEGETABLE MARROW	60	7-inch-long, white fruit with pale green, white-tinged interior; English variety; closed habit.	JLH LED
PALEFACE	50	Tastes like the Cousa variety; pale greenish white, cylindrical fruit.	STO
TOMBONCINO	50	Very long neck with curving bulb end; vining type.	SEE
WHITE EGYPTIAN	65–75	9–10 inches, elongated, plump, pale green; distinctive bush plant.	SEED
ZUCCHINI ROUND	50	Bright yellow fruit; bush habit.	DEG

SUMMER SQUASH (SPACE SAVERS)

VARIETY	DAYS	DESCRIPTION	SOURCES (p. 385)
GOLD SLICE (hybrid)	48	Golden yellow crookneck type; tolerant of cooler soils.	LIB
GREEN MAGIC II (hybrid)	48	Dark green zucchini; compact, 18-inch plant.	PAR
PARK'S CREAMY (hybrid)	55	6–8-inch–long, creamy yellow straightneck; 18-inch–tall plant; withstands extreme temperatures.	PAR
SUNDROPS (hybrid)	45–55	Oval, yellow squash with 3-inch diameter; compact, bushy plant; All-American winner.	JUN LED PAR POR

VARIETY	DAYS	DESCRIPTION	SOURCES (p. 385)

SUMMER SQUASH (OTHER TYPES)

VARIETY	DAYS	DESCRIPTION	SOURCES (p. 385)
BONITA (hybrid)	43	Although this fruit is in the same class as zucchini, it's quite different. Best eaten at 3–5 inches long, it's often fried with the flowers attached. This squash is great in Mexican cooking.	PAR
BUTTERBLOSSOM (hybrid)	45–85	This zucchini plant is grown for its enormous numbers of large, firm male flowers, which are stuffed by cooks. Keep the fruit picked to encourage new flower growth.	COM LED ORN
COSTA ROMANESCA	80	An Italian variety, the fruit is 8 inches thick by 2 feet long and fluted. It's usually fried whole with the flower still attached.	RED
FOO GWA (Chinese Bitter Melon, Balsam Pear)	60	This light green, bumpy fruit turns golden when ripe, with red flesh. The vine grows best in warm, moist soil.	JLH THE
KUTA (hybrid)	48	Pick this light green fruit when it's under 6 inches long. It's low in calories and fat. Mature plants turn dark green.	PAR
LAGINARIA LONGISSIMA	65	Pick when halfway ripe; vining Italian variety.	NIC
LEBANESE LIGHT GREEN	40–50	Pick the small fruit, though it's still fine when it weighs 1–2 pounds. Variety withstands tough climatic conditions.	BOU
MAO GWA (Chinese Fuzzy Gourd)	85	The small, green, downy fruit has white flesh. Pumpkinlike vine needs warmth and rich, light, moist soil.	JLH THE
NEW GUINEA BUTTER VINE	60	Pick this easy-to-grow squash at about 10 inches long and fry like eggplant. Mature fruit can be stuffed.	BURG
TATUME (Mexican)	52	6-inch-long, pear-shaped, green fruit with tough skin; vining Mexican variety.	HOR POR
ZAHRA (hybrid)	46	Blocky, tapered fruit; pick at 3–4 inches; pale green Cousa type; Middle Eastern style.	JOH
ZAPPALITO DEL TRONCO (South American)	94	Pick the squash at 2½–4 inches. If left to mature, treat this fruit like a winter squash. Plants are bushy.	BOU GAR JLH
ZUCHETTA RAMPICANTE	58	12–15 inches long, curved, trumpet-shaped; Italian heirloom variety; edible blossoms.	ORN PIN SHE

SQUASH, WINTER

BOTANICAL NAME: *Cucurbita maxima* and *C. moschata*

DAYS TO MATURITY: 50–220.

PLANTING TIME: Plant seeds in the ground after the last frost, when night temperatures are remaining above 50°F.

SOIL: Rich and well-manured; pH 6.0–7.5.

NUTRIENTS: Fertilize the plants with nitrogen only during the growth period before blooming.

WATER: Give squash plenty of water.

LIGHT: Full sun.

SPACING: Sow seeds 1 inch deep, 10 feet apart.

HARVEST: Let winter squashes mature fully on the vines until their skins are extremely hard. Cut them from the vine, leaving a 2–3-inch stem on each squash.

STORAGE: Cure the squashes in the sun for a week or more; store them in a cool, dry place over the winter.

Winter Squash Growing Tip

Squash Basics

Before harvesting winter squash for storage, push your thumbnail against the squash as hard as you can. If the outer skin doesn't break easily, the squash will keep a long time. If you can cut the skin with little effort, it will probably rot in storage. In the latter case, cook the squash within a few days.

VARIETY	DAYS	DESCRIPTION	SOURCES (p. 385)
WINTER SQUASH (ACORN)			
AUTUMN QUEEN	71	Dark green rind, orange flesh; same size as Table King; semibush plant.	LIB STO
BUSH TABLE QUEEN (Acorn Bush)	82	4x5 inches, green, deeply ribbed rind, orange flesh; semibush plant.	ALL BURP BURR DEG HEN SOU
EARLY ACORN (hybrid)	75	5 dark green, medium-large fruit per semibush plant.	BURP
EAT–IT–ALL	75–80	You can eat all of this fruit, including the seeds. With green rind and light orange flesh, it measures 5x4 inches. Variety is a bush type.	BURP
EBONY (Improved Table Queen)	85–90	5x6 inches; stores well.	BOU BURR BUT COM HIG JOH JUN LED LEJ LIB ORG PIN SHE TER VER

VARIETY	DAYS	DESCRIPTION	SOURCES (p. 385)
WINTER SQUASH (ACORN) *(continued)*			
FISHER'S EARLY ACORN	85	8x6 inches, dark green, sharp ridges.	FIS
JERSEY GOLDEN ACORN	50–60	Golden rind, light orange meat; semibush plant; Plant Variety Patented (PVP).	BURP ORN
ROYAL ACORN (Mammoth Table Queen)	82	6x7 inches, 3–4 pounds; dull, dark green rind.	DEG PON SEED TIL TWI WIL
SNOW WHITE	80	Snow white rind, buttery white flesh; mellow flavor.	PIN
TABLE ACE (hybrid)	70–78	4½x5½ inches, black-green rind, bright orange flesh; semibush type.	BURR COM GUR HEN JUN LED LIB PAR PIN POR STO TWI
TABLE GOLD	90	4½x4 inches, bright orange rind, pale orange flesh; bushy plant.	HEN LIB STO
TABLE KING	75–80	6x5 inches; hard ribbed, dark green rind and thick, golden flesh; bush type; Plant Variety Patented (PVP).	BURP FAR GAR LIB STO TER VER
TABLE QUEEN (OP) (Acorn, Des Moines)	85	4½x5–6 inches, light yellow flesh; trailing vine type.	ABU ALL BURR DEG FAR GUR JUN MEY NIC PON ROS SOU STO TIL TWI VER WIL WILL
TAY BELLE (hybrid)	68–70	Green to jet black rind; semibush plant.	STO
WHITE SWAN	90	6x5 inches, creamy white rind, pale yellow flesh; heavy-yielding vine type; Plant Variety Patented (PVP).	ORN STO

WINTER SQUASH (BUTTERCUP—FLATTENED GLOBE, TURBAN-SHAPED)

VARIETY	DAYS	DESCRIPTION	SOURCES (p. 385)
ARGENTINE PRIMITIVE	100	Parent of Buttercup; heirloom variety.	ORG
BLACK FOREST	95	Buttonless Buttercup; dark green rind, deep orange, medium-dry flesh; 4–5 fruits per plant.	JOH
BUTTERCUP (OP)	90–105	3–5 pounds, 4½x6½ inches; dark green rind with silvery white stripes; thick, orange flesh.	ABU ALL BURP BURR COM DEG FAR FIS GAR GUR HEN JOH, JUN LIB NIC PIN PON SEE SEED SOU STO TER TIL TWI VER WILL
CHESTNUT	105	3–4 pounds, medium-small; "turbanless" Buttercup; dark slate green rind and thick, deep orange flesh; stores well.	JOH
HEART OF GOLD	90	Shaped like a Sweet Dumpling; green-striped ivory rind and fine-grained, orange flesh; semibush.	GUR
HOME DELIGHT (hybrid)	95–100	The 3-pound fruit has dark green rind and dry, yellow flesh. Plant produces a few lateral shoots.	STO
HONEY DELIGHT (hybrid)	95–110	4–6 pounds; forest green rind with moss green stripes, rich, orange meat; Japanese Kabocha type; stores well.	JOH ORN PIN

VARIETY	DAYS	DESCRIPTION	SOURCES (p. 385)

WINTER SQUASH (BUTTERCUP—FLATTENED GLOBE, TURBAN-SHAPED)
(continued)

VARIETY	DAYS	DESCRIPTION	SOURCES (p. 385)
MOOREGOLD	90–95	7x5 inches, 1–3 pounds; bright orange rind, bright orange flesh; vining type; keeps a long time.	GAR JUN
SWEET DUMPLING	90–100	4 inches long, up to 2 pounds; teacup shape; ivory rind with dark green stripes, orange flesh; no need to cure; stores 3–4 months; medium-length vining type.	ABU DEG GAR GUR HEN JOH LIB ORG ORN PIN SEED SHE STO TER THO VER
SWEET MAMA (hybrid)	85	Squat fruit with dark gray-green rind and medium-thick flesh; 2–3 pounds; short vine; All-American winner.	FAR NIC ORN PAR POR STO TWI VER
SWEET MEAT	85–115	10–14 inches long, 7–15 pounds; slate-gray rind; stores well.	ABU GAR NIC ORN PIN TER

WINTER SQUASH (BUTTERNUT—BOTTLE-SHAPED)

VARIETY	DAYS	DESCRIPTION	SOURCES (p. 385)
BURPEE'S BUTTERNUT	85	10x5 inches, 1–2 pounds; buff-colored rind, orange flesh; nutty flavor.	WILL
BUTTER BOY (hybrid)	80	2¾ pounds; rich, reddish orange flesh.	BURP
BUTTERNUT	90–100	5x12 inches; creamy brown rind, bright orange flesh.	ALL BUT LEJ MEY POR
BUTTERNUT SUPREME (hybrid)	87	12x5 inches; medium uniform, thick neck.	STO TWI
BUTTERNUT WALTHAM (OP)	85–110	3½x9 inches, 3–5 pounds; creamy tan rind, deep, orange flesh; small seed cavity; keeps well; All-American winner.	ABU BOU BURP BURR COM DEG FAR GOU GUR HEN JOH JUN LED LIB ORG PAR PIN PON ROS SEE SEED SOU STO TWI VER WIL WILL
PONCA	83–110	8x12 inches; creamy tan rind; about half the size of Waltham.	BURR SEE SHE VER
ULTRA BUTTERNUT (hybrid)	89	18x4 inches, 8½–10 pounds; extralong, thick neck.	STO
ZENITH (hybrid)	85–120	2½–4½ pounds; small seed cavity.	DEG FAR LIB STO TER TWI WIL

WINTER SQUASH (HUBBARD)

VARIETY	DAYS	DESCRIPTION	SOURCES (p. 385)
BABY BLUE HUBBARD (Silver Bell)	90	3–4 pounds; light blue rind, orange flesh; keeps well.	ABU GAR ORN
BABY GREEN HUBBARD	100	5–6 pounds; keeps well.	FIS
BLUE BALLET	95	A scaled-down Blue Hubbard, at 4 pounds; blue-gray rind, bright orange, fiberless flesh; stores well; 2 fruit per plant.	JOH

VARIETY	DAYS	DESCRIPTION	SOURCES (p. 385)
WINTER SQUASH (HUBBARD) *(continued)*			
BLUE HUBBARD (New England)	100–120	12–20 pounds; bluish gray rind, bright yellow-orange flesh; keeps well.	ALL BURP COM DEG FAR GAR HEN JLH LED LEJ LIB ORG ORN PIN SEE STO TER VER
GENUINE HUBBARD (True Hubbard)	90–115	10x12 inches, 12–15 pounds; dark bronze-green rind, yellow-orange flesh.	ABU BURP
GOLDEN HUBBARD (OP) (Red Hubbard, Delicious Golden Hubbard)	90–100	10x9 inches; slightly warted, reddish orange rind with grayish stripes, yellow-orange flesh.	ALL DEG GAR ORN PIN PON SEE STO TIL TWI VER WILL
GREEN HUBBARD	100–120	9x14 inches, 9–12 pounds; oval-shaped, pale green, moderately warted rind; 1790 heirloom variety.	ALL DEG LIB MEY ORG SEED TIL VER
GREEN HUBBARD IMPROVED	95–105	9x14 inches, 12 pounds; bronzy green, warted rind, orange-yellow flesh.	BOU ROS STO WILL
LITTLE GEM	80	3–5 pounds; miniature Golden Hubbard type.	GLE
MOUNTAINEER	90	4–5 pounds; slate-blue rind; Montana variety; great short season choice.	FIS HIG
SUGAR HUBBARD	100	15 pounds, with blue-green rind.	ABU
WARTED HUBBARD (OP) (Chicago)	105–110	12 pounds, 10x15 inches; dark slate green, heavily warted rind, orange-yellow flesh; keeps well.	BURR JUN STO TWI
WINTER SQUASH (SPACE SAVERS)			
ALL SEASONS (hybrid)	50	A bush Buttercup; 5 inches long; bright orange rind, orange flesh; long-keeping.	GUR LIB PAR
BURPEE'S BUTTERBUSH	75	This storable squash weighs 1¾ pounds and has deep reddish orange flesh. Plant grows 3–4 feet long and bears 4–5 fruit.	BURP PIN
BUSH BUTTERCUP	88–100	3–5 pounds; round; thick, orange flesh; stores well when ripe.	ALL COM FIS LIB TIL
BUTTERBALL (hybrid) (Sakata)	95	5–6 pounds; heavy in starch and sugar, low in moisture; short vines; keeps well.	NIC VER
BUTTERNUT BUSH	95	10–12 inches long; small seed cavity; rich orange flesh.	PON
CREAM OF THE CROP (hybrid)	85	3-pound acorn squash with creamy white rind and pale flesh; compact, bushy plant; long-keeping All-American winner.	BURR COM FAR JOH JUN LIB PAR POR TER TWI WILL
EARLY BUTTERNUT (hybrid)	75	7 inches long; rich orange flesh; bush type; short season variety; storable All-American winner.	COM FAR HEN JUN LIB NIC PAR PIN POR STO TWI VER WIL WILL
EMERALD	90	Buttercup squash with gray-green rind and thick, orange flesh; keeps well.	JUN

VARIETY	DAYS	DESCRIPTION	SOURCES (p. 385)

WINTER SQUASH (SPACE SAVERS) *(continued)*

VARIETY	DAYS	DESCRIPTION	SOURCES (p. 385)
GOLDEN BUSH BUTTERCUP	90	3–5 pounds; golden orange rind with some green.	FIS
GOLDEN DEBUT (hybrid)	105	Orange Butterball type with edible skin and yellow flesh; oblate; 2–3 pounds; green rind turns orange-red at maturity.	VER
GOLD NUGGET	80–85	1–2 pounds; red-orange rind with faint stripes, thick, deep orange flesh; round and sometimes oblate; bush type; stores well.	FIS GAR HIG ORN
TABLE GOLD	90	Harvest this acorn squash when it's 2x3 inches and yellow. It's bright orange when ripe. Variety is a bush type.	GUR TWI
TABLE KING	70–80	5x6-inch, 1½-pound acorn squash with dark green rind and golden yellow flesh; 6–8 fruit per plant; All-American winner; Plant Variety Patented (PVP).	GAR LED TWI

WINTER SQUASH (OTHER TYPES)

VARIETY	DAYS	DESCRIPTION	SOURCES (p. 385)
ACOMA SQUASH	90–100	10–15 pounds; thick, orange flesh; 8-foot vine; ancient Southwestern variety.	PLA
AKIKARA	90	Pink, slightly warted rind, dark orange flesh; Plains Indian heirloom variety.	ORG
AYOTE CASCARA DURA	100	This Honduran variety has an extremely hard shell and nearly black flesh. Roast and eat the seeds.	JLH
BLUE BANANA (Gray Banana, Green Banana)	105–120	24x6 inches, greenish gray rind; pie squash.	ROS SEE TIL
BLUE KURI	100	4–5 pounds; green rind and thick, yellow flesh; Japanese squash derived from Hubbard.	ABU
BOSTON MARROW	100	7–15 inches long, 20 pounds; bright orange rind, yellow flesh.	LED SEE
CHURIMEN	85	Flat and globular, with very dark green, bumpy rind and yellow flesh; Japanese squash.	DEG
DELICA (hybrid)	85–92	4–6-pound, flattened globe with dark green rind and thick, yellow flesh.	GAR TIL
DELICATA (Peanut)	95–100	8x3 inches, 1–2 pounds; creamy yellow with dark green stripes; vining type, sweet potato squash; stores well.	ABU BOU DEG GAR GUR HEN JOH JUN ORG PIN PLA PON SEE TER
DINOSAUR GOURD	100	12–15 inches long; club-shaped, with spikes.	SEE
GILL'S GOLDEN PIPPIN	85	Miniature, orange acorn squash, deeply ribbed, with yellow flesh.	JLH SEE

VARIETY	DAYS	DESCRIPTION	SOURCES (p. 385)

WINTER SQUASH (OTHER TYPES) *(continued)*

VARIETY	DAYS	DESCRIPTION	SOURCES (p. 385)
GOLD CUSHAW	105–118	8–12-pound, curved fruit, with cream-colored rind and a long neck; large vines; keeps well; 1880s heirloom variety.	SEED
GOLDEN DELICIOUS	103–105	6–7 pounds; bright orange rind, golden flesh; heart-shaped; keeps well.	ALL STO
GOLD NUGGET	85–95	Deep golden orange rind, orange flesh; 18-inch bush type; 6–12 fruit per plant; keeps well.	ORN SEE TIL
GOLDPAK BANANA	110	8–10 pounds, pink rind.	SEE
GREEN DELICIOUS	100–103	8x10 inches; dark green rind, bright orange flesh.	LIB STO
GREEN HOKKAIDO (Truly Hokkaido)	98–105	Round and slightly ribbed; slate green rind, yellow flesh; Japanese variety.	JOH ORG
GREEN STRIPED CUSHAW	110	Bulb-shaped crookneck; 10–12 pounds, 18x10 inches; whitish green rind with mottled green stripes, light yellow flesh; pre-1893 heirloom variety.	GUR HEN LED PIN SOU
KIKUZA	100	4–5 pounds; ribbed, light mocha rind; rare variety from south China.	NIC
MARBLEHEAD YAKIMA	90	8–25-pound, nearly round squash with gray-green rind; 1896 heirloom variety; keeps well.	ABU
PASTA (hybrid)	90	Spaghetti squash; 12 inches long, cylindrical; creamy white rind.	BURP LED LIB NIC
PINK BANANA JUMBO	105	Up to 30x7 inches and 70 pounds; thick, yellow-orange flesh; limited storage.	BURR DEG GLE GUR HEN LIB POR SEE WIL
QUEENSLAND BLUE	110	8 pounds; striking blue rind; keeps well.	SEE
RED KURI (Orange Kokkaido, Baby Red Hubbard, Uchiki Kuri)	92–95	Bright red-orange rind; teardrop shape; Japanese variety.	DEG GAR JOH ORG ORN SEE
SANTO DOMINGO SQUASH	90	The 12-pound, yellow-and-green-striped squash has pale yellow flesh and can be picked young and used as summer squash. Keep this drought-tolerant variety in a cool, dry place.	PLA
STRIPETTI (hybrid)	95	This crossbreed of Delicata and Vegetable Spaghetti squash stores 2–3 months.	STO
SUGAR LOAF	95–105	Delicata squash; 7–9x3–4 inches; dark green and tan stripes, golden flesh; stores well.	BURR GAR GOU JLH JOH LIB NIC SEED TER
SWEET KEEPER	100	10–12 pounds; cheesebox shape; deep orange flesh; Pacific Northwest heirloom variety; vining type of pie squash.	SEED
TAHITIAN MELON SQUASH	85–220	Grown mainly in California, this squash weighs up to 40 pounds and has a very high sugar content. Its rampant vines need space.	ABU GUR HEN LEJ PAR POR SEED

VARIETY	DAYS	DESCRIPTION	SOURCES (p. 385)
WINTER SQUASH (OTHER TYPES) *(continued)*			
TETSUKABUTO (hybrid)	100	These 8-inch, round, glossy green squashes with deep orange flesh taste like yams. There are 50 or more fruit per vine of this Japanese variety.	GLE PIN
TEXAS INDIAN MOSCHATA	100	Shaped like a flattened pumpkin, this 10–15-pound squash has a tan to orange rind. From Gila, Texas, the variety has a large vine.	SEED
TIVOLI (hybrid)	100	3–4-pound Spaghetti squash with a light yellow rind; bush type; 3–5 fruit per plant.	COM DEG GAR GUR HEN JUN LED LIB PAR PIN TWI WILL
TURKS TURBAN (OP) (Mexican Hat)	110	8x10-inch, striped, spotted, turban-shaped fruit.	BURR DEG GAR GUR HEN JUN LED LIB MEY PON POR TWI
UPPER GROUND SWEET POTATO SQUASH	100	Resembles a no-neck Butternut; orange-yellow flesh; drought-resistant, long-running vines; Kentucky heirloom variety.	SOU
VALENCIANO	100	Gray, squat fruit with a ribbed, hard shell and thick flesh; French heirloom variety.	ORG
VEGETABLE SPAGHETTI (OP) (Spaghetti Squash)	90–110	This 3–4-pound, oblong squash with yellow rind is low in calories and fat and an excellent substitute for spaghetti. Harvest for fall storage.	ABU BURG BURP BURR BUT COM FIS GAR GLE GUR HEN HIG JOH JUN LED LIB ORG PAR PIN PLA PON POR RED ROS SEE SEED SOU STO TIL TWI VER WIL WILL

SWEET POTATOES

BOTANICAL NAME: *Ipomoea batatas*

DAYS TO MATURITY: 90–150.

PLANTING TIME: Plant sweet potato from slips in the spring.

SOIL: Light, sandy, and shallow; pH 5.5–6.5.

NUTRIENTS: Add fish emulsion only to the planting soil. This vegetable doesn't need much to keep it happy.

WATER: Sweet potato can tolerate dry soil once it's established.

LIGHT: Full sun.

SPACING: Give it plenty of spreading room. Plant slips 9–12 inches apart. Space rows 3 feet apart.

HARVEST: When the foliage begins to yellow, carefully dig out the tubers. Dry them in the sun for several hours, then cure (let them dry and harden) for about a week.

STORAGE: Store at 55–60°F in a dry area. They will keep about 10 weeks.

SWEET POTATOES

Sweet Potato Growing Tip

Sweet Potato in a Box

Try growing sweet potato in a box or tub. Select a container that's at least 12 inches deep and 15 inches wide. Use a light, porous soil mix. Place a 4-foot stake in the center to support the vine. The vines will grow up, then out and down the sides of the container. Harvest the tubers at the end of the season.

VARIETY	DAYS	DESCRIPTION	SOURCES (p. 385)
SWEET POTATOES			
BEAUREGARD	100	Light purple skin, dark orange flesh; extremely high yields.	PAR
CENTENNIAL	90–100	Bright copper skin, deep orange flesh; uniform, medium-size roots; vining type.	BURP FAR GUR HEN JUN PAR VER
GEORGIA JET	90–100	Red skin, deep orange flesh; short season choice.	BURP GUR HEN JUN VER
JEWELL	100	Bright copper skin, deep orange flesh; keeps well.	GUR HEN JUN POR
PORTO RICO	110	Pale yellow skin, deep orange flesh; bush type.	BURP GUR HEN VER
VARDAMAN	100–110	Golden yellow skin, deep orange flesh; compact bush type.	BURP GUR HEN PAR POR VER

TOMATOES

BOTANICAL NAME: *Lycopersicon esculentum*

DAYS TO MATURITY: 50–100.

PLANTING TIME: Tomatoes should not be planted until the night temperatures are above 55°F. Low temperatures—below 55°F—prevent fruit set.

SOIL: Enrich the bed with well-rotted manure or garden compost, and dig deeply; pH 5.5–7.5.

NUTRIENTS: Once the fruits begin to swell, feed the plants with fish emulsion every two weeks. Too much nitrogen produces much growth but little fruit.

WATER: Regular and adequate watering is required; maintain an even moisture by mulching.

LIGHT: Full sun.

SPACING: Sow seeds ½ inch deep, 2–3 feet apart. For row gardening, space rows 4 feet apart.

HARVEST: Tomatoes are ready when they develop their full color. Lift each tomato until its stem snaps.

STORAGE: Use fresh, frozen, dried, or canned.

TOMATOES

Tomato Growing Tips

Improving Fruit Set

A battery-operated toothbrush can improve the fruit set of your tomatoes! Use it to give individual clusters of flowers a daily vibration, which will scatter pollen from top to bottom. The best time to jiggle your tomatoes is midday, when the air is warm and the humidity is low.

Extending the Season

Keep from losing tomatoes, peppers, and eggplants to the first frost by laying a wide strip of black plastic over each row or cage at night. These strips will protect the fruit and extend the season by as much as three weeks.

Too Much Foliage

Sometimes tomato plants keep producing foliage but seem reluctant to switch gears and start churning out ripe, juicy tomatoes. Too much nitrogen, too much water, and too much shade in the first stages of growth often cause this. To help the plant move on to the fruiting stage, pluck out the terminal shoots and withhold water. This checks root growth so the plant can put all of its energy into fruit production.

Root Pruning

To force tomatoes to ripen, prune their roots by cutting into the soil halfway around the plant with a long knife. Killing some roots puts stress on the plant and triggers the ripening mechanism.

Use Grass Clippings

Grass clippings make a great mulch, but most gardeners won't use this material on warm weather crops because it usually retards fruiting. Research shows, however, that if grass clippings are applied after the first flower clusters set, overall yields increase significantly. Tomatoes mulched with grass clippings also need less watering during the season.

Vertical Supports

Portable 4x5-foot racks made of rough-hewn redwood laths can be used to support sprawling cucumbers, melons, squash, or tomatoes. A hinged 1x2-inch brace will allow you to angle the rack as you wish.

TOMATOES

Larger Tomatoes

Here's how to have a beer with your tomato plants. When their fruits begin to appear, poke a ring of holes around the base of each plant, using a pencil or some stiff wire. Penetrate at least 6 inches into the ground. Fill the holes with beer. Repeat at two-week intervals for large, juicy, delicious tomatoes.

Wire Mesh

Wire mesh stretched horizontally along 1-foot posts will hold sprawling vines off the ground. In time, the vines spread together over the wire to produce a huge raised tomato patch (Figure 9-2). You can also use wire mesh cages to contain tomatoes.

Hanging Tomatoes

You can stretch your garden space by hanging a few tomato plants from the eaves of your house. Plant Small Fry, Sugar Lump, and similar varieties in 6-inch pots. Fill the containers with potting mix, keep the plants moist, and fertilize them every two weeks with fish emulsion. Hang with rope slings.

Ripening Green Tomatoes

To protect unripe tomatoes from that first frost, pick the green tomatoes and wrap them immediately in newspaper or packing tissue. Then store them in a cool, dry place. They will ripen over a few weeks.

Blossom End Rot Solution

Blossom end rot starts as a small, sunken spot at the base of a tomato that expands as the fruit grows. The cause is a combination of water stress and calcium deficiency within the plant. During the day, young tomatoes draw little sap from their leaves, but at night, root pressure forces sap up the plant, giving the developing fruits their share. If the tomato plant is water-stressed at night, the system breaks down and the fruit gets little calcium. Tissue at its base is damaged, setting the stage for blossom end rot.

To keep harm to a minimum, feed your plants with a good organic fertilizer. Also, don't let the soil dry out, especially when the weather is hot and dry. If the plants are on the point of wilting by the end of the day, water then to make sure there is sufficient moisture at night.

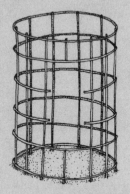

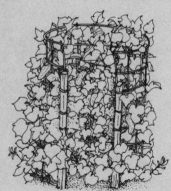

figure 9-2

VARIETY	DAYS	DESCRIPTION	SOURCES (p. 385)

TOMATOES (LARGE)

VARIETY	DAYS	DESCRIPTION	SOURCES (p. 385)
ABRAHAM LINCOLN (ORIGINAL)	70–87	Indeterminate fruit is slightly larger than regular Abraham Lincoln. This 1923 heirloom variety bears until frost.	SOU TOMA
ABRAHAM LINCOLN (REGULAR)	77	Indeterminate; 1–2-pound, dark red, solid meat, with very few seeds; bears until frost; 1923 heirloom variety.	TOM TOMA
BEEFEATER VFN (hybrid)	60–85	Indeterminate; up to 2 pounds, red, almost seedless; Italian beefsteak variety.	STO
BEEFMASTER VFN (hybrid)	80	Indeterminate; up to 2 pounds, oblate, deep red; beefsteak type, but more tolerant of cracking; tolerant of disease.	ALL COM DEG GUR HEN LED LIB MEY PAR PIN POR TOM TOMA TWI VER WIL
BEEFSTEAK (Crimson Cushion)	80–100	Indeterminate; large, oblate, red.	ALL BURR DEG LEJ PIN ROS SEE TOM TOMA
BEEFSTEAK IMPROVED	80	Indeterminate; large, smooth, round, 17 ounces or more.	THO
BETTER BOY VFN (hybrid)	70–75	Indeterminate; bright red, up to 1 pound; tolerant of disease.	ALL BURG BURP BURR COM DEG GUR HEN LED LEJ LIB MEY NIC PAR PIN PON POR STO TOM TOMA TWI VER WIL WILL
BIG BEEF VFFNTA (hybrid)	73	Indeterminate; a 10–12-ounce, red globe; Italian beefsteak type; disease-resistant All-American winner.	ALL BURG BURP LED LIB MEY PAR POR SHE STO TER THO TOMA TWI VER WILL
BIG BOY (hybrid) (Burpee's Big Boy)	80	Indeterminate; a bright red, semiglobe, up to 2 pounds; heavy bearing variety.	BURG BURP COM DEG FAR GUR HEN JUN LED MEY PAR STO TOM TOMA TWI
BIG PICK VFFNT (hybrid)	70–80	Indeterminate; large, red; resistant to disease; bears all season long.	GUR HEN TOMA
BRAGGER VF (hybrid)	75	Determinate; deep red, up to 2 pounds; resistant to cracking and splitting.	FAR HEN TOM TOMA
BURGESS COLOSSAL (hybrid)	90	Indeterminate; 6-inch diameter and up to 2½ pounds; deep, flat shape; red, golden, crimson, and yellow colors.	BURG TOM
BURGESS GIANT BEEFSTEAK	85	Indeterminate; large, red, flat, 10–12-ounce tomato with few seeds.	BURG TOM
BURGESS STUFFING	78	Determinate; 3½x2¾ inches; hollow, bell-pepper shape, few seeds.	BURG TOMA
BURPEE'S BIG EARLY (hybrid)	62	Indeterminate; bright scarlet up to 1 pound; produces all season long.	LED TOM TOMA
BURPEE'S BIG GIRL VF (hybrid)	78	Indeterminate; bright red, up to 1 pound; no cracking.	BURG BURP LED PON TOM TOMA
BURPEE'S SUPER-STEAK VFN (hybrid)	80	Indeterminate; red, flat-round, 1–2 pounds; resistant to wilts and root-knot nematodes.	BURG GOU JUN LED THO TOM TOMA

VARIETY	DAYS	DESCRIPTION	SOURCES (p. 385)
TOMATOES (LARGE) *(continued)*			
CHAMPS OF NEW JERSEY	77	Especially big.	TOM
DELICIOUS (Burpee's Delicious)	77	Indeterminate; beefsteak type; up to 3 pounds, small seed cavity; little cracking.	BURP GUR HEN LED LIB PON SOU TOM TOMA
DOUBLE RICH	65–70	Indeterminate; red, up to 1 pound; has twice the vitamin C of others.	JLH SEED
EARLY GIANT (hybrid)	65	Indeterminate; red, oblate; bears until October.	WIL
GIANT TREE	88–90	Indeterminate; crimson, oblate, 1½–2 pounds; low in acid; Italian potato-leaf type plant.	TOMA
GOLIATH	85	Indeterminate; beefsteak-shaped, red, up to 3 pounds; 1800s heirloom variety.	TOMA
HEAVY WEIGHT VF (hybrid)	80	This red globe weighs up to 1½ pounds and ripens even during cool summers.	TOMA
JUMBO JIM (hybrid)	80	Indeterminate; dark red, 4½x3¼ inches, up to 2 pounds.	TOM
LADY LUCK VFNT (hybrid)	78	Indeterminate; red, up to 1 pound; resistant to disease and well adapted.	BURP TOM
MAMMOTH WONDER	75	Indeterminate; deep scarlet globe; up to 1½ pounds; crack-resistant.	TOM
MONSTER	85	Indeterminate; red and very big.	TOM
OREGON STAR	80–85	Indeterminate; red, up to 2 pounds; larger sister of Oregon Pride.	NIC TER
PONDEROSA RED	90	Indeterminate; deep red, up to 2 pounds; does best in a long, warm growing season; 1891 heirloom variety.	DEG JLH LED LIB SEE TOM VER
RED SIBERIAN (Big's Red Siberian, Big Red)	72	Indeterminate; bright red, round; 3–4-inch diameter, 8–12 ounces.	HEN HIG
RIO GRANDE	90	Determinate; large, red, up to 5 pounds; tolerates hot days and cool nights; fruit ripens all at once.	JLH ORN
SUPER BEEFSTEAK VFN	80	Indeterminate; red, 17 ounces or more.	GUR JUN ORN PON TOM
TRIP–L–CROP (Italian Tree)	85–90	Indeterminate; 3x5–6 inches, up to 1 pound; crimson; a ladder is required to harvest this vine.	BURG SOU TOM TOMA
ULTRA BOY VFN (hybrid)	72	Indeterminate; red globe, up to 1 pound.	STO TOM TOMA
ULTRA MAGNUM VFT (hybrid)	68	Indeterminate; dark red globe, 14 ounces; good cracking tolerance; resistant to disease.	STO
WANDA'S POTATO TOP	70	12–18 ounces.	SEE
WONDER BOY VFN (hybrid)	68–80	Indeterminate; red, up to 1 pound; resistant to disease.	BURR COM TOM TOMA WIL

VARIETY	DAYS	DESCRIPTION	SOURCES (p. 385)
TOMATOES (EARLY SEASON)			
ALICANTE (OP)	68	Indeterminate; midsize, red.	THO
ALISA CRAIG (OP)	70	Indeterminate; deep red, medium-size; Scottish variety.	BOU
AMATEUR'S DREAM	65	Indeterminate; round, red, large.	HIG
ANGORA	68–80	This indeterminate, medium-size, brilliant red tomato has grayish white fuzz on its stems and leaves.	GLE SEED TOMA
BALL EXTRA EARLY (hybrid)	55	Indeterminate; midsize, round, red.	TOMA
BASKET VEE (OP)	70	Determinate; beefsteak type; red, 8½–9 ounces; usually free of cracks.	STO TOM
BEST OF ALL	70	Indeterminate; medium-size, red; heirloom variety.	SEED
BETTER GIRL VFN (hybrid)	68	Determinate; red, 7 ounces.	TOM
BIG SET VFN (hybrid)	65	Determinate; red, 8–9 ounces; tolerates disease and sets well under adverse conditions.	TOM
BINGO	70	Determinate; large, red globe; moderate crack resistance; tolerant of disease.	POR WIL
BLACK TOMATO	70	The fruit is so red, it looks black. This indeterminate variety sets under adverse conditions.	GLE
BONITA (hybrid)	70	Determinate; red, 7-ounce globe; tolerant to disease.	TWI
BURPEEANA EARLY (hybrid)	70	Indeterminate; red; for greenhouse or garden.	TOM
BURPEE'S EARLY PICK VF (hybrid)	62	Bright scarlet, up to ½ pound; widely adapted but highly recommended for the West Coast.	BURP TOM TOMA
BUSH BEEFSTEAK	62–65	Determinate; rich red, 8 ounces; few seeds; grows well under adverse conditions.	STO TOM TOMA WILL
CABOT	70	Determinate; midsize, brilliant red; short season variety.	TOM
CARMELLO VFNT (hybrid)	70	Indeterminate; large fruit; cracking- and disease-resistant French variety.	ORN SHE
CELEBRITY VFFNT (hybrid)	70–80	Determinate; 7–12-ounce red globe; resistant to disease and cracking; All-American winner.	BURG BURP BURR COM DEG FAR GUR HEN JOH LED LIB MEY NIC PAR PIN POR STO TER TOM TOMA TWI VER WIL WILL
CHAMPION (hybrid)	65	Indeterminate; red, 10 ounces; resistant to disease.	LIB NIC VER
COLDSET	68	Determinate; bloodred, 3–4-inch diameter, 5–6 ounces; short season canning variety.	ABU GUR HEN HIG TOM
DAYBREAK (hybrid)	65	Determinate; 8–10-ounce red globe; tolerant to disease.	JOH MEY

VARIETY	DAYS	DESCRIPTION	SOURCES (p. 385)

TOMATOES (EARLY SEASON) *(continued)*

VARIETY	DAYS	DESCRIPTION	SOURCES (p. 385)
DEL ORO VFFNA (hybrid)	70	Determinate; red, round canning variety.	TOM TOMA
EARLIANA (hybrid)	66	Indeterminate; scarlet, oblate, 6 ounces; 1900 heirloom variety.	ABU TOM
EARLIBRIGHT	60	Determinate; crimson, 4–6 ounces; short season variety.	HIG TOM
EARLIROUGE	63	Determinate; red, 6½ ounces; ripens from the inside out; low in acid.	ABU HIG JOH PLA STO TOM TOMA
EARLY CASCADE VF (hybrid)	52–66	Indeterminate; bright red, 4–6 ounces; very resistant to disease.	ALL FAR GUR JOH LED NIC TER TOM TOMA
EARLY GIRL (hybrid)	50–62	Indeterminate; red, 4–6 ounces; resistant to cracking.	ALL BURG BURP DEG FAR GAR GUR HEN MEY NIC ORN PAR POR TIL TOM TOMA VER
EARLY GIRL IMPROVED VFN	60	Indeterminate; red, 4–6 ounces; resistant to disease.	LIB PIN
EARLY PICK (hybrid)	62	Indeterminate; bright red, oblate, 4–6 ounces; resistant to verticillium wilt.	DEG
ENCHANTMENT (hybrid)	70	Indeterminate; 3-inch diameter, oval, glossy crimson; resistant to disease; heavy yields.	PIN POR SHE
EROS	70	Determinate; red, midsize German variety.	ABU
FANTASTIC (hybrid)	68–72	Indeterminate; 6–8-ounce, red globe; widely adapted.	BURG BURR COM FAR LIB PON STO TER TOM TOMA
FIREBALL	60–64	Determinate; red, oblate, 5 ounces; short season variety.	STO TOM WILL
FIRST LADY (hybrid)	60	Indeterminate; red, oblate to globe shape, 4–5 ounces; resistant to cracking and disease.	BURR COM DEG FAR JUN LED LIB NIC PAR PIN POR TOMA WILL
FLORIDA MH-1	70	Determinate; red, jointless; resistant to disease.	TOM
GARDENER VF	63	Indeterminate; red, sweet-tart flavor.	SOU
GLASNOST	62	Indeterminate; shiny, reddish orange; 3-inch diameter, 6–10 ounces.	HIG
GOOD 'N EARLY VFT (hybrid)	62	Determinate; oblate, 7 ounces, red.	BURP TOM
HARBINGER (OP)	70	Indeterminate; medium-size, red fruit; an old variety.	BOU
HEARTLAND (hybrid)	68	Semi-indeterminate; 8–10 ounces, oblate; resistant to disease.	VER
HEATWAVE (hybrid)	68	Determinate; red, round, 6–7 ounces; resistant to disease; does especially well in warm areas.	BURP POR ROS TOMA TWI
HIGHLANDER VF	68	Determinate; 5-ounce, bright scarlet globe.	TOM

VARIETY	DAYS	DESCRIPTION	SOURCES (p. 385)

TOMATOES (EARLY SEASON) *(continued)*

VARIETY	DAYS	DESCRIPTION	SOURCES (p. 385)
IMUR PRIOR BETA	70	Salad tomato.	SEE
JACKPOT VFN (hybrid)	68–71	Determinate; red, 8–9 ounces; free of blemishes; resistant to gray leaf spot and other diseases.	POR TOM TOMA WIL
JOHNNY'S 361 (hybrid)	64	Determinate; beefsteak type; red, slightly flattened, 8 ounces; resistant to disease.	JOH
JUNG'S IMPROVED WAYAHEAD	63	Determinate; scarlet, almost perfectly round.	JUN
JUNG'S SUPER SELECT QUALITY WAYAHEAD	70	Determinate; scarlet.	JUN
LANDRY'S RUSSIAN (OP)	70	Midsize, medium red; short season variety from Canada.	DEG
LUCKY LADY (hybrid)	70	Red.	TOM
MANITOBA	60	Determinate; red, 6½ ounces.	GAR STO TOM
MARKET MIRACLE	65	Semi-determinate; round, red, 8–12 ounces; Siberian variety.	HIG
MARMANDE VF	65–67	Semi-determinate; beefsteak type; scarlet, 8 ounces; sets in cool weather; French variety.	GOU ORN SEE TOMA
MARMANDE EXTRA	70	Determinate; red; will grow in greenhouse or garden.	TOM
MARMANDE SUPER (OP)	70–75	Semi-determinate; irregularly shaped, red, 5-inch diameter.	BOU SEED THO
MATADOR (hybrid) (The Tasty Tom)	68	Indeterminate; semibeefsteak type; produces over a long period.	THO
MERCED (hybrid)	69	Determinate; bright red, 9-ounce globe; resistant to disease; widely adapted.	POR
MONEYMAKER	70	Indeterminate; red globe; good variety for humid areas.	BOU SEE
MORCROSS SURPRISE (hybrid)	70	Indeterminate; red, flattened; resistant to cracking; tolerant to fusarium wilt.	TOMA
MORETON (hybrid)	70	Slightly flattened, brilliant red.	GOU
MOSKVICH	60	Indeterminate; deep red, 4–6-ounce globe; heirloom variety from Eastern Siberia.	JOH
MOUNTAIN BOY	60	Large, scarlet, 3–3½-inch fruit; self-pruning plant.	FIS
MOUNTAIN SPRING VF (hybrid)	65–72	Determinate; dark red, 9-ounce globe; resistant to cracking and blossom end rot.	LIB STO TOM TOMA TWI
NEW YORKER	60	Determinate; bright scarlet, 3–5 ounces; sets fruit under cool conditions.	STO TOM TOMA VER
NORTHERN EXPO-SURE VFNTA (hybrid)	65	Determinate; red, 8 ounces; short season variety for cool growing areas.	TOMA

VARIETY	DAYS	DESCRIPTION	SOURCES (p. 385)

TOMATOES (EARLY SEASON) *(continued)*

VARIETY	DAYS	DESCRIPTION	SOURCES (p. 385)
ODESSA	58	Determinate; 4–6 ounces; Ukrainian variety.	ABU HIG
OLD BROOKS	60	Indeterminate; red; intense flavor.	TOM TOMA
OREGON SPRING	58–70	Determinate; red, almost seedless; 4-inch diameter, 6–8 ounces; tolerant of cold and disease.	GAR HIG JOH NIC PIN SEE SEED SHE TIL TOM TOMA
PERESTROIKA	67	Indeterminate; solid, red-orange, 8–10 ounces, few seeds.	HIG
PERON (Sprayless)	68	Indeterminate; scarlet, 8 ounces; resistant to cracking.	GLE SEE SEED TOM TOMA
PILGRIM (hybrid)	68	Determinate; 6–8 ounces; hardy, resistant to disease and cracking.	VER
PORTERS EARLY BROOKPACT	70	Red; highly tolerant of cold.	GLE HIG TOM
PRAIRIE FIRE	53–65	Determinate; a crossbreed of beefsteak and the Sub-artic variety; red, 3-inch diameter, 3–4 ounces.	FIS HIG TER
PRESIDENT VFNT (hybrid)	68–75	Determinate; oblate, red, 7 ounces; resistant to disease.	BURR DEG POR TOM
PRITCHARD'S SCARLET TOPPER	70	Red, 5 ounces.	SEE
PUSA RUBY	60	Deep red tomato with good keeping qualities and disease resistance; East Indian variety.	GLE RED
QUICK PICK VFFNT (hybrid)	60–68	Indeterminate; medium-size, red fruit; heavy yields.	PAR TOMA
QUINTE (Easy Peel)	70	Determinate; crimson, 7 ounces; easy to peel; tolerant of verticillium.	TOM
RED CLOUD	70	This determinate, red variety likes to grow under plastic. It will withstand humid conditions.	TOM
RED HOUSE FREE STANDING	75–85	Determinate; round, red, 6–8 ounces; resistant to fusarium wilt and cracking; tolerant of heat (great for hot summers).	SEED
RED LIGHTNING	55	Determinate; scarlet, 4 inches in diameter; short season variety.	FIS
RED STAR	70	Determinate; solid red; long storage life.	TOM
ROADSIDE RED VF (hybrid)	65	Determinate; red, 8-ounce, flat globe; bush beefsteak type; resistant to disease.	STO
ROCKY MOUNTAIN (hybrid)	60	Determinate; scarlet, 3-inch diameter, sets even in cold weather.	FIS
RUSHMORE VF (hybrid)	66	Determinate; dark red; good disease resistance; withstands cool springs and hot summers.	TOM TOMA
SANTA CRUZ KADA	70	Bred for cool, foggy, coastal California climates.	SEE

VARIETY	DAYS	DESCRIPTION	SOURCES (p. 385)
TOMATOES (EARLY SEASON) *(continued)*			
SASHA'S ALTAI	59	Indeterminate; slightly flattened, bright red; 3 inches in diameter, 5–8 ounces; Siberian variety.	HIG
SCOTIA	60	Determinate; red, 4 ounces; sets in cool weather.	STO TOM WILL
SHIRLEY (hybrid)	68	Indeterminate; medium-size, red; resistant to disease.	THO
SHOW ME (hybrid)	70	Red; disease and crack resistance.	TOM
SIOUX	70	Indeterminate; deep red globe; no cracks or acidity.	DEG TOM
SPITFIRE	70	Determinate; large, flat, intensely red globe; crack resistance and disease tolerance.	WIL
SPRING GIANT VFN (hybrid)	60–70	Determinate; bright red, 10-ounce globe; All-American winner.	ROS TOM TOMA
SPRINGSET VF (hybrid)	65	Determinate; oblate, red, medium-size fruit; resistant to cracking.	ALL PIN TOM TOMA
STARFIRE	56–60	Determinate; round, deep red, ½ pound; likes light, sandy soil.	GAR STO TOM WILL
STARSHOT	55	Determinate; round, bright red, 3 ounces; tolerant to disease.	PIN STO
STOKES PAK VFN (hybrid)	67	Red, 9 ounces; tolerant to disease.	STO
SUMMER FLAVOR BRAND 4000 VF (hybrid)	65–70	Determinate; red, medium-large globe; tolerant to disease.	TWI
SUMMER FLAVOR BRAND VARIETY 4200 (hybrid)	65–70	Determinate; large, oblate globe; tolerant to disease; sets well under many conditions.	TWI
SUMMERSET VF (hybrid)	63	Determinate; deep red, 7½-ounce globe.	STO
SUMMERTIME FN	70	Determinate; red; sets fruit in July and August heat.	TOM
SUNRISE VF (hybrid)	67	Determinate; bright red, 7¼-ounce, flat globe; tolerant to disease.	STO TOM
SUPER CHIEF VF (hybrid)	65	Determinate; bright red, 8 ounces; tolerant to disease.	GUR TOMA
SUPER FANTASTIC VF (hybrid)	70	Indeterminate; round, red, large fruit; well adapted to all parts of the country.	MEY TOMA
SUREFIRE (hybrid)	65–70	Determinate; red, round; resists cracking and stores well.	POR
SURPRISE VF (hybrid)	65	Indeterminate; red globe; resistant to cracking.	DEG TOM
TERRIFIC VFN (hybrid)	70	Indeterminate; oblate, red, 8–10 ounces; produces all season; resistant to cracking and disease.	POR TOM TOMA WIL

VARIETY	DAYS	DESCRIPTION	SOURCES (p. 385)

TOMATOES (EARLY SEASON) *(continued)*

VARIETY	DAYS	DESCRIPTION	SOURCES (p. 385)
THE JUICE VF (hybrid)	65–72	Determinate; red, 6–8 ounces; juicing or canning variety.	TOMA
THESSALONIKI	66–72	Indeterminate; red, baseball-size fruit; resistant to cracking and disease; Greek variety.	GLE SEED TOM
TOMATO NO. 670	65	Determinate; scarlet; resists sunburn and cracking.	GLE
ULTRA GIRL VFN (hybrid)	56	Semi-determinate; bright red, 7–9 ounces; tolerance to cracking and multiple diseases.	STO TOM
ULTRASONIC VFT (hybrid)	65	Determinate; bright red, 12-ounce globe; resistant to disease.	STO
ULTRA SWEET VFT (hybrid)	62	Determinate; bright red, 10-ounce globe; disease-resistant; beefsteak type.	STO
VALIANT	70	Indeterminate; red, 8-ounce globe.	COM
VALLEY GIRL (hybrid)	69	Determinate; red, 7–8-ounce globe; tolerant to cracking; sets fruit under heat or cold stress.	JOH
WEST VIRGINIA '63	70	Indeterminate; red, 8-ounce globe; resistant to cracking and wilt.	BURG TOM TOMA
WHIRLAWAY (hybrid)	70	Determinate; medium-large, red fruit; resistant to common diseases and cracking.	POR

TOMATOES (MIDSEASON)

VARIETY	DAYS	DESCRIPTION	SOURCES (p. 385)
ACE 55 VF	80	Semi-determinate; oblate, bright red; widely adapted; tolerant to disease.	LED MEY ORN TOMA WIL
ACE 55 VF IMPROVED	80	Semi-determinate; large, scarlet; resistant to disease.	ROS
ACE–HY VFN (hybrid)	70–75	Determinate; large, oblate, red fruit; especially adapted to California.	TOM TOMA
ALL STAR VFA (hybrid)	72	Determinate; red, 7-ounce globe; widely adapted; highly resistant to disease.	TOMA
AVALANCHE (hybrid)	77	Indeterminate; up to ¾ pound; resistant to cracking and fusarium wilt.	TOM
BIG'S RED SIBERIAN	72	Indeterminate; round, bright red, 3–4 inches in diameter, 8–12 ounces.	HIG
BLAZER (hybrid)	70	Determinate; red, oblate; resistant to disease; widely adapted.	POR TOM
BONNEYVEE (hybrid)	71	Determinate; red, 6½ ounces; tolerant to cracking.	TOM
BONNY BEST (hybrid) (John Baer)	70–78	Indeterminate; slightly flattened, red, 5–8 ounces; 1908 heirloom variety.	ABU ALL HIG NIC PIN PLA SEE TOM TOMA WILL
BURBANK	80	Indeterminate; 4–5 tomatoes per pound; heirloom variety developed by botanist Luther Burbank.	ORG SEE SEED TOM

VARIETY	DAYS	DESCRIPTION	SOURCES (p. 385)

TOMATOES (MIDSEASON) *(continued)*

VARIETY	DAYS	DESCRIPTION	SOURCES (p. 385)
BURGESS STUFFING TOMATO	78	Bright red, hollow, 3¼ inches wide, 2¾ inches tall.	BURG
BURPEE HYBRID VF	72	Indeterminate; rich red, 7–10 ounces; resistant to cracking and catfacing.	BURP MEY TOM TOMA
CAL ACE VF	80	Determinate; large, firm, smooth, red; adapted to arid regions.	TOM TOMA
CALYPSO	80	Determinate; red, firm fruit; resistance to foliage diseases; good variety for humid areas.	TOM
CAMPBELL 17	80	Determinate; red.	TOM
CAMPBELL 19 VF	75	Determinate; red, 8–10 ounces.	TOM
CAMPBELL 1327 VF	70–75	Determinate; oblate, rich red, 7–10 ounces; resists cracking; sets under adverse conditions.	BURR LED MEY STO TOM TOMA WIL
CARNIVAL VFFNTA (hybrid)	70	Determinate; slightly flattened, red, 7–8-ounce globe; resistant to disease; widely adapted.	LIB POR TOM TOMA
CAVLIER VFNTA (hybrid)	68–71	Determinate; red, 12 ounces; good tolerance to cracking; resistant to disease.	PIN TOMA
CHAMPION VFNT (hybrid)	70	Indeterminate; large, red fruit; high yields.	POR TOMA
CHEROKEE VF	80	Indeterminate; large, slightly flattened, red fruit.	TOM
COLONIAL (hybrid)	78	Determinate; oblate, deep red, 7 ounces; disease resistance; widely adapted.	TWI
DONA (hybrid)	60–71	Indeterminate; crimson, 5–7-ounce, flattened globe; French variety.	COO GAR GOU POR SHE TOMA
DUKE VFA (hybrid)	74–78	Determinate; large, 8 ounces; does well in a wide range of growing conditions.	TOMA TWI
EARLY ROUGE	75	Indeterminate; medium-size, red fruit; resists cracking.	SEED
EMPIRE (hybrid)	78	Determinate; red, 10–11 ounces; resistant to cracking; tolerant to disease.	MEY TWI
ENTERPRISE VFFNTA (hybrid)	72	Determinate; deep red, 8–9 ounces; disease resistance.	TOMA
FANTASTIC (hybrid)	68–72	Indeterminate; red, 6–8-ounce globe; widely adapted.	BURG BURR COM FAR LIB PON STO TER TOM TOMA
FARMERS 112 (hybrid)	80	Determinate; red.	TOM
FLORAMERICA (hybrid)	70–80	Determinate; deep red, flattened globe, up to 1 pound; tolerant to 17 tomato diseases; All-American winner.	ALL BURG BURR DEG FAR JUN LED LIB MEY POR TOM TOMA TWI VER WIL WILL
GARDEN PEACH	80	This indeterminate, red variety is the original long-keeping tomato.	TOM

VARIETY	DAYS	DESCRIPTION	SOURCES (p. 385)

TOMATOES (MIDSEASON) *(continued)*

VARIETY	DAYS	DESCRIPTION	SOURCES (p. 385)
GERMAN	72	Indeterminate; ribbed, flattish round, red; beefsteak type.	JOH
GLAMOUR	75–77	Indeterminate; oblate, red, 6–8 ounces; resistant to cracking.	ALL DEG SEE TOM TOMA WILL
GLASNOST	70–75	Determinate; deep red, 6-ounce globe; Siberian variety.	TOMA
GURNEY GIRL IMPROVED VFNT (hybrid)	75	Indeterminate; red, 6–8 ounces; strong disease resistance.	GUR
HARVESTVEE VF	75	Determinate; red, 9½ ounces; tolerant to catfacing, blossom end rot, and blotching.	STO TOM
HAWAIIAN VFNT (hybrid)	70	Indeterminate; red, 10 ounces; tolerant to heat and disease.	TOMA
HAYSLIP (OP)	72–79	Determinate; oblate, red, 6 ounces; disease-resistant; tolerant to blossom end rot, black shoulder, catfacing, and cracking.	TOM TOMA
HEARTLAND VFN (hybrid)	68–70	Semi-indeterminate; red, 6–8 ounces.	TOMA
HEAVYWEIGHT (hybrid)	80	Indeterminate; red, 8-ounce globe; resistant to disease.	TOM
HEINZ 1350 VF	75	Determinate; slightly flattened, bright red, 6 ounces; resistant to cracking; widely adapted.	LIB PON SOU STO TER TOM TOMA
HEINZ 1370	75	Determinate; red; interior develops slowly; does best in long season areas.	TOM
HEINZ 1439 VF	72	Determinate; medium red, 8 ounces; tolerant to cracking.	BURR STO TOM WIL WILL
HEINZ 1765 VF	73	Determinate; dark red, 9-ounce globe; tolerant to cracking and fusarium.	STO TOM
HOMESTEAD FWR	80	Semi-determinate; bright red fruit.	LEJ
HOMESTEAD 24	80	Determinate; red; variety for humid areas.	TOM
HOMESTEAD 500 F	80	Determinate; slightly flat, red.	TOM TOMA WIL
HYBRID ACE VFN	75	Determinate; large, red fruit; well adapted to hot, dry areas.	TOMA
JET STAR VF (hybrid)	72	Indeterminate; red, 8-ounce globe; low acidity; tolerant to disease and resistant to cracking.	TOM TOMA WIL
KOOTENAI	78–83	Determinate; red, 2–3 inches in diameter; Russian variety.	PLA TER
LORISSA VFNT	80	Semi-determinate; deep red fruit; disease-tolerant French variety.	ORN
MAGNUM	75	Indeterminate; huge, red fruit.	THO

VARIETY	DAYS	DESCRIPTION	SOURCES (p. 385)

TOMATOES (MIDSEASON) *(continued)*

VARIETY	DAYS	DESCRIPTION	SOURCES (p. 385)
MANALUCIE	80	Indeterminate; red; slow to mature; resistant to disease.	TOM TOMA
MANAPAL F	85	Indeterminate; medium-size fruit; resistant to disease; suited to humid areas.	TOM TOMA
MARGLOBE	75	Determinate; red, 10 ounces; old variety; widely adapted.	ALL COM DEG GLE LED LEJ MEY ORG SEE TOM WIL
MARGLOBE VF IMPROVED	75	Determinate; oblate, red, 6 ounces; resistant to cracking.	LIB ROS TOMA
MARGLOBE SELECT	77	Indeterminate; midsize, firm, red; widely adapted.	PAR TOM TOMA
MARS	75	Determinate; medium-size, red fruit with thicker skin than most.	SEED
MOIRA	76	Determinate; round, 6 ounces; does well under adverse conditions.	TOM
MONEYMAKER	80	Indeterminate; medium-size, intensely red; good variety for humid areas.	TOM
MONTE CARLO VFN (hybrid)	75	Indeterminate; red globe, up to 1 pound; resists cracking, catfacing, sunscald, and blossom end rot.	TOM TOMA
MOUNTAIN DELIGHT VFFA (hybrid)	77	Determinate; oblate, red, 8 ounces; resistant to disease.	BURR GUR HEN LED LIB MEY PAR TOMA TWI
MOUNTAIN FRESH VF (hybrid)	76	Determinate; red, firm, 8 ounces; resistant to cracking.	TOMA
MOUNTAIN PRIDE VF (hybrid)	77	Determinate; oblate, red, 6–7 ounces; widely adapted.	LIB MEY STO TOM TOMA TWI WIL
MOUNTAIN SUPREME VF (hybrid)	76	Determinate; red, 6–8 ounces; early blight resistance.	TOMA
MT. ATHOS	80	Large, blocky fruit; Greek variety.	ABU
NEPAL	80	Indeterminate; deep red, 10–12-ounce globe; disease-resistant Himalayan variety.	HIG JOH TOM TOMA
OLD BROOKS	80	Indeterminate; medium to large, round, red; bears all season long; heirloom variety.	TOMA
OLOMOVIC	75–85	Semi-determinate; red, 4–5-ounce, flattened globe; sets in cooler summer areas; Czechoslovak heirloom variety.	ABU SEED
OLYMPIC (hybrid)	72	Determinate; oblate, red, 8 ounces; tolerant to disease.	MEY TWI
OPAL'S HOMESTEAD	80	Red, up to 1 pound; old strain from Kentucky.	ABU
PIK-RED VFN (hybrid) (Red Pak)	71	This determinate variety yields a brilliant red, 6–7-ounce globe. The plants can be grown close together.	TIL TOMA WIL
POLE KING (hybrid)	75	Indeterminate; red, 8 ounces, thick walls; resistant to disease; sets under adverse conditions.	TOM TWI

VARIETY	DAYS	DESCRIPTION	SOURCES (p. 385)

TOMATOES (MIDSEASON) *(continued)*

VARIETY	DAYS	DESCRIPTION	SOURCES (p. 385)
POPOVICH	72	Siberian variety.	HIG
PORTER	78	This indeterminate variety yields a bright red, egg-shaped and -sized tomato that does well in any kind of soil, isn't affected by heat, and doesn't crack.	POR TOMA WIL
PORTER'S PRIDE (Improved Porter)	70–72	Indeterminate; round, scarlet, 3 ounces.	POR TOM TOMA
PRESIDENT VFN (hybrid)	68–74	Determinate; red, large globe; tolerant to disease.	FAR TOMA
PRITCHARD (Scarlet Topper)	75	Determinate; scarlet, ¼–½-pound globe; small core and seed cavity; adapted to heavy soils; 1932 heirloom variety.	SOU TOM
RAMAPO VF (hybrid)	72	Indeterminate; round, crimson, ½–1-pound; sets under adverse conditions; resists disease and cracking.	DEG LED TOM TOMA
RED CUP	75	Indeterminate; red, 2–4 ounces, 3 lobes; hollow tomato for stuffing.	TOM TOMA
RED STAR (hybrid)	74	Determinate; red, 7-ounce globe; resistant to cracking.	TWI
ROYAL FLUSH	70	Determinate; large, meaty, red; widely adapted; resistant to disease.	LIB
RUSSIAN RED	74	Determinate; round, red, ¼–½-pound; tolerates lower temperatures; New Zealand variety.	GLE TOM
RUTGERS IMPROVED VF	73	Indeterminate; red, ½–¾-pound globe with few seeds; ripens from the inside out.	TOM
RUTGERS 39 VF	80	Indeterminate; red, ¼–½ pound; resistant to disease and cracking.	TOM
RUTGERS VF (hybrid)	73–90	Indeterminate; oblate, red, 6 ounces; resistant to cracking and disease.	BOU BURP COM DEG FAR GLE HEN JLH LEJ LIB MEY ROS SEE SOU TOM TOMA VER WIL
SALSA VFT (hybrid)	72	Semi-determinate; round, red, 5 ounces; French variety; grows in greenhouse or garden.	TOMA
SIMBA VFNT (hybrid)	75	Indeterminate; large, red fruit; resistant to cracking and disease; suited to greenhouse or garden.	POR TOM TOMA
SOLAR SET VFF (hybrid)	70–72	Determinate; bright red, 8–9 ounces; resistant to disease and tolerant to heat; sets even in high temperatures and humidity.	TOMA
STOKESDALE	72	Determinate; large, rich red fruit; heavy yields.	TOM
ST. PIERRE	78–82	Large, red, thin-skinned fruit; produces well under adverse conditions of weeds, little water, and cool weather.	RED SEED

VARIETY	DAYS	DESCRIPTION	SOURCES (p. 385)
TOMATOES (MIDSEASON) *(continued)*			
SUMMER FLAVOR BRAND 5000 VFFN (hybrid)	70–80	Determinate; large, oblate, red fruit; tolerant to disease; widely adapted.	TOMA TWI
SUMMER FLAVOR BRAND 6000 VFF (hybrid)	70–80	Determinate; large, red globe; tolerant to disease.	TWI
SUNCOAST VFF	72	Determinate; deep red, 8 ounces; resistant to gray leaf spot.	TOMA
SUNNY VFA (hybrid)	70–80	Determinate; medium to large, red fruit; cracking and disease resistance.	DEG POR TOMA
SUNRIPE VFN (hybrid)	75	Determinate; very large, bright red fruit; resistant to cracking.	TOMA
SUPER SIOUX	70–75	Indeterminate; oblate, red; does well in hot, dry areas.	BURR HOR SEE TOM TOMA
SUPERSONIC BVFF (hybrid)	80	Indeterminate; large, red, slightly flattened globe; good crack and disease resistance.	COM
SUPERSONIC VF	79	Indeterminate; red, 9-ounce, flattened globe.	TOM TOMA
TOM BOY	80	Indeterminate; red, ¾–1 pound; beefsteak type.	TOM
TROPIC VFN	80	Indeterminate; deep red, 9 ounces, thick walls; variety for hot, humid, or disease-prone areas.	POR SOU TOM TOMA
URBANA VF	78	Scarlet fruit; high yields.	TOM
URIBIKANY	70–78	Determinate; light red, 3–4-ounce, somewhat flattened globe; Czechoslovak variety.	HIG SEED
VERI BEST (hybrid)	75	Indeterminate; 10 ounces, round; resistant to disease and cracking.	VER
VICTOR	80	This determinate, All-American winning, red variety is hard to find.	TOM
WALTER	79	Determinate; dark red, 7 ounces; resistant to cracking; tolerant to fusarium.	TOM TOMA
WALTER VILLEMAIRE (Walter Improved)	75	Determinate; uniform, red, 8 ounces; resistant to disease.	SOU
WEST VIRGINIA '63	70–72	Indeterminate; red; widely adapted; good disease and cracking resistance.	TOM
WILLAMETTE (OP)	68–72	Determinate; round, red, 3-inch diameter; well adapted to western valley areas.	NIC ORG SEE SEED
WISCONSIN CHIEF (Wisconsin 55)	72	Determinate; oblate, deep red; tolerant to disease.	JUN

VARIETY	DAYS	DESCRIPTION	SOURCES (p. 385)
TOMATOES (LATE SEASON)			
BRIGADE	121	Determinate; blocky to square, medium-size, red fruit; produces well.	DEG
CAL ACE VF	85	Determinate; red semiglobe; sets well under adverse weather conditions; resistant to disease.	BURR
DAD'S MUG	85–95	Indeterminate; blocky, large, mug-shaped, pink to red; few seeds; stores well; heirloom variety.	SEE TOM TOMA
EARLYPAK NO. 7	81	Determinate; 2¾x2½ inches, bright scarlet.	BURR
FLORADADE VFN (OP)	77–83	Determinate; red, 7-ounce globe; resistant to disease.	BURR TOM TOMA
FLORADEL	85	Indeterminate; somewhat globe-shaped, large, medium red; resistant to cracking and disease.	TOM WIL
HOMESTEAD 24	80–83	Determinate; red, 8-ounce globe; sets under wide range of conditions.	SOU TOMA WIL
INDIAN RIVER	85	Indeterminate; scarlet globe; resistant to disease; good variety for warm, humid areas.	TOM
J. MORAN	95	Indeterminate; large, red; good for canning.	TOM
JEFF DAVIS	90	Disease-resistant variety for hot, humid areas.	SEE
LANDREY'S	90–100	Indeterminate; 8 ounces, round; tolerant of drought and poor soil; resistant to cracking.	PLA
LARGE	110	Indeterminate; large, red, round; no cracking; resistant to disease; heirloom variety.	TER
LIBERTY (hybrid)	80	Determinate; red, 6–7 ounces; widely adapted; resistant to disease.	TWI
LISA KING (OP)	95–100	Determinate; 8–10 ounces, red; resistant to cracking, sunscald, fruit rots, and blossom end rot; heirloom variety.	TER
MANALUCIE F	80–87	Indeterminate; large, red globe; resistant to disease.	TOMA
MORTGAGE LIFTER RED VFN (Red Mortgage Lifter)	83	This indeterminate variety ripens red and bears until frost. It is resistant to disease.	SOU
MOUNTAIN PRIDE VF (hybrid)	90	Determinate; large, red globe; disease-resistant variety.	COM
PARAGON (hybrid)	82	Determinate; large, red globe; disease-resistant variety.	JOH
PEARSON	80	Determinate; large, red; tolerates heat well.	TOM
PEARSON A–1 IMPROVED	80–93	Determinate; scarlet, ¼–½-pound globe; resistant to fusarium.	BURR ORG ROS TOM WIL
RED CALABASH	85	Indeterminate; ruffled shape, thin skin; 4 fruit per pound; ugly tomato that tastes good.	SEED

VARIETY	DAYS	DESCRIPTION	SOURCES (p. 385)

TOMATOES (LATE SEASON) *(continued)*

VARIETY	DAYS	DESCRIPTION	SOURCES (p. 385)
RED ROSE	90	Indeterminate; red; a cross between Brandywine and Rutgers.	TOM
RUTGERS SELECT	80	Indeterminate; dark red, 8-ounce globe with thick walls and small seed cells; resistant to cracking; widely adapted.	DEG LED PAR TOM TOMA
SEPTEMBER DAWN F	85	Large fruit; resists cracking and fusarium.	TOMA
STONE	81	Indeterminate; slightly ridged and flattened, 7 ounces; good resistance to drought; pre-1913 heirloom variety.	PIN SEE SOU
VOYAGER (hybrid)	82	Determinate; big, red globe.	JOH

TOMATOES (PINK)

VARIETY	DAYS	DESCRIPTION	SOURCES (p. 385)
ARKANSAS TRAVELER (Arkansas Pink)	76–89	Indeterminate; pink, 3–4 inches in diameter, 6–8 ounces; resistant to disease; does well in hot or humid areas; pre-1900 Southern heirloom variety.	SEED SOU TOM TOMA
BLUE RIDGE	90	Indeterminate; pink; North Carolina heirloom.	TOM
BRADLEY	80	Determinate; pink; resistant to fusarium.	TOM
BRANDYWINE	74	Indeterminate; dark reddish pink, ½ pound; not disease resistant; 1885 Amish heirloom variety.	ABU COO GLE JOH ORG PIN SEE SEED SOU TOM TOMA
BRIMMER (Pink Brimmer)	83–100	Indeterminate; purplish pink, 4-inch diameter, 2½ pounds; no core and very few seeds; 1905 Virginia heirloom variety.	SEED SOU
CHEROKEE PURPLE	78–82	This indeterminate, pre-1890 Cherokee people heirloom variety is an odd but interesting tomato. The medium-large, flattened globe is dusky pink to pinkish brown. There's green gel inside when it's less ripe.	JOH SOU
DUTCHMAN	85	Indeterminate; purplish pink, large, oblate; no acidity; heirloom variety.	GLE TOM TOMA
EARLY DETROIT	78	Determinate; large, pink globe.	TOM
EVA PURPLE BALL	78	Indeterminate; round, pink-purple, 4–5 ounces; good variety for hot, humid areas; resistant to disease and cracking; 1800s German heirloom variety.	SOU
EVERBEARING	80	Indeterminate; pink; bears until frost.	TOM
GERMAN HEAD	80	Indeterminate; large, pink, well-shaped beefsteak type; heirloom variety.	GLE TOM TOMA
GERMAN JOHNSON (German Johnson Pink)	80–90	Indeterminate; irregularly shaped, pink-red, 1 pound; Southern heirloom variety.	SOU TOMA
GIANT BELGIUM	90	This indeterminate variety's dark pink, 2–5-pound tomatoes can be used to make a dessert wine.	GLE TOM TOMA

VARIETY	DAYS	DESCRIPTION	SOURCES (p. 385)
TOMATOES (PINK) *(continued)*			
GRANDE ROSE VFT (hybrid)	68	Large, pink, 12-ounce beefsteak type; resistant to disease.	STO
GREGORI'S ALTAI	67	Indeterminate; purple-red, 8–10 ounces; beefsteak type from mountains near China.	HIG TOMA
GRUSHOVKA	67	Determinate; rose, 3-inch diameter, 6–8 ounces; Russian variety.	HIG
ISPOLIN	70	This indeterminate variety's round, pink tomatoes weigh 1–2 pounds each. Ispolin means "giant" in Russian.	HIG
JUNE PINK (Pink Earliana)	68	Indeterminate; rose-pink; grows in clusters of 6–10 tomatoes; low disease resistance; 1900 heirloom variety.	TOM SOU
LONG KEEPER (Burpee's Long Keeper)	75–78	This semi-determinate variety's 4–7-ounce, pale pink fruit ripens to red-orange. It may be stored unwrapped for up to 3 months.	ALL BURG BURP COM FAR GAR GUR HEN HIG JUN LED LIB PIN PON SOU TER TOM TOMA WILL
MAC PINK	90	Determinate; pink, smooth, firm fruit.	TOM
MARITIME PINK	69	Indeterminate; deep rose-pink, 5–7 ounces.	HIG
MICADO VIOLETTOR	80	Indeterminate; medium-size, pink; old variety from Australia.	SEED
MISSION DYKE	70	Indeterminate; medium pink, 8–10 ounces; resistant to disease and drought.	GLE SOU TOM
MORTGAGE LIFTER (Radiator Charlie's)	79–85	Indeterminate; slightly flattened, pink-red, 2½–4 pounds, few seeds.	GLE SEE SOU TOM TOMA
OLYMPIC	76	Indeterminate; pink, firm fruit; resistant to cracking.	TOM
OZARK PINK	65–80	Indeterminate; pink, 7-ounce, flattened globe; good shelf life; good variety for hot, humid, disease-prone areas.	SEED SOU
PERESTROIKA	67	Indeterminate; round, red-orange, 8–10 ounces, very few seeds.	HIG
PINK GIRL VFT (hybrid)	71–85	Indeterminate; pink, 8-ounce globe; widely adapted; tolerant to cracking.	GUR HEN LIB PAR PON TOM TOMA
PINK ODORIKO	76	Indeterminate; deep rose-red, round; resistant to disease; Japanese variety.	SHE
PONDERHEART	90	Semiglobe; no acidity; Japanese variety.	GLE TOM
PONDEROSA (OP) (Beefsteak Pink)	80–95	Indeterminate; oblate, purplish pink, 2 pounds, rather rough skin; low acidity.	DEG LIB NIC POR TOM TOMA VER WIL WILL
PORTER IMPROVED PINK	80	Indeterminate; pink, 5–6 tomatoes per pound; resistant to cracking.	SEED

VARIETY	DAYS	DESCRIPTION	SOURCES (p. 385)

TOMATOES (PINK) *(continued)*

VARIETY	DAYS	DESCRIPTION	SOURCES
PRUDEN'S PURPLE	67	Indeterminate; flattened, vivid dark pink, red flesh, more than 1 pound; widely adapted.	JOH PIN
RUBY RAKES	85	Pink, 10–14 ounces; easy to peel.	SEE
SPARTAN PINK 10	85	Pink; resistant to fusarium.	TOM
TAPPY'S FINEST	77	Indeterminate; somewhat flattened, pink-red, 14–16 ounces; small core; seed originally from Italy; West Virginia heirloom.	SOU
TENNESSEE PEACH FUZZ	85	Dark pink, 2–inch diameter, unusual skin texture.	SEE
THE 1884	90	Indeterminate; pink; 1884 West Virginia heirloom.	TOM
TRAVELER 76	76	Indeterminate; smooth, pink, 6 ounces; resistant to disease; widely adapted.	SOU TOM
ULTRA PINK VFT (hybrid)	64	Indeterminate; rosy pink, 10-ounce globe.	STO
WATERMELON BEEFSTEAK	75	Indeterminate; oblong, pink, 2 pounds or more; acid-free, purplish red flesh.	GLE TOM TOMA
WINSALL	80	Indeterminate; slightly flattened, large, pink; 1924 heirloom variety.	SOU

TOMATOES (ORANGE/YELLOW/GOLD)

VARIETY	DAYS	DESCRIPTION	SOURCES
BRANDYWINE YELLOW	90	Indeterminate; yellow version of the pink variety.	SEE TOM
BREAK O'DAY	85	Indeterminate; orange-red, large.	TOM
CARO RED	80	Indeterminate; orange-red globe; rich in vitamin A.	TOM
CARO RICH (OP)	72–80	Indeterminate; carrot-colored, 4–6 ounces; low acidity.	GLE NIC ORG SEE SEED TOM TOMA
DAD'S SUNSET	80	Yellow, 4–6 ounces, meaty.	SEE
DJENA LEE'S GOLDEN GIRL	80	Indeterminate; golden-orange; 1920 Minnesota heirloom variety (pronounced *zshena*).	SOU
GOLD DUST	61	Determinate; midsize, orange globe; bears early and heavily in cold or heat stress.	JOH
GOLDEN BOY (hybrid)	80	Indeterminate; large, deep yellow globe.	COM LEJ PIN TOM TOMA VER WIL
GOLDEN DELIGHT	57–65	Determinate; full-size, butter yellow, 3–5-ounce fruit; low acidity; resistant to cracking.	ABU TER TOM
GOLDEN PONDEROSA, C&O	78	One round, large, golden yellow tomato weighs more than 1 pound. This 1891 heirloom variety was traded by the employees of the C&O Railroad. It has no disease tolerance.	SOU

VARIETY	DAYS	DESCRIPTION	SOURCES (p. 385)

TOMATOES (ORANGE/YELLOW/GOLD) *(continued)*

VARIETY	DAYS	DESCRIPTION	SOURCES
GOLDEN QUEEN	79–83	Indeterminate; slightly flattened, bright yellow, 6 ounces; no acidity; 1882 heirloom variety.	STO TOM TOMA
GOLDEN SUNBURST	85	Indeterminate; yellow, ¾–1 pound.	TOM
GOLDEN SUNRAY (OP)	80	Yellow globe; no cracking; resistant to fusarium.	TOM
GOLDEN SUNRISE	78	Indeterminate; medium-size, golden yellow.	THO
GOLDEN TREASURE	70–100	This indeterminate variety's fruit measures 2¼–2½ inches in diameter. It ripens to golden yellow and will store for up to 3 months on a shelf.	TER
GOLDIE	90	Indeterminate; huge, flattish round, golden; no acidity; heirloom variety.	GLE ORN
HUGH'S	89–90	Indeterminate; pale yellow, up to 2½ pounds, thin skin; beefsteak type; requires a long growing season; Indian heirloom variety.	SOU TOMA
IDA GOLD	59	Determinate; brilliant orange, 2–3 ounces; low acidity; Idaho variety.	GAR HIG SEE TOM
JUBILEE (OP) (Burpee's Jubilee, Golden Jubilee, Orange Jubilee)	72–80	Indeterminate; orange-yellow, ½-pound globe; no acidity; All-American winner.	ALL BURP BURR DEG FAR LED LIB NIC ORN POR TIL TOM TOMA WIL WILL
LEMON BOY VFN (hybrid)	72–100	Indeterminate; bright lemon yellow, 3–4 inches in diameter, 8–10 ounces.	BURP DEG HEN JLH LIB NIC PAR POR STO TER TOM TOMA VER WILL
MANDARIN CROSS (hybrid)	71–90	Indeterminate; orange-yellow, 9 ounces; low acidity; Japanese variety; not for cooler climates.	ABU ORN SHE TOMA
MOON GLOW	72	Indeterminate; medium-size, orange-yellow globe with blunt point; no acidity; keeps well.	GLE TOM
MOUNTAIN GOLD VFF	70–72	Determinate; yellow-gold, 3½-inch, 9-ounce globe; resistant to disease; long shelf life; Plant Variety Patented (PVP).	BURR SOU STO TOM TOMA
OLD FLAME	80	Indeterminate; big, sunny yellow shot through with red; beefsteak type; resistant to cracking; no acidity; heirloom variety.	HEN SHE
OLD GERMAN	90	Indeterminate; yellow with red center, more than 1 pound, few seeds; does not tolerate drought; Virginia heirloom variety.	SOU
OLD WYANDOTTE	85	Yellow, 8–10 ounces; resistant to disease.	SEE
OLGA'S YELLOW ROUND CHICKEN	75	Indeterminate; bright orange, round, 5–6 ounces; slightly acid.	HIG
ORANGE QUEEN	65–70	Determinate; bright orange, 4–6 ounces; low acidity.	SEED STO
PERSIMMON	80–88	Indeterminate; oblate, deep orange, up to 2 pounds; resembles a ripe persimmon; heirloom variety.	COO SEE SEED SOU

VARIETY	DAYS	DESCRIPTION	SOURCES (p. 385)
TOMATOES (ORANGE/YELLOW/GOLD) *(continued)*			
PINK GRAPEFRUIT	60–70	Indeterminate; midsize, yellow skin, pink flesh.	GLE TOM TOMA
RUFFLED YELLOW	80–85	Indeterminate; accordion-shaped, yellow, hollow.	GLE SEE SEED TOMA
SUNRAY VFF (OP)	80	Indeterminate; orange-yellow, 3-inch-diameter globe.	GLE MEY
TANGERINE	80–85	Indeterminate; deep yellow-orange beefsteak type; shaped like a tangerine; heirloom variety.	TOM TOMA
TAXI	64–70	Determinate; oblate, taxicab yellow, 4–6 ounces; widely adapted.	COO HIG JOH SEED TER TOM
VALENCIA	76	Indeterminate; round, bright orange, 8–10 ounces, few seeds; Maine heirloom variety.	HIG JOH TOM TOMA
VICTORY	72	Indeterminate; slightly flattened, red-orange, 6–8 ounces; Sakhalin island variety.	HIG
WINTER KEEPER	75–80	Light orange-red when ripe, with red flesh; stores 8–12 weeks.	SEED
YELLOW BELGIUM	85	Indeterminate; large, yellow-orange; low acidity; heirloom variety.	JLH SEED TOM
YELLOW BRANDYWINE	90–100	Indeterminate; large, yellow, 12–24 ounces.	TOMA
YELLOW PERFECTION	75	Indeterminate; brilliant yellow, 1 ounce, thin skin; British heirloom variety.	SEED
YELLOW STUFFER	76	This indeterminate variety produces a bright yellow stuffing tomato that looks like a bell pepper.	DEG GLE GUR JLH LED LIB PAR POR STO TOM TOMA

TOMATOES (CONTAINER VARIETIES)

VARIETY	DAYS	DESCRIPTION	SOURCES (p. 385)
BASKET KING (hybrid)	55	Determinate; round, 1¾-inch diameter; good variety for hanging baskets.	TOM TOMA
BETTER BUSH VFN (hybrid)	72	3x3-foot plant; 3–4-inch-diameter tomatoes.	PAR
BROOKPACK	55	Strong, dwarf plant; bright red, 8–9-ounce, flattened globe; resistant to cold.	HIG
BURGESS EARLY SALAD (hybrid)	45	Plant is 6–8 inches high, with 2-foot spread. The bright red tomatoes measure 1½x1¼ inches. There are about 300 tomatoes per plant. Variety bears in hot weather, up until frost.	BURG
BURPEE'S PIXIE (hybrid) (Pixie)	52	Determinate; 14–18-inch, strong plant; 1¾-inch-diameter, scarlet tomatoes.	ALL PON TOM TOMA
CALIFORNIA SUN VFN (hybrid)	70	Dwarf, indeterminate variety; 3–4 feet tall; red, 7–8-ounce tomatoes.	TOMA
CHERRY EXPRESS (hybrid)	71	10-inch-tall plant; 1¾-inch, large cherry tomato; tolerant to cracking and verticillium.	STO

VARIETY	DAYS	DESCRIPTION	SOURCES (p. 385)
TOMATOES (CONTAINER VARIETIES) *(continued)*			
CHERRY GOLD	45	6x6-inch plant; deep golden yellow cherry tomatoes.	STO
CHERRY PINK (hybrid)	68	Bushy dwarf plant; 1½-inch, cherry pink fruit.	STO
DWARF CHAMPION	73	24-inch, potato-leaf plant; rose-pink, 5-ounce tomatoes; low acidity.	STO TOM
ELDELROT (Red Supreme)	70	This bushy European variety does not keep well in wet weather. It bears medium-size fruit.	ABU
FLORAGOLD BASKET	85	One 12-inch pot can hold 3 plants. This determinate variety yields tiny, yellow cherry tomatoes.	TOMA
FLORIDA BASKET	70	This determinate variety is good for hanging baskets. The plant trails 4–6 inches over the edge and yields 1-inch tomatoes.	TOM TOMA
FLORIDA PETIT (OP)	59	These determinate 1½-inch tomatoes can be grown in a 4-inch pot.	TOM
GERMAN DWARF BUSH	45	Determinate, rugged plant; resists 28°F temperature; 2-inch, red tomatoes.	GLE TOM
GOLDEN BABY	60	Small, bushy plant; yellow cherry tomatoes.	LIB
GOLDEN PIGMY	70	This 12-inch plant yields yellow tomatoes the size of marbles.	ORN
HUSKY GOLD VF	70	Stocky, 48-inch plant; vibrant golden orange, 5–7-ounce fruit with orange interior; disease-tolerant All-American winner.	BURP LED LIB MEY POR STO THO TOM TOMA TWI VER
HUSKY PINK VF	72	Rose-pink version of Husky Gold.	LED LIB NIC PAR STO TOM TOMA VER
HUSKY RED VF	68	Dark red version of Husky Gold; recommended for tubs or cages.	LED LIB PAR STO TOM TOMA VER
IRION (Olomovic)	70	Bush plant; cherry-size tomatoes; Czechoslovak variety.	ABU
LEMON BUSH	70	Bush plant; light yellow, almost white, tomatoes about the size of small lemons; susceptible to blight.	GLE
LUNCH BOX VF (hybrid)	62	Bush plant; egg-size, two-bite, crimson tomato.	STO
MICRO-TOM	85	This determinate variety grows 5–8 inches tall. The miniature tomatoes are about the size of croutons and can be grown in 4-inch pots.	BURG GUR PIN TOM TOMA
NIAGARA BELLE (hybrid)	68	Dwarf plant; dark red, 1¼-ounce, 1¾-inch, large cherry tomatoes.	STO
ORANGE PIXIE VFT (hybrid)	52	Determinate, disease-resistant, 18-inch plant; yellow-orange, 1¼-inch tomatoes.	TOMA
PATIO PRIZE VFN (hybrid)	52–67	Determinate; red, 5 ounces.	PAR POR

VARIETY	DAYS	DESCRIPTION	SOURCES (p. 385)

TOMATOES (CONTAINER VARIETIES) *(continued)*

VARIETY	DAYS	DESCRIPTION	SOURCES
PATIO VF (hybrid)	50–70	Determinate, 24–30-inch plant; oblate, red, 2-inch, 4-ounce fruit.	ALL COM DEG LED LIB TOM TOMA WIL
PIXIE HYBRID II	52	Determinate; 18-inch plant; improved Pixie with disease resistance; bright scarlet, 1¾-inch fruit.	JUN ORN TOMA WILL
PRAIRIE FIRE	52	Dwarf plant; very red, 3-inch-diameter fruit.	FIS
PRESTO	60	Small, open vine; round, bright red, 1½–2-inch fruit; bears all season long.	GOU
RED ROBIN	55–63	Determinate; 6–12 inches tall; 1¼-inch, red tomatoes; no disease resistance.	DEG ORN PAR STO TOMA
SIBERIA	48–55	The determinate, 2½-foot plant sets in low temperatures–about 60 fruit per plant. A tomato measures 1½ inches, 3–4 ounces.	ABU TOMA
SMALL FRY VFN (hybrid)	65–72	Determinate; compact vine; round, red, 1-inch cherry tomatoes; All-American winner.	BURG COM JUN LED LIB STO TOM TOMA
STAKELESS BUSH	78–80	18-inch plant; deep red, 8-ounce tomatoes; tolerant to fusarium.	BURR STO TOM TOMA
STOKESALASKA	55	18-inch plant; 1¾-ounce, red, thin-skinned fruit.	STO TOM TOMA
STUPICE	52–62	The indeterminate plant sets 3–6-ounce, red-orange fruit. This Czechoslovak variety won honors in the San Francisco Bay Area.	ABU HIG SOU
SUB-ARTIC CHERRY (Sub-Artic Plenty)	58–59	This determinate variety produces clusters of red, 2-ounce fruit–about 300 tomatoes per plant.	HIG TOMA
SUMMERPINK VF (hybrid)	63	This bush yields 7½–8-ounce, pastel pink globes.	STO
SUPER BUSH VFN (hybrid)	63–85	Determinate; 16-inch plant; red, 6-ounce fruit; resistant to disease.	LED PIN SHE TOM TOMA
TIGERETTE CHERRY	68	Dwarf plant; red and yellow striped, 2¾-inch fruit.	STO
TINY TIM	45–60	Determinate; 6x6-inch plant; round, bright red, ¾-inch cherry tomatoes.	ALL BURG COM GLE LED SEE STO TOM TOMA WILL
TOMATO NO. 506	62	Determinate; 18-inch plant; brilliant red tomatoes; resistant to cracking, sunburn, and drought.	GLE
TOY BOY VF (hybrid)	68	Determinate; 14-inch plant; red, 1½-inch tomatoes.	COM POR TOMA
TUMBLER HYBRID	49	These round, bright red cherry tomatoes measure 1¼ inches in diameter. Each determinate plant produces up to 6 pounds of tomatoes.	BURP THO
WENDY	65	Semi-determinate; round, yellow, 2-inch fruit; New Zealand variety.	HIG
WINDOWBOX	60	Tiny plant.	SEE

VARIETY	DAYS	DESCRIPTION	SOURCES (p. 385)

TOMATOES (CONTAINER VARIETIES) *(continued)*

VARIETY	DAYS	DESCRIPTION	SOURCES
YELLOW CANARY (hybrid)	55–63	The 6-inch plant tolerates low light but has no disease tolerance. Its 1-ounce, cherry-type fruit is golden yellow.	PAR STO TOMA
YELLOW PIGMY	45	Small, compact plant; yellow version of Tiny Tim.	GLE

TOMATOES (SMALL FRUITED)

VARIETY	DAYS	DESCRIPTION	SOURCES
ABUNDANT CHERRIES	65	Medium-size fruit.	ORG
AURORA	65	Indeterminate; round, scarlet, 2–3-ounce fruit; variety from Krasnoyarsk, Siberia.	HIG
BASKET PAK	76	Indeterminate; rich red fruit, 1½ inches in diameter; bears heavily all season.	TOM TOMA
BAXTER'S BUSH CHERRY	60–72	Determinate; grows to 4 feet; round, red, 1-inch fruit.	LIB TOM TOMA
CAMP JOY	65	Indeterminate; 1–1½-inch, red fruit.	SHE
CHEERIO	65	Determinate; medium-large, bright red cherry type; tolerates cold and adverse weather conditions.	TOM
CHELLO YELLOW CHERRIES	63	Determinate; glossy golden yellow, 1-inch fruit; bears all season long.	SHE TOMA
CHERRY ELITE (hybrid)	77	Determinate; 1¼-inch fruit; tolerant to cracking.	TOM
CHERRY GOLD	70	Determinate; golden yellow fruit.	TOM
CHERRY GRANDE VF (hybrid)	55–74	Determinate; red, 1½-inch fruit; widely adapted.	STO TOM TOMA TWI
CHERRY SALAD	50	Determinate; self-pruning plant; red fruit with a 1–1½-inch diameter.	FIS
CURRANT DROPS	55	Variety is indeterminate. Put a cloth under the plant and shake to harvest these pea-size tomatoes.	SEE
EARLY CASCADE VF (hybrid)	60	Indeterminate; red, 2-inch, somewhat heart-shaped fruit; tolerant to disease.	TER WILL
EARLY CHERRY	55	Determinate; bright red, 1½-inch fruit; sets crop even in cool weather.	TER
EARLY TEMPTATION (hybrid)	50	Determinate; 2–3-ounce fruit.	TOM
ENCHANTMENT VFFN (hybrid)	70	Indeterminate; egg-shaped, 3–4-ounce fruit; resistant to disease.	TOMA
FAKEL	72	Indeterminate; intensely red, 2½ inches; Russian variety.	NIC
FOX CHERRY	90	Indeterminate; large, red cherry tomatoes.	SEED

VARIETY	DAYS	DESCRIPTION	SOURCES (p. 385)

TOMATOES (SMALL FRUITED) *(continued)*

VARIETY	DAYS	DESCRIPTION	SOURCES
GALINA'S	59	Indeterminate; round, yellow, 1-inch, ½-ounce.	GLE HIG
GARDENER'S DELIGHT (Sugar Lump)	50–80	Indeterminate; bite-size, ½–¾-inch; heirloom variety.	BOU BURP COO GAR PAR PIN SEE SEED THO TOM TOMA
GARDEN PEACH	75–85	This indeterminate heirloom variety yields abundant clusters of small to medium-size, yellow tomatoes with pink blush.	SEE TOMA
GEM STATE	58	Determinate; red, 2 ounces, 1½–2 inches; heavy yields; cool weather variety.	HIG JOH SEE TOM
GLACIER	45–54	Determinate; spreading plant; red, 2-inch tomatoes.	GLE PLA TOM
GOLD CURRENT	70	Indeterminate; small, yellow cherry tomatoes; self-sowing.	SEED
GOLDEN PEARL TOMATO	67	Indeterminate. These grapelike, golden yellow cherry tomatoes are grown in the wine country of California and served in fine restaurants. This crack-resistant, indeterminate, heirloom variety bears over a long season.	SHE
GOLDEN TOMBOY	75	Indeterminate; miniature, yellow tomatoes with green shoulders; 10 fruits per cluster.	DEG
GOLD NUGGET (OP)	50–80	Determinate; golden yellow, 1–1¼ inches in diameter, almost seedless; sets well under cool conditions.	COO HIG JOH NIC ORN PIN SEE SEED TOM TOMA
GREEN GRAPE	70	Semi-determinate; 1¾-inch, greenish yellow fruit.	ABU GLE SEE SOU TOM TOMA
HIGH COUNTRY	60	Indeterminate; red, medium-size, 3–4 ounces, scarlet; thick enough to use in pastes.	HIG
HUSKY CHERRY RED (hybrid)	65	This dwarf, indeterminate plant yields red, 1-inch tomatoes in large clusters. They can be grown in containers.	LED TOMA WILL
LOOMIS POTATO LEAF CHERRY	70	Indeterminate; red, cherry-size tomatoes.	GLE TOM
MINI ORANGE	66	Indeterminate; bright orange, 1½ inches; good resistance to tomato hornworm; fine variety for hot, humid areas.	GLE SOU
MOSCOW	62	Indeterminate; red, 3–4 ounces, 2½ inches.	HIG
MOUNTAIN BELLE VF (hybrid)	65	Determinate; round to slightly oval, bright red, 1¼ inches; resistant to cracking.	TOMA
ORANGE PIXIE VFT (hybrid)	70	Determinate; orange, 1½ inches.	TOM
OTRAOLNY	70	Indeterminate; somewhat oblong, 3–4 ounces, red; slightly acid bite; variety from Krasnoyarsk, Siberia.	HIG
PARTY	70	Cherry-size.	SEE

VARIETY	DAYS	DESCRIPTION	SOURCES (p. 385)
TOMATOES (SMALL FRUITED) *(continued)*			
PEACEVINE CHERRY	75	Indeterminate; also called the "mellow tomato" because it is high in gamma-aminobutyric acid, a bodily sedative; cherry-size tomatoes.	SEED
PEARLY PINK CHERRY	70	Indeterminate; small, slightly oval, dark pink.	JLH
PINK CHERRY	70	Indeterminate; round, ¾-inch, pinkish-red.	ABU GLE TOM TOMA
PINK DROPLET	70	Medium-size bush; rich pink cherry tomatoes.	SEED
PINK PEAR	75	Indeterminate; little, pear-shaped, pink tomato.	TOM
POMME D'AMOUR	75	Indeterminate; oversize pink cherry tomato; 1820s heirloom variety from the Canary Islands.	SEED TOM
PRIZE OF THE TRIALS	75–80	Indeterminate; orange, apricot-size cherry tomatoes; resistant to cracking.	SEED
PURPLE CALABASH	90	Indeterminate; small, purple-pink, ruffled tomato; low-quality heirloom variety.	GLE JLH SEE TOM
RED CHERRY, LARGE (OP)	70–75	Indeterminate; red, 1¼ inches in diameter.	ABU BURG BURR BUT GLE GUR LED LIB NIC ROS TER TOM TOMA WIL
RED CHERRY, SMALL (Old Fashioned Red Cherry)	72	Indeterminate; red, ⅞-inch; resistant to disease, fruitworm, and high temperatures; pre-1840 heirloom variety.	ALL BURG COM MEY PIN RED SOU STO TOM
RED CURRANT	70–75	To harvest this indeterminate variety's tiny fruit, spread a cloth beneath the plant and shake.	COO DEG JLH JOH SEED TOM
RED PEACH	75	Indeterminate; small, red tomato with slightly fuzzy skin.	STO TOM
RED PEAR	73	Indeterminate; clusters of pear-shaped, 1-inch, red fruit bears over a long season; resistant to disease.	BURG COO DEG GLE HEN JOH ORN SEE STO TOM
RED PLUM	75	Indeterminate; scarlet, plum-shaped tomato, good for preserving.	BURG GLE ORN SEE STO TOM TOMA
RED ROBIN	55–63	Determinate; red, 1–1¼ inches; no disease tolerance.	TOMA
RIESENSTRAUBE	76	The red, ¾-ounce, 1½x1¼-inch fruit has a rounded pear shape with a sharply pointed end. The name of this indeterminate German heirloom variety means "giant bunch of grapes."	SOU
RUBY PEARL (hybrid)	67	Indeterminate; grape-size, ruby red; resistant to cracking; widely adapted; Chinese variety.	SHE
SPRINT (Kotlas)	59	Indeterminate; round, red, 2 ounces; tolerant to cold and disease.	JOH TOM
SPRINTER (hybrid)	65	Determinate; 2 inches in diameter.	TOMA
STARSHOT	55	Round, 3 ounces, 2 inches; tolerant to verticillium.	STO

VARIETY	DAYS	DESCRIPTION	SOURCES (p. 385)
TOMATOES (SMALL FRUITED) *(continued)*			
STUPICE	52	Indeterminate; 1–2 ounces, red; tolerant of cold; voted first-rate in San Francisco Bay Area; almost 90 tomatoes per plant; Czechoslovak variety.	HIG SEED TER TOMA
SUB-ARTIC CHERRY	45	1¾ inches, red; grows under adverse conditions; about 300 fruit per plant.	GLE JLH
SUB-ARTIC MAXI	64	Determinate; bright red, 3 ounces; tolerant of cold.	HIG STO TOM WILL
SUB-ARTIC PLENTY	58–62	Determinate; red, 1½–2 inches, 2 ounces; widely adapted.	GUR HEN HIG JOH TOM
SUGAR CHERRY	76	Indeterminate; currant type; ¾-inch, orange-red; sets in clusters of 12.	SOU
SUN CHERRY (hybrid)	60	Indeterminate; red, 1¼ inches, less than 1 ounce; sets in long, 20-fruit clusters; 10 percent sweeter than most other cherry types.	JOH
SUNDROP	76	Indeterminate; 1⅞–2 inches, 2 ounces, deep orange; resistant to cracking.	DEG JLH
SUN GOLD (hybrid)	57	Indeterminate; bite-size, bright tangerine color; high sugar content; tolerant to disease.	JOH TER THO TOMA
SUPER SWEET 100 (hybrid)	70	This indeterminate variety produces its scarlet, cherry-size fruit in long clusters right up until frost.	BURP JUN LED PAR VER
SWEET CHELSEA VFTMV (hybrid)	67	Indeterminate; cherry red, 1 ounce, 1¾ inches; resistant to cracking; produces until frost.	COM DEG ORN PIN STO TOM TOMA TWI VER
SWEET CHERRY	65	Indeterminate; clusters of bright red, 1-inch tomatoes.	FIS
SWEETIE (OP)	65–70	Indeterminate; large clusters of small, round, red fruit.	COM DEG HEN LIB NIC SEE TER TOMA WILL
SWEET MILLION VFT (hybrid)	67	Indeterminate; ½–¾ ounces, red; resistant to diseases and cracking.	GOU JUN ORN PAR PIN STO TER TOMA VER WILL
SWEET 100	65–70	This indeterminate variety's red, cherry-size tomatoes grow in clusters and reappear until fall.	BURP COM COO GUR HEN LIB MEY ORN POR SHE STO THO TIL TOM TOMA TWI
SWIFT	54	Determinate; brick red, 2¾-ounce, 2-inch globes; sets in low temperatures; resists cracking.	STO TOM
WASHINGTON CHERRY	60	Determinate; red, 1–1¼-ounce globes; widely adapted.	JOH TOM
WHIPPERSNAPPER	52	Determinate; oval, pinkish-red, about 1 inch long; more than 100 fruit per plant.	GAR HIG JOH TOM
WICKLINE CHERRY	85–90	Indeterminate; pinkish-red, egg-shaped, 1x1½ inches; tolerant of cool, wet conditions; Pennsylvania heirloom variety.	SOU
WILD CHERRY	70	Indeterminate; red, dime-size tomato; Mexican variety.	TOM

VARIETY	DAYS	DESCRIPTION	SOURCES (p. 385)

TOMATOES (SMALL FRUITED) *(continued)*

VARIETY	DAYS	DESCRIPTION	SOURCES
YELLOW CHERRY	70	Indeterminate; ½-inch diameter, light yellow.	ORG STO TOM TOMA
YELLOW CURRANT (OP)	65	Indeterminate; yellow version of South American wild red currant; ⅛ ounce.	COO GLE JOH NIC TOM TOMA
YELLOW MARBLE	65	Indeterminate; marble-size, yellow.	SEE
YELLOW PEACH	65	Indeterminate; light yellow with fuzzy skin.	TOM
YELLOW PEAR	70–78	Indeterminate; clusters of 1¾x2-inch, pear-shaped, bright yellow fruit; 1805 heirloom variety.	ABU ALL BURP COO DEG GAR GLE GOU HEN HIG JOH MEY NIC ORN POR SEE SEED SHE SOU STO TOM TOMA WIL WILL
YELLOW PING PONG	65	Indeterminate; Ping-Pong-ball size, golden yellow.	SEE
YELLOW PLUM	78–85	Indeterminate; 1½–2x½-inch, plum-shaped, yellow.	BURG DEG GLE LED ORN ROS SEE TOM TOMA

TOMATOES (PASTE)

VARIETY	DAYS	DESCRIPTION	SOURCES
ANDINO	70	Determinate; 3–4 ounces, red, plum-shaped; grows well in Northern California.	TOM
ARTELA (hybrid)	70	Semi-determinate; cylindrical, meaty fruit.	COO
AZTECA VFN (hybrid)	68	Determinate; bright red, 2½–3 ounces; green shoulders; resistant to disease.	STO
BELLSTAR	70–74	Determinate; red, 4–6 ounces.	GAR HIG JOH STO TOM TOMA
BIG RAY'S ARGENTINA PASTE	70	Similar to Super Italian Paste.	SEE
CANNER'S DELIGHT	65	Determinate; red; 6 fruits per pound; productive variety.	SEED
CAPRI VF (hybrid)	70	Determinate; plum-shaped, bright red, 2¾-inch diameter; 3⅛ ounces.	STO
CARROT	70	Long, thin tomato.	SEE
CHICO III (Chico Grande Improved)	62–85	Determinate; red, 2 ounces; sets well in high temperatures.	JUN TER TIL TOM
COMSTOCK'S SAUCE 'N SLICE	92	Indeterminate; oblong, red; resistant to disease.	COM
CRIMSONVEE VF	72	Determinate; medium-size, square, dark crimson; tolerant to cracking.	STO
DE BARRAO II	67	Semi-determinate; pear-shaped, 3-inch, 6–8-ounce fruit; Russian variety; stores well.	HIG
FULL FLAVOR PASTE	70	Determinate; pear-shaped, bright red.	SEED
GIANT ITALIAN PLUM	70	Indeterminate; red, about 1 pound, few seeds.	TOM

VARIETY	DAYS	DESCRIPTION	SOURCES (p. 385)
TOMATOES (PASTE) *(continued)*			
GIANT PASTE	72	Indeterminate; rounded oval, plum type, red, 6–10 ounces.	JOH
HEINZ 2653 VF	68	Determinate; red, 3 ounces; often ripens all at once.	TOM
HIGH COUNTRY	60	Determinate; pear-shaped, medium-size, scarlet.	FIS
HUNGARIAN ITALIAN	79	Determinate; red, 2–3 ounces; bears until frost.	SEE SOU
HYBRID 882	76	Determinate; red, 2⅛–2½x2¾–2⅞ inches; 3½ ounces.	JOH
LAKETA	75	Indeterminate; long, pointed bloodred; no acidity.	TOM
LA ROMA VF (Roma Hybrid)	62	Determinate; 3–4 ounces, red.	TOM TOMA
LA ROSSA (hybrid)	78	Determinate; 2–2⅛x3–3⅜ inches, 4 ounces; long plum type.	JOH PIN
MACERO II VF	75	Determinate; large, elongated, pear-shaped, red.	TOM
MARMANDE VF (Vleestomaat)	60–70	Semi-determinate; flat, scarlet; sets well even in cool conditions; French variety.	COO WILL
MARZANO BIG RED	75	Determinate; plum-shaped, red, 2 ounces; good variety for humid areas.	TOM
MH 6203 VF	76	Medium-size vine; medium-size, blocky, plum-shaped, bright red fruit; popular in California.	STO
MIKARDA SWEET	67	Indeterminate; clear red, pear-shaped, 3–4 inches, 5–7 ounces.	HIG
MILANO (hybrid)	70	Determinate; plum-shaped, red; Italian variety.	SHE TOM
MT. ROMA VF	68	Determinate; 2–3 ounces, red; produces even in cold areas.	HIG
NAPOLI VF	65–76	Determinate; elongated, bright red, 2½ ounces.	DEG GLE TOM TOMA WILL
NEW ZEALAND PASTE (New Zealand Pear)	80	Indeterminate; pink, with the size and shape of a Bartlett pear; some tolerance to heat and drought; New Zealand heirloom variety.	GLE TOMA
NOVA	65–75	Determinate; deep red, elongated, 3x1¼ inches, 2 ounces; susceptible to blight; some tolerance to fusarium.	ABU GAR HIG SEE SEED TOM
OREGON PRIDE	70–75	Heart-shaped to Roma-shaped, 1½ pounds, red, seedless.	TER
OROMA	85–90	Determinate; cylindrical, 3–3½ inches long, 4 ounces; sets in clusters of 4–7 fruit.	TER
PEASANT	67	Determinate; Roma-shaped, 3–4 ounces, thick walls; Siberian variety; yields about 100 tomatoes per plant.	HIG
POLISH PASTE	75–85	Indeterminate; pear-shaped, large.	SEED

VARIETY	DAYS	DESCRIPTION	SOURCES (p. 385)

TOMATOES (PASTE) *(continued)*

VARIETY	DAYS	DESCRIPTION	SOURCES (p. 385)
PRINCIPE BORGHESE	75	Determinate; plum-shaped, with a pointed end, 2 ounces, few seeds.	ABU COO JLH RED SEE SEED TOM
RED ROCK	75	Large, round, chunky tomato for paste.	ORG
ROMA VF	75–78	Determinate; bright red, 3 inches long, pear-shaped.	ABU ALL BURG BURP BURR COM DEG FAR HEN LED LEJ LIB MEY NIC PAR PIN PON SEE SEED SOU STO TOM TOMA VER WIL WILL
ROPRECO	70	Determinate; brilliant red, about 10 tomatoes per pound; good short season variety.	ORG SEED
ROSSOL	70	Determinate; large, 2–3-ounce paste tomato.	SEED TOM
ROYAL CHICO VFN	75–80	Determinate; bright red, 3½ ounces.	TOM TOMA
SAN MARZANO	75–80	Indeterminate; pear-shaped, 3½ inches long; intense flavor.	ABU BURG BUT COO GLE JLH LIB ORG PIN ROS STO TOM TOMA WILL
SAN MARZANO LARGE	75	Indeterminate; deep red, 2 ounces, pear-shaped.	TOM
SAN PABLO	75	Determinate; red, 2 ounces, plum type.	TOM
SAN REMO (hybrid)	76	Indeterminate; shape of a fat, elongated sausage; crimson; resistant to verticillium and fusarium; Italian variety.	SHE
SAUCEY	75–85	Determinate; blunt, plum-shaped, red; concentrated clusters of 5–10 tomatoes.	TER
SAUSAGE	78	Indeterminate; red paste tomato, up to 6 inches long; heirloom variety.	GLE TOM TOMA
SHOWELL'S RED	80	Indeterminate; large, red-orange paste tomato.	SEED
SQUARE PASTE TOMATO	74	Determinate; 2-inch diameter, square-round, crimson red; fruit ripens all at once; tolerant to disease; resistant to cracking.	STO TOM TOMA
SUPER ITALIAN PASTE	75	Indeterminate; 4x6 inches, red.	SEE
SUPER ROMA VF	70	Determinate; plum-shaped, red, nearly seedless; resistant to disease.	THO
VEEPICK VF	73	Determinate; elongated, flat sides, blunt ends, 3¼x2 inches; peels easily.	STO TOM
VEEROMA VF	72	Determinate; medium red Roma type; resistant to cracking.	STO TOM
VIVA ITALIA FVNSTA (hybrid)	76–80	Determinate; red, 5½ inches long, 3 ounces; resistant to disease; widely adapted.	BURP BURR GOU LED LIB NIC PAR POR TER TOMA VER WILL
YELLOW BELL	60	Indeterminate; 3x1½ inches, creamy yellow; survives cool, wet conditions; rare Tennessee heirloom variety.	SOU

VARIETY	DAYS	DESCRIPTION	SOURCES (p. 385)
TOMATOES (GREENHOUSE)			
BOA	75	Beefsteak type; red, with semigreen shoulders; medium vigor; good tolerance to cracking; resistant to disease.	STO TWI
BUFFALO (hybrid)	75	Beefsteak type; 10 ounces, red, no green shoulders; disease-resistant, vigorous, tall vine.	JOH
CARUSO (hybrid)	75	This short, open plant sets and yields under cooler greenhouse temperatures.	STO
COBRA (hybrid)	75	Large, firm, 8 ounces; beefsteak type; resistant to disease.	STO TWI
DOMBO (hybrid) (Jumbo)	75	Red, 5–8 ounces; 12 fruit clusters per plant; tolerant to disease.	STO TOM
FURON (hybrid)	75	Red, 6½–7 ounces; tolerant to disease.	STO
GREENHOUSE 109 VT (hybrid)	78	Indeterminate; large, smooth, red fruit; vigorous, high yielding plants.	TOMA
GREENHOUSE 656 VFFNT (hybrid)	75	Indeterminate; midsize fruit; good yields.	TOMA
HYBRID PINK CR–864	75	These rose-pink, 8-ounce globes are recommended as cooler, early spring crops. (They may crack in extreme heat.) Variety has good tolerance to fusarium crown rot.	STO
HYBRID PINK KR–381	75	Extralarge, pink, 8½ ounces; tolerant to fusarium crown rot.	STO
MATCH	75	8½-ounce, red globes with green shoulders; tolerant to fusarium crown rot and russeting; for summer growing.	STO
MEDALLION	75	This red, 8½-ounce beefsteak type is a spring or fall crop. Plants are open and tolerant to fusarium crown rot.	STO
SIERRA (hybrid)	75	Oblate, red, 7 ounces; resistant to disease.	JOH
TREND	75	Deep red, 7½ ounces, similar to Jumbo in shape; a fall crop.	STO
VENDOR VF	75	Bright red, 8-ounce globe; semicompact plant; some disease tolerance.	HIG
VENDOR VFT	75	6 ounces, red, no green shoulders; disease tolerance.	STO TOM

TOMATOES (HEART-SHAPED)

VARIETY	DAYS	DESCRIPTION	SOURCES (p. 385)
ANNA RUSSIAN	70	Indeterminate; large, pinkish red, up to 1 pound; wispy vine; heirloom variety.	TOMA
DINNER PLATE	90–100	Indeterminate; red, 1½–2 pounds; heirloom variety.	SEED TOM TOMA

VARIETY	DAYS	DESCRIPTION	SOURCES (p. 385)

TOMATOES (HEART-SHAPED) *(continued)*

VARIETY	DAYS	DESCRIPTION	SOURCES
GIANTISSIMO	85	Indeterminate; red, 2½ pounds, few seeds.	NIC
GRIGHTMIRES PRIDE	65	Indeterminate; large, pinkish red; low acidity; Yugoslavian variety.	WILL
JUNG'S GIANT OXHEART	90	Indeterminate; deep pink, almost solid meat, with few seeds.	JUN
MARVEL STRIPED	90–110	Indeterminate; large, orange skin with red stripes, multicolored flesh; Mexican variety.	SEED
MONIX (hybrid)	70–75	Determinate; 3–4 ounces, red; resistant to cracking; Dutch seed.	TER
MOTHER RUSSIA	72	Indeterminate; a perfect heart, 4 inches in diameter, 10–12 ounces, pink, dense, meaty; Russian variety.	HIG
OXHEART ORANGE	85–90	Indeterminate; meaty, golden orange tomato.	GLE TOM TOMA
OXHEART PINK	90–95	Indeterminate; pink, up to 2 pounds, almost seedless.	BURG COM DEG FAR TOM TOMA
OXHEART YELLOW	75–90	Indeterminate; bright yellow, up to 1 pound; low disease tolerance; 1915 heirloom variety.	SEE TOM
VERNA ORANGE	84	Indeterminate; huge, orange; semihollow seed cavity; Indiana heirloom variety.	SOU

TOMATOES (WHITE)

VARIETY	DAYS	DESCRIPTION	SOURCES
GREAT WHITE	85	Indeterminate; large, white beefsteak type; heirloom variety.	GLE TOM TOMA
WHITE BEAUTY (Snowball)	80–84	Indeterminate; 8 ounces, ivory skin and paper white flesh; low acidity; low disease resistance.	BURG FAR GLE SEE SOU TOM TOMA
WHITE POTATO LEAF	80	Indeterminate; large, white tomato.	TOM
WHITE WONDER	85	Indeterminate; medium-size, creamy white skin and flesh; low acidity.	GUR HEN JLH JUN SOU TOM

TOMATOES (TOMATILLO—GROUND CHERRY, HUSK TOMATO)

VARIETY	DAYS	DESCRIPTION	SOURCES
AUNT MOLLY'S	65–70	This ground cherry from Poland turns golden orange and drops to the ground when ripe. It has papery husk like a tomatillo. Store it for up to 3 months.	TER
COSSACK PINEAPPLE	60	These bite-size berries ripen to pineapple yellow. The 12–18-inch plant has spreading lateral branches.	SOU
GOLDIE	75	Ground cherry; ½–¾-inch diameter; golden fruit inside papery husk; prolific plant.	JOH JUN SOU TOM TOMA

VARIETY	DAYS	DESCRIPTION	SOURCES (p. 385)

TOMATOES (TOMATILLO—GROUND CHERRY, HUSK TOMATO) *(continued)*

VARIETY	DAYS	DESCRIPTION	SOURCES (p. 385)
GROUND CHERRY (Strawberry Tomato, Goldenberry, Cape Gooseberry)	70–100	The 2¼-inch fruit ripens to yellow inside thin, papery husks.	ABU BURG COM COO DEG FAR FIS HOR RED SEE STO TOM VER
INDIAN STRAIN	55	This tomatillo is smaller and sweeter than most.	TER
MEXICAN STRAIN	65	Tomatillo; 2 inches in diameter; heavy yields.	TER
TOMATILLO (Toma Verde, Mexican Green, Green Husk, Tomate Verde)	60–95	The tomatillo is a member of the tomato family, though not a real tomato. Round, green tomatillos have papery husks. They are used in Mexican dishes.	ABU BURP COM COO GAR HEN JOH LIB PIN PLA POR RED SEE SEED SOU TER TIL TOMA VER WIL
TOMATILLA DE MILPA (Tomatillo Purple, The Purple Field, Purple de Milpa)	70	1–2-inch, 2–3-ounce, purple-tinged fruit with sharp flavor; rambling plant.	ABU RED SOU TOM
VERDE PUEBLA	90	Tennis-ball-size tomatillos in papery husks.	GUR
YELLOW HUSK (Ground Cherry)	70–85	Cherry-size, deep golden yellow, very sweet fruit; resistant to heat and drought.	FIS GUR TOMA WILL

TOMATOES (OTHER VARIETIES/TYPES)

VARIETY	DAYS	DESCRIPTION	SOURCES (p. 385)
BANANA LEGS	72–75	Elongated, 2-ounce fruit; low acidity.	SEED
BIG RAINBOW	90–102	Indeterminate; 2-pound bicolored beefsteak; light yellow shoulders, golden orange center, ruby red at blossom end; heirloom variety.	COO SOU TOMA
COSTOLUTO GENOVESE (Ribbed Genova)	78–80	Fruit is 3 inches, 5 ounces, slightly ribbed, and scarlet. This determinate variety comes in 2 sizes, medium and large. A Northern Italian heirloom variety, it does well in hot weather.	RED SEE SEED SHE SOU TOMA
EGG TOMATO	75	Egg-size tomato with solid, red flesh; no acidity; keeps indefinitely.	GLE
EVERGREEN TOMATO (Emerald Evergreen)	70–72	Indeterminate; green when ripe; low acidity.	GLE SEE TOM TOMA
GEORGIA STREAK	91	Indeterminate; beefsteak type; yellow and red, inside and out; Georgia heirloom variety.	SOU
GRANDMA OLIVER'S GREEN	75	Indeterminate; bright green flesh, skin tinged amber when ripe.	TOM
GREEN ZEBRA	86	Indeterminate; ripens to yellow-gold with alternating dark green stripes; emerald green flesh; elongated globe; some slightly ridged at shoulder; 3 ounces.	SOU
JERSEY DEVIL	80	Indeterminate; red, 2–6 ounces; long, tapering to a point; sweet, with few seeds.	TOM

VARIETY	DAYS	DESCRIPTION	SOURCES (p. 385)

TOMATOES (OTHER VARIETIES/TYPES) *(continued)*

VARIETY	DAYS	DESCRIPTION	SOURCES (p. 385)
JERSEY GIANT	80	Indeterminate; red, 4–12 ounces; Jersey Devil type, but larger and less slender; irregular yet crack-free.	TOM
LIBERTY BELL	80	Indeterminate; red, bell-shaped stuffing tomato with a small core; no acidity.	GLE TOM
MARVEL STRIPED	80	Golden orange-red, 1 pound or more; needs long growing season; does not do well in cool, wet conditions; Chilean variety.	ABU
M'SIA	80	2–2½ inches across, slightly asymmetrical yet almost round, with faint ribbing and slight nipple at end; Malaysian variety.	RED
OLYMPIC FLAME	90	Red and yellow, 12–24 ounces; resistant to disease.	SEE
PINEAPPLE	80	This indeterminate variety is yellow with red streaks starting at the bottom. The tomato looks like a peach when cut up.	GLE TOM TOMA
PRUDEN'S PURPLE	85	Indeterminate; large, deep red with purple tint; resists cracking from overwatering.	SEED
RED STUFFER	75–85	Indeterminate; bright red, round, 3 inches in diameter; completely hollow.	SEED
STRIPED CAVERN	80	Bicolored, hollow tomato.	SEE
STRIPED GERMAN	78	Indeterminate; flat, medium to large, red and yellow, with ribbed shoulders; German variety.	JOH
THAI ROUND GREEN (Green Tomato)	65	Used in Oriental cooking, this fruit resembles a green tomato.	THE
TIGERELLA (OP) (Mr. Stripey)	55–65	Indeterminate; red and yellow stripes, 1½–2 inches; English variety.	ABU GLE JLH SEE SEED THO TOM TOMA
ZAPOTEC RIBBED (Zapotec Pleated)	80–85	Indeterminate; 2–4 pounds, 3½ inches in diameter, pink, hollow, ruffled; Mexican variety.	SEED

TURNIPS

BOTANICAL NAME: *Brassica rapa*

DAYS TO MATURITY: 28–80.

PLANTING TIME: Plant turnips four to six weeks before the last frost. In regions where winter temperatures rarely fall below 25°F, start successive planting in late summer.

SOIL: Turnips do best in loamy soils but will grow in any soil supplied with phosphates. Avoid fresh manure; pH 5.5–7.0.

NUTRIENTS: The only fertilizing turnips might need is a light application of organic nitrogen when the plants are 5–6 inches high.

WATER: Keep well watered.

LIGHT: Full sun.

SPACING: Sow seeds ½ inch deep, 4 inches apart. Rows should be 12–15 inches apart.

HARVEST: Gather your turnips when they are young and tender—about 2–2½ inches in diameter. Grasp the tops, and pull them up.

STORAGE: Hardy varieties can stay in the ground until you need them. Alternatively, you can cut the tops off and store turnips boxed in layers of dry sand or peat.

Turnip Growing Tip

Aborted Roots

Sometimes turnips go to seed in the spring before good roots can form because the plants have been overexposed to 40°F temperatures. To avoid this problem, plant them in the spring four to six weeks before the last frost. In areas where late spring and summer have many days in the 80s, plant for a fall harvest.

VARIETY	DAYS	DESCRIPTION	SOURCES (p. 385)
TURNIPS (WHITE)			
ALL SEASONS	28	This globe-shaped root with white flesh stays sweet even in hot weather.	SEE
CROISSY (de Croissey)	40	Elongated, 6–9 inches at harvest size; creamy white, resembling a daikon radish; resistant to disease.	PIN SEE
GILFEATHER	80–82	This large, white globe with green shoulders is a Vermont heirloom variety. Its green tops resemble kale.	COO PIN VER
JUST RIGHT (hybrid)	60	White globe, 5–6 inches across; glossy, tender greens in 28 days; for fall sowing; bolts easily.	BURG POR TWI
MARKET EXPRESS (hybrid)	38	Harvest these white globes young for baby turnips or let them grow to be 2–3 inches in diameter. The dark green tops are hairless.	JOH ORN SHE
PRESTO	30	Small, pure white; fast-growing Japanese variety.	NIC
SNOWBALL	40	Snow white, 3-inch globe with white flesh.	BOU
TOKYO CROSS (hybrid)	35	White globe, up to 6 inches across; good resistance to viruses; All-American winner.	BURP FIS GUR HEN JUN MEY PIN POR TWI VER WILL
TOKYO MARKET	28–56	White globe; Japanese variety; for spring or fall sowing.	DEG GLE NIC
VERTUS	50–60	Cylindrical, white; 12–18-inch-tall tops; use when young.	GOU

TURNIPS

VARIETY	DAYS	DESCRIPTION	SOURCES (p. 385)

TURNIPS (WHITE) *(continued)*

VARIETY	DAYS	DESCRIPTION	SOURCES
WHITE EGG	50–55	Egg-shaped, 2 inches, pure white; winter variety.	COM JLH SEE TIL
WHITE KNIGHT (hybrid)	60–75	Pure white semiglobe.	LIB
WHITE LADY (hybrid)	34–45	Semiround, 2½ inches in diameter; 20-inch tops; widely adapted; some bolting tolerance.	ORN PAR POR STO TWI
YORII SPRING	38	Small, white, flattened globe; Japanese variety.	GAR HIG

TURNIPS (PURPLE TOP)

VARIETY	DAYS	DESCRIPTION	SOURCES
PURPLE-TOP WHITE GLOBE (OP)	45–60	5-inch diameter; bright purple top, creamy white bottom; pre-1890 heirloom variety.	ABU ALL BURG BURR BUT COM DEG FIS GAR GUR HEN HIG JOH JUN LED LEJ LIB MEY PAR PIN PON POR ROS SEE SEED SOU STO TER TIL TWI VER WIL WILL
ROYAL CROWN (hybrid)	52	White semiglobe, 14 ounces, 4 inches across; 21-inch, purple tops.	GUR HEN MEY PAR PIN TWI
ROYAL GLOBE II (hybrid)	50	White globe; purple top, bright glossy green tops.	LIB POR
STRAP LEAF PURPLE-TOP FLAT (Purple Top Flat Strapleaf)	47	White, flattened globe, 2–4½ inches in diameter; purple-red tops; pre-1845 heirloom variety.	TIL

TURNIPS (OTHER COLORS)

VARIETY	DAYS	DESCRIPTION	SOURCES
AMBER	75	6-inch, yellowish globe with yellow flesh; for fall sowing.	MEY POR SEE
DE MILAN (Milan Early Red Top, Red Milan)	35	Harvest the white globe at 2x4 inches, as a baby turnip. This French variety thrives in cool weather. Tops are rosy red.	GOU PIN SEE SHE
EARLY ITALIAN WHITE RED TOP	60	Sow seeds in early spring. Pick the turnips when they are 3–4 inches wide.	WILL
GOLDEN BALL (Orange Jelly)	45–65	Round, yellow, 4 inches across; yellow flesh; 1859 heirloom variety.	ABU BOU GLE JLH NIC ORN WILL
OHNO SCARLET (OP)	55	The red, irregularly shaped roots have white flesh. The 15–18-inch, green tops have red veins.	ORN SEE
SCARLET BALL	30	The slightly flattened, deep scarlet semiglobe with white flesh looks like a beet. The green foliage of this Japanese variety has red veins.	GLE NIC
SCARLETT QUEEN (hybrid)	45	Scarlet semiglobe, 4½ inches in diameter, with white flesh; resistant to downy mildew.	ORN PAR
TSUGARU SCARLET (hybrid)	55	Globe with red skin and white flesh; 20-inch-tall tops.	GLE

VARIETY	DAYS	DESCRIPTION	SOURCES (p. 385)

TURNIPS (OTHER COLORS) *(continued)*

VARIETY	DAYS	DESCRIPTION	SOURCES
YELLOW GLOBE	70	Light yellow globe; keeps well in winter.	COM

TURNIPS (FOR GREENS ONLY)

VARIETY	DAYS	DESCRIPTION	SOURCES
ALL TOP (hybrid)	50	Does not form roots; large, broad, smooth, green leaves on sturdy, green stems.	PAR TWI
SEVEN TOP (OP) (Winter Greens, Southern Prize, Foliage Turnip)	45	Tops will grow to 18–22 inches tall, but harvest them young. This pre-1880 Southern heirloom variety grows a tough root.	COM LED LIB MEY SOU STO TWI WIL
SHOGOIN	35–70	Globe-shaped roots; 18–20-inch, upright tops.	COM DEG LEJ NIC POR ROS TER VER WIL
TOPPER (hybrid)	60–80	Seven Top type; 28 inches tall; thick, smooth, lobed, dark green leaves.	LIB TWI
TURNIP TOPS GREEN	60	The smooth, green leaves should be cut at 6 inches. They will grow back for more cutting.	WILL

WATERMELON

BOTANICAL NAME: *Citrullus vulgaris*

DAYS TO MATURITY: 65–100.

PLANTING TIME: Transplant watermelon outside when night temperatures reach 55°F and daytime temperatures are no lower than 80°F. In the warmer parts of the state, you can plant in the ground in springtime.

SOIL: Light, sandy; pH 6.0.

NUTRIENTS: Feed the plants every six weeks with fish emulsion.

WATER: Water thoroughly in dry weather. Keep a 6-inch-deep trench around each plant to fill as needed. Do not keep the soil soaked, and do not overhead water.

LIGHT: Full sun.

SPACING: All melons spread (except the bush variety) and need plenty of space. Sow seeds 1 inch deep, 12 inches apart. For row gardening, space rows 4–6 feet apart.

HARVEST: Thump them: ripe melons have a dull sound. The discolored spots on the melon bellies turn from white to pale yellow when the fruits are ready.

STORAGE: Use fresh or pickled.

WATERMELON

Watermelon Growing Tips

Off the Ground

To make midget watermelons even sweeter, set each small melon up on a small can, such as a tomato sauce can. This makes them ripen faster and helps increase the sugar content.

Vertical Melon Patch

You can grow a vertical watermelon patch in your garden by running nylon cord up an open A-frame. Tie the cord to a wire strung across the bottom. As the vines grow, attach them to the cord with garbage-bag ties. Train them upward until they grow over the top of the structure and then let them ramble down the other side. The growing fruits will balance each other and hence won't pull the vines down. Even though the melons are heavy, most of them will hang. To keep them from blowing down in the wind, you can support them with slings made from garden netting or panty hose.

VARIETY	DAYS	DESCRIPTION	SOURCES (p. 385)
WATERMELON (ICEBOX)			
EARLY MIDGET	65	5–6 pounds; light green rind with dark stripes, red flesh; 8 fruit per vine.	PLA
GARDEN BABY (hybrid)	70	Round, 6–8 pounds; bright red flesh.	VER
GOLDEN MIDGET	65	With red flesh and black seeds, this melon measures 8 inches in diameter. The green rind turns golden yellow when ripe.	SEE
JADE STAR (hybrid)	85	15 pounds, round to oval; dark green rind, bright red flesh with small, brown seeds; resistant to fusarium.	FAR GUR TER
MALALI	90	8–10 pounds; very thin rind, red flesh with tan, black-ringed seeds; requires a hot summer.	SEED
MICKEYLEE	75–80	6½–7 pounds, round, 6½ inches in diameter; hard, light green rind, dark red flesh; tolerant to disease; Plant Variety Patented (PVP).	BURR GAR LIB PIN STO WIL WILL
MINILEE	78	4–15 pounds; tough, light green rind, intensely red flesh, with few seeds; tolerant to disease; Plant Variety Patented (PVP).	POR WIL
NEW HAMPSHIRE MIDGET	68	Nearly round, 6x5½ inches.	VER

VARIETY	DAYS	DESCRIPTION	SOURCES (p. 385)

WATERMELON (ICEBOX) (continued)

VARIETY	DAYS	DESCRIPTION	SOURCES (p. 385)
SUGAR BABY (OP)	68–96	6–12 pounds, 6–8 inches across, round; hard, dark green rind, dark red flesh with few seeds; widely adapted.	ABU ALL BOU BURG BURP BURR BUT COM DEG GAR GOU HEN JOH JUN LED LEJ MEY ORG PIN PLA PON POR ROS SHE SOU STO TER TWI VER WIL WILL
SUGAR DOLL (hybrid)	72	Round, 8–10 pounds, 8–inch diameter; dark green rind, red flesh.	LED
SWEET BABY (hybrid)	60–86	8–15 pounds, 8½–9-inch diameter; tough, dark green rind, bright red flesh with small, brown seeds; tolerant to fusarium.	SEED TWI
TIGER BABY	80	Oval, 7–10 pounds, 7x9½ inches; light gray-green rind with medium green stripes, pink-red flesh; tolerant to fusarium.	LED STO TWI WILL
YOU SWEET THING (hybrid)	70	12–13 pounds, round; striped rind, rose-colored flesh with a high sugar content.	NIC

WATERMELON (OBLONG, GREEN RIND)

VARIETY	DAYS	DESCRIPTION	SOURCES (p. 385)
AMISH MOON AND STARS	90	This oblong, 25–30-pound melon's dark green rind has large, yellow moons and small stars. The foliage is covered with yellow stars. The reddish pink flesh contains brown seed, slightly mottled with beige.	ABU BOU PIN SHE
FAMILY FUN (hybrid)	80	13–15 pounds; tough rind, red flesh; tolerant to disease.	GLE NIC
FAR NORTH	70	6–8 pounds; bright red flesh, black seeds.	FIS
KLECKLEY SWEET (Monte Carlo)	87	25–40 pounds, square ends; bright scarlet flesh.	JLH
KLECKLEY SWEET IMPROVED (Wonder Melon)	85	Long melon with thin rind and bright red flesh.	COM
KLONDIKE PEACOCK IMPROVED	80–90	20–22 pounds, rounded to blocky in shape; thin, tough rind, bright orange-red flesh.	ROS
KLONDYKE WILT RESISTANT NO. 6	85	35 pounds; dark green rind.	MEY
MOON AND STARS, LONG MILKY WAY	95	Elongated, 35 pounds; dark green rind speckled with bright yellow, pinpoint stars; bright red flesh.	SOU
NORTHERN SWEET (4th of July)	68	15 pounds; deep red flesh.	SEE
PEACOCK WR–60	88	20–25 pounds; bright red flesh, almost black seeds.	WIL
STONE MOUNTAIN (OP)	85–90	Oval, 30–40 pounds; medium-thick, dark green rind, scarlet flesh, with few seeds; resistant to fusarium.	SEE SOU

VARIETY	DAYS	DESCRIPTION	SOURCES (p. 385)

WATERMELON (OBLONG, GREEN RIND) *(continued)*

VARIETY	DAYS	DESCRIPTION	SOURCES
TOM WATSON	90	35–40 pounds, 22x12 inches; deep red flesh with large, brown seeds.	WIL

WATERMELON (OBLONG, GRAYISH RIND)

VARIETY	DAYS	DESCRIPTION	SOURCES
CALHOUN GRAY (OP)	85	20–25 pounds, 10x24 inches; improved Charleston Gray type; bright red flesh; resistant to fusarium wilt.	TWI WIL
CHARLEE	87	23 pounds, 17x18 inches; red flesh with large black seeds; tolerant to disease; Plant Variety Patented (PVP).	WIL
CHARLESTON GRAY 5	90	30–40 pounds; resistant to disease.	BURG
CHARLESTON GRAY 133 (OP)	85	More wilt-resistant and uniform in shape than the original.	BURR LIB TWI WIL
CHARLESTON GREY (Charleston Gray)	85–90	20–40 pounds, 24x10 inches; tough, green-gray rind, deep red flesh; tolerant to disease; heirloom variety.	BURP BURR HEN LED LEJ MEY PON POR ROS SEE VER
CHUBBY GRAY	90	28–30 pounds, blocky, oblong; gray rind, red flesh; Plant Variety Patented (PVP).	WIL
TOP YIELD (hybrid)	80	Oblong, 25–35 pounds; thick, gray-green rind, red flesh with small seeds; resistant to anthracnose and tolerant to fusarium.	TWI

WATERMELON (OBLONG, STRIPED)

VARIETY	DAYS	DESCRIPTION	SOURCES
ALLSWEET (OP)	90–104	25–45 pounds; dark green rind with dark stripes, bright red flesh; Crimson Sweet type; tolerant to disease.	BURR LED POR TWI WIL
AU JUBILANT (OP)	90–95	25–30 pounds; light green rind with dark stripes, deep red flesh; Jubilee type; Plant Variety Patented (PVP).	TWI WIL
CALSWEET	92	Blocky, 25–30 pounds; light green rind with dark stripes, intensely red flesh with dark seeds; resistant to fusarium; Plant Variety Patented (PVP).	TWI WIL
CANADA SUPER-SWEET (hybrid)	70	22 pounds; light green rind with dark stripes; tolerant to fusarium.	STO
CONGO	90	30–40 pounds; tough, medium green rind with dark stripes; bright red flesh, with gray-white seeds; resistant to anthracnose; All-American winner.	BURP MEY WIL
DESERT STORM (hybrid)	80–85	22–25 pounds; tough, medium green rind with darker green stripes, red flesh, with small, mottled brown seeds; tolerant to fusarium wilt.	WIL
EARLY JUBILEE	85	As large and flavorful as the standard Jubilees; tolerant to disease.	LED

VARIETY	DAYS	DESCRIPTION	SOURCES (p. 385)

WATERMELON (OBLONG, STRIPED) *(continued)*

VARIETY	DAYS	DESCRIPTION	SOURCES (p. 385)
FIESTA (hybrid)	85	22–26 pounds; light green rind with dark green broken stripes, dark red flesh.	BURR TWI WIL
GARRISON	85–90	34–45 pounds, 12x24 inches; deep red flesh, tan seeds with dark tips; resistant to anthracnose.	WIL
HUCK FINN (hybrid)	85	20–25 pounds; dark green rind with dark stripes, reddish pink flesh, small seeds.	WIL
JUBILEE	95	25–40 pounds, 13x24 inches; bright red flesh, dark seeds; resistant to some anthracnose.	BURR HEN LED MEY POR ROS WIL
JUBILEE II	95	30 pounds; dark red flesh; resistant to disease.	WIL
JUBILEE REGISTERED (OP)	95	24–30 pounds; light green rind with dark green stripes, bright red flesh; resistant to fusarium; produced from Florida foundation seed to maintain genetic purity.	BURR TWI
KLONDYKE SUGAR	78–90	25 pounds; scarlet flesh with a high sugar content.	BURG
LONG CRIMSON	85	25–28 pounds; bright red flesh, black seeds; Plant Variety Patented (PVP).	WIL
LOUISIANA SWEET	90	23–30 pounds; medium green rind with dark green stripes, brilliant red flesh; midsize black-stippled seeds; tolerant to disease; Plant Variety Patented (PVP).	WIL
MIRAGE (hybrid)	85	25–30 pounds; light green rind with dark stripes; deep red flesh; tolerant to fusarium wilt.	DEG WIL
NANCY	90	25 pounds, 14x16 inches; green striped rind, pink-red flesh, white seeds; average disease tolerance; excellent drought resistance; 1885 Georgia heirloom variety.	WIL
PARKER (hybrid)	80–85	22–25 pounds; tough, tricolored, thin rind, red flesh; tolerant to fusarium.	WIL
PATRIOT (hybrid)	80–85	22–25 pounds; light green rind with medium green stripes, red flesh with small, mottled brown seed; tolerant to fusarium.	WIL
RATTLESNAKE (Garrisonian)	90	35–40 pounds, 22x10 inches; bright rose flesh.	GUR WIL
REGENCY (hybrid)	82	20–25 pounds; medium green striped rind, bright red flesh; tolerant to fusarium.	TWI
ROYAL JUBILEE (hybrid)	90	25–30 pounds; medium green striped rind, bright red flesh, medium-small seeds; resistant to fusarium.	BURR POR TWI WIL
ROYAL MAJESTY (hybrid)	80	30 pounds, 11x24 inches; bright red flesh, small, dark seeds; tolerant to fusarium.	TWI
ROYAL SWEET (hybrid)	85	20–25 pounds; medium green striped rind, bright red flesh, small, dark seeds; resistant to fusarium.	TWI WIL

VARIETY	DAYS	DESCRIPTION	SOURCES (p. 385)
WATERMELON (OBLONG, STRIPED) *(continued)*			
RUBY GEM	85	10–20 pounds; green and white striped rind.	SEED
SANGRIA (hybrid)	85	20–26 pounds; deep green patterned rind, bright red flesh, medium-size, dark seeds; tolerant to disease.	BURR JUN LIB POR TWI WILL
STAR BRITE (hybrid)	85	29 pounds; tough, light green rind with dark green stripes, red flesh, large seeds; tolerant to disease.	WIL
STOKES SUGAR (hybrid)	70	15 pounds; medium green rind with indistinct stripes, deep rose flesh.	STO
STRAWBERRY	85	15–25 pounds, 8x20 inches; dark green rind with darker green stripes, strawberry-red flesh ripens to ½ inch of rind; good disease resistance; Florida heirloom variety.	SOU
STRIPED BLUE RIBBON KLONDIKE	80	20 pounds; moderately tough rind with irregular stripes, deep red flesh.	ROS
SUGAR BOWL (hybrid)	82	20–25 pounds; distinctively striped rind, deep red flesh.	BURP
SUMMER FESTIVAL	88	10–15 pounds; light green rind with green veins, bright red-pink flesh.	LIB
SUMMER FLAVOR BRAND VARIETY 400 (hybrid)	85	25 pounds; medium green rind with broad, dark stripes, bright red flesh.	TWI
SUMMER FLAVOR BRAND VARIETY 410 (hybrid)	85	25 pounds; medium green rind with broad, dark stripes, bright red flesh.	TWI
SUMMER FLAVOR BRAND VARIETY 610 (hybrid)	90	25–30 pounds; medium green striped rind, deep red flesh.	TWI
SUMMER FLAVOR BRAND VARIETY 700 (hybrid)	85	22–28 pounds; light green rind with dark stripes, bright red flesh.	TWI
SUMMER FLAVOR BRAND VARIETY 710 (hybrid)	85	30 pounds; light green rind with narrow, green stripes, bright red flesh.	TWI
SUNNY'S PRIDE (hybrid)	85	22–26 pounds; dark green rind with broken, light green stripes, bright red flesh, dark brown seeds; tolerant to disease.	WIL
SUN SWEET (OP)	85	18–24 pounds; striped rind, bright red flesh; tolerant to disease; Plant Variety Patented (PVP).	TWI
SWEET FAVORITE (hybrid)	64–79	10–20 pounds; red flesh, small seeds; high sugar content; variety for cool areas; All-American winner.	COM HEN JOH JUN STO TWI WILL
SWEET NORTHERN PRIZE	100	7–12 pounds; thinly striped rind ripens almost to black, small, brown seeds; resistant to drought; good variety for short season areas.	SEED

VARIETY	DAYS	DESCRIPTION	SOURCES (p. 385)

WATERMELON (OBLONG, STRIPED) *(continued)*

VARIETY	DAYS	DESCRIPTION	SOURCES
SWEET PRINCESS	90	25 pounds; tough, thick rind, deep pink-red flesh, with exceptionally small seeds; some disease tolerance.	WIL
TOP YIELD (hybrid)	82	20 pounds; bright red flesh, small seeds; resistant to anthracnose and fusarium.	TWI

WATERMELON (ROUND, GREEN)

VARIETY	DAYS	DESCRIPTION	SOURCES
ASAHI MIYAKO (Asahi Sugar)	80	12–15 pounds; dark green rind; Japanese variety.	GLE
BLACK DIAMOND (OP) (Cannonball, Florida Giant, Shipper)	75–95	40–70 pounds; very tough, dark green rind, deep red flesh, with large, dark brown seeds.	BURG BURR DEG FAR GUR HEN JUN LED MEY PON ROS SEE TWI VER WIL
BLACK DIAMOND YELLOW BELLY	90	30–40 pounds, 17x19 inches; bright red flesh, black seeds, yellow belly.	BURR POR WIL
BLACKSTONE	85–89	25–35 pounds; red flesh, black stippled seeds.	WIL
COLE'S EARLY (Harris Earliest)	75	Dark green rind; 1892 heirloom variety.	ABU
FORDHOOK (hybrid) (Burpee's Fordhook)	75	12–14 pounds; glossy, dark green rind, bright red flesh, few seeds.	BURP
GLORY SUGAR (hybrid)	79	10 pounds; very dark green rind, red flesh.	PIN
KING & QUEEN WINTER (Winter Melon, Winterkeeper)	80–90	15–20 pounds; 8x12 inches; light green rind, bright red flesh.	BURR DEG HEN NIC PLA RED VER
LEDMON	85	20 pounds; thin, dark rind, pink-red flesh; resistant to disease; heirloom variety.	SOU
MOON AND STARS, PLANETS AND STARS	100	The rind of this 25-pound melon has characteristic yellow stars with much smaller moons than Amish Moon and Stars. Foliage is covered with yellow stars. Ivory seeds have brown tips.	ORN PIN SOU
VERONA	80	30–40 pounds; Black Diamond type; medium rose flesh, black seeds.	WIL

WATERMELON (ROUND, STRIPED)

VARIETY	DAYS	DESCRIPTION	SOURCES
AU PRODUCER	90	20–25 pounds; light green rind with dark green stripes, pink-red flesh; resistant to disease; Plant Variety Patented (PVP).	TWI WIL
BIG CRIMSON	90	30 pounds; larger than but otherwise identical to Crimson Sweet; Plant Variety Patented (PVP).	WIL

VARIETY	DAYS	DESCRIPTION	SOURCES (p. 385)
WATERMELON (ROUND, STRIPED) *(continued)*			
CARMEN (hybrid)	86	22–25 pounds; medium green rind with dark stripes, red flesh, dark seeds; Crimson Sweet type; resistant to disease.	LIB TWI
CRIMSON SWEET (OP)	80–96	23–27 pounds; 10x12 inches; tough, light green rind with dark green stripes, dark red flesh; tolerant to disease; high sugar content; All-American winner.	ABU BOU BURG BURP BURR COM DEG GUR HEN JUN LED LIB MEY PON POR ROS SOU STO TER TWI WIL
CRIMSON TIDE (hybrid)	84	22–26 pounds; bright red flesh; tolerant to disease.	TWI
DIXIELEE (OP)	90–92	20–30 pounds; tough, light green rind with dark green stripes.	TWI WIL
DIXIE QUEEN (hybrid)	90	30–50 pounds, 12x15 inches; deep red flesh; tolerant to fusarium wilt.	BURG MEY POR SEE
DIXIE QUEEN II (hybrid)	85	Midsize; light green rind with dark green stripes and blotches, red flesh, very few seeds; resistant to wilt.	LED
JUBILATION (hybrid)	84	22–27 pounds; striped rind, medium bright red flesh; resistant to disease.	TWI
NAVAJO SWEET	90	10–20 pounds; pale green rind with dark green stripes.	BURR SEE
NORTHERN SWEET (Early Northern Sweet)	68–78	10–15 pounds; dark red-orange flesh; 1932 heirloom variety.	ABU BURG
RUBY DIAMOND	70–80	20–40 pounds; Black Diamond type; thin, dark green rind, red flesh; tolerant to fusarium.	SEED
SUPER SWEET	90	15 pounds; markings similar to Crimson Sweet; tolerant to disease.	BURR

WATERMELON (OTHER COLORS/TYPES)

VARIETY	DAYS	DESCRIPTION	SOURCES
CREAM OF SASKATCHEWAN	85	Round, up to 10 pounds; pale green rind with darker stripes, creamy white flesh, black seeds; good variety for cool growing areas.	JLH
FUNBELL (hybrid)	85	4–5 pounds; rind's dark green stripes ripen to yellow; deep red flesh.	GUR HEN
GOLDEN CROWN (hybrid)	75	7 pounds; golden rind, red flesh, small seeds; All-American winner.	BURP JUN PAR TWI
HOPI RED (OP)	70	Small to medium; red flesh; antique heirloom variety.	ABU
ICE CREAM, BLACK SEEDED	82	10 pounds; pale green rind with green lines; pink-red flesh; pre-1885 heirloom variety.	SOU
SUN	70	Golden rind, pink to red flesh.	ORN

VARIETY	DAYS	DESCRIPTION	SOURCES (p. 385)

WATERMELON (GIANT)

VARIETY	DAYS	DESCRIPTION	SOURCES
CAROLINA CROSS 183	100	At 200 pounds or more, with a thick rind, this melon needs lots of room to grow and good loamy soil, plus long, hot summers.	BURG BURP FAR GUR HEN LED NIC
COBB GEM	100	130 pounds; grayish black rind, red flesh.	GLE GUR HEN WIL
MOUNTAIN HOOSIER	85	Oblong, 75–80 pounds; dark green rind, deep red flesh, white seeds with black rims and tips; 1937 heirloom variety.	SOU
WHITE SEEDED WATSON	90–95	75–100 pounds; shiny blue-green rind, red flesh; large leaves that prevent sunburn; 1900 heirloom variety.	SEED WIL

WATERMELON (SPACE SAVERS)

VARIETY	DAYS	DESCRIPTION	SOURCES
BABY FUN (hybrid)	82	Midsize, slightly oval; extrasweet; compact vine; tolerates fusarium.	JUN
BUSH BABY II (hybrid)	80	10 pounds; bright red flesh; compact dwarf plant.	PAR
BUSH JUBILEE	95	13 pounds; disease-resistant bush variety; Plant Variety Patented (PVP).	LED MEY PON POR
BUSH SNAKESKIN	100	Oval, 25 pounds; bush plant.	SEED
BUSH SUGAR BABY	80	Oval, 8–12 pounds, 8½–10 inches long; scarlet flesh, medium-small seeds.	BURP BURR
CHARLESTON GRAY BUSH	90	22–40 pounds; gray rind, deep red flesh; resistant to disease; 3–5-foot vine.	DEG
GARDEN BABY (hybrid)	70–75	Round, 6–7-inch diameter; dark green rind; compact vine.	JOH LIB PIN TER TIL
SUGAR BUSH	80	6–8 pounds; medium green rind with dark veining, bright scarlet flesh; 6 square feet needed to grow a 3½-foot vine.	DEG VER
SWEET TREAT (Sweetheart)	85	9–14 pounds; bush type with 5-foot vine; light green rind with dark stripes, scarlet flesh, medium-size seeds.	JUN

WATERMELON (YELLOW/ORANGE FLESH)

VARIETY	DAYS	DESCRIPTION	SOURCES
ARIKARA	85	Dark green rind, pink to yellow flesh, many seeds; heirloom variety from the Arikara Indians.	ABU
AU GOLDEN PRODUCER (OP)	89	Globe, 25 pounds; light green skin with dark green stripes, golden orange flesh; some disease tolerance; Plant Variety Patented (PVP).	LED LIB STO
DESERT KING YELLOW	85	Round to oblong; yellow rind, yellow flesh, grayish black seeds; resistant to drought; will not sunburn.	GUR JLH PLA ROS WIL

VARIETY	DAYS	DESCRIPTION	SOURCES (p. 385)
WATERMELON (YELLOW/ORANGE FLESH) *(continued)*			
EARLY MOONBEAM	80	8–10 pounds; thin rind, yellow flesh; good short season variety.	SEED
GOLDEN HONEY (Golden Honey Sweet)	80	Oblong, 15–30 pounds; dark green mottled and striped rind, golden yellow-orange flesh.	DEG POR SEED
KAHO	85	Oval, 3 pounds; pale green rind with dark stripes, orange-yellow flesh; Chinese variety.	RED
MOON AND STARS, YELLOW FLESHED	95–100	15–40 pounds; dark green rind with yellow splashes for stars and larger splashes for moons, white seeds; some disease and drought tolerance; 1900 heirloom variety.	SEE SEED SHE SOU
ORANGEGLO	85	50 pounds; pale green rind, orange flesh, cream-colored seeds with dark rings and tips.	WIL
PONY YELLOW (hybrid)	75–85	Up to 8 pounds; thin, medium green rind with dark stripes, lemon-yellow flesh.	PIN
SUNSHINE (hybrid)	75	Oval, midsize; striped rind, bright yellow flesh; tolerant to hollow heart.	JOH
TASTIGOLD	80	Round, 22–24 pounds; gray rind, yellow flesh with small, black seeds; good tolerance to wilt.	WIL
TENDERSWEET ORANGE	85–90	35–50 pounds, 18x12 inches; dark green rind with mottled stripes, orange flesh, white seeds.	BURR GLE HEN POR ROS WIL
TENDERSWEET YELLOW	80	30–40 pounds; dark green rind, golden yellow flesh.	SEE
TOHONO O' ODHAM	85	Oval, 40 pounds; green striped rind, yellow flesh; Indian variety.	GLE
WILHITE'S TENDERGOLD	80	22–28 pounds; dark green striped rind, yellow flesh, black seeds.	WIL
YELLOW BABY (hybrid)	70–75	10 pounds, 7-inch diameter; thin, extrahard, light green rind with dark stripes, bright yellow flesh with a few small seeds; All-American winner.	PAR SHE STO
YELLOW CRIMSON	80	Round; striped rind, yellow flesh, black seeds; Plant Variety Patented (PVP).	WIL
YELLOW CUTIE (hybrid)	68	Oval, 3–4 pounds; striped rind, yellow flesh; resistant to disease and heat.	NIC
YELLOW DOLL (hybrid)	70–75	Round, 5–8 pounds; green striped rind, bright yellow flesh with small black seeds; semicompact vines.	BURG COM HEN JUN LED LIB NIC ORG POR TER TWI WIL WILL
YELLOW FLESH BLACK DIAMOND (Wilhite's Yellow Flesh Black Diamond)	90	60–70 pounds; thin, tough, glossy, dark green rind, yellow flesh with small grayish black seeds.	GUR ROS WIL
YELLOW GEM SWEET	78–82	Nearly round; green and light green striped rind, bright yellow flesh.	SEED

VARIETY	DAYS	DESCRIPTION	SOURCES (p. 385)

WATERMELON (YELLOW/ORANGE FLESH) *(continued)*

VARIETY	DAYS	DESCRIPTION	SOURCES
YELLOW ROSE (hybrid)	75	Oblong, 12–15 pounds; yellow flesh.	LIB PON

WATERMELON (SEEDLESS—TRIPLOID)

VARIETY	DAYS	DESCRIPTION	SOURCES
HONEY RED SEEDLESS	65	Round, 8 inches across; light green rind, bright red flesh.	PAR
HYBRID SEEDLESS	80	Oval, 20–24 pounds; striped rind.	BURG FAR
JACK OF HEARTS (hybrid)	85	Oval, 11–13 pounds; light green rind with dark green stripes, bloodred flesh; especially sweet.	BURG JUN LED LIB NIC POR STO VER
KING OF HEARTS	82	Round, 14–18 pounds; dark green rind, bright red flesh.	GUR
NOVA (hybrid)	84	Round to oval, 10–13 pounds; light green rind with dark green stripes, deep red flesh.	JOH
REDBALL SEEDLESS	80	Round, 12 pounds; glossy green rind, red flesh.	BURP
RUBY	85	Round, 15–20 pounds; medium green rind with dark green stripes, bright red flesh.	LIB
SSUPERSWEET BRAND VARIETY 2532 (hybrid) (Triploid)	90	12–15 pounds; thick, tough, light green rind with dark stripes.	TWI
SSUPERSWEET BRAND VARIETY 3731 (hybrid) (Triploid)	90	Round, 12–14 pounds; medium green rind with dark green stripes, red flesh; tolerant to disease.	TWI
SSUPERSWEET BRAND VARIETY 5032 (hybrid) (Triploid)	90	12–16 pounds; light green rind with dark green stripes, bright red flesh; Crimson Sweet type.	TWI
SSUPERSWEET BRAND VARIETY 5244 (hybrid) (Triploid)	90	Oblong, 14–18 pounds; light green rind with dark green stripes, bright red flesh; tolerant to disease.	TWI
SWEET HEART (hybrid)	85	Round; 8–10 pounds, 8–9 inches in diameter; red flesh.	PAR
TIFFANY	70–75	Round, 18–24 pounds; medium green rind with dark green stripes, dark red flesh.	WIL
TRISTAR SWEET 1	78	Oval, 20 pounds; green rind with dark green stripes, bright red flesh; tolerant to disease.	LIB

WATERMELON (EDIBLE SEEDS)

VARIETY	DAYS	DESCRIPTION	SOURCES
GIZA (No. 1 Egyptian)	80	Very large edible seeds.	JLH SEE
KILY EDIBLE SEEDED (hybrid) (Wanli)	80	The globe-shaped melon is grown for its large, very thick seeds. Variety is resistant to disease.	GLE

General Growing Tips

Learning some of gardening's many shortcuts will help the novice gardener grow bigger, juicier crops, and knowledge of some vegetable-growing esoterica will make the work easier for even the experienced gardener. Here are some of the best tips around.

Keeping Vegetables Growing

Okra, cucumbers, beans, and, to a certain extent, zucchini tend to stop producing if the fruits are allowed to stay on the vines. Pick okra and cucumbers every day even if you don't want to eat them. To encourage continual production, pick zucchini at the fingerling (finger-size) stage.

Computer Gardening

Many gardeners enlist their computers' help. Computer programs can establish planting schedules and display layouts based on garden size, food needs, and frost dates. Some software plans vegetable rotation; a few programs offer advice on plant selections for particular climates.

Paper Pulp Pots

No space for vegetables? Then try farming in 12–18-inch paper pulp pots, available at most nurseries. Fill these tubs with a blend of commercially prepared peat moss and vermiculite. Cole crops (of the genus *Brassica*), greens, peppers, and tomatoes grow especially well. The pots are inexpensive and light enough for easy transport from place to place.

Season Extension

There's probably never been a season-extender like an umbrella. Each can protect several plants. At night, push the waterproof dome down until it firmly touches the soil on all sides. On warm days, lift the umbrella up several inches so air can circulate and the plants won't cook.

Pot Vegetables

Surprisingly, according to Dr. John White, a Pennsylvania floriculturist, and Dr. Peter A. Feretti, an All-America Selections judge, you can grow the following vegetables in 6-inch pots:

Vegetable	Plants per 6-inch pot
beet	4–5
chard	3–4
cherry tomato	1
eggplant	1
lettuce, leaf	6–10

Vegetable	Plants per 6-inch pot
lettuce, semiheading	4–6
pepper	1
radish	6–8

The Cook's Garden

To grow a cook's garden that will provide all the vegetables you can eat in less than 54 square feet, plant baby vegetables. The new generation of gourmet varieties will charm you and draw raves from those who share your meals. Summer baby Bibb lettuce, Little Gem romaine, Lollo Rossa loose-leaf lettuce, and baby cabbage are just a fraction of your choices.

Healthy Vegetables

Here are some quick nutrition facts about the vegetables you grow in your garden.

• Kale has the highest calcium content of any vegetable.

• Hot red peppers are the vegetable highest in vitamins A and C.

• Crisphead lettuce is the lowest in calories.

• Pumpkin and squash seeds have the most iron.

• Sunflower seeds are high in fat and fiber.

Hanging Gardens

Vegetables such as Pot Luck cucumber, Florida Basket tomato, and Dusky eggplant thrive in hanging baskets, producing fruit all summer long. Just fill the containers with a soilless mix and plant.

Try the Unusual

To grow some distinctive vegetables, try the long skinny asparagus bean (Chinese long bean), the winged pea (asparagus pea), scarlet runner beans, pear tomatoes, or peppers. There are a number of varieties: Butler, Desiree, Goliath, Prizewinner, Tiny Yellow Pear, and the narrow Italian sweet pepper.

Ethnic Gardening

Gourmet cooks love to sample the flavors of French, Italian, Northern European, Chinese, and Japanese vegetables, but it used to be difficult to find them. Fortunately, it's possible to grow these special regional vegetables in your own garden.

APPENDIX A

SEED CATALOG SOURCES

CODE

CODE

ABU   Abundant Life Seed Foundation
P.O. Box 722
Port Townsend, WA 98368
Order: 206/385.7192
Office: 206/385.5660
Fax: 206/385.7455
$2 donation for catalog
Open pollinated seed

ALL   Allen, Sterling & Lothrop
191 U.S. Route One
Falmouth, ME 04105
Order: 207/781.4142
$1 for mailing

BOU   Bountiful Gardens
18001 Shafer Ranch Road
Willits, CA 95490
Order: 707/459.6410
Free to U.S. addresses
$2 to foreign addresses
Open pollinated varieties, rare varieties
John Jeavons is the mini-farm director.

BURG   Burgess Seed and Plant Co.
905 Four Seasons Road
Bloomington, IL 61701
Order: 309/663.9551
$1 catalog

BURP   W. Atlee Burpee & Co.
300 Park Avenue
Warminster, PA 18974
Order: 800/888.1447
Fax: 215/674.4170
Free catalog

BURR   D. V. Burrell Seed Growers Co.
Rocky Ford, CO 81067
Order: 719/254.3318
Fax: 719/254.3319
Free catalog
This commercial grower also lists small
quantities for the home gardener.

BUT   Butterbrooke Farm
78 Barry Road
Oxford, CT 06478-1529
Order: 203/888.2000
Send a self-addressed, stamped envelope
for price list.
Specializes in pure, untreated, short
maturity seeds

COM   Comstock, Ferre & Co.
Box 125
Wethersfield, CT 06109
Order: 203/529.6255
$3 catalog
Specializes in seeds—packets
to pounds

CODE

COO The Cook's Garden
P.O. Box 535
Londonderry, VT 05148
Order: 802/824.3400
Fax: 802/824.3027
$1 catalog
This company specializes in culinary
vegetables, European salad greens, and hard-
to-find vegetables. It also has trial tests of the
varieties in the catalog.

DEG DeGiorgi Seed Company
6011 N Street
Omaha, NE 68117-1634
Order: 800/858.2580
Fax: 402/731.8475
Information: 402/731.3901
$2 catalog
Vegetable and flower seeds, garden products

FAR Farmer Seed and Nursery
Dept. 58 Reservations Center
1706 Morrissey Drive
Bloomington, IL 61704
Order: 507/334.1623
Free catalog
Vegetable and flower seeds, garden products

FIS Fisher's Seeds
P.O. Box 236
Belgrade, MT 59714
Order: 406/388.6052
Free catalog
High altitude and short season varieties of
both vegetables and flowers

GAR Garden City Seeds
1324 Red Crow Road
Victor, MT 59875-9713
Order: 406/961.4837
$1 catalog
This is an excellent source of high altitude,
short season vegetable varieties as well as
herbs, and it's filled with gardening tips.
Seeds are certified as organically grown.

GLE Glecker's Seedmen
Metamora, OH 43540
Free catalog
Specializes in unusual seeds from around
the world

CODE

GOU The Gourmet Gardener
8650 College Boulevard, Dept. 205TC
Overland Park, KS 66210
Order: 913/345.0490
$2 catalog
The company preselects seeds that are widely
adapted. This is a good source for gourmet and
European vegetables.

GUR Gurney's Seed & Nursery Co.
110 Capital Street
Yankton, SD 57079
Order: 605/665.1930
Fax: 605/665.9718
Customer service: 605/665.1671
Free catalog
Old-fashioned catalog, fun for browsing

HEN Henry Field's Seed & Nursery Co.
415 North Burnett
Shenandoah, IA 51602
Order: 605/665.9391
Fax: 605/665.2601
Customer service: 605/665.4491
Free catalog
Seeds and gardening products

HIG High Altitude Gardens
P.O. Box 1048
Hailey, ID 83333
Order: 208/788.4363
Fax: 208/788.3452
Free catalog
High altitude and short season varieties as well
as classics and heirlooms; tomato varieties from
around the world

HOR Horticultural Enterprises
P.O. Box 810082
Dallas, TX 75381-0082
Free catalog
Specializes in hot peppers and books about them

JLH J. L. Hudson, Seedman
P.O. Box 1058
Redwood City, CA 94064
$1 catalog
An ethnobotanical catalog of seeds

CODE

JOH Johnny's Selected Seeds
Foss Hill Road
Albion, ME 04910-9731
Order: 207/437.4301
Free catalog
Beautiful color catalog with a great selection of
vegetables and flowers, plus heirloom varieties

JUN J. W. Jung Seed Co.
Randolph, WI 53957
Order: 414/326.4100
Customer service: 414/326.3123
Free catalog
Old-fashioned in design; good selection of
vegetable and flower seeds

LED Oral Ledden & Sons
P.O. Box 7
Sewell, NJ 08080-0007
Order: 609/468.1000
Free catalog
Good selection of vegetable and flower seeds

LEJ Le Jardin du Gourmet
P.O. Box 75
St. Johnsbury Center, VT 05863-0075
Order: 800/659.1446
Fax: 802/748.9592
Free catalog
Confusing but interesting catalog

LIB Liberty Seed Company
P.O. Box 806
New Philadelphia, OH 44663
Order: 216/364.1611
Fax: 216/364.6415
Free catalog
Good selection of vegetable and flower seeds,
plus books

MEY The Meyer Seed Company
600 S. Caroline Street
Baltimore, MD 21231
Order: 410/256.8128
Fax: 410/256.6045
Free catalog
Sells seed by the ounce or pound

CODE

NIC Nichols Garden Nursery
1190 North Pacific Highway
Albany, OR 97321-4598
Order: 503/928.9280
Fax: 503/967.8406
Free catalog
Numerous herbs and rare seed varieties, plus
gardening books and supplies

ORG Organic Seeds
Southern Oregon Organics
1130 Tetherow Road
Williams, OR 97544
Order: 503/846.7173
Free catalog
Limited list of organic seeds

ORN Ornamental Edibles
3622 Weedin Court
San Jose, CA 95132
Order: 408/946.SEED
Fax: 408/946.4297
Free catalog
Specialty seeds by mail

PAR Park Seed
Cokesbury Road
Greenwood, SC 29648-0046
Free catalog
Full color, lots of selection

PIN Pinetree Garden Seeds
P.O. Box 300
New Gloucester, ME 04260
Order: 207/926.3400
Free catalog
Good selection of vegetable and flower seeds, as
well as gardening products and books

PLA Plants of the Southwest
Route 6, Box 11A
Santa Fe, NM 87501
Order: 505/471.2212
Free catalog
Excellent source for plants native to the
Southwest and California; limited vegetable list

CODE

CODE

PON   Pony Creek Nursery
P.O. Box 16
Tilleda, WI 54978
Order: 715/787.3889
Free catalog
Newspaper-style catalog with limited seed
varieties

POR   Porter & Son, Seedsmen
P.O. Box 104
Stephenville, TX 76401-0104
Free catalog
Good vegetable selection

RED   The Redwood City Seed Company
P.O. Box 361
Redwood City, CA 94064
Order: 415/325.SEED
$1 catalog
Some unusual varieties

ROS   Roswell Seed Co.
P.O. Box 725
Roswell, NM 88202
Order: 505/662.7701
Fax: 505/623.2885
Free catalog
Good selection of vegetable varieties that can
be bought by the ounce or pound

SEE   Seeds Blum
Idaho City Stage
Boise, ID 83706
Fax: 208/338.5658
$3 catalog
Well worth the price, this is a very different cat-
alog, with lots of unusual vegetable and herb
varieties, plus books and other items.

SEED   Seeds of Change
P.O. Box 15700
Santa Fe, NM 87506-5700
Free catalog
The catalog is full of useful information and
varieties of vegetables, herbs, and flowers. All
the seeds are organic.

SHE   Shepherd's Garden Seeds
6116 Highway 9
Felton, CA 95018
Order: 408/335.6910
Fax: 408/335.2080
Free catalog
A must-see catalog. Lots of friendly horti-
cultural help from the garden staff when you
telephone. Unique varieties of vegetables,
herbs, and flowers.

SOU   Southern Exposure Seed Exchange
P.O. Box 170
Earlysville, VA 22936
Order: 804/973.4703
Fax: same
$3 catalog
Many heirloom varieties and good descriptions

STO   Stokes
P.O. Box 548
Buffalo, NY 14240-0548
Order: 716/695.6980
Fax: 716/695.9649
Free catalog
A complete gardening catalog

SUN   Sunrise Enterprises
P.O. Box 330058
West Hartford, CT 06133-0058
$2 catalog
Oriental seeds

TER   Territorial Seed Company
20 Palmer Avenue
Cottage Grove, OR 97424
Order: 503/942.9547
Fax: 503/942.9881
Free catalog
Lots of information, vegetable and herb varieties

THE   The Good Earth Seed Company
P.O. Box 5644
Redwood City, CA 94063
Free catalog
Oriental vegetables

CODE

CODE

THO Thompson & Morgan Inc.
P.O. Box 1308
Jackson, NJ 08527-0308
Order: 800/274.7333
Fax: 908/363.9356
Information: 908/363.2225
Free catalog
Full-color catalog with vegetables and flowers

TIL Tillinghast Seed Co.
P.O. Box 738
La Conner, WA 98257
Order: 206/466.3329
Free catalog
Read the interesting history of this Northwest
seed company on the back of the catalog.

TOM The Tomato Seed Company Etc.
P.O. Box 1400
Tryon, NC 28782
Free catalog
Myriad tomato varieties, old and new

TOMA Tomato Growers Supply Company
P.O. Box 2237
Fort Myers, FL 33902
Order: 813/768.1119
Fax: 813/768.3475
Free catalog
Tomatoes, tomatoes, and more tomatoes (some
peppers, too)

TWI Otis S. Twilley Seed Co., Inc.
P.O. Box 65
Trevose, PA 19053
Order: 800/622.7333
Fax: 215/245.1949
Information: 215/639.8800
Free catalog
Full-color catalog chock-full of vegetables,
herbs, and flowers, plus gardening products

VER Vermont Bean Seed Co.
P.O. Box 250
Fair Haven, VT 05743
Order: 802/273.3400
Free catalog
Plenty of vegetable varieties

WIL Willhite Seed Company
Poolville, TX 76487
Order: 800/828.1840
Fax: 817/599.5843
Information: 817/599.8656
Free catalog
Full-color catalog with numerous vegetables,
especially melons

WILL William Dam Seeds
P.O. Box 8400
Dundas, Ontario
Canada L9H 6M1
Order: 905/628.6641
Fax: 905/627.1729
Free catalog

County Farm Advisors
Vegetable Crops Cooperative Extension

Alameda County

Advisor: Richard Molinar
224 W. Winton Avenue, Room 174
Hayward, CA 94544-1220
510/670.5200, fax: 510/670.5231

Amador County

No specific contact for vegetable crops
Director: Lucrecia Farfan-Ramirez
12380 Airport Road, Martell, Jackson, CA 95642
209/223.6482, fax: 209/223.3312

Butte County

No specific contact for vegetable crops
Director: Bob Willoughby
2279 Del Oro Avenue, Suite B, Oroville, CA 95965
916/538.7201, fax: 916/538.7140

Calaveras County

No specific contact for vegetable crops
Director: Ken Churches
891 Mountain Ranch Road, San Andreas, CA 95249
209/754.6477, fax: 209/754.6472

Colusa County

Advisor: Mike Murray
P.O. Box 180, Colusa, CA 95932
916/458.2105, fax: 916/458.4625

Contra Costa County

Advisor: Janet Caprile
1700 Oak Park Boulevard, Building A–2
Pleasant Hill, CA 94523
510/646.6540, fax: 510/646.6708

El Dorado County

No specific contact for vegetable crops
Director: Mario Moratorio
311 Fair Lane, Placerville, CA 95667
916/621.5502, fax: 916/642.0803

Fresno County

Advisor: Pedro Ilic
1720 S. Maple Avenue, Fresno, CA 93702
209/488.3285, fax: 209/488.1975

Glenn County

Advisor: Mike Murray
P.O. Box 697, Orland, CA 95963
916/865.1107, fax: 916/865.1109

Humboldt/Del Norte Counties

Advisor: Deborah Giraud
Agriculture Center Building
5630 S. Broadway, Eureka, CA 95501-6998
707/445.7351, fax: 707/444.9334

Imperial County

Advisor: Keith Mayberry
1050 E. Holton Road, Holtville, CA 92250-9615
619/352.9474, fax: 619/352.0846

Inyo/Mono Counties

No specific contact for vegetable crops
Director: Richard Scott
207 W. South Street, Bishop, CA 93514
619/873.7854, fax: 619/872.1610

Kern County

Advisor: Greg Browne
1031 S. Mt. Vernon Avenue, Bakersfield, CA 93307
805/861.2631, fax: 805/834.9359

Kings County

Advisor: Michelle Le Strange
680 N. Campus Drive, Hanford, CA 93230
209/582.3211, fax: 209/582.5166

Lake County

Advisor: Rachel Elkins
Agriculture Center
883 Lakeport Boulevard, Lakeport, CA 95453
707/263.2281, fax: 707/263.2399

Lassen County

Advisor: Dan Marcum
Memorial Building, Susanville, CA 96130
916/257.6363, fax: 916/257.6129

Los Angeles County

Advisor: Yvonne Freeman
2615 S. Grand Avenue, Suite 400, Los Angeles, CA 90007
213/744.4340, fax: 213/745.7513

Madera County

No specific contact for vegetable crops
Director: Ron Vargas (acting)
328 Madera Avenue, Madera, CA 93637
209/675.7879, fax: 209/675.0639

Marin County

No specific contact for vegetable crops
Director: Ellen Rilla
1682 Novato Boulevard, Suite 150B, Novato, CA 94947
415/899.8620, fax: 415/899.8619

Mariposa County

No specific contact for vegetable crops
Director: Wain Johnson
5009 Fairgrounds Road, Mariposa, CA 95338-9435
209/966.2417, fax: 209/966.2056

Mendocino County

Advisor: Glenn McGourty
Agriculture Center, Courthouse, Ukiah, CA 95482
707/463.4495, fax: 707/463.4477

Merced County

No specific contact for vegetable crops
Director: Jim Farley (acting)
2145 W. Wardrobe Avenue, Merced, CA 95340
209/385.7403, fax: 209/722.8856

Modoc (Tulelake) County

Advisor: Harry Carlson
P.O. Box 638, Tulelake, CA 96134
916/667.2719, fax: 916/667.5265

Monterey County

Advisors: Bill Chaney, Steve Koike,
Kurt Schulbach, John Inman
118 Wilgart Way, Salinas, CA 93901
408/758.4637, fax: 408/758.3018

Napa County

No specific contact for vegetable crops
Director: John Wagenknecht (acting)
1436 Polk Street, Napa, CA 94559-2597
707/253.4221, fax: 707/253.4434

Nevada/Placer Counties

Advisor: Garth Veerkamp
11477 E Avenue, Auburn, CA 95603
916/889.7385, fax: 916/889.7397

Orange County

No specific contact for vegetable crops
Director: Anne Cotter
1000 S. Harbor Boulevard, Anaheim, CA 92805
714/477.7150, fax: 714/477.7171

Plumas/Sierra Counties

No specific contact for vegetable crops
Director: Holly George
208 Fairgrounds Road, Quincy, CA 95971
916/283.6270, fax: 916/283.4210

Riverside County

Advisor: Jose Aguiar (for Indio)
83–612 Avenue 45, Suite 7, Indio, CA 92201
619/863.8293, fax: 619/775.9049

Advisor: Aziz Baameur
21150 Box Springs Road, Moreno Valley, CA 92387
909/683.6491, fax: 909/788.2615

Advisor: Les Ede (for Palo Verde)
160 N. Broadway, Blythe, CA 92225
619/922.5171, fax: 619/922.0367

Sacramento County

Advisor: Peggy Mauk
4145 Branch Center Road, Sacramento, CA 95827
916/366.2013, fax: 916/366.4133

San Benito County

Advisor: Richard Smith
649-A San Benito Street, Hollister, CA 95023
408/637.5346, fax: 408/637.7111

San Diego County

Advisors: Wayne Schrader, Faustino Munoz
Building 4, 5555 Overland Avenue, San Diego, CA 92123
619/694.2854, fax: 619/694.2849

San Joaquin County

Advisor: Bob Mullen
420 S. Wilson Way, Stockton, CA 95205
209/468.2085, fax: 209/462.5181

San Mateo/San Francisco Counties

Advisor: Ann King
625 Miramontes Street, Suite 200
Half Moon Bay, CA 94019
415/726.9059, fax: 415/726.9267

Santa Barbara County

Advisors: Frank Laemmlen, Louie Valenzuela (for Santa Maria)
624 W. Foster Road, Santa Maria, CA 93455
805/934.6240, fax: 805/934.6333

Santa Clara County

Advisors: Nancy Garrison, Craig Kolodge
2175 The Alameda, San Jose, CA 95126
408/299.2634, fax: 408/246.7016

Santa Cruz County

Advisor: Norm Welch
1432 Freedom Blvd., Watsonville, CA 95076-2796
408/425.2591, fax: 408/761.4106

Shasta County

Advisor: Richard Buchner
1851 Hartnell Avenue, Redding, CA 96002-2217
916/224.4900, fax: 916/224.4904

Shasta/Lassen Counties

Advisor: Dan Marcum
P.O. Box 9, McArthur, CA 96056-0009
916/336.5784, fax: same, call first

Siskiyou County

Advisor: Steve Orloff
1655 S. Main Street, Yreka, CA 96097
916/842.2711, fax: 916/842.6931

Solano County

Advisor: Larry Clement
2000 W. Texas Street, Fairfield, CA 94533-4498
707/421.6790, fax: 707/429.5532

Sonoma County

Advisor: Paul Vossen
2604 Ventura Avenue, Room 100
Santa Rosa, CA 95403-2894
707/527.2621, fax: 707/527.2623

Stanislaus County

Advisor: Jesus Valencia
733 County Center III Court, Modesto, CA 95355
209/525.6654, fax: 209/525.4619

Sutter/Yuba Counties

No specific contact for vegetable crops
Director: Chuck Wilson
142-A Garden Highway, Yuba City, CA 95991
916/741.7515, fax: 916/673.5368

Tehama County

No specific contact for vegetable crops
Director: Ray Lyon
P.O. Box 370 (1754 Walnut), Red Bluff, CA 96080
916/527.3101, fax: 916/628.5495

Trinity County

No specific contact for vegetable crops
Director: Ray Lyon
P.O. Box 370 (Fairgrounds), Hayfork, CA 96041
916/628.5495, fax: same

Tulare County

Advisors: Manuel Jimenez, Michelle Le Strange
Agriculture Building, County Civic Center
Visalia, CA 93291-4584
209/733.6363, fax: 209/733.6720

Tuolumne County

No specific contact for vegetable crops
Director: Don Appleton
2 S. Green Street, Sonora, CA 95370
209/533.5695, fax: 209/532.8978

Ventura County

Advisor: Harry Otto
702 County Square Drive, Ventura, CA 93003-5404
805/645.1456, fax: 805/648.9221

Yolo County

Advisor: Gene Miyao
70 Cottonwood Street, Woodland, CA 95695
916/666.8143, fax: 916/666.8736

APPENDIX C

VEGETABLE PLANTING GUIDE

VEGETABLE	DEPTH TO PLANT SEED (INCHES)	NUMBER OF SEED TO SOW PER FOOT	DISTANCE BETWEEN PLANTS (INCHES)	DISTANCE BETWEEN ROWS (INCHES)	NUMBER OF DAYS TO GERMINATION	SEED SOIL TEMPERATURE			WEEKS NEEDED TO GROW TO TRANSPLANT SIZE	DAYS TO MATURITY
						NEEDS COOL SOIL	TOLERATES COOL SOIL	NEEDS WARM SOIL		
Artichokes	½	–	60	72	7–14		•		4–6	1 year
Asparagus	1½	–	18	36	7–21		•		1 year	3 years
Beans, bush lima	1½–2	5–8	3–6	24–30	7–12			•	–	60–80
Beans, pole lima	1½–2	4–5	6–10	30–36	7–12			•	–	85–90
Beans, bush snap	1½–2	6–8	2–3	18–30	6–14			•	–	45–65
Beans, pole snap	1½–2	4–6	4–6	36–48	6–14			•	–	60–70
Beets	½–1	10–15	2	12–18	10–14		•		–	55–65
Broccoli	½	4–6	14–18	24–30	3–10		•		5–7	60–80 (trans.)
Brussels sprouts	½	4–6	12–18	24–30	3–10		•		4–6	80–90 (trans.)
Cabbage	½	4–6	12–20	24–30	4–10		•		5–7	65–95 (trans.)
Carrots	¼	15–20	1–2	14–24	10–17		•		–	60–80
Cauliflower	½	4–6	18	24–30	4–10		•		5–7	55–65 (trans.)
Celery	⅛	4–6	8	24–30	9–21	•			10–12	90–120 (trans.)
Chard	1	4–6	4–8	18–24	7–10		•		–	55–65
Chives	½	4–6	8	10–16	8–12		•		–	80–90
Collards	¼	4–6	10–15	24–30	4–10		•		4–6	65–85 (trans.)
Corn	2	3–4	10–14	30–36	6–10			•	–	60–90
Cucumbers	1	2–4	12	48–72	6–10			•	4	55–65
Eggplant	¼–½	4–6	18	36	7–14			•	6–9	75–95 (trans.)
Endive	½	4–6	9–12	12–24	5–9		•		4–6	60–90

VEGETABLE PLANTING GUIDE *(continued)*

VEGETABLE	DEPTH TO PLANT SEED (INCHES)	NUMBER OF SEED TO SOW PER FOOT	DISTANCE BETWEEN PLANTS (INCHES)	DISTANCE BETWEEN ROWS (INCHES)	NUMBER OF DAYS TO GERMINATION	SEED SOIL TEMPERATURE			WEEKS NEEDED TO GROW TO TRANSPLANT SIZE	DAYS TO MATURITY
						NEEDS COOL SOIL	TOLERATES COOL SOIL	NEEDS WARM SOIL		
Kale	½	6–10	8–12	18–24	3–10		•		4–6	55–80
Kohlrabi	½	8–12	3–4	18–24	3–10		•		4–6	60–70
Leeks	½–1	8–12	2–4	12–18	7–12		•		10–12	80–90 (trans.)
Lettuce, head	¼–½	4–8	12–14	18–24	4–10	•			3–5	55–80
Lettuce, leaf	¼–½	6–10	4–6	12–18	4–10	•			3–5	45–60
Muskmelon	1	3–4	12	48–72	4–8			•	3–4	75–100
Mustard	½	8–10	2–6	12–18	3–10		•		–	40–60
Okra	1	4–6	15–18	28–36	7–14			•	–	50–60
Onions, plants	2–3	–	2–3	12–24	–	•			–	95–120 (trans.)
Onions, seed	½	10–15	2–3	12–24	7–12	•			8	100–165
Onions, sets	1–2	10–15	2–3	12–24	–	•			–	95–120
Parsley	¼–½	–	3–6	12–20	14–28		•		8	85–90
Parsnips	½	8–12	3–4	16–24	15–25		•		–	100–120
Peas	2	6–7	2–3	18–30	6–15	•			–	65–85
Peppers	¼	4–6	18–24	24–36	10–20			•	6–8	60–80 (trans.)
Potatoes	4	1	12	24–36	8–16		•		–	90–105 (trans.)
Pumpkins	1–1½	2	30	72–120	6–10			•	–	70–110
Radishes	½	14–16	1–2	6–12	3–10		•		–	20–50
Rhubarb	–	crown	36	60	–		•		–	second season
Rutabaga	½	4–6	8–12	18–24	3–10		•		–	80–90
Salsify	½	8–12	2–3	16–18	–	•			–	110–150
Shallot	1	bulb	2–4	12–18	–		•		–	60–75
Spinach	½	10–12	2–4	12–14	6–14	•			–	40–65
Spinach, Malabar	½	4–6	12	12	10–14		•		–	70
Spinach, New Zealand	1½	3–4	18	24	5–10		•		–	70–80
Spinach, Tampala	¼–½	6–10	4–6	24–30	–		•		–	21–42
Squash, summer	1	3–4	16–24	36–60	3–12			•	–	50–60
Squash, winter	1	1–2	24–48	72–120	6–10			•	–	85–120
Sweet potatoes	–	plants	12–18	36–48	–			•	–	120
Tomatoes	½	–	18–36	36–60	6–14			•	5–7	55–90 (trans.)
Turnips	½	12–14	1–3	15–18	3–10	•			–	45–60
Watermelon	1	3–4	12–16	60	3–12			•		80–100